A People and A Nation

Brief Eighth Edition

A People and A Nation

A HISTORY OF THE UNITED STATES

Volume 1 To 1877

Brief Eighth Edition

MARY BETH NORTON
Cornell University

CAROL SHERIFF
College of William and Mary

DAVID M. KATZMAN
University of Kansas

DAVID W. BLIGHT
Yale University

HOWARD P. CHUDACOFF
Brown University

FREDRIK LOGEVALL
Cornell University

BETH BAILEY
Temple University

DEBRA MICHALS
Merrimack College

 WADSWORTH
CENGAGE Learning

Australia • Brazil • Japan • Korea • Mexico • Singapore • Spain • United Kingdom • United States

WADSWORTH
CENGAGE Learning™

A People and A Nation: A History of the United States Volume 1 To 1877, Brief Eighth Edition

Mary Beth Norton, Carol Sheriff, David M. Katzman, David W. Blight, Howard P. Chudacoff, Fredrik Logevall, Beth Bailey, Debra Michals

Sponsoring Editor: Ann West

Development Manager: Jeffrey Greene

Assistant Editor: Megan Curry

Editorial Assistant: Megan Chrisman

Senior Editor: Lisa Ciccolo

Senior Marketing Manager: Katherine Bates

Marketing Coordinator: Lorreen Pelletier

Marketing Communications Manager: Christine Dobberpuhl

Content Project Manager, Editorial Production: Aimee Chevrette Bear

Art and Design Manager: Jill Haber

Print Buyer: Miranda Klapper

Senior Rights Acquisition Account Manager: Katie Huha

Text Designer: Cia Boynton

Senior Photo Editor: Jennifer Meyer Dare

Photo Researcher: Bruce Carson

Cover Design Manager: Tony Saizon

Cover Image: King, Samuel (1748–1819). Ezra Stiles (1727–1795), 1771. Oil on Canvas

Cover Credit: Yale University Art Gallery, Bequest Charles Jenkins Foote/Art Resource, NY

Compositor: Macmillan Publishing Solutions

For product information and technology assistance, contact us at
**Cengage Learning Academic Resource Center,
1-800-423-0563**
For permission to use material from this text or product, submit all requests online at **www.cengage.com/permissions**.
Further permissions questions can be e-mailed to
permissionrequest@cengage.com

Library of Congress Control Number: 2008933839

Student Edition:

ISBN-13: 978-0-547-17559-1

ISBN-10: 0-547-17559-0

Wadsworth
25 Thomson Place
Boston, MA 02210
USA

Cengage Learning products are represented in Canada by Nelson Education, Ltd.

For your course and learning solutions, visit
www.cengage.com.

Purchase any of our products at your local college store or at our preferred online store **www.ichapters.com**.

Printed in the United States of America
1 2 3 4 5 6 7 13 14 12 11 10

Brief Contents

Contents

16

Reconstruction: An Unfinished Revolution, 1865–1877   409

Maps

Figures

Tables

Preface to the Brief Eighth Edition

CREATION OF THE BRIEF EDITION

Nearly three decades have passed since the publication of the first brief edition of *A People and a Nation*. In that initial brief edition, as well as each subsequent one, the intent was to preserve the uniqueness and integrity of the complete work while condensing it. This Brief Eighth Edition once again reflects the scholarship, readability, and comprehensiveness of the full-length version. It also maintains the integration of social, cultural, political, economic, and foreign relations history that has been a hallmark of *A People and a Nation*.

Starting with this edition, a new editor, Dr. Debra Michals, has worked with us, ensuring that the changes in content and organization incorporated in the full-length Eighth Edition were retained in the condensation. The authors attained reductions by paring down details rather than deleting entire sections. The Brief Eighth Edition thus contains fewer statistics, fewer quotations, and fewer examples than the unabridged version. A sufficient number of quotations and examples are retained, however, to maintain the richness in style created by the authors.

The Brief Eighth Edition is available in both one-volume and two-volume formats. The two-volume format is divided as follows: Volume 1 contains Chapters 1 through 16, beginning with a discussion of three cultures—American, African, and European—that intersected during the exploration and colonization of the New World and ending with a discussion of the Reconstruction era. Volume 2 contains Chapters 16 through 33, beginning its coverage at Reconstruction and extending the history of the American people to the present. The chapter on Reconstruction appears in both volumes to provide greater flexibility in matching a volume to the historical span covered by a specific course.

CHANGES IN THIS EDITION

While the following Preface to the full-length Eighth Edition elaborates on specific content changes, we note here that the authors paid increased attention to the following: the history of children and childhood; the environment, including the past impact of hurricanes; the American West, subject of a completely new chapter; and the social and religious diversity of America's population, developed through territorial incorporation as well as through immigration. We have further widened our lens to include more coverage of America's place in the world. These emphases as well as the updated scholarship on which they are based, are fully retained in the Brief Eighth Edition. New to this edition are focus questions that follow each chapter's introduction to call students' attention to key issues in the chapter. These questions are answered at the end of each chapter.

Although each author feels answerable for the whole of *A People and a Nation*, we take primary responsibility for particular chapters: Mary Beth Norton, Chapters 1–8; Carol Sheriff, Chapters 9, 11–13; David Blight, Chapters 10, 14–16;

Howard P. Chudacoff, Chapters 17–21 and 24; Fredrik Logevall, Chapters 22, 23, 26, 28, and shared responsibility for 30–33; Beth Bailey, Chapters 25, 27, 29, and shared responsibility for 30–33.

LEARNING AND TEACHING AIDS

This edition of *A People and a Nation* includes a number of useful learning and teaching aids. These ancillaries are designed to help students get the most from the course and to provide instructors with useful course management and presentation tools.

Website Tools

The **Instructor Website** features the **Instructor's Resource Manual** written by George C. Warren of Central Piedmont Community College. For each chapter, there is a brief list of learning objectives, a comprehensive chapter outline, ideas for classroom activities, discussion questions and several suggested paper topics, and a lecture supplement. Also available on the Instructor Website are primary sources with instructor notes in addition to hundreds of maps, images, audio and video clips, and PowerPoint slides for classroom presentation created by Barney Rickman of Valdosta State University. The **HM Testing™** CD-ROM provides flexible test-editing capabilities for the Test Items written by George Warren.

HistoryFinder, a new Houghton Mifflin technology initiative, helps instructors create rich and exciting classroom presentations. This online tool offers thousands of online resources, including art, photographs, maps, primary sources, multimedia content, Associated Press interactive modules, and ready-made Power-Point slides. HistoryFinder's assets can easily be searched by keyword, or browsed from pull-down menus by topic, media type, or by textbook. Instructors can then browse, preview, and download resources straight from the website.

The **Student Website** contains a variety of tutorial resources including the **Study Guide** written by George Warren, ACE quizzes with feedback, interactive maps, primary sources, chronology exercises, flashcards, and other interactivities. The Website for this edition of *A People and a Nation* features **Audio Summaries,** audio files that are downloadable as MP3 files. These audio summaries help students review each chapter's key points.

Please contact your local Houghton Mifflin sales representative for more information about these learning and teaching tools in addition to the **Rand McNally Atlas of American History,** WebCT and Blackboard cartridges, and transparencies for United States History.

ACKNOWLEDGMENTS

Author teams rely on review panels to help create and execute successful revision plans. For the revision of this Brief Eighth Edition, we were guided by the many historians whose thoughtful insights and recommendations helped us with the preparation of the full-length Eighth Edition. Their names appear in the preface to that edition that follows.

Finally, we want to thank the many people who have contributed their thoughts and labors to this work, especially the talented staff at Houghton Mifflin.

For the authors, Mary Beth Norton, coordinating author.

In this eighth edition, *A People and a Nation* has undergone both reorganization and revision, while still retaining the narrative strength and focus that have made it so popular with students and teachers alike. In the years since the publication of the seventh edition, new materials have been uncovered, new interpretations advanced, and new themes have come to the forefront of American historical scholarship. All the authors—joined by one new member, Carol Sheriff—have worked diligently to incorporate those findings into this text.

Like other teachers and students, we are always re-creating our past, restructuring our memory, and rediscovering the personalities and events that have influenced us, injured us, and bedeviled us. This book represents our continuing rediscovery of America's history—its diverse people and the nation they created and have nurtured. As this book demonstrates, there are many different Americans and many different memories. We have sought to present as many of them as possible, in both triumph and tragedy, in both division and unity.

ABOUT A PEOPLE AND A NATION

A People and a Nation, first published in 1982, was the first major textbook in the United States to fully integrate social and political history. From the outset, the authors have been determined to tell the story of *all* the people of the United States. This book's hallmark has been its melding of social and political history, its movement beyond history's common focus on public figures and events to examine the daily life of America's people. All editions of the book have stressed the interaction of public policy and personal experience, the relationship between domestic concerns and foreign affairs, the various manifestations of popular culture, and the multiple origins of America and Americans. We have consistently built our narrative on a firm foundation in primary sources—on both well-known and obscure letters, diaries, public documents, oral histories, and artifacts of material culture. We have long challenged readers to think about the meaning of American history, not just to memorize facts. Both students and instructors have repeatedly told us how much they appreciate and enjoy our approach to the past.

As has been true since the first edition, each chapter opens with a dramatic vignette focusing on an individual or a group of people. These vignettes introduce key themes, which then frame the chapters in succinct introductions and summaries. Numerous maps, tables, graphs, and charts provide readers with the necessary geographical and statistical context for observations in the text. Carefully selected illustrations—many of them unique to this book—offer readers visual insight into the topics under discussion, especially because the authors have written the captions. In this edition, as in all previous ones, we have sought to incorporate up-to-date scholarship, readability, a clear structure, critical thinking, and instructive illustrative material on every page.

THEMES IN THIS BOOK

Several themes and questions stand out in our continuing effort to integrate political, social, and cultural history. We study the many ways Americans have defined themselves—gender, race, class, region, ethnicity, religion, sexual orientation—and the many subjects that have reflected their multidimensional experiences. We highlight the remarkably diverse everyday lives of the American people—in cities and on farms and ranches, in factories and in corporate headquarters, in neighborhoods and in legislatures, in love relationships and in hate groups, in recreation and in work, in the classroom and in military uniform, in secret national security conferences and in public foreign relations debates, in church and in voluntary associations, in polluted environments and in conservation areas. We pay particular attention to lifestyles, diet and dress, family life and structure, labor conditions, gender roles, migration and mobility, childbearing, and child rearing. We explore how Americans have entertained and informed themselves by discussing their music, sports, theater, print media, film, radio, television, graphic arts, and literature, in both "high" culture and popular culture. We study how technology has influenced Americans' lives, such as through the internal combustion engine and the computer.

Americans' personal lives have always interacted with the public realm of politics and government. To understand how Americans have sought to protect their different ways of life and to work out solutions to thorny problems, we emphasize their expectations of governments at the local, state, and federal levels; governments' role in providing answers; the lobbying of interest groups; the campaigns and outcomes of elections; and the hierarchy of power in any period. Because the United States has long been a major participant in world affairs, we explore America's participation in wars, interventions in other nations, empire-building, immigration patterns, images of foreign peoples, cross-national cultural ties, and international economic trends.

WHAT'S NEW IN THIS EDITION

Planning for the eighth edition began at a two-day authors' meeting at the Houghton Mifflin headquarters in Boston. There we discussed the most recent scholarship in the field, the reviews of the seventh edition solicited from instructors, and the findings of our own continuing research. For this edition, we added a new colleague, Carol Sheriff, who experienced the intellectual exhilaration and rigor of such an authors' meeting for the first time. Sheriff, a member of the History Department at the College of William and Mary, has written extensively on antebellum America, especially in the north, and she has taken on the responsibility for those chapters in the eighth edition.

This edition builds on its immediate predecessor in continuing to enhance the global perspective on American history that has characterized the book since its first edition. From the "Atlantic world" context of European colonies in North and South America to the discussion of international terrorism, the authors have incorporated the most recent globally oriented scholarship throughout the volume. Significantly, the eighth edition includes an entirely new chapter on the American west in the years before the Civil War and the discussion of the west has been expanded throughout. The treatment of the history of children and childhood has been increased, as has the discussion of environmental history, including the devastating impact of hurricanes in North America and the Caribbean from the earliest days of European settlement. As in the seventh edition, we have worked to strengthen our treatment of the diversity of America's people by examining differences within the broad ethnic categories commonly employed and by paying greater attention to immigration, cultural and intellectual infusions from around the world, and America's growing religious diversity. We have also stressed the incorporation of different peoples into the United States through territorial acquisition as well as through immigration. At the same time, we have integrated the discussion of such diversity into our narrative, so as not to artificially isolate any group from the mainstream. We have added three probing questions at the end of each chapter's introduction to guide students' reading of the pages that follow.

As always, the authors reexamined every sentence, interpretation, map, chart, illustration, and caption, refining the narrative, presenting new examples, and bringing to the text the latest findings of scholars in many areas of history, anthropology, sociology, and political science. More than one-third of the chapter-opening vignettes are new to this edition.

"LEGACIES" AND "LINKS TO THE WORLD"

Each chapter contains two brief feature essays: "Legacies" (introduced in the sixth edition) and "Links to the World" (introduced in the seventh edition). Legacies follow chapter summaries and offer compelling and timely answers to students who question the relevance of historical study by exploring the historical roots of contemporary topics. New subjects of Legacies are: Kennewick Man/Ancient One, Blue Laws, women's political activism, the township and range system, descendants of early Latino settlers, "Big Government," the Lost Cause, the Cowboy myth, recorded music, Guantanamo Bay, atomic proliferation, and the all-volunteer military. Numerous other Legacies have been updated.

"Links to the World" examine both inward and outward ties between America (and Americans) and the rest of the world. The "Links" appear at appropriate places in each chapter to explore specific topics at considerable length. Tightly constructed essays detail the often little-known connections between developments here and abroad. The topics range broadly over economic, political, social, technological, medical, and cultural history, vividly demonstrating that the geographical region that is now the United States has never lived in isolation from other peoples and countries. New to this edition are Links on smallpox inoculations, the Amistad case, Russian Populism, European influence on American workers' compensation, and *National Geographic.* Each Link highlights global interconnections with unusual and lively examples that will both intrigue and inform students.

SECTION-BY-SECTION CHANGES IN THIS EDITION

Mary Beth Norton, who had primary responsibility for Chapters 1 through 8 and served as coordinating author, augmented her discussion of the age of European expansion with new information on Muslim power and the allure of exotic spices; she also expanded the treatment of Spanish colonization and settlements in the Caribbean. She incorporated extensive new scholarship on early Virginia into Chapter 2. In addition to reorganizing part of Chapter 3 to bring more coherence to the discussion of the origins of slavery in North America, she added demographic information about enslaved people (both Indians and Africans) and those who enslaved and transported them, stressing in particular the importance of African women in South Carolina rice cultivation. She added material on transported English convicts, Huguenot immigrants, Acadian exiles, iron-making, land riots, the Stono Rebellion, the Seven Years' War in western Pennsylvania, the experiences of common soldiers in the Revolution, Shays's Rebellion, and the Jay Treaty debates. In Chapter 8 she created new sections on Indians in the new nation and on revolutions at the end of the century, including among them the election of Thomas Jefferson.

Carol Sheriff completely reorganized the contents of Chapters 9, 11, and 12, clarifying chronological developments and including much new material. Chapter 9 now covers politics through 1823 in order to emphasize the impact of the War of 1812 in accelerating regional divisions. It has expanded coverage of popular political practice (including among non-voters), the separation of church and state, the Marshall Court, the First and Second Barbary Wars, and the incorporation of the Louisiana Territory and its residents into the United States. Chapter 11, retitled "The Modernizing North," consolidates information previously divided between two chapters and augments it with new discussions of daily life before commercial and industrial expansion, rural-urban contrasts, children and youth culture, male and female common laborers, and the origins of free-labor ideology. Chapter 12 focuses on reform and politics in the age of Jackson, with expanded attention to communitarian experiments, abolitionism (including African Americans in the movement), women's rights, and religion, including revivalism in general and the Second Great Awakening in particular. The entirely new Chapter 13, "The Contested West," combines material that was previously scattered in different locations with a great deal of recent scholarship on such topics as the disjunction between the ideal and reality of the West, exploration and migration, cultural diversity in the West, cooperation and conflict among the West's peoples, and the role of the federal government in regional development. In all her reorganized chapters she relied on a base created by David M. Katzman, an original member of the author team who had responsibility for this section in the seven earlier editions.

David W. Blight, who had primary responsibility for Chapters 10 and 14 through 16, extensively reorganized Chapter 10 (previously Chapter 13), on the South, in part to reflect its new chronological placement in the book. The chapter now covers material beginning in 1815 rather than 1830 and contains a section on Southern expansion and Indian removal. In his chapters he has added material on the Taos revolt, enslaved children, "Bleeding Kansas," Harriet Scott, Louisa May Alcott, union sentiment in the South, the conduct of the war, and economic and social conditions in the postwar North and South. He has revised Chapter 16 to emphasize economic as well as political change in the era of Reconstruction.

Howard P. Chudacoff, responsible for Chapters 17 through 21 and 24, has increased the coverage of Indians, Exodusters, and Hispanics in the West, and of western Progressivism. His treatment of popular culture now stresses its lower-class, bottom-to-top origins. He added information on the history of childhood, vaudeville, and the movies; and he revised discussions of monetary policy, Progressivism, Populism, and urban and agrarian protests. He also has included more coverage of racism and those who combated it, such as Ida B. Wells, and on women and the Ku Klux Klan. Business operation and regulation receive new attention in his chapters, as do Calvin Coolidge, consumerism, and baseball.

Fredrik Logevall, with primary responsibility for Chapters 22, 23, 26, and 28, continued throughout his chapters to work to establish the wider international context for U.S. foreign affairs. He added considerable new material on the Middle East (especially in Chapter 28) and incorporated recent scholarship on the Vietnam War. He also updated the treatment of the Spanish-American War with new information on the sinking of the *Maine* and on the Philippine insurrection. His discussion of World War I now includes consideration of the antagonistic relationship of Woodrow Wilson and V.I. Lenin; and he has given more attention to American economic and cultural expansion in the 1920s and 1930s. He has furthermore expanded his treatment of American reactions to the Spanish Civil War.

Beth Bailey, primarily responsible for Chapters 25, 27, and 29, added information on women, the left, and popular culture (especially film and the production code) during the 1930s. She expanded coverage of the European front in World War II and of divisions within the United States during the war. In Chapter 29, she thoroughly reorganized the section on civil rights to clarify the chronology and key points of development, and she also included new information on emerging countercultures and the beats, union activities, and the Eisenhower administration.

Bailey and Logevall shared responsibility for Chapters 30 through 33. In Chapter 30 Freedom Summer is given enhanced attention and the section on civil rights has been reorganized to emphasize a clear chronology. These chapters contain new material on the women's movement and the barriers women faced before 1970s reforms, recent immigration, neoconservatism, anti-Vietnam War protests, Nixon's presidency, the Supreme Court, the 1982 Israeli invasion of Lebanon, and the 1991 Iraq War. Chapter 33 in particular has been thoroughly revised to include the latest demographic data on Americans and their families, along with discussions of the struggles over science and religion, hurricane Katrina, the Bush administration's domestic policies, and especially the Iraq War.

TEACHING AND LEARNING AIDS

The supplements listed here accompany the Eighth Edition of *A People and a Nation.* They have been created with the diverse needs of today's students and instructors in mind.

FOR THE INSTRUCTOR

- Houghton Mifflin's **HistoryFinder** is a new online tool developed to help instructors create rich and exciting presentations for the U.S. history survey class. HistoryFinder offers thousands of online resources, including art, photographs, maps, primary sources, multimedia content, Associated Press interactive modules, and ready-made PowerPoint slides. HistoryFinder's assets can easily be searched by keyword topic, media type, or by textbook chapter. It is then possible to browse, preview, and download resources straight from the website into the instructor's own PowerPoint collection.

- **The Instructor Website**, at HM HistorySPACE(tm), includes a variety of resources that will help instructors engage their students in class and assess their understanding inside and outside the classroom. The Instructor Website includes the **Instructor's Resource Manual,** written by George C. Warren, of Central Piedmont Community College. For each chapter, there is a brief list of learning objectives, a comprehensive chapter outline, ideas for classroom activities, discussion questions and several suggested paper topics, and a lecture supplement. Also available on the Instructor Website is a complete set of PowerPoint slides created by Barney Rickman of Valdosta State University, to assist in instruction and discussion of key topics and materials for each chapter.

- The **HM Testing™ CD-ROM** provides flexible test-editing capabilities for the Test Items written by George Warren of Central Piedmont Community College. Included in the Test Bank are multiple choice, identification, geography, and essay questions.

- Houghton Mifflin's **Eduspace Course** for *A People and a Nation* offers a customizable course management system powered by Blackboard along with homework assignments that engage students and encourage in-class discussion. Assignments include gradable homework exercises, writing assignments, primary sources with questions, and Associated Press Interactives. Eduspace also provides a gradebook and communication capabilities, such as live chats, threaded discussion boards, and announcement postings. The Eduspace course also includes an interactive version of *A People and a Nation* with direct links to relevant primary sources, quizzes, and more.

FOR THE STUDENT

- The **Student Website**, at HM HistorySPACE™, contains a variety of review and self-assessment resources to help students succeed in the U.S. history survey course. ACE quizzes with feedback, interactive maps, primary sources, chronology exercises, flashcards, and other activities are available for each chapter. Audio files provide chapter summaries in MP3 format for downloading and listening to at any time.

- **Study Guides** (Volumes I and II), written by George Warren, provide learning objectives, vocabulary exercises, identification suggestions, skill-building activities, multiple choice questions, essay questions, and map exercises in two volumes.

Please contact your local Houghton Mifflin sales representative for more information about these learning and teaching tools in addition to the **Rand McNally Atlas of American History,** WebCT and Blackboard cartridges, and transparencies for United States History. Your sales representative can also provide more information about **BiblioBase for U.S. History,** a database of hundreds of primary sources from which you can create a customized course pack.

ACKNOWLEDGMENTS

The authors would like to thank the following persons for their assistance with the preparation of this edition: Shawn Alexander, Marsha Andrews, Edward Balleisen, Philip Daileader, Katherine Flynn, John B. Heiser, Danyel Logevall, Daniel Mandell, Clark F. Norton, Mary E. Norton, Anna Daileader Sheriff, Benjamin Daileader Sheriff, Selene Sheriff, Seymour Sheriff.

At each stage of this revision, a sizable panel of historian reviewers read drafts of our chapters. Their suggestions, corrections, and pleas helped guide us through this momentous revision. We could not include all of their recommendations, but the book is better for our having heeded most of their advice. We heartily thank:

Marynita Anderson, Nassau Community College/SUNY
Stephen Aron, UCLA and Autry National Center
Gordon Morris Bakken, California State University, Fullerton
Todd Forsyth Carney, Southern Oregon University
Kathleen S. Carter, High Point University
Robert C. Cottrell, California State University, Chico
Lawrence Culver, Utah State University
Lawrence J. DeVaro, Rowan University
Lisa Lindquist Dorr, University of Alabama
Michelle Kuhl, University of Wisconsin, Oshkosh
Martin Halpern, Henderson State University
John S. Leiby, Paradise Valley Community College
Edwin Martini, Western Michigan University
Elsa A Nystrom Kennesaw State University
Chester Pach, Ohio University
Stephen Rockenbach, Northern Kentucky University
Joseph Owen Weixelman, University of New Mexico

The authors once again thank the extraordinary Houghton Mifflin people who designed, edited, produced, and nourished this book. Their high standards and acute attention to both general structure and fine detail are cherished in the publishing industry. Many thanks, then, to Patricia Coryell, vice president, publisher, history and social science; Suzanne Jeans, publisher, history and political Science; Sally Constable and Ann West, senior sponsoring editors; Ann Hofstra Grogg, freelance development editor; Jeff Greene, senior development editor; Jane Lee, senior project editor, Katherine Bates, senior marketing manager; Pembroke Herbert, photo researcher; Jill Haber, art and design manager, Charlotte Miller, art editor; and Evangeline Bermas, editorial assistant.

M.B.N.
C.S.
D.B.
H.C.
F.L.
B.B.

Three Old Worlds Create a New

F ive years later, Alvar Nuñez Cabeza de Vaca still recalled the amazement he encountered in northern Mexico in mid-February 1536. "I reached four Christians on horseback who registered great surprise at seeing me so strangely dressed and in the company of Indians. They . . . neither spoke to me nor dared to ask anything."

Cabeza de Vaca, two Spaniards, and an enslaved North African named Estevan had just walked across North America. They, along with about six hundred others, left Spain in June 1527 on an ill-fated expedition. After exploring near Tampa Bay, eighty of the men, including Cabeza de Vaca, were shipwrecked in late 1528 on the coast of modern Texas. Most of the survivors—alternately abused, aided, and enslaved by local Indians—died. Cabeza de Vaca reached the mainland, where he survived as a traveling trader, exchanging seashells for hides and flint.

In January 1533 he stumbled on the other three. Guided by Indians, they walked south in September 1534; turned inland and headed north, exploring the upper reaches of the Rio Grande; then walked almost to the Pacific before turning south once more. Vaca described the diets, living arrangements, and customs of many villages, thus providing modern historians and anthropologists with an invaluable record of native cultures as they first encountered Europeans. For thousands of years before 1492, human societies in the Americas developed in isolation from the rest of the world. That ended in the Christian fifteenth century. As Europeans sought treasure and trade, peoples from different cultures came into contact for the first time and were profoundly changed. Their interactions over the next 350 years involved cruelty and kindness, greed and deception, trade and theft, sickness and enslavement. The history of the

This icon will direct you to interactive activities and study materials on A People And A Nation, Brief Edition
website: **www.cengage.com/history/norton/ peoplenationbrief8e**

1

Chronology

12,000–10,000 B.C.E.	Paleo-Indians migrate from Asia to North America across the Beringia land bridge.	**1494**	Treaty of Tordesillas divides land claims between Spain and Portugal in Africa, India, and South America.
7000 B.C.E.	Cultivation of food crops begins in America.	**1496**	Last Canary Island falls to Spain.
ca. 2000 B.C.E.	Olmec civilization appears.	**1497**	Cabot reaches North America.
ca. 300–600 C.E.	Height of influence of Teotihuacán.	**1513**	Ponce de León explores Florida.
ca. 600–900 C.E.	Classic Mayan civilization exists.	**1518–30**	Smallpox epidemic devastates the Indian population of the West Indies and Central and South America.
1000 C.E.	Ancient Pueblos build settlements in modern states of Arizona and New Mexico.	**1519**	Cortés invades Mexico.
1001	Norse establish a settlement in Vinland.	**1521**	Tenochtitlán surrenders to Cortés; Aztec Empire falls to Spaniards.
1050–1250	Height of influence of Cahokia. Prevalence of Mississippian culture in modern midwestern and southeastern United States.	**1524**	Verrazzano sails along Atlantic coast of the United States.
		1534–35	Cartier explores the St. Lawrence River.
1300s	Aztecs rise to power.	**1534–36**	Vaca, Estevan, and two companions walk across North America.
1450s–80s	Portuguese explore and colonize islands in the Mediterranean Atlantic and São Tomé in Gulf of Guinea.	**1539–42**	de Soto explores the southeastern United States.
		1540–42	Coronado explores the southwestern United States.
1477	Publication of Marco Polo's *Travels*, describing China.	**1587–90**	Raleigh's Roanoke colony vanishes.
1492	Columbus reaches the Bahamas.	**1588**	Harriot publishes *A Briefe and True Report of the New Found Land of Virginia*.

colonies that would become the United States must be seen in this context of European exploration and exploitation.

The continents that European sailors reached in the late fifteenth century had their own histories, which the intruders largely ignored. The residents of the Americas were the world's most skillful plant breeders; they developed vegetable crops more nutritious and productive than in Europe, Asia, or Africa. They invented systems of writing and mathematics. As in Europe, their societies rose and fell as leaders succeeded or failed in expanding their power. But the arrival of Europeans immeasurably altered Americans' struggles with one another.

After 1400 European nations tried to acquire valuable colonies and trading posts around the world. Initially interested in Asia and Africa, Europeans eventually focused on the Americas. Even as Europeans slowly achieved dominance, their fates were shaped by Americans and Africans. In the Americas of the fifteenth and sixteenth centuries, three old worlds came together to produce a new.

- **What were the key characteristics of the three worlds that met in the Americas?**
- **What impact did their encounter have on each of them?**
- **What were the crucial initial developments in that encounter?**

AMERICAN SOCIETIES

Human beings originated on the continent of Africa, where humanlike remains about 3 million years old have been found in what is now Ethiopia. Over many millennia, the growing population dispersed to other continents. Because the climate was far colder than it is now, much of the earth's water was concentrated in huge rivers of ice called glaciers. Sea levels were lower, and land masses covered a larger proportion of the earth's surface. Scholars long believed that the earliest inhabitants of the Americas crossed a land bridge known as Beringia (at the site of the Bering Strait) approximately 12,000 to 14,000 years ago. Yet new archaeological discoveries suggest that parts of the Americas may have been settled earlier, possibly in three successive waves beginning 30,000 years ago. When, about 12,500 years ago, the climate warmed and sea levels rose, Americans were separated from the connected continents of Asia, Africa, and Europe.

Ancient America

The first Americans are called Paleo-Indians. Nomadic hunters of game and gatherers of wild plants, they spread throughout North and South America, probably as bands of extended families. By about 11,500 years ago the Paleo-Indians were making stone projectile points, which they attached to wooden spears to kill and butcher bison (buffalo), woolly mammoths, and other large mammals. But as the Ice Age ended and the human population increased, all the large American mammals except the bison disappeared.

Consequently, by approximately 9,000 years ago, the residents of what is now central Mexico began cultivating food crops, especially maize (corn), squash, beans, avocados, and peppers. As knowledge of agricultural techniques improved, vegetables proved a more reliable food source than hunting and gathering. Most Americans adopted a sedentary life so they could tend fields regularly. Some established permanent settlements; others moved several times a year among fixed sites. They cleared forests through controlled burning, which created cultivable lands by killing trees and fertilizing the soil with ashes and also opened meadows for deer and other wildlife. Although they traded such items as shells, flint, salt, and copper, none of the American cultures became dependent on other groups for survival.

Wherever agriculture dominated, civilizations flourished. With steady supplies of grains and vegetables, such societies could broaden their focus from subsistence to trade, accumulating wealth, producing ornamental objects, and creating elaborate rituals. In North America, the cultivation of nutritious crops seems to have led to the development of all the major civilizations: first the large city-states of Mesoamerica (modern Mexico and Guatemala) and then the urban clusters known collectively as the Mississippian culture (in present-day United States). Each later collapsed after reaching the limits of its food supply.

Mesoamerican Civilizations

Scholars know little about the first major Mesoamerican civilization, the Olmecs, who about 4,000 years ago lived in cities near the Gulf of Mexico. The Mayas and Teotihuacán, which developed approximately 2,000 years later, are better recorded. Teotihuacán, founded in the Valley of Mexico about 300 B.C.E. (Before the Common

Era), became one of the largest urban areas in the world with 100,000 people in the fifth century C.E. (Common Era). Pilgrims traveled long distances to visit Teotihuacán's impressive pyramids and the great temple of Quetzalcoatl—the feathered serpent, primary god of central Mexico.

On the Yucatán Peninsula, in today's eastern Mexico, the Mayas built urban centers containing pyramids and temples, studied astronomy, and created an elaborate writing system. Their city-states engaged in near-constant warfare with one another, which, combined with inadequate food supplies, caused the collapse of the most powerful cities by 900 C.E. and ended the classic era of Mayan civilization.

Pueblos and Mississippians

Ancient native societies in what is now the United States learned to grow maize, squash, and beans from Mesoamericans. The Hohokam, Mogollon, and ancient Pueblo peoples of the modern states of Arizona and New Mexico subsisted by combining hunting and gathering with agriculture in an arid region with unpredictable rainfall. Hohokam villagers constructed extensive irrigation systems, but relocated when water supplies failed. Between 900 and 1150 C.E., Chaco Canyon, at the juncture of perhaps 400 miles of roads, served as a trading and processing center for turquoise. Yet aridity caused the Chacoans to migrate to other sites.

Almost simultaneously, the unrelated Mississippian culture flourished in what is now the midwestern and southeastern United States. Relying largely on maize, squash, nuts, pumpkins, and venison, the Mississippians lived in settlements organized hierarchically. Their largest urban center was the City of the Sun (now called Cahokia), near modern St. Louis. Located on rich farmland near the confluence of the Illinois, Missouri, and Mississippi Rivers, Cahokia was a focal point for religion and trade. At its peak (in the eleventh and twelfth centuries C.E.), the City of the Sun covered more than 5 square miles and had a population of about twenty thousand—small by Mesoamerican standards but larger than other northern communities or London.

The sun-worshipping Cahokians developed an accurate calendar. The city's main pyramid, today called Monks Mound, remains the largest earthwork ever built in the Americas. Yet following 1250 C.E. the city was abandoned, and archaeologists believe that climate change and the degradation of the environment, caused by overpopulation and the destruction of nearby forests, contributed to its collapse.

Aztecs

Aztec histories tell of its peoples' migration into the Valley of Mexico during the twelfth century. They record that their primary deity, Huitzilopochtli—a war god represented by an eagle—directed them to establish their capital on an island where they saw an eagle eating a serpent. That island city became Tenochtitlán, the center of a society composed of hereditary classes of warriors, merchants, priests, common folk, and slaves.

The Aztecs (who called themselves Mexica) conquered their neighbors, forcing them to pay tribute in textiles, gold, foodstuffs, and human sacrifices to Huitzilopochtli. They also engaged in ritual combat for further sacrificial victims. In the Aztec year Ten Rabbit (1502), at the coronation of Motecuhzoma II (the Spaniards mispronounced his name as Montezuma), thousands were sacrificed by having their hearts torn from their bodies.

NORTH AMERICA IN 1492

Over the centuries, the Americans who lived north of Mexico adapted their once-similar ways of life to different climates and terrains, thus creating the diverse culture areas that the Europeans encountered (see Map 1.1). Scholars often refer to such culture areas by language group (such as Algonquian or Iroquoian). Bands that lived in environments not suited to agriculture followed a nomadic lifestyle typified by the Paiutes and Shoshones, who inhabited the Great Basin (now Nevada and Utah). Because finding sufficient food was difficult, hunter-gatherer bands were small, usually composed of one or more related families. Where large game was plentiful, as in present-day central and western Canada and the Great Plains, bands were somewhat larger.

In favorable environments, larger groups like the Chinooks of present-day coastal Washington and Oregon combined agriculture with gathering, hunting, and fishing. Residents of the interior (for example, the Arikaras of the Missouri River valley) hunted large animals while cultivating maize, squash, and beans. The peoples of contemporary eastern Canada and the northeastern United States combined hunting, fishing, and agriculture.

Gendered Division of Labor

Societies that relied primarily on hunting large animals, such as deer and bison, assigned that task to men, allotting food preparation and clothing production to women. Before acquiring horses from the Spaniards, women—occasionally assisted by dogs—carried the family's belongings whenever their band relocated. The sexual division of labor was universal among hunting peoples. Yet agricultural societies assigned work in divergent ways. The Pueblo peoples defined agricultural labor as men's work. In the east, clusters of peoples speaking Algonquian, Iroquoian, and Muskogean languages allocated most agricultural chores to women, although men cleared the land. In farming societies, women gathered wild foods and prepared food for consumption or storage, where men were responsible for hunting.

Almost universally, women cared for young children, while older youths learned adult skills from their same-sex parent. Children enjoyed a lot of freedom. Young people chose their own marital partners, and in most societies couples could easily divorce. Infants and toddlers were nursed until the age of two or older, and taboos prevented couples from having sexual intercourse during that period.

Social Organization

Similarly, southwestern and eastern agricultural peoples lived in villages, sometimes with a thousand or more inhabitants. The Pueblos resided in multistory buildings constructed on terraces along the sides of cliffs or other easily defended sites. Northern Iroquois villages (in modern New York State) were composed of large, rectangular, bark-covered structures, or long houses; the name Haudenosaunee, which the Iroquois called themselves, means "People of the Long House." In the present-day southeastern United States, Muskogeans and southern Algonquians lived in large thatched houses. Most of the eastern villages were surrounded by wooden palisades and ditches to fend off attackers.

GREENLAND

Bering Strait

ARCTIC

Baffin Island

Davis Strait

ARCTIC

SUB-ARCTIC

NORTHWEST COAST

SUB-ARCTIC

PLATEAU

PACIFIC
OCEAN

GREAT
PLAINS

NORTHEAST

ATLANTIC
OCEAN

GREAT
BASIN

PRAIRIES

CALIFORNIA

SOUTHEAST

SOUTHWEST

NORTHEAST
MEXICO

CARIBBEAN

MESOAMERICA

Primary mode of subsistence:
- Agriculture
- Hunting
- Hunting-gathering
- Fishing

Map 1.1   Native Cultures of North America

The natives of the North American continent effectively used the resources of the regions in which they lived. As this map shows, coastal groups relied on fishing, residents of fertile areas engaged in agriculture, and other peoples employed hunting (often combined with gathering) as their primary mode of subsistence.

Jacques Le Moyne, an artist accompanying the French settlement in Florida in the 1560s, produced some of the first European images of North American peoples. His depiction of native agricultural practices shows the gendered division of labor: men breaking up the ground with fish-bone hoes before women drop seeds into the holes. But Le Moyne's version of the scene cannot be accepted uncritically: Unable to abandon a European view of proper farming methods, he erroneously drew plowed furrows in the soil.   (Collection of Mary Beth Norton)

In all agricultural societies, each dwelling housed an extended family defined matrilineally (through a female line of descent). Mothers, their married daughters, and their daughters' husbands and children lived together. Matrilineal descent did not imply matriarchy, or the wielding of power by women, but denoted kinship and linked extended families into clans. The nomadic bands of the Prairies and Great Plains were most often related patrilineally (through the male line).

War and Politics

Long before Europeans arrived, residents fought one another for control of the best hunting and fishing territories, the most fertile agricultural lands, or the sources of essential items, such as salt (for preserving meat) and flint (for making knives and arrowheads). Bands of Americans protected by wooden armor literally stood face to face in battle, because their clubs and throwing spears were only effective at close quarters. They began to shoot arrows from behind trees only when they confronted

European guns. Captives were sometimes enslaved, but slavery was never an important labor source in pre-Columbian America.

Political structures varied considerably. Among Pueblos, the village council, composed of ten to thirty men, was the highest political authority; no government structure connected the villages. The Iroquois had an elaborate system incorporating villages into nations and nations into a confederation. A council comprising representatives from each nation made the crucial decisions of war and peace. Women more often assumed leadership roles among agricultural peoples than among nomadic hunters. Female sachems (rulers) led Algonquian villages in what is now Massachusetts, but women never became heads of hunting bands. Iroquois women did not become chiefs, yet older women chose the village chief and could both start wars (by calling for the capture of prisoners to replace dead relatives) and stop them (by refusing to supply warriors with foodstuffs).

Religion
All the American peoples were polytheistic, worshiping a multitude of gods. The major deities of agricultural peoples like the Pueblos and Muskogeans were associated with cultivation, and festivals centered on planting and harvest. The important gods of hunters like those on the Great Plains and Prairies were associated with animals. Women held the most prominent religious positions in agricultural societies where they were also the chief food producers, whereas in hunting societies men took the lead in religious and political affairs.

A variety of cultures, comprising more than 10 million people speaking over one thousand different languages, inhabited America north of Mexico when Europeans arrived. The hierarchical kingdoms of Mesoamerica bore little resemblance to the nomadic hunting societies of the Great Plains or to the agriculturalists of the Northeast or Southwest. They did not consider themselves one people, nor did they think of uniting to repel European invaders.

AFRICAN SOCIETIES

Fifteenth-century Africa housed a variety of cultures. In the north, along the Mediterranean Sea, lived the Berbers, who were Muslims, or followers of the Islamic religion. On the east coast of Africa, Muslim city-states engaged in extensive trade with India, the Moluccas (part of modern Indonesia), and China. Sustained contact and intermarriage among Arabs and Africans created the Swahili language and culture. Waterborne commerce passed between the eastern Mediterranean and East Asian city-states; land commerce followed the Silk Road, the long land route across Central Asia.

South of the Mediterranean coast in the African interior lie the great Saharan and Libyan Deserts. The introduction of the camel in the fifth century C.E. made long-distance travel possible, and as Islam expanded after the ninth century, commerce controlled by Muslim merchants helped spread similar religious and cultural ideas throughout the region. Below the deserts, the continent is divided between tropical rain forests (along the coasts) and grassy plains (in the interior). South of the Gulf of Guinea, the grassy landscape came to be dominated by Bantu-speaking peoples, who left their homeland in modern Nigeria about two thousand years ago.

West Africa (Guinea)

West Africa was a land of tropical forests and savanna grasslands where fishing, cattle herding, and agriculture supported the inhabitants for at least ten thousand years before Europeans arrived in the fifteenth century. The northern region of West Africa, or Upper Guinea, was heavily influenced by the Islamic culture of the Mediterranean. Trade via camel caravans between Upper Guinea and the Muslim Mediterranean was sub-Saharan Africa's major connection to Europe and West Asia. In return for salt, dates, silk, and cotton cloth, Africans exchanged ivory, gold, and slaves.

Upper Guinea runs northeast-southwest from Cape Verde to Cape Palmas. The people of its northernmost region, the so-called Rice Coast (present-day Gambia, Senegal, and Guinea), fished and cultivated rice in coastal swamplands. The Grain Coast, the next region to the south, was thinly populated and, with only one good harbor (modern Freetown, Sierra Leone), was not easily accessible from the sea. Its people concentrated on farming and raising livestock.

In Lower Guinea, south and east of Cape Palmas, most Africans were farmers who practiced traditional religions. Believing that spirits inhabited particular places, they developed rituals intended to ensure good harvests. With individual villages linked into hierarchical kingdoms, decentralized political and social authority characterized the region at the time of initial European contact.

Complementary Gender Roles

Like American society, West African societies assigned different tasks to men and women. In general, the sexes shared agricultural duties. Men also hunted, managed livestock, and did most of the fishing. Women were responsible for childcare, food preparation, manufacture, and trade. They managed local and regional networks through which families, villages, and small kingdoms exchanged goods.

Lower Guinea had similar social systems organized on the basis of what anthropologists have called the dual-sex principle. Each sex handled its own affairs: male political and religious leaders governed men; females ruled women. Many West African societies practiced polygyny (one man's having several wives, each of whom lived separately with her children). Thus few adults lived permanently in marital households, but the dual-sex system ensured that their actions were scrutinized by their own sex.

Throughout Guinea, religious beliefs stressed complementary male and female roles. Both women and men served as heads of the cults and secret societies that directed village spiritual life. Young women were initiated into the Sandé cult, young men into Poro. Although West African women rarely held formal power over men, female religious leaders governed their sex within the Sandé cult, enforcing conformity to accepted norms.

Slavery in Guinea

West African law recognized individual and communal land ownership, but men seeking wealth needed labor—wives, children, or slaves—who could work the land. West Africans enslaved for life were vital to the economy. Africans could be enslaved for criminal acts, but more often slaves were enemy captives or people who enslaved themselves or their children in payment for debts. An African slave owner had the right to the products of a slave's labor, although slave status did not always descend to the next generation. Some slaves were held as chattel, and whatever they produced belonged entirely to slave owners; others could trade in products raised in their spare time, retaining a portion of their profits; and still others achieved prominent political or military positions. All, however, could be traded at the will of their owners.

West Africans were agricultural peoples, skilled at tending livestock, hunting, fishing, and manufacturing cloth. Both men and women enjoyed an egalitarian relationship and worked communally in family groups or with members of their sex. Carried as captives to the Americas, they became essential laborers for European settlers who showed little respect for their traditions.

EUROPEAN SOCIETIES

In the fifteenth century, European society was also largely agricultural. In the hierarchical European societies, a few families wielded autocratic power over the majority. English society was organized as a series of interlocking hierarchies; that is, each person (except those at the very top or bottom) was superior to some, inferior to others. At the bottom were people held in bondage. Although Europeans were not subjected to perpetual slavery, Christian doctrine permitted the enslavement of "heathens" (non-Christians) and serfdom, which tied some Europeans to the land or to specific owners. In short, Europe's kingdoms resembled those of Africa or Mesoamerica but differed from the more egalitarian societies found in America north of Mexico.

Work, Politics, and Religion

Most Europeans, like most Africans and Americans, lived in small villages. European farmers, called peasants, owned or leased separate landholdings but worked the fields communally. Because fields had to lie unplanted every second or third year to regain fertility, a family could not be assured of food unless all villagers shared the work and the crops. Men did fieldwork; women helped at planting and harvest. In some regions men concentrated on herding livestock. Women's duties consisted primarily of childcare and household tasks, including preserving food, milking cows, and caring for poultry. If a woman's husband was a city artisan or storekeeper, she might assist him in business. Because Europeans kept domesticated animals (pigs, goats, sheep, and cattle) for meat, hunting had little economic importance and was primarily a sport for male aristocrats.

Men dominated European society. A few women—notably Queen Elizabeth I of England—achieved power by birthright, but most were excluded from positions of political authority. They also held inferior social, religious, and economic positions, yet wielded power over children and household servants. European children were tightly controlled and subjected to harsh discipline.

Christianity was the dominant European religion. In the West, authority rested in the Catholic Church, based in Rome and led by the pope, who directed a male clergy. Although Europeans were nominally Catholic, many adhered to local belief systems that the church deemed heretical. Still, Europe's Christian nations from the twelfth century on publicly united to drive nonbelievers (especially Muslims) from their domains and from the holy city of Jerusalem, triggering a series of wars known as the Crusades. Nevertheless, in the fifteenth century Muslims dominated the commerce and geography of the Mediterranean, especially after they conquered Constantinople (capital of the Christian Byzantine empire) in 1453. Few would have predicted that Christian Europeans would ever pose a challenge.

Effects of Plague and Warfare

When the fifteenth century began, European nations were recovering from the devastating Black Death epidemic, which seems to have reached Europe from China, brought by traders. The disease recurred with severity in the 1360s and 1370s. Although the impact of the Black Death varied regionally, the best estimate is that one-third of Europe's people died. A precipitous economic decline followed, as did severe social, political, and religious disruption.

As plague ravaged the population, England and France waged the Hundred Years' War (1337–1453), initiated because English monarchs claimed the French throne. The war interrupted overland trade routes connecting England and Antwerp (in modern Belgium) to Venice, a Christian trading center, and thence to India and China. Needing a new way to reach their northern trading partners, eastern Mediterranean merchants forged a maritime route to Antwerp. Using a triangular, or lateen, sail (rather than square rigging) improved ships' maneuverability, enabling vessels to sail from the Mediterranean and north around the European coast. The perfection of navigational instruments like the astrolabe and the quadrant allowed sailors to estimate their position (latitude) by measuring the relationship of the sun, moon, or certain stars to the horizon.

Political and Technological Change

After the Hundred Years' War, European monarchs consolidated their political power and raised revenues through increased taxation of an already hard-pressed peasantry. In England, Henry VII in 1485 founded the Tudor dynasty and began uniting a previously divided land. In France, Charles VII's successors unified the kingdom. Most successful were Ferdinand of Aragón and Isabella of Castile; in 1492 they defeated the Muslims, who had lived in Spain and Portugal for centuries, and established a strongly Catholic Spain by expelling Jews and Muslims.

The fifteenth century also brought technological change to Europe. Movable type and the printing press, invented in Germany in the 1450s, made information more accessible, including information in books about fabled lands across the seas. The most important was Marco Polo's *Travels,* published in 1477, which recounted a Venetian merchant's adventures in thirteenth-century China and described that nation as bordered on the east by an ocean. That led Europeans to believe they could reach China by sea. A transoceanic route, if it existed, would allow northern Europeans to circumvent the Muslim and Venetian merchants who controlled their access to Asian goods.

Motives for Exploration

Technological advances and newly powerful national rulers made possible the European explorations of the fifteenth and sixteenth centuries. Each country craved easy access to African and Asian goods—silk, dyes, perfumes, jewels, sugar, gold, and especially spices, which were desirable for seasoning food and as possible medicines.

Their allure stemmed largely from their rarity, their extraordinary cost, and their mysterious origins. They passed through so many hands en route to London or Seville that no European knew exactly where they came from. Acquiring products directly would improve a country's income and its standing relative to other countries.

Spreading Christianity around the world supplemented the economic motive. Fifteenth-century Europeans saw no conflict between materialistic and spiritual goals. Explorers and colonizers—especially Roman Catholics—sought to convert "heathen" peoples and also hoped to increase their nation's wealth via direct trade with Africa, China, India, and the Moluccas.

EARLY EUROPEAN EXPLORATIONS

To reach Asia, seafarers also required knowledge of the sea, its currents and winds. Wind would power their ships. But where would Atlantic breezes carry their square-rigged ships, which needed the wind directly behind the vessel?

Sailing in the Mediterranean Atlantic The answers would be found in the Mediterranean Atlantic, the expanse of the Atlantic Ocean south and west of Spain and bounded by the Azores (on the west) and the Canaries (on the south), with the Madeiras in their midst. Europeans reached all three sets of islands during the fourteenth century. Sailing to the Canaries from Europe was easy because strong Northeast Trade winds blew southward along the Iberian and African coastlines. The voyage took just a week.

The Iberian sailor attempting to return home from the Canaries, however, faced a major obstacle: the winds now blew directly at him. Rowing and tacking back and forth against the wind were tedious and ineffectual. So, mariners began sailing "around the wind"—literally, sailing as directly against the wind as possible without being forced to tack. In the Mediterranean Atlantic, a mariner would head northwest into the open ocean until—weeks later—he reached the winds that would carry him home, the so-called Westerlies.

This solution became the key to successful exploration of both the Atlantic and the Pacific Oceans. Faced with a contrary wind, a sailor just sailed around it until he found a wind to carry him in the proper direction.

Islands of the Mediterranean Atlantic During the fifteenth century, Iberian sailors regularly visited the three island groups. The uninhabited Azores were settled by Portuguese migrants who raised wheat for sale in Europe and sold livestock to passing sailors. By the 1450s Portuguese colonists who settled the uninhabited Madeiras were employing slaves (probably Jews and Muslims brought from Iberia) to grow sugar for export. By the 1470s Madeira had developed into a colonial plantation economy. For the first time in history, a region had been settled explicitly to cultivate a valuable crop—sugar—for sale elsewhere. Because the work was so backbreaking, only a supply of enslaved laborers (who could not quit) could ensure the system's success.

The Canaries had indigenous residents—the Guanche people, who traded animal skins and dyes with Europeans. After 1402 the French, Portuguese, and Spanish sporadically attacked the islands. The Guanches resisted but were weakened by

European diseases. The seven islands fell to Europeans, who carried Guanches as slaves to the Madeiras or the Iberian Peninsula. Spain conquered the last island in 1496 and devoted it to sugar plantations.

Portuguese Trading Posts in Africa

For other Europeans, the islands of the Mediterranean Atlantic were stepping-stones to Africa. In 1415 Portugal seized control of Ceuta, a Muslim city in North Africa (see Map 1.2). Prince Henry the Navigator, son of King John I of Portugal, dispatched ships southward along the African coast, attempting to discover an oceanic route to Asia. Not until after his death did Bartholomew Dias round the southern tip of Africa (1488) and Vasco da Gama finally reach India (1498), where at Malabar he located the richest source of peppercorns in the world.

Although West African states resisted European penetration of the interior, they let the Portuguese establish trading posts along their coasts. The African kingdoms charged the traders rent and levied duties on imports. The Portuguese gained, too, profiting from transporting African gold, ivory, and slaves to Europe. By bargaining with African masters to purchase slaves and carrying those bondspeople to Iberia, the Portuguese introduced black slavery to Europe.

Lessons of Early Colonization

In the 1480s the Portuguese colonized São Tomé, an island in the Gulf of Guinea. With Madeira at its sugar-producing capacity, the soil of São Tomé proved ideal, and plantation agriculture there expanded rapidly. Planters imported large numbers of slaves to work the cane fields, thus creating the first economy based primarily on the bondage of black Africans.

By the 1490s, Europeans had learned three key colonization lessons in the Mediterranean Atlantic. First, they learned how to transplant crops and livestock to exotic locations. Second, they discovered that native peoples could be conquered (like the Guanches) or exploited (like the Africans). Third, they developed a model of plantation slavery and a system for supplying many such workers. The stage was set for a pivotal moment in world history.

VOYAGES OF COLUMBUS, CABOT, AND THEIR SUCCESSORS

Christopher Columbus understood the lessons of the Mediterranean Atlantic. Born in 1451 in the Italian city-state of Genoa, this self-educated son of a wool merchant was by the 1490s an experienced sailor and mapmaker. Drawn to Portugal and its islands, especially Madeira, he voyaged at least once to the Portuguese outpost on the Gold Coast, where he became obsessed with gold and witnessed the economic potential of the slave trade.

Like all accomplished seafarers, Columbus knew the world was round. But he thought that China lay only 3,000 miles from the southern European coast. Thus, he argued, it would be easier to reach Asia by sailing west. Experts scoffed, accurately predicting that the two continents lay 12,000 miles apart. When Columbus in 1484 asked the Portuguese rulers to back his plan, they rejected what appeared to be a crazy scheme.

Map 1.2   European Explorations in America

In the century following Columbus's voyages, European adventurers explored the coasts and parts of the interior of North and South America.

Columbus's Voyage

Jealous of Portugal's successes in Africa, Ferdinand and Isabella of Spain agreed to finance Columbus's risky voyage. In part they hoped the profits would pay for a new expedition to conquer Muslim-held Jerusalem. On August 3, 1492, in command of three ships—the *Pinta,* the *Niña,* and the *Santa Maria*—Columbus sailed from the Spanish port of Palos.

Just over two months later, the vessels found land approximately where Columbus had predicted (see Map 1.2). On October 12, he and his men landed on an island in the Bahamas, which its inhabitants called Guanahaní but he renamed San Salvador. Later he explored the islands now known as Cuba and Hispaniola, which their residents, the Taíno people, called Colba and Bohío. Because he thought he had reached the East Indies, Columbus referred to the inhabitants as Indians.

Columbus's Observations

Three themes predominate in Columbus's log. First, he insistently asked the Taínos where he could find gold, pearls, and spices. They replied (via signs) that such products were on other islands, on the mainland, or in interior cities. He came to mistrust such answers, noting, "They will tell me anything I want to hear."

Second, Columbus wrote about the strange and beautiful plants and animals. His interest was not soley aesthetic. "There are many plants and trees here that could be worth a lot in Spain for use as dyes, spices, and medicines," he observed and planned to carry home "a sample of everything I can" for experts to examine.

Third, Columbus described the people, seizing some to take back to Spain. The Taínos were, he said, handsome, gentle, and friendly, though they told him of fierce people on nearby islands who raided their villages. Columbus believed the Taínos to be likely converts to Catholicism and potentially "good and skilled servants." Thus the records of the first encounter between Europeans and America revealed themes that would be of enormous significance for centuries. Europeans wanted to extract profits from the Americas by exploiting natural resources—plants, animals, and people. Columbus made three more voyages to the region, and until his death in 1506, he mistakenly believed he had reached Asia. Because the Florentine Amerigo Vespucci, who explored the South American coast in 1499, was the first to publish the idea that a new continent had been discovered, Martin Waldseemüller in 1507

This map, produced in 1489 by Henricus Marcellus, represents the world as Christopher Columbus knew it, for it incorporates information obtained after Bartholomew Dias, a Portuguese sailor, rounded the Cape of Good Hope at the southern tip of Africa in 1488. Marcellus did not try to estimate the extent of the ocean separating the west coast of Europe from the east coast of Asia.   (© British Library Board. All Rights Reserved. Add. 15760, f.68–f69v)

labeled the land America in his map (reproduced on page 00). By then, Spain, Portugal, and Pope Alexander VI had signed the Treaty of Tordesillas (1494), confirming Portugal's dominance in Africa—and later Brazil—in exchange for Spanish preeminence in the rest of the Americas.

Norse and Other Northern Voyagers

About the year 1001, Leif Ericsson and other Norse people sailed to North America across the Davis Strait, which separated their Greenland villages from Baffin Island (located northeast of Hudson Bay; see Map 1.1) by 200 nautical miles, settling at a site they named Vinland. Attacks by residents forced them out after a few years. In the 1960s, archaeologists determined that the Norse had established an outpost at what is now L'Anse aux Meadows, Newfoundland, but Vinland was probably located farther south.

Some historians argue that in the 1480s European sailors probably located the rich fishing grounds off the Newfoundland coast but kept the information secret. Fifteenth-century seafarers voyaged between the European continent, England, Ireland, and Iceland. The mariners who explored the region that would become the United States and Canada built on their knowledge.

The winds that the northern sailors confronted posed problems on their outbound journeys. But mariners soon learned that the strongest winds shifted southward during the winter and that, by departing from northern ports in spring, they could steer northward to catch easterly breezes. Thus, those taking the northern route usually reached America along the coast of what is now Maine or the Canadian Maritime Provinces.

John Cabot's Explorations

The European generally credited with "discovering" North America is Zuan Cabboto, known today as John Cabot. More precisely, Cabot brought to Europe the first formal knowledge of the northern continental coastline and claimed the land for England. Like Columbus, Cabot was a master mariner from the Italian city-state of Genoa. Calculating that England, which traded with Asia through a network of intermediaries, would be eager to sponsor exploratory voyages for a possible alternative route, he gained financial backing from King Henry VII. He sailed from Bristol in late May 1497, reaching his destination about a month later. Scholars disagree about the location of Cabot's landfall but recognize the importance of his month-long exploration of the coast of modern Newfoundland.

The voyages of Columbus, Cabot, and others brought the Eastern and Western Hemispheres together. The Portuguese explorer Pedro Álvares Cabral reached Brazil in 1500; Cabot's son Sebastian landed in North America in 1507; France financed Giovanni da Verrazzano in 1524 and Jacques Cartier in 1534; and in 1609 and 1610 Henry Hudson explored the North American coast for the Dutch West India Company. All were hoping to find the legendary, nonexistent "Northwest Passage" through the Americas, an easy route to Asia's riches. Although they did not plant colonies in the Western Hemisphere, their discoveries interested European nations in exploring North and South America.

SPANISH EXPLORATION AND CONQUEST

Only Spain began colonization immediately. On his second voyage in 1493, Columbus brought to Hispaniola seventeen ships loaded with twelve hundred men, seeds, plants, livestock, chickens, and dogs. The settlement named Isabela (in the modern Dominican Republic) and its successors became the staging area for the Spanish invasion of America.

Cortés and Other Explorers

At first, Spanish explorers fanned out around the Caribbean basin. In 1513 Juan Ponce de León reached Florida, and Vasco Núñez de Balboa crossed the Isthmus of Panama to the Pacific Ocean, followed by Pánfilo de Narváez and others who traced the Gulf of Mexico. In the 1530s and 1540s, conquistadores explored other regions claimed by Spanish monarchs. Francisco Vásquez de Coronado journeyed through the southwestern portion of what is now the United States while Hernán de Soto explored the Southeast. Francisco Pizarro, who ventured into western South America, acquired the richest silver mines in the world by conquering the Incas. But the most important conquistador was Hernán Cortés, who in 1521 seized control of the Aztec Empire.

Cortés landed a force on the Mexican mainland in 1519 to search for rumored wealthy cities. Near the coast, local Mayas presented him with young enslaved women. One of them, Malinche (whom the Spaniards baptized as a Christian and renamed Doña Marina), became Cortés's translator, bore him a son, Martín—one of the first *mestizos,* or mixed-blood children—and eventually married one of his officers.

Capture of Tenochtitlán

Traveling toward the Aztec capital, Cortés, with Malinche's help, recruited peoples whom the Aztecs had long subjugated. The Spaniards' strange beasts (horses, livestock) and noisy weapons (guns, cannon) awed their new allies. Yet the Spaniards, too, were awed. Years later, Bernal Díaz del Castillo recalled his first sight of Tenochtitlán: "We were amazed . . . on account of the great towers and cues [temples] and buildings rising from the water, and all built of masonry."

The Spaniards also brought smallpox to Tenochtitlán, transporting an epidemic that had begun on Hispaniola. The disease peaked in 1520, fatally weakening Tenochtitlán's defenders. Largely as a consequence, Tenochtitlán surrendered in 1521, and the Spaniards built Mexico City on its site while Cortés seized a treasure of gold and silver. Thus, the Spanish monarchs controlled the richest, most extensive empire Europe had known since ancient Rome.

Spanish Colonization

Spain established the model of colonization based on three major elements that other countries would later imitate. First, the Crown sought tight control over the colonies, imposing a hierarchical government that allowed little autonomy to American jurisdictions. That included carefully vetting and limiting prospective emigrants and insisting that colonies import all manufactured goods from Spain. Roman Catholic priests attempted to ensure their religious conformity.

Second, men constituted most of the first colonists. Although some Spanish women later immigrated to America, the men took primarily Indian—and later, African—women as wives or concubines, a development often encouraged by colonial administrators. They thereby began the racially mixed population that characterizes much of Latin America today.

Third, the colonies' wealth was based on the exploitation of the native population and slaves from Africa. Spaniards took over the autocratic rule once assumed by native leaders, who exacted labor and tribute from their subjects. Cortés established the *encomienda* system, which granted Indian villages to conquistadors as a reward for service, thus legalizing slavery in all but name.

In 1542, after an outcry from sympathetic Spaniards, a new legal code forbade the conquerors from enslaving Indians while still allowing them to collect money and goods from tributary villages. That, combined with the declining Indian population, led the *encomenderos* to import Africans as their controlled labor force. They employed Indians and Africans primarily in gold and silver mines, on sugar plantations, and on horse, cattle, and sheep ranches. African slavery was more common in the Greater Antilles (the major Caribbean islands) than on the mainland.

Many demoralized residents of Mesoamerica accepted the Christian religion brought to New Spain by Franciscan and Dominican friars. Spaniards leveled cities, constructing Roman Catholic cathedrals and monasteries on sites once occupied by Aztec, Incan, and Mayan temples. Indians were exposed to European customs and religious rituals designed to assimilate Catholic and pagan beliefs. Friars juxtaposed the cult of the Virgin Mary with that of the corn goddess, and the Indians melded aspects of their world-view with Christianity, in a process called syncretism. Thousands of Indians embraced Catholicism, at least partly because it was the religion of their new rulers.

Gold, Silver, and Spain's Decline

The New World's gold and silver, initially a boon, ultimately brought about the decline of Spain as a major power. China gobbled up roughly half of the total output of New World mines. In the 1570s, the Spanish dispatched silver-laden galleons annually from Acapulco (on Mexico's west coast) to trade at their new settlement at Manila, in the Philippines, which gained them easy access to luxury Chinese goods, such as silk and spices.

This unprecedented wealth led to rapid inflation, which caused Spanish products to be overpriced in international markets and imported goods to become cheaper in Spain. The once-profitable Spanish textile-manufacturing industry collapsed, as did many other businesses. The seemingly endless income from American colonies emboldened Spanish monarchs to spend lavishly on wars against the Dutch and the English.

Late-sixteenth- and early-seventeenth-century monarchs repudiated the state debt, wreaking havoc on national finances. When the South American gold and silver mines faltered in the mid-seventeenth century, Spain's economy crumbled, ending its international importance.

THE COLUMBIAN EXCHANGE

A mutual transfer of diseases, plants, and animals (called the Columbian Exchange by historian Alfred Crosby; see Figure 1.1) resulted directly from the European voyages of the fifteenth and sixteenth centuries and Spanish colonization. Many large mammals, such as cattle and horses, were native to the connected continents of Europe, Asia, and Africa, but the Americas had no domesticated beasts larger than llamas. Vegetable crops of the Americas—particularly maize, beans, squash, cassava, and potatoes—were more nutritious and produced higher yields than those of Europe and Africa. In time, native peoples learned to raise and consume European livestock, and Europeans and Africans planted and ate American crops. The diets of all three peoples were enriched, helping the world's population to double over the next three hundred years. About three-fifths of all crops cultivated worldwide today were first grown in the Americas.

Smallpox and Other Diseases

Diseases carried from Europe and Africa devastated the Americas. Indians fell victim to microbes that had long infested other continents, killing hundreds of thousands of Europeans but leaving survivors with some immunity. When Columbus landed on

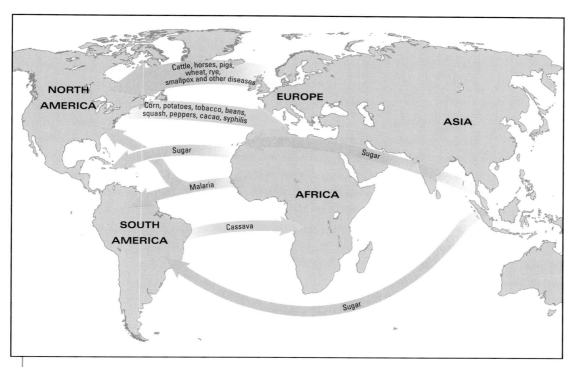

Figure 1.1 Major Items in the Columbian Exchange

As European adventurers traversed the world in the fifteenth and sixteenth centuries, they initiated the Columbian Exchange of plants, animals, and diseases. These events changed the lives of the peoples of the world forever, bringing new foods and new pestilence to both sides of the Atlantic.

Hispaniola in 1492, approximately half a million people resided there. Fifty years later, there were fewer than two thousand native inhabitants.

Although measles, typhus, influenza, malaria, and other illnesses severely afflicted native peoples, the greatest killer was smallpox. Historians estimate that over time, alien diseases could have reduced the precontact American population by as much as 90 percent. The epidemics recurred at twenty- to thirty-year intervals, appearing either in tandem or in quick succession. Large numbers of deaths further strained native societies, rendering them more vulnerable to droughts, crop failures or other challenges. A great epidemic, probably viral hepatitis, swept through the coastal villages north of Cape Cod from 1616 to 1618, wiping out up to 90 percent of the population. Because of this dramatic depopulation, a few years later English colonists were able to establish settlements virtually unopposed.

The Americans, however, probably gave the Europeans syphilis, a virulent venereal disease. The first recorded European case occurred in Barcelona, Spain, in 1493, after Columbus's return from the Caribbean. Although less likely than smallpox to be fatal, syphilis was debilitating. Carried by soldiers, sailors, and prostitutes, it spread through Europe and Asia, reaching China by 1505.

Sugar, Horses, and Tobacco
The exchange of three commodities significantly altered Europe and the Americas. The ravenous European demand for sugar, a luxury foodstuff, led Columbus to take Canary Island sugar canes to Hispaniola in 1493. By the 1520s, plantations in the Greater Antilles worked by African slaves regularly shipped sugar to Spain. Half a century later, Portugal's Brazil colony (founded in 1532) was producing sugar for the European market on a larger scale, and after 1640, sugar cultivation became the crucial component of English and French Caribbean colonization.

Horses—which Columbus brought to America in 1493—fell into the hands of North American Indians during the seventeenth century. Through trade and theft, horses spread among the peoples of the Great Plains by 1750. Lakotas, Comanches, and Crows, among others, used horses for transportation and hunting, calculated their wealth in number of horses owned, and waged war primarily on horseback. After acquiring horses, their mode of subsistence shifted from hunting various animals, combined with gathering and agriculture, to one based almost entirely on buffalo hunting.

In America, Europeans encountered tobacco, which at first they believed to be medicinal. Smoking and chewing the "Indian weed" became a European fad after it was planted in Turkey in the sixteenth century. Despite the efforts of King James I of England, who in 1604 pronounced smoking "hatefull to the Nose, harmfull to the brain, [and] dangerous to the Lungs," tobacco's popularity climbed.

EUROPEANS IN NORTH AMERICA

Europeans were initially more interested in exploiting North America's natural resources than in establishing colonies. John Cabot reported that fish were plentiful near Newfoundland, so the French, Spanish, and Portuguese rushed to take advantage of abundant codfish, which were prized in European markets. In the early 1570s, the English joined the Newfoundland fishery, selling salt cod to the Spanish

Maize

Maize, to Mesoamericans, was a gift from Quetzalcoatl, the plumed serpent god. Cherokees told of an old woman whose blood produced the prized stalks after her grandson buried her body in a field. For the Abenakis, the crop began when a beautiful maiden ordered a youth to drag her by the hair through a burned-over field. The long hair turned into silk, the flower on corn stalks. Both tales' symbolic association of corn and women supports archaeologists' recent suggestion that—in eastern North America at least—female plant breeders were responsible for substantial improvements in the productivity of maize.

Sacred to the Indian peoples who grew it, maize was a main part of their diet. They dried the kernels; ground into meal, maize was cooked as a mush or baked as flat cakes, the forerunners of modern tortillas. Although European invaders initially disdained maize, they soon learned that it could be cultivated under many conditions—from sea level to twelve thousand feet, from regions with abundant rainfall to dry lands. So Europeans, too, came to rely on corn, growing it in their American settlements and their homelands.

Maize cultivation spread to Asia and Africa. Today China is second only to the United States in corn production, and corn is more widely grown in Africa than any other crop. Still, the United States produces 45 percent of the world's corn, and it is the nation's single largest crop. More than half of American corn is consumed by livestock. Much of the rest is processed into syrup used as a sweetener or into ethanol, a gasoline additive that reduces both pollution and dependence on fossil fuels. Of the ten thousand products in a modern American grocery store, about one-fourth rely on corn. Currently this crop provides one-fifth of all the calories consumed by the earth's peoples.

TVRCICVM
FRVMENTVM.
Turckisch korn.

The earliest known European drawing of maize, the American plant that was to have such an extraordinary impact on the entire world.
(Typ 565.42.409 F[B], Department of Printing and Graphic Arts, Houghton Library, Harvard University Library)

in exchange for Asian goods. The English became dominant in the region, which by century's end was the focal point of valuable European commerce.

Trade Among Indians and Europeans

Fishermen quickly realized that they could increase profits by exchanging cloth and metal goods, such as pots and knives, for native trappers' beaver pelts, used to make fashionable hats in Europe. Initially, Europeans traded from ships along the coast. Later, male adventurers set up outposts on the mainland.

Indians similarly desired European goods that could make their lives easier and establish their tribal superiority. Some bands concentrated entirely on trapping for the European market and abandoned their traditional economies. The Abenakis of Maine, for example, trapped beaver to sell to French traders and became partially dependent on food supplied by their southern neighbors, the Massachusett tribe. In exchange, the Massachusetts sought European metal tools which they preferred over their handmade stone implements. The pelt trade wiped out beaver in some regions. The disappearance of their dams led to soil erosion, which later increased when European settlers cleared forests for farmland.

A watercolor by John White, an artist with Raleigh's second preliminary expedition (and who later was governor of the ill-fated 1587 colony). He identified his subjects as the wife and daughter of the chief of Pomeioc, a village near Roanoke. Note the woman's elaborate tattoos and the fact that the daughter carries an Elizabethan doll, obviously given to her by one of the Englishmen.   (© Trustees of the British Museum)

Contest Between Spain and England

In the mid-sixteenth century, English "sea dogs" like John Hawkins and Sir Francis Drake raided Spanish treasure fleets from the Caribbean. Their actions helped foment a war that in 1588 culminated in the defeat of the Spanish Armada off the English coast. English leaders started to consider planting colonies in the Western Hemisphere, thereby gaining better access to trade goods while preventing Spain from dominating the Americas.

The first English colonial planners hoped to reproduce Spanish successes by dispatching to America men who would exploit the native peoples for their nation's benefit. In the mid-1570s, a group that included Sir Walter Raleigh promoted a scheme to establish outposts that could trade with the Indians and provide bases for attacks on New Spain. Approving the idea, Queen Elizabeth I authorized Raleigh to colonize North America.

Roanoke

After two preliminary expeditions, in 1587 Sir Walter Raleigh sent 117 colonists to the territory he named Virginia, after Elizabeth, the Virgin Queen. They established a settlement on Roanoke Island, in what is now North Carolina, but in 1590 a resupply ship found the colonists had vanished, leaving only the word *Croatoan* (the name of a nearby island) carved on a tree. Recent tree-ring studies have shown that the North Carolina coast experienced a severe drought between 1587 and 1589 that may have led colonists to abandon Roanoke.

Harriot's *Briefe and True Report*

The reason becomes clear in Thomas Harriot's *A Briefe and True Report of the New Found Land of Virginia,* published in 1588. Harriot, a noted scientist traveling with the second voyage to Roanoke, revealed that, although explorers depended on villagers for food, they needlessly antagonized them by killing some of them for what Harriot admitted were unjustifiable reasons.

Harriot advised later colonizers to treat the native peoples more humanely. But his book's description of America's economic potential demonstrated why that advice would rarely be followed. Harriot stressed three points: the availability of familiar European commodities, such as grapes, iron, copper, and fur-bearing animals; the potential profitability of exotic American products, such as maize and tobacco; and the relative ease of manipulating the native population. Should the Americans resist, Harriot asserted, England's disciplined soldiers and superior weaponry would quickly deliver victory.

Harriot's *Briefe and True Report* depicted for English readers a bountiful land of profitable opportunities. The people residing there would, he thought, "in a short time be brought to civilitie" through conversion to Christianity, admiration for European superiority, or conquest—if they did not die from disease. But European dominance of North America was never fully achieved as Harriot and his compatriots intended.

Summary

Initial contact among Europeans, Africans, and Americans that ended near the close of the sixteenth century began approximately 250 years earlier when Portuguese sailors explored the Mediterranean Atlantic and the West African coast. Those seamen established commercial ties that brought African slaves first to Iberia and then to the islands the Europeans conquered and settled. The Mediterranean Atlantic and its island sugar plantations nurtured the mariners. Except for the Spanish, early explorers regarded the Americas primarily as a barrier blocking them from their goal of an oceanic route to the riches of China and the Moluccas. European fishermen were the first to realize that the northern coasts had valuable products of fish and furs to offer.

The Aztecs experienced hunger after Cortés's invasion, and their great temples were destroyed as the Spaniards used their stones (and Indian laborers) to construct cathedrals. The conquerors employed first American and later, enslaved African workers, to till the fields, mine the precious metals, and herd the livestock that generated immense profits.

The initial impact of Europeans on the Americas proved devastating in just decades. Europeans' diseases killed millions, and their livestock, along with other imported animals and plants, irrevocably modified the American environment. Europe, too, was changed: American foodstuffs like corn and potatoes improved nutrition, and American gold and silver first enriched, then ruined, the Spanish economy.

By the late sixteenth century, fewer people resided in North America than had lived there before Columbus's arrival. The Indians, Africans, and Europeans who lived there inhabited a new world that combined in unprecedented ways foods, religions, economies, ways of life, and political systems that had developed separately for millennia. Understandably, conflict permeated that process.

Kennewick Man/Ancient One

On July 28, 1996, Will Thomas, a college student wading in the Columbia River near Kennewick, Washington, felt a skull underfoot. Shocked, Thomas initially believed he had found a recent murder victim. Soon the skeleton was determined to be about 9,200 years old. During the next decade, the skeleton, dubbed Kennewick Man (by the press) or Ancient One (by local Indian tribes), was featured on television news shows and in magazines.

The oldest nearly complete skeleton found in the United States, the remains became the subject of a major federal court case. At issue was the interpretation of the Native American Graves Protection and Repatriation Act (NAGPRA), adopted by Congress in 1990 to prevent the desecration of Indian gravesites and to provide for the return of bones and sacred objects to native peoples. It defined the term *Native American* as "of, or relating to, a tribe, people, or culture that is indigenous to the United States." Led by the Umatillas, area tribes prepared to reclaim and rebury the remains. But eight anthropologists filed suit in federal court, contending that bones of such antiquity were unlikely to be linked to modern tribes and requesting access to them for scientific study.

Although the U.S. government supported the tribes' claims, in late August 2002 a federal judge ruled in favor of the anthropologists, in a decision upheld on appeal two years later. He declared that the Interior Department had erred in concluding that all pre-1492 remains found in the United States should automatically be considered Native American. The Umatillas protested, contending that he clearly contradicted Congress's intent in enacting NAGPRA. In June 2006 Umatilla leaders visited the bones at a Seattle museum to honor and pray for them.

The debate over the skeleton reveals one facet of the continuing legacy of the often-contentious relationship between the nation's indigenous inhabitants and later immigrants.

Chapter Review

AMERICAN SOCIETIES

What led to the development of major North American civilizations in the centuries before Europeans arrived?

Paleo-Indians were the first known people on the North American continent about 11,000 years ago. When the Ice Age ended, and the prevalence of mammals decreased, many native peoples in what is now central Mexico began cultivating food crops for survival, including maize (corn), squash, beans, avocados, and peppers. As agricultural methods improved, vegetables became a more reliable and nutritious food source, leading most early Americans to abandon nomadic ways and settle to tend crops. Agricultural success facilitated the rise of civilizations, since with steady food supplies, people could broaden their focus from farming to trade to accumulating wealth. Food supply, however, was so keenly linked to a civilization's success that the first large city-states of MesoAmerica and Mississippian culture later collapsed from lack of adequate food.

NORTH AMERICA IN 1492

What were the gender dimensions of native cultures?

Like Europeans, Native American societies assigned various tasks and responsibilities to members along gender lines. Societies that were predominantly hunting assigned women to making food and clothing. Agricultural peoples varied in their gendered division of labor; some, like the Pueblos, defined farming as men's work, while others, like the Algonquian, Iroquoian, and Muskogean, gave women most agricultural chores, and men hunted and cleared the land. Women just about everywhere raised children. Agricultural families were defined matrilineally, through the female line of descent, and women assumed more leadership roles than in nomadic hunter peoples. They never became chiefs, but older women chose chiefs and could start or stop wars.

AFRICAN SOCIETIES

What was the nature of slavery in Africa?

Slavery enabled upwardly mobile farmers to expand their labor force and potentially gain wealth. People became enslaved due to criminal acts, or more typically, either because they were captured by enemies or agreed to enslave themselves or family members to repay debts. Unlike the form of slavery that would develop in America, slave status did not always pass to the next generation. African slavery varied from complete chattel to allowing slaves to participate in trade or even achieve prominent military or political posts.

EUROPEAN SOCIETIES

What were the motives behind fifteenth and sixteenth century European explorations?

While technological advances and powerful rulers facilitated explorations, the driving force behind them was the quest for a transoceanic trade route that would provide direct access to African and Asian goods such as silks, dyes, jewels, sugar, gold, and spices. This would allow northern Europeans to bypass the Muslim and Venetian merchants who served as middle men for these items. Rulers also believed that the more they controlled access to these much-desired products, the better their nation's standing would be relative to other countries. The other motivation was to spread Christianity and convert those they considered to be heathen peoples.

EARLY EUROPEAN EXPLORATIONS

What lessons learned during early colonization would influence future European settlement in the sixteenth century?

By the end of the fifteenth century, Europeans learned how to transport crops and livestock to their exotic new world conquests. They recognized that native peoples could be conquered, exploited, and forced to labor. The Portuguese colony of Madeira was the first in history to be settled to cultivate a cash crop—

sugar—for exportation. This experience, and others like it, led to the creation of the plantation slavery model, as well as a system for supplying slave labor to do the backbreaking work of cultivating crops, without the ability to quit.

VOYAGES OF COLUMBUS, CABOT, AND THEIR SUCCESSORS

How did the voyages of Columbus, Cabot, and others inspire further exploration and settlement of what became America?

Explorers initially launched their expeditions partly seeking a northwest passage to Asia and partly hoping to discover gold, spices, and other riches they could claim for their sponsoring nations. Columbus, for example, found plants and trees that he envisioned Spain might use for dyes, spices, and medicines. He and many other explorers looked to America as a source of future profits, and their discoveries did indeed inspire further exploration by European nations, though for most, colonization would lag for generations.

SPANISH EXPLORATION AND CONQUEST

What model of colonization did Spain establish that other nations would later follow?

Spain sought immediately to colonize America and developed a model based on three key concepts that would later be adopted by other European colonizing nations. First, Spain's monarchy maintained firm control over its colonies with virtually no autonomy granted to American colonies. Second, men made up the majority of early colonists, taking first Indian, and later African, women as wives or concubines. Third, the development of the colonies and its subsequent wealth was based on exploiting native people and African slaves as labor.

THE COLUMBIAN EXCHANGE

What were the results of contact between native populations and European settlers and explorers?

Native Americans and Europeans exchanged diseases, plants, and animals when they came into contact on the North American continent in the fifteenth and sixteenth centuries. Native American vegetable crops were more nutritious than those in Europe and Africa, while Europeans brought livestock that helped enrich Indians' diets, too. The Spanish also brought horses to their American territories, which aided the shift in native society from hunting various animals combined with some farming and gathering, to almost exclusively hunting buffalo as their main form of subsistence. The exchange of diseases, however, had severe consequences. Europeans brought many diseases from typhus to malaria to hepatitis, all of which devastated tribal populations, but none as much as small pox. Dramatic Indian depopulation in what became New England enabled settlers to claim land and establish colonies almost uncontested. Europeans, meanwhile acquired syphilis from Native Americans, which was debilitating, but not usually fatal.

EUROPEANS IN NORTH AMERICA

What were the reasons behind the failure of England's, Portugal's, and France's initial attempts at colonization?

In a nutshell, all three failed because colonists were unable to be self-sustaining and at the same time, did little to diminish the hostility of native peoples. In fact, while many colonists relied on Indians for food, they also heightened animosities by antagonizing them or, as one British scientist wrote, killing some with little cause. Ironically, the solution this scientist, Thomas Harriot, proposed was on the one hand to treat native people with greater humanity, but on the other hand, to take advantage of the fact that they are easily manipulated toward whatever ends Europeans sought. And if they resisted, he recommended the use of military force, and he hoped conversion to Christianity would civilize them and make such conquest unnecessary.

SUGGESTIONS FOR FURTHER READING

Alfred W. Crosby, *The Columbian Exchange: Biological and Cultural Consequences of 1492* (1972)

John H. Elliott, *Empires of the Atlantic World: Britain and Spain in America, 1492–1830* (2006)

Alvin Josephy Jr., ed., *America in 1492* (1992)

Charles C. Mann, *1491: New Revelations of the Americas Before Columbus* (2005)

D. W. Meinig, *Atlantic America, 1492–1800* (1986)

Samuel Eliot Morison, *The Southern Voyages, A.D. 1492–1616* (1974); *The European Discovery of America: The Northern Voyages, A.D. 1500–1600* (1971)

John Thornton, *Africa and Africans in the Making of the Atlantic World, 1400–1680* (1992)

Europeans Colonize North America | 1600–1650

Captain William Rudyerd seemed like the sort of man Puritan colonies in the Americas would prize, so when his older brother urged planners of a new settlement to appoint him master general, they agreed. Rudyerd followed the dissenting English faith and vigorously trained the settlers to defend themselves. But he also vigorously defended his status and wreaked havoc in the fragile community. He beat to death a servant suffering from scurvy (who he thought was merely lazy) and quarreled with settlers, whom he believed failed to show him the respect due to a gentleman of noble birth.

One of Rudyerd's antagonists was the Reverend Lewis Morgan, with whom the captain argued about religious books and church services. Their disagreements escalated into insults. "Your foul-mouthed answer deserves rather sharp retribution than any equal respect from a gentleman," the captain once haughtily told the minister.

Similar conflicts occurred elsewhere, as gentlemen accustomed to unquestioning deference learned that in the colonies their social standing could be challenged. But in Rudyerd and Morgan's colony the disputes were especially dangerous because they lived on Providence Island, an isolated Puritan outpost off the coast of modern Nicaragua.

Providence Island, founded by Puritan adventurers in 1630—the same year as the Massachusetts Bay colony—sought to establish an English beachhead in the tropics as an entrée to colonizing the Central American mainland. Yet its perilous location amid Spanish settlements, failure to establish a local economy, and, ultimately, its desperate attempts to stay afloat by serving as a base for English privateers caused its downfall. The latter riled the Spaniards, who attacked in 1635 and 1640. In May 1641 a Spanish fleet of seven ships carrying two thousand

This icon will direct you to interactive activities and study materials on A People And A Nation, Brief Edition website: **www.cengage.com/history/norton/ peoplenationbrief8e**

Chronology

1533	Henry VIII divorces Catherine of Aragón. English Reformation begins.
1558	Elizabeth I becomes queen.
1565	St. Augustine (Florida), the oldest permanent European settlement in present-day United States, is founded.
1598	Oñate conquers the Pueblos in New Mexico for Spain.
1603	James I becomes king.
1607	Jamestown, the first permanent English settlement in North America, is founded.
1608	Quebec is founded by the French.
1610	Santa Fe, New Mexico, is founded.
1611	First Virginia tobacco crop is harvested.
1614	Fort Orange (Albany) is founded by the Dutch.
1619	Virginia House of Burgesses, the first representative assembly in the English colonies, is established.
1620	Plymouth colony, the first permanent English settlement in New England, is founded.

1622	Powhatan Confederacy attacks Virginia.
1624	Dutch settle on Manhattan Island (New Amsterdam).
	English colonize St. Kitts, the first island in Lesser Antilles to be settled by Europeans.
	James I revokes the Virginia Company's charter.
1625	Charles I becomes king.
1630	Massachusetts Bay colony is founded.
1634	Maryland is founded.
1636	Williams is expelled from Massachusetts Bay and founds Providence, Rhode Island.
	Connecticut is founded.
1637	Pequot War occurs in New England.
1638	Hutchinson is expelled from Massachusetts Bay and goes to Rhode Island.
ca. 1640	Sugar cultivation begins on Barbados.
1642	Montreal is founded by the French.
1646	Treaty ends hostilities between Virginia and Powhatan Confederacy.

soldiers and sailors captured the island, and survivors scattered to other Caribbean settlements, English mainland colonies, or back to England.

By this time, Spain no longer predominated in the Americas, and by the 1640s, France, the Netherlands, and England had permanent colonies in North America. The French and Dutch colonies, like the Spanish outposts, were settled largely by European men who interacted with indigenous peoples, using their labor or seeking to convert them to Christianity. Like the conquistadors, French and Dutch merchants (on the mainland) and planters (in the Caribbean) hoped to make a quick profit and perhaps return home. The English were similarly interested in profiting from North America, but pursued profits differently.

Unlike other Europeans, most English settlers came to stay. In the area that would later be known as New England, they arrived in family groups and re-created the European agricultural economy and family life to an extent impossible in colonies where single men predominated.

The first permanent English colonies survived because of contacts with nearby Indians. The settlers learned to grow such unfamiliar American crops as maize and squash. They also developed extensive trading relationships with native peoples and with other colonies. Needing field laborers, they first used English indentured servants, then African slaves. Thus the early history of the region that became the United States and the English Caribbean is best understood as a series of complex interactions among various European, African, and American peoples and environments.

The *history companion* powered by Eduspace®
Your primary source for interactive quizzes, exercises, and more to help you learn efficiently.
http://history.college.cengage.com/students

- Why did different groups of Europeans choose to migrate to the Americas?
- How did different native peoples react to their presence?
- In what ways did the English colonies in the Chesapeake and New England differ, and in what ways were they alike?

SPANISH, FRENCH, AND DUTCH NORTH AMERICA

Spaniards established the first permanent European settlement within the modern United States, but others had tried earlier. Twice in the 1560s Huguenots (French Protestants) escaping persecution planted colonies on the southern Atlantic coast. A passing ship rescued the starving survivors of the first, located in present-day South Carolina. The second, near modern Jacksonville, Florida, was destroyed in 1565 by a Spanish expedition commanded by Pedro Menéndez de Avilés, who sought Spanish domination of the strategically important region. Menéndez set up a small outpost, which he named St. Augustine—now the oldest continuously inhabited European settlement in the United States.

The local Guale and Timucua nations initially allied with the powerful newcomers and welcomed Franciscan friars. The relationship fractured quickly, as natives resisted Spanish authority. Still, the Franciscans offered the Indians spiritual solace for the diseases and troubles besetting them after the Europeans' invasion. Eventually they gained numerous converts across Florida and the islands along the Atlantic coast.

New Mexico   In 1598, drawn by rumors of rich cities, Juan de Oñate, a Mexican-born adventurer, led about five hundred soldiers and settlers to New Mexico. At first, the Pueblo peoples greeted them cordially. But when the Spaniards used torture, murder, and rape to extort food and clothing from the villagers, the residents of Acoma killed several soldiers, including Oñate's nephew, Juan de Zaldívar. The invaders responded ferociously, killing more than eight hundred people and capturing the remainder. All the captives above age twelve were enslaved for twenty years, and men older than twenty-five had one foot amputated. Other Pueblo villages surrendered.

Oñate's bloody victory proved illusory. New Mexico held little wealth and was too far from the Pacific coast to help protect Spanish sea-lanes. Many Spaniards returned to Mexico, and officials considered abandoning the isolated colony, which was 800 miles north of the nearest Spanish settlement. Instead, they maintained a small military outpost and a few Christian missions there, with the capital at Santa Fe (founded in 1610). As in southern regions, Spanish leaders were granted *encomiendas* guaranteeing them control over Pueblo villagers' labor. But in the absence of mines or fertile agricultural lands, such grants yielded little profit.

Quebec and Montreal   On the Atlantic coast, the French focused on the area that Jacques Cartier had explored in the 1530s. They tried to establish permanent bases along the Canadian coast but failed until 1605, when they founded Port Royal. In 1608 Samuel de Champlain set

TABLE 2.1 The Founding of Permanent European Colonies in North America, 1565–1640

Colony	Founder(s)	Date	Basis of Economy
Florida	Pedro Menéndez de Avilés	1565	Farming
New Mexico	Juan de Oñate	1598	Livestock
Virginia	Virginia Co.	1607	Tobacco
New France	France	1608	Fur trading
New Netherland	Dutch West India Co.	1614	Fur trading
Plymouth	Separatists	1620	Farming, fishing
Maine	Sir Ferdinando Gorges	1622	Fishing
St. Kitts, Barbados, et al.	European immigrants	1624	Sugar
Massachusetts Bay	Massachusetts Bay Company	1630	Farming, fishing, fur trading
Maryland	Cecilius Calvert	1634	Tobacco
Rhode Island	Roger Williams	1636	Farming
Connecticut	Thomas Hooker	1636	Farming, fur trading
New Haven	Massachusetts migrants	1638	Farming
New Hampshire	Massachusetts migrants	1638	Farming, fishing

up a trading post at an interior site that the Iroquois called Stadacona, which he renamed Quebec. It was the most defensible spot in the St. Lawrence River valley, a stronghold that controlled access to the continent's heartland. In 1642 the French established a second post, Montreal, at the falls of the St. Lawrence.

Previously, fishermen were the major transporters of North American beaver pelts to France, but the new posts quickly took over (see Table 2.1). Only a few Europeans resided in New France; most were men, and some married Indian women. The colony's leaders gave land grants along the river to wealthy seigneurs (nobles), who imported tenants to work their farms. A few Frenchmen brought their wives and took up agriculture; still, more than twenty-five years after Quebec's founding, it had just sixty-four resident families along with traders and soldiers. Northern New France never grew much beyond the river valley between Quebec and Montreal (see Map 2.1). Thus it differed from New Spain, characterized by scattered cities and direct supervision of Indian laborers.

Jesuit Missions in New France

Missionaries of the Society of Jesus (Jesuits), a Roman Catholic order dedicated to converting nonbelievers to Christianity, first arrived in Quebec in 1625. The Jesuits, whom the Indians called Black Robes, tried to persuade indigenous peoples to live near French settlements and adopt European agricultural methods. Failing that, they tried to introduce Catholicism without insisting that Indians fundamentally alter their traditions. Accordingly, the Black Robes learned Indian languages and traveled to remote regions, where they lived among hundreds of potential converts.

Jesuits sought to gain the confidence of influential men and to undermine the authority of village shamans, the traditional religious leaders. Immune to smallpox

Map 2.1   European Settlements and Indian Tribes in Eastern North America, 1650

The few European settlements established in the East before 1650 were widely scattered, hugging the shores of the Atlantic Ocean and the banks of its major rivers. By contrast, America's native inhabitants controlled the vast interior expanse of the continent, and Spaniards had begun to move into the West.

(having survived it already), Jesuits explained epidemics among the Indians as God's punishment for sin. It helped that shamans' traditional remedies proved ineffective against the new pestilence. Perhaps most important, they amazed the villagers by communicating with each other over long distances through marks on paper (letters). The Indians' desire to harness the extraordinary power of literacy made them receptive to the missionaries' spiritual message.

Over time, the Jesuits gained thousands of converts. Catholicism offered women the inspiring role model of the Virgin Mary, personified in Montreal and Quebec by communities of nuns who taught and ministered to Indian women and children. Many converts altered the native customs of premarital sexual relationships and easy divorce because Catholic doctrine prohibited both. Yet they resisted strict European child-rearing practices. Jesuits recognized that aspects of native culture could be compatible with Christianity. Their conversion efforts were further aided by their lack of interest in labor tribute or land.

New Netherland

Jesuit missionaries had little competition from other Europeans, but French fur traders faced direct challenges. In 1614, only five years after Henry Hudson explored the river that now bears his name, his sponsor, the Dutch West India Company, established an outpost (Fort Orange) at the site of present-day Albany, New York. The Dutch, too, sought beaver pelts, and their presence close to Quebec threatened French regional domination. The Netherlands, at the time the world's greatest commercial power, sought trade rather than colonization. Thus New Netherland remained small. The colony's southern anchor was New Amsterdam, founded in 1624 on Manhattan Island.

New Netherland was the small outpost of the Dutch West India Company's vast commercial empire extending to Africa, Brazil, the Caribbean, and modern-day Indonesia. Autocratic directors-general ruled the colony, garnering little loyalty. Even an offer in 1629 of large land grants, or patroonships, to anyone bringing fifty settlers to the province failed to attract takers. (Only one such tract—Rensselaerswyck, near Albany—was ever developed.) As late as the mid-1660s, New Netherland had only about five thousand inhabitants. Some were Swedes and Finns in the former colony of New Sweden (founded in 1638 on the Delaware River; see Map 2.1), which the Dutch took over in 1655.

Indian allies of New France and New Netherland clashed partly because of fur-trade rivalries. In the 1640s the Iroquois, who traded chiefly with the Dutch and lived in modern upstate New York, went to war against the Hurons, who traded primarily with the French and lived in present-day Ontario. The Iroquois wanted to become the major pelt supplier and safeguard their hunting territories. With guns supplied by the Dutch, they virtually exterminated the Hurons, whose population was already decimated by smallpox. The Iroquois thus established themselves as a major force in the region.

THE CARIBBEAN

In the first half of the seventeenth century, the Spanish concentrated on colonizing the Greater Antilles—Cuba, Hispaniola, Jamaica, and Puerto Rico. They ignored many smaller islands, partly because of resistance from inhabitants and partly

Wampum

Native North Americans highly valued small cylindrical beads made from whelk and quahog shells, known as wampum. For centuries, the white and purple beads were strung to make necklaces and ornamental belts, but with the Europeans' arrival, wampum became a currency.

Wampum's transformation occurred not only because the Indians would trade deerskins and beaver pelts for the beads but also because Dutch and English settlers lacked access to currency from their homelands. Wampum filled a need as a handy medium of exchange, especially in the early settlement decades.

Whelk (white) and quahog (purple) shells were found primarily along the shores of Long Island Sound, where Narragansetts, Montauks, Niantics, and other local peoples gathered them in summer. In winter, women fashioned the hard shells into beads, a time-consuming and skilled task. But Europeans' metal tools allowed a rapid increase in the quantity and quality of wampum. Some villages abandoned hunter-gatherer modes of subsistence and settled permanently in shell-rich areas to focus on the manufacture of wampum year-round.

Wampum played a key role in the early economies of New Netherland and New England. Dutch settlers in Manhattan traded such manufactured goods as guns, kettles, axes, or knives with the wampum makers, then used wampum to purchase furs and skins from the Iroquois. In 1627 Isaac de Rasière, a Dutch trader, introduced wampum to English colonists at Plymouth. Ten years later, the Massachusetts Bay colony made wampum legal tender for paying debts under 12 pennies, at a rate of six white beads or three purple beads to 1 penny. Wampum were often strung on thin cords in set amounts worth English equivalents from 1 penny to 5 shillings (60 pennies) in white beads, or 2 pennies to 10 shillings (120 pennies) in purple beads. Wampum became an initial, indispensable link in the commerce between Europe and North America.

Before Europeans arrived in North America, wampum—which required great skill to make—served primarily ceremonial purposes for native peoples, as in the Four Huron Nations wampum belt presented to Samuel de Champlain in 1611 to signify the alliance of France and the Hurons. But several decades later, after Dutch and English colonists came to rely on it as a medium of exchange and European tools made it easier to manufacture, wampum became far more utilitarian in design and appearance. (Right: Time Life Pictures/Getty Images; below: Image #18491 Wampum Beads by Craig Chesek, courtesy the Library, American Museum of Natural History)

because the mainland offered greater wealth for less effort. But the tiny islands attracted other European powers as bases from which to attack Spanish vessels loaded with American gold and silver and as sources of valuable tropical products such as dyes and fruits.

Warfare and Hurricanes

England was the first northern European nation to establish a permanent foothold in the smaller Caribbean islands (the Lesser Antilles), settling on St. Christopher (St. Kitts) in 1624, then on other islands, such as Barbados (1627) and Providence (1630). France colonized Guadeloupe and Martinique by defeating the Caribs, whereas the Dutch easily gained control of tiny St. Eustatius (strategically located near St. Kitts). Along with indigenous inhabitants, Europeans worried about conflicts with Spaniards and each other. Many colonies changed hands during the seventeenth century: the English drove the Spanish out of Jamaica in 1655, and the French soon assumed over half of Hispaniola, creating the colony of St. Domingue (modern Haiti).

Great windstorms, called *hurakán* by the Taíno people (hurricanes in English), also posed a danger. Almost every year in late summer one or two islands suffered significant hurricane damage. Survivors expressed awe at the destructive storms, which repeatedly forced them to rebuild and replant.

Sugar Cultivation

Sugar was the main reason Europeans sought control of these imperiled volcanic islands. Europeans loved sugar with its sweet taste and quick energy boost. Sugar entered Europe at approximately the same time as coffee and tea—the stimulating, addictive, and bitter Asian drinks improved by sweetening.

After experimenting with tobacco, cotton, and indigo, English residents of Barbados discovered in the early 1640s that the island's soil and climate were ideal for sugar cane. At the time, sugar came primarily from the Madeiras, the Canaries, São Tomé, and Brazil. Barbadians initially copied the Brazilians' machinery and small-scale production methods, which used servants and slaves. But by the mid-1650s, substantial planters increased the size of their landholdings, built sugar mills, and purchased more laborers.

Sugar remained the most valuable American commodity for more than a century. In the 1700s, sugar grown by slaves in British Jamaica and French St. Domingue dominated the world market. Yet, the future economic importance of the American colonies lay on the mainland, not the Caribbean.

ENGLISH INTEREST IN COLONIZATION

After Raleigh's Roanoke colony failed, it was two decades before the English attempted to settle North America again. When they tried in 1606, they found success using a settlement model unlike those of other European powers. England sent large numbers of men and women to set up agriculturally-based colonies on the mainland. Two major developments prompted approximately 200,000 English people to move to North America in the seventeenth century.

Social and Economic Change

The first was dramatic social and economic change. In the 150 years after 1530, largely as a result of nutritious American crops, England's population doubled. More people competed for food, clothing, and other goods; this led to inflation. Wages also fell as the supply of workers increased. Some English people—especially those with sizable landholdings that could produce food and clothing fibers for the growing population—gained substantially. Others, particularly landless laborers and those with small land holdings, fell into poverty. When landowners raised rents, seized lands that peasants had long used in common (enclosure), or combined small holdings into large units, they forced tenants out. Consequently, the population of cities swelled. London more than tripled in size to 375,000 by 1650.

Landless and homeless people filled the streets. Fearing overcrowding, officials concluded that colonies established in North America could siphon off England's "surplus population." Likewise, many English people hoped to improve their circumstances by migrating to a land-rich, apparently empty continent and its nearby islands. Similarly attracted were younger sons of gentlemen who were excluded from inheriting land by wealthy families' practice of primogeniture, which reserved all real estate for the eldest son.

English Reformation

The sixteenth century also witnessed a religious transformation that eventually led many English dissenters to leave. In 1533 Henry VIII, wanting a male heir and infatuated with Anne Boleyn, sought to annul his twenty-year marriage to Spanish-born queen Catherine of Aragón, despite the birth of a daughter. When the pope refused, Henry founded the Church of England and—with Parliament's concurrence—proclaimed himself its head. English people welcomed the schism, for many disliked the English Catholic Church. Initially, the reformed Church of England differed little from the Catholic Church, but under Henry's daughter Elizabeth I (child of his later marriage to Anne Boleyn), new currents of religious belief affected the English church.

These currents were the Protestant Reformation, led by Martin Luther, a German monk, and John Calvin, a French cleric and lawyer. Challenging the Catholic doctrine that priests were intermediaries between laypeople and God, Luther and Calvin insisted that people could interpret the Bible for themselves. They rejected Catholic rituals and the elaborate church hierarchy. They also asserted that the key to salvation was faith in God, rather than the Catholic combination of faith and good works. Calvin went further, stressing the need for total submission to God's will.

Puritans and Separatists

Elizabeth I tolerated diverse forms of Christianity as long as she was acknowledged as head of the Church of England. During her reign (1558–1603), Calvin's ideas gained influence. By the late sixteenth century, many English Calvinists—those who came to be called Puritans, because they wanted to purify the church, or Separatists, because they wanted to leave it—believed that the English Reformation had not gone far enough. Henry had simplified the church hierarchy; they wanted to abolish it. Henry had subordinated the church to the state; they wanted a church free from political interference. Puritans and Separatists wanted to confine church membership to persons they believed God had selected for salvation before birth.

Paradoxically, a key article of their faith insisted that people could not know if they were "saved" because mortals could not comprehend or affect their predestination to heaven or hell. Thus pious Puritans and Separatists daily confronted serious dilemmas: If one was predestined and could not alter one's fate, why attend church or do good works? They admitted that their judgments as to eligibility for church membership only approximated God's unknowable decisions. And they reasoned that God gave the elect the ability to accept salvation and lead a good life. Therefore, piety and good works could indicate one as saved.

Stuart Monarchs　Elizabeth I's Stuart successors, her cousin James I (1603–1625) and his son Charles I (1625–1649), exhibited less tolerance for Puritans and Separatists. As Scots, they also had little respect for the representative government that developed in England under the Tudors (see Table 2.2). Wealthy landowners in Parliament had grown accustomed to having considerable influence on government policies. But James I publicly declared the divine right of kings, the notion that a monarch's power came from God and that his subjects had a duty to obey him.

TABLE 2.2　Tudor and Stuart Monarchs of England, 1509–1649

Monarch	Reign	Relation to Predecessor
Henry VIII	1509–1547	Son
Edward VI	1547–1553	Son
Mary I	1553–1558	Half-sister
Elizabeth I	1558–1603	Half-sister
James I	1603–1625	Cousin
Charles I	1625–1649	Son

Both James I and Charles I sought to enforce religious conformity. Because Puritans, Separatists, and the remaining English Catholics challenged many important precepts of the English church, the Stuart monarchs authorized the removal of dissenting clergy. In the 1620s and 1630s, some English Puritans, Separatists, and Catholics decided to move to America, where they hoped to practice their religion freely. Some fled to avoid arrest and imprisonment.

THE FOUNDING OF VIRGINIA

The motivation for England's first permanent colony in the Western Hemisphere was, however, economic. A group of merchants and wealthy gentry in 1606 obtained a royal charter for the Virginia Company, organized as a joint-stock company. Such enterprises pooled the resources of many small investors through stock sales, spreading out the risks and typically providing quick returns. But colonies required significant capital and commonly suffered from a shortfall in financing. Although investors anticipated great profits, the joint-stock company, then as later, proved a poor vehicle for establishing colonies.

Jamestown and Tsenacomoco

In 1607 the Virginia Company dispatched 104 men and boys to a region near the Chesapeake Bay called Tsenacomoco by its native inhabitants. In May they established a settlement called Jamestown on a swampy peninsula in a river. Ill equipped for survival, the colonists fell victim to dissension and disease. The gentlemen and soldiers at Jamestown expected to rely on local Indians for food and tribute, but they refused. Moreover, the settlers arrived in the midst of a severe drought (now known to be the worst for 1,700 years), which persisted until 1612.

The weroance (chief) of Tsenacomoco, Powhatan, had inherited the rule over six Algonquian villages and subsequently controlled twenty-five others (see Map 2.1). In late 1607 negotiations with colonial leader Captain John Smith, the weroance tentatively agreed to an alliance with the Englishmen. In exchange for foodstuffs, Powhatan wanted guns, hatchets, and swords which would give him a technological advantage over his people's enemies.

The fragile relationship soon foundered on mutual mistrust. The wereoance relocated his primary village in early 1609 to a place the newcomers could not access easily. Without Powhatan's assistance, the settlement experienced a "starving time" (winter 1609–1610). Many died, and at least one colonist resorted to cannibalism. In spring 1610 the survivors left on a newly arrived ship but en route encountered a new governor, more settlers, and supplies, so they returned to Jamestown. To gain the upper hand, settlers in 1613 kidnapped Powhatan's daughter, Pocahontas. In captivity, she converted to Christianity and married colonist John Rolfe. He had fallen in love, but she probably married him for diplomatic reasons; their union initiated peace between the English and Powatans. Funded by the Virginia Company, she and Rolfe sailed to England to promote the colony. She died at Gravesend in 1616, leaving an infant son who returned to Virginia as a young adult.

Although their royal charter claimed a wider territory, the Jamestown settlers saw their Virginia as corresponding to Tsenacomoco. Beyond that lay the Powhatans' enemies. English people relied on the Powhatans as guides and interpreters in trading with the Powhatans' partners. For more than half a century, settlement in Virginia was confined to Tsenacomoco.

Algonquian and English Cultural Differences

In Tsenacomoco and elsewhere on the North American coast, English settlers and local Algonquians focused on their cultural differences, although both groups similarly held deep religious beliefs, subsisted primarily through agriculture, accepted social and political hierarchy, and observed well-defined gender roles. English men regarded Indian men as lazy because they did not cultivate crops and spent much of their time hunting (a sport, not work, in English eyes). Indian men thought English men effeminate because they did woman's work of cultivation.

Among Algonquians like Powhatans, political power and social status did not pass through the male line, instead flowing through sisters' sons. English gentlemen inherited their position from their father. English political and military leaders

tended to rule autocratically, whereas Algonquian leaders (even Powhatan) had limited authority over their people. Accustomed to powerful kings, the English overes-
timated the chiefs' ability to make treaties that would bind their people.

Furthermore, Algonquians and English had different notions of property ownership. Most Algonquian villages held their land communally. It could not be
bought or sold absolutely. English villagers had once used land in common, but in
the previous century had become accustomed to individual farms. The English also
refused to accept Indians' claims to traditional hunting territories, insisting that
only cultivated land could be owned or occupied. Ownership of such "unclaimed"
property, the English believed, lay with the English monarchy, in whose name John
Cabot had claimed North America in 1497.

In the early years of colonization, English settlers often anticipated living peacefully alongside indigenous peoples, but on English terms. They expected native peoples to adopt English customs and convert to Christianity. They showed little

A comparison of the portrait of Sir Walter Raleigh and his son (left), with that of an Algonquian Indian
drawn by John White, from Raleigh's Roanoke expedition (right), shows a dramatic difference in standard dress styles which for many must have symbolized the apparent cultural gap between Europeans
and Americans. Yet the fact that both men (and the young boy) were portrayed in similar stances, with
arms akimbo, demonstrated that all were high-status individuals. In Europe, only aristocrats were
represented in such a domineering pose.   (Left: National Portrait Gallery, London; right: © Trustees of the British Museum)

respect for the Indians when English interests were at stake, as demonstrated once settlers found a salable commodity in Virginia.

Tobacco Cultivation

That commodity was tobacco. In 1611 John Rolfe planted seeds of a tobacco strain from the Spanish Caribbean, which was superior to the strain Indians grew. Nine years later, Virginians exported 40,000 pounds of cured leaves, and by the late 1620s shipments jumped to 1.5 million pounds. Escalating demand from Europe and Africa meant high prices and substantial profits. The price later fell sharply and fluctuated annually in response to increasing supply and international competition.

Tobacco cultivation made Virginia prosper and immeasurably altered life for everyone. It required abundant land because a field could produce only about three satisfactory crops before needing to lie fallow for several years to regain its fertility. Thus applicants asked the Virginia Company for large land grants. Virginians established farms some distance from one another along the riverbanks—a settlement pattern convenient for tobacco cultivation but dangerous for defense.

Indian Assaults

Opechancanough, Powhatan's brother and successor, watched the English colonists' expansion and attempts to convert natives to Christianity. Recognizing the danger, he attacked along the James River on March 22, 1622. By day's end, 347 colonists (about one-quarter) lay dead. Only a timely warning from two Christian converts saved Jamestown from destruction.

Reinforced by shipments of men and arms from England, Virginia's settlers repeatedly attacked Opechancanough's villages. A peace treaty was signed in 1632, but in April 1644 the elderly Opechancanough assaulted the invaders one last time; then in 1646, survivors formally subordinated themselves to England.

End of the Virginia Company

The 1622 assault killed the Virginia Company, which remained unprofitable due to internal corruption and the heavy cost of supporting the settlers. Before its demise, the company developed two precedent-setting policies. First, to attract settlers, in 1617 it established the headright system, giving each arrival who paid his or her own way a land grant of 50 acres; those who financed the passage of others received similar headrights. To English farmers who owned little or no land, the headright system offered a powerful incentive to move to Virginia. To wealthy gentry, it promised the possibility of vast agricultural enterprises. Two years later, the company authorized landowning men of major Virginia settlements to elect representatives to an assembly called the House of Burgesses. This was similar to their long-held English right of electing members of Parliament and controlling local governments.

When James I revoked the charter in 1624, transforming Virginia into a royal colony, he continued the headright policy but abolished the assembly. Virginians protested, and by 1629 the House of Burgesses was functioning again. Two decades after the first permanent English settlement in North America, the colonists successfully insisted on governing themselves locally. Thus England's American possessions differed from the autocratic rule in the Spanish, Dutch, and French colonies.

LIFE IN THE CHESAPEAKE

Tobacco quickly became as important in the second English Chesapeake colony: Maryland. Given by Charles I to George Calvert, first Lord Baltimore, as a personal possession (proprietorship), it was settled in 1634. (Virginia and Maryland border the Chesapeake Bay—see Map 2.1—and are referred to collectively as the Chesapeake.) The Calvert family envisioned the colony as a haven for their persecuted fellow Catholics. Cecilius Calvert, second Lord Baltimore, became the first colonizer to offer religious freedom to all Christian settlers, codified in 1649 in Maryland's Act of Religious Toleration.

In everything but religion the two Chesapeake colonies resembled each other. Tobacco planters spread out along the riverbanks because the rivers offered dependable water transportation. Each farm or group of farms had its own wharf where oceangoing vessels could load or discharge cargo.

Demand for Laborers Planting, cultivation, harvesting, and curing tobacco were repetitious, time consuming, and labor intensive. Above all, successful Chesapeake farms required workers, but with their numbers reduced by war and disease, Indians could not supply such needs. Nor were enslaved Africans available: traders could more easily and profitably sell slaves to Caribbean sugar planters. By 1650 barely three blacks, some of them free, lived in Virginia.

Chesapeake tobacco farmers thus looked primarily to England for labor. Because of the headright system (which Maryland adopted in 1640), a tobacco farmer could obtain land and labor by importing English workers. He could use his profits to pay for the passage of more workers and thereby gain more land. Success could even move him into the region's new planter gentry.

Male laborers, along with a few women, immigrated to America as indentured servants; that is, in return for their passage, they contracted to work from four to seven years. Indentured servants accounted for 75 to 85 percent of the approximately 130,000 English immigrants to Virginia and Maryland during the seventeenth century. The rest were young couples with one or two children.

Roughly three-quarters of servants were males aged fifteen to twenty-four; only one in five or six was female. Most young men came from farming or laboring families, often from areas experiencing severe social disruption. Some had moved several times within England before relocating to America. Often they came from the middling ranks—what their contemporaries called the "common sort."

Conditions of Servitude From a distance, America seemed to offer opportunities for advancement unavailable in England. Servants who fulfilled their indenture earned freedom dues consisting of clothes, tools, livestock, casks of corn and tobacco, and sometimes land. Yet servants typically worked six days a week, ten to fourteen hours a day, in sweltering climates. Masters could discipline or sell them, and they faced severe penalties for running away. Laws did offer some protection. Masters were to supply them with sufficient food, clothing, and shelter and not beat them excessively. Cruelly treated servants could seek court assistance, sometimes winning verdicts directing their transfer to more humane masters or release from indenture.

Immigrants first had to survive "seasoning," a bout with disease (probably malaria) that usually occurred during colonists' first Chesapeake summer. They often endured recurrences of malaria, along with dysentery, typhoid fever, and other illnesses. About 40 percent of male servants did not survive to become freedmen. Even men of twenty-two who survived their seasoning could expect to live only about another twenty years.

For those who endured, opportunities were real. Until the late seventeenth century, former servants often became independent farmers (freeholders), living a modest but comfortable existence. But in the 1670s tobacco prices entered a fifty-year period of stagnation and decline, while land grew increasingly scarce and expensive. In 1681 Maryland dropped its requirement that servants receive land with their freedom dues, forcing many freed servants to live as wage laborers or tenant farmers. By 1700 the Chesapeake was no longer a land of opportunity.

Standard of Living

Life in the early Chesapeake was hard. Farmers (and sometimes their wives) toiled in the fields alongside servants. Because hogs needed little tending, Chesapeake households subsisted mainly on pork and corn, a filling but not sufficiently nutritious diet. Families supplemented by eating fish, shellfish, wildfowl, and vegetables they grew, such as lettuce and peas. The difficulty of safely preserving food for winter consumption magnified the health problems caused by epidemic disease.

Few households had more than farm implements, bedding, and basic cooking and eating utensils. Chairs, tables, candles, and knives and forks were luxury items. The ramshackle houses commonly had just one or two rooms. Colonists devoted their income to their farms and imported necessities such as cloth or tools from England.

Chesapeake Families

The predominance of males (see Figure 2.1), the incidence of servitude, and the high mortality rates produced unusual patterns of family life. Female servants normally could not marry while indentured because masters feared pregnancies would deprive them of workers. Many male ex-servants could not marry at all because of the scarcity of women. In contrast, nearly every free Chesapeake woman married, and widows usually remarried within months of a husband's death. Because of high infant mortality and marriages delayed by servitude or broken by death, Chesapeake women commonly reared only one to three healthy children, where English women normally had at least five.

Thus Chesapeake families were few, small, and short lived. In one Virginia county, more than three-quarters of the children had lost at least one parent by age twenty-one. Those children were put to work as soon as possible on the farms of parents, stepparents, or guardians. Their schooling, if any, was haphazard; whether Chesapeake-born children learned to read or write depended largely on whether their parents were literate and took the time to teach them.

Age and Sex Composition

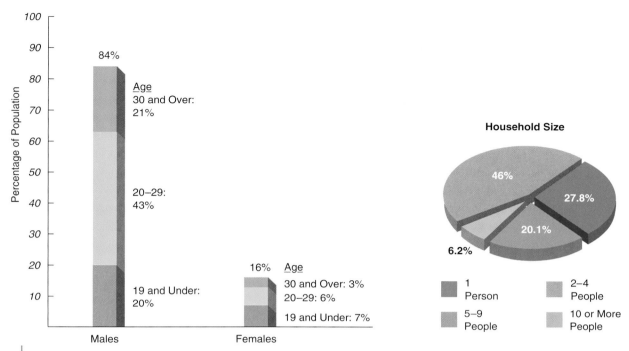

Figure 2.1   Population of Virginia, 1625

The only detailed census taken in the English mainland North American colonies during the seventeenth century was prepared in Virginia in 1625. It listed a total of 1,218 people, constituting 309 households living in 278 dwellings, so some houses contained more than one family. The chart shows, on the left, the proportionate age and gender distribution of the 765 individuals for whom full information was recorded, and on the right, the percentage variation in the sizes of the 309 households. The approximately 42 percent of the residents of the colony who were servants were concentrated in 30 percent of the households. Nearly 70 percent of the households had no servants at all.

(*Source of data:* Robert V. Wells, *The Population of the British Colonies in America Before 1776: A Survey of Census Data* [Princeton: Princeton University Press, 1975], Tables V-5 and V-6 and pp. 165–166)

Chesapeake Politics   Throughout the seventeenth century, immigrants composed a majority of the Chesapeake population. Most members of Virginia's House of Burgesses and Maryland's House of Delegates (established in 1635) were immigrants; they also dominated the governor's council, which simultaneously served as the highest court, part of the legislature, and executive adviser to the governor. A cohesive, native-born ruling elite emerged only in the early eighteenth century.

In the seventeenth-century Chesapeake, most property-owning white males could vote and chose as their legislators (burgesses) the local elites who seemed to be the natural leaders. But because most such men were immigrants lacking strong ties to one another or to the colonies, the assemblies did not create political stability, and were instead contentious.

THE FOUNDING OF NEW ENGLAND

Economic motives also drew men and women to New England, known as North Virginia before Captain John Smith renamed it in 1616. Due to environmental factors and the Puritans' organization of the New England colonies, the northern settlements turned out vastly different than their southern counterparts.

Contrasting Regional Demographic Patterns In late 1634, royal bureaucrats ordered London's port officials to collect information on travelers departing for the colonies. The records for 1635 document the departure of fifty-three vessels—twenty to Virginia, seventeen to New England, eight to Barbados, five to St. Kitts, two to Bermuda, and one to Providence Island. Almost five thousand people set sail, two thousand for Virginia, about twelve hundred for New England, and the rest for island destinations. Nearly three-fifths were between the ages of fifteen and twenty-four.

But among those bound for New England, such youths constituted less than one-third of the total; nearly 40 percent were older, and another third were younger. Whereas women made up just 14 percent of those going to Virginia, they composed almost 40 percent of the passengers to New England. New England migrants often traveled in family groups, brought more goods and livestock, and often journeyed with others from the same region. Their lives in North America must have been less lonely than those of their southern counterparts.

Contrasting Regional Religious Patterns Many New England colonists were inspired to migrate by religion. Puritan congregations became key institutions in colonial New England, whereas neither the Church of England nor Catholicism had much impact on the early development of the Chesapeake. Catholic and Anglican bishops in England largely ignored their coreligionists in America, and Chesapeake congregations languished. Not until the 1690s did the Church of England take firmer root in Virginia; by then it also replaced Catholicism as Maryland's established church.

Pious Puritans regularly reassessed the state of their souls. Many devoted themselves to self-examination and Bible study, and families prayed together daily under the guidance of the husband and father. Yet because even the most pious could never be certain that they were among the elect, anxiety troubled Puritans. It lent a special intensity to their beliefs and their concern with proper behavior—their own and that of others.

Separatists Separatists who thought the Church of England too corrupt to be salvaged became the first religious dissenters to move to New England. In 1609 a Separatist congregation relocated to Leiden, in the Netherlands, where they found religious freedom as well as tolerance for faiths and behaviors they abhorred. Hoping to isolate their families from corrupting influences, these people, who came to be known as Pilgrims, received permission from the Virginia Company to colonize its northern territory.

In September 1620 more than one hundred people, only thirty of them Separatists, sailed from England on the crowded *Mayflower*. In December they landed in

America, farther north than intended. They moved into the empty dwellings of an Indian village whose inhabitants perished in the epidemic of 1616–1618, at a harbor named Plymouth by John Smith in 1616.

Pilgrims and Pokanokets

Because they landed outside the jurisdiction of the Virginia Company, some non-Separatists aboard questioned the authority of the colony's leaders. In response, the Mayflower Compact, which substituted for a charter, was signed in November 1620 on shipboard to establish a Civil Body Politic which bound all settlers to the colony's leaders and laws . Male settlers elected a governor and made all decisions at town meetings. Later, Plymouth created an assembly to which landowning male settlers elected representatives.

The residents of Plymouth were poorly prepared to subsist in the new environment. Only half of the *Mayflower's* passengers lived to spring. The survivors owed much to the Pokanokets (a branch of the Wampanoags), who controlled the area. Pokanoket villages suffered terrible losses in a recent epidemic, so to protect themselves from the powerful Narragansetts of the southern New England coast, the Pokanokets allied themselves with the newcomers. In spring 1621, their leader, Massasoit, agreed to a treaty, and during the colony's first difficult years the Pokanokets supplied settlers with foodstuffs. The colonists also relied on Squanto, an Indian who served as a conduit between native peoples and Europeans. Captured by fishermen in the early 1610s and taken to Europe, Squanto learned to speak English. After returning, he became the settlers' interpreter and taught them about the environment.

Massachusetts Bay Company

Before the 1620s ended, another group of Puritans (Congregationalists, who hoped to reform the Church of England from within) launched the colonial enterprise that would dominate New England. Under the leadership of Charles I, who became king in 1625, the Church of England attempted to suppress Puritan practices. Some Congregationalist merchants, concerned about their prospects in England, sent colonists to Cape Ann (north of Cape Cod) in 1628. The following year the merchants obtained a royal charter, constituting themselves as the Massachusetts Bay Company.

The new joint-stock company quickly attracted Puritans of the "middling sort" who feared they could no longer practice their religion freely in their homeland. The Congregationalist merchants transferred the Massachusetts Bay Company's headquarters to New England. The settlers would then be able to handle their affairs, secular and religious, as they pleased. Like Plymouth settlers, they expected to profit from cod fishing and additionally from timber exports.

Governor John Winthrop

In October 1629, the Massachusetts Bay Company elected John Winthrop, a member of the lesser English gentry, as its governor. (Until his death twenty years later, he served continuously in one leadership post or another.) Winthrop organized the initial segment of the great Puritan migration. In 1630 over one thousand English men and women moved to Massachusetts, most to Boston. By 1643 nearly twenty thousand more followed.

On board the *Arbella,* en route to New England in 1630, John Winthrop preached a sermon, "A Model of Christian Charity," outlining his expectations for the colony. He stressed the communal nature of the endeavor where differences in status or wealth—although retained—would not imply worth. Instead, he explained that God had planned the world so that "every man might have need of other, and from hence they might be all knit more nearly together." In America, Winthrop asserted, "we shall be as a city upon a hill—the eyes of all people are upon us."

Winthrop foresaw in Puritan America a true commonwealth in which each person put the good of the whole ahead of his or her own. Although that society would be characterized by social inequality and hierarchies of status and power, Winthrop hoped its members would live by the precepts of Christian love. Early New England and its Caribbean counterpart, Providence Island, had some bitter quarrels and unchristian behavior, though remarkably, in New England the ideal persisted for generations.

Covenant Ideal

Puritans embraced the doctrine of the covenant, believing God had made a contract with them when they were chosen for their special mission to America. In turn they covenanted with one another to work together. The founders of churches, towns, and colonies in Anglo America often drafted formal documents outlining the principles on which their institutions would be based. The Pilgrims' Mayflower Compact was a covenant as was the Fundamental Orders of Connecticut (1639), which defined the basic law for settlements along the Connecticut River valley in 1636.

The leaders of Massachusetts Bay likewise transformed their company charter into the basis for a covenanted community based on mutual consent. Under pressure from landowning male settlers, they gradually changed the General Court—officially the company's small governing body—into a colonial legislature. They also granted the status of freeman, or voting member, to all property-owning, adult, male church members. Less than two decades after the Puritans arrived in Massachusetts Bay, the colony had a functioning system of self-government composed of a governor and a two-house legislature. The General Court also established a judicial system modeled on England's, although with very different laws.

New England Towns

The colony's method of distributing land furthered the communal ideal. In Massachusetts groups of men—often from the same English village—applied together for grants of land on which to establish towns (novel governance units that did not exist in England). Receiving a grant, these men then determined how the land would be distributed. Understandably, they copied their home villages, first laying out lots for houses and a church. They then gave each family parcels of land around the town center and reserved the best and largest plots for the most distinguished among them, including the minister. People with low status in England received smaller, less desirable allotments. Still, every man and even a few single women obtained land.

Towns developed quickly, evolving in three distinct ways. Some, chiefly isolated agricultural settlements in the interior, tried to sustain Winthrop's vision of community life based on diversified family farms. A second group, the coastal towns like Boston and Salem, became bustling seaports, focal points for trade and places of entry for new immigrants. The third category, commercialized agricultural towns, grew up in the Connecticut River valley, where easy water transportation enabled farmers to sell surplus goods.

Pequot War and Its Aftermath

Migration into the Connecticut valley ended the Puritans' relative freedom from clashes with nearby Indians. Relocating under the direction of their minister, Thomas Hooker, their new settlements were far from other English towns, although the wide river promised ready access to the ocean. The site, however, fell within territory controlled by the powerful Pequots.

The Pequots' dominance stemmed from their role as primary intermediaries in the trade between the New England Algonquians and the Dutch in New Netherland. With the arrival of the English, however, previously subordinate bands could now trade directly with Europeans. Clashes between Pequots and English colonists began earlier, but the establishment of settlements in the Connecticut valley pushed them toward war. After two English traders were killed (not by Pequots), the English raided a Pequot village. The Pequots then attacked the new town of Wethersfield in April 1637, killing nine and capturing two. To retaliate, a Massachusetts Bay expedition attacked and burned the main Pequot town on the Mystic River. The Englishmen and their Narragansett allies slaughtered at least four hundred Pequots, mostly women and children, capturing and enslaving most of the survivors.

For the next four decades, the New England Indians accommodated themselves to the European invasion. They traded with newcomers and sometimes worked for them, but resisted incorporation into English society. Native Americans persisted in using traditional farming methods, which did not employ plows or fences, and women continued to be the chief cultivators. When Indian men learned European trades, they chose those—like broom making, basket weaving, and shingle splitting— that most resembled their customary occupations and ensured independence. The one European practice they adopted was keeping livestock, for domesticated animals provided excellent sources of meat once hunting territories became English farms and wild game disappeared.

Missionary Activities

Most colonists showed little interest in converting the Algonquians to Christianity. Only a few Massachusetts clerics, notably John Eliot and Thomas Mayhew, seriously undertook missionary work. Eliot insisted that converts reside in towns, farm the land in English fashion, assume English names, wear European-style clothing and shoes, cut their hair, and stop observing a wide range of their own customs. He met with little success. Only eleven hundred Indians (out of many thousands) lived in the fourteen "Praying Towns" Eliot established, and just 10 percent were formally baptized.

The missions in New France, however, were more successful. Puritan services lacked Catholicism's beautiful ceremonies and special appeal for women, and Calvinist Puritans could not offer assurances of a heavenly afterlife. Yet on the island of Martha's Vineyard, Thomas Mayhew converted substantial numbers of Indians to Calvinist Christianity, partly by allowing Wampanoag Christians to lead traditional lives and by training their men as ministers.

While conversion often alienated new Christians from their relatives and traditions, many Indians hoped to use the Europeans' religion to cope with the dramatic changes the intruders had wrought. The combination of disease, alcohol, new trading patterns, and loss of territory disrupted customary ways of life. Shamans had little success in restoring tradition. Many Indians must have concluded that the Europeans' ideas could help them survive.

John Winthrop's description of a great smallpox epidemic that swept through southern New England in the early 1630s reveals the relationship among smallpox, conversion to Christianity, and English land claims. "Divers of them, in their sickness, confessed that the Englishmen's God was a good God; and that if they recovered, they would serve him," he noted in his diary in 1633. But by July, Winthrop observed that most Indians within a 300-mile radius of Boston had died of the disease, declaring "the Lord hath cleared our title to what we possess."

LIFE IN NEW ENGLAND

New England's colonizers lived differently than their Algonquian neighbors and Chesapeake counterparts. Algonquian bands usually moved four or five times annually to fully utilize their environment. In spring, women planted the fields, and once crops were established, they gathered wild foods while men hunted and fished. Villagers returned for harvest, separated for fall hunting, and wintered together in a sheltered spot. Women probably determined the timing of these moves because their activities used the environment more intensively than did men's.

English people lived year-round in the same location. Household furnishings resembled those of Chesapeake residents, but New Englanders' diets were somewhat more varied. They replowed fields, believing it was less arduous to employ manure as fertilizer than to clear new fields every few years. Furthermore, they fenced their croplands to keep out the cattle, sheep, and hogs that were their chief sources of meat. Animal crowding more than human crowding caused New Englanders to spread out across the countryside.

New England Families Because Puritans commonly moved in family groups, the age range in early New England was wide; and because many more women migrated to New England than to the tobacco colonies, the population could immediately reproduce itself. Lacking tropical diseases, New England was, after the difficult early years, healthier than the Chesapeake and the mother country. Adult male migrants to the Chesapeake lost about a decade from their English life expectancy of fifty to fifty-five years; their Massachusetts counterparts gained five or more years.

Consequently, New England families were numerous, large, and long lived. Most men married; immigrant women married young (at age twenty, on the average); and marriages lasted longer and produced more children likely to live to maturity. Seventeenth-century New England women raised five to seven children compared to one to three for Chesapeake women.

The presence of many children, combined with the Puritans' stress on reading the Bible, led to concern for the education of youth. That people lived in towns meant small schools could be established; girls and boys were taught basic reading by their parents or a school "dame," and boys could then learn writing and eventually arithmetic and Latin. Whereas early Chesapeake parents commonly died before their children married, New England parents exercised much control over their adult offspring. Young men could not marry without acreage and depended on their fathers for that land. Daughters, too, needed a dowry of household goods from their parents. Parents relied on their children's labor and often seemed reluctant to see them marry. These needs sometimes led to generational conflicts, though children generally obeyed their parents' wishes.

Impact of Religion

Puritans controlled the governments of Massachusetts Bay, Plymouth, Connecticut, and other early northern colonies. Congregationalism was the only officially recognized religion; except in Rhode Island, founded by Massachusetts dissenters, other sects had no freedom of worship. In Massachusetts Bay and New Haven, church membership was a prerequisite for voting. Early colonies taxed residents to build meetinghouses and pay ministers' salaries, but only in New England were provisions of criminal codes based on the Old Testament. Massachusetts's first bodies of law (1641 and 1648) incorporated regulations drawn from scriptures; New Haven, Plymouth, New Hampshire, and Connecticut later copied those codes. Colonists were required to attend religious services, and people who expressed contempt for ministers or their preaching could be punished with fines or whippings.

Strict Puritan codes of conduct meant colonists could be tried for drunkenness, card playing, dancing, or idleness, although frequent prosecutions suggest that New Englanders often enjoyed such activities. Couples who had sex during their engagement (as revealed by the birth of a baby less than nine months after their wedding) were fined and publicly humiliated. Men, and a handful of women, who engaged in behaviors that today would be called homosexual were seen as especially sinful, and some were executed.

In New England, church and state were thus intertwined. Puritans objected to secular interference in religious affairs yet expected the church to influence politics and social life. They also believed that the state was obliged to support and protect their one true church. Although they came to America seeking religious freedom, they saw no contradiction in refusing that freedom to others.

Roger Williams

Roger Williams, a Separatist who migrated to Massachusetts Bay in 1631, quickly ran afoul of Puritan orthodoxy. He told fellow settlers that the king of England had no right to grant them land already occupied by Indians, that church and state should be kept separate, and that Puritans should not impose their beliefs on others. In October 1635, the Massachusetts General Court tried Williams for challenging the validity of the colony's charter and for maintaining that New England Congregationalists had not separated sufficiently from England's corrupt institutions and practices.

Convicted and banished, Williams journeyed in early 1636 to the head of Narragansett Bay, where he founded the town of Providence on land he obtained from the Narragansetts and Wampanoags. Providence and other towns in what became Rhode Island tolerated all religions, including Judaism. Along with Maryland, Williams' tiny colony presaged the religious freedom that eventually became a hallmark of the United States.

Anne Hutchinson

Mistress Anne Hutchinson presented a more sustained challenge to Massachusetts' leaders. A skilled medical practitioner popular with Boston women, she admired John Cotton, a minister who stressed the covenant of grace, or God's free gift of salvation. Most Massachusetts clerics emphasized the need for good works, study, and reflection to receive God's grace. (In its most extreme form, such a doctrine could verge on the covenant of works, or the idea that people could earn their salvation.) Mistress Hutchinson began holding women's meetings in her home. She emphasized the covenant of grace and asserted that the elect could be assured of salvation and communicate directly with God, which lessened the importance of the institutional church.

In November 1637, Puritan officials charged Hutchinson with maligning the colony's ministers by accusing them of preaching the covenant of works. For two days she defended herself, matching scriptural references with John Winthrop. But then Hutchinson boldly declared that God had spoken to her and would curse the Puritans if they harmed her. Excommunicated, she was exiled to Rhode Island in 1638, along with her family and some faithful followers. Several years later, after moving to New Netherland, she and most of her children were killed by Indians.

Authorities in Massachusetts perceived Anne Hutchinson as a threat to religious orthodoxy and traditional gender roles. Puritans believed in the equality before God of all souls, but they considered actual women inferior to men. The magistrates' comments during Hutchinson's trial reveal that they were almost as outraged by her masculine behavior as by her religious beliefs. A minister told her, "You have stepped out of your place, you have rather been a Husband than a Wife and a preacher than a Hearer."

To New England authorities, an orderly society required the submission of wives to husbands as well as the obedience of subjects to rulers and ordinary folk to gentry. English people intended to make many changes by colonizing North America, but not to the gendered division of labor, the assumption of male superiority, or the maintenance of social hierarchies.

Blue Laws

Seventeenth-century New England colonies enacted statutes, now referred to as *blue laws*, preventing residents from working or engaging in recreation on Sundays, when they were supposed to attend church. Colonists were fined for plowing their fields, pursuing wandering livestock, drinking in taverns, or playing such games as shuffleboard. More harshly treated were thieves who took advantage of church attendance to break into homes.

The term *blue laws* appears to have been coined by the Reverend Samuel Peters, a loyalist, in his *General History of Connecticut*, published in 1781. Peters used *blue laws* to refer to Connecticut's early legal code in general, defining it as "bloody Laws; for they were all sanctified with whippings, cutting off the ears, burning the tongue, and death." Eventually, *blue laws* acquired its current meaning of legislation regulating behavior on Sundays. States continued to enact such statutes throughout the nineteenth century, but as in the colonial period, enforcement varied.

Still, they remained on the books. A 1961 Supreme Court decision, *McGowan v. Maryland*, upheld that state's law restricting what could be sold on Sundays because of its secular purpose—promoting the "health, safety, recreation, and general well-being" of the populace. Whereas colonial legislators were attempting to prevent Sunday work, modern Americans seem more concerned about halting Sunday shopping. Not until 1991 did the last state (North Dakota) repeal a law requiring stores to be closed on Sundays, and only in May 2003 did New York State remove its ban on Sunday liquor sales.

Today a website, *www.BlueLaws.net*, urges readers to join its "Keep Sunday Special Campaign," arguing that Sunday closing laws are "pro-family, pro-environment and pro-labor." Its plea to "restore the observance of the Lord's Day in our nation" shows the continuing legacy of the seventeenth century.

Summary

By the mid-seventeenth century, Europeans came to North America and the Caribbean to stay and indelibly altered their lives and those of native peoples. Europeans killed Indians with weapons and diseases and had varying success in converting them to Christianity. Contacts with indigenous peoples taught Europeans to eat new foods and recognize—however reluctantly—other cultural patterns. The survival and prosperity of many European colonies depended heavily on the cultivation of American crops (maize and tobacco) and an Asian crop (sugar), thus attesting to the importance of post-Columbian ecological exchange.

To a greater extent than their European counterparts, the English transferred the society and politics of their homeland to a new environment. Their sheer numbers, coupled with their need for vast quantities of land for cultivating crops and raising livestock, inevitably led to conflict with Indian neighbors. New England and the Chesapeake differed in the sex ratio and age range of their immigrant populations, their diverse economies, their settlement patterns, and the impact of their religious beliefs. Yet their expansions engendered similar internal and external conflicts. Both regions would become embroiled in increasingly fierce rivalries besetting the European powers that would affect Americans of all races until after the mid-eighteenth century, when the Anglo-American colonies won their independence.

Chapter Review

SPANISH, FRENCH, AND DUTCH NORTH AMERICA

How did the Jesuits' treatment of Native Americans differ from that of explorers and other settlers?

Spanish and other settlers typically sought to dominate the native populations, controlling their labor and often enslaving them, sometimes through the use of violence. The French Jesuits who settled New France (Montreal and Quebec) tried to convert Indians to Christianity while not insisting that they abandon their traditions. These missionaries learned Indian languages and lived among potential converts, and Indians' desire for literacy made them willing to listen to spiritual messages. And while they tried to undermine the authority of shamans and encouraged converts to abandon premarital sex and easy divorce, Jesuits also recognized the compatibility of some aspects of native culture with Christianity. This somewhat flexible approach, combined with their lack of interest in land or tribute, made at least some Indians receptive to conversion.

THE CARIBBEAN

What made the Caribbean islands initially desirable for colonization?

While Spain focused on larger islands that offered the potential for greater wealth with less effort, other countries explored smaller islands, initially as a base to attack Spanish vessels transporting gold, silver, and other valuable commodities from the Americas. The second reason for settling on the smaller islands was sugar cultivation. Sugar was in high demand in Europe, particularly since the sweetener improved the taste of coffee and tea and provided a sweet, yet quick, energy boost. Soil on volcanic islands such as Barbados proved ideal for sugar cane and later mills added an additional, and British-controlled, source of sugar.

ENGLISH INTEREST IN COLONIZATION

What two developments prompted England to make a second attempt at colonization in the early seventeenth century?

First, dramatic population growth in England, partly as a result of more nutritious American food exports, increased competition for food, clothing, shelter, and jobs. That, in turn, spurred inflation, reduced wages, and made upward mobility increasingly impossible for those at the lower end of the socioeconomic spectrum. Officials looked to the prospect of colonizing North America as a way to reduce England's population and related woes. Second, the Protestant Reformation sparked new forms of Christianity that diverged from the Church of England, and while Elizabeth I tolerated such dissent, her successors, the Stuart monarchs, did not. Ultimately, seeking to practice freely their religious beliefs (and avoid imprisonment), some English Puritans, Separatists, and Catholics fled to America.

The Founding of Virginia

How did English cultural traditions clash with those of Native Americans in Virginia?

While both were deeply religious, Englishmen considered Indian men lazy because they let women cultivate crops while they hunted, which the British regarded as a sport and not work. Native Americans thought Englishmen were effeminate because they farmed, which Indians considered women's work. Political power in Algonquian culture passed through sisters' sons rather through the father, as was the custom in England. Because the British were used to powerful kings, they assumed Indian chiefs held the same autocratic control and ability to make treaties, where in reality, they had limited authority. Most importantly, where the English believed in individual farms and private land ownership, the Algonquians held land communally as a village.

Life in the Chesapeake

What were the myths and realities of indentured servitude in the Chesapeake?

Chesapeake tobacco farmers filled their extensive demand for labor with indentured servants from England—typically young men who worked for four to seven years in exchange for their passage. Indentured servitude for these young men represented a slim chance at upward mobility. Most gained "freedom dues" at the completion of their contract, including clothes, tools, livestock, casks of corn and tobacco, and sometimes land. But they worked long hours, six or seven days a week, doing intense physical labor in hot climates. Masters could discipline or sell them, and if indentured servants fled, they faced extreme penalties, although some did win verdicts against cruel masters calling for their transfer or release from indenture. Exposure to disease combined with intense labor so that only 60 percent of indentured men lived to become freedmen, and many who did, lived only another twenty years.

The Founding of New England

What were John Winthrop's expectations for the Massachusetts Bay Company colony?

First elected governor in 1629, John Winthrop was instrumental in organizing the first Puritan migration from England to the colony. While in transit, he delivered his famous sermon, calling for the new colony to serve as a moral and spiritual example for the rest of the world, a "city upon a hill." He urged colonists to mediate status differences and unite around their communal interests. He envisioned a true commonwealth, where people put the common good ahead of their own and be governed by Christian brotherhood.

Life in New England

What was the impact of religion on colonial life in New England?

Although Puritans fled England to practice their faith freely, in New England, they offered no such freedom of worship to those who dissented from their beliefs.

Puritans controlled the government in many early northern colonies and made Congregationalism the only recognized religion, with church membership and voting rights linked. Colonists were punished with fines or whippings for missing religious services. In addition, strict behavioral codes meant colonists were tried for drunkenness, card playing, dancing, or idleness. Couples who had sex during their engagement (as revealed by the birth of a baby less than nine months after their wedding) were fined and publicly humiliated. People who behaved in ways that today would be called homosexual were sometimes executed. Separatists such as Roger Williams or Anne Hutchinson, who challenged Puritan orthodoxy, were tried and banished—Williams founded Providence based on religious tolerance and was subsequently joined by Hutchinson. Beyond challenging church authority, Hutchinson violated gender norms by preaching.

SUGGESTIONS FOR FURTHER READING

Virginia DeJohn Anderson, *Creatures of Empire: How Domestic Animals Transformed Early America* (2004)

Richard S. Dunn, *Sugar and Slaves: The Rise of the Planter Class in the English West Indies, 1624–1713* (1972)

Alison Games, *Migration and the Origins of the English Atlantic World* (1999)

David D. Hall, *Worlds of Wonder, Days of Judgment: Popular Religious Belief in Early New England* (1989)

Karen O. Kupperman, *Indians & English: Facing off in Early America* (2000)

Mary Beth Norton, *Founding Mothers & Fathers: Gendered Power and the Forming of American Society* (1996)

Helen C. Rountree, *Pocahontas, Powhatan, Opechancanough: Three Indian Lives Changed by Jamestown* (2005)

David J. Weber, *The Spanish Frontier in North America (1992)*

Keith Wrightson, *English Society, 1580–1680* (1982)

North America in the Atlantic World

She was starving. Offered a piece of boiled horse's foot by a compassionate neighbor, the slave gulped it down and seized another piece from a child. Later, she recalled, "Thus the Lord made that pleasant refreshing, which another time would have been an abomination." But Mary Rowlandson's mistress then threatened to kill her, saying she disgraced the household by begging for food.

What brought the wife of the Reverend Joseph Rowlandson of Lancaster, Massachusetts, to such distress? On February 10, 1676, in the conflict that New Englanders called King Philip's War, a force of Wampanoags, Narragansetts, and Nipmucks killed fourteen townspeople (including her daughter) and captured twenty-three others. Carried away, she endured their hardships in the wintry countryside of western Massachusetts and southern New Hampshire. She became the slave of Quinnapin, a Narragansett sachem, and his three wives, one of whom, Weetamoo, was herself a sachem and her mistress. Both were eventually killed by the colonists after the death of their leader, the Wampanoag known as King Philip, in August 1676. Months earlier, in May, Mary Rowlandson had been ransomed for £20—roughly equivalent to $500 today.

Mary Rowlandson's famous 1682 narrative, *The Sovereignty and Goodness of God,* exposes the sufferings she shared with her captors and her inability to understanding or sympathize with them. When Weetamoo's baby died, she remarked coldly that "there was one benefit in it, that there was more room" in the wigwam. Her narrative illustrates the contentious relationships between Anglo New Englanders and their native neighbors.

Much of the tension was related to the mainland colonies' involvement in a growing international network. North America, like England, was becoming embedded in a worldwide matrix

This icon will direct you to interactive activities and study materials on A People And A Nation, Brief Edition website: **www.cengage.com/history/norton/peoplenationbrief8e**

Chronology

1642–46	English Civil War occurs.
1649	Charles I is executed.
1651	First Navigation Act is passed to regulate colonial trade.
1660	Stuarts are restored to throne. Charles II becomes king.
1663	Carolina is chartered.
1664	English conquer New Netherland. New York is founded. New Jersey is established.
1670s	Marquette, Jolliet, and La Salle explore the Great Lakes and Mississippi valley for France.
1675–76	Bacon's Rebellion disrupts Virginia government. Jamestown is destroyed.
1675–78	King Philip's War devastates New England.
1680–1700	The Pueblo revolt temporarily drives the Spaniards from New Mexico.
1681	Pennsylvania is chartered.
1685	James II becomes king.
1686–88	Dominion of New England is established, superseding all charters of colonies from Maine to New Jersey.

1688–89	James II is deposed in the Glorious Revolution. William and Mary ascend to the throne.
1689	Glorious Revolution in America: Massachusetts, New York, and Maryland overthrow colonial governors.
1688–99	King William's War is fought on northern New England frontier.
1691	New Massachusetts charter is issued.
1692	Witchcraft crisis in Salem: nineteen people are hanged.
1696	Board of Trade and Plantations is established to coordinate English colonial administration. Vice-admiralty courts are established in America.
1701	Iroquois adopt neutrality policy toward France and England.
1702–13	Queen Anne's War is fought by French and English.
1711–13	Tuscarora War (North Carolina) leads to capture or migration of most Tuscaroras.
1715	Yamasee War nearly destroys South Carolina.
1718	New Orleans is founded in French Louisiana.

of trade and warfare. Oceangoing vessels now crisscrossed the globe, carrying European goods to America and Africa, Caribbean sugar to New England and Europe, Africans to the Americas, and New England fish and wood products—and occasionally Indian slaves—to the Caribbean. North American colonies expanded their territorial claims and diversified their economies after the mid-seventeenth century.

Three developments shaped life in mainland English colonies between 1640 and 1720: escalating conflicts with Indians and other European colonies, the expansion of slavery, and changes in the colonies' political and economic relationships with England.

The explosive growth of the slave trade significantly altered the Anglo-American economy. Mariners and ship owners transporting human cargoes profited handsomely, as did planters who could afford slaves. Initially the slave trade involved Indians and already enslaved Africans from the Caribbean, but it soon focused on cargoes from Africa. The large influx of West African slaves expanded agricultural productivity, fueled the international trading system, and dramatically reshaped colonial society.

The burgeoning North American economy attracted new attention from colonial administrators. After the Stuarts were restored to the throne in 1660 (having lost it briefly because of the English Civil War), London bureaucrats attempted to supervise American settlements to ensure the mother country benefited from their economic growth.

As English settlements expanded, they came into violent conflict with powerful Indian nations, the Dutch, the Spanish, and the French. All European colonies confronted significant crises during the 1670s. By 1720, war—between Europeans and Indians, among Europeans, and among Indians allied with colonial powers—had become a familiar feature of American life. No longer isolated, the people and products of the North American colonies had become integral to the world trading system and enmeshed in its conflicts.

- What were the consequences of the transatlantic slave trade in North America and Africa?
- How did English policy toward the colonies change from 1650 to 1720?
- What were the causes and results of new friction between Europeans and native peoples?

THE GROWTH OF ANGLO-AMERICAN SETTLEMENTS

Between 1642 and 1646 civil war between supporters of King Charles I and the Puritan-dominated Parliament engulfed England. Parliament triumphed, leading to the execution of the king in 1649 and interim rule by the parliamentary army's leader, Oliver Cromwell, during the so-called Commonwealth period. But after Cromwell's death, Parliament decided to restore the monarchy if Charles I's son agreed to restrictions on his authority (see Table 3.1). Assuming the throne in 1660, Charles II rewarded nobles and other supporters with huge land tracts on the North American mainland, thereby establishing six of the thirteen polities that would form the American nation: New York, New Jersey, Pennsylvania (including Delaware), and North and South Carolina (see Map 3.1). These became known as the Restoration colonies. All were proprietorships, where one man or several men owned the soil and controlled the government.

TABLE 3.1   Restored Stuart Monarchs of England, 1660–1714

Monarch Reign	Relation to Predecessor
Charles II 1660–1685	Son
James II 1685–1688	Brother
Mary 1688–1694	Daughter
William 1688–1702	Son-in-law
Anne 1702–1714	Sister, sister-in-law

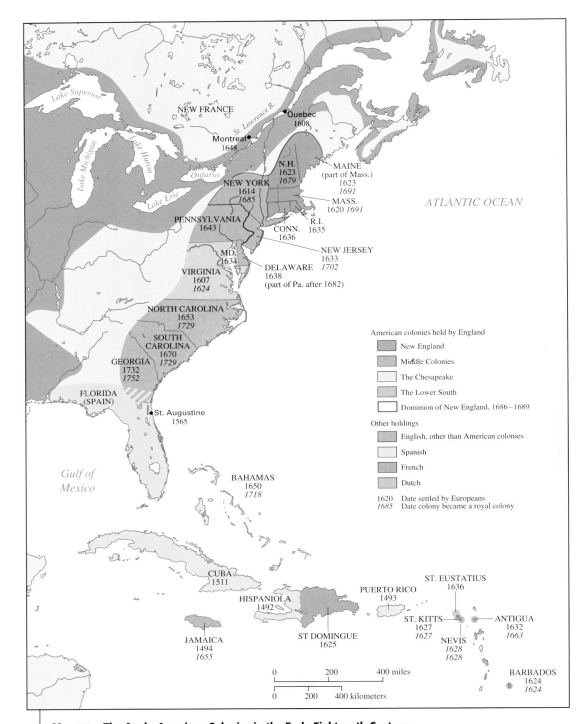

Map 3.1   The Anglo-American Colonies in the Early Eighteenth Century

By the early eighteenth century, the English colonies nominally dominated the Atlantic coastline of North America. But the colonies' formal boundary lines are deceiving because the western reaches of each colony were still largely unfamiliar to Europeans and because much of the land was still inhabited by Native Americans.

TABLE 3.2   **The Founding of English Colonies in North America, 1664–1681**

Colony	Founder(s)	Date	Basis of Economy
New York (formerly New Netherland)	James, duke of York	1664	Farming, fur trading
New Jersey	Sir George Carteret, John Lord Berkeley	1664	Farming
North Carolina	Carolina proprietors	1665	Tobacco, forest products
South Carolina	Carolina proprietors	1670	Rice, indigo
Pennsylvania (incl. Delaware)	William Penn	1681	Farming

New York

In 1664 Charles II gave his brother James, the duke of York, the region between the Connecticut and Delaware Rivers, including the Hudson valley and Long Island. That the Dutch had settled there mattered little; the English and the Dutch were engaged in sporadic warfare. In August James's warships anchored off Manhattan Island, demanding and achieving New Netherland's surrender. Although in 1672 the Netherlands briefly retook the colony, the Dutch permanently ceded it in 1674.

In 1664 a significant minority of English people (mostly Puritans who had come to Long Island from New England) already lived in the territory James renamed New York, along with the Dutch, Indians, Africans, Germans, Scandinavians, and other Europeans (see Table 3.2). The Dutch West India Company had imported slaves, intending some for resale in the Chesapeake, although many remained in New Netherland as laborers. At the time of the English conquest, almost one-fifth of Manhattan's approximately fifteen hundred inhabitants were of African descent.

Recognizing the population's diversity, James's representatives moved cautiously in establishing English authority. The Duke's Laws, a 1665 legal code, applied solely to English settlements on Long Island and was only later extended to the entire colony. James initially maintained Dutch local government, confirmed Dutch land titles, and allowed Dutch residents to maintain customary legal practices. Each town could decide which church (Dutch Reformed, Congregational, or Church of England) to support with its taxes. Much to the dismay of English residents, there was no provision for a representative assembly. James distrusted legislative bodies, and not until 1683 did he agree to an elected legislature. The English takeover thus had little immediate effect. The colony's population barely reached eighteen thousand by 1698. Until the 1720s, New York City remained a commercial backwater within Boston's orbit.

New Jersey

In 1664, the duke of York regranted the land between the Hudson and Delaware Rivers—East and West Jersey—to his friends Sir George Carteret and John Lord Berkeley. That left the duke's own colony hemmed in between Connecticut to the east and the Jerseys to the west and south, hindering its economic growth. He failed to promote migration, while the Jersey proprietors quickly attracted settlers by promising generous land grants, limited freedom of religion, and—without the Crown's authorization—a representative assembly. Many Puritan New Englanders migrated to the Jerseys, along with Barbadians and Dutch New Yorkers. By 1726, New Jersey had 32,500 inhabitants, only 8,000 fewer than New York.

Within twenty years, the Society of Friends, also called Quakers, purchased Carteret's share (West Jersey) and portions of Berkeley's (East Jersey). Rejecting religious hierarchies, Quakers believed that anyone could be saved by receiving God's "inner light" and that all people were equal in God's sight. With no formally trained clergy, this new, small sect allowed men and women to speak in meetings or become a "public Friend" and spread God's word. Quakers proselytized throughout the Atlantic world in the 1650s. Authorities rejected their radical egalitarianism, and Quakers encountered persecution everywhere.

Pennsylvania

In 1681, Charles II granted the region between Maryland and New York to his friend William Penn, a prominent Quaker. Penn held the colony as a personal proprietorship, one that earned profits for his descendants until the American Revolution. Penn also saw his province as a haven for persecuted coreligionists. He offered land to settlers on liberal terms, promised religious toleration (although only Christians could vote), guaranteed English liberties, and pledged to establish a representative assembly. He also publicized the availability of land in Pennsylvania through promotional tracts in German, French, and Dutch.

By mid-1683, more than three thousand people—among them Welsh, Irish, Dutch, and Germans—had already moved to Pennsylvania, and within five years the population reached twelve thousand. Philadelphia, situated on the navigable Delaware River, drew merchants and artisans from throughout the English-speaking world. Quakers seeking religious freedom arrived from mainland and Caribbean colonies, bringing experience on American soil and trade connections. Pennsylvania's fertile lands enabled residents to export surplus flour and other foodstuffs to the West Indies. Philadelphia acquired more than two thousand citizens and challenged Boston's commercial dominance.

Penn attempted to treat native peoples fairly. He learned to speak the language of the Delawares (or Lenapes), from whom he bought land to sell to European settlers. Penn also established strict trade regulations and forbade the sale of alcohol to Indians. His policies attracted native peoples who moved to Pennsylvania in the late seventeenth century to escape clashes with English colonists in Maryland, Virginia, and North Carolina. Ironically, the same toleration that attracted Native Americans also brought non-Quaker Europeans—notably the Scots-Irish, Germans, and Swiss— who showed little respect for Indian claims to the soil.

Carolina

Granted by Charles II in 1663, the southernmost proprietary colony stretched from the southern boundary of Virginia to Spanish Florida. Strategically, a successful English settlement there would prevent Spaniards from pushing farther north. The fertile, semitropical land also promised to produce such exotic and valuable commodities as figs, olives, wines, and silk. The proprietors named their new province Carolina in honor of Charles. The Fundamental Constitutions of Carolina, which they asked political philosopher John Locke to draft, outlined a colony governed by landholding aristocrats and characterized by a structured distribution of political and economic power.

Carolina quickly developed two distinct population centers, which in 1729 split into separate colonies under royal rule. Virginia planters settled the Albemarle region that became North Carolina and established a society like their own, based on cultivating tobacco and exporting forest products. The other population center, which eventually formed South Carolina, developed at Charles Town, founded in 1670. Many of its early residents were sugar planters from overcrowded Barbados who expected to reestablish plantation agriculture and escape hurricanes. They were disappointed: sugar would not grow in Carolina, and they experienced a destructive hurricane in 1686.

The settlers raised corn and cattle, which they sold to Caribbean planters. They also depended on trade with nearby Indians for commodities they could sell elsewhere, mostly deerskins and Indian slaves, which were shipped to the Caribbean and northern colonies. Indians sold captured enemies to the English settlers. During the first decade of the eighteenth century, South Carolina exported approximately 54,000 deerskins annually, which peaked at 160,000 a year. Before 1715, Carolinians exported 30,000 to 50,000 Indian slaves.

The Chesapeake

The English Civil War retarded the development of the earlier English settlements. Struggles between supporters of the king and Parliament caused military clashes in Maryland and political upheavals in Virginia. Once the war ended and immigration resumed, the colonies expanded again. Some settlers, especially those on the Virginia coast and southern border, raised grain, livestock, and flax to be sold to English and Dutch merchants. Tobacco growers began importing increasing numbers of English indentured servants as farms grew into plantations. No longer fearing Indian attacks after the defeat of the Powhatan Confederacy in 1646, they eagerly sought to enlarge their landholdings.

Chesapeake tobacco planters also started to acquire slaves. Most came from a population that historian Ira Berlin has termed *Atlantic creoles*—people (perhaps of mixed race) who came from other European Atlantic settlements, primarily Iberian outposts. Not all Atlantic creoles who came to the Chesapeake were bondspeople; some were free or indentured. With their arrival, the Chesapeake became a society with slaves, where slavery coexisted with other labor systems.

New England

In New England, migration ceased after the English Civil War began in 1642. While Puritans were challenging the king and then governing England as a commonwealth, they had little incentive to leave their homeland. Yet the Puritan colonies' population grew dramatically by natural increase. By the 1670s, New England's population more than tripled to approximately seventy thousand, putting pressure on available land. Colonial settlement spread into the Massachusetts and Connecticut interior, and many later generations migrated—north to New Hampshire or Maine, south to New York or New Jersey, west beyond the Connecticut River—to find sufficient farmland. Others learned such skills as blacksmithing or carpentry to support themselves in the growing towns.

Those who remained in the small, densely populated older New England communities experienced witchcraft accusations and trials after 1650. The accused allies of the Devil were thought to harness spirits for good or evil. A witch might engage in fortunetelling, prepare healing potions or charms, or cause the death of a child or animal. Only New England witnessed many witch trials (about one hundred before 1690). Most of the accused were middle-aged women who had angered their neighbors. Historians have concluded that daily interactions in close-knit communities fostered quarrels that led some colonists to believe others had diabolically caused certain misfortunes. Even so, judges and juries were skeptical: only a few of the accused were convicted, and fewer were executed.

Colonial Political Structures

By the last quarter of the seventeenth century, almost all Anglo-American colonies had well-established political and judicial structures. In New England, property-holding men or the legislature elected the governors; in other regions, the king or proprietor appointed them. A council, elected or appointed, advised the governor, as well as serving as the upper legislative house and the appeals court. Each colony also had local justices of the peace and county courts, and most jurisdictions elected local governing bodies.

A DECADE OF IMPERIAL CRISES: THE 1670s

Between 1670 and 1680, New France, New Mexico, New England, and Virginia experienced bitter conflicts as their interests collided with those of America's original inhabitants.

New France and the Iroquois

In the mid-1670s Louis de Buade de Frontenac, the governor-general of Canada, decided to expand New France south and westward to establish a trade route to Mexico and gain control of the valuable fur trade. Accordingly, he encouraged the explorations of Father Jacques Marquette, Louis Jolliet, and René-Robert Cavelier de La Salle in the Great Lakes and Mississippi valley regions. His goal led to conflict with the powerful Iroquois Confederacy, composed of five Indian nations—the Mohawks, Oneidas, Onondagas, Cayugas, and Senecas. (In 1722 the Tuscaroras became the sixth.)

Under the terms of a unique defensive alliance forged early in the sixteenth century, a representative council made war decisions for the entire Iroquois Confederacy. Before the arrival of Europeans, the Iroquois waged wars primarily for captives to replenish their population. Foreigners brought ravaging disease by 1633, intensifying the need for captives. Simultaneously, Europeans inspired a new economic motive for warfare: the desire to dominate the fur trade and gain unimpeded access to European goods. The war with the Hurons in the 1640s initiated a series of conflicts with other Indians known as the Beaver Wars, in which the Iroquois fought to control the lucrative peltry trade. Iroquois did not trap beaver; instead, they raided other villages for pelts or attacked Indians carrying furs to European outposts. The

Iroquois then traded that booty for European-made blankets, knives, guns, alcohol, and other items.

In the mid-1670s, and for the next twenty years, the French repeatedly attacked Iroquois villages, seeing them as a threat to France's plans to trade with western Indians. Depleted by constant warfare, the confederacy in 1701 negotiated a neutrality treaty with France and other Indians. For the next half-century the Iroquois maintained their power through trade and diplomacy, especially focusing on a covenant chain alliance with New York.

French Expansion

The wars against the Iroquois in the 1670s were crucial to French Canada's plan to penetrate the North American heartland. Unlike the Spaniards, French adventurers did not subjugate the Indians they encountered or initially claim large territories. Still, when France decided to strengthen its presence near the Gulf of Mexico by founding New Orleans in 1718, the Mississippi posts became the glue of empire. *Coureurs de bois* (literally, "forest runners") used the interior waterways to carry French goods between Quebec and Louisiana to outposts such as Michilimackinac (at the junction of Lakes Michigan and Huron), Kaskaskia (in present-day Illinois), and Fort Rosalie (Natchez) on the lower Mississippi River.

Indians, such as the Choctaws, Chickasaws, and Osages, gained access to valuable trade goods by tolerating the minimal European presence. The largest French settlements in the region, known as *le pays de Illinois* ("the Illinois country"), barely totaled three thousand in population. Located south of modern St. Louis and north of Fort Chartres, the settlements produced wheat for export to New Orleans. The shortage of European women led to interracial unions between French men and Indian women and created a mixed-race people known as *metís*.

Pueblo Peoples and Spaniards

In New Mexico, too, events of the 1670s led to a crisis with long-term consequences. Under Spanish domination, Pueblo peoples added Christianity to their beliefs while retaining traditional rituals. But as decades passed, Franciscans adopted brutal and violent tactics to erase the native religion. Priests and colonists who held *encomiendas* also placed heavy labor demands on the population. In 1680, the Pueblos revolted under the leadership of Popé, a respected shaman, driving the Spaniards out of New Mexico. Although Spain restored its authority by 1700, Spanish governors now stressed cooperation with native peoples, no longer violating their cultural integrity or enslaving them. The Pueblo revolt constituted the most successful and longest-sustained Indian resistance in colonial North America.

Contemporary engraving of John Verelst's 1710 portrait of the Mohawk chief known as Hendrick to Europeans (his Indian name was rendered as "Dyionoagon" or "Tee Yee Neen Ho Ga Row"). Hendrick and three other Iroquois leaders visited London in 1710, symbolically cementing the Covenant Chain negotiated in 1677. His primarily European dress and the wampum belt in his hand accentuate his identity as a cross-cultural diplomatic emissary.   (Anne S.K. Brown Military Collection, Brown University Library)

When Spaniards expanded their territorial claims to the east and north, they followed the strategy they used in New Mexico, establishing military outposts (presidios) and Franciscan missions. The army maintained order among the subject Indians—to protect them from attack and ensure the availability of their labor—and guarded the boundaries of New Spain from possible incursions, especially by the French. The friars concentrated on conversions and allowed religious syncretism. By the late eighteenth century, Spain claimed a vast territory that stretched from California (first colonized in 1769 to prevent Russian sea-otter trappers from taking over the region) through Texas (settled after 1700) to the Gulf Coast. Throughout that region, the Spanish presence consisted of a mixture of missions and presidios dotting the countryside, sometimes at considerable distances from one another.

King Philip's War

In the 1670s in the densely settled English colonies, hostilities developed as the expanding Anglo-American population sought more land. In both New England and Virginia settlers began to encroach on territories that belonged to Native Americans.

By the early 1670s the growing settlements in southern New England surrounded Wampanoag ancestral lands on Narragansett Bay. The local chief, Metacom, or King Philip, was troubled by territorial loss and the impact of European culture and Christianity on his people. Philip led attacks on nearby communities in June 1675. Other Algonquian peoples, among them Nipmucks and Narragansetts, joined King Philip's forces. In the fall, they attacked settlements in the northern Connecticut River valley, and the war spread to Maine when the Abenakis joined the conflict. In early 1676 the Indian allies devastated villages like Lancaster, where they captured Mary Rowlandson and others, and attacked Plymouth and Providence; later, Abenaki assaults forced the abandonment of most Maine settlements. Altogether, the alliance wholly or partially destroyed twenty-seven of ninety-two towns and attacked forty others, pushing the line of English settlement back toward the east and south.

In summer 1676, the Indian coalition ran short of food and ammunition. On June 12, the Mohawks—ancient Iroquois enemies of New England Algonquians—devastated a major Wampanoag encampment while most of the warriors were attacking an English town. After King Philip was killed that August, the southern alliance crumbled. Fighting continued on the Maine frontier for another two years until the English and Abenakis agreed to end the conflict in 1678.

In addition to the Wampanoags, Nipmucks, Narragansetts, and Abenakis who were captured and sold into slavery, still more died of starvation and disease. New Englanders had broken the power of the southern coastal tribes. Thereafter southern Indians lived in small clusters, subordinated to the colonists and often working as servants or sailors. Only on Martha's Vineyard did Christian Wampanoags preserve their cultural identity.

The settlers may have won King Philip's War, but an estimated one-tenth of the adult male population was killed or wounded. Proportional to population, it was the most costly conflict in American history. New Englanders did not fully rebuild abandoned interior towns for thirty years, and not until the American Revolution did the region's per capita income reach pre-1675 levels.

Bacon's Rebellion

In the early 1670s, ex-servants unable to acquire land avidly eyed the territory reserved by treaty for Virginia's Indians. Governor William Berkeley resisted starting a war, and dissatisfied colonists rallied behind a recent immigrant, the gentleman Nathaniel Bacon, who shared their frustrations about the lack of available land. Using as a pretext the July 1675 killing of an indentured servant by Doeg Indians, settlers attacked the Doegs and the Susquehannocks, a more powerful nation. In retaliation, Susquehannocks raided outlying farms early in 1676.

The governor outlawed Bacon and his men; the rebels held Berkeley hostage until they won authorization to attack the Indians. As the chaotic summer of 1676 wore on, Bacon alternately pursued Indians and battled the governor. In September Bacon's forces burned Jamestown to the ground. But when Bacon died of dysentery the following month, the rebellion collapsed. Even so, in 1677 a new treaty opened much of the disputed territory to settlement. The end of Bacon's Rebellion pushed most of Virginia's Indians west beyond the Appalachians.

THE ATLANTIC TRADING SYSTEM

In the 1670s and 1680s, the Chesapeake's prosperity rested on tobacco, which required an ample labor supply. But fewer English men and women proved willing to indenture themselves. Population pressures had eased in England, and the Restoration colonies gave migrants other settlement options. Furthermore, fluctuating tobacco prices and the scarcity of land made the Chesapeake less appealing. Wealthy Chesapeake tobacco growers found the answer to their labor problem in the Caribbean sugar islands, where Dutch, French, English, and Spanish planters were accustomed to purchasing African slaves.

Why African Slavery?

Slavery had been practiced in Europe and Islamic lands for centuries. European Christians justified enslaving heathen peoples, especially those of exotic origin, in religious terms, arguing it might lead to their conversion. Muslims, too, enslaved infidels and imported tens of thousands of black African bondspeople into North Africa and the Middle East. Others believed that wartime prisoners could be enslaved. Consequently, when Portuguese mariners encountered African societies holding slaves, they purchased bondspeople. Starting in the 1440s, Portugal imported large numbers of slaves into the Iberian Peninsula; by 1500, enslaved Africans composed about one-tenth of the population of Lisbon, Portugal, and Seville, Spain. In 1555 some were taken to England, and soon residents of London and Bristol became accustomed to black slaves on the streets.

Iberians exported African slavery to New Spain and Brazil. Because the Catholic Church prevented the formal enslavement of Indians in those domains and free laborers would not do difficult jobs in mines or on sugar plantations, African bondspeople became mainstays of the Caribbean and Brazilian economies. The first African slaves in the Americas were imported from Angola, Portugal's early trading partner, and the Portuguese word *Negro* came into use as a descriptor.

English people had few moral qualms about enslaving other humans. Slavery was sanctioned in the Bible and widely practiced by contemporaries. Yet their early attempts to define slave status indicate that seventeenth-century English colonists lacked clear conceptual categories for race or slave. For example, the 1670 Virginia law that first tried to define the enslaveable declared that "all servants not being christians imported into this colony by shipping shall be slaves for their lives." Such nonracial phrasing reveals that Anglo-American settlers had not fully developed the meaning of *race* and *slave;* that would come over time.

Atlantic Slave Trade

North American mainland planters could not have obtained enslaved workers without the rapid development of an Atlantic trading system. Although this elaborate Atlantic economic system has been called the triangular trade, people and products did not move across the ocean in easily diagrammed patterns. Rather, a complex web of exchange inextricably tied the peoples of the Atlantic world together (see Map 3.2).

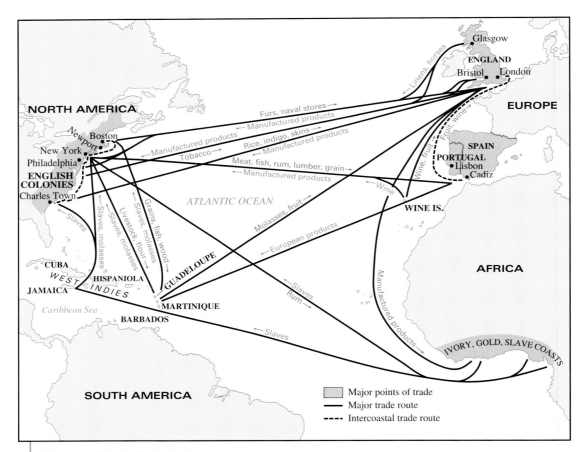

Map 3.2   Atlantic Trade Routes

By the late seventeenth century, an elaborate trade network linked the countries and colonies bordering the Atlantic Ocean. The most valuable commodities exchanged were enslaved people and the products of slave labor.

The expanding trade network between Europe and its colonies was fueled by the sale and transport of slaves, the exchange of commodities produced by slave labor, and the need to feed and clothe bound laborers. By the late seventeenth century, the basis of the European economy shifted from the Mediterranean and Asia to the Atlantic, with commerce in slaves and the products of slave labor as its core.

Chesapeake tobacco and Caribbean and Brazilian sugar were shipped to Europe, where they were in demand. The profits paid for African laborers and European manufactured goods. The African coastal rulers received their payment for slave cargoes in European manufactures and East Indian textiles. Europeans purchased slaves from Africa for resale in their colonies and acquired sugar and tobacco from America and dispatched their manufactures everywhere.

Europeans fought bitterly to control the lucrative trade. The Portuguese, who first dominated it, were supplanted by the Dutch in the 1630s. In the Anglo-Dutch wars, the Dutch lost to the English, who controlled the trade through the Royal African Company. Holding a monopoly on English trade with sub-Saharan Africa until 1712, the company maintained forts and trading posts, dispatched to West Africa hundreds of ships and transported about 100,000 slaves to England's Caribbean colonies. After the company's monopoly expired, independent traders carried most of the Africans imported into the colonies.

West Africa and the Slave Trade

Most of the enslaved people carried to North America originated in West Africa, some from the Rice and Grain Coasts, many others from the Gold and Slave Coasts and the Bight of Biafra (modern Nigeria) and Angola (see Map 1.2). Certain coastal rulers served as intermediaries, allowing permanent slave-trading posts and supplying resident Europeans with slaves. Such rulers simultaneously controlled inland peoples' access to desirable trade goods, such as textiles, iron bars, alcohol, tobacco, guns, and cowry shells from the Maldive Islands (in the Indian Ocean), used as currency. At least 10 percent of all slaves exported to the Americas passed through Ouidah, Dahomey's slave-trading port.

The slave trade's centralizing tendencies helped create such powerful eighteenth-century kingdoms as Dahomey and Asante (formed from the Akan States). Yet rulers in parts of Upper Guinea, especially modern Gambia and Senegal, resisted involvement. Traffic in slaves destroyed smaller polities and disrupted economic and demographic patterns. Agricultural production intensified, especially in rice-growing areas, to supply slave ships with foodstuffs. Because prisoners of war constituted most of the exported slaves, successful traders were also successful warriors. Some nations even initiated conflicts specifically to acquire captives.

New England and the Caribbean

New England produced only one item England wanted: tall trees for masts on sailing vessels. To buy English manufactures, New Englanders needed profits earned elsewhere, especially in the Caribbean. By the late 1640s, decades before the Chesapeake became dependent on *production* by slaves, New England already relied on *consumption* by slaves and owners. The sale of cheap foodstuffs (primarily corn and salt fish) to feed the slave population and wood products for barrels to Caribbean sugar planters provided New England farmers and merchants with a major source of income.

Shopkeepers in the New England interior and the middle colonies bartered with local farmers for grains, livestock, and barrel staves, then traded those items to merchants in port towns. Such merchants dispatched ships to the Caribbean, where they exchanged their cargoes for molasses, sugar, fruit, dyestuffs, and slaves. Fully reloaded, the ships then returned to Boston, Newport, New York, or Philadelphia. Americans distilled molasses into rum, the only part of the trade that could be termed triangular. Rhode Islanders took rum to Africa and traded it for slaves, whom they carried to Caribbean islands to exchange for more molasses to produce more rum.

Slaving Voyages

Tying the system together was the voyage (commonly called the middle passage) that brought Africans to the Americas. That voyage could be fatal for the enslaved. About 10 to 20 percent of the captives died en route; on long or disease-ridden voyages, mortality rates could be higher. Another 20 percent died either before the ships left Africa or shortly after arriving in the Americas. Europeans in the trade also died at high rates, chiefly through exposure to such diseases as yellow fever and malaria. One in every four or five European sailors died on voyages, and just 10 percent of the men sent to the Royal African Company's forts in Lower Guinea lived to return to England.

Sailors signed on to slaving voyages reluctantly. Slave merchants were notoriously greedy and captains brutal—to sailors and slaves. Unfortunately, sailors, often the subject of abuse, in turn abused bondspeople. Yet through contact with the enslaved, they learned the value of freedom, and sailors became known for their fierce attachment to independence.

SLAVERY IN NORTH AMERICA AND THE CARIBBEAN

Barbados, America's first slave society (an economy wholly dependent on enslavement), spawned others. As the island's population expanded, about 40 percent of the early English residents dispersed to other colonies, carrying their laws, commercial contacts, and slaveholding practices with them. A large proportion of the first Africans imported into North America came via Barbados. In addition to the many Barbadians who settled in Carolina, others moved to the southern regions of Virginia, New Jersey, and New England.

African Enslavement in the Chesapeake

Newly arrived Africans in the Chesapeake were typically assigned to outlying parts of plantations (called quarters) until they learned some English and the routines of tobacco cultivation. Such Africans—primarily men—lived with ten to fifteen workers housed together in one or two buildings, supervised by an Anglo-American overseer. Each man was expected to cultivate two acres of tobacco a year. Their lives must have been filled with toil and loneliness, for few spoke the same language, and all were expected to work six days a week. Many used their Sunday off to cultivate gardens or to hunt or fish to supplement their meager diet. Only rarely could they form families, because of the scarcity of women.

Slaves usually cost about two and a half times more than indentured servants, but they supplied a lifetime of service, assuming they survived—which large numbers, weakened by the voyage and sickened by new diseases, did not. Those with enough money could acquire slaves, accumulate greater wealth, and establish large plantations worked by hundreds of bondspeople, whereas the less affluent could not even buy indentured servants. Anglo-American society in the Chesapeake thus became increasingly stratified, as the gap between rich and poor planters steadily widened.

So many Africans were imported into Virginia and Maryland that by 1710 people of African descent composed one-fifth of the population. Even with continuing imports, a decade later American-born slaves outnumbered their African-born counterparts in the Chesapeake, a trend that continued thereafter.

In 1726, William Smith, an employee of the Royal African Company, sketched this musician playing a traditional marimba-like instrument called a *balafo*. Later in the eighteenth century, Virginians described slaves playing the same instrument, thus showing that African music came to North America with the enslaved multitudes. (University of Chicago Library, Special Collections Research Center)

African Enslavement in South Carolina

Africans who came with their masters from Barbados to South Carolina in 1670 composed one-quarter to one-third of Carolina's early population. The Barbadian slaveowners quickly discovered that African-born slaves' skills were well suited to South Carolina's semitropical environment. African-style dugout canoes became the chief means of transportation in the colony, which was crossed by rivers with large islands offshore. Fishing nets copied from African models proved more efficient. Baskets that enslaved laborers wove and gourds that they hollowed out came into general use as food and drink containers. Finally, Africans adapted their cattle herding techniques in America. Because meat and hides initially constituted a chief export, Africans contributed significantly to South Carolina's prosperity.

After 1700 South Carolinians began importing slaves directly from Africa. By 1710 African-born slaves outnumbered those born in the Americas, and they made up a majority of the enslaved population in South Carolina until midcentury. The similarity of the South Carolinian and West African environments, coupled with the substantial African-born population, ensured the survival of more aspects of West African culture than elsewhere. Only in South Carolina did enslaved parents give their children African names and develop a dialect that combined English and African terms. (Known as Gullah, it has survived to the present in isolated areas.) And in South Carolina African women became the primary petty traders, dominating the markets of Charles Town as they did in Guinea.

Rice and Indigo

Slave importation coincided with the successful introduction of rice in South Carolina. English people knew nothing about rice production, but people from Africa's Rice Coast had spent their lives working with the crop. Rice-growing techniques from West Africa, especially cultivation in inland swamps and tidal rivers, were widely adopted. South Carolinians preferred slaves from the Rice Coast, and they preferred women. That was possibly due to women's crucial role in cultivating rice in West Africa, where they sowed and weeded the crop, pounded harvested rice with a mortar and pestle to remove the hulls and bran, and then winnowed to separate the grains from the chaff. South Carolinians utilized the West African system of pounding rice by hand until the late eighteenth century.

Every field worker on rice plantations was expected to cultivate three to four acres a year. Most were female, because many enslaved men were assigned to jobs like blacksmithing or carpentry. Planters also expected slaves to grow part of their own food. Under the task system of predefined work assignments, experienced slaves could complete their tasks by early afternoon; after that and on Sundays, they were free to work their gardens or rest. One scholar has suggested this unique task system in South Carolina in the early eighteenth century resulted from negotiations between slaves familiar with rice cultivation and masters who desperately needed their expertise.

Developers of South Carolina's second cash crop—indigo—also used the task system and drew on slaves' specialized skills. Indigo, the only source of blue dye for the growing English textile industry, was much prized. Eliza Lucas, who managed her father's plantations, experimented with indigo cultivation during the early 1740s. Drawing on the knowledge of slaves and overseers from the Caribbean, she developed the planting and processing techniques later adopted colony-wide. South Carolina indigo never matched the quality of that from the Caribbean, but indigo plantations flourished because Parliament offered a bounty on every pound exported to Great Britain.

Indian Enslavement in North and South Carolina

In 1708 enslaved Indians composed about 14 percent of the South Carolina population. The lucrative traffic in Indian slaves significantly affected South Carolina's relationship with its indigenous neighbors. Native Americans knew they could find a ready market for captive enemies in Charles Town and used it to rid themselves of potential rivals. Yet as settlers and traders shifted their priorities, first one set of former allies, then another, found themselves enslaved.

The trade in Indian slaves began when the Westos (originally known as the Eries), migrated south from the Great Lakes in the mid-1650s, fleeing their Iroquois enemies after the Beaver Wars. The Westos raided Spain's lightly defended Florida missions and sold Indian captives to Virginians. With the establishment of Carolina, the proprietors monopolized trade with the Westos, which infuriated settlers shut out of the commerce in slaves and deerskins. The planters secretly financed attacks on the Westos, wiping them out by 1682. Southeastern Indians protected themselves from these slave raids—continued by other native peoples—by subordination to either the English or Spanish or by coalescing into larger political units, such as those later known as Creeks, Chickasaws, or Cherokees.

At first the Carolinians did not directly conflict with neighboring Indians. But in 1711 the Tuscaroras, an Iroquoian people, attacked a Swiss-German settlement at New Bern, North Carolina, which had expropriated their lands. South Carolinians and their Indian allies combined to defeat the Tuscaroras. Afterward, more than a thousand Tuscaroras were enslaved, and the remainder drifted northward, where they joined the Iroquois Confederacy.

Four years later, the Yamasees, who helped overcome the Tuscaroras, turned on their English allies. In what seems a long-planned retaliation for abuses by traders and threats to their lands, the Yamasees enlisted the Creeks and other Muskogean peoples to attack outlying English settlements. In spring and summer 1715, English and African refugees by the hundreds streamed into Charles Town. The Yamasee-Creek offensive was thwarted when reinforcements arrived from the north, colonists hastily armed African slaves, and Cherokees joined the fight. Afterward, Carolinian involvement in the Indian slave trade ceased because their native neighbors moved away for self-protection. Then, the native peoples of the Carolinas could regroup and rebuild, for they were no longer subjected to slavers' raids.

Slaves in Spanish and French North America

Few Indians or Africans were enslaved in any of Spain's North American territories, which had no plantations or cash crops. In 1693, Florida officials offered freedom to Carolina fugitives who converted to Catholicism. Hundreds of runaways accepted the offer, although not all won their liberty. Many settled in a town founded for them near St. Augustine, Gracia Real de Santa Teresa de Mose, headed by former slave Francisco Menéndez.

In early Louisiana, too, slaves—some Indians, some Atlantic creoles—at first composed only a tiny proportion of the residents. But a growing European population demanded more, and after 1719 French officials dispatched more than six thousand Africans. The residents failed to develop a plantation economy, but they angered the Natchez Indians by taking their lands. In 1729 the Natchez, assisted by newly arrived slaves, attacked, killing more than 10 percent of the European population. The French struck back, slaughtering the Natchez and their allies. Throughout the century, Louisiana remained a society with slaves rather than a slave society.

Enslavement in the North

Bondspeople in the northern mainland colonies were Atlantic creoles from the Caribbean, native peoples from the Carolinas and Florida, and local Indians sentenced to slavery for crime or debt. The intricate involvement of northerners in the commerce surrounding the slave trade ensured that many people of African descent lived north of Virginia, and that "Spanish Indians" became part of the New England population. Some bondspeople resided in urban areas, especially New York, which in 1700 had a larger black population than any mainland city. Women tended to work as domestic servants, men as unskilled laborers on the docks.

Yet even in the North most bondspeople worked in the country doing agricultural tasks. Dutch farmers in the Hudson Valley and northern New Jersey were likely to rely on enslaved Africans, as were the owners of large landholdings in the Rhode Island's Narragansett region. Some toiled in new enterprises, such as ironworks, alongside hired laborers and indentured servants. While slavery did not greatly contribute to the northern economy, individual slaveholders benefited from the institution and wanted to preserve it.

Slave Resistance

As slavery increased, so did slaves' resistance. Typically that meant malingering or running away, but occasionally bondspeople planned rebellions. Seven times before 1713 the English Caribbean experienced major revolts. The first mainland slave revolt occurred in New York in 1712. The rebels set a fire and ambushed anyone trying to put it out, killing eight and wounding twelve. Of the rebels caught and tried, eighteen were executed, with their decapitated bodies left rotting outdoors as a warning.

IMPERIAL REORGANIZATION AND THE WITCHCRAFT CRISIS

English officials seeking new sources of revenue focused on the expanding Atlantic trade in slaves and the products of slave labor. Parliament and the Stuart monarchs drafted laws to harness proceeds of the trade for the benefit of the mother country.

Mercantilism and the Navigation Acts

Like other European nations, England based its commercial policy on mercantilism, the theory that viewed the economic world as a collection of national states, whose governments competed for shares of a finite amount of wealth. What one nation gained, another lost. Each nation sought economic self-sufficiency and a favorable balance of trade by exporting more than it imported. Colonies played an important role, supplying the mother country with valuable raw materials and its market for the mother country's manufactured goods.

Parliament's Navigation Acts—passed between 1651 and 1673—established three principles that accorded with mercantilist theory. First, only English or colonial merchants could legally trade in the colonies. Second, certain valuable American products could be sold only in the mother country or other English colonies. Initially, these enumerated goods included wool, sugar, tobacco, indigo, ginger, and dyes, and later, rice, naval stores (masts, spars, pitch, tar, and turpentine), copper, and furs. Third, foreign goods for sale in the colonies had to be shipped through England, with English import duties paid. Years later, new laws established a fourth principle: the colonies could not export items (such as wool clothing or iron) that competed with English products.

These laws adversely affected Chesapeake planters, who were barred from seeking foreign markets for their staple crops. The statutes initially helped sugar producers of the English Caribbean by driving Brazilian sugar from the home market, but later prevented English planters from selling sugar elsewhere. The laws, however, stimulated a lucrative colonial shipbuilding industry, especially in New England. And the northern and middle colonies produced many unenumerated goods—fish, flour, meat and livestock, and barrel staves—that could be traded directly to the French, Spanish, or Dutch Caribbean islands if they were carried in English or American ships.

English authorities soon learned that enforcing mercantilist laws would be difficult. The American coast's many harbors were havens for smugglers, and colonial officials often looked the other way when illegally imported goods were sold. Because American juries had already demonstrated a tendency to favor local smugglers, Parliament in 1696 established American vice-admiralty courts, which operated without juries and adjudicated violations of the Navigation Acts.

Colonial Autonomy Challenged

By the early 1680s Massachusetts, Plymouth, Connecticut, and Rhode Island operated independently, subject neither to the direct authority of the king nor to a proprietor. Whereas Virginia was a royal colony and New Hampshire (1679) and New York (1685) gained that status, all other mainland settlements were proprietorships, over which England exercised little control. In all English colonies, free adult men who owned property expected to have an influential voice in their government, especially about decisions concerning taxation.

When James II became king in 1685, he and his successors sought to tighten the reins of colonial government and reduce the colonies' political autonomy. English officials were convinced that New England was a hotbed of smuggling. Moreover, Puritans denied religious freedom to non-Congregationalists and maintained laws incompatible with English practice. The charters of all the colonies from New Jersey to Maine were revoked, and a Dominion of New England was established in 1686 (see Map 3.1). Sir Edmund Andros, the governor, had immense power: Parliament dissolved all the assemblies, and Andros needed only the consent of an appointed council to make laws and levy taxes.

Glorious Revolution in America

New Englanders endured Andros's autocratic rule for more than two years. Then, James II's power crumbled when he angered his subjects by levying taxes without parliamentary approval and by converting to Catholicism. In April 1689, Boston's leaders jailed Andros and his associates. The following month they received news of the bloodless coup known as the Glorious Revolution, in which James was replaced in late 1688 by his daughter Mary and her husband, the Dutch prince William of Orange. With Protestants William and Mary in power, the Glorious Revolution affirmed the supremacy of Parliament and Protestantism.

In other colonies, the Glorious Revolution inspired revolt. In Maryland the Protestant Association overturned the government of the Catholic proprietor, and in New York a militia officer of German origin, Jacob Leisler, assumed control of the government. Bostonians, Marylanders, and New Yorkers saw themselves as carrying out the colonial phase of the English revolt.

But William and Mary also believed that England should exercise tighter control over its unruly American possessions. Consequently, only the Maryland rebellion received royal sanction, primarily because of its anti-Catholic thrust. In New York, Leisler was hanged for treason, and Massachusetts became a royal colony with an appointed governor. The province retained its town meeting system and continued to elect its council, but the 1691 charter eliminated the religious test for voting and holding office. A parish of the Church of England appeared in Boston.

King William's War

A war with the French and their Algonquian allies compounded New England's difficulties. King Louis XIV of France allied himself with the deposed James II, and England declared war on France in 1689. (In Europe, this conflict was known as the War of the League of Augsburg, but the colonists called it King William's War.) Even before war broke out in Europe, Anglo-Americans and Abenakis clashed over English settlements in Maine that had been reoccupied after the 1678 truce and were expanding. Attacks wholly or partially destroyed several towns, and colonial expeditions against Montreal and Quebec in 1690 failed miserably. Even the Peace of Ryswick (1697), which ended the war in Europe, did not bring peace to the northern frontiers. Maine could not be resettled for decades because of the continuing conflict.

The 1692 Witchcraft Crisis

For eight months in 1692, witchcraft accusations spread through rural Essex County, Massachusetts—the area most threatened by the Indian attacks in southern Maine and New Hampshire. Before the crisis ended, 14 women and 5 men were hanged, 1 man was pressed to death with stones, 54 people confessed to being witches, and more than 140 people were jailed. The crisis began in late February when several children and young women in Salem Village formally charged older female neighbors with torturing them in spectral form. Other accusers and confessors chimed in, among them some female domestic servants orphaned in the Maine war. These young women offered fellow New Englanders a compelling explanation for the troubles afflicting them: their province was under direct assault not only by the Indians and their French allies but also by the Devil and his allied witches.

Among others, the afflicted people accused prominent men from the Maine frontier who had traded with or failed to defeat the Indians. Their leader, accusers declared, was the Reverend George Burroughs, a Harvard graduate who had ministered in Maine and Salem Village and was suspected of bewitching soldiers sent to combat the Abenakis. The colony's magistrates, who were also its political and military leaders, were willing to believe such accusations because it freed them from any responsibility for New England's troubles.

In October, the worst phase of the crisis ended when the governor dissolved the special court established to try the suspects. He and prominent clergymen regarded the descriptions of spectral torturers as "the Devil's testimony," and the Devil could not be trusted. Most critics did not think the afflicted were faking, that confessions were false or that witches did not exist. Rather, they questioned whether guilt could be legally established by the evidence. During the final trials in 1693, almost all the defendants were acquitted, and the governor pardoned the few found guilty.

New Imperial Measures

In 1696 England created the fifteen-member Board of Trade and Plantations, the chief government organ concerned with the American colonies. The board gathered information, reviewed Crown appointments, scrutinized legislation passed by colonial assemblies, supervised trade policies, and advised ministries on colonial issues.

The Wonders of the Invisible World.

OBSERVATIONS

As well *Historical* as *Theological*, upon the NATURE, the NUMBER, and the OPERATIONS of the

DEVILS.

Accompany'd with,

I. Some Accounts of the Grievous Molestations, by DÆMONS and WITCHCRAFTS, which have lately annoy'd the Countrey; and the Trials of some eminent *Malefactors* Executed upon occasion thereof: with several Remarkable *Curiosities* therein occurring.

II. Some Counsils, Directing a due Improvement of the terrible things, lately done, by the Unusual & Amazing Range of EVIL SPIRITS, in Our Neighbourhood: & the methods to prevent the *Wrongs* which those *Evil Angels* may intend against all sorts of people among us; especially in Accusations of the Innocent.

III. Some Conjectures upon the great EVENTS, likely to befall, the WORLD in General, and NEW-ENGLAND in Particular; as also upon the Advances of the TIME, when we shall see BETTER DAYES.

IV A short Narrative of a late Outrage committed by a knot of WITCHES in *Swedeland*, very much Resembling, and so far Explaining, *That* under which our parts of *America* have laboured!

V. THE DEVIL DISCOVERED: In a Brief Discourse upon those TEMPTATIONS, which are the more Ordinary *Devices* of the Wicked One.

By **Cotton Mather**.

Boston Printed by *Benj. Harris* for *Sam. Phillips.* 1693.

The Reverend Cotton Mather of Boston, twenty-nine years old in 1692 at the time of the Salem witchcraft crisis, rushed this book—*The Wonders of the Invisible World*—into print shortly after the trials ended. He tried to explain to his fellow New Englanders the "Grievous Molestations by Daemons and Witchcrafts which have lately annoy'd the Countrey" by providing both brief trial narratives and examples of similar recent occurrences elsewhere, most notably in Mohra, Sweden.   (Image courtesy of The Massachusetts Historical Society)

It had no powers of enforcement and shared jurisdiction with the customs service, the navy, and a member of the ministry. Although this reform improved colonial administration, supervision of the American provinces remained decentralized and haphazard.

Most colonists resented alien officials who arrived to implement the policies of king and Parliament, but they adjusted to them and to the Navigation Act's trade restrictions. They fought another of Europe's wars—the War of the Spanish Succession, called Queen Anne's War in the colonies—from 1702 to 1713, without enduring the stresses of the first, despite the heavy economic burdens the conflict imposed. Colonists who allied with the royal government were given offices and land grants and made up court parties that supported English officials. Others, who were without well-placed friends or who defended colonial autonomy, formed the opposition, or country interest. By the end of the first quarter of the eighteenth century, most men in both groups were American born. They were from elite families whose wealth derived in the South from staple-crop production and in the North from commerce.

Exotic Beverages

Seventeenth-century colonists developed a taste for tea (from China), coffee (from Arabia), chocolate (from Mesoamerica), and rum. Demand for these once-exotic beverages helped reshape the world economy after the mid-seventeenth century. Approximately two-thirds of the people who migrated across the Atlantic before 1776 were involved, primarily as slaves, in the production of tobacco, calico, and these four drinks. These exotic beverages profoundly affected culture, too, as they moved from luxury to necessity.

Each beverage had its own pattern of consumption. Chocolate, brought to Spain from Mexico and consumed hot at intimate gatherings, became the drink of aristocrats. Coffee became the morning beverage of English and colonial businessmen, who praised its caffeine for keeping drinkers alert. Coffee was served in new public coffeehouses, patronized by men, which opened first in London in the late 1660s and then in Boston in the 1690s. By the mid-eighteenth century, tea, consumed at home in the afternoon at tea tables presided over by women, supplanted coffee in England and America. In contrast, rum was the drink of the masses, made possible by new technology and the increasing production of sugar.

Cacao plantations in the South American tropics multiplied to meet the rising chocolate demand. Rum involved Americans in every phase of its production and consumption. The sugar grown on Caribbean plantations was transported to the American mainland in barrels and ships made from North American wood. There the syrup was turned into rum at 140 distilleries. Americans drank an estimated four gallons per person annually, but exported much of the rum to Africa, where it could purchase more slaves to produce more sugar to make more rum.

Thus these beverages linked the colonies to the world and altered their economic and social development.

The frontispiece of Peter Muguet, *Tractatus De Poto Caphe, Chinesium The et de Chocolata,* 1685. Muguet's treatise visually linked the three hot, exotic beverages recently introduced to Europeans. The drinks are being consumed by representatives of the cultures in which they originated: a turbaned Turk (with coffeepot in the foreground), a Chinese man (with teapot on the table), and an Indian drinking from a hollowed, handled gourd (with a chocolate pot and ladle on the floor in front of him).

(Library of Congress)

Americans of African Descent

After the 1670s, the rise of southern economies based on the enslavement of Africans, coupled with employment of enslaved Africans in northern colonies, dramatically altered the American population. By 1775, more than a quarter-million Africans had been imported into the territory that later became the United States, constituting about 20 percent of the population at the time of the Revolution.

According to the 2000 census, 12.5 percent of Americans today claim descent from African ancestors. Because the legal importation of African slaves ended in 1808 and because the United States attracted few voluntary African migrants until the late twentieth century, most of today's African Americans have colonial ancestors. Conversely, most European Americans are descended from the massive European migrations of the nineteenth and early twentieth centuries.

The modern African American population includes people with various skin colors, reflecting many past interracial sexual relationships, coerced and voluntary. African Americans, free and enslaved, have had children with Europeans and Indians since the colonial period; more recently, they have intermarried with Asian immigrants. State miscegenation laws, enacted from the early American republic until 1967—when they were struck down by the Supreme Court—forbade legal marriages between people of European descent and those of other races. That forced the non-European groups to seek marital partners among themselves.

The 2000 census allowed Americans to define themselves as members of more than one race. African American leaders opposed this change, fearing a diminution of political clout. Previous laws defined people with any African ancestry as black; on census forms people of African descent have now proved less willing to define themselves as multiracial. Their racial self-definition thus continues to be influenced by a legacy of discrimination.

Summary

The seventy years from 1650 to 1720 established the basic economic and political patterns in mainland colonial society. In 1650 two isolated centers of English population, New England and the Chesapeake, existed along the seaboard, along with the tiny Dutch colony of New Netherland. In 1720 nearly the entire North American east coast was in English hands and Indian control east of the Appalachian Mountains had largely been broken by King Philip's War, Bacon's Rebellion, the Yamasee and Tuscarora wars, and Queen Anne's War. West of the mountains, the Iroquois reigned supreme. Most of the population was American born, except for African-born people in South Carolina and the Chesapeake. Economies originally based on trade in fur and skins had become more complex and linked with the mother country; and political structures had become more uniform. Yet the adoption of large-scale slavery and production of tobacco, rice, and indigo in the Chesapeake and Carolinas differentiated them from northern colonies. They had become slave societies, heavily reliant on a system of perpetual servitude.

The northern colonies, too, counted on profits from the Atlantic trading system, the key element of which was traffic in slaves, primarily Africans. New England sold corn, salt fish, and wood products to the West Indies, where slaves consumed the foodstuffs and from where planters shipped sugar and molasses in barrels made from staves crafted by northern farmers. Pennsylvania and New York also found the Caribbean islands a ready market for their livestock, grains, and wheat flour.

Meanwhile, the Spanish expanded their influence throughout the Gulf Coast and, after midcentury, north to California. The French moved to dominate the length of the Mississippi River and the Great Lakes region. Both Spanish and French colonists lived near Indian nations and depended on their labor and goodwill. The extensive Spanish and French presence to the south and west of English settlements made future conflicts among European powers in North America inevitable.

By 1720, key elements of the imperial administrative structure that would govern the English colonies until 1775 were in place. Anglo-Americans' commitment to autonomous local government would later lead them into conflict with Parliament and the king.

Chapter Review

THE GROWTH OF ANGLO-AMERICAN SETTLEMENTS

Why did New York's development lag behind that of other British colonies in the seventeenth century?

Several factors were critical to a colony's growth. Leaders who encouraged migration and settlement, often through land grants and freedom of religion as well as the prospect of a representative assembly, typically had the best results. Granted to James the Duke of York in 1664, New York remained a shadow of Boston until well into the 1720s largely because James, unlike William Penn of Pennsylvania and other proprietors, made none of these moves. Instead, his colony remained hemmed in by Connecticut and New Jersey, which each made successful overtures to draw populations helpful to development. Instead, James retained Dutch local government, land title, and legal practices that had been in place when he came to power and refused a legislative assembly—which many English colonists wanted—until 1683.

A DECADE OF IMPERIAL CRISES: THE 1670S

How did settlers' interests collide with those of Native Americans?

Settlers' and Native Americans' interests clashed in two pivotal areas: control of trade and desire for more land. New France and the Iroquois Confederacy clashed over control of the valuable fur trade, which the Iroquois had fought hard to attain. Bitter battles and attacks lasted for twenty years, before culminating in a neutrality treaty. Similarly, in the densely settled New England colonies in the 1670s, hostilities developed as Anglo-Americans sought more land and tried to grab it away from Native Americans, fueling the deadly and destructive King Phillips' War. And in Virginia, Bacon's Rebellion also focused on seizing desirable interior land from Indians, ultimately attacking them and pushing them further west.

THE ATLANTIC TRADING SYSTEM

How was slavery at the center of the expanding trade network between Europe and the colonies?

First, the Chesapeake developed around tobacco farming, which required a vast supply of workers. Fewer English workers were available as population pressures in England eased and Restoration colonies offered land and other opportunities to would-be settlers. Tobacco growers instead turned to slave labor, as did other plantation colonies, thereby expanding the sale and transport of slaves. In addition, commodities produced by slave labor helped boost exports and trade networks, while the need to feed and clothe slaves stimulated new business opportunities for other colonies, particularly New England, which grew economically by selling cheap foodstuffs to feed slaves. And the slave trade itself created a global economic network and tensions among European nations seeking to control the lucrative trade.

SLAVERY IN NORTH AMERICA AND THE CARIBBEAN

What skills did African slaves bring to America that proved vital to the development of colonial South Carolina?

African-born slaves had several skills that were crucial to the economic development of South Carolina. From a similarly semi-tropical climate, these slaves adapted dugout canoes from their homeland that became a key means of transportation in the many rivers of the Carolinas. Their fishing nets also proved more efficient. African cattle herding techniques aided in producing the meat and hides that were an early export from the region. Slaves, particularly women, also knew how to cultivate rice, which was rapidly becoming a staple crop in South Carolina. The area's other crash crop—indigo (the only source of blue dye for the growing English textile industry)—similarly drew on the knowledge of slaves transported to South Carolina from the Caribbean, where indigo plantations flourished.

IMPERIAL REORGANIZATION AND THE WITCHCRAFT CRISIS

How did mercantilism benefit some colonies economically and hurt others?

Mercantilism was grounded in the notion that the world contained a finite amount of wealth, and that if one nation gained, another had to lose. For England, that meant exporting more than it imported and using the colonies to facilitate its prosperity. England controlled colonial trade through the Navigation Acts (passed between 1651 and 1673), which allowed only English merchants to trade in the colonies, permitted American products to be sold only to England or other English colonies, and required foreign goods bound for the colonies to ship through England and pay related duties. Later, it additionally prevented colonists from exporting anything that competed with English goods. For Chesapeake planters, these policies had a negative affect, preventing them from selling staple crops in foreign markets. English sugar producers in the Caribbean were initially helped, as their Brazilian competitors were driven from the market, but later hurt when they were prevented from selling their sugar elsewhere. New England benefitted from the emergence of a lucrative shipbuilding industry, while the northern and middle colonies gained from trading goods not outlined in the Navigation Acts, including fish, flour, meat, livestock, and barrels.

SUGGESTIONS FOR FURTHER READING

Wesley Frank Craven, *The Colonies in Transition, 1660–1713* (1968)

David Eltis, *The Rise of African Slavery in the Americas* (1998)

Alan Gallay, *The Indian Slave Trade: The Rise of the English Empire in the American South, 1670–1717* (2002)

Andrew Knaut, *The Pueblo Revolt of 1680* (1995)

Jill Lepore, *The Name of War: King Philip's War and the Origins of American Identity* (1998)

David S. Lovejoy, *The Glorious Revolution in America* (1972)

Edmund S. Morgan, *American Slavery, American Freedom: The Ordeal of Colonial Virginia* (1975)

Jennifer L. Morgan, *Laboring Women: Reproduction and Gender in New World Slavery* (2004)

Mary Beth Norton, *In the Devil's Snare: The Salem Witchcraft Crisis of 1692* (2002)

Betty Wood, *The Origins of American Slavery* (1997)

American Society Transformed

"I f god Spers [spares] you in this Cuntrie but a few years you will blis the day you left" Alexander McAllister told his cousin in late 1770. McAllister, who as a youth moved to North Carolina with his parents, urged friends and family in his Scottish Highlands hometown in Argyleshire to come to North America. He noted that at his adopted home at Cross Creek (near modern Fayetteville, North Carolina) anyone could easily grow corn, wheat, barley, rye, oats, potatoes, and tobacco, and other immigrants had harvested "plenty of Corn for them Selves and famile and seemes to be very well Satisfied."

McAllister's letters were central to a network of correspondents that brought five thousand Scots to North America in the two decades after the mid-1750s. When Scots arrived in North Carolina with letters of introduction, McAllister helped them find land and supplies, even while knowing that "the best [land] is taken up many years ago" and that newcomers' early years would be hard. McAllister's own prosperity illustrated what some might achieve: by the late 1780s, having fathered numerous children by two wives, he owned forty slaves and more than 2,500 acres. He served as an elder of the Presbyterian church, a member of the colonial assembly, and a state senator.

Highland Scots were part of a massive eighteenth-century migration of Europeans and Africans that by 1770 had changed the American population and landscape. The British colonies south of New England drew the most newcomers, who swelled the population, altered political balances, and introduced new sects. Unwilling immigrants (slaves and transported convicts), too, clustered in the middle and southern colonies.

Several key themes marked colonial development in the mideighteenth century: the new ethnic diversity, the increasing importance of urban centers, the creation of a prosperous urban

This icon will direct you to interactive activities and study materials on *A People And A Nation*, Brief Edition website: **www.cengage.com/history/norton/peoplenationbrief8e**

Chronology

1690	Locke's *Essay Concerning Human Understanding,* a key example of Enlightenment thought, is published.	**1741**	New York City conspiracy reflects whites' continuing fears of slave revolts.
1721–22	Smallpox epidemic in Boston leads to the first widespread adoption of inoculation in America.	**1747**	Princeton University is founded, joining Harvard, Yale, and other earlier institutions of higher learning.
1732	Georgia is founded.	**1751**	Franklin's *Experiments and Observations on Electricity,* an important American contribution to Enlightenment science, is published.
1733	John Peter Zenger is tried for and acquitted of seditious libel in New York.		
1739	Stono Rebellion (South Carolina) leads to increased white fears of slave revolts.	**1760s**	Baptist congregations take root in Virginia.
		1760–75	This is the peak of eighteenth-century European and African migration to the English colonies.
	George Whitefield arrives in America; Great Awakening broadens.	**1765–66**	Hudson River land riots pit tenants and squatters against large landlords.
1739–48	King George's War disrupts the American economy.	**1767–69**	Regulator movement (South Carolina) tries to establish order in the backcountry.
1740s	Black population of the Chesapeake begins to grow by natural increase, contributing to the rise of large plantations.	**1771**	North Carolina Regulators are defeated by the eastern militia at Battle of Alamance.

elite, rising consumption, and the new significance of internal markets. Where exports continued to dominate French and British mainland colonies, settlers along the Atlantic and Gulf coasts were tied to an international commercial system that fluctuated wildly, as expanding populations demanded greater quantities and types of goods and Europe could not keep up. Consequently, colonists increasingly depended on their own resources.

Intermarried networks of wealthy families developed in Europe's American possessions by the 1760s. Most colonists of the "lesser sort" worked with their hands from dawn to dusk and could neither read nor write. Well-off, educated elites, however, participated in transatlantic intellectual life, such as the Enlightenment, lived in comfortable houses, and enjoyed leisure activities. Divisions were most pronounced in British America, the largest and most prosperous settlement, where by the last half of the century, social and economic distance among different ranks of Anglo-Americans had widened and sparked new conflicts.

In 1720 much of North America remained under Indian control. But by 1770, settlements of Europeans and Africans ruled by Great Britain filled most of the region between the Appalachian Mountains and the Atlantic Ocean. After defeating France in the Seven Years' War (see pages 112–113), the British dominated North America's extensive rivers and lakes. Spanish missions extended from present-day northern California to the Gulf Coast. Such changes transformed Europe's North American possessions.

- What were the effects of demographic and economic changes in the mainland colonies?
- What were the key elements of eighteenth-century colonial culture?
- What developments at midcentury began the process of political and religious change?

POPULATION GROWTH AND ETHNIC DIVERSITY

Dramatic population growth characterized British mainland colonies in the eighteenth century. About 250,000 European and African Americans resided in the colonies in 1700. Thirty years later, that number more than doubled, reaching 2.5 million by 1775. Only modest population changes occurred in French and Spanish North America. At the end of the eighteenth century, Texas had just 2,500 Spanish residents, and the largest Spanish colony, New Mexico, included only 20,000. The total European population of the mainland French colonies expanded from 15,000 in 1700 to about 70,000 in the 1760s, but concentrations of French settlers existed only along the St. Lawrence River between Quebec and Montreal and in New Orleans.

Migration was important, but most of the population growth in Anglo America resulted from natural increase. Once the difficult early decades of settlement passed and the sex ratio evened out in the South (after 1700), the American population doubled every twenty-five years. Because of women's youthful age at the onset of childbearing (early twenties for European Americans, late teens for African Americans), married women became pregnant every two or three years and bore five to ten children. With a large proportion of children reaching maturity, about half of the American population was under sixteen years old in 1775. (By contrast, only about one-quarter of the American population was under sixteen in 2005.)

Involuntary Migrants from Africa

More Africans than Europeans came to the Americas, the overwhelming majority as slaves. Of at least 11 million slaves brought to the Americas during slavery, by 1775 only 260,000 were imported into the region that became the United States. The height of the trade occurred in the eighteenth century, when about half of all slaves crossed the Atlantic, primarily in British or Portuguese vessels. Furthermore, in the slaveholding South America and Caribbean, a surplus of males and appallingly high mortality rates meant that only a continuing influx of slaves could maintain a consistent work force. On the mainland, only South Carolina, where rice cultivation was difficult and unhealthful (chiefly because malaria-carrying mosquitoes bred in the rice swamps), required a similar influx of slaves.

The involuntary migrants came from various ethnic groups and regions of Africa (see Map 4.1). More than 40 percent embarked from West Central Africa (modern Congo and Angola), nearly 20 percent from the Bight of Benin (modern Togo, Benin, and southwestern Nigeria), about 13 percent from the Bight of Biafra (today's Cameroon, Gabon, and southeastern Nigeria), and approximately 9 percent from the Gold Coast (modern Ghana and neighboring countries). Smaller proportions came from East Africa and the Windward and Rice Coasts (modern Senegal, Gambia, and Sierra Leone).

Standard slave-trading practice of loading an entire cargo at one port and selling them in another meant that people from the same area were often taken to the Americas together. That was heightened by planter partiality for particular ethnic groups. Virginians favored Igbos from the Bight of Biafra, whereas South Carolinians and Georgians selected Senegambians and people from West Central Africa. Louisiana planters first chose slaves from the Bight of Benin but later bought many from West Central Africa.

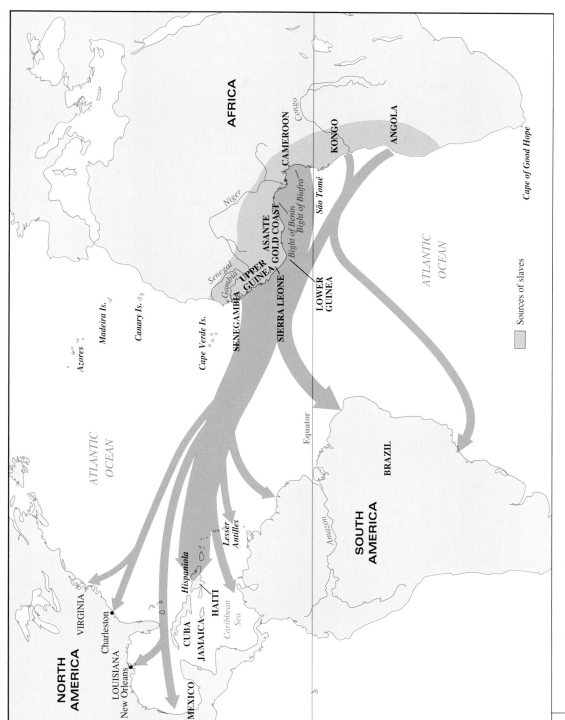

Map 4.1 Major Origins and Destinations of Africans Enslaved in the Americas
As this schematic map shows, enslaved Africans were drawn from many regions of western Africa (with some coming from the interior of the continent) and were shipped to areas throughout the Americas.

Possibly tens of thousands of enslaved Africans were Muslims, some of whom were literate in Arabic and came from aristocratic families. The discovery of noble birth could lead to slaves' being returned home. For example, Job Ben Solomon, a slave trader from Senegal, had been captured by raiders while selling bondspeople in Gambia and sent to Maryland in 1732. A letter he wrote in Arabic so impressed his owners that he was liberated the next year. Despite the 260,000 slaves brought to the mainland, American-born people of African descent came to dominate the enslaved population because of natural increase after 1740. Although about 40 percent of imported Africans were male, women and children composed a majority of slave imports. Females were valued for their productive and reproductive capacities. A planter who owned female slaves could watch his labor force expand steadily through the births of their children, designated as slaves in every colony. In the Chesapeake, the number of bondspeople rose rapidly because the imports were added to an enslaved population that also grew through natural increase. Work routines involved in cultivating tobacco, coupled with a roughly equal sex ratio, reduced slave mortality and increased fertility. Even in unhealthful South Carolina, American-born slaves outnumbered the African born as early as 1750.

Newcomers from Europe

About 500,000 Europeans moved to British North America during the eighteenth century, most after 1730. Influenced by mercantilist thought, British authorities regarded an industrious population at home as an asset. They deported undesirables—vagabonds and Jacobite rebels (supporters of the deposed Stuart monarchs)—but otherwise discouraged emigration. Instead they recruited German and French Protestants to the colonies by promising free land and religious toleration, even financing the passage of some groups. After 1740 they relaxed citizenship requirements to a small fee, seven years' residence, adherence to Protestant beliefs, and an oath of allegiance to the king.

The most successful migrants came prepared, having learned from their correspondents like McAllister that land and resources were abundant and that they would need capital. People who arrived penniless did less well; approximately 40 percent fell into that category, immigrating as bound laborers. Worse off were the 50,000 migrants who came as criminals convicted of offenses such as theft and murder. Many unskilled and perhaps one-third female, they were often dispatched to Maryland, where they worked in tobacco fields or as ironworkers or household servants. Little is known about their fate, but some who committed further crimes in the colonies became notorious in newspaper accounts.

Scots-Irish, Scots, and Germans

One of the largest immigrant groups came from Ireland or Scotland, largely in family units. About 70,000 Scots-Irish descendants of Presbyterian Scots who had settled in Northern Ireland during the seventeenth century joined 35,000 who came to America from Scotland (see Table 4.1). Another 45,000, both Protestants and Catholics, migrated from southern Ireland. High rents, poor harvests, and religious discrimination (in Ireland) pushed people from their homeland. Such immigrants usually landed in Philadelphia or New Castle, Delaware, and moved to the Pennsylvania

TABLE 4.1   Who Moved to America from England and Scotland in the Early 1770s, and Why?

	English Emigrants	Scottish Emigrants	Free American Population
Destination			
13 British colonies	81.1%	92.7%	—
Canada	12.1%	4.2%	—
West Indies	6.8%	3.1%	—
Age Distribution			
Under 21	26.8%	45.3%	56.8%
21–25	37.1%	19.9%	9.7%
26–44	33.3%	29.5%	20.4%
45 and over	2.7%	5.3%	13.1%
Sex Distribution			
Male	83.8%	59.9%	—
Female	16.2%	40.1%	—
Unknown	4.2%	13.5%	—
Traveling with Families or Alone			
With families	20.0%	48.0%	—
Alone	80.0%	52.0%	—
Known Occupation or Status			
Gentry	2.5%	1.2%	—
Merchandising	5.2%	5.2%	—
Agriculture	17.8%	24.0%	—
Artisanry	54.2%	37.7%	—
Laborer	20.3%	31.9%	—
Why They Left			
Positive reasons (e.g., desire to better one's position)	90.0%	36.0%	—
Negative reasons (e.g., poverty, unemployment)	10.0%	64.0%	—

Note: Between December 1773 and March 1776, the British government questioned individuals and families leaving ports in Scotland and England for the American colonies to learn who they were, where they were going, and why they were leaving. This table summarizes just a few of the findings of the official inquiries, which revealed a number of significant differences between the Scottish and English emigrants.

Source of data: Bernard Bailyn, *Voyagers to the West* (New York: Knopf, 1986), Tables 4.1, 5.2, 5.4, 5.7, 5.23, and 6.1.

backcountry along the Susquehanna River. Later migrants moved to the backcountry of Maryland, Virginia, and the Carolinas. Frequently unable to afford land, they lived illegally on acreage belonging to Indians, land speculators, or colonial governments and gained a reputation for lawlessness, hard drinking, and fighting.

Migrants from Germany and German-speaking areas of Switzerland numbered about 85,000 between 1730 and 1755. They, too, usually came in family groups and landed in Philadelphia. By century's end, they accounted for one-third of Pennsylvania's residents. Many Germans moved west and then south into the backcountry of Maryland and Virginia, as well as of Charles Town and the southern interior. The Germans belonged to a wide variety of Protestant sects, adding to the already substantial religious diversity of Pennsylvania. So many Germans had arrived by

In December 1729, probably in New York's Hudson Valley, an unknown artist portrayed J. M. Stolle, the son of a Palatine immigrant who came to North America from Germany in 1709. The young man's fancy clothing and the column and balustrade in the background suggest that the artist wanted to convey an image of the family's economic success, though whether that image was accurate is unknown.   (National Gallery of Art, Washington, D.C. Gift of Edgar William and Bernice Chrysler Garbisch)

1751 that Benjamin Franklin feared they would Germanize Pennsylvania. They "will never adopt our Language or Customs," he predicted, inaccurately.

The most concentrated period of colonial migration fell between 1760 and 1775, when more than 220,000 free and enslaved people arrived—nearly 10 percent of the population of British North America. Tough economic times led many to seek a better life in America; simultaneously, the slave trade burgeoned. Late-arriving free immigrants had little choice but to remain in cities or move to the edges of settlement; land elsewhere was fully occupied. In the settlement periphery, they became the tenants of, or bought property from, land speculators.

Maintaining Ethnic and Religious Identities   Half of the colonial population south of New England had non-English origins by 1775. Assimilation into Anglo-American culture depended on settlement patterns, group size, and the migrants' cultural ties. The French Protestants (Huguenots) who migrated to Charles Town or New York City were unable to sustain either their language or religious practices for more than two generations, whereas Huguenots settling in the Hudson Valley remained recognizably French and Calvinist for a century. By contrast, the equally small group of colonial Jews maintained a distinct identity wherever they settled. In places like New York and Newport, Rhode Island, they established synagogues and preserved their religion.

Members of larger migrant groups (Germans, Irish, and Scots) found it easier to sustain European ways. Some ethnicities dominated certain localities. When migrants from different countries settled the same region, ethnic antagonisms surfaced. One German clergyman in Pennsylvania, for example, claimed that Scots-Irish were "lazy, dissipated and poor." Anglo-American elites fostered antagonisms to maintain their political and economic power and frequently subverted naturalization laws to deprive even long-resident immigrants a voice in government.

Ultimately, elites would need the support of non-English Americans. When they moved toward revolution in the 1770s, they quite deliberately began speaking of the rights of man, rather than English liberties, to enlist recruits.

ECONOMIC GROWTH AND DEVELOPMENT

The dramatic population increase in Anglo America caused its economies to grow, despite the vagaries of international markets. By contrast, the population and economy of New Spain's northern Borderlands stagnated. The isolated settlements produced few exports (notably, hides); residents typically exchanged goods illegally with French and English colonies rather than with Spanish Mexico or the Caribbean.

French Canada exported large quantities of furs and fish, but the government's trade monopoly ensured that most of the profits ended up in the home country. The Louisiana colony required substantial government subsidies, despite its active internal trade. Of France's American possessions, only the Caribbean islands flourished.

Population and Economic Growth

In British North America, the rising population increasingly demanded more goods and services; this led to the development of small-scale colonial manufacturing and a complex internal trade network. Roads, bridges, mills, and stores were built to serve new settlements. A lively coastal trade developed; more than half of the vessels leaving Boston by the late 1760s sailed to other mainland colonies, collecting exports and distributing imports and American-made goods. For the first time, the American population generated sufficient demand to encourage manufacturing enterprises, enabling the colonies to move away from dependence on European goods.

Iron making became the largest indigenous industry, surpassing England's by 1775. Located primarily in New Jersey, Pennsylvania, and the Chesapeake, ironworks required large investments and substantial work forces—usually indentured servants, convicts, and slaves—who dug the ore, chopped and hauled trees, then burned them to make charcoal, which was used to smelt and refine the ore. The work was dirty, dangerous, and difficult; convicts and servants often fled, but enslaved men gained valuable skills and could accumulate property because supervisors compensated them for extra work above assigned tasks. Colonial prosperity nevertheless depended chiefly on overseas demand for tobacco, rice, indigo, fish, and timber products. By selling these items, colonists earned credit to purchase English and European imports. If demand for American exports slowed, the colonists' income dropped.

Wealth and Poverty

Despite fluctuations, the American economy grew during the eighteenth century, in part due to higher earnings from exports. That, in turn produced better standards of living for property-owning Americans. Early in the century, as the price of British manufactures fell, households began acquiring amenities such as chairs and earthenware dishes. Diet also improved as trade brought more varied foodstuffs. After 1750, luxury items like silver plate could be found in wealthy homes, and the middling sort purchased imported English ceramics and teapots. Even the poorest property owners had more and better household goods.

Wealthy Americans improved their position relative to other colonists. Native-born elite families who dominated America by 1750 had begun the century with sufficient capital to take advantage of the changes caused by population growth. They were the urban merchants who exported raw materials and imported luxury goods, the large landowners who rented small farms to immigrant tenants, the slave traders, and the owners of rum distilleries. The rise of this moneyed group made mid-eighteenth-century America more socially and economically stratified.

New arrivals did not have the same opportunities for advancement as their predecessors. Still, at least two-thirds of rural householders owned their own land by 1750. But in cities, laboring families lived on the edge of destitution. By the 1760s, applicants for assistance overwhelmed public, urban poor-relief systems, and some cities established workhouses or almshouses to accommodate the growing number of poor, among them recent immigrants, the elderly and infirm, and widows, especially those with small children.

New England and King George's War

In New England, three elements influenced economic development: the landscape, shipping, and the impact of imperial wars. New England's farms produced little to sell other than livestock and timber; the region also had the lowest average wealth per freeholder in the colonies. But there were wealthy merchants who profited from trade with the Caribbean in salt fish and molasses (see Figure 4.1).

Boston, by the 1730s a major shipbuilding center, was greatly affected when British vessels clashed with Spanish ships in the Caribbean in 1739, sparking what became known in America as King George's War (Europeans called it the War of the Austrian Succession). The war initially energized Boston's economy, for ships—and sailors—were in great demand. Merchants profited by supplying military expeditions. But costly losses in Caribbean battles against Canada and an expensive victory in capturing the French Louisbourg fortress (in modern Nova Scotia) led to heavy

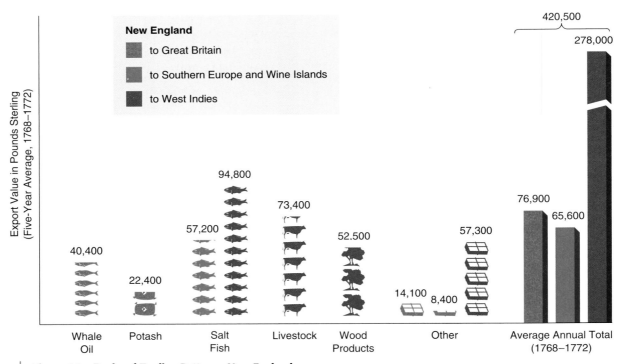

Figure 4.1   Regional Trading Patterns: New England

New England's major exports—salt fish, livestock, and wood products—were sold primarily in the West Indies.

(*Source:* James F. Shepherd and Gary M. Walton, *Shipping, Maritime Trade, and the Economic Development of Colonial North America* [Cambridge: Cambridge University Press, 1972]. Copyright 1972. Used by permission of Cambridge University Press.)

taxation of Massachusetts residents. After the war, the shipbuilding boom ended, the economy stagnated, taxes remained high, and widows and children crowded Boston's relief rolls. Britain even returned Louisbourg to France in the Treaty of Aix-la-Chapelle (1748).

Middle Colonies and the Chesapeake

King George's War affected the middle colonies and the Chesapeake more positively, thanks to the prevalence of commercial farming in the region's fertile soil. An average Pennsylvania farm family consumed only 40 percent of what it produced, selling the rest. New York and New Jersey both had many tenant farmers who leased acreage, often paying rent by sharing crops with landlords. Prosperous landlords and farmers profited from wartime demand for grain and flour, especially from the Caribbean (see Figure 4.2). After the war, several poor harvests in Europe caused flour prices to skyrocket. Philadelphia and New York, with grain- and livestock-producing areas, led the foodstuffs trade. Some Chesapeake planters began to convert tobacco fields to wheat and corn (see Figure 4.3). Tobacco remained the largest single export from mainland colonies, yet grain cultivation significantly changed Chesapeake settlement by encouraging the development of port towns (like Baltimore), where merchants and shipbuilders would handle the new trade.

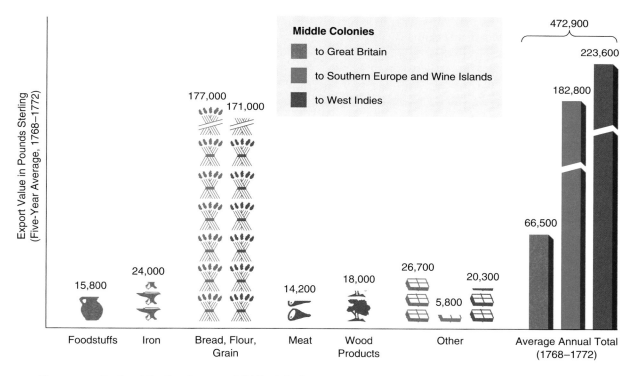

Figure 4.2   Regional Trading Patterns: Middle Colonies

The middle colonies' major trading partners were the West Indies, the Wine Islands, and southern Europe. Bread, flour, and grains were the region's most valuable exports.

(*Source:* James F. Shepherd and Gary M. Walton, *Shipping, Maritime Trade, and the Economic Development of Colonial North America* [Cambridge: University Press, 1972]. Used by permission of Cambridge University Press.)

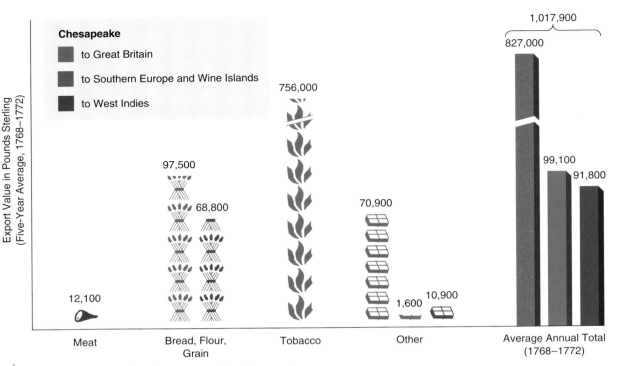

Figure 4.3   Regional Trading Patterns: The Chesapeake

Tobacco—legally exported only to Great Britain under the terms of the Navigation Acts—was the Chesapeake's dominant product. Grain made up an increasing proportion of the crops this region sold to other destinations.

(*Source:* James F. Shepherd and Gary M. Walton, *Shipping, Maritime Trade, and the Economic Development of Colonial North America* [Cambridge: Cambridge University Press, 1972]. Copyright 1972. Used by permission of Cambridge University Press.)

Carolina and Georgia   The Lower South, too, depended on staple crops and an enslaved labor force but had a distinctive pattern of economic growth. After Parliament in 1730 removed rice from the list of enumerated products, South Carolinians traded directly with Europe. Rice prices doubled by the late 1730s (see Figure 4.4). But the outbreak of King George's War disrupted trade. Rice prices plummeted, and South Carolina entered a decade-long depression. Rising European demand for South Carolina's exports restored prosperity by the 1760s. But throughout the century the colony's rice and indigo crops—and sugar cane in the Caribbean islands—were periodically devastated by hurricanes that caused some overextended planters to go bankrupt. Still, the Lower South grew faster than other regions and had the highest average wealth per freeholder in mainland Anglo America by the American Revolution.

The newest mainland settlement, Georgia, was chartered in 1732 as a haven for previously imprisoned English debtors; its founder, James Oglethorpe, envisioned Georgia as a garrison where farmers would defend the southern flank of English settlement against Spanish Florida. The charter prohibited slavery, but neighboring Carolina rice planters had the restriction removed in 1751. Thereafter, Georgia developed into a rice-planting slave society resembling South Carolina.

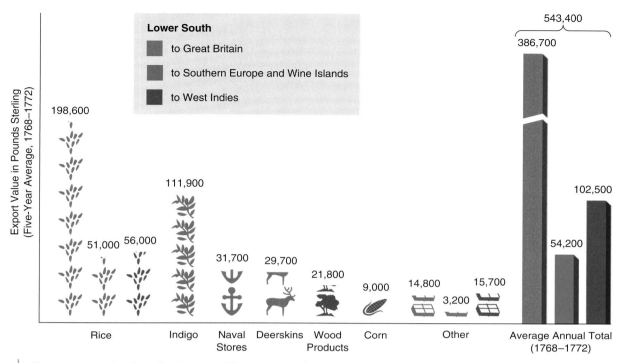

Figure 4.4   Regional Trading Patterns: The Lower South

Rice and indigo, sold primarily in the mother country, dominated the exports of the Lower South.

(*Source:* James F. Shepherd and Gary M. Walton, *Shipping, Maritime Trade, and the Economic Development of Colonial North America* [Cambridge: Cambridge University Press, 1972]. Copyright 1972. Used by permission of Cambridge University Press.)

Regional economic variations show that the British mainland colonies were not a unified whole. Despite increasing coastal trade, individual colonies' fortunes depended on the shifting markets of Europe and the Caribbean. Without an unprecedented crisis in the British imperial system (discussed in Chapter 5), it seems unlikely they could have been persuaded to join in a common endeavor. Even with that impetus, unity proved difficult to maintain.

COLONIAL CULTURES

By 1750, Britain's American possessions were marked by a denser, more diverse population than a half-century earlier, as well as by visible extremes of wealth and poverty, especially in cities. Native-born colonial elites sought to distinguish themselves from ordinary folk as they consolidated their hold on local power.

Genteel Culture

Colonists who acquired wealth through trade, agriculture, or manufacturing spent their money ostentatiously, dressing fashionably, traveling in horse-drawn carriages, and hosting lavish parties. They built large houses with rooms for dancing, cardplaying, or drinking tea. Sufficiently well-off to enjoy leisure time (a first for North America), they attended concerts and the theater, gambled at horse races, and played billiards and other games. They also cultivated polite manners. Although the effects of accumulated wealth were most pronounced in Anglo America, elite families in New Mexico, Louisiana, and Quebec as well set themselves off from the lesser sort. Together these wealthy families deliberately constructed a genteel culture quite different from that of ordinary colonists.

Men from such families prided themselves on their possessions, their positions in colonial society, their education, and their intellectual connections to Europe. Many had been tutored by private teachers; some attended college. (Harvard, the first colonial college, founded in 1636, was joined by William and Mary in 1693 and Yale in 1701.) In the seventeenth century, only aspiring clergymen attended college, but by the mid-eighteenth century, as colleges broadened their curricula to include mathematics, science, law, and medicine, young men from elite or upwardly mobile families enrolled. American women were mostly excluded from advanced education, except those tutored at nunneries in Canada or Louisiana.

The Enlightenment

The intellectual current known as the Enlightenment deeply affected the clergymen who headed colonial colleges and their students. Around 1650, European thinkers analyzed nature to determine the laws governing the universe. They employed experimentation and abstract reasoning to discover general principles behind phenomena like the motions of planets. Enlightenment philosophers emphasized acquiring knowledge through reason, challenging unquestioned assumptions. John Locke's *Essay Concerning Human Understanding* (1690) disputed the notion that human beings were imprinted with innate ideas at birth. All knowledge, Locke asserted, derived from observations. Belief in witchcraft, astrology, and similar phenomena thus came under attack.

The Enlightenment supplied educated, wealthy people in Europe and America with a common vocabulary and unified world-view—one that believed the enlightened eighteenth century was better and wiser than previous ages. It joined them in the common endeavor of making sense of God's creation. Thus American naturalists like John and William Bartram supplied European scientists with information about New World plants and animals for newly formulated classification systems. A prime example of America's participation in the Enlightenment was Benjamin Franklin, who retired from a successful printing business in 1748 at age forty-two, devoting himself to scientific experimentation and public service. His *Experiments and Observations on Electricity* (1751) established the basic theory of electricity still used today.

Enlightenment rationalism affected politics, too. Locke's *Two Treatises of Government* (1691) and works by French and Scottish philosophers challenged a divinely sanctioned, hierarchical political order originating in the power of fathers over families. Men created governments and could alter them, Locke declared. A ruler who broke the social contract and failed to protect people's rights could legitimately be ousted from power by peaceful—or violent—means. Enlightenment theorists proclaimed God's natural laws governed even the power of monarchs.

Smallpox Inoculation

Smallpox, the world's greatest killer of human beings, repeatedly ravaged North American colonists and Indians. Thus, when the vessel *Seahorse* arrived in Boston from the Caribbean in April 1721 with smallpox-infected people on board, New Englanders feared the worst and quarantined the ship. It was too late: smallpox escaped into the city, and by June several dozen people were infected.

But the Reverend Cotton Mather, a member of London's Royal Society (an Enlightenment organization), had read years earlier of a medical technique previously unknown to Europeans but widely employed in North Africa and the Middle East. Called inoculation, it involved taking pus from the pustules (or poxes) of an infected person and inserting it into a cut on the arm of a healthy individual. With luck, that person would experience a mild case and gain lifetime immunity. Mather's interest was further piqued by his slave Onesimus, a North African who had been inoculated as a youth and who described the procedure in detail.

With the disease coursing through the city, Mather promoted inoculation to the local medical community. But nearly all the city's doctors ridiculed his ideas, except Zabdiel Boylston, a physician and apothecary. The two men inoculated their children and about two hundred others. After the epidemic ended, Bostonians could see the results: of those inoculated, just 3 percent had died; among the thousands of others who contracted the disease, mortality was 15 percent. Even Mather's most vocal opponents supported inoculation thereafter.

Thus, through transatlantic links forged by the Enlightenment and enslavement, American colonists learned to combat the deadliest disease. Although Americans feared smallpox might be used as a biological weapon by its enemies after the attacks of September 11, 2001, no such incident has occurred. Today, thanks to a campaign by the World Health Organization, smallpox has been eradicated.

An Historical

ACCOUNT

OF THE

SMALL-POX

INOCULATED

IN

NEW ENGLAND,

Upon all Sorts of Persons, *Whites, Blacks,* and of all Ages and Constitutions.

With some Account of the Nature of the Infection in the NATURAL and INOCULATED Way, and their different Effects on HUMAN BODIES.

With some short DIRECTIONS to the UNEXPERIENCED in this Method of Practice.

Humbly dedicated to her Royal Highness the Princess of WALES, by *Zabdiel Boylston,* Physician.

LONDON:

Printed for S. CHANDLER, *at the* Cross-Keys *in the* Poultry. M.DCC.XXVI.

Several years after he and Cotton Mather combated a Boston smallpox epidemic by employing inoculation, Zabdiel Boylston published this pamphlet in London to spread the news of their success. The dedication to the Princess of Wales was designed to indicate the royal family's support of the procedure. (Picture Research Consultants and Archives)

Oral Cultures

The world in which such ideas were discussed was small. Books and newspapers were scarce until the 1750s, and many Anglo-Americans could not read or write. Youngsters who learned to read were usually taught at home by parents, older siblings, or local widows who needed extra income. More fortunate boys (and genteel girls after the 1750s) might learn to write in private schools. Few Americans other than some Church of England missionaries in the South tried to instruct enslaved children. And only the most zealous Indian converts learned Europeans' literacy skills.

Thus the cultures of colonial North America were primarily oral, communal, and local. Face-to-face conversation was the major means of communication. Different locales developed divergent cultural traditions, and racial and ethnic variations heightened those differences.

Religious and Civic Rituals

Church attendance was perhaps the most important ritual. In early New England Congregational (Puritan) churches, men and women sat on opposite sides of a central aisle, arranged by age, wealth, and church membership. By the mid-eighteenth century, wealthy husbands and wives sat in privately owned pews; their children, servants, slaves, and the less fortunate still sat in sex-segregated fashion at the rear, sides, or balcony of the church. In eighteenth-century Virginia, planter families purchased pews, and in some parishes landed gentlemen strode into church as a group just before the service, deliberately drawing attention to their exalted position. In Quebec City, formal processions of men into the parish church celebrated Catholic feast days; each participant's rank determined his place in the procession. By contrast, Quaker meetinghouses in Pennsylvania and elsewhere used an egalitarian but sex-segregated seating system. The various seating and entrance rituals symbolized social rank and local values.

Communal culture also centered on civic involvement. In New England, governments proclaimed official days of thanksgiving (for good harvests, military victories, etc.) and days of fasting and prayer (during difficulties such as droughts or epidemics). Everyone was expected to participate. Because able-bodied men between ages sixteen and sixty were required to serve in local militias, monthly musters also brought the community together.

In the Chesapeake, important rituals occurred on court and election days. When the county court met, men came to file lawsuits, appear as witnesses, or serve as jurors. Court attendance provided civic education; from the proceedings men learned what behavior was expected of them. Elections served the same purpose, for property-holding men voted in public. An election official, often flanked by the candidates for office, would call each voter forward to declare his preference. Voters would then be thanked by the gentleman selected, often treated later to rum at nearby taverns.

Throughout colonial North America, the public punishment of criminals served to both humiliate the offender and remind the community of proper behavioral standards. Public hangings, whippings, and sitting in the stocks expressed community outrage and restored harmony. Judges often assigned penalties that shamed miscreants. When a New Mexico man assaulted his father-in-law, he was directed to pay medical expenses and kneel before him publicly to beg his forgiveness.

Even after being pardoned of capital offenses, New Englanders were frequently ordered to wear nooses around their necks for years, as a reminder to all of their violation of community norms.

Rituals of Consumption

By 1770 Anglo-American households allocated roughly one-quarter of their spending to consumer goods, which fostered new rituals centered on consumption and created what historians have termed an empire of goods. In the seventeenth century, settlers acquired necessities by bartering with neighbors or ordering from a home-country merchant. By the middle of the eighteenth century, specialized shops selling nonessentials proliferated in cities like Philadelphia and New Orleans. In 1770 Boston had more than five hundred stores, offering millinery, sewing supplies, tobacco, gloves, tableware, and the like. Even small towns had one or two retail establishments. Colonists would set aside time to go shopping, a novel and pleasurable leisure activity that marked the beginning of consumption rituals.

Colonists took pleasure in owning and displaying lovely objects for neighbors and kin to see: hanging a mirror prominently, displaying a ceramic bowl on a table, turning fabric into special clothing. A rich man might hire an artist to paint his family using the objects, thereby creating a record to be displayed.

Tea and Madeira

Tea drinking, a consumption ritual dominated by women, played an important role in Anglo America. Households with aspirations to genteel status sought the necessary items for the proper tea consumption: pots, cups, strainers, sugar tongs, bowls, and special tables. Tea provided a focal point for socializing and, because of its cost, served as a status symbol. Wealthy women regularly entertained friends at afternoon tea parties. Because tea also appeared healthful, even poor households consumed it, although without the fancy equipment of their wealthier neighbors.

Another genteel drink was Madeira wine, imported from the Portuguese islands. By 1770 Madeira had become the favored drink of the elite, expensive to purchase and consume properly. Opening the bottle, letting it breathe, decanting and serving it with appropriate glassware were all accomplished with elaborate ceremony. After the 1750s, urban dwellers could buy wines at specialized stores. Much of it must have been smuggled, because more wines were advertised than were recorded in customs records.

Rituals on the Middle Ground

Other rituals provided an opportunity for the disparate cultures of colonial North America to interact. Particularly important rituals developed on what the historian Richard White has termed the *middle ground*—the psychological and geographical space in which Indians and Europeans encountered each other, primarily via trade or warfare.

When Europeans sought to trade with Indians, they encountered an indigenous exchange system that stressed gift giving over buying and selling. Successful bargaining required French and English traders to present Indians with gifts (cloth, rum, gunpowder, and other items) before negotiating with them for pelts and skins. Only after those gifts were reciprocated could formal trading begin. Rum became a crucial component, as traders concluded that drunken Indians would sell their furs more cheaply, and some Indians refused to hunt or trade unless they first received rum. Alcohol abuse hastened the deterioration of villages already devastated by disease and dislocation.

Intercultural rituals also developed to deal with murders. Where Europeans sought primarily to punish the murderer, Indians regarded Europeans' eye for an eye revenge as only one possible response. Compensation could also be accomplished by capturing another Indian or a colonist to take the dead person's place or by "covering the dead"—providing the deceased's family with compensatory goods. Eventually, the French and the Algonquians evolved an elaborate ritual borrowed from both societies' traditions: murders were investigated and murderers identified, but deaths were covered by trade goods rather than blood revenge.

COLONIAL FAMILIES

Families constituted the basic units of colonial society, serving as the mechanism for production and consumption. Never-married adults were extremely rare. Yet family forms varied widely, and not all were headed by couples.

Indian and Mixed-Race Families As Europeans consolidated their hold on North America, Indians had to adapt. Bands reduced by disease and warfare recombined into new units; for example, the Catawbas emerged in the 1730s in the western Carolinas by merging several earlier peoples including the Yamasees and Guales. Likewise, European authorities reshaped Indian family forms. Whereas many Indian societies had permitted easy divorce, European missionaries frowned on it; and societies that had allowed polygynous marriages (including New England Algonquians) redefined them to designate one wife as legitimate and others as concubines.

With continued high mortality rates, extended kin took on new importance in Indian societies, with other relatives—even occasionally nonkin—assuming child-rearing responsibilities when parents died. Once Europeans established dominance in any region, Indians were unable to pursue traditional modes of subsistence, pushing them into unusual family structures and new economic strategies. In New England, for instance, Algonquian husbands and wives survived by working separately and often living apart (perhaps wives as domestic servants, husbands as sailors). Some native women married African American men, due to sexual imbalances in both populations. In New Mexico, detribalized Navajos, Pueblos, and Apaches employed as servants by Spanish settlers clustered in the small Borderlands towns. Known as *genizaros,* they lost contact with Indian cultures, instead living on the fringes of Latino society.

Wherever the population contained relatively few European women, sexual liaisons occurred between European men and Indian women. The resulting mixed-race population of *mestizos* and *métis* worked as a familial middle ground to ease other cultural interactions. In New France and the Anglo-American backcountry, such families resided in Indian villages, and their children sometimes became prominent

Native American leaders. By contrast, in the Spanish Borderlands the offspring of Europeans and *genízaros* were shunned.
Largely denied legal marriage, they bore generations of illegitimate children of various racial mixtures, giving rise in Latino
society to multiple labels describing degrees of skin color with
a precision unknown in English or French America.

European American Families

To eighteenth-century Anglo-
Americans, the word *family* meant
everyone in one household (in-
cluding servants and slaves). In 1790 the average home in the
United States contained 5.7 free people; few included extended kin, such as grandparents. Family members worked
together to produce goods for consumption or sale. The
head of the household represented it to the outside world,
voting in elections, managing the finances, and holding legal
authority over the rest of the family—his wife, his children,
and his servants and slaves.

In English, French, and Spanish America, the vast majority of European families supported themselves by cultivating
crops and raising livestock. While the work differed by region
and crop produced, household tasks were allocated by sex.

The mistress oversaw her female helpers in what Anglo-
Americans called indoor affairs, preparing food, cleaning the
house, doing laundry, and often making clothes. Along with
cooking, food preparation involved cultivating a garden, harvesting and preserving vegetables, salting and smoking meat,
drying apples and pressing cider, milking cows, and making
butter and cheese. The head of the household and his male
helpers, managed outdoor affairs, cultivating the fields,
building fences, chopping wood, harvesting and marketing
crops, caring for livestock, and butchering cattle and hogs.
Farm work was so extensive that a married couple could not
do it alone; if childless, they needed servants or slaves.

African American Families

Most African American families
lived as components of European
American households. More than
95 percent of colonial African Americans were held in perpet-
ual bondage, sometimes on farms with only a few other slaves. In South Carolina, a
majority of the population was of African origin; in Georgia, about half; and in the
Chesapeake, 40 percent. Portions of the Carolina low country were nearly 90 percent
African American by 1790.

Where African Americans lived determined the shape of their families. In the
North, the scarcity of other blacks made it difficult for bondspeople to form stable
households. In the Chesapeake, men and women who regarded themselves as married (slaves could not legally wed) frequently lived on different quarters or different

In eighteenth-century Spain, the existence of
mixed-race North American families aroused
great curiosity, creating a market for so-called
casta paintings, which illustrated different
sorts of multiracial households. In 1763 the
Mexican artist Miguel Cabrera depicted a
Spanish father and an Indian mother, who
have produced a *mestiza* daughter. Real
families resembling this idealized picture
would have been seen in New Mexico.
(© The Gallery Collection / Corbis)

plantations. Children generally resided with their mothers. On large Carolina and Georgia rice plantations, enslaved families usually lived together and accumulated property by working for themselves after completing daily tasks. Some Georgia slaves sold surplus produce, earning money for nice clothing or such luxuries as tobacco, but rarely enough for their freedom.

Forms of Resistance

Because all British colonies legally permitted slavery, bondspeople had few options for escaping servitude other than fleeing to Florida, where the Spanish offered protection. Some recently arrived Africans stole boats or ran off to join Indians or establish independent communities on the frontier. Among American-born slaves, family ties strongly affected such decisions. As one South Carolina planter wrote, slaves "love their families dearly and none runs away from the other." Consequently, many owners sought to keep families together. In the Chesapeake, where family members often lived separately, affectionate ties could cause slaves to run away, especially if family members were sold.

Although colonial slaves rarely rebelled collectively, they resisted in other ways. Bondspeople rejected owners' attempts to commandeer their labor on Sundays without compensation. Extended-kin groups protested excessive punishment of relatives and sought to live near one another. If parents and children were separated by sale, other relatives helped with child rearing. Just as among Indians, the extended family served a more important function for African Americans than for European Americans.

Most slave families carved out some autonomy, especially in their working and spiritual lives, and particularly in the Lower South. Some African Americans preserved traditional beliefs or Islamic faith, while others converted to Christianity, comforted by its assurances that everyone would be free and equal in heaven. South Carolina and Georgia slaves jealously guarded their ability to control their time after completing their tasks. Even on Chesapeake tobacco plantations, slaves planted gardens and trapped or fished to supplement their meager diet. Late in the century, some Chesapeake planters began to hire slaves out, often allowing the workers to keep some of their earnings.

City Life

In cities, African and European Americans resided together in unsegregated neighborhoods. (In 1760s Philadelphia, one-fifth of the work force was enslaved, and by 1775 blacks composed nearly 15 percent of New York City's population.) Such cities were tiny by today's standards. In 1750 the largest cities, Boston and Philadelphia, had just seventeen thousand and thirteen thousand inhabitants, respectively. Unlike their rural counterparts, city dwellers purchased food and wood, and men's jobs frequently took them away from their household, giving them greater contact with the broader world.

By the 1750s, most major cities had at least one weekly newspaper. Anglo-American newspapers mixed local reports with the latest advices from London (usually two to three months old). People who could not afford to buy newspapers could either read them (or listen to them read aloud) at taverns and coffeehouses. Urban contact with the outside world, however, meant sailors sometimes brought deadly diseases into port. Boston, New York, Philadelphia, and New Orleans endured small-pox and yellow fever epidemics, which Europeans and Africans in the countryside largely escaped.

POLITICS: STABILITY AND CRISIS IN BRITISH AMERICA

Early in the eighteenth century, Anglo-American political life exhibited new stability. Despite substantial immigration, most mainland residents were born in America. Men from genteel families dominated the political structures, for voters (free male property holders) typically deferred to their well-educated betters in elections.

Colonial Assemblies   Throughout the Anglo-American colonies, political leaders sought to increase the powers of elected assemblies relative to that of governors and other appointed officials. Assemblies began to claim privileges associated with the British House of Commons, such as initiating tax legislation and controlling the militia. Assemblies also influenced British appointees by threatening to withhold their salaries. In some colonies (Virginia and South Carolina, for example), elite assemblymen presented a united front to royal officials, but in others (such as New York), they fought among themselves bitterly. To win hotly contested elections, New York's genteel leaders began competing for commoners' votes. Yet in 1733 the New York government imprisoned a newspaper editor, John Peter Zenger, who had criticized it, on the charge of seditious libel. Arguing that the truth could not be defamatory, his lawyer helped establish the free-press principle in American law.

Assemblymen saw themselves as acting to prevent encroachments on the colonists' liberties, for example, by preventing governors from imposing oppressive taxes. By midcentury, they were comparing the structure of their governments to Britain's balanced polity, equating their governors with the monarch, their councils with the aristocracy, and their assemblies with the House of Commons. All three were believed essential to good government, but Anglo-Americans viewed governors and appointed councils as Britain's representatives and potential threats to colonial ways of life. Many colonists saw the assemblies, however, as the people's protectors. And the assemblies regarded themselves as the people's representatives.

In reality, the assemblies, controlled by dominant families whose members were reelected year after year, rarely responded to poorer constituents' concerns. They also did not reapportion themselves to provide representation for new settlements; this led to grievances among backcountry dwellers, especially non-English ethnic groups. The colonial ideal of the assembly as the defender of liberty was a myth. In truth, the most ably represented were wealthy male colonists, particularly the assembly members themselves.

At midcentury, the political structures that had stabilized in a period of relative calm confronted a series of crises—ethnic, racial, economic, and regional—that exposed internal tensions and foreshadowed the disorder of the revolutionary era. They demonstrated that the political accommodations achieved after the Glorious Revolution could no longer adequately govern Britain's American empire.

Slave Rebellions in South Carolina and New York

Early on Sunday, September 9, 1739, about twenty enslaved men, most likely Catholics from Kongo, gathered near the Stono River south of Charles Town. September fell in the midst of the rice harvest (and thus a stressful time for male Africans, less accustomed than women to rice cultivation), and September 8 was, to Catholics, the birthday of the Virgin Mary. Seizing guns and ammunition, the slaves killed storekeepers and nearby planter families. Then, joined by other slaves, they headed toward Florida in hopes of finding refuge. By midday, however, the militia attacked the nearly one hundred fugitives, killing some and dispersing the rest. A week later, most of the remaining conspirators were captured and executed. But for two years rumors about escaped renegades haunted the colony.

After the Stono Rebellion, laws governing African Americans were stiffened throughout British America. In New York City, the site of the first mainland slave revolt in 1712, the Stono news combined with fears of Spain generated by the outbreak of King George's War to set off a reign of terror in the summer of 1741. Colonial authorities suspected a biracial gang of thieves and arsonists of fomenting a slave uprising under the guidance of a white schoolteacher thought to be a Spanish priest. By summer's end, thirty-one blacks and four whites had been executed for participating in the alleged plot. The Stono Rebellion and the New York conspiracy confirmed Anglo-Americans' deepest fears about the dangers of slaveholding and revealed the assemblies' inability to prevent internal disorder.

Rioters and Regulators

By midcentury, with most fertile land east of the Appalachians purchased or occupied, conflicts over land titles and conditions of landholding increased. In 1746, for example, violence erupted when the East proprietors claimed farmers' land as theirs and demanded annual payments, called quit-rents. The most serious land riots occurred along the Hudson River in 1765–1766. Late in the seventeenth century, the governor of New York had granted huge tracts in the lower Hudson valley to prominent families. They then divided these estates into small farms, which they rented to poor Dutch and German migrants who regarded tenancy as a step toward independence.

After 1740, though, New Englanders increasingly migrated to the region, resisting tenancy and often squatting. In the mid-1760s the Philipse family sued farmers who had lived on Philipse land for two decades. The courts ordered squatters to make way for tenants with valid leases. Instead, a diverse group of farmers rebelled, terrorizing proprietors and tenants and on one occasion battling a county sheriff and his posse. The rebellion lasted nearly a year, ending when British troops captured its leaders.

Violent conflicts erupted in the Carolinas as well when the Regulator movements of the late 1760s (South Carolina) and early 1770s (North Carolina) pitted backcountry farmers against wealthy eastern planters who controlled colonial governments. In South Carolina, Scots-Irish settlers protested their lack of an adequate voice in political affairs. For months they policed the countryside in vigilante bands known as Regulators, complaining of lax and biased law enforcement. North Carolina Regulators, who objected to heavy taxation, lost a battle with eastern militiamen at Alamance in 1771.

A CRISIS IN RELIGION

The most widespread crisis was religious. From the mid-1730s through the 1760s, waves of religious revivalism—today known as the First Great Awakening—swept over various colonies, primarily New England (1735–1745) and Virginia (1750s–1760s). Orthodox Calvinists sought to combat Enlightenment rationalism, which denied innate human depravity. The economic and political uncertainty accompanying King George's War made colonists receptive to evangelists' messages. With no prior religious affiliation, many recent immigrants and backcountry residents became potential converts.

The Great Awakening began in New England, where descendants of the Puritan founding generation still composed the membership of Congregational churches. While church members were predominantly female, men and women responded with equal fervor. In the mid-1730s, the Northampton, Massachusetts, preacher and theologian Reverend Jonathan Edwards gained new youthful adherents with a Calvinist-based message that individuals could attain salvation, only by recognizing their depraved nature and surrendering completely to God's will.

George Whitefield

The effects of such conversions remained isolated until 1739, when George Whitefield, a Church of England clergyman, who led celebrated revivals in England, arrived in America. A gripping orator, Whitefield toured the British colonies for fifteen months, effectively generating the Great Awakening by preaching to large audiences from

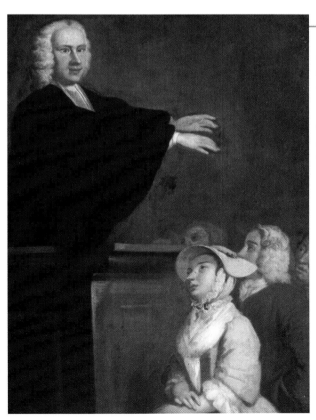

Reverend George Whitefield, the charismatic evangelist who sparked the First Great Awakening in the mainland British colonies, attracted harsh critics as well as avid admirers. Here an English cartoonist satirizes him as a money-grubbing charlatan who hoodwinks his gullible followers into believing that he is a "Pious Churchman" motivated by "Holy Zeal." Whitefield's crossed eyes, obvious in this image as in others, played a prominent role in contemporary depictions of him. (The Granger Collection, New York)

Georgia to New England. The historian Harry Stout has termed him *the first modern celebrity* because of his skillful self-promotion and clever manipulation of both listeners and the newspapers. Everywhere he traveled, his fame preceded him. Readers snapped up books by and about him, among the first colonial bestsellers. Thousands of free and enslaved folk from Boston to Savannah heard him speak and experienced conversion. Whitefield's journey created new interconnections among the previously distinct colonies.

Regular clerics initially welcomed Whitefield and his American-born imitators, but soon concluded that the revived religion ran counter to their own doctrine. They disliked the emotional style of the revivalists, who lured churchgoers away from their usual church services. Particularly troublesome to the orthodox were the female exhorters who publicly proclaimed their right to expound God's word.

Impact of the Awakening

Opposition to the Awakening heightened rapidly, further splintering the already fragmented American Protestantism. Major denominations split into Old Lights—traditional clerics and their followers—and New Lights—the evangelicals. New sects such as Methodists and Baptists also gained adherents. Paradoxically, the angry fights and the rapid rise in the number of distinct denominations eventually inspired an American willingness to tolerate religious diversity. Since no single sect could make an unequivocal claim to orthodoxy, they had to coexist if they were to exist at all.

Most significantly, the Awakening challenged traditional social patterns, in particular the colonial tradition of deference. Itinerant preachers, only a few of whom were ordained, claimed they understood God's will better than elite college-educated clerics. They and their followers divided the world into the saved and the damned, without respect to gender, age, or status. New Lights also defended the rights of individuals to dissent from a community consensus, thereby challenging fundamental tenets of colonial political life. The egalitarian themes of the Awakening simultaneously attracted ordinary folk and repelled the elite.

Virginia Baptists

By the 1760s Baptists gained a foothold in Virginia, but their beliefs clashed with genteel lifestyles. They rejected as sinful the horseracing, gambling, and dancing that occupied the gentry's leisure time. They dressed plainly, in contrast to the gentry's opulence. They addressed one another as Brother and Sister regardless of social status, and they elected their congregation's leaders. Their monthly great meetings, which attracted hundreds of people, introduced new public rituals that rivaled weekly Anglican services.

Strikingly, almost all the Virginia Baptist congregations included free and enslaved members, and some had African American majorities. Church rules applied equally to all members; interracial sexual relationships, divorce, and adultery were forbidden. Congregations forbade masters from breaking up slave couples through sale. Biracial committees investigated complaints about members' misbehavior. Churches excommunicated slaves for stealing from their masters and masters for physically abusing their slaves.

By injecting an egalitarian strain into Anglo-American life at midcentury, the Great Awakening had important social and political consequences, calling into question habitual modes of behavior in the secular as well as the religious realm.

"Self-Made Men"

Americans universally celebrate the ideal of the self-made man (always someone explicitly *male*) of humble origins who gains wealth through extraordinary efforts. Most commonly cited as examples are nineteenth-century businessmen such as Andrew Carnegie (a poor immigrant from Scotland) and John D. Rockefeller (born on a hardscrabble farm in upstate New York).

The initial exemplars, though, lived in the eighteenth century. Benjamin Franklin's *Autobiography* chronicled his method for achieving success after beginning life as the seventeenth child of a Boston candle maker. From such humble origins Franklin became a wealthy, influential man active in science, politics, education, and diplomacy. Yet Franklin's tale is rivaled by that of a man apparently born a slave in South Carolina. He acquired literacy, worked as a sailor, purchased his freedom, became an influential abolitionist, married a wealthy Englishwoman, and published a popular autobiography that predated Franklin's. His first master called him Gustavus Vassa, but when publishing his *Interesting Narrative* in 1789, he called himself Olaudah Equiano.

In his *Narrative*, Equiano said he was born in Africa in 1745, kidnapped at the age of eleven, and transported to Barbados and then to Virginia, where a British naval officer purchased him. For years, scholars and students have relied on that account for its insights into the experience of the middle passage. But evidence recently uncovered by Vincent Carretta, although confirming much of Equiano's autobiography, shows that Equiano twice identified his birthplace as Carolina and was three to five years younger than he claimed. Carretta speculates that the *Narrative* gained its credibility from Equiano's African birth and that admitting his real age would have raised questions about his early life.

Equiano, or Vassa, thus truly made himself, just as Benjamin Franklin and many others have done. (Franklin tended to omit, rather than alter, inconvenient parts of his personal history, for example, his having fathered an illegitimate son.) Equiano used information undoubtedly gleaned from acquaintances who *had* experienced the middle passage to craft an accurate depiction of its horrors. In the process he became one of the first Americans to explicitly reinvent himself.

Summary

Over the half-century before 1770, British North America was transformed, partly by the many newcomers from Germany, Scotland, Ireland, and Africa, who brought their languages, customs, and religions with them. The European immigrants were concentrated in the growing cities and backcountry. By contrast, enslaved migrants from Africa lived and worked within 100 miles of the Atlantic coast. In many colonial South areas, 50 to 90 percent of the population was of African origin.

The economic life of Europe's North American colonies proceeded on two levels. On the farms, plantations, and ranches where most colonists resided, arduous labor dominated people's lives while providing the goods for consumption or sale. Simultaneously, an intricate international trade network affected the economies of the British, French, and Spanish colonies. The bitter wars fought by European nations during the eighteenth century both created new opportunities for overseas sales and disrupted traditional markets. The few who reaped the profits of international commerce were the wealthy class of merchants and landowners who dominated colonial life. A century and a half after Europeans first settled in North America, the colonies mixed diverse European, American, and African traditions into a novel cultural blend.

Europeans who interacted regularly with peoples of African and American origin—and with Europeans from other nations—developed new methods of accommodating intercultural differences while also creating ties within their own potentially fragmenting communities. Initially, many colonists continued to identify themselves as French, Spanish, or British rather than as Americans, but in the 1760s some Anglo-Americans began to realize that their interests did not necessarily coincide with those of Great Britain.

Chapter Review

POPULATION GROWTH AND ETHNIC DIVERSITY

What spurred population growth in the thirty years before 1775?

Immigration—particularly Scots-Irish and Germans—contributed to some of the population growth among European Americans, but the largest single factor was natural increase (live births). Once the difficult years of early settlement passed and the sex ratio evened out in the South, the population doubled every twenty-five years. Natural increase also boosted the African American enslaved population after 1740, and in some regions the slave population was further augmented by new imports.

ECONOMIC GROWTH AND DEVELOPMENT

How were the colonies' economic fate increasingly linked to world markets?

Simply put, as colonial population grew, the increased demand for goods and products sparked the development of small-scale American manufacturing and broader trade networks. Moreover, selling tobacco, rice, indigo, fish, and timber overseas provided the resources for colonists to import what they did not produce and to prosper individually and regionally. But as colonies became more entwined in overseas trade, their fortunes were increasingly tied to the ups and downs of those economies. The outbreak of King George's War, for example, disrupted the rice trade and caused prices to plummet.

COLONIAL CULTURES

How did rituals function in colonial America?

Cultural rituals played a central role in colonial life, both to create community and reinforce social status. Church rituals were among the most important, but also the most revealing, with seating arrangements often made by sex, class, age, or wealth. Civic rituals likewise generated community involvement and revealed what society expected of its members. In New England, everyone was expected to participate in official holidays or local militia musters; in the Chesapeake, rituals centered on court or election days; and public punishment of criminals throughout North America was a ritual designed to reinforce behavioral standards.

Even simple rituals, such as tea-drinking, reinforced gender norms but also distinctions of wealth and status. Finally, colonists created middle ground rituals to facilitate trade with Indians, who had vastly different customs. Europeans seeking to trade with Indians engaged in the gift-giving system typical of native cultures before trade could begin.

COLONIAL FAMILIES

How did European American families differ from those of Indians or African Americans?

Anglo Americans used the word "family" to describe everyone in a household: parents, children, extended kin, and slaves. Families typically supported themselves by farming, with each member assigned a task according to gender norms. (Women did indoor work and related tasks; men did outdoor work.) Indian families were more fluid; before contact with Europeans, they permitted divorce, for example. After contact, extended kin became more important, particularly as families were decimated by disease. Shortages of European women in some colonies fueled increased inter-marriages, with children raised in Indian villages rather than among settlers. Most African Americans were enslaved, and their families subsumed under European American households. In the Chesapeake, slaves who considered themselves married (despite laws prohibiting slave marriage) often lived in different quarters or plantations with children residing with mothers (and potentially sold off at any time.) On large Georgia or Carolina rice plantations, slave families often lived together.

POLITICS: STABILITY AND CRISIS IN BRITISH AMERICA

What were the myths and realities of colonial assemblies?

Anglo-American assemblymen believed they safeguarded colonists' liberties from encroachments by the British government, such as oppressive taxation. Regarding Britain's appointed councils and governors as potential threats, colonists looked to assemblies as their protectors. In truth, elite, wealthy families dominated the assemblies and paid little regard to constituents' concerns, nor did they reapportion themselves so that new settlements would gain representatives, which angered backcountry residents and non-English immigrants.

A CRISIS IN RELIGION

What was the social and political impact of the Great Awakening?

Socially, the Great Awakening challenged traditional norms and patterns. Women, for example, began to claim an equal right to preach, and Protestant denominations further split into the "Old Lights"—who followed traditional teachings and ministers—and the "New Light evangelicals. In the end, the rise of new denominations promoted greater tolerance for religious diversity, but at the time, it sparked animosity. The Great Awakening's egalitarianism also challenged the colonial tradition of deference, in which people knew their place and respected their so-called "betters." New Lights attracted ordinary people as followers and preachers, and argued that the world was divided into the saved and the damned without respect to gender, age or status.

SUGGESTIONS FOR FURTHER READING

Marilyn Baseler, *"Asylum for Mankind": America 1607–1800* (1998)

Richard R. Beeman, *The Varieties of Political Experiences in Eighteenth-Century America* (2004)

James F. Brooks, *Captives and Cousins: Slavery, Kinship, and Community in the Southwest Borderlands* (2002)

William E. Burns, *Science and Technology in Colonial America* (2005)

Richard Bushman, *The Refinement of America: Persons, Houses, Cities* (1992)

Rhys Isaac, *The Transformation of Virginia, 1740–1790* (1982)

Jill Lepore, *New York Burning: Liberty, Slavery, and Conspiracy in Eighteenth-Century Manhattan* (2005)

John J. McCusker and Russell R. Menard, *The Economy of British America, 1607–1789* (1985)

Harry S. Stout, *The Divine Dramatist: George Whitefield and the Rise of Modern Evangelicalism* (1991)

Stephanie G. Wolf, *As Various as Their Land: The Everyday Lives of 18th Century Americans* (1992)

Severing the Bonds of Empire

The well-born Scotswoman Janet Schaw chose an inopportune time to visit her older brother in North America. Sailing from Edinburgh in October 1774, she arrived in the West Indies in January 1775, where she visited Scottish planter families and did some shopping before sailing on to meet her brother in North Carolina. There she encountered "rusticks" who had, in her opinion, a "rooted hatred" for the mother country and were forming "schemes" detrimental to Britain and America.

Janet Schaw soon learned that an American congress had forbidden "every kind of diversion, even card-playing." When Wilmington residents held a ball before the ban took effect, she compared it to seventeenth-century Dutch paintings of comic, carousing peasants. She also reported that "the Ladies have burnt their tea in a solemn procession," but added, "the sacrifice was not very considerable, as I do not think any one offered above a quarter of a pound." All the "genteel" merchants, she observed, "disapprove of the present proceedings," and were planning to leave. She concluded that the trouble in the colonies had been caused by "mistaken notions of moderation" in parliamentary policy. Janet returned to Scotland within the year; her brother's property was later confiscated by the state for refusing an oath of allegiance, but he remained in his new homeland until his death.

In retrospect, John Adams identified 1760 to 1775 as the era of the true American Revolution. The Revolution, Adams declared, ended before the fighting started, for it was "in the Minds of the people," involving not the actual wartime victory but a shift of allegiance from Britain to America. Today, not all historians would concur. But none would deny the importance of the events of those crucial years, which divided Americans politically and pointed the colonies toward independence.

This icon will direct you to interactive activities and study materials on A People And A Nation, Brief Edition website: **www.cengage.com/history/norton/peoplenationbrief8e**

Chronology

1754	Albany Congress meets to try to forge colonial unity.
	Fighting breaks out with Washington's defeat at Fort Necessity.
1756	Britain declares war on France; Seven Years' War officially begins.
1759	British forces take Quebec.
1760	American phase of war ends with fall of Montreal to British troops.
	George III becomes king.
1763	Treaty of Paris ends Seven Years' War.
	Pontiac's allies attack British forts in the West.
	Proclamation of 1763 attempts to close land west of the Appalachians to English settlement.
1764	Sugar Act lays new duties on molasses and tightens customs regulations.
	Currency Act outlaws paper money issued by the colonies.
1765	Stamp Act requires stamps on all printed materials in the colonies.
	Sons of Liberty is formed.
1766	Stamp Act is repealed.
	Declaratory Act insists that Parliament can tax the colonies.
1767	Townshend Acts lay duties on trade within the empire and sends new officials to America.
1768	Fort Stanwix treaty opens Kentucky to Anglo-American settlement.
1768–70	Townshend duties are resisted; boycotts and public demonstrations divide merchants and urban artisans.
1770	Lord North becomes prime minister.
	Townshend duties are repealed, except for tea tax.
	Boston Massacre kills five colonial rioters.
1772	Boston Committee of Correspondence is formed.
1773	Tea Act aids the East India Company.
	Boston Tea Party protests the Tea Act.
1774	Coercive Acts punish Boston and Massachusetts as a whole.
	Quebec Act reforms government of Quebec.
	First Continental Congress is called.

During the 1760s and early 1770s, an ever-widening split occurred between Great Britain and Anglo America. In the long history of British settlement in the Western Hemisphere, tension had occasionally marred the relationship between individual provinces and the mother country. Still, it rarely persisted for long and was not widespread, except during the crisis following the Glorious Revolution in 1689. In the 1750s, however, a series of events beginning with the Seven Years' War drew the colonists' attention toward their relations with Great Britain.

Britain's overwhelming victory in that war, confirmed by treaty in 1763, forever altered the balance of power in North America. France was ousted from the continent and Spain from Florida, with major consequences for interior indigenous peoples and British colonists. Indians, who were expert at playing European powers against one another, lost a major diplomatic tool. Anglo-Americans no longer feared the French on their northern and western borders or the Spanish in the Southeast. The coastal British colonies would never have risked breaking with their mother country, some historians contend, had France still controlled the Mississippi River and the Great Lakes.

The British victory in 1763 left Great Britain with a massive war debt that needed to be repaid. Consequently, Parliament for the first time imposed revenue-raising taxes on the colonies in addition to the customs duties that had long regulated trade. That exposed differences in the political thinking of Americans and Britons that had previously been obscured by a shared political vocabulary.

During the 1760s and early 1770s, Anglo-American men and women resisted new tax levies and Britain's attempts to tighten controls over provincial governments. The colonies' elected leaders became increasingly suspicious of Britain's motives. They laid aside old antagonisms to coordinate their responses to these measures. As late as summer 1774, though, most were seeking a solution within the empire; few harbored thoughts of independence.

- **What were the causes and consequences of the Seven Years' War?**
- **What British policies did Americans protest, and what theories and strategies did they develop to support those protests?**
- **Was a war for independence inevitable by the end of 1773? Why or why not?**

RENEWED WARFARE AMONG EUROPEANS AND INDIANS

In the mid-eighteenth century, British colonies along the Atlantic seaboard were surrounded by potentially hostile neighbors: Indians everywhere, the Spanish in Florida and the Gulf of Mexico, the French along the rivers and lakes stretching from the St. Lawrence to the Mississippi. Spanish outposts posed little threat, since Spain was no longer a major power. However, France's forts and settlements dominated the North American interior. In all three Anglo-French wars between 1689 and 1748 Britain could not shake France's hold on the American frontier. Under the Peace of Utrecht, which ended Queen Anne's War in 1713, England won control of such peripheral northern areas as Newfoundland, Hudson's Bay, and Acadia (Nova Scotia). But Britain made no territorial gains in King George's War (see Table 5.1).

Iroquois Neutrality   During Queen Anne's War and King George's War, the Iroquois Confederacy maintained a neutrality policy first developed in 1701. While British and French forces vied for nominal control of North America, the confederacy skillfully manipulated the Europeans, refusing to commit warriors to either side despite gifts from both. The Iroquois continued a long-standing conflict with Cherokees and Catawbas in the South, thus giving young warriors combat experience and replacing population

TABLE 5.1 The Colonial Wars, 1689–1763

American Name	European Name	Dates	Participants	American Sites	Dispute
King William's War	War of the League of Augsburg	1689–97	England, Holland versus France, Spain	New England, New York, Canada	French power
Queen Anne's War	War of the Spanish Succession	1702–13	England, Holland, Austria versus France, Spain	Florida, New England	Throne of Spain
King George's War	War of the Austrian Succession	1739–48	England, Holland, Austria versus France, Spain, Prussia	West Indies, New England, Canada	Throne of Austria
French and Indian War	Seven Years' War	1756–63	England versus France, Spain	Ohio country, Canada	Possession of Ohio country

losses with new captives. They also cultivated peaceful relationships with Pennsylvania and Virginia, partly to obtain the colonists' imprimatur for their domination of the Shawnees and Delawares. And they forged ties with Algonquians of the Great Lakes region, thereby making themselves indispensable go-betweens for commerce between the Atlantic coast and the West. Thus the Iroquois consolidated their control over the interior north of Virginia and south of the Great Lakes.

But the region inhabited by the Shawnees and Delawares (now western Pennsylvania and Virginia, and eastern Ohio) provided the spark that set off a major war. In a significant reversal of previous patterns, that conflict spread from America to Europe, decisively resolving the contest for North America.

Trouble began in the 1740s, when at two treaty conferences Iroquois negotiators, claiming to speak for the Delawares and Shawnees, ceded large land tracts to Pennsylvania officials. Squatters (mainly Scots-Irish and Germans, but also some Anglo-Americans) had negotiated individual agreements with the Delawares for settlement rights; some paying rent to native "landlords." But the agreements reached by agents of the Penn family and the Iroquois ignored local Indians and squatters, all of whom were told to move. Disgruntled Delawares and Shawnees migrated west, where they joined other displaced eastern Indians.

The region to which they moved, claimed by both Virginia and Pennsylvania, was coveted by wealthy Virginians, who, organized as the Ohio Company, received a huge land grant in 1749. The company's agents established trading posts in the west, hoping to control the crucial area where the Allegheny and Monongahela Rivers join to form the Ohio (see Map 5.1). But the French relied on the Ohio River for direct access to its posts on the Mississippi. Thus, in the early 1750s, Pennsylvania fur traders, Ohio Company representatives, the French military, squatters, Iroquois, Delawares, and Shawnees jostled for position in the region. A 1752 raid by the French and their native allies on a trading outpost situated at modern Cleveland rid the region of Pennsylvanians, but the Virginians posed a challenge. Accordingly, in 1753 the French pushed southward, building fortified outposts at strategic points.

Albany Congress

In response to the French threat, delegates from seven northern and middle colonies gathered in Albany, New York, in June 1754. They sought two goals: to persuade the Iroquois to abandon their neutrality and to coordinate colonial defense. The Iroquois saw no reason to change a policy that served them well for half a century. And although the Albany Congress adopted a Plan of Union (which would have established an elected intercolonial legislature with the power to tax), their provincial governments rejected the plan, fearing a loss of autonomy.

While the Albany Congress delegates deliberated, the war began. Virginia Governor Robert Dinwiddie sent a small militia troop to build a palisade at the forks of the Ohio. When a substantial French force arrived there, the Virginia militia surrendered and left. The French then constructed the more elaborate Fort Duquesne. Learning of the confrontation, the inexperienced young officer who commanded Virginia reinforcements pressed on, attacking a French detachment and becoming trapped in his crudely built Fort Necessity at Great Meadows, Pennsylvania. After a day-long battle (on July 3, 1754), during which more than one-third of his men were killed or wounded, twenty-two-year-old George Washington surrendered.

Map key:

Total population of
English colonies: ca. 1.5 million

Extent of settlement

Scale:
0   100   200 miles
0   100   200   300 kilometers

Map 5.1 European Settlements and Indians, 1754

By 1754 Europeans had expanded the limits of the English colonies to the eastern slopes of the Appalachian Mountains. Few independent Indian nations still existed in the East, but beyond the mountains they controlled the countryside. Only a few widely scattered English and French forts maintained the Europeans' presence there.

Seven Years' War

Washington's blunder helped ignite a war that would encompass nearly the entire world. In July 1755, a few miles south of Fort Duquesne, the French and Indians jointly attacked British and colonial troops. In the devastating defeat, General Edward Braddock was killed. The Pennsylvania frontier was repeatedly attacked by Delawares for two more years. Settlers felt betrayed because the Indians attacking them—their former neighbors—had once been (an observer noted) "allmost dayly familiars at their houses."

Britain declared war on France in 1756, thus formally beginning the Seven Years' War. Even before then, Britons and New Englanders feared that France would try to retake Nova Scotia, where most of the population was descended from seventeenth-century French settlers who had intermarried with local Mikmaqs. Afraid that the approximately twelve thousand French Nova Scotians would abandon their neutrality policy, British commanders in 1755 forced about seven thousand from their homeland—the first large-scale modern deportation, now called ethnic cleansing. Ships crammed with Acadians sailed to each mainland colony. Many families were separated, some forever. After 1763 the survivors relocated, some to Canada, others to France or its Caribbean islands. Many settled in Louisiana, where they became known as Cajuns (derived from *Acadian*).

British officers tried unsuccessfully to coerce the colonies into supplying men and materiel to the army. When William Pitt, the civilian official spearheading the war effort in 1757, agreed to reimburse the colonies' wartime expenditures and placed recruitment in local hands, he gained American support. Many colonial militiamen served alongside red-coated regulars from Britain; the two groups maintained an antagonistic relationship, however.

In July 1758, British forces recaptured the fortress at Louisbourg, winning control of the entrance to the St. Lawrence River. In the fall, the Delawares and Shawnees accepted British peace overtures, and the French abandoned Fort Duquesne. Then, in September 1759, General James Wolfe's regulars defeated the French and took Quebec. Sensing a British victory, the Iroquois abandoned neutrality, hoping to gain a postwar advantage by allying with Britain. A year later, the British captured Montreal, the last French stronghold, and the American phase of the war ended.

In the Treaty of Paris (1763), France ceded its major North American holdings to Britain. Spain, an ally of France toward war's end, gave Florida to the victors. France ceded Louisiana west of the Mississippi to Spain, in partial compensation for its ally's losses elsewhere. The British thus gained control of the continent's fur trade. No longer would the English seacoast colonies have to worry about the threat to their existence posed by France's extensive North American territories.

1763: A TURNING POINT

Indigenous peoples of the interior first felt the impact of Britain's victory. After Britain gained the upper hand in the American war in 1758, Creeks and Cherokees lost their ability to force concessions by threatening to turn to France or Spain. In desperation, and retaliation for British atrocities, Cherokees attacked the Carolina and Virginia frontiers in 1760. Though initially victorious, the Indians were defeated the following year. Late in 1761, a treaty allowed the construction of British forts in Cherokee territories and opened a large tract to European settlement.

The First Worldwide War

Today we call two twentieth-century conflicts world wars, but the contest that historians term the *Great War for the Empire* was actually the first worldwide war. It began in spring 1754 in southwestern Pennsylvania, over whether Britain or France would build a fort at the forks of the Ohio. That it eventually involved combatants around the world attests to the growing importance of European nations' overseas empires and the increasing centrality of North America to their struggles for dominance.

The contest at the forks of the Ohio helped to reinvigorate a conflict between Austria and Prussia that sent European nations scrambling for allies. Eventually England, Hanover, and Prussia lined up against France, Austria, Russia, Sweden, Saxony, and, later, Spain. The war in Europe would last seven years. In 1763 these nations signed a peace treaty that returned the continent to its prewar status, but in the rest of the world, Britain vanquished France and Spain.

In the Caribbean, Britain seized the French islands of Guadeloupe and Martinique, and took Havana from Spain. In North America, the British recaptured the French fortress of Louisbourg and conquered Quebec. In Africa, Britain overwhelmed France's slave-trading posts in Senegambia. In India, British forces won control of Bengal by defeating a local ruler and French soldiers. Three years later, the British beat a French army at Pondicherry; four months after France lost Canada, its influence in India was also extinguished. At the very end of the war, a British expedition took Manila in the Philippines from Spain.

Thus the war that started in the American backcountry revealed the steadily growing links between North America and the rest of the world. Winners and losers had to pay for this first worldwide war. Financial struggles in Britain and France, produced revolutions abroad (for Britain, in America) and at home (for France).

In 1771 the artist Dominic Serres, the Elder, depicted British naval vessels attacking the French fortress at Chandernagore in India in 1757 (at left in background). Cannon fire from the warships was critical to the British victory, one of the keys to the conquest of India during the Seven Years' War.

(© National Maritime Museum, Greenwich, London)

Neolin and Pontiac

In the Ohio country, the Ottawas, Chippewas, and Potawatomis reacted angrily when Great Britain, no longer facing French competition, raised prices on trade goods and ended traditional gift-giving practices. As settlers moved into the Monongahela and Susquehanna valleys, a shaman named Neolin urged Indians to oppose European settlement and influence on their culture. Contending that Indian peoples were destroying themselves by dependence on European goods (especially alcohol), Neolin advocated peaceful, armed, and unified resistance. If Indians west of the mountains collectively rejected the invaders, Neolin declared, the Master of Life would replenish the depleted deer herds and look kindly on his people.

Heeding Neolin's call, in spring 1763 Ottawa war chief Pontiac forged an unprecedented alliance among Hurons, Chippewas, Potawatomis, Delawares, Shawnees, and Mingoes (Pennsylvania Iroquois). Pontiac then besieged Fort Detroit while war parties attacked other British outposts in the Great Lakes. Detroit withstood the siege, but by late June the forts west of Niagara and north of Fort Pitt had fallen. Indians then raided the Virginia and Pennsylvania frontiers throughout the summer, but failed to take Niagara, Fort Pitt, or Detroit. In early August, colonial militiamen defeated a combined Indian force at Bushy Run, Pennsylvania. Pontiac concluded the Detroit siege in late October; a treaty ending the war was negotiated three years later.

For nearly eighty years European settlers and Indians in Penn's Woods avoided major conflicts. But the Indian attacks and the settlers' response—especially the massacre of several defenseless Conestoga Indian families in December 1763 by fifty Scots-Irish men known as the Paxton Boys—revealed that violence in the region would become endemic.

Benjamin West, the first well-known American artist, engraved this picture of a prisoner exchange at the end of Pontiac's Uprising, with Colonel Henry Bouquet supervising the return of settlers abducted during the war. In the foreground, a child resists leaving the Indian parents he had grown to love. Many colonists were fascinated by the phenomenon West depicted—the reluctance of captives to abandon their adoptive Indian families. (Ohio Historical Society)

Proclamation of 1763

London officials had no experience managing an area as vast as the territory it acquired from France, which included French settlers along the St. Lawrence and many Indian communities. In October the ministry issued the Proclamation of 1763, designating the headwaters of rivers flowing into the Atlantic from the Appalachians as the temporary western boundary for colonial settlement (see Map 5.1). Its promulgators expected to prevent clashes by forbidding colonists to move onto Indian lands. But it infuriated colonists who had squatted west of the line and land speculation companies from Pennsylvania and Virginia.

After 1763, the latter groups (which included such men as George Washington, Thomas Jefferson, Patrick Henry, and Benjamin Franklin) lobbied vigorously to have their claims validated by colonial governments and London administrators. At a treaty conference at Fort Stanwix, New York, in 1768, they negotiated with Iroquois representatives to push the boundary farther west and south. The Iroquois, still claiming to speak for the Delawares and the Shawnees, agreed to the deal, which yielded valuable trade goods and did not affect their own territories. While the Virginia land companies eventually gained the support of the House of Burgesses, they never made headway in London because administrators worried that western expansion would require funds they did not have.

George III

Financing Britain's debt from the Seven Years' War—and defending the newly acquired territories—bedeviled King George III, who in 1760 succeeded his grandfather, George II. During the crucial years between 1763 and 1770, when the rift with the colonies widened and various political crises beset England, the twenty-two-year-old king replaced ministries rapidly. Although determined to assert the power of the monarchy, George III stubbornly regarded adherence to the status quo as the hallmark of patriotism.

Selected as prime minister in 1763, George Grenville confronted a financial crisis: England's indebtedness had nearly doubled since 1754, from £73 million to £137 million. Pre-war annual expenditures amounted to no more than £8 million; now the yearly interest on the debt came to £5 million. Grenville's ministry needed funds, but the British people were already heavily taxed. Because the colonists benefited from wartime expenditures, Grenville concluded that Anglo-Americans should pay a larger share of the empire's costs.

Theories of Representation

Americans believed that they could be represented only by men who lived nearby and for whom they or their property-holding neighbors voted. Grenville and his English contemporaries, however, believed that Parliament—king, lords, and Commons acting together—represented all British subjects, even overseas, whether or not they could vote.

In Parliament, the particular constituency that chose a member of the House of Commons had no special claim on that member's vote, nor did the member have to live near his constituents. According to this theory, called virtual representation, all Britons—including colonists—were represented in Parliament. Thus their consent to acts of Parliament could be presumed. In the colonies, however, members of the assemblies' lower houses were viewed as specifically representing the regions that elected them. Before Grenville proposed to tax the colonists, the two notions coexisted. But events of the 1760s revealed their incompatibility.

Real Whigs

Colonists had become accustomed to a central government with limited authority. Consequently, they believed that a good government was one that largely left them alone, a view matching the theories of British writers known as the Real Whigs. Drawing on a tradition of dissent reaching back to John Locke, the Real Whigs stressed the dangers inherent in a powerful government, particularly a monarchy. Some favored republicanism, which proposed to eliminate monarchs and rest power more directly on the people. Real Whigs warned the people to guard against government's attempted encroachments on their liberty and property.

As Britain tightened the reins in the 1760s and early 1770s, many Americans saw parallels in their circumstances and the Real Whigs' ideology. Excessive and unjust taxation, they believed, could destroy their freedoms, and they saw oppressive designs behind the actions of Grenville and his successors. In the mid-1760s, however, colonial leaders merely questioned the wisdom of Grenville's proposed laws.

**Sugar and
Currency Acts**

In 1764 Parliament passed the Sugar and Currency Acts. The Sugar Act (also known as the Revenue Act) revised existing customs regulations and laid new duties on some foreign imports into the colonies. Its key provisions, advocated in London by influential Caribbean planters, aimed at discouraging American rum distillers from smuggling French West Indian molasses, thereby improving the market for British sugar. Although the Sugar Act resembled the Navigation Acts, it broke with tradition by deliberately seeking to raise revenue rather than channel American trade through Britain. The Currency Act outlawed most colonial issues of paper money, because British merchants had complained that Americans paid debts in inflated local currencies.

The Sugar and Currency Acts were imposed on an already depressed economy. A business boom accompanied the Seven Years' War, but prosperity ended in 1760 when the war shifted overseas. Atlantic trade routes were disrupted, merchants found few buyers for imported goods, and the loss of the military's demand for foodstuffs hurt American farmers. The bottom dropped out of the European tobacco market, threatening the livelihood of Chesapeake planters. Sailors and artisans had little work. Thus, the prospect of increased import duties and inadequate currency aroused merchants' hostility.

Without precedent for a united campaign against acts of Parliament, Americans in 1764 took uncoordinated steps. Eight colonial legislatures sent petitions to Parliament requesting the Sugar Act's repeal. They argued that its commercial restrictions would hurt Britain as well as the colonies and that they had not consented to its passage. The law remained in force.

THE STAMP ACT CRISIS

The Stamp Act (1765), Grenville's most important revenue proposal, required tax stamps on most printed materials, placing the heaviest burden on merchants and the colonial elite, who used printed matter more than ordinary folk. Anyone who purchased a newspaper, made a will, accepted a government appointment, or borrowed money would have to pay the tax. Never before had a revenue measure of such scope been proposed for the colonies. The act also required that tax stamps be purchased with scarce sterling coin. Violators would be tried by vice-admiralty courts, where judges rendered decisions, leading Americans to fear the loss of their right to trial by a jury of their peers. Finally, such a law broke with the colonial tradition of self-imposed taxation.

**James Otis's *Rights of
the British Colonies***

The young Massachusetts attorney James Otis Jr., penned the most important pamphlet protesting the Sugar Act and proposed Stamp Act: *The Rights of the British Colonies Asserted and Proved*. Otis exposed the dilemma that confounded the colonists for the next decade. How could they oppose certain acts of Parliament without questioning Parliament's authority over them? On the one hand, Otis asserted, Americans were "entitled to all the natural, essential, inherent, and inseparable rights" of Britons, including the right not to be taxed without their consent. On the other, Otis admitted that, under the British system after the Glorious Revolution, "the power of parliament is uncontrollable but by themselves, and we must obey . . . till they will be pleased to relieve us."

Otis's first contention implied that Parliament could not constitutionally tax the colonies because Americans were not represented in its ranks. Yet his second point accepted the prevailing theory of British government: that Parliament was the sole, supreme authority in the empire. Otis tried to find a middle ground by proposing colonial representation in Parliament, but the British believed that colonists were already virtually represented in Parliament, and colonists realized that a handful of colonial delegates to London would be outvoted. When Americans learned of the act's adoption in the spring of 1765, they reacted indecisively. Few colonists publicly favored the law, but petitions failed to prevent its adoption. Perhaps Otis was correct: the only course was to pay the stamp tax, reluctantly but loyally.

Patrick Henry and the Virginia Stamp Act Resolves

A twenty-nine-year-old lawyer serving his first term in the Virginia House of Burgesses, Patrick Henry was appalled by his fellow legislators' unwillingness to oppose the Stamp Act. "Alone, unadvised, and unassisted, on a blank leaf of an old law book," he took action and wrote the Virginia Stamp Act Resolves.

Little in Henry's earlier life foreshadowed his political success. The son of a prosperous Scots immigrant to western Virginia, Henry had little formal education. After marrying at eighteen, he failed at farming and storekeeping before turning to the law to support his wife and six children. Henry lacked legal training, but his oratorical skills made him an effective advocate first for his clients and later for his political beliefs.

In 1795 the artist Lawrence Sully painted the only known life portrait of Patrick Henry. The old man's fierce gaze reflects the same intensity that marked his actions thirty years earlier, when he introduced the Virginia Stamp Act Resolves in the House of Burgesses. (Mead Art Museum, Amherst College. Bequest of Herbert L. Pratt, Class of 1985, Acc. No. AC1945.115)

Patrick Henry introduced his seven proposals near the end of the legislative session, when many burgesses had already departed. The few remaining burgesses adopted five of Henry's resolutions by a bare majority. But some colonial newspapers printed Henry's seven original resolutions as if they had been uniformly passed by the House. One was rescinded and two others were never debated or voted on.

The four propositions adopted by the burgesses asserted that colonists had never forfeited their rights as British subjects, which included consent to taxation. The other resolutions went further. The repealed resolution claimed the burgesses had the exclusive right to tax Virginians, and the two never considered asserted that Virginians need not obey tax laws passed by other legislative bodies (namely, Parliament).

Continuing Loyalty to Britain

Though vying for their rights, the colonists did not seek independence. Maryland lawyer Daniel Dulany, whose *Considerations on the Propriety of Imposing Taxes on the British Colonies* was the most widely read pamphlet of 1765, expressed the consensus: "The colonies are dependent upon Great Britain, and the supreme authority vested in the king, lords, and commons, may justly be exercised to secure, or preserve their dependence." But, warned Dulany, there was a crucial distinction between "dependence and inferiority" and "absolute vassalage and slavery."

Over the next ten years, America's political leaders searched for a way to control their internal affairs, especially taxation, but remain under British rule. The notion that Parliament could exercise absolute authority over colonial possessions inhered in the British theory of government. Even Britain's harshest critics of the 1760s and 1770s questioned only the wisdom of specific policies, not the principles on which they rested. In effect, the Americans (perhaps unrealistically) wanted British leaders to revise their fundamental understanding of their government.

Anti–Stamp Act Demonstrations

In August, the Loyal Nine, a Boston social club of printers, distillers, and other artisans, organized an anti–Stamp Act demonstration. Hoping to show that people from all ranks opposed the act, they approached leaders of the city's rival laborers' associations, based in Boston's North End and South End neighborhoods. The two gangs, composed of unskilled workers and poor tradesmen, were often at odds, but the Loyal Nine convinced them to lay aside their differences for the demonstration.

On August 14, the demonstrators hung an effigy of Andrew Oliver, the province's stamp distributor, from a tree on Boston Common. That night a crowd led by about fifty well-dressed tradesmen paraded the effigy around the city. The crowd tore down a small building they thought was intended as the stamp office, making a bonfire near Oliver's house and tossing the beheaded effigy onto the flames. Demonstrators broke Oliver's windows and threw stones at officials. During the melee, the North End and South End leaders toasted their union. Oliver publicly promised not to fulfill the duties of his office.

But another crowd action twelve days later, aimed at Oliver's brother-in-law, Lieutenant Governor Thomas Hutchinson, drew no praise from respectable Bostonians. On the night of August 26, a mob attacked the homes of several customs officers and destroyed Hutchinson's elaborately furnished townhouse. But Hutchinson took some comfort in the fact that "the encouragers of the first mob never intended matters should go this length and the people in general express the utmost detestation of this unparalleled outrage."

Americans' Divergent Interests

Few colonists sided with Britain during the 1760s, but groups had divergent goals. The skilled craftsmen who composed the Loyal Nine and merchants, lawyers, and other educated elites preferred orderly demonstrations. For the city's laborers, economic grievances may have been paramount. Certainly, their "hellish Fury" as they wrecked Hutchinson's house suggests resentment against his display of wealth.

Colonists, like Britons, had a long tradition in which disfranchised people took to the streets to redress grievances. But the Stamp Act controversy for the first time drew ordinary urban folk into transatlantic politics, including recent non-English-speaking immigrants targeted by the double taxation of foreign-language newspapers. Matters that previously concerned only the gentry or colonial legislators were now discussed everywhere.

The entry of unskilled workers, slaves, and women into imperial politics threatened and aided elite men who wanted to oppose British measures. Anti–Stamp Act demonstrations occurred in areas stretching from Halifax in the north to the Caribbean island of Antigua in the south. They were so successful that, by November 1, when the law was to take effect, not one stamp distributor would carry out his duties. But wealthy men recognized that mobs composed of the formerly powerless could endanger their own dominance of the society.

Sons of Liberty

They therefore attempted to channel resistance into acceptable forms through a newly created intercolonial association, the Sons of Liberty. Composed of merchants, lawyers, and prosperous tradesmen, the Sons of Liberty by early 1766 linked protest leaders from New York to those in Charleston, South Carolina, to those in Portsmouth, New Hampshire. With taverns as key settings for exchanging news and opinions, many members were tavern owners.

In Charleston (formerly Charles Town) in October 1765, a crowd shouting, "Liberty Liberty and stamp'd paper" forced the resignation of the South Carolina stamp distributor. But the Charleston chapter of the Sons of Liberty was horrified when in January 1766 local slaves paraded through the streets similarly crying, "Liberty!" Freedom from slavery was not what elite slave owners had in mind.

In Philadelphia, resistance leaders were dismayed when an angry mob threatened to attack Benjamin Franklin's house. The city's laborers believed Franklin to be partly responsible for the Stamp Act because he obtained the post of stamp distributor for a friend. But Philadelphia's artisans—the foundation of the opposition there and elsewhere—were loyal to Franklin, considered one of their own, and protected his home. The resulting split between Philadelphia's better-off tradesmen and common laborers prevented an alliance as successful as Boston's.

Opposition and Repeal   During fall and winter 1765–1766, Stamp Act opposition mounted. Colonial legislatures petitioned Parliament to repeal the hated law, and courts closed because they could not obtain the stamps needed for legal documents. In October, nine colonies sent delegates to a general congress, the Stamp Act Congress, in New York to draft a protest statement stressing the law's adverse economic effects rather than its rights violations. Meanwhile, the Sons of Liberty held mass meetings to rally public support. Finally, American merchants organized nonimportation associations to pressure British exporters, expecting that since one-quarter of all exports went to the colonies by 1760, London merchants might lobby for repeal, especially if sales suffered.

In March 1766, Parliament repealed the Stamp Act. The nonimportation agreements had the anticipated effect of allying wealthy London merchants to the colonies. But the main factor in winning repeal than was the appointment of a new prime minister. Lord Rockingham, who replaced Grenville in summer 1765, opposed the Stamp Act as an unwise and divisive law. But Rockingham linked repeal to passage of a Declaratory Act, which asserted Parliament's authority to tax and legislate for Britain's American possessions.

News of the repeal arrived in Newport, Rhode Island, in May, and the Sons of Liberty dispatched messengers throughout the colonies. They organized celebrations, stressing unwavering loyalty to Britain. Their goal achieved, the Sons of Liberty dissolved.

RESISTANCE TO THE TOWNSHEND ACTS

In summer 1766, another ministry change in London revealed how fragile the colonists' victory had been. The new prime minister, William Pitt, fostered cooperation between the colonies and Britain during the Seven Years' War. But when Pitt fell ill, Charles Townshend became the dominant force in the ministry. An ally of Grenville, Townshend renewed efforts to obtain funds from Britain's American possessions (see Table 5.2).

The duties Townshend proposed in 1767 seemed to extend the existing Navigation Acts by focusing on trade goods like paper, glass, and tea. But they differed first, by

TABLE 5.2   British Ministries and Their American Policies

Head of Ministry	Major Acts
George Grenville	Sugar Act (1764) Currency Act (1764) Stamp Act (1765)
Lord Rockingham	Stamp Act repealed (1766) Declaratory Act (1766)
William Pitt/Charles Townshend	Townshend Acts (1767)
Lord North	Townshend duties (except for the tea tax) repealed (1770) Coercive Acts (1774) Quebec Act (1774)

applying to British imports, not those from foreign countries. Second, the revenues would pay some royal officials in the colonies, thereby eliminating assemblies' ability to threaten to withhold salaries from uncooperative officials. Additionally, Townshend's scheme established an American Board of Customs Commissioners and vice-admiralty courts at Boston, Philadelphia, and Charleston. This angered merchants, whose profits would be threatened by more vigorous enforcement of the Navigation Acts.

John Dickinson's Farmer's Letters

Passage of the Townshend Acts drew a quick response from the colonies. One series of widely published essays, *Letters from a Farmer in Pennsylvania*, by prominent lawyer John Dickinson, expressed a broad consensus. Dickinson contended that Parliament could regulate colonial trade but could not raise revenue. By distinguishing between trade regulation and taxation, Dickinson avoided the sticky issue of consent and colonial subordination to Parliament. But his argument obligated the colonies to assess Parliament's motives in passing trade laws before deciding whether to obey them.

The Massachusetts assembly responded to the Townshend Acts by circulating a letter calling for unity among colonial legislatures and a joint petition of protest. When Lord Hillsborough, recently named secretary of state for America, learned of the letter, he ordered Massachusetts governor Francis Bernard to insist that the assembly recall it and directed other governors to prevent their assemblies from discussing it. Hillsborough's order motivated colonial assemblies to unite in opposing this new threat to their prerogatives. In late 1768, the Massachusetts legislature resoundingly rejected recall by a vote of 92 to 17. Bernard immediately dissolved the assembly, and other governors followed suit.

Rituals of Resistance

The number of votes cast against recalling the circular letter—92—assumed ritual significance for the resistance. The number 45 was already symbolic because John Wilkes, a radical Londoner sympathetic to the American cause, had been jailed for publishing an essay entitled *The North Briton*, No. 45. In Boston, the silversmith Paul Revere made a punchbowl weighing 45 ounces that held 45 gills (half-cups). Charleston's tradesmen decorated a tree with 45 lights, set off 45 rockets, and carrying 45 candles, met at a tavern where 45 tables were set with 45 bowls of wine, 45 bowls of punch, and 92 glasses.

Such public rituals taught illiterate Americans about the reasons for resistance. When Boston's revived Sons of Liberty invited hundreds of residents to dine with them each August 14 to commemorate the first Stamp Act demonstration, crowds listened. Likewise, the public singing of songs supporting the American cause helped to spread the word.

The Sons of Liberty and other American leaders made a deliberate effort to involve ordinary folk in the campaign against the Townshend duties. Most important, they urged colonists of all ranks and both sexes to sign agreements not to purchase or consume British products. The new consumerism that had linked colonists economically now supplied them with a ready method of displaying their allegiance.

Daughters of Liberty

As the primary purchasers of textiles and household goods, women played a central role in the nonconsumption movement. More than three hundred Boston matrons publicly promised not to buy or drink tea, "Sickness excepted." As Janet Schaw later noted, the women of Wilmington, North Carolina, burned their tea after walking through town in a solemn procession. Women exchanged recipes for tea substitutes or drank coffee instead. The best known of the protests, the so-called Edenton Ladies Tea Party, was actually a meeting of prominent North Carolina women who pledged to work for the public good and support resistance to British measures.

In many towns, young women calling themselves Daughters of Liberty met to spin in public squares to persuade other women to make homespun and wear homespun clothing, thereby ending the colonies' dependence on British cloth. These patriotic displays served the same purpose as the male rituals involving the numbers 45 and 92. When young ladies from well-to-do families sat outdoors at spinning wheels all day, eating only American food, drinking local herbal tea, and listening to patriotic sermons, they served as political instructors, a role they accepted with pride.

Divided Opinion Over Boycotts

Colonists were by no means united in support of nonimportation and nonconsumption. Resistance to the Townshend Acts exposed new splits in American ranks. The most significant rifts divided urban artisans and merchants, allies in 1765.

The Stamp Act boycotts helped revive a depressed economy by stimulating demand for local products and reducing merchants' inventories. But in 1768 and 1769, merchants enjoyed boom times and had no incentive to support a boycott. Artisans, however, supported nonimportation, recognizing that the absence of British goods would create a market for their own manufactures. Thus tradesmen formed the core of the crowds that coerced both importers and their customers by picketing stores, publicizing offenders' names, and sometimes destroying property.

Such tactics were effective: colonial imports from England dropped dramatically in 1769, especially in New York, New England, and Pennsylvania. But these tactics also aroused heated opposition. Some Americans who supported resistance questioned the use of violence to force others to join the boycott. The threat to private property inherent in the campaign frightened wealthier and more conservative men and women. Political activism by ordinary colonists challenged the ruling elite's domination, as many feared in 1765.

Disclosures that leading merchants had violated the nonimportation agreement caused dissension in the ranks of boycotters, so Americans were relieved when news arrived in April 1770 that the Townshend duties had been repealed, except the tea tax. A new prime minister, Lord North, persuaded Parliament that duties on trade within the empire were ill advised. The other Townshend Acts remained in force, but provisions for paying officials' salaries and tightening customs enforcement now appeared less objectionable.

CONFRONTATIONS IN BOSTON

On the day Lord North proposed repeal of the Townshend duties, a confrontation between civilians and soldiers in Boston led to five Americans' deaths. The decision to base the American Board of Customs Commissioners in Boston ultimately caused the confrontation that patriots called the Boston Massacre.

Mobs targeted the customs commissioners on their arrival in November 1767. In June 1768 their seizure of the patriot leader John Hancock's sloop *Liberty* on suspicion of smuggling caused a riot in which prominent customs officers' property was destroyed. The ministry brought in troops to maintain order. The assignment of two regiments to their city confirmed Bostonians' worst fears about the oppressive potential of British power. Guards on Boston Neck, the entrance to the city, checked travelers and their goods. Redcoat patrols roamed the city, questioning and sometimes harassing passersby. Parents feared for the safety of daughters, who were subjected to soldiers' coarse sexual insults. Additionally, many redcoats sought off-duty employment, competing for unskilled jobs with the city's workingmen. The two groups brawled repeatedly in taverns and on the streets.

Boston Massacre

On the evening of March 5, 1770, a crowd of laborers threw snowballs at soldiers guarding the Customs House. Against orders, the sentries fired on the crowd, killing four and wounding eight, one of whom died days later. Reportedly the first to die was Crispus Attucks, a sailor of mixed Nipmuck and African origins. Resistance leaders idealized Attucks and the other dead rioters as martyrs for liberty, holding a solemn funeral and later commemorating March 5 annually.

Despite the political benefits patriots derived from the massacre, they probably did not approve the crowd action that provoked it. Since the destruction of Hutchinson's house in August 1765, men allied with the Sons of Liberty supported orderly demonstrations. Thus, when the soldiers were tried in November, John Adams and Josiah Quincy Jr., both unwavering patriots, acted as their defense attorneys. Almost all were acquitted, and the two convicted were released after being branded on the thumb. Undoubtedly this favorable outcome persuaded London officials not to retaliate against the city.

A British Plot?

For more than two years after the Boston Massacre, a superficial calm emerged. In June 1772, Rhode Islanders angry with overzealous customs enforcement by the British naval schooner *Gaspée* attacked and burned it in Narragansett Bay near Providence. Because the perpetrators were never identified, there were no adverse consequences for the colony. The most outspoken newspapers, such as the *Boston Gazette,* the *Pennsylvania Journal,* and the *South Carolina Gazette,* published essays drawing on Real Whig ideology and accusing Great Britain of scheming to oppress the colonies. After the Stamp Act's repeal, the protest leaders praised Parliament; following repeal of the Townshend duties, they warned of impending tyranny. The single ill-chosen stamp tax now seemed part of a plot against American liberties. Essayists pointed to the stationing of troops in Boston and the growing number of vice-admiralty courts as evidence of plans to enslave the colonists. Indeed, patriot writers repeatedly used the word *enslavement.* Most free colonists had direct knowledge of slavery, and the threat of enslavement by Britain must have had peculiar force.

Although some colonists were increasingly convinced that they should seek freedom from parliamentary authority, they continued to acknowledge their British identity and allegiance to George III. They began to envision a system that would enable

Shortly after the Boston Massacre, Paul Revere printed this illustration of the confrontation near the Customs House on March 5, 1770. Offering visual support for the patriots' version of events, it showed the British soldiers firing on an unresisting crowd (instead of the aggressive mob described at the soldiers' trial) and—even worse—a gun firing from the building itself, which has been labeled Butchers Hall.
(Anne S.K. Brown Military Collection, Brown University Library)

them to be ruled by their own elected legislatures while remaining subordinate to the king. But any such scheme violated Britons' conception of their government, which posited that Parliament (which they believed encompassed the king as well as lords and commons) wielded sole, undivided sovereignty over the empire. Then, in fall 1772, the North ministry implemented the Townshend Act that would pay governors and judges from customs revenues. In early November, voters at a Boston town meeting established a Committee of Correspondence to publicize the decision by exchanging letters with other Massachusetts towns. Heading the committee was Samuel Adams.

Samuel Adams and Committees of Correspondence

Fifty-one in 1772, Samuel Adams was about a decade older than other American resistance leaders. He had been a Boston tax collector, a member and clerk of the Massachusetts assembly, an ally of the Loyal Nine, and one of the Sons of Liberty. Adams drew a sharp contrast between a corrupt, vice-ridden Britain and the colonies, peopled by simple, liberty-loving folk. An experienced political organizer, Adams' Committee of Correspondence sought to create an informed consensus among Massachusetts residents.

Until 1772, the protest movement was confined largely to the seacoast and major cities and towns. Adams wanted to widen the movement's geographic scope. Accordingly, the Boston town meeting directed the Committee of Correspondence "to state the Rights of the Colonists and of this Province in particular"; to list "the Infringements and Violations thereof that have been, or from time to time may be made"; and to send copies to other towns. The statement of colonial rights declared that Americans had absolute rights to life, liberty, and property. The idea that "a British house of commons, should have a right, at pleasure, to give and grant the property of the colonists" was "irreconcileable" with "the first principles of natural law and Justice . . . and of the British Constitution." They complained of taxation without representation, unnecessary troops and customs officers on American soil, the use of imperial revenues to pay colonial officials, and the expanded jurisdiction of vice-admiralty courts.

The document, which was printed as a pamphlet for distribution to the towns, exhibited none of the hesitation of 1760s' claims against Parliament. No longer were resistance leaders—at least in Boston—preoccupied with defining the limits of parliamentary authority, nor did they mention obedience to Parliament. They placed American rights first, loyalty to Great Britain a distant second.

The towns' response to the pamphlet must have thrilled Samuel Adams. While some disagreed with Boston's assessment, most aligned with the city. The town of Holden declared that "the People of New England have never given the People of Britain any Right of Jurisdiction over us." The citizens of Petersham commented that resistance to tyranny was "the first and highest social Duty of this people." Beliefs like these made the next crisis in Anglo-American affairs the last.

TEA AND TURMOIL

The tea tax was the sole Townshend duty in effect by 1773. After 1770, some Americans continued to boycott English tea; others resumed drinking it. As explained in Chapter 4, tea figured prominently in the colonists' diet and social lives, so the boycott meant giving up a favorite beverage and altering habitual forms of socializing.

Reactions to the Tea Act

In May 1773, Parliament passed the Tea Act to save the East India Company from bankruptcy. The company, which held a monopoly on British trade with the East Indies, was important to the British economy and to the prominent British politicians who invested in it. Under the act, only the East India Company's agents could legally sell tea in America. That enabled the company to avoid intermediaries and lower its prices to compete with smugglers. Resistance leaders, however, interpreted the measure as designed to make them admit Parliament's right to tax them, since the less expensive tea would still be taxed. Others saw the Tea Act as the first step in an East India Company monopoly on all colonial trade. Residents of the four cities to receive the first tea shipments prepared to respond to this perceived threat to their freedom.

In New York City, tea ships never arrived. In Philadelphia, Pennsylvania's governor persuaded the captain to return to Britain. In Charleston, the tea was unloaded; some was destroyed, the rest sold in 1776 by the new state government. The only confrontation occurred in Boston, where both sides—the town meeting and Governor Thomas Hutchinson, two of whose sons were tea agents—rejected compromise.

The first of three tea ships, the *Dartmouth,* entered Boston harbor on November 28. Customs laws required cargo to be landed and the duty paid within twenty days of arrival; otherwise, it would be seized and sold at auction. After several mass meetings, Bostonians voted to post guards to prevent the tea from being unloaded. Hutchinson refused to permit the vessels to leave the harbor.

On December 16, one day before the cargo would have been confiscated, more than five thousand people (nearly a third of the city's population) crowded into Old South Church. Chaired by Samuel Adams, the meeting hoped to convince Hutchinson to send the tea back. But he refused. In the early evening Adams reportedly announced "that they had now done all they could for the Salvation of their Country." Cries rang out from the crowd: "Boston harbor a tea-pot tonight!" Within minutes, about sixty men crudely disguised as Indians assembled at the wharf, boarded the ships, and dumped the cargo into the harbor. By 9 P.M. 342 chests of tea worth approximately £10,000 floated on the water.

Among the "Indians" were many Boston artisans, including the silversmith Paul Revere. Five masons, eleven carpenters and builders, three leatherworkers, a blacksmith, two barbers, a coachmaker, a shoemaker, and twelve apprentices have been identified as participants. That their ranks also included four farmers from outside Boston, ten merchants, two doctors, a teacher, and a bookseller illustrated the resistance movement's widespread support.

Coercive and Quebec Acts

Responding to the Tea Party, in March 1774, Parliament adopted the first of four laws that became known as the Coercive, or Intolerable, Acts. It ordered Boston's port closed until the tea was paid for, prohibiting all but coastal trade in food and firewood. Later that spring, Parliament passed three other punitive measures. The Massachusetts Government Act altered the province's charter, substituting an appointed council for the elected one, increasing the governor's powers, and forbidding most town meetings. The Justice Act provided that a person accused of committing murder while suppressing a riot or enforcing the laws could be tried outside the colony. Finally, the Quartering Act allowed military officers to commandeer privately owned buildings to house troops.

Parliament then turned to reforming Quebec's government. Intended to ease strains emerging since the British conquest of the French colony, the Quebec Act granted greater religious freedom to Catholics—alarming Protestant colonists, who equated Roman Catholicism with despotism. It also reinstated French civil law, which had been replaced by British procedures in 1763, and it established an appointed council (rather than an elected legislature). Finally, to protect northern Indians against Anglo-American settlement, the act annexed to Quebec the area west of the Appalachians, east of the Mississippi River, and north of the Ohio River—thereby

Women's Political Activism

In the twenty-first century, female citizens of the United States participate at every level of American politics. But before the 1760s, American women were seen as having no political role; they often apologized for even talking about political issues. A male essayist expressed the consensus in the mid-1730s: "the Governing Kingdoms and Ruling Provinces are Things too difficult and knotty for the fair Sex, it will render them grave and serious, and take off those agreeable Smiles that should always accompany them."

But that changed when colonists resisted new British taxes and laws in the mid- to late 1760s. Because women made purchasing decisions for American households and because in the case of spinning and cloth manufacture their labor could replace imported clothing, it was vital for them to participate in the resistance. For the first time in American history, women of all ranks took political stands, deciding whether to boycott British goods. The groups they established to promote home manufactures—dubbed *Daughters of Liberty*—constituted the first American women's political organizations.

Since then, American women have taken part in many political movements, among them antislavery societies, suffrage organizations, the Women's Christian Temperance Union, and the civil rights movement. The legacy of revolutionary-era women continues today in such groups as the National Women's Political Caucus and Concerned Women for America. Contemporary Americans would find it impossible to imagine their country without female activists of all political affiliations.

removing the region from the jurisdiction of the seacoast colonies. Wealthy colonists who hoped to develop the Ohio country now faced the prospect of dealing with officials in Quebec.

To resistance leaders, the Coercive Acts and the Quebec Act proved what they had feared since 1768: that Britain had a deliberate plan to oppress them. If Boston's port could be closed, why not Philadelphia's or New York's? If the royal charter of Massachusetts could be changed, why not that of South Carolina? If the Catholic Church could receive favored status in Quebec, why not everywhere?

The Boston Committee of Correspondence urged all colonies to boycott British goods. But Rhode Island, Virginia, and Pennsylvania suggested that another inter-colonial congress be convened to consider an appropriate response, and in mid-June 1774 Massachusetts acquiesced. Even the most ardent patriots remained loyal Britons and hoped for reconciliation. Americans were approaching the brink of confrontation, but had yet to reach an irrevocable break. So the colonies agreed to send delegates to a Continental Congress in Philadelphia in September.

Summary

Twenty years earlier, at the outbreak of the Seven Years' War in the western Pennsylvania wilderness, no one could have predicted such a dramatic change for Britain's mainland colonies. Yet that conflict simultaneously removed France from North America and created a huge debt for Britain, developments with major implications for the imperial relationship.

After the war ended in 1763, the number of colonists who defined themselves as political actors increased substantially. Once linked unquestioningly to Great Britain, they began to develop an American identity. Their concept of the political process differed from that of the mother country, and they held a different definition of what constituted representation and consent to government actions. After a long train of events, they understood that their economic interests did not necessarily coincide with those of Great Britain. Parliamentary acts such as the Stamp and Townshend Acts elicited colonial responses that produced further responses from Britain. Tensions escalated and climaxed when Bostonians destroyed the East India Company's tea. From then on, there would be no turning back.

In late summer 1774, Americans were committed to resistance but not independence. During the next decade, they would forge the bonds of a new American nationality.

Chapter Review

RENEWED WARFARE AMONG EUROPEANS AND INDIANS

What was at stake in the Seven Years' War?

The Seven Years' War was ultimately a contest over land between the British, French, Native Americans, and some settlers. All parties vied for control of large tracts of western land. The Iroquois, believing themselves the voice of the Delawares and Shawnees, negotiated to cede the land to Pennsylvania; the two tribes then moved west onto land claimed by Virginia and Pennsylvania, while France sought to hold and expand its possessions along the Ohio River, which it relied on for trade. After battling with Indians, the French continued to push southward in its land grabbing, and Anglo-American colonists gathered to address the French threat. England declared war and, after winning the protracted battle, the issue of land between European nations was settled when France ceded most of its North American territories to Britain.

1763: A TURNING POINT

How did colonists' ideas about government differ from those of the British in the 1760s?

British authorities believed that Parliament—which included the king, lords, and Commons—represented all British subjects regardless of where they lived and voting status. In this system of virtual representation, the people's consent to Parliament's actions was assumed. Americans, on the other hand, increasingly believed in direct representation, that they could only be represented by men who lived nearby and whom they elected. Moreover, the lower houses were specifically linked to the interests and needs of the regions that elected them. Living on the other side of the ocean, colonists were also accustomed to a central government with limited authority, and embraced the Real Whig notion that good government was one that left them alone to manage their affairs. As England imposed taxes and greater control over the colonies beginning in 1763, many Americans felt their freedom was endangered and questioned whether authority should lie with the monarchy or the people.

THE STAMP ACT CRISIS

How did the Stamp Act raise issues that would lead to the American Revolution?

Angry about the heavy taxes and questioning Britain's right to impose them, colonists began to wonder how they might resist Parliament yet remain British subjects. At issue for essayists such as James Otis was that as British subjects, they were entitled to the right to consent to taxation—which had not been granted under the Stamp Act. On the other hand, Parliament was a supreme authority to which they must give complete consent. Other leaders, such as Patrick Henry and the Virginia House of Burgesses, were unwilling to relinquish the right to consent to taxation, and some sought representation in Parliament. For ten years, Americans struggled with how to control their internal affairs yet remain under British rule. Protests led to the act's repeal in 1766, but questions about government nonetheless remained.

RESISTANCE TO THE TOWNSHEND ACTS

How did the Sons of Liberty politicize ordinary Americans during resistance to the Townshend Acts?

Ordinary Americans were not accustomed to being involved in political affairs, which they understood as matters handled by elites. But the Sons of Liberty made a conscious effort to draw people from all ranks into their anti-Townshend campaign, partly because they needed widespread participation for their boycott of British products designed in protest to the act. To rally a wider populace, they created rituals that would teach illiterate Americans about the reasons for resistance, including commemorating previous demonstrations with elaborate public celebrations including singing. Women helped, too, by spinning their own textiles outdoors in public, symbolically displaying their patriotism and pride for all to see.

CONFRONTATIONS IN BOSTON

How do Samuel Adams's Committees of Correspondence mark a turning point in Americans' political thinking?

An original member of the Sons of Liberty, Adams wanted to widen the movement's scope beyond its stronghold in New England cities and seacoast towns and create consensus among Massachusetts residents for the cause of liberty. The pamphlet he produced for the Boston Committee of Correspondence in 1772 was widely distributed. It stated the rights of colonists to life, liberty, and property, and it outlined complaints against England for taxation without representation, unnecessary troops and customs officers on American soil, the use of imperial revenues to pay colonial officials, and the expanded jurisdiction of vice-admiralty courts. Far more radical than earlier documents, this one did not seek to define the limits of Parliamentary authority but instead declared colonists' allegiance to America first and England a distant second. This new articulation, along with the pamphlet's widespread popularity, marked an important ideological moment.

TEA AND TURMOIL

| **How did the Tea Act push the country to the brink of revolution?**

  When Parliament imposed the Tea Act on the colonies in May 1773, it was attempting to save the East India Tea Company from bankruptcy, but colonists interpreted the move as an effort to make them admit Parliament's right to tax them. Citizens in several cities wanted to prevent the tea from being unloaded from ships; in Boston that effort led to a protest in which the tea was dumped in the harbor by men dressed as Indians. In response, Parliament adopted punitive laws, known as the Coercive or Intolerable Acts, ordering the city to pay for the tea and closing the port to food and other shipments until it did. Other acts reorganized the state's government and forbade town meetings, and allowed officers to commandeer private buildings to house troops. Colonists saw such measures as proof that Britain would oppress them. They considered boycotts and other measures, with colonies sending delegates to a Continental Congress in Philadelphia in 1774 to consider what to do next.

SUGGESTIONS FOR FURTHER READING

Fred Anderson, *The War That Made America: A Short History of the French and Indian War* (2005)

Bernard Bailyn, *The Ideological Origins of the American Revolution* (1967)

T. H. Breen, *The Marketplace of Revolution: How Consumer Politics Shaped American Independence* (2004)

Gregory Dowd, *War Under Heaven: Pontiac, the Indian Nation, and the British Empire* (2002)

Marc Egnal, *A Mighty Empire: The Origins of the American Revolution* (1988)

Merrill Jensen, *The Founding of a Nation: A History of the American Revolution, 1763–1776* (1968)

Pauline R. Maier, *From Resistance to Revolution: Colonial Radicals and the Development of American Opposition to Britain, 1765–1776* (1972)

Gary B. Nash, *The Unknown American Revolution: The Unruly Birth of Democracy and the Struggle to Create America* (2005)

William A. Pencak and Daniel K. Richter, eds., *Friends & Enemies in Penn's Woods: Indians, Colonists, and the Racial Construction of Pennsylvania* (2004)

Timothy Shannon, *Indians and Colonists at the Crossroads of Empire: The Albany Congress of 1754* (1999)

A Revolution, Indeed 1774–1783

The Shawnee chief Blackfish named his new captive Sheltowee, or Big Turtle, and adopted him as his son. In February 1778, Blackfish's warriors had caught the lone hunter, Daniel Boone, who then persuaded his fellow frontiersmen to surrender to the Shawnees (British allies). Boone had moved his family from North Carolina to Kentucky three years earlier as the Revolutionary War began. His contemporaries and some historians have questioned Boone's allegiances during the Revolution. His encounter with the Shawnees highlights ambiguities of revolutionary-era loyalties.

The Shawnees sought captives to cover the death of their chief, Cornstalk, killed months earlier while a prisoner of American militiamen in the Ohio country. Half of the twenty-six men taken were adopted into Shawnee families; those less willing to conform to Indian ways were dispatched as prisoners to the British fort at Detroit. Boone, who assured Blackfish that in the spring he would negotiate the surrender of women and children at his Boonesborough settlement, watched and waited. In June 1778 he escaped to warn the Kentuckians of an impending attack.

When Shawnees and their British allies appeared outside the Boonesborough stockade in mid-September, Boone agreed to negotiate. Although the settlers refused to move back across the mountains, fragmentary evidence suggests that they promised allegiance to the British to avert a battle. But discussions dissolved into a melee, with Indians besieging the fort for a week before withdrawing. That threat gone, Boone was charged with treason and court-martialed by the Kentucky militia. Although he was later cleared, questions about the incident and its aftermath haunted him for the rest of his life.

This icon will direct you to interactive activities and study materials on A People And A Nation, Brief Edition website: **www.cengage.com/history/norton/peoplenationbrief8e**

131

Chronology

1774	First Continental Congress meets in Philadelphia, adopts Declaration of Rights and Grievances.
	Continental Association implements economic boycott of Britain; committees of observation are established to oversee boycott.
1774–75	Provincial conventions replace collapsing colonial governments.
1775	Battles of Lexington and Concord, first shots of war are fired.
	Second Continental Congress begins.
	Washington is named commander-in-chief.
	Dunmore's proclamation offers freedom to patriots' slaves who join British forces.
1776	Paine publishes *Common Sense*, advocating independence.

	British evacuate Boston.
	Declaration of Independence is adopted.
	New York City falls to British.
1777	British take Philadelphia.
	Burgoyne surrenders at Saratoga.
1778	French alliance brings vital assistance to America.
	British evacuate Philadelphia.
1779	Sullivan expedition destroys Iroquois villages.
1780	British take Charleston.
1781	Cornwallis surrenders at Yorktown.
1782	Peace negotiations begin.
1783	Treaty of Paris, granting independence to the United States, is signed.

Where did Boone's loyalties lie? To the British, the Americans, or other Kentuckians? His actions made all three seem possible. Had he betrayed the settlers to Shawnees, seeking to establish British authority in Kentucky? Had he, as he claimed, twice deceived the Shawnees? Or was the survival of the fragile settlements his highest priority? Kentucky was a borderland where British, Indians, and American settlers vied for control. Boone and other Appalachian backcountry residents did not always face clear-cut choices as they struggled under precarious circumstances.

The American Revolution uprooted thousands of families, disrupted the economy, reshaped society by forcing many colonists into permanent exile, led Americans to develop new conceptions of politics, and created a nation from thirteen separate colonies. The struggle for independence required revolutionary leaders to accomplish three separate but related tasks. First, they had to transform a consensus favoring loyal resistance into a coalition supporting independence. They pursued various measures (ranging from persuasion to coercion) to enlist European Americans in the patriot cause, while seeking neutrality from Indians and slaves.

Second, to win independence, patriot leaders needed international recognition and aid, particularly from France. Thus they dispatched to Paris the most experienced American diplomat, Benjamin Franklin, who skillfully negotiated the Franco-American alliance of 1778, crucial to gaining independence.

Only the third task directly involved the British. George Washington, commander-in-chief of the American army, soon recognized that his primary goal should be not to win battles but to survive to fight another day. The British military concentrated on winning battles, as they had in other European wars, and did not consider the difficulties of their main goal, retaining the colonies' allegiance.

- What choices of allegiance confronted residents of North America after 1774? Why did people of various descriptions make the choices they did?
- What military strategies did the British and American forces adopt?
- Why did the Americans win the war?

GOVERNMENT BY CONGRESS AND COMMITTEE

When the fifty-five delegates to the First Continental Congress convened in Philadelphia in September 1774, they knew that any measures they adopted would likely enjoy widespread support. That summer, participants at well-publicized open meetings throughout the colonies promised (in the words of Johnson County, North Carolina, freeholders) to "strictly adhere to, and abide by, such Regulations and Restrictions as the Members of said General Congress shall agree to." Most congressional delegates were selected by extralegal provincial conventions whose members were chosen at local gatherings, because governors had forbidden regular assemblies to conduct formal elections. By designating delegates to the Congress, Americans openly defied British authority.

First Continental Congress

The colonies' leading political figures—mostly lawyers, merchants, and planters representing every colony but Georgia—attended the Philadelphia Congress. The Massachusetts delegation included Samuel Adams, the Boston resistance organizer, and his younger cousin John, an ambitious lawyer. Among others, New York sent the talented, young attorney John Jay. Virginia elected Richard Henry Lee, Patrick Henry, and George Washington. These men became the chief architects of the new nation.

The congressmen faced three tasks when they convened at Carpenters' Hall on September 5: defining American grievances, developing a resistance plan, and articulating their constitutional relationship with Great Britain. Radical congressmen, like Lee of Virginia, argued that colonists owed allegiance only to George III and that Parliament had no legitimate authority over them. Conservatives, like Pennsylvania's Joseph Galloway and his allies, proposed a union requiring Parliament and a new American legislature to consent jointly to all laws pertaining to the colonies. After heated debate, delegates narrowly rejected Galloway's proposal, but did not embrace the radicals' position either.

Finally, they accepted wording proposed by John Adams. The crucial clauses in the Congress's Declaration of Rights and Grievances declared that Americans would obey Parliament, but only voluntarily, and would resist all taxes in disguise, like the Townshend duties. Remarkably, this position, which would have seemed radical years before, represented a compromise in fall 1774.

Continental Association

The delegates agreed on the laws they wanted repealed (notably the Coercive Acts) and implemented an economic boycott while petitioning the king for relief. They adopted the Continental Association, which called for nonimportation of British goods (effective December 1, 1774), nonconsumption of British products (effective March 1, 1775), and nonexportation of American goods to Britain and the British West Indies (effective September 10, 1775).

More comprehensive than previous economic measures, the provisions of the association appealed to different groups and regions. The nonimportation agreement's inclusive language banned commerce in slaves and manufactures; this accorded with the Virginia gentry's desire to halt or slow the arrival of enslaved Africans. (Leading Virginians believed slave importations discouraged free Europeans with useful skills from immigrating.) Delaying nonconsumption until three months after implementing nonimportation allowed northern urban merchants time to sell items they acquired legally before December 1. The novel tactic of nonexportation and its postponement for nearly a year served other interests. In 1773 small farmers in Virginia already vowed to stop exporting tobacco to raise prices in the glutted market. The next year, the association accomplished the same end while letting them profit from higher prices for their 1774 crop. It similarly benefited northern exporters of wood products and foodstuffs to the Caribbean with a final sales season before the embargo.

Committees of Observation

To enforce the Continental Association, the Congress recommended the election of committees of observation and inspection in every American locality. By specifying that committee members be chosen by all men qualified to vote, the Congress guaranteed them a broad popular base. The seven thousand to eight thousand committeemen became local leaders of the American resistance.

Initially charged with overseeing implementation of the boycott, within six months these committees became de facto governments. They examined merchants' records, publishing the names of those who continued importing British goods. They promoted home manufactures, encouraging simple modes of dress and behavior that symbolized Americans' commitment to liberty. Because expensive leisure-time activities were believed to reflect vice and corruption, the Congress urged Americans to forgo dancing, gambling, horseracing, cardplaying, and cockfighting.

The committees gradually extended their authority. They attempted to identify opponents of American resistance, developing spy networks, circulating copies of the Continental Association for signatures, and investigating questionable remarks and activities. Suspected dissenters were urged to support the colonial cause publicly; if they refused, the committees had them watched, restricted their movements, or tried to force them to move away. People engaging in casual political exchanges one day could find themselves charged with treasonable conversation the next.

Provincial Conventions

Meanwhile, during the winter and early spring of 1775, colonial governments were collapsing. Only a few legislatures met without challenges to their authority. In most colonies, popularly elected provincial conventions took over the government, sometimes replacing legislatures or holding concurrent sessions. In late 1774 and early 1775, these conventions approved the Continental Association, elected delegates to the Second Continental Congress (scheduled for May), organized militias, and gathered arms.

Royal officials suffered constant humiliation. Courts were prevented from meeting; taxes were paid to the conventions' agents rather than to provincial tax collectors; and militiamen would muster only when committees ordered. During the six months preceding the battles at Lexington and Concord, independence was being won at the local level. Not many Americans fully realized what was happening. Most continued to proclaim loyalty to Great Britain.

CONTEST IN THE BACKCOUNTRY

While the committees of observation consolidated their authority in the East, some colonists headed west. Ignoring the Proclamation of 1763, pronouncements by colonial governors, and the threat of Indian attacks, land-hungry folk—many of them recent immigrants from Ireland and soldiers who demobilized in North America after the Seven Years' War—swarmed onto lands along the Ohio River and its tributaries after the mid-1760s. Sometimes they purchased property from opportunists with dubious grants; often, they claimed land as squatters. Britain's 1771 decision to abandon (and raze) Fort Pitt removed final restraints on settlement there and rendered the Proclamation of 1763 unenforceable. By late 1775, thousands of new homesteads dotted the backcountry from western Pennsylvania south through Virginia and eastern Kentucky into western North Carolina.

Distrust and Warfare Few backcountry folk viewed the region's native peoples positively. Frontier dwellers had little interest in the small-scale trade that had once sustained an uneasy peace; they wanted land for crops and livestock pastures.

Headed by a new governor, Lord Dunmore, in 1774 Virginia asserted its title to the developing backcountry. During spring and early summer, tensions mounted as Virginians surveyed Kentucky land on the south side of the Ohio River—territory claimed by the Shawnees. Lord Dunmore's war consisted of one large-scale confrontation between Virginia militia and some Shawnee warriors. Neither won, but in the immediate aftermath thousands of settlers—including Daniel Boone and his associates—flooded across the mountains.

When the Revolutionary War began, the loyalties of Indians and settlers in the backcountry remained fluid and uncertain. Hostile to each other, the side each would take in the imperial struggle might depend on which could better serve their interests. Understanding that, the Continental Congress moved to reoccupy Fort Pitt and establish other garrisons in the Ohio country. With this protection, up to twenty thousand settlers poured into Kentucky and western Pennsylvania by 1780.

Native Americans' grievances against the European American newcomers predisposed many to ally with Great Britain. Yet some chiefs urged caution: the British abandonment of Fort Pitt (and them) suggested that Britain might not protect them in the future. Furthermore, Britain hesitated to make immediate use of its potential native allies and initially sought from the Indians only a promise of neutrality.

Patriots also sought the Indians' neutrality. In 1775 the Second Continental Congress sent a message to Indian communities, describing the war as "a family quarrel between us and Old England" and requesting that they "not join on either side." The Iroquois pledged neutrality. But the Cherokees led by Chief Dragging Canoe hoped to use the family quarrel to regain land. In summer 1776, they attacked settlements in western Virginia and the Carolinas. After a militia campaign destroyed many Cherokee towns, Dragging Canoe and some followers fled to the West, establishing new villages. Other Cherokees agreed to a treaty that ceded more of their land.

Frontier Hostilities   Shawnees and Cherokees continued to attack backcountry settlements throughout the war, but dissent within their ranks crippled these efforts. The British victory over France in 1763 destroyed the Indians' ability to maintain independence by playing European powers against one another. Only a few communities (among them the Stockbridge Indians of New England and the Oneidas in New York) unwaveringly supported the American revolt; most others either remained neutral or sporadically aligned with the British. In 1778 and early 1779 a frontier militia force under George Rogers Clark captured British posts in modern Illinois (Kaskaskia) and Indiana (Vincennes). The revolutionaries could never overtake the redcoats' stronghold at Detroit. Backcountry warfare between settlers and Indians persisted long after the Revolution ended. Indeed, the Revolutionary War itself constituted a brief chapter in the ongoing struggle for control of the region west of the Appalachians, which began in 1763 and continued into the next century.

CHOOSING SIDES

In 1765 Stamp Act protests were supported by most colonists in the Caribbean, Nova Scotia, and the future United States. Although provisions of the 1764 Sugar Act benefited Britain's Caribbean possessions, the Stamp Act levied higher duties on them than on the mainland colonies. When the act took effect, though, islanders loyally paid the duties. Eventually many colonists in North America and the West Indies questioned the aims and tactics of the resistance movement.

Nova Scotia and the Caribbean   Northern mainland and southern island colonies depended on Great Britain militarily and economically. Despite the British victory in the Seven Years' War, they felt vulnerable to French counterattack. Additionally, sugar planters—on some islands outnumbered by their bondspeople twenty-five to one—feared potential slave revolts. Neither region had a large population of European descent or strong political structures. Fewer people lived in Halifax in 1775 than in the late 1750s, and with successful men heading to England, the sugar islands had just a few resident planters to provide leadership.

Nova Scotians and West Indians had economic reasons for supporting the mother country. In the mid-1770s the northerners finally broke into the Caribbean market with their dried and salted fish. They also began to reduce New England's domination of the northern coastal trade, and they benefited from Britain's retaliatory measures against the rebels' commerce. British sugar producers relied on their trade monopoly within the empire, for more efficient French planters could sell sugar for one-third less. Further, the West Indian planters' lobbyists in London won the islands' exclusion from some Townshend Act provisions.

Patriots

Many residents of the thirteen colonies supported resistance, then independence. Active revolutionaries accounted for about two-fifths of the European American population and included small and middling farmers, members of dominant Protestant sects, Chesapeake gentry, merchants, city artisans, elected officeholders, and people of English descent. Wives usually adopted their husbands' political beliefs, but not always. Although all supported the Revolution, they pursued divergent goals within the broader coalition. Some sought limited political reform; others, extensive political change; and still others, social and economic reforms. (The ways their concerns interacted are discussed in Chapter 7.)

Loyalists

About one-fifth of the European American population remained loyal to Great Britain, firmly rejecting independence. Most loyalists long opposed the men who became patriot leaders for varying reasons. British-appointed government officials; Anglican clergy and lay Anglicans in the North; tenant farmers; members of persecuted religious sects; backcountry southerners who rebelled against eastern rule in the late 1760s and early 1770s; and non-English ethnic minorities, especially Scots—all feared the power of those who controlled the colonial assemblies and who had previously shown little concern for their welfare. Joined by merchants whose trade depended on imperial connections and by former British military men who settled in America after 1763, they formed a loyalist core.

During the war, loyalists congregated in cities held by the British army. When those posts were evacuated at war's end, loyalists scattered throughout the British Empire—Britain, the Bahamas, and especially Canada. In Nova Scotia, New Brunswick, and Ontario roughly seventy thousand former Americans laid the foundations of British Canada.

Neutrals

Between patriots and loyalists, there remained in the middle perhaps two-fifths of the European American population. Some, like the Quakers, were sincere pacifists. Others opportunistically shifted their allegiance to whichever side happened to be winning. Still others cared little about politics and obeyed whoever was in power. Such colonists resisted British and Americans alike when their demands seemed too heavy—when taxes became too high or when calls for militia service were too frequent. They made up a large proportion of the backcountry population, where Scots-Irish settlers had little love for either the patriot gentry or English authorities.

To patriots, apathy or neutrality was as heinous as loyalism. By winter 1775–1776, the Second Continental Congress recommended that "disaffected" persons be disarmed and arrested. State legislatures passed laws prescribing severe penalties for suspected loyalists or neutrals. Many began to require voters (or, in some cases, all free adult men) to take oaths of allegiance; refusal usually meant banishment to England or extra taxes. After 1777 many states confiscated the property of banished persons, using it to fund the war. The patriots' policies ensured that their scattered and persecuted opponents could not band together against the revolutionary cause.

Slaves

In New England, with few resident bondspeople, revolutionary fervor was widespread, and free African Americans enlisted in patriot militias. The middle colonies, where slaves constituted a small but substantial proportion of the population, were more divided but largely revolutionary. In Virginia and Maryland, where free people constituted a slender majority, the potential for slave revolts raised occasional but not disabling fears. By contrast, South Carolina and Georgia, where slaves composed more than half of the population, were less enthusiastic about resistance. Georgia sent no delegates to the First Continental Congress and reminded representatives at the second to consider its circumstances, "with our blacks and tories [loyalists] within us," when voting on independence.

Bondspeople faced a dilemma during the Revolution. Their goal was *personal* independence, but how best could they escape from slavery? To most slaves, supporting the British held promise. In late 1774 and early 1775, slaves offered to assist the British army in return for freedom.

Slaveowners' worst fears were realized in November 1775, when Virginia's royal governor, Lord Dunmore, offered to free slaves and indentured servants willing to join the British forces. About one thousand African Americans rallied to the British; although many perished in a smallpox epidemic, three hundred survived to reach occupied New York City under British protection. Because other commanders renewed Dunmore's proclamation, tens of thousands of runaway slaves eventually joined the British. At war's end, at least nine thousand left with the redcoats.

Although slaves did not pose a serious threat early on, patriots turned rumors of slave uprisings to their advantage. In South Carolina, resistance leaders argued that the Continental Association could protect masters from their slaves. Undoubtedly many wavering Carolinians were drawn into the revolutionary camp by fear that divisiveness among free people would encourage rebellion by the bondspeople.

Patriots could never completely ignore threats posed by loyalists, neutrals, slaves, and Indians. Occasionally backcountry militiamen refused to turn out for duty on the seacoast because they feared Indian attacks in their absence. Sometimes southern troops refused to serve in the North because they would not leave their regions unprotected against a slave insurrection. But the unlikelihood of a large-scale slave revolt, coupled with dissension in Indian communities and the patriots' successful campaign to disarm and neutralize loyalists, ensured that the revolutionaries would control the countryside.

War and Independence

On January 27, 1775, Lord Dartmouth, secretary of state for America, wrote to General Thomas Gage in Boston, urging decisive action. On April 14, Gage responded by sending an expedition to confiscate colonial military supplies stockpiled at Concord.

New Nations

The American Revolution not only created the United States but led to the formation of three other nations: English-dominated Canada, Sierra Leone, and Australia.

In northern North America before the Revolution, only Nova Scotia had a sizable number of English-speaking settlers. Largely New Englanders, they were recruited after 1758 to repopulate the region forcibly taken from exiled Acadians. During and after the Revolution, loyalist families, especially from northern and middle colonies, moved to the region that is now Canada, which remained under British rule. Some exiles settled in Quebec as well. In a few years, loyalist refugees transformed the sparsely populated former French colony, laying the foundation for the modern bilingual (but majority English-speaking) Canadian nation.

Sierra Leone, too, was founded by colonial exiles—African Americans who had fled to the British army during the war, many of whom ended up in London. Seeing the refugees' poverty, charitable merchants—calling themselves the Committee for Relief of the Black Poor—developed a plan to resettle the African Americans elsewhere. The refugees rejected the Bahamas, fearing reenslavement there. They accepted a return to the land of their ancestors. In early 1787, vessels carrying about four hundred settlers reached Sierra Leone in West Africa, where representatives of the Black Poor Committee acquired land. The first years were difficult, and many newcomers died of disease and deprivation. But in 1792 they were joined by several thousand other loyalist African Americans who originally moved to Nova Scotia. The influx ensured the colony's survival; it remained a part of the British Empire until its independence in 1961.

At the Paris peace negotiations in 1782, American diplomats rejected British suggestions that the United States continue to serve as a dumping ground for convicts. Britain thus needed another destination for people sentenced for crimes such as theft, assault, and manslaughter. It sent them halfway round the world to Australia, which Captain James Cook claimed in 1770. Britain continued this practice until 1868, but voluntary migrants also arrived. The modern nation was created from a federation of separate colonial governments on January 1, 1901.

Thus the founding event in the history of the United States links the nation to the formation of its northern neighbor and to new nations in West Africa and the Asian Pacific.

The New York Public Library / Art Resource, NY

National Library of Australia

139

Battles of Lexington and Concord

Bostonians dispatched two messengers, William Dawes and Paul Revere (later joined by Dr. Samuel Prescott), to rouse the countryside. When the British vanguard of several hundred men approached Lexington at dawn on April 19, they found just seventy militiamen—about half of the town's adult male population—mustered on the common. Realizing they could not halt the redcoats, the Americans' commander ordered his men to withdraw. But as they dispersed, a shot rang out; British soldiers then fired. When they stopped, eight Americans lay dead, and another ten wounded. The British moved on to nearby Concord.

There the militia contingents, joined by men from nearby towns, were larger. At the North Bridge three British men were killed and nine wounded. Thousands fired from houses and from behind trees as British forces retreated to Boston. By day's end, the redcoats suffered 272 casualties, including 70 deaths. The arrival of reinforcements and the American militia's lack of coordination prevented heavier British losses. The patriots suffered just 93 casualties.

First Year of War

By the evening of April 20, thousands of American militiamen gathered around Boston, summoned by local committees. Many did not stay long, but those who remained were organized into formal units. Officers under the command of General Artemas Ward of the Massachusetts militia ordered that latrines be dug, the water supply protected, supplies purchased, military discipline enforced, and defensive fortifications constructed.

For nearly a year the two armies stared at each other across siege lines. The redcoats attacked only once, on June 17, when they drove the Americans from trenches atop Breed's Hill in Charlestown. In that misnamed Battle of Bunker Hill, the British incurred their greatest wartime losses: over 800 wounded and 228 killed. The Americans lost less than half that number.

During the same eleven-month period, patriots captured the British Fort Ticonderoga on Lake Champlain, acquiring much-needed cannon. Trying to bring Canada into the war, patriots also mounted a northern campaign that ended in disaster at Quebec in early 1776 when troops were ravaged by smallpox. But the long lull in fighting between the main armies at Boston during the war's first year gave both sides time to regroup and strategize.

British Strategy

Lord North and his new American secretary, Lord George Germain, made three central assumptions about the war. First, they concluded that patriot forces could not withstand assaults by trained British regulars. Convinced that the 1776 campaign would begin and end the war, they dispatched Great Britain's largest force ever: 370 transport ships carrying 32,000 troops and tons of supplies, accompanied by 73 naval vessels and 13,000 sailors. Among the troops were thousands of German mercenaries, soldiers who hired out to the highest bidder.

Second, British officials and officers adopted a conventional strategy of capturing major American cities and defeating the rebel army with minimal casualties. Third, they assumed that military victory would retain the colonies' allegiance.

All three assumptions proved false. London officials also missed the significance of the American population's dispersal over an area 1,500 miles long and more than 100 miles wide. Although Britain would control each of America's largest ports at some time during the war, less than 5 percent of the population lived in those cities. Furthermore, with a vast coastline, commerce was easily rerouted. Hence, the loss of cities did little to damage the American cause.

Most of all, London officials did not initially understand that military triumph would not necessarily lead to political victory. Securing the colonies would require Americans to return to their original allegiance. After 1778 the ministry adopted a strategy to achieve that through the expanded use of loyalist forces and the restoration of civilian authority in occupied areas. But the policy came too late.

Second Continental Congress

Great Britain had a bureaucracy to supervise the war. Americans had only the Second Continental Congress. The delegates who convened in Philadelphia on May 10, 1775, had to assume the mantle of intercolonial government. As summer passed, Congress organized the colonies for war. It authorized the printing of money, established a committee to supervise foreign relations, and strengthened the militia. Most important, it created the Continental Army.

Until Congress met, the Massachusetts provincial congress supervised Ward and the militiamen encamped at Boston. But that army, composed of men from all over New England, heavily drained local resources. Consequently, Massachusetts asked the Continental Congress to direct the army and choose a commander-in-chief. John Adams proposed the appointment of a Virginian "whose Skill and Experience as an Officer, whose independent fortune, great Talents and excellent universal Character, would command the Approbation of all America": George Washington. Congress unanimously concurred.

George Washington

Washington had not participated prominently in the pre-revolutionary agitation. Devoted to the American cause, he was dignified, conservative, and respectable—a man of unimpeachable integrity. The younger son of a Virginia planter, Washington did not expect to inherit substantial property and planned to work as a surveyor. But the early death of his older brother and his marriage to the wealthy widow Martha Custis made George Washington one of Virginia's largest slaveholders. After his mistakes early in the Seven Years' War, he repaired his reputation by rallying the troops and maintaining calm during Braddock's defeat in 1755.

Washington had remarkable stamina and leadership ability. More than six feet tall (when most men were five inches shorter), he displayed a commanding presence. Even a loyalist admitted that Washington could "atone for many demerits by the extraordinary coolness and caution which distinguish his character."

British Evacuate Boston

Washington took command of the army outside Boston in July 1775. By March 1776, when the arrival of cannon from Ticonderoga enabled him to pressure the redcoats, his army was prepared. Yet an assault on Boston proved unnecessary. Sir William Howe, the new commander, wanted to transfer his men to New York City. The patriots' cannon decided the matter. On March 17, the British and their loyalist allies abandoned Boston forever.

Although at war for months, American leaders denied seeking a break with Great Britain until a pamphlet published in January 1776 advocated that step.

Common Sense

Thomas Paine's *Common Sense* exploded, quickly selling tens of thousands of copies. The author, a radical English printer who had lived in America only since 1774, called for independence and challenged many common American assumptions about government and the colonies' relationship to Britain. He advocated the establishment of a republic, a government by the people with no king or nobility. Paine insisted that Britain had exploited the colonies. And for the frequent assertion that an independent America would be weak and divided, he substituted unlimited confidence in America's strength once freed from European control.

By late spring, independence had become inevitable. On May 10, the Second Continental Congress recommended that individual colonies form new governments, replacing colonial charters with state constitutions. On June 7, Richard Henry Lee of Virginia, seconded by John Adams of Massachusetts, introduced the crucial resolution: "that these United Colonies are, and of right ought to be, free and independent States, . . . and that all political connection between them and the State of Great Britain is, and ought to be, totally dissolved." Congress did not immediately adopt Lee's resolution, postponing a vote until early July. Meanwhile, a five-man committee—including Thomas Jefferson, John Adams, and Benjamin Franklin—was directed to draft a declaration of independence.

Jefferson and the Declaration of Independence

The committee assigned primary responsibility for writing the declaration to Thomas Jefferson, who was known for his eloquence. The thirty-four-year-old Virginia lawyer and member of the House of Burgesses was educated at the College of William and Mary and in the law offices of a prominent attorney. His knowledge of history and political theory was evident in the declaration and his draft of the Virginia state constitution. While Jefferson wrote and debated in Philadelphia, his beloved wife Martha suffered a miscarriage at their home, Monticello. Not until after her 1782 death from complications following the birth of their sixth (but only third surviving) child, did Jefferson fully commit to public service.

The draft of the declaration reached Congress on June 28, 1776. The delegates voted for independence four days later, then debated the declaration's wording for two days, adopting it with changes on July 4. The Declaration of Independence concentrated on George III (see the appendix), accusing the king of attempting to destroy representative government in the colonies and of oppressing Americans.

The declaration's chief long-term importance lay in the ringing statements of principle that have since served as the American ideal: "We hold these truths to be self-evident: That all men are created equal; that they are endowed by their Creator with certain unalienable rights; that among these are life, liberty and the pursuit of happiness; that, to secure these rights, governments are instituted among men, deriving their just powers from the consent of the governed; that whenever any form of government becomes destructive of these ends, it is the right of the people to alter or to abolish it, and to institute new government."

When the delegates in Philadelphia voted to accept the Declaration of Independence, they were committing treason. Therefore, when they concluded with the assertion that they "mutually pledge[d] to each other our lives, our fortunes, and our sacred honor," they spoke the truth.

THE STRUGGLE IN THE NORTH

In late June 1776, ships carrying Sir William Howe's troops from Halifax appeared off the New York coast (see Map 6.1). On July 2, redcoats landed on Staten Island. Washington marched his army of seventeen thousand from Boston to defend Manhattan. Because Howe waited until more troops arrived from England, Americans could prepare to defend the city.

New York and New Jersey

Still inexperienced, Washington and his men made major mistakes, losing battles at Brooklyn Heights and on Manhattan Island. The city fell to the British, who captured nearly three thousand American soldiers. Washington retreated into Pennsylvania, and British forces took most of New Jersey. Occupying troops met little opposition; the revolutionary cause appeared in disarray. "These are the times that try men's souls," wrote Thomas Paine in his pamphlet *The Crisis*.

The British then forfeited their advantage as redcoats in New Jersey went on a rampage of rape and plunder. Determined to strike back, Washington crossed the Delaware River at night to attack a Hessian encampment at Trenton early on December 26. The patriots captured more than nine hundred Hessians and killed another thirty; only three Americans were wounded. Days later, Washington attacked

Map 6.1 The War in the North, 1775–1777

The early phase of the Revolutionary War was dominated by British troop movements in the Boston area, the redcoats' evacuation to Nova Scotia in the spring of 1776, and the subsequent British invasion of New York and New Jersey.

George Washington at the Battle of Princeton, 1779, by Charles Willson Peale. Two years after the battle, Peale created this heroic image of the Continental Army's commander, intended (as were all his portraits of revolutionary leaders) to instill patriotic sentiments and pride in its viewers.   (Courtesy of the Pennsylvania Academy of the Fine Arts, Philadelphia. Gift of Maria McKean Allen and Phebe Warren Downs through the bequest of their mother, Elizabeth Wharton McKean)

at Princeton. Gaining command of the field, Washington set up winter quarters at Morristown, New Jersey.

Campaign of 1777

British strategy for 1777 aimed to isolate New England from the other colonies. General John Burgoyne would lead an invading force down the Hudson River from Canada to rendezvous near Albany with a similar force moving east. The combined forces would then link up with Howe's troops in New York City. But Howe was planning to capture Philadelphia. In 1777 the British armies in America operated independently; the result was disaster.

Howe took Philadelphia, but he delayed before beginning the campaign, took six weeks to transport his troops by sea, and ended up only 40 miles closer to Philadelphia than when he started. This gave Washington time to prepare a defense. At Brandywine Creek and Germantown, the two armies clashed. Although the British won both engagements, the Americans handled themselves well. The redcoats captured Philadelphia in late September but to little effect. The campaign season was nearly over; the revolutionary army had gained confidence in itself and its leaders; and, far north, Burgoyne was going down to defeat.

Burgoyne and his men set out from Montreal in mid-June. An easy triumph at Fort Ticonderoga in July was followed in August by two setbacks—the redcoats and Indians marching east along the Mohawk River turned back after a battle at Oriskany, New York; and in a clash near Bennington, Vermont, American militiamen nearly wiped out eight hundred of Burgoyne's German mercenaries. After several skirmishes, Burgoyne was surrounded near Saratoga, New York. On October 17, 1777, he surrendered his force of more than six thousand men.

Iroquois Confederacy Splinters

The August 1777 battle at Oriskany divided the Iroquois Confederacy. Although the Six Nations had pledged neutrality, two influential Mohawk leaders, siblings Mary and Joseph Brant, believed the Iroquois should ally with the British to protect their territory from land-hungry colonists. The Brants won over the Senecas, Cayugas, and Mohawks, but the Oneidas preferred the Americans and brought the Tuscaroras with them. The Onondagas split into three factions, one on each side and one supporting neutrality. At Oriskany, some Oneidas and Tuscaroras joined patriot militiamen in fighting their Iroquois brethren, shattering three-hundred years of friendship.

The collapse of Iroquois unity had significant consequences. In 1778 Iroquois warriors allied with the British raided frontier villages in Pennsylvania and New York. The following summer, the Americans dispatched an expedition to burn Iroquois crops and settlements. The devastation led many bands to seek food and shelter north of the Great Lakes during the winter of 1779–1780. Many Iroquois settled permanently in Canada.

Burgoyne's surrender at Saratoga brought joy to patriots, discouragement to loyalists and Britons. Most important, the American victory at Saratoga drew France into the conflict. The American Revolution gave the French an opportunity to avenge their defeat in the Seven Years' War. Even before Benjamin Franklin arrived in Paris in late 1776, France covertly supplied the revolutionaries with military necessities. Indeed, 90 percent of the gunpowder Americans used during the war's first two years came from France, transported via the French Caribbean island of Martinique.

Franco-American Alliance of 1778

Benjamin Franklin worked tirelessly to strengthen ties between the two nations. Adopting a plain style of dress, Franklin played on the French image of Americans as virtuous farmers. In 1778 the countries signed two treaties. In the Treaty of Amity and Commerce, France recognized American independence and established trade ties. In the Treaty of Alliance, France and the United States promised—assuming that France would declare war on Britain, which it soon did—that neither would negotiate peace without consulting the other. France also abandoned claims to Canada and to North American territory east of the Mississippi River. The most visible symbol of Franco-American cooperation was the Marquis de Lafayette, a young nobleman who volunteered for service with George Washington in 1777 and fought with American forces.

With the alliance, France aided Americans openly, sending troops, naval vessels, arms, ammunition, clothing, and blankets. And Britain now had to fight France in the Caribbean and elsewhere, in addition to its battles on the American mainland. Spain's entry into the war in 1779 as an ally of France (but not of the United States) transformed the Revolution into a global war. The French aided Americans throughout the conflict, but in its last years that assistance proved vital.

Joseph Brant, the Iroquois leader who helped to persuade the Mohawks, Senecas, and Cayugas to support the British in the latter stages of the Revolution, as painted by Charles Willson Peale in 1797.
(Independence National Historic Park Collection)

LIFE IN THE ARMY AND ON THE HOME FRONT

Only in the first months of the war was the revolutionaries' army manned primarily by the semimythical citizen-soldier, who exchanged his plow for a gun. After a few months, early arrivals went home. They reenlisted only briefly when the contending armies neared their farms and towns. In such militia units, elected officers and the soldiers who chose them reflected social hierarchies in their regions of origin, yet also retained a flexibility absent from the Continental Army, composed of men in formally organized statewide units led by appointed officers.

Continental Army

Continental soldiers, unlike militiamen, were primarily young, single, or propertyless men who enlisted for long periods or for the war's duration, partly for monetary bonuses or land. They saw in military service an opportunity to assert their masculinity and claim postwar citizenship and property-owning rights. As the fighting dragged on,

Barzillai Lew, a free African American born in Groton, Massachusetts, in 1743, served in the Seven Years' War before enlisting with patriot troops in the American Revolution. An accomplished fifer, Lew fought at the Battle of Bunker Hill. Like other freemen in the north, he cast his lot with the revolutionaries, in contrast to southern bondspeople, who tended to favor the British. (Courtesy of Mae Theresa Bonitto)

bonuses grew larger. To meet quotas, towns and states recruited everyone, including recent immigrants; about 45 percent of Pennsylvania soldiers were of Irish origin and about 13 percent were German.

Dunmore's proclamation led Congress in January 1776 to modify an earlier policy prohibiting African Americans in the regular army. Recruiters in northern states turned increasingly to slaves, who were often promised freedom after the war. Southern states initially resisted, but later all except Georgia and South Carolina enlisted black soldiers. Approximately five thousand African Americans served in the Continental Army, typically in racially integrated units where they were assigned tasks that others shunned, such as burying the dead, foraging for food, and driving wagons. Overall, they composed about 10 percent of the regular army, although rarely serving in militia units.

American wives and widows of poor soldiers came to the army with their menfolk because they were too impoverished to survive alone. Such camp followers—roughly 3 percent of the total number of troops—worked as cooks, nurses, and launderers for rations and low wages. The women, along with civilian commissaries and militiamen who floated in and out at irregular intervals, were difficult to manage, especially since they were not subject to military discipline.

Officer Corps

The officers of the Continental Army developed intense pride and commitment to the revolutionary cause. The realities of warfare were often messy and corrupt, but officers drew strength from a developing image of themselves as professionals who sacrificed for the nation. When Benedict Arnold, an officer who fought heroically for the patriot cause early in the war, defected to the British, they made his name a metaphor for villainy.

Unlike poor women, officers' wives did not travel with the army but made extended visits while the troops were in camp (usually during winter). They brought food, clothing, and household furnishings to make their stay more comfortable, and they entertained each other and their menfolk at teas, dinners, and dances. Socializing created friendships later renewed when some of their husbands became the new nation's leaders.

Hardship and Disease

Ordinary soldiers endured more hardships than officers. Wages were small, and often the army could not meet the payroll. Rations (a daily allotment of bread, meat, vegetables, milk, and beer) did not always appear, and men had to forage for food. Clothing and shoes were often poor quality. When conditions deteriorated, troops threatened mutiny (though only a few followed through) or, more often, simply deserted. Punishments for desertion or offenses such as theft and assault were harsh; convicted soldiers were sentenced to hundreds of lashes, whereas officers were publicly humiliated, deprived of their commission, and discharged in disgrace.

Endemic disease in the camps—dysentery, various fevers, and, early in the war, smallpox—made matters worse. Most native-born colonists had neither been exposed to smallpox nor been inoculated and were vulnerable when smallpox spread through the northern countryside in early 1774. The disease ravaged Bostonians during the British occupation, troops attacking Quebec in 1775–1776, and African Americans who fled to join Lord Dunmore (1775) or Lord Cornwallis (1781). Most British soldiers had already survived smallpox (which was endemic in Europe), so it posed little threat to redcoat troops.

Recognizing smallpox's potential to decimate the revolutionaries' ranks, Washington ordered that the regular army be inoculated in Morristown in early 1777. Some would die from the risky procedure and survivors would be incapacitated for weeks. Yet inoculation, coupled with the increasing numbers of foreign-born (and mostly immune) enlistees, helped protect Continental soldiers later in the war, contributing to the eventual American victory.

Home Front
Men who enlisted in the army or served in Congress were away from home for long periods of time. In their absence their womenfolk, who previously had handled only the indoor affairs of the household, shouldered outdoor affairs as well. John and Abigail Adams took pride in Abigail's developing skills as a "farmeress." Like other female contemporaries, Abigail Adams stopped calling the farm *yours* in letters to her husband and began referring to it as *ours*. Most women did not work in the fields, but they supervised field workers and managed their families' resources.

Wartime disruptions affected all Americans. People suffered from shortages of necessities like salt, soap, and flour. Severe inflation added to the country's woes. Soldiers on both sides plundered farms and houses, looking for food or salable items; they burned fence rails in fires and took horses and oxen for their wagons. Moreover, they carried smallpox and other diseases wherever they went. Women had to decide whether to deliberately risk their children's lives by inoculating them with smallpox or to chance youngsters' contracting the disease "in the natural way." Many chose the former and were relieved when their children survived.

VICTORY IN THE SOUTH

In early 1778, in the wake of the Saratoga disaster, British military leaders reassessed their strategy. Loyalist exiles in London persuaded them to shift the field of battle southward, contending that loyal southerners would welcome the redcoat army as liberators. The South could then serve as a base for attacking the middle and northern states.

South Carolina and the Caribbean
Sir Henry Clinton oversaw the regrouping of British forces in America. He ordered the evacuation of Philadelphia in June 1778 and sent a convoy that captured the French Caribbean island of St. Lucia, thereafter a key British base. He also dispatched a small expedition to Georgia. When Savannah and then Augusta fell into British hands, Clinton became convinced that a southern strategy would

Map 6.2   The War in the South

The southern war—after the British invasion of Georgia in late 1778—was characterized by a series of British thrusts into the interior, leading to battles with American defenders in both North and South Carolina. Finally, after promising beginnings, Cornwallis's foray into Virginia ended with disaster at Yorktown in October 1781.

succeed. In late 1779 he sailed down the coast from New York to besiege Charleston, the most important city in the South (see Map 6.2). Although afflicted by smallpox, Americans trapped there held out for months. On May 12, 1780, General Benjamin Lincoln surrendered the entire southern army—5,500 men. The redcoats then spread through South Carolina, establishing garrisons at key points. Hundreds of South Carolinians proclaimed renewed loyalty to the Crown.

Success of the southern campaign depended on controlling the seas, for the British armies were widely dispersed and travel by land was difficult. The Royal Navy dominated the American coastline, but French naval power posed a threat. American privateers infested Caribbean waters, seizing cargoes to and from the British islands. Furthermore, after late 1778 France picked off those islands one by one, including Grenada—second only to Jamaica in sugar production. In early 1781 the British captured St. Eustatius (the Dutch island that was the main conduit for moving military supplies from Europe to America). But the victory might well have cost them the war, for Admiral Sir George Rodney failed to pursue the French fleet under Admiral François de Grasse when it subsequently sailed from the Caribbean to Virginia, where it played a major role in the battle at Yorktown.

The redcoats never established control of the areas they seized in South Carolina or Georgia. Patriot bands operated freely, and the fall of Charleston spurred them to greater exertions. Patriot women in four states formed the Ladies Association, raising funds to purchase shirts for needy soldiers. Recruiting efforts were stepped up.

Nevertheless, the war in South Carolina went badly for the patriots throughout 1780. At Camden in August, forces under Lord Cornwallis, the new British commander, crushed a reorganized southern army led by Horatio Gates. Thousands of enslaved African Americans joined the redcoats. Running away from their patriot masters individually and as families, they disrupted farming in the Carolinas and Georgia in 1780 and 1781. Tens of thousands of slaves were lost to their owners. Not all of them won their freedom. Many served the redcoats as scouts and guides or as laborers in camps or occupied cities like New York.

Greene and the Southern Campaign

After the Camden defeat, Washington (who remained in the North to contain the British army occupying New York) appointed General Nathanael Greene to command the southern campaign. Greene was appalled by conditions in South Carolina. His troops needed clothing, blankets, and food. He told a friend that incessant guerrilla warfare had "so corrupted the principles of the people that they think of nothing but plundering one another."

Greene moved cautiously. He adopted a conciliatory policy toward the many Americans who had switched sides, a wise choice in a region where people changed their allegiance up to seven times in less than two years. He ordered his troops to treat captives fairly and not loot loyalist property. He helped the shattered provincial congresses of Georgia and South Carolina reestablish civilian authority in the interior—a goal the British were never able to accomplish. With only sixteen hundred regulars, Greene could not afford to have frontier militia companies occupied in defending their homes from Indian attack. He accordingly pursued diplomacy to keep Indians out of the war. Although royal officials initially won some Indian allies, by war's end, only the Creeks remained allied with Great Britain.

Even before Greene took command in December 1780, the tide was turning. In October, at King's Mountain, a backcountry force defeated a large party of redcoats and loyalists. Then in January 1781 Greene's trusted aide Daniel Morgan brilliantly routed the British regiment Tarleton's Legion at Cowpens. Greene confronted the main body of British troops under Lord Cornwallis at Guilford Court House, North Carolina, in March. Although Cornwallis controlled the field at day's end, most of his army was destroyed. Greene returned to South Carolina, where he forced the redcoats to abandon their interior posts and retire to Charleston.

Surrender at Yorktown

Cornwallis headed north into Virginia, where he joined forces with redcoats commanded by the American traitor Benedict Arnold. He then withdrew to the peninsula between the York and James Rivers, where he fortified Yorktown. Washington moved more than seven thousand French and American troops south from New York City. When De Grasse's fleet arrived in time to defeat the Royal Navy vessels sent to relieve Cornwallis, the British general was trapped (see Map 6.2). On October 19, 1781, Cornwallis surrendered.

When news of the defeat reached London, Parliament voted to cease offensive operations in America, authorizing peace negotiations. Washington returned with the main army to the environs of New York, where in March 1783, his underpaid—and, they thought, underappreciated—officers threatened to mutiny unless Congress guaranteed them adequate compensation. Washington, warned in advance of the so-called Newburgh Conspiracy, defused the crisis with a well-reasoned and patriotic speech. At the end of the year, he resigned as commander-in-chief. Still, Washington established an enduring precedent: civilian control of the American military.

The war had been won but at terrible cost. More than 25,000 American men died, about one-quarter of them from battle. The rest were declared missing or died of disease or as prisoners of war. In the South, years of guerrilla warfare and the loss of thousands of runaway slaves shattered the economy. Indebtedness soared, and local governments were crippled, as few people could pay taxes. Some formerly wealthy planters descended into insolvency.

Treaty of Paris

Yet Americans all rejoiced when they learned of the signing of the preliminary peace treaty at Paris in November 1782. American diplomats—Benjamin Franklin, John Jay, and John Adams—ignored their instructions from Congress to be guided by France and negotiated directly with Great Britain. Their instincts were sound: the French government was more an enemy to Britain than a friend to the United States. French ministers worked secretly to try to prevent the establishment of a strong, unified

Revolutionary Origins

Many historians today would contend that the American Revolution was not truly revolutionary, if *revolution* means overturning an earlier power structure. The United States won its independence and established a republic, both radical events in the eighteenth century, but essentially the same men who led the colonies also led the new country (with the exception of British officials and appointees). In contrast, the nearly contemporary French Revolution witnessed the execution of the monarch and many aristocrats, and a significant redistribution of authority. So the legacy of the American Revolution appears radical and conservative by comparison.

Throughout the more than two hundred years since the Revolution, varying groups have frequently declared that they are acting in the spirit of the Revolution. People protesting discriminatory policies against women and minorities (usually liberals) invoke the created-equal language of the Declaration of Independence. Left-wing organizations rail against concentrations of wealth and power in a few hands. Those protesting higher taxes (usually conservatives wanting a reduced role for government) often adopt the symbolism of the Boston Tea Party. Right-wing militias arm themselves, preparing to defend their homes against a malevolent government, just as they believe the minutemen did in 1775. In 2006 so-called minutemen formed vigilante groups to guard the United States– Mexico border against illegal aliens. The message of the Revolution can be invoked to support extralegal demonstrations of any description, from invasions of military bases by antiwar protesters to demonstrations outside abortion clinics. But the Revolution can also be invoked to oppose such street protests, because—some would argue—in a republic, change should come peacefully, via the ballot box.

Just as Americans in the eighteenth century disagreed over the meaning of their struggle, so the legacy of revolution remains contested early in the twenty-first century.

government in America. Spain's desire to lay claim to the region between the Appalachian Mountains and the Mississippi River further complicated the negotiations. But the American delegates proved adept at power politics, achieving their main goal: independence as a united nation. Weary of war, the new British ministry made so many concessions that Parliament ousted it shortly after peace terms were approved.

The treaty, signed on September 3, 1783, granted independence to a nation named the United States of America. Generous boundaries delineated that new nation: to the north, approximately the present-day boundary with Canada; to the south, the 31st parallel (about the modern northern border of Florida); to the west, the Mississippi River. Florida, which Britain had acquired in 1763, reverted to Spain (see Map 7.2). The Americans also gained unlimited fishing rights off Newfoundland. In ceding so much land, Great Britain ignored the territorial rights of its Indian allies. British diplomats also poorly served loyalists and British merchants. The treaty's ambiguously worded clauses regarding prewar debts and postwar treatment of loyalists proved impossible to enforce.

Summary

The victorious Americans could reflect on their achievement with satisfaction. Having unified the mainland colonies, they claimed their place in the family of nations and forged a successful alliance with France. With an inexperienced army, they defeated the world's greatest military power. They won only a few actual victories—most notably at Trenton, Saratoga, and Yorktown—but their army survived to fight again. Ultimately, the Americans simply wore their enemy down.

In winning the war, Americans abandoned their British identity, excluding from their new nation loyalist neighbors unwilling to break with the mother country. They established republican governments at state and national levels and created new national loyalties. They also claimed most of the territory east of the Mississippi River and south of the Great Lakes, thereby greatly expanding land open to settlement and threatening traditional Indian dominance of the interior.

In the future Americans faced new challenges: ensuring the survival of their republican polity in a world dominated by bitter rivalries among Britain, France, and Spain.

Chapter Review

GOVERNMENT BY CONGRESS AND COMMITTEE

How did the first Continental Congress redefine America's relationship to England?

Congressmen meeting at the First Continental Congress in September 1774 were not ready for a complete break from England, but they did outline America's grievances, develop a resistance plan, and define America's relationship to Great Britain. Debate covered the spectrum of opinion from the radical call to obey only the king and not Parliament to the more conservative view that would have Parliament and a new American legislature jointly enacting colonial laws. In the end, the group compromised and agreed in the Declaration of Rights and Grievances to obey Parliament on a voluntary basis (rather than as subjects) and resist all taxes.

CONTEST IN THE BACKCOUNTRY

Where did backcountry Indians' loyalties lay at the onset of the Revolution?

Initially, Indians were inclined to ally with Great Britain, given the hostility they experienced from European American settlers in the backcountry. But other chiefs had their doubts: England had abandoned them in vacating Fort Pitt years earlier. Both the Americans and the British sought a pledge of neutrality, and while some, such as the Iroquois, agreed, others, such as the Cherokees and Shawnees, attacked backcountry settlements in western and the Carolinas hoping to use the conflict to regain lost land. A few Indian communities supported the Americans, but most others remained neutral or sporadically sided with the British.

CHOOSING SIDES

How did people choose sides in the conflict with England?

Not everyone supported complete and total independence from Great Britain. In fact, only two-fifths of the European American population of the thirteen colonies were Patriots seeking to separate from England—among them small and middling farmers, Chesapeake gentry, merchants, city artisans, elected officeholders— and even then, their specific goals varied. Loyalists who opposed the break with England represented one-fifth of the population, and included Anglican clergy parishioners in the North; tenant farmers; members of persecuted religious sects; backcountry southerners; ethnic minorities, especially Scots; and merchants who relied on British trade. Two-fifths of the population remained neutral, including pacifist groups such as the Quakers. Finally, free blacks in the North and slaves in the middle colonies took the Patriots' side, while southern bondspeople thought they'd have a better chance at personal freedom by allying with the British, and some offered to join the British in exchange for their freedom.

WAR AND INDEPENDENCE

How did Thomas Paine's *Common Sense* potentially reshape the war's purpose?

While Americans had been at war with Great Britain for months, most leaders denied seeking a complete break from England and focused on achieving some autonomy and a redress for various grievances. In January 1776, Paine's widely popular pamphlet called for independence and the establishment of a republic (a government by the people with no king or nobility). He argued that once America broke from European control, it would become strong and prosperous. Within months of its publication, the Second Continental Congress passed a resolution that the colonies should be free and all ties to Great Britain dissolved, and they charged several men, among them Thomas Jefferson, to write a Declaration of Independence.

THE STRUGGLE IN THE NORTH

What was France's role in the American Revolution?

Initially, France secretly sent military supplies to the Americans and regarded the revolution as a chance to avenge its defeat to Britain in the Seven Years' War. Once Americans won the Battle of Saratoga, the French openly supported them, sending naval vessels, ammunition, and troops. France's assistance proved vital to American victory in the final years of the war. Americans and the French signed two treaties in 1778, the Treaty of Amity and Commerce, which recognized American independence and set up trade relations; and the Treaty of Alliance, which promised neither side would negotiate peace (in conflicts with Britain) without consulting the other. France also abandoned claims to Canada and to North American territory east of the Mississippi River.

LIFE IN THE ARMY AND ON THE HOME FRONT

How was the Continental Army staffed?

Only in the war's earliest months were battlefields filled by militia men, who left their fields to fight. After that, American leaders organized an army comprising young, single, often propertyless men who enlisted for a period of time for money or land. Towns were required to send their quota of soldiers and did so by enlisting everyone, including recent immigrants. Initially, African Americans were banned from the army, but by 1776, that prohibition was lifted, as northern recruiters promised slaves their freedom after the war. About five thousand enlisted, composing 10 percent of the army, though they were typically in segregated units and often given tasks others rejected, such as burying the dead. Wives and widows of poor soldiers often followed the camps, too, working as cooks, nurses, and launderers for rations or low wages.

VICTORY IN THE SOUTH

How did the decision to ignore the Treaty of Alliance prove wise in negotiating the peace with England after the American Revolution?

In the 1778 Treaty of Alliance, Americans agreed not to make peace with England without consulting France first (and vice versa). During the signing of a preliminary peace treaty in Paris in 1782 ending the American Revolution, diplomats Benjamin Franklin, John Jay, and John Adams ignored Congress's instructions to let Paris lead the way and trusted their instincts about France's true motives. French ministers had secretly tried to prevent a strong government from taking hold in America. War-weary Britain not only gave America its independence, but also ceded vast tracts of land and unlimited fishing rights off Newfoundland.

SUGGESTIONS FOR FURTHER READING

Robert McCluer Calhoon, *The Loyalists in Revolutionary America, 1760–1781* (1973)

Colin Calloway, *The American Revolution in Indian Country* (1995)

Stephen Conway, *The War of American Independence, 1775–1783* (1995)

Sylvia Frey, *Water from the Rock: Black Resistance in a Revolutionary Age* (1991)

Pauline Maier, *American Scripture: Making the Declaration of Independence* (1997)

Charles Niemeyer, *America Goes to War: A Social History of the Continental Army* (1997)

Mary Beth Norton, *Liberty's Daughters: The Revolutionary Experience of American Women, 1750–1800* (2d ed., 1996)

Cassandra Pybus, *Epic Journeys of Freedom: Runaway Slaves of the American Revolution and their Global Quest for Liberty* (2006)

Charles Royster, *A Revolutionary People at War: The Continental Army and American Character, 1775–1783* (1980)

Richard W. Van Alstyne, *Empire and Independence: The International History of the American Revolution* (1965)

Forging a National Republic

On December 26, 1787, a group of Federalists—supporters of the proposed Constitution—gathered in the frontier town of Carlisle, Pennsylvania. The men planned to fire a cannon in celebration of their state convention's ratification vote two weeks earlier, but a crowd of Antifederalists stopped them. First, the Antifederalists blocked the cannon. Then, they attacked the Federalists, who fled as the angry Antis burned a copy of the Constitution.

The next day, Federalists fired their cannon and read the ratification proclamation. Antifederalists paraded and burned effigies of two Federalists. When Federalist officials arrested several demonstrators for rioting, the Antifederalist-dominated militia broke them out of jail. For weeks, participants argued in the Carlisle newspaper about what the demonstrations meant. Federalists proclaimed that the respectable celebrants acted with "good order." Replying, Antifederalists pronounced the Federalists "an unhallowed riotous mob," claiming that the Constitution's supporters declared themselves "friends of government" but, through advocacy of a government that aimed to suppress people's liberties, they revealed they were secretly aristocrats.

The Carlisle riots presaged violent disputes over the new Constitution in Albany, New York; Providence, Rhode Island; and other cities. In a struggle that began in 1775 and persisted until century's end, Americans argued over how to implement republican principles and who best represented the people. In a world where relatively few property-holding men had the right to vote, people often expressed their political opinions in the streets.

Republicanism—the idea that governments should be based on the consent of the people—originated with political theorists in ancient Greece and Rome. Republics, theorists declared, were

This icon will direct you to interactive activities and study materials on A People And A Nation, Brief Edition website: **www.cengage.com/history/norton/peoplenationbrief8e**

Chronology

1776	Second Continental Congress directs states to draft constitutions.	**1786**	Annapolis Convention meets and discusses reforming government.
	Abigail Adams advises her husband to "Remember the Ladies."	**1786–87**	Shays's Rebellion in western Massachusetts raises questions about the future of the republic.
1777	Articles of Confederation are sent to states for ratification.	**1787**	Royall Tyler's *The Contrast*, the first successful American play, is performed.
	Vermont becomes first jurisdiction to abolish slavery.		Northwest Ordinance organizes the territory north of Ohio River and east of Mississippi River.
1781	Articles of Confederation are ratified.		Constitutional Convention drafts a new form of government.
1783	Treaty of Paris is signed, formalizing American independence.	**1788**	Hamilton, Jay, and Madison write *The Federalist* to urge ratification of the Constitution by New York.
1784	Diplomats sign treaty with Iroquois at Fort Stanwix, but Iroquois repudiate it two years later.		Constitution is ratified.
1785	Land Ordinance of 1785 provides for surveying and sale of national lands in Northwest Territory.	**1789**	William Hill Brown publishes *The Power of Sympathy,* the first American novel.
1785–86	United States negotiates treaties at Hopewell, South Carolina, with Choctaws, Chickasaws, and Cherokees.		Massachusetts orders towns to support public schools.
		1800	Weems publishes his *Life of Washington.*

desirable yet fragile government forms. Unless citizens were virtuous—that is, sober, moral, and industrious—and agreed on key issues, republics were doomed. When Americans left the British Empire, they abandoned the idea that the best system of government balanced participation by a king, the nobility, and the people. Instead, they embraced republicanism, in which the people were sovereign. Still, during and after the war, Americans wondered how to ensure political stability, how to foster consensus, and how to create and sustain a virtuous republic.

Leaders attempted to inculcate virtue in their fellow American countrymen and countrywomen. After 1776, literature, theater, art, architecture, and education pursued moral goals. Women's education became important, for mothers of the republic's children were responsible for ensuring the nation's future. Almost all white men assumed that women, African Americans, and Indians should have no role in politics; the first two groups were regarded as household dependents, the last as outside the polity. Still, they disagreed on how many of their number should be included in the political process and how their new governments should be structured.

Then there were Thomas Jefferson's words in the Declaration of Independence: "all men are created equal." Given that statement of principle, how could white republicans justify holding African Americans in perpetual bondage? Some freed their slaves or voted for state laws abolishing slavery. Others denied that blacks were men in the same sense as whites.

The most important task facing Americans was constructing a unified national government. Before 1765, many circumstances divided the British mainland colonies: diverse economies, varying religious traditions and ethnic compositions, competing western land claims, and different polities. But the Revolutionary War brought them together, creating a new nationalistic spirit that replaced loyalties to state and region.

However, America's first national government, under the Articles of Confederation, proved weak and decentralized. Political leaders tried another approach in drafting the Constitution in 1787. Some historians have argued that the Articles of Confederation and the Constitution reflect opposing political philosophies, the Constitution representing an aristocratic counterrevolution against the democratic Articles. The two documents are more accurately viewed as successive attempts to solve the same problems—the relationship of states and nation and the extent to which authority should be centralized. Both applied theories of republicanism to questions of governance; neither was entirely successful in resolving those difficulties.

- **What were the elements of the new national identity? How did women, Indians, and African Americans fit into that identity?**
- **What problems confronted the new nation's leaders as they attempted to establish the first modern republic?**
- **How and why were those problems resolved differently at different times?**

CREATING A VIRTUOUS REPUBLIC

When the colonies declared independence, John Dickinson recalled, many years later, "there was no question concerning forms of Government, no enquiry whether a Republic or a limited Monarchy was best. . . . We knew that the people of this country must unite themselves under some form of Government and that this could be no other than the republican form"—in short, self-government by the people. But how should that goal be implemented?

Varieties of Republicanism

Three definitions of republicanism emerged in the new United States. Ancient history and political theory informed the first, held chiefly by the educated elite (such as the Adamses of Massachusetts). The histories of popular governments in Greece and Rome suggested that republics could succeed only if they were small and homogeneous. According to classical republican theory, unless a republic's citizens were virtuous men willing to forgo personal profit for the best interests of the nation, the government would collapse. In return for sacrifices, a republic offered equality of opportunity. Rank would be based on merit rather than inherited wealth and status. Society would be governed by members of a "natural aristocracy," men whose talent elevated them from possibly humble beginnings to positions of power.

A second definition, advanced by other elites and some skilled craftsmen, drew on economic theory. Instead of perceiving the nation as composed of people nobly sacrificing for the common good, this version of republicanism followed Scottish theorist Adam Smith in emphasizing individuals' pursuit of rational self-interest. When republican men sought to improve their own economic and social circumstances, the nation would benefit. Republican virtue would be achieved through the pursuit of private interests, rather than through subordination to communal ideals.

The third notion of republicanism was less influential but more egalitarian than the others. Men who advanced the third version of republicanism, among them Thomas Paine, called for widening men's political participation. They wanted government to respond directly to the needs of ordinary folk, rejecting that the "lesser sort" should defer to their "betters." They were democrats in the modern sense. For them, the untutored wisdom of the people embodied republican virtue.

All three strands of republicanism contrasted America's industrious virtue with the corruption of Britain and Europe. In the first version, that virtue manifested itself in frugality and self-sacrifice; in the second, it would prevent self-interest from becoming vice; in the third, it was the justification for including propertyless free men as voters. Most agreed that a virtuous country would be composed of hardworking citizens who would dress and live simply, elect wise leaders, and forgo conspicuous consumption of luxury goods.

Virtue and the Arts

As citizens of the United States constructed their republic, they expected to replace the vices of monarchical Europe—immorality, selfishness, and lack of public spirit—with the virtues of republican America. They sought to embody republican principles in their governments and in their culture, expecting painting, literature, drama, and architecture to convey nationalism and virtue.

Americans faced a crucial contradiction, however. To some republicans, fine arts were manifestations of vice, signaling luxury and corruption. Why did a frugal farmer need a painting or a novel? Why should anyone spend hard-earned wages to see a play in a lavish theater? The first American artists and authors wanted to produce works embodying virtue, but many viewed those works as corrupting, regardless of their content.

Still, authors and artists tried. In Royall Tyler's *The Contrast* (1787), the first successful American play, Colonel Manly's virtuous conduct was contrasted with Billy Dimple's reprehensible behavior. The era's most popular book, Mason Locke Weems's *Life of Washington,* published in 1800 after George Washington's death, was intended to "hold up his great Virtues . . . to the imitation of Our Youth." The famous tale Weems invented—six-year-old George bravely admitting cutting down his father's favorite cherry tree—ended with George's father exclaiming, "Such an act of heroism in my son, is worth more than a thousand trees."

Painting and architecture were also expected to exemplify moral standards and instill patriotism. The period's most prominent artists, Gilbert Stuart and Charles Willson Peale, painted portraits of upstanding republican citizens. John Trumbull's canvases depicted historical milestones such as the Battle of Bunker Hill and Cornwallis's surrender at Yorktown. When the Virginia government asked Thomas Jefferson, then minister to France, for advice on designing the state capitol in Richmond, Jefferson recommended copying a simple but noble Roman building, the Maison Carrée at Nîmes. Ideals he set forth would guide American architecture for a generation: simplicity of line, harmonious proportions, a feeling of grandeur.

Despite the artists' efforts (or perhaps because of them), some Americans detected signs of luxury and corruption by the mid-1780s. The resumption of European trade after the war brought imported fashions for men and women. Elite

Novels

In novels, poems, paintings, plays, and histories, citizens of the United States explored their new national identity. Ironically, the standards against which they measured themselves and the models they followed were primarily British.

This was especially true of the most widely read literary form: the novel. In the mid-eighteenth century, the Englishman Samuel Richardson composed the first fictional works that today are called novels. Richardson's novels—*Pamela* (1740), *Clarissa* (1748), and *Sir Charles Grandison* (1753)—revolved around the courtship and sexual relationships of young adults. Those themes permeated the most popular early American novel, Susanna Haswell Rowson's *Charlotte: A Tale of Truth*, and other novels. Changing mores in the late eighteenth century freed English and American youth from parental supervision of their marital decisions. That freedom also rendered girls vulnerable to new dangers of deception and seduction by unscrupulous suitors. Young women were the most avid readers of novels, especially as women's literacy rates increased.

One of the best-selling novels of its time, *Charlotte*, had the subtitle *A Tale of Truth* despite no known factual basis. First published in London in 1791, Rowson's novel was reprinted in Philadelphia three years later and went through more than 160 editions. *Charlotte* focuses on a naive young woman who elopes, pregnant and unmarried, with her seducer, only to be deserted when a beautiful, rich, and virtuous rival appears. After giving birth, Charlotte dies in her father's arms. "Oh my dear girls," Rowson cautions readers, "pray for fortitude to resist the impulses of inclination, when it runs counter to the precepts of religion and virtue."

Generations of young American women sobbed over Charlotte's fate, visiting Trinity churchyard in lower Manhattan, where a real-life counterpart of the fictional heroine was reputed to be buried. Their tears and women's preference on both sides of the Atlantic for such sentimental novels linked the young readers and their nation to the former mother country from which they were nominally so eager to separate.

This "Eighth American Edition" (such statements on the title pages of early novels can rarely be trusted because some printings were pirated) of Susanna Rowson's *Charlotte Temple* included a "portrait" of its entirely fictional heroine. That engraving thus reinforced the subtitle, *A Tale of Truth.* (AC7.R7997.791c 1804, Houghton Library, Harvard University Library)

families again attended balls and concerts. Parties no longer seemed complete without gambling and cardplaying. Social clubs for young people multiplied. Especially alarming was the establishment in 1783 of the Society of the Cincinnati, a hereditary association for Revolutionary War officers and their firstborn sons. Although organizers hoped to advance the citizen-soldier, opponents feared that the group would become the nucleus of a native-born aristocracy. All these developments challenged the United States' self-image as a virtuous republic.

Educational Reform

Americans' concern for the infant republic's future focused their attention on children. Education was previously seen as the concern of individual families. Now schooling would serve a public purpose. If young people were to resist vice and become useful citizens, they would need education. The nation's survival depended on it. The 1780s and 1790s thus witnessed two major changes in educational practice.

First, some northern states began using tax money to support public elementary schools. In 1789 Massachusetts became one of the first states to require towns to offer free public elementary education. Second, since mothers would have to be educated if they were to instruct children adequately, Massachusetts insisted that elementary schools teach girls as well as boys. Throughout the United States, private academies were founded to provide advanced schooling to teenage girls from well-to-do families. Colleges remained closed to women, but a few fortunate girls could study history, geography, rhetoric, and mathematics.

Judith Sargent Murray

Judith Sargent Murray of Gloucester, Massachusetts, became the chief theorist of women's education in the early republic. Murray argued that women and men had equal intellectual capacities, but inadequate education might make women seem less intelligent. Therefore, concluded Murray, boys and girls should be offered equivalent schooling. She further contended that girls should be taught to support themselves: "Independence should be placed within their grasp."

Murray's views were part of a general rethinking of women's position that resulted from the Revolution. Men and women realized that female patriots had made important contributions toward independence. Consequently, Americans considered new ideas about women's roles in republican society.

Women and the Republic

The best-known expression of those ideas appeared in a letter Abigail Adams addressed to her husband in March 1776. "In the new Code of Laws which I suppose it will be necessary for you to make I desire you would Remember the Ladies," she wrote.

Judith Sargent Stevens (later Murray), by John Singleton Copley, ca. 1770–1772. The eventual author of tracts advocating improvements in women's education sat for this portrait two decades earlier, during her first marriage. Her clear-eyed gaze suggests both her intelligence and her seriousness of purpose. (Terra Foundation for American Art, Chicago / Art Resource, NY)

"Remember all Men would be tyrants if they could. . . . If perticuliar [sic] care and attention is not paid to the Laidies [sic] we are determined to foment a Rebelion, and will not hold ourselves bound by any Laws in which we have no voice, or Representation." With these words, Abigail Adams deliberately applied the ideology developed to combat parliamentary supremacy. She argued that, because men were "Naturally Tyrannical," the United States should reform marriage laws, which subordinated wives to their husbands, giving men control of family property and denying wives the right to independent legal action.

Abigail Adams did not ask for woman suffrage, but others claimed that right. In 1776, the New Jersey state constitution defined voters as "all free inhabitants" who met property qualifications. They thereby unintentionally gave the vote to property-holding white spinsters and widows and free black landowners. Qualified women and African Americans regularly voted in New Jersey's local and congressional elections until 1807, when they were disfranchised by the state legislature. That women voted at all was evidence of their altered perception of their place in the nation's political life.

Even after the war, European Americans still viewed women in traditional terms, affirming their primary function as wives, mothers, and mistresses of households. Because wives could not own property or participate directly in economic life, women came to be seen as the embodiment of self-sacrificing republicanism. Through new female-run charitable associations, better-off women assumed public responsibilities, among them caring for poor widows and orphans. Thus men were freed to pursue their economic self-interests, while wives and daughters fulfilled the family's obligation to the common good. The ideal republican man was an individualist, seeking advancement for himself and his family. The ideal republican woman always put the well-being of others first.

THE FIRST EMANCIPATION AND THE GROWTH OF RACISM

Revolutionary ideology exposed a primary contradiction in American society. There were 700,000 African Americans residing in the new nation, roughly 20 percent of the population. European and African Americans saw the irony in slaveholders' claims that they sought to prevent Britain from "enslaving" them. In 1773 Dr. Benjamin Rush called slavery "a vice which degrades human nature," warning ominously that "the plant of liberty is of so tender a nature that it cannot thrive long in the neighborhood of slavery."

African Americans used revolutionary ideology to their advantage. In 1779 slaves from Portsmouth, New Hampshire, asked the state legislature "from what authority [our masters] assume to dispose of our lives, freedom and property?" The same year, several bondsmen in Fairfield, Connecticut, petitioned the legislature for their freedom, characterizing slavery as a "dreadful Evil." How could men who were "nobly contending in the Cause of Liberty," they asked, continue "this detestable Practice?"

Emancipation and Manumission

Both legislatures responded negatively, but the postwar years witnessed the gradual abolition of slavery in the North. Vermont banned slavery in its 1777 constitution. Responding to lawsuits filed by enslaved men and women, Massachusetts courts ruled in 1783 that the state constitution prohibited slavery. Other states north of Maryland adopted emancipation laws between 1780 (Pennsylvania) and 1804 (New Jersey). New Hampshire did not abolish slavery, but only eight slaves were reported on the 1800 census and none in 1810. Although no southern state adopted emancipation laws, the legislatures of Virginia (1782), Delaware (1787), and Maryland (1790 and 1796) loosened earlier laws restricting slaveowners' ability to free their bondspeople. South Carolina and Georgia never considered any such acts, and North Carolina insisted that manumissions (emancipations of individual slaves) be approved by county courts.

Revolutionary ideology thus had limited impact on the economic interests of large slaveholders. Only in northern states—societies with slaves, not slave societies—could state legislatures abolish slavery. Even there, legislators' concern for the property rights of slave owners led them to favor gradual over immediate emancipation. For example, New York's law freed children born into slavery after July 4, 1799, but only once they reached their mid-twenties. Laws failed to emancipate the existing slave population. Although emancipation laws forbade the sale of slaves to jurisdictions where slavery remained legal, slaveowners regularly circumvented such provisions. As late as 1840 the census recorded the presence of slaves in several northern states.

A sailor of African descent posed proudly for this portrait around 1790. Unfortunately, neither the name of the sailor nor the name of the artist is known today.   (Private collection, photograph courtesy of Hirschl and Adler Galleries, New York)

Growth of Free Black Population

The number of free people of African descent in the United States grew dramatically in the initial post-Revolution years. Most slaves emancipated before the war were mulattos, born of unions between bondswomen and their masters, who manumitted the children. Wartime escapees from plantations, slaves who served in the American army, and those emancipated by owners or by state laws contributed to the nearly 60,000 free people of color by 1790. Ten years later they numbered more than 108,000, nearly 11 percent of the total African American population.

In the Chesapeake, manumissions were speeded by economic changes, such as declining soil fertility and the shift from tobacco to grain production. Because grain cultivation was less labor-intensive than tobacco growing, planters had excess slaves. They occasionally solved that problem by freeing less productive or more favored bondspeople. The enslaved also negotiated agreements with owners allowing them to live and work independently until they could purchase themselves. Virginia's free black population more than doubled between 1790 and 1810; also by 1810, nearly one-quarter of Maryland's African American population was no longer in bondage.

Freedpeople's Lives

Beginning in the 1780s, rural freedpeople headed to northern port cities, such as Boston and Philadelphia. With better employment opportunities, especially in domestic service, women outnumbered male migrants by three to two. Some freedmen also worked in domestic service, but larger numbers were unskilled laborers and sailors. A few women and many men (nearly one-third of those in Philadelphia in 1795) were skilled workers or retailers. They exchanged the surnames of former masters for names like Newman or Brown and established independent two-parent families. They also began to occupy distinct neighborhoods, probably due to discrimination.

Even whites who recognized African Americans' right to freedom were unwilling to accept them as equals. Laws discriminated against freedpeople as they had against slaves. Several states—among them Delaware, Maryland, and South Carolina—adopted laws denying property-owning black men the vote. South Carolina forbade free blacks from testifying against whites in court. New Englanders used indenture contracts to control freed youths, who were often denied public education. Freedmen found it difficult to purchase property and find good jobs.

Gradually, freedpeople developed their own institutions. In Charleston, mulattos formed the Brown Fellowship Society, which provided insurance for them, financed a school, and helped support orphans. In 1794 former slaves in Philadelphia and Baltimore, led by the Reverend Richard Allen, founded societies that eventually formed the African Methodist Episcopal (AME) denomination. AME churches sponsored schools and, along with African Baptist, African Episcopal, and African Presbyterian churches, became cultural centers for free blacks.

Development of Racist Theory

Before the revolution, European Americans regarded slaves as inferior. Influential writers argued that African slaves' seemingly debased character derived from their enslavement, rather than enslavement's being the consequence of inherited inferiority.

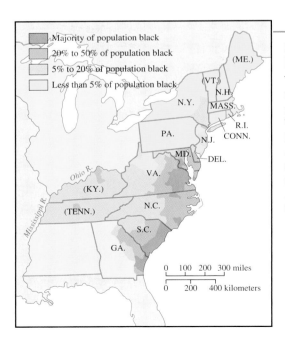

Map 7.1   African American Population, 1790: Proportion of Total Population

The first census clearly indicated that the African American population was heavily concentrated in just a few areas of the United States, most notably in coastal regions of South Carolina, Georgia, and Virginia. Although there were growing numbers of blacks in the backcountry—presumably taken there by migrating slaveowners—most parts of the North and East, with the exception of the immediate vicinity of New York City, had few African American residents. (*Source:* From Lester J. Cappon et al., eds., *Atlas of Early American History: The Revolutionary Era, 1760–1790.* Copyright © 1976 by Princeton University Press. Reprinted by permission of Princeton University Press.)

In the Revolution's aftermath, slaveowners needed to defend human bondage against the proposition that "all men are created equal." Consequently, they argued that people of African descent were less than fully human and that the principles of republican equality applied only to European Americans.

Egalitarian thinking among European Americans downplayed status distinctions within their own group and differentiated all whites from people of color—Indians and African Americans. Decades earlier, Indians began referring to themselves as *red*. Experience as slaves on American soil forged the identity African or black from the various ethnic and national affiliations of people who survived the transatlantic crossing. Among the first to term themselves *Africans* were oceanic sailors—men whose contacts with Europeans caused them to construct a unified, separate identity. Thus in the revolutionary era whiteness, redness, and blackness—along with the superiority of the first and the inferiority of the latter two—developed as contrasting concepts.

With this racism came first the assertion that, as Thomas Jefferson insisted in 1781, blacks were "inferior to the whites in the endowments both of body and mind." (He was less certain about Indians.) There followed the belief that blacks were congenitally lazy, even though owners often argued that slaves were natural workers. Third was the notion that blacks were sexually promiscuous and that African American men lusted after European American women. The specter of interracial sexual intercourse involving black men and white women haunted early American racist thought. Significantly, the more common sexual exploitation of enslaved women by their masters aroused little concern.

African Americans challenged these racist notions. In 1791 Benjamin Banneker, a free black mathematical genius, sent Thomas Jefferson a copy of his latest almanac (including astronomical calculations) to show blacks' mental powers. Jefferson admitted Banneker's intelligence, but said Banneker was exceptional and he needed more evidence before he would change his mind about the inferiority of people of African descent.

A White Men's Republic

Laws from the 1770s on linked whiteness and male citizenship rights. Some historians have argued that the subjugation of blacks, Indians, and women was a necessary precondition for theoretical equality among white men. Identifying common racial antagonists helped create white solidarity and lessen the threat to gentry power posed by the enfranchisement of poorer men. Moreover, excluding women from politics reserved power for men, specifically the "better sort." After the Revolution the division of American society between slave and free was transformed into a division between blacks—some of whom were free—and whites.

DESIGNING REPUBLICAN GOVERNMENTS

In May 1776, the Second Continental Congress directed states to devise new republican governments to replace the provincial conventions and committees that had met since colonial governments collapsed in 1774 and 1775. Thus American men devoted little attention to their national government—an oversight they would later remedy.

State Constitutions

At the state level, political leaders had trouble defining a constitution and concluded that legislative bodies should not draft their constitutions. Following Vermont in 1777 and Massachusetts in 1780, they elected conventions exclusively to draft constitutions. Thus states sought authorization from the people—the theoretical sovereigns in a republic—before establishing new governments. After preparing new constitutions, delegates submitted them to voters for ratification.

Framers of state constitutions concerned themselves with outlining the distribution of and limitations on government power. If authority was not confined within reasonable limits, states might become tyrannical, as Britain had.

Under colonial charters, Americans learned to fear the power of the governor—usually the appointed agent of the king or proprietor—and to see the legislature as their defender. Accordingly, the first state constitutions typically provided for the governor to be elected annually (commonly by the legislature), limited the number of terms he could serve, and gave him little independent authority. Simultaneously, they expanded the legislature's powers. Every state except Pennsylvania and Vermont retained a two-house structure, with members of the upper house having longer terms and meeting higher property-holding standards than members of the lower house. They also redrew electoral districts to reflect population patterns. Finally, most states lowered property qualifications for voting. Thus the revolutionary era witnessed the first deliberate attempt to broaden the base of American government.

Limiting State Governments

But the state constitutions' authors worried about what might happen if tyrants were elected. They consequently included limitations on government authority to protect the inalienable rights of citizens. Seven constitutions contained a bill of rights, and others had similar clauses. Most guaranteed freedom of the press, rights to fair trials, and protection against general search warrants. An independent judiciary was charged with upholding such rights. Most states also guaranteed freedom of religion but with restrictions. For example, seven states required that officeholders be Christians, and some supported churches with tax money.

In general, constitution makers put greater emphasis on preventing state governments from becoming tyrannical than on making them effective wielders of political authority. Establishing such weak political units, especially in wartime, practically ensured that the constitutions would need revision in the 1780s.

Revising State Constitutions

The revised constitutions increased the powers of the governor and reduced those of the legislature. By the mid-1780s, some political leaders concluded that the best way to limit government power was to balance legislative, executive, and judicial powers, a design called checks and balances. The national Constitution drafted in 1787 also embodied that principle.

Yet the constitutional theories applied at the state level did not immediately influence Americans' conception of national government. Because American officials initially focused on the war, the Continental Congress evolved by default. Not until late 1777 did Congress send the Articles of Confederation—which outlined a national government—to the states for ratification, and those Articles simply made law the unplanned arrangements of the Continental Congress.

Articles of Confederation

The chief organ of national government was a unicameral (one-house) legislature in which each state had one vote. Its powers included conducting foreign relations, mediating interstate disputes, controlling maritime affairs, regulating Indian trade, and valuing state and national coinage. The United States was described as a "league of friendship" in which each state "retains its sovereignty, freedom and independence, and every Power, Jurisdiction and right, which is not by this confederation expressly delegated to the United States, in Congress assembled."

The Articles required unanimous consent of state legislatures for ratification or amendment. A clause concerning western lands proved troublesome. The draft accepted by Congress allowed states to retain land claims from their original charters. But states with definite western boundaries (such as Maryland and New Jersey) wanted other states to cede to the national government their landholdings west of the Appalachian Mountains. They feared states with large claims could expand and overpower smaller neighbors. Maryland refused to accept the Articles until 1781, when Virginia surrendered its western holdings to national jurisdiction (see Map 7.2). Other states followed, establishing the principle that unorganized lands would be held by the nation.

The unicameral legislature, whether it was called the Second Continental Congress (until 1781) or the Confederation Congress (thereafter), was too inefficient to govern effectively. The Articles' authors had not given adequate thought to the distribution of power within the national government or to the relationship between the Confederation and the states. Congress was a legislative body and a collective executive (there was no judiciary), but it had no independent income and no authority to compel the states to accept its rulings. Under the Articles, national government lurched from crisis to crisis. (See the appendix for the text of the Articles of Confederation.)

TRIALS OF THE CONFEDERATION

Finance posed the most persistent problem. Because legislators levied taxes reluctantly, Congress and the states first tried to finance the war by printing currency. Although the money was backed only by good faith, it circulated freely and without excessive depreciation during 1775 and most of 1776. Demand for military supplies and civilian goods was high, stimulating trade and local production.

Financial Affairs

But in late 1776, as the American army suffered reverses in New York and New Jersey, prices rose and inflation set in. State governments fought inflation by controlling wages and prices and requiring acceptance of paper currency equally with specie (coins). States also borrowed funds, established lotteries, and levied taxes. Their efforts were futile, as was Congress's attempt to stop printing currency and rely on state

BRITISH NORTH AMERICA

Lake Superior

NORTHWEST

Lake Michigan

Lake Huron

Lake Ontario

Lake Erie

TERRITORY

ME.
(part of Mass.)

N.H.

MASS.

CONN.

R.I.

N.Y.

PA.

N.J.

MD.   DEL.

Ohio R.

SPANISH
LOUISIANA

Mississippi R.

Tennessee R.

VA.

N.C.

S.C.

GA.

SPANISH
FLORIDA

Area of thirteen colonies
after cessions, 1802

N.Y. cedes to Congress, 1782

Va. cedes to Congress, 1784

N.C. cedes to Congress, 1790

S.C. relinquishes claims to Ga.,
1787 (Beaufort Convention)

Ga. cedes to Congress, 1802

Massachusetts Cessions

Mass. cedes to Congress, 1785

Mass. relinquishes sovereignty and
jurisdiction to N.Y., 1786 (Hartford
Agreement); Mass. retains title to land

Mass. relinquishes all claims to N.Y.,
1786 (Hartford Agreement)

Connecticut Cessions

Conn. relinquishes claims to Pa., 1782
(Congressional arbitration)

Conn. cedes to Congress, 1786

Conn. cedes Western Reserve
to Congress, 1800

Map 7.2   Western Land Claims and Cessions, 1782–1802

After the United States achieved independence, states competed with one another for control of valuable lands to which they had possible claims under their original charters. That competition led to a series of compromises among the states or between individual states and the new nation, indicated on this map.

Figure 7.1 Depreciation of Continental Currency, 1777–1780

The depreciation of Continental currency accelerated in 1778, as is shown in this graph measuring its value against 100 silver dollars. Thereafter, its value dropped almost daily.

(*Source for data:* John J. McCusker, "How Much Is That in Real Money? A Historical Price Index for Use as a Deflator of Money Values in the Economy of the United States," *Proceedings of the American Antiquarian Society* 101, pt. 2 [1991], Table C-1.)

* Currency abandoned in April 1780

contributions. By early 1780 it took 40 paper dollars to purchase 1 silver dollar. Continental currency was worthless (see Figure 7.1).

In 1781, faced with the collapse of the monetary system, Congress undertook ambitious reforms. After establishing a department of finance under the wealthy Philadelphia merchant Robert Morris, it asked states to amend the Articles of Confederation to allow a national duty of 5 percent on imported goods. Morris put national finances on a solid footing, but the customs duty was never adopted. The states' resistance reflected fear of a powerful central government.

Foreign Affairs

Because the Articles denied Congress the power to establish a national commercial policy, foreign trade exposed the new government's weaknesses. After the war, Britain, France, and Spain restricted American trade with their colonies. Congress watched helplessly as British goods flooded the United States while American produce could not be sold in the British West Indies, once its prime market. Although Americans reopened commerce with other European countries and started a profitable trade with China in 1784, neither substituted for access to closer and larger markets.

Congress furthermore had difficulty dealing with the Spanish on the nation's southern and western borders. Spain in 1784 closed the Mississippi River to American navigation. Congress, through its Department of Foreign Affairs, opened negotiations with Spain in 1785, but talks collapsed the following year after Congress divided: southerners and westerners insisted on navigation rights, whereas

THE COMMISSIONERS.

A British cartoon ironically reflected Americans' hopes for postwar trade, hopes that were dashed after 1783. The Indian woman symbolizing America sits on a pile of tobacco bales, with rice and indigo casks bound for Europe nearby. The artist was satirizing the failed 1778 British peace commission and Britons' willingness to make concessions to the rebellious colonies, but his image captured Americans' belief in the importance of their produce.   (Chicago History Museum / Chicago Historical Society)

northerners were willing to abandon that claim for commercial concessions in the West Indies.

Peace Treaty Provisions

Provisions of the 1783 Treaty of Paris, too, caused problems. Article four, which promised payment of prewar debts (most owed by Americans to British merchants), and Article five, which recommended that states allow loyalists to recover their confiscated property, aroused opposition. States passed laws denying British subjects the right to sue for recovery of debts or property in American courts. Another reason for state opposition was that sales of loyalists' property and possessions had helped finance the war. Because many purchasers were prominent patriots, states hesitated to question the legitimacy of their property titles.

The refusal of state and local governments to comply with Articles four and five gave Britain an excuse to maintain military posts on the Great Lakes. Furthermore, Congress's inability to enforce the treaty disclosed its lack of power, even in an area—foreign affairs—in which it had authority under the Articles. Concerned nationalists argued that failure to enforce the treaty challenged the republic's credibility.

ORDER AND DISORDER IN THE WEST

Although British and American diplomats did not discuss tribal claims, the United States assumed that the Treaty of Paris cleared its title to all land east of the Mississippi except that held by Spain. Recognizing that land cessions should be obtained from the most powerful tribes, Congress initiated negotiations with northern and southern Indians.

Indian Relations

At Fort Stanwix, New York, in 1784, American diplomats negotiated a treaty with chiefs who claimed to represent the Iroquois; and at Hopewell, South Carolina, in late 1785 and early 1786, they negotiated with emissaries from the Choctaw, Chickasaw, and Cherokee nations. In 1786 the Iroquois repudiated the Fort Stanwix treaty, denying that the negotiators were authorized to speak for the Six Nations. The confederacy threatened new attacks on frontier settlements, but the treaty stood by default. By 1790 the once-dominant confederacy was confined to a few scattered reservations. In the South, too, the United States took the treaties as confirmation of its sovereignty. European Americans poured over the southern Appalachians, provoking the Creeks to declare war. In 1790, they came to terms with the United States.

Western nations, such as the Shawnees, Chippewas, Ottawas, and Potawatomis, rejected Iroquois hegemony as early as the 1750s. After Iroquois power collapsed, they formed a confederacy and demanded negotiations with the United States. As a united front, they hoped to avoid the piecemeal surrender of land by individual bands and villages. But in the postwar world, Indian nations could no longer play European and American powers against one another. France was gone, Spanish territory lay far to the west and south, and British power was confined to Canada. Only the United States remained.

Ordinance of 1785

Shortly after state land cessions were completed, Congress organized the Northwest Territory, bounded by the Mississippi River, the Great Lakes, and the Ohio River (see Map 7.2). Ordinances passed in 1784, 1785, and 1787 outlined the process through which the land could be sold and governments organized.

To ensure orderly development, Congress in 1785 wanted the land surveyed into townships 6 miles square, each divided into thirty-six sections of 640 acres (1 square mile). Revenue from the sale of the sixteenth section of each township would support public schools—the first federal aid to education in American history. One dollar was the minimum price per acre; the minimum sale was one section. The resulting minimum outlay, $640, was unaffordable for ordinary Americans, except veterans who received part of their army pay in land warrants. Proceeds from western land sales constituted the first independent revenues available to the national government.

Northwest Ordinance

The most important of the three land policies—the Northwest Ordinance of 1787—contained a bill of rights guaranteeing freedom of religion and the right to a jury trial, forbidding cruel and unusual punishments, and nominally prohibiting slavery.

Eventually, that prohibition became an important symbol for antislavery northerners, but at the time it had little effect. Some residents already held slaves, and Congress would not deprive them of their property. The ordinance also allowed slaveowners to reclaim runaways who took refuge in the territory—the first national fugitive slave law. It prevented slavery from taking deep root by discouraging slaveholders from moving into the territory, but enslavement was not abolished until 1848.

The ordinance of 1787 also specified how territorial residents could organize state governments and seek admission to the Union. Early in the nation's history, therefore, Congress established a policy of admitting new states on the same basis as the old. Having suffered under the rule of a colonial power, congressmen understood the importance of preparing the new nation's first "colony" for eventual self-government.

In 1787 the ordinance was largely theoretical. Miamis, Shawnees, and Delawares refused to acknowledge American sovereignty and attacked pioneers who ventured too far north of the Ohio River. In 1788 the Ohio Company, to which Congress had sold a large tract of land at reduced rates, established the town of Marietta at the juncture of the Ohio and Muskingum Rivers. But Indians prevented the company from extending settlement into the interior.

Not until after the Articles of Confederation were replaced with a new constitution could the United States muster sufficient force to implement the Northwest Ordinance. Thus, although the ordinance is often viewed as one of the few lasting accomplishments of the Confederation Congress, it existed within a context of political impotence.

FROM CRISIS TO THE CONSTITUTION

Under the Articles of Confederation, Congress could not levy taxes, force states to establish a uniform commercial policy, or enforce treaties. Partly as a result, the economy slid into a depression within a year after the war's end. Exporters of staple crops (especially tobacco and rice) and importers of manufactured goods suffered from postwar restrictions that European powers imposed on American commerce. Although recovery began by 1786, some estimates suggest that between 1775 and 1790 America's per capita gross national product declined by nearly 50 percent.

Economic Change and Commercial Reform   The near-total cessation of foreign commerce in nonmilitary items during the war stimulated domestic manufacturing. Despite the influx of European goods after 1783, the postwar period witnessed stirrings of American industrial development. Because of continuing population growth, the domestic market assumed greater economic importance. Moreover, foreign trade patterns shifted from Europe toward the West Indies. Foodstuffs to the French and Dutch Caribbean islands became America's largest export, replacing tobacco (and thus accelerating the Chesapeake's conversion to grain). South Carolina resumed large-scale slave importation, as planters sought to replace workers lost to wartime disruptions. Yet without British subsidies, American indigo could not compete with Caribbean indigo, and rice planters struggled to find new markets.

Representatives of Virginia and Maryland met at Mt. Vernon (George Washington's plantation) in March 1785 to negotiate an agreement about trade on the Potomac River, which divided the two states. The successful meeting led to an invitation to other states to discuss trade policy at a convention in Annapolis, Maryland. Nine states named representatives to the meeting in September 1786; only five delegations attended. Consequently, they issued a call for another convention in Philadelphia nine months later "to devise such further provisions as shall . . . appear necessary to render the constitution of the federal government adequate to the exigencies of the Union."

Shays's Rebellion

An armed rebellion in Massachusetts convinced doubting states that reform was needed. Men from several western counties, many of them veterans from leading families, violently opposed the high taxes levied by the eastern-dominated legislature to pay war debts. Such obligations consisted largely of securities issued during the war to soldiers in lieu of pay and to others for supplies and loans. During the hard times following the war, many veterans and creditors sold the securities at heavy discounts. The state legislature nevertheless levied taxes to pay off the securities (plus interest) at full price in specie by decade's end. Men with little prospect of obtaining specie without selling their land responded furiously when the state moved to collect the taxes.

Daniel Shays, a former Continental Army officer, led the disgruntled westerners. On January 25, 1787, about fifteen hundred of Shay's troops assaulted the Springfield federal armory. The militiamen defending the armory fired on their former comrades-in-arms, who withdrew after suffering twenty-four casualties. Some (including Shays) fled the state; two were hanged; and most escaped punishment by paying small fines and taking oaths of allegiance to Massachusetts. The state legislature reduced the burden on landowners with new import duties and by easing tax collections.

Terming Massachusetts *tyrannical* and styling themselves *Regulators,* Shaysites insisted that "whenever any encroachments are made either upon the liberties or properties of the people, if redress cannot be had without, it is virtue in them to disturb government." Thus they linked their rebellion to the earlier independence struggle.

Constitutional Convention

To political leaders, the rebellion confirmed the need for a stronger federal government. After most states appointed delegates, the Confederation Congress belatedly endorsed the convention, "for the sole and express purpose of revising the Articles of Confederation." In mid-May 1787, fifty-five men, representing every state but Rhode Island, assembled in Philadelphia.

Most delegates to the Constitutional Convention were substantial men of property: merchants, planters, physicians, generals, governors, and especially lawyers. They wanted to give the national government new authority over taxation and foreign commerce, but also sought to advance their states' interests. Many had been state legislators, and some helped draft state constitutions. Most were born in America; many came from families that arrived a century earlier. More than half had attended college. The youngest delegate was twenty-six, the oldest—Benjamin

Franklin—eighty-one. George Washington was elected presiding officer. A dozen men did the bulk of the convention's work; among them, Virginia's James Madison deserves the title *Father of the Constitution*.

Madison and the Constitution

The shy James Madison was thirty-six years old in 1787. A Princeton graduate raised in western Virginia, he served on the local Committee of Safety and was elected to the provincial convention, the state's lower and upper houses, and the Continental Congress (1780–1783). Although Madison returned to serve in the Virginia state legislature in 1784, he kept up with national politics, partly through correspondence with his friend Thomas Jefferson.

Madison systematically prepared for the Philadelphia meeting. He bought more than two hundred books on history and government, analyzing their accounts of past confederacies and republics. He summed up his research in a paper entitled "Vices of the Political System of the United States." After listing the flaws he perceived in the current government (among them "encroachments by the states on the federal authority" and lack of unity), Madison revealed his guiding belief that government had to be constructed so that it could not become tyrannical or fall under the influence of a particular faction. Rejecting the notion that republics had to be small, Madison asserted that a large, diverse republic was preferable. Because the nation would include many factions, no one of them could control the government. Political stability would result from compromises among contending parties.

Virginia and New Jersey Plans

The so-called Virginia Plan, introduced on May 29 by Edmund Randolph, embodied Madison's conception of national government. The plan provided for a two-house legislature, the lower house elected directly by the people and the upper house selected by the lower; representation in both houses proportional to property or population; an executive elected by Congress; a national judiciary; and congressional veto over state laws. Had it been adopted intact, it would have created a government in which national authority reigned unchallenged and state power was diminished. Proportional representation in both houses would also have given large states a dominant voice in national government.

Many delegates believed the Virginia Plan went too far toward national consolidation. After two weeks of debate, disaffected delegates—particularly those from small states—united under William Paterson of New Jersey. On June 15 Paterson presented an alternative, the New Jersey Plan, calling for strengthening the Articles rather than overhauling the government. Paterson proposed retaining a unicameral Congress in which each state had an equal vote, but giving Congress new powers of taxation and trade regulation. Although the convention initially rejected Paterson's position, he and his allies won several victories in subsequent months.

Debates over Congress

The delegates agreed that the new national government should have a two-house (bicameral) legislature. Further, they concurred that the people should be directly represented in at least one house. But they differed on three key questions: Should representation in both houses of Congress be proportional to population? How was representation to be apportioned among the states? How were the members of the two houses to be elected?

The last issue proved the easiest to resolve. Delegates thought it "essential" that the lower branch of Congress be elected directly by the people and "expedient" that members of the upper house be chosen by state legislatures. If the convention had not agreed to allow state legislatures to elect senators, the Constitution would have run into significant opposition among state leaders. The plan also placed the election of one house of Congress one step removed from the "lesser sort," whose judgment wealthy convention delegates did not wholly trust.

The delegates accepted without much debate the principle of representation proportional to population in the House of Representatives. But small states wanted equal representation in the Senate, which would give them relatively more power at the national level. Large states supported a proportional plan that would give them more votes in the upper house. For weeks the convention deadlocked. A committee appointed to devise a compromise recommended equal representation in the Senate, with a proviso that all appropriation bills originate in the lower house. A breakdown was only averted when the convention accepted a suggestion that a state's two senators vote as individuals rather than as a unit.

Slavery and the Constitution

The remaining question of how to apportion representation in the lower house divided the nation along sectional lines. Delegates concurred that a census should be conducted every decade to determine the nation's population and that Indians who paid no taxes should be excluded. Delegates from states with large slave populations wanted African and European inhabitants counted equally; delegates from states with few slaves wanted only free people counted. Slavery thus became linked to the new government. Delegates resolved the dispute with a formula developed by the Confederation Congress in 1783 to allocate financial assessments among states: three-fifths of slaves would be included in population totals. (The formula reflected delegates' judgment that slaves were less efficient producers of wealth than free people, not that they were 60 percent human and 40 percent property.)

Although the words *slave* and *slavery* do not appear in the Constitution (the framers used such euphemisms as "other persons"), the document contained direct and indirect protections for slavery. The three-fifths clause, for example, assured white southern male voters congressional representation out of proportion to their numbers and a disproportionate influence on the selection of the president, because the number of each state's votes in the electoral college (see below) was determined by the size of its congressional delegation. In return for southerners' agreement that commercial regulations could be adopted by a simple majority vote (rather than two-thirds), New Englanders agreed that Congress could not end the importation of slaves for twenty years. The fugitive slave clause required states to return runaways to their masters. By guaranteeing national assistance to states threatened with "domestic violence," the Constitution promised aid in putting down future slave revolts and incidents like Shays's Rebellion.

Congressional and Presidential Powers

With the questions of slavery and representation resolved, delegates concurred that the national government needed the authority to tax and to regulate foreign and interstate commerce. But instead of giving Congress the wide latitude of the Virginia Plan, delegates enumerated congressional powers and then granted Congress the "necessary and proper" authority to carry them out. Discarding the Virginia Plan's congressional veto, the convention implied but did not explicitly authorize a national judicial veto of state laws. The Constitution plus national laws and treaties would constitute "the supreme law of the land; and the judges in every state shall be bound thereby," Article VI declared ambiguously. Delegates drafted a long list of actions forbidden to states, and—contrary to many state constitutions—they provided that religious tests could never be required of U.S. officeholders.

The convention placed primary responsibility for foreign affairs with a new official, the president, who was also designated commander-in-chief of the armed forces. That raised the question, unspecified in the Constitution's text, of whether the president (or Congress) acquired special powers in wartime. With the Senate's consent, the president could appoint judges and other federal officers. To select the president, delegates established the electoral college, whose members would be chosen in each state by legislatures or voters. If a majority of electors failed to unite behind one candidate, the House of Representatives (voting as states, not as individuals) would choose the president. The chief executive would serve for four years but be eligible for reelection.

The key to the Constitution was the distribution of political authority, that is, the separation of powers among executive, legislative, and judicial branches of the national government and the division of powers between states and nation (called *federalism*). Two-thirds of Congress and three-fourths of the states had to concur on amendments. The branches balanced one another, their powers deliberately entwined to prevent each from acting independently. The president could veto congressional legislation, but that veto could be overridden by two-thirds majorities in both houses, and his treaties and major appointments required the Senate's consent. Congress could impeach the president and federal judges, but courts would have the final say on interpreting the Constitution. These checks and balances would keep the government from becoming tyrannical, but at times, they prevented the government from acting quickly and decisively. Furthermore, the Constitution drew such a vague line between state and national powers that the United States fought a civil war in the next century over that issue.

The convention held its last session on September 17, 1787. Of the forty-two delegates present (others left weeks earlier), three refused to sign the Constitution, two partly because it lacked a bill of rights. Benjamin Franklin urged unity, admitting, "I confess that there are several parts of this constitution which I do not at present approve." Yet he encouraged its acceptance "because I expect no better, and because I am not sure, that it is not the best." Only then was the Constitution made public. (See the appendix for the full text of the Constitution.)

OPPOSITION AND RATIFICATION

Later that month, the Confederation Congress submitted the Constitution to the states. The ratification clause provided for the new system to take effect after approval by special conventions in at least nine states. Thus the national Constitution, unlike the Articles of Confederation, would rest directly on popular authority.

As states elected delegates to the special conventions, newspaper essays and pamphlets defended or attacked the Philadelphia convention's decisions. Every newspaper in the country printed the Constitution, and most supported its adoption. Although most citizens concurred that the national government should have more power over taxation and foreign and interstate commerce, some believed that the proposed government held the potential for tyranny. As happened in Carlisle, Pennsylvania, the debate frequently spilled into the streets.

Federalists and Antifederalists

The Constitution's supporters called themselves Federalists. Building on classical republicanism, they envisioned a virtuous, self-sacrificing republic led by a manly aristocracy of talent. They argued that when good men drawn from the elite were in charge, the carefully structured government would prevent tyranny. A republic could be large if the government's design kept any one group from controlling it. The separation of powers among legislative, executive, and judicial branches and the division of powers between states and nation would accomplish that.

The Federalists termed those who opposed the Constitution Antifederalists, thus casting them in a negative light. While recognizing the need for a national source of revenue, Antifederalists feared a too-powerful central government. They saw the states as the chief protectors of individual rights; consequently, weakening the states could bring the onset of arbitrary power. Antifederalist arguments often listed potential abuses of government authority.

Heirs of the Real Whig ideology of the late 1760s and early 1770s, Antifederalists stressed the need for constant popular vigilance to avert oppression. Indeed, some Antifederalists promulgated those ideas prior to the centralizing, nationalistic Revolution—Samuel Adams, Patrick Henry, and Richard Henry Lee led the opposition to the Constitution. Joining them were small farmers preoccupied with guarding their property against excessive taxation, backcountry Baptists and Presbyterians, and upwardly mobile men who would benefit from an economic and political system less tightly controlled than that the Constitution envisioned.

Bill of Rights

Antifederalists focused on the Constitution's lack of a bill of rights. Even if the new system weakened the states, critics believed, people could be protected from tyranny by specific guarantees of rights. The Constitution did contain some prohibitions on congressional power. For example, the writ of habeas corpus, which prevented arbitrary imprisonment, could not be suspended except in "cases of rebellion or invasion." But Antifederalists found such constitutional provisions to be few and inadequate. They wanted a bill of rights.

Letters of a Federal Farmer, perhaps the most widely read Antifederalist pamphlet, listed the rights that should be protected: freedom of the press and religion, trial by jury, and guarantees against unreasonable searches. From Paris, Thomas Jefferson added his voice to the chorus, declaring, "A bill of rights is what the people are entitled to against every government on earth."

Ratification

Many state conventions were persuaded when Federalists promised that a national government with the power to tax foreign commerce would lessen the financial burdens that prompted Shays's Rebellion and protests in other states. Four of the first five states to ratify did so unanimously, but serious disagreements then surfaced. Massachusetts, where Antifederalist forces were bolstered by a backlash against the state's heavy-handed treatment of the Shays rebels, ratified by a majority of only 19 of 355 votes and recommended amendments identifying rights. In June 1788, when New Hampshire ratified, the requirement of nine states was satisfied. But New York and Virginia had not yet voted, and everyone realized the new Constitution could not succeed without those key states.

Pro-Constitution forces won by ten votes in the Virginia convention, which recommended adding rights specifications. In New York, James Madison, John Jay, and Alexander Hamilton, writing collectively as Publius, published *The Federalist,* eighty-five essays explaining the theory behind the Constitution and answering its critics. Their arguments, coupled with Federalists' promise to add a bill of rights, helped win the battle. On July 26, 1788, New York ratified the Constitution by just three votes. Although the last states—North Carolina and Rhode Island—did not join the Union until November 1789 and May 1790, respectively, the new government was a reality.

Celebrating Ratification

Americans in many cities celebrated ratification with parades on July 4, 1788, linking the acceptance of the Constitution to the adoption of the Declaration of Independence. The processions dramatized the history and unity of the new nation, seeking to counteract the dissent that had engulfed such towns as Carlisle, Pennsylvania. The processions aimed to educate people about the significance of the new Constitution and instruct them about leaders' hopes for industry and frugality on the part of a virtuous public.

About five thousand people participated in the Philadelphia parade. Floats portraying such themes as "The Grand Federal Edifice" stretched for a mile and a half. More than forty groups of tradesmen sponsored floats. Marchers representing the first pioneers and Revolutionary War troops paraded with farmers and artisans, followed by lawyers, doctors, clergymen, and congressmen. Symbolizing the nation's future, students from the University of Pennsylvania and other schools bore a flag labeled *The Rising Generation.*

The Township and Range System

Anyone flying over the American countryside west of the Appalachians today can see the township and range system inscribed on the landscape. Roads cross the land in straight lines, meeting at 90-degree angles, carving the terrain into a checkerboard. Originated in the Land Ordinance of 1785, that system organized land sales in the Northwest Territory.

English and native peoples traditionally bounded their lands by natural landmarks such as hills, streams, large trees, and rock outcroppings. That system was known as *metes and bounds*. Some early colonial settlers employed surveyors, who created lots of varying sizes divided by lines laid out abstractly on the soil. Sometimes those lines related to natural features, such as the long, narrow lots in French Canada that fronted on the St. Lawrence River. But because North America was settled piecemeal, no one system dominated until the Land Ordinance of 1785. Thereafter, the ordinance's system became the template for the U.S. government's land distribution.

After a surveyor established an east-west baseline and a north-south meridian on a particular tract, he laid out rectangular townships composed of thirty-six numbered square-mile sections. He ignored natural features; potential buyers would learn for themselves which sections had rivers, hills, or assets like salt licks. The initial policy of selling equally priced sections broadened by 1832 to allow individuals to purchase as few as 40 acres and, after 1854, included price variations. As the United States expanded westward, the township and range system followed, democratizing access to land and opening land for settlement.

The legacy of the Land Ordinance of 1785 for the American people and nation still marks the landscape west of the Ohio River.

Summary

During the 1770s and 1780s the nation began to develop an economy independent of Britain and attempted to protect the national interest, defend its borders, and promote trade. Some Americans outlined artistic and educational goals for a properly virtuous people. The formulation of American racist thought was also an integral part of the developing Union. Emphasizing race (rather than status as slave or free) as a determinant of African Americans' standing allowed men who now termed themselves *white* to define republicanism to exclude most men but themselves. White women, viewed primarily as household dependents, had a limited role in the republic, as mothers of the next generation and selfless contributors to the nation's welfare.

In 1775 most Americans believed that "that government which governs best governs least," but by the late 1780s many changed their minds. Drafters and supporters of the Constitution concluded that a more powerful central government was needed. During ratification debates, they contended that their proposals were just as republican as the Articles of Confederation.

Both sides adhered to republican principles, but Federalists embraced classical republicanism, stressing the community over the individual. Antifederalists wanted a weak central government, protection of individual rights, and a loosely regulated economy. The Federalists won when the Constitution was adopted, however narrowly. The 1790s, the first decade under the Constitution, would witness hesitant steps toward creating a true nation, the United States of America.

Chapter Review

CREATING A VIRTUOUS REPUBLIC

How were notions of republican virtue gendered in post-revolutionary America?

Leaders wanted the new United States to be a republican form of government, and while they debated the specifics, they agreed that in a republic, citizens were virtuous men willing to forgo personal profit for the best interests of the nation. The notion of virtue—the absence of vice or corruption—became increasingly important and inspired educational reform to help children become useful citizens. Some argued that since childrearing was women's role, they, too, would need education to help raise virtuous future citizens. Since women could not own property or participate in politics, their role was as the embodiment of self-sacrificing republicanism, using their nurturing skills to run charitable associations aiding the poor and others. This, in turn, conveyed virtue on their families and freed men to pursue their economic self-interests. The ideal republican male sought upward mobility for himself and his family, while the ideal republican woman put the needs of others first.

THE FIRST EMANCIPATION AND THE GROWTH OF RACISM

What contributed to the growing number of free blacks in America after the revolution?

Northern states, which were less reliant on slave labor, increasingly freed slaves after court challenges from blacks about the contradictions between forced bondage and the Declaration of Independence. Other former slaves obtained their freedom by escaping during the war, by enlisting, or by state emancipation laws. Some slaveholders also manumitted slaves. Postwar economic changes also spurred manumissions, particularly in the Chesapeake, where the shift from tobacco to grain production meant far fewer slaves were required.

DESIGNING REPUBLICAN GOVERNMENTS

How did Americans' former experience as British subjects influence the state governments they established?

Americans feared tyranny as well as the power of the governor, and as such, early state constitutions sought to limit governors' power through annual elections and term limitations. They further provided little independent authority for governors while expanding that granted to legislatures, typically in a two-house structure. And states put more power in the hands of the people by redrawing election districts to reflect the population and reducing property requirements for voting. To protect citizens' rights, several states included a bill of rights guaranteeing freedom of the press, rights to fair trials and sometimes freedom of religion even if officeholders had to be Christians. Ultimately, the emphasis on preventing tyranny made states weak politically. Subsequent revisions to state constitutions in the mid-1780s increased the power of the governor and reduced that of the legislature via a system of checks and balances.

TRIALS OF THE CONFEDERATION

How did fears of a strong central government ultimately tie the hands of the Confederation Congress?

The Articles of confederation limited congressional power in a number of areas that, in turn, led to policy problems for the new nation. First, because of state resistance to a large central government, a much-needed customs duty was never adopted. Second, Congress's limited ability to establish a national commercial policy left it unable to take action when Britain, France, and Spain restricted American trade. Third, Congress had little power to enforce the 1783 Treaty of Paris promising payment of prewar debts (owed by Americans to British merchants) and allowing loyalists to recover confiscated property. States passed various laws prohibiting both, which gave the British an excuse to maintain military posts on the Great Lakes. Worse, the inability to enforce the treaty hurt the republic's credibility in foreign affairs.

ORDER AND DISORDER IN THE WEST

What was the significance of the Northwest Ordinance?

One of the lasting accomplishments of the First Continental Congress, the Northwest Ordinance of 1787 effectively outlined how territories west of the Mississippi would be organized, how land could be divided and sold, how new states would be admitted to the Union, as well as the rights of people living there. It included a bill of rights guaranteeing freedom of religion and the right to a jury trial, and it forbade cruel and unusual punishments and nominally prohibited slavery. While the ordinance did not deprive those with slaves of their property and included the first fugitive slave law, it did discourage slaveholders from moving into the territory and prevented slavery from taking hold on a large scale.

FROM CRISIS TO THE CONSTITUTION

How did the question of slavery become linked to the new U.S. Constitution?

Slavery came into play at the Constitutional Convention as states debated how their populations should be counted in determining the number of representatives each would get in the lower house of Congress. Slave states wanted their bondsmen fully counted, while those from states with few slaves wanted only free people counted. The dispute was resolved by a formula known as the three-fifths compromise, noting that three-fifths of slaves would be included in population totals in censuses conducted every decade. While the words *slave* and *slavery* are not used in the Constitution, it nonetheless included direct and indirect protections for slavery, among them assistance in putting down revolts, returning fugitive slaves to masters, and agreeing not to end the importation of slaves for twenty years.

OPPOSITION AND RATIFICATION

What were the differences between Federalists and Antifederalists in the Constitution debate?

Federalists supported ratification of the Constitution and believed a strong national government led by a talented elite would prevent tyranny. Moreover, they agued that dividing power between the legislative, executive, and judicial branches, as well as between states and the nation, would prevent a tyrant from rising up. Antifederalists, so dubbed by their opponents, feared a too-powerful central government and saw states as protectors of individual rights. As such, they supported state sovereignty, and while they agreed on the need for central currency and taxation, Antifederalists were concerned that the Constitution did not include a bill of rights to safeguard people's individual rights.

SUGGESTIONS FOR FURTHER READING

Richard Beeman et al., eds., *Beyond Confederation: Origins of the Constitution and American National Identity* (1987)

Carol Berkin, *A Brilliant Solution: Inventing the American Constitution* (2002)

Ira Berlin and Ronald Hoffman, eds., *Slavery and Freedom in the Age of the American Revolution* (1983)

Cathy N. Davidson, *Revolution and the Word: The Rise of the Novel in America* (1987)

Edith Gelles, *Portia: The World of Abigail Adams* (1992)

Peter S. Onuf, *Statehood and Union: A History of the Northwest Ordinance* (1987)

Jack N. Rakove, *Original Meanings: Politics and Ideas in the Making of the Constitution* (1996)

Leonard L. Richards, *Shays's Rebellion: The American Revolution's Final Battle* (2002)

David Waldstreicher, *In the Midst of Perpetual Fetes: The Making of American Nationalism, 1776–1820* (1997)

Gordon S. Wood, *The Creation of the American Republic, 1776–1787* (1969)

The Early Republic: Conflicts at Home and Abroad

In late 1798, the wealthy Philadelphia matron Deborah Norris Logan became the target of widespread criticism. Her husband, Dr. George Logan, who supported Jefferson, had undertaken a personal peace mission to France, fearing war between the United States and its former ally. When Logan's wife defended him, she endured a campaign unlike anything experienced by an American woman. Her treatment suggests the political symbolism now embodied by women, the growing division between the Federalist and Republican factions, and the significance of foreign affairs in the early republic.

First to attack was the Federalist newspaper editor William Cobbett, who observed with sly sexual innuendo in his *Porcupine's Gazette* in July that "it is said that JEFFERSON went to his friend Doctor Logan's farm and spent three days there, soon after the Doctor's departure for France. *Query:* What did he do there?" Later Cobbett suggested that George and Deborah Logan should be publicly shamed—him, presumably, for treason and her, Cobbett implied, for adultery. Republican newspapers leaped to Deborah's defense, attacking the vulgarity of suggestions about her and Vice President Jefferson.

At first Deborah Logan secluded herself at her country estate, but on Jefferson's advice she returned to Philadelphia to prove she was "not afraid nor ashamed to meet the public eye." As reports emerged that her husband had some success in quelling hostilities, she reveled in the praise subsequently showered on him. George Logan was enthusiastically welcomed home by Jeffersonian partisans. However, in January 1799, Congress, controlled by Federalists, adopted the so-called Logan Act, still in effect, which forbids private citizens from undertaking diplomatic missions.

The Logan controversy was one of many battles in the 1790s. The fight over ratifying the Constitution presaged wide divisions

This icon will direct you to interactive activities and study materials on *A People And A Nation*, Brief Edition website: **www.cengage.com/history/norton/peoplenationbrief8e**

Chronology

1789	Washington is inaugurated as first president. Judiciary Act of 1789 organizes the federal court system. French Revolution begins.		Pinckney's Treaty with Spain establishes the southern boundary of the United States. Treaty of Greenville with the Miami Confederacy opens Ohio to settlement.
1790	Hamilton's *Report on Public Credit* proposes the assumption of state debts.	**1796**	First contested presidential election: Adams is elected president, Jefferson vice president.
1791	First ten amendments (Bill of Rights) are ratified. First national bank is chartered.	**1798**	XYZ affair arouses American opinion against France. Sedition Act penalizes dissent. Virginia and Kentucky Resolutions protest suppression of dissent.
1793	France declares war on Britain, Spain, and the Netherlands. Washington's neutrality proclamation keeps the United States out of war. Democratic and Republican societies, the first grassroots political organizations, are founded.	**1798–99**	Quasi-War with France occurs. Fries's Rebellion in Pennsylvania protests taxation.
1794	Wayne defeats the Miami Confederacy at Fallen Timbers. Whiskey Rebellion in western Pennsylvania protests taxation.	**1800**	Franco-American Convention ends the Quasi-War. Gabriel's Rebellion threatens Virginia slaveowners.
1795	Jay Treaty with England resolves issues remaining from the Revolution.	**1801**	Thomas Jefferson is elected president by the House of Representatives after a stalemate in the electoral college.

over the major political, economic, and diplomatic questions confronting the young republic: the extent to which authority should be centralized, the relationship between national power and states' rights, the formulation of foreign policy in an era of continual warfare in Europe, and the limits of dissent. Americans had not anticipated the acrimonious disagreements that rocked the 1790s or the difficulties that would develop as the United States attempted to deal with Indian nations within its borders.

Most important, Americans could not understand the division of citizens into two competing factions. In republics, they believed, the rise of such factions signified decay and corruption. Yet on numerous occasions, Federalist and Republican leaders sought to mobilize their supporters, thereby reworking the nation's political practice if not its theory. As the decade closed, Americans were still grappling with the implications of partisan politics, as evidenced by the 1800 election.

- **What major challenges confronted the new republic?**
- **What issues caused disputes among the nation's citizens?**
- **How did Americans react to those disputes?**

BUILDING A WORKABLE GOVERNMENT

At first, consensus appeared possible, as the nation's celebratory mood after the Constitution's ratification carried into Congress's first session. Only a few Antifederalists ran for office in 1788, and even fewer were elected. Thus the First Congress consisted chiefly of men who supported a strong national government. The drafters of the Constitution deliberately left key issues undecided, so the nationalists' domination of Congress meant that their views prevailed.

First Congress

Congress faced four immediate tasks when it convened in April 1789: raising revenue, responding to states' calls for a bill of rights, setting up executive departments, and organizing the judiciary.

James Madison, representing Virginia in the House of Representatives, became influential in Congress. He persuaded Congress to adopt the Revenue Act of 1789, imposing a 5 percent tariff on certain imports. Thus the First Congress achieved an effective national tax law.

Bill of Rights

Madison opposed additional limitations on the national government and believed it unnecessary to guarantee people's rights explicitly given the government's limited powers. But he recognized that Congress should respond to amendments proposed in state ratifying conventions. Accordingly, he introduced nineteen amendments; the states ratified ten, which became part of the Constitution on December 15, 1791 (see the appendix for the Constitution and all amendments). Their adoption defused Antifederalist opposition.

The First Amendment prohibited Congress from passing laws restricting the right to freedom of religion, speech, press, peaceable assembly, or petition. The Second Amendment guaranteed the right "to keep and bear arms" because of the need for a "well-regulated Militia." It was based on the expectation that most able-bodied men would serve as citizen-soldiers, eliminating the need for a permanent army. The Third Amendment limited the conditions under which troops could be quartered in private homes. The next five pertained to judicial procedures. The Fourth Amendment prohibited "unreasonable searches and seizures"; the Fifth and Sixth established the rights of accused persons; the Seventh specified the conditions for jury trials in civil (as opposed to criminal) cases; and the Eighth forbade "cruel and unusual punishments." The Ninth and Tenth Amendments reserved to the people and the states other unspecified rights and powers.

Executive and Judiciary

Congress also considered the organization of the executive branch. It agreed to continue the three administrative departments established under the Articles of Confederation: War, Foreign Affairs (renamed State), and Treasury. Congress instituted two lesser posts: the attorney general—the nation's official lawyer—and the postmaster general. Controversy arose over whether the president alone could dismiss officials whom he appointed with Senate approval. Ultimately, the House and Senate agreed that he had such authority. That established the principle that heads of executive departments are accountable solely to the president.

The far-reaching Judiciary Act of 1789 defined the jurisdiction of the federal judiciary and established a six-member Supreme Court, thirteen district courts, and three circuit courts of appeal. Its most important provision, Section 25, allowed appeals from state to federal courts when cases raised certain constitutional questions. It presumed that Article VI of the Constitution, which stated that federal statutes and treaties were "the supreme Law of the Land," implied the right of appeal from state to federal courts, yet the Constitution did not explicitly permit such actions. In the nineteenth century, judges and legislators committed to states' rights would challenge Section 25's constitutionality.

During its first decade, the Supreme Court handled few cases of any importance, and several members resigned. But in a 1796 decision, *Ware v. Hylton,* the Court for the first time declared a state law unconstitutional. That same year it also reviewed the constitutionality of an act of Congress, upholding its validity in the case of *Hylton v. U.S.* The most important case of the decade, *Chisholm v. Georgia* (1793), established that states could be sued in federal courts by citizens of other states. Five years later, the Eleventh Amendment to the Constitution overturned that decision.

Debate over Slavery

Constitutional provisions forbade Congress from prohibiting the importation of slaves for twenty years, but in 1790 three Quakers groups petitioned Congress to end slavery. Southerners asserted that had they thought that the federal government would consider interfering with slavery, they would never have ratified the Constitution. Southern legislators insisted, as they would for the next seven decades, that slavery was integral to the Union and that abolition would cause bigger problems, primarily how to deal with a sizable population of freed people.

Some northern congressmen—and Benjamin Franklin—contested the southerners' position. But Congress accepted a committee report denying it the power to halt slave importations before 1808 or emancipate slaves at any time, that authority "remaining with the several States alone."

DOMESTIC POLICY UNDER WASHINGTON AND HAMILTON

George Washington did not seek the presidency. In 1783 he returned to Mount Vernon as a Virginia planter. But his fellow countrymen never regarded Washington as just another citizen. Americans concurred that only Washington had sufficient stature to serve as the republic's first president, an office designed with him in mind. The unanimous vote of the electoral college formalized that consensus. Washington could not ignore his country's call and headed to New York City, the nation's capital.

Washington's First Steps

Washington acted cautiously during his first months in office in 1789, knowing he would set future precedents. When the title by which he should be addressed aroused controversy (Vice President John Adams favored His Highness, the President of the United States of America, and Protector of their Liberties), Washington said nothing. The accepted title became simply Mr. President. By using the heads of executive departments as chief advisers, he created the cabinet. Washington also exercised his veto power over congressional legislation sparingly—only if he believed a bill was unconstitutional.

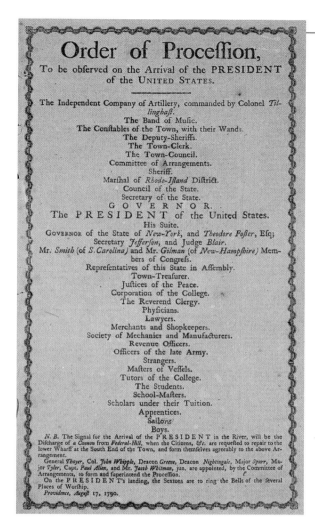

Order of Procession,

To be observed on the Arrival of the PRESIDENT of the UNITED STATES.

The Independent Company of Artillery, commanded by Colonel *Tillinghaſt*.
The Band of Muſic.
The Conſtables of the Town, with their Wands.
The Deputy-Sheriffs.
The Town-Clerk.
The Town-Council.
Committee of Arrangements.
Sheriff.
Marſhal of *Rhode-Iſland* Diſtrict.
Council of the State.
Secretary of the State.
GOVERNOR.
The PRESIDENT of the United States.
His Suite.
GOVERNOR of the State of *New-York*, and *Theodore Foſter*, Eſq;
Secretary *Jefferſon*, and Judge *Blair*.
Mr. *Smith* (of *S. Carolina)* and Mr. *Gilman* (of *New-Hampſhire)* Members of Congreſs.
Repreſentatives of this State in Aſſembly.
Town-Treaſurer.
Juſtices of the Peace.
Corporation of the College.
The Reverend Clergy.
Phyſicians.
Lawyers.
Merchants and Shopkeepers.
Society of Mechanics and Manufacturers.
Revenue Officers.
Officers of the late Army.
Strangers.
Maſters of Veſſels.
Tutors of the College.
The Students.
School-Maſters.
Scholars under their Tuition.
Apprentices.
Sailors.
Boys.

N. B. The Signal for the Arrival of the PRESIDENT in the River, will be the Diſcharge of *a Cannon* from *Federal-Hill*, when the Citizens, *&c.* are requeſted to repair to the lower Wharff at the South End of the Town, and form themſelves agreeably to the above Arrangement.
General *Thayer*, Col. *John Whipple*, Deacon *Greene*, Deacon *Nightingale*, Major *Spurr*, Major *Tyler*, Capt. *Paul Allen*, and Mr. *Jacob Whitman*, jun. are appointed, by the Committee of Arrangements, to form and ſuperintend the Proceſſion.
On the PRESIDENT's landing, the Sextons are to ring the Bells of the ſeveral Places of Worſhip.
Providence, Auguſt 17, 1790.

When George Washington toured the nation during his first term in office, he was greeted by local leaders in elaborately orchestrated rituals. The organizers of the ceremony at Providence, Rhode Island, on August 17, 1790, issued this broadside to inform participants of their plans for a formal procession. While some Americans gloried in such displays of pomp, others feared they presaged the return of monarchy.   (The Huntington Library and Art Collections, San Marino, California)

Washington's first major task was to choose the heads of the executive departments. For the War Department he selected Henry Knox of Massachusetts, who was his artillery general during the Revolution. For the State Department, he selected fellow Virginian Thomas Jefferson, who had been minister to France. For secretary of the treasury, Washington chose the brilliant, ambitious Alexander Hamilton.

Alexander Hamilton

The illegitimate son of a Scottish aristocrat and a woman whose husband divorced her for adultery and desertion, Hamilton was born in the British West Indies in 1757. He spent his early years in poverty, working as a mercantile clerk after his mother's death when he was eleven. In 1773 Hamilton enrolled at King's College (later Columbia University) in New York City. In late 1774, the seventeen-year-old contributed a pamphlet to the prerevolutionary publication wars. A devoted patriot, Hamilton volunteered for the American army, where in 1777, Washington appointed him as an aide, and they developed great mutual affection.

At twenty-three, Hamilton wed Elizabeth Schuyler, daughter of a wealthy New York family. After the war, he practiced law in New York City and served as a delegate to the Annapolis Convention and the Constitutional Convention. His contributions to *The Federalist* in 1788 made him one of the republic's chief political thinkers.

As treasury secretary and presidential adviser, Hamilton's primary loyalty lay with the nation. With no natal ties to any state, Hamilton neither sympathized with nor fully understood demands for local autonomy. His fiscal policies aimed at consolidating national power, and he openly favored close ties with Britain.

Second, Hamilton cynically believed people to be motivated by self-interest. He placed no reliance on people's capacity for virtuous, self-sacrificing behavior. This set him apart from those Americans who believed that public-spirited citizens would pursue the common good rather than private gain. Hamilton's beliefs influenced the way he tackled the new nation's tangled finances.

National and State Debts

Congress ordered the new treasury secretary to assess the public debt. The country's war debts fell into three categories: those owed by the nation to foreign governments and investors, mostly France (about $11 million); those owed by the national government to merchants, soldiers, and revolutionary bondholders (about $27 million); and, finally, those owed by state governments (roughly $25 million). Regarding the national debt, Americans recognized that, if their new government were to succeed, it would have to repay financial obligations incurred while winning independence.

State debts were another matter. Some—notably, Virginia, Maryland, North Carolina, and Georgia—had already paid off most war debts by levying taxes and handing out land grants in lieu of money. They opposed taxing their citizens so the national government could assume other states' debts. Massachusetts, Connecticut, and South Carolina still had sizable unpaid debts and welcomed national assumption. Consolidating state debt in the hands of the national government would help concentrate power at the national level.

Hamilton's Financial Plan

In his first *Report on Public Credit* in January 1790, Hamilton proposed that Congress assume outstanding state debts, combine them with national obligations, and issue new securities covering principal and accumulated unpaid interest. Hamilton hoped to ensure that holders of the public debt—many of them wealthy merchants and speculators—had a stake in the new government's survival. Opposition coalesced around James Madison, whose state of Virginia had mostly eliminated its war debt and who wanted to avoid rewarding wealthy speculators who purchased debt certificates at a fraction of their value from needy veterans and farmers.

The House initially rejected the assumption of state debts, but the Senate adopted Hamilton's plan largely intact. Compromises followed, in which the assumption bill became linked to another major issue: location of the permanent national capital. Deals were struck. A site on the Potomac River became the capital, and the first part of Hamilton's program became law in August 1790.

First Bank of the United States

Four months later, Hamilton submitted to Congress a second report on public credit, recommending the chartering of a national bank modeled on the Bank of England. The Bank of the United States, to be chartered for twenty years, was to be capitalized at $10 million. Just $2 million would come from public funds; private investors would supply the rest. The bank would act as collecting and disbursing agent for the Treasury, and its notes would become the nation's currency. But did the Constitution give Congress the power to establish such a bank?

Interpreting the Constitution

James Madison thought not. He pointed out that Constitutional Convention delegates rejected a clause authorizing Congress to issue corporate charters. President Washington sought other opinions. Attorney General Edmund Randolph and Secretary of State Thomas Jefferson agreed with Madison. Jefferson referred to Article I, Section 8, of the Constitution, which gave Congress the power "to make all Laws which shall be necessary and proper." The key word, Jefferson argued, was *necessary*: Congress could do what was needed, but not what was merely desirable. Thus Jefferson formulated the strict-constructionist interpretation of the Constitution.

Hamilton's *Defense of the Constitutionality of the Bank,* presented in February 1791, expounded a broad-constructionist view of the Constitution. Hamilton argued that Congress could choose any means not specifically prohibited by the Constitution to achieve a constitutional end. He reasoned: if the end was constitutional and the means was not *un*constitutional, then the means was constitutional.

Washington concurred, and the bill became law. The bank proved successful, as did the debt program. The new nation's securities became desirable investments for citizens and wealthy foreigners, especially those in the Netherlands. The influx of new capital, coupled with the high prices that American grain now commanded in European markets, eased farmers' debt burdens and contributed to a new prosperity.

Report on Manufactures

In December 1791, Hamilton presented to Congress his *Report on Manufactures,* his third and final economic prescription. Hamilton argued that the nation could never be truly independent as long as it relied heavily on Europe for manufactured goods. He urged Congress to promote the immigration of technicians and laborers and to support industrial development through limited use of protective tariffs. Many of Hamilton's ideas were implemented in later decades, but congressmen in 1791 believed that America's future lay in agriculture and the carrying trade. Congress rejected Hamilton's report.

That year Congress tried another of Hamilton's suggestions, an excise tax on whiskey distilled within the United States. Although proceeds from the Revenue Act of 1789 covered the interest on the national debt, the national government required additional income to fund state debts. A whiskey tax affected few westerners—farmers who grew corn and distillers who turned it into whiskey—and might also reduce whiskey consumption. (Eighteenth-century Americans, notorious for their heavy drinking, consumed about twice as much alcohol per capita as Americans do today.) Moreover, western farmers and distillers were Jefferson's supporters, and Hamilton saw the benefits of taxing them rather than his merchant allies.

Whiskey Rebellion   News of the tax sparked protests on Pennsylvania's frontier. Residents were upset that the government that protected them inadequately from Indian attacks was proposing to tax them disproportionately. Unrest continued for two years on the frontiers of Pennsylvania, Maryland, and Virginia. Large groups drafted petitions protesting the tax, deliberately imitated 1760s' crowd actions, and occasionally harassed tax collectors.

President Washington stayed restrained until violence erupted in July 1794, when western Pennsylvania farmers resisted two excise tax collectors. When about seven thousand rebels convened on August 1 to plot the destruction of Pittsburgh, Washington took action to prevent a repeat of Shays's Rebellion. On August 7, he told insurgents to disperse and summoned nearly thirteen thousand militia from Pennsylvania and neighboring states. By the time federal forces marched westward in October and November, the disturbances ceased. Troops met no resistance and arrested only twenty suspects. Two were convicted of treason, but Washington pardoned both.

The importance of the Whiskey Rebellion lay in the forceful message it conveyed. The national government, Washington demonstrated, would not allow violent resistance to its laws. In the republic, people dissatisfied with laws should peacefully try to amend or repeal them.

THE FRENCH REVOLUTION AND THE DEVELOPMENT OF PARTISAN POLITICS

By 1794 some Americans were beginning to seek change through electoral politics. In a monarchy, formal opposition groups, commonly called factions, were expected. In a government of the people, however, sustained factional disagreement was taken as a sign of corruption, but that did not halt partisanship.

Republicans and Federalists   Jefferson and Madison became convinced as early as 1792 that Hamilton's policies favoring wealthy commercial interests over agriculture aimed at imposing a corrupt, aristocratic government on the United States. Characterizing themselves as the true heirs of the Revolution, they charged that Hamilton was plotting to subvert republican principles and began calling themselves and their followers Republicans. Hamilton likewise accused Jefferson and Madison of attempting to destroy the republic. Hamilton and his supporters called themselves Federalists to link themselves with the Constitution.

Washington tried to remain aloof from the political dispute dividing his chief advisers. The growing controversy persuaded him to promote political unity by seeking office again in 1792. But beginning in 1793, developments in foreign affairs magnified the disagreements, for France (America's wartime ally) and Great Britain (America's most important trading partner) resumed the periodic hostilities that originated a century earlier.

French Revolution

In 1789 Americans welcomed news of the French Revolution. The French people's success in limiting, and then overthrowing, an oppressive monarchy enabled Americans to see themselves as the vanguard of an inevitable trend that would reshape the world in republican terms. But by the early 1790s violence in France continued, and political leaders rapidly succeeded each other. Executions mounted; the king was beheaded in early 1793. Although many Americans, including Jefferson and Madison, retained sympathy for the revolution, others, among them Alexander Hamilton, cited France as an example of the perversion of republicanism.

Debates within the United States intensified when the newly republican France became enmeshed in conflict with other European nations. Seeking to keep neighboring monarchies from intervening, and hoping to spread republicanism, French leaders declared war on Austria and then, in 1793, on Britain, Spain, and Holland. That posed a dilemma for Americans. The 1778 Treaty of Alliance with France bound them as allies "forever." Yet the United States was connected to Great Britain through a shared history and language and renewed economic ties. Americans still purchased most of their manufactured goods from Great Britain, and because U.S. revenues depended heavily on import tariffs, the nation's economic health required uninterrupted trade with England.

Edmond Genêt

The situation intensified in April 1793, when Edmond Genêt, a representative of the French government, arrived in Charleston, South Carolina. As he traveled to New York City, he recruited Americans for expeditions against British and Spanish colonies. Washington wondered: Should he receive Genêt, thus officially recognizing the French revolutionary government? Or should he proclaim neutrality?

Washington resolved his dilemma by receiving Genêt but also issuing a proclamation that the United States would adopt "a conduct friendly and impartial toward the belligerent powers." Federalist newspapers defended the proclamation, while Republicans only reluctantly accepted the enormously popular neutrality policy.

Genêt's faction fell from power in Paris, and he sought political asylum in the United States. But the domestic divisions Genêt helped to widen were perpetuated by clubs called Democratic societies, formed by Americans sympathetic to the French Revolution and worried about the Washington administration.

Democratic Societies

More than forty Democratic societies organized between 1793 and 1800. Members saw themselves as heirs of the Sons of Liberty with the same goal: protecting people's liberties against encroachments by corrupt, self-serving rulers. They protested government fiscal and foreign policy and proclaimed their belief in the equal rights of man, particularly free speech, free press, and free assembly. The Democratic societies comprised chiefly artisans and craftsmen, although professionals, farmers, and merchants also joined. They communicated through newspapers and allied with congressional Republicans.

The rapid spread of citizens' groups outspokenly critical of the administration disturbed Hamilton and Washington. Calling them dangerously subversive, the groups' "real design," a Federalist newspaper asserted, was "to involve the country in war, to assume the reins of government and tyrannize over the people." The counter-attack climaxed in the fall of 1794, when Washington accused the societies of fomenting the Whiskey Rebellion. As the first organized political dissenters in the United States, the Democratic societies alarmed officials, who had not yet accepted that organized loyal opposition was one component of a free government.

PARTISAN POLITICS AND RELATIONS WITH GREAT BRITAIN

In 1794 George Washington dispatched Chief Justice John Jay to London to negoti-ate unresolved questions in Anglo-American relations. The United States wanted to establish freedom of the seas and to assert its right, as a neutral nation, to trade freely with both combatants. Further, Great Britain still held posts in the American Northwest, thus violating the 1783 peace treaty. Settlers there believed that the British were responsible for renewed warfare with neighboring Indians. The Americans also hoped for a commercial treaty and sought compensation for the slaves who left with the British army after the war.

Jay Treaty Debate
Britain agreed to evacuate western forts and ease restric-tions on American trade to England and the West Indies. The treaty established two arbitration commissions—one to deal with prewar debts Americans owed to British creditors and the other to hear claims for captured American merchant ships—but Britain refused slaveowners com-pensation for lost bondspeople. Most Americans, including the president, expressed dissatisfaction with some treaty clauses.

The Senate debated the Jay Treaty in secret, and the public only learned its pro-visions after ratification in late June 1795. Protests followed, in newspaper essays and popular gatherings that asked Washington to reject the treaty. Southern planters criticized the lack of compensation for runaway slaves and objected to the commis-sion on prewar debts, which might make them pay debts dating back to the 1760s. Federalists countered with their own meetings and publications, contending that the Jay Treaty would prove preferable to no treaty at all. The president signed the treaty in mid-August. One opportunity remained to prevent it from taking effect: Congress had to appropriate funds, and, according to the Constitution, appropria-tion bills had to originate in the House of Representatives.

Washington delayed submitting the treaty to the House until March 1796, fu-tilely hoping that opposition would have dissipated. During the debate, Republicans argued against the appropriations, and they asked Washington to give the House all negotiation documents. In resisting the request, Washington established a power still used today—executive privilege, in which the president may withhold informa-tion from Congress if he deems it necessary.

The treaty's opponents initially commanded a congressional majority, but soon pressure mounted for appropriating the necessary funds, fostered by a Federalist campaign targeting middle-state congressmen whose districts would benefit from approval. Petitions contended that failure to fund the treaty would lead to war with Britain, thus endangering Pennsylvania frontier settlements and New York and

New Jersey commercial interests. Further, Federalists linked the Jay Treaty with the more popular Pinckney's Treaty. In 1795 Thomas Pinckney of South Carolina negotiated a treaty with Spain giving the United States navigation privileges on the Mississippi River and the right to land and store goods at New Orleans tax free. The overwhelming support for Pinckney's Treaty helped to overcome opposition to the Jay Treaty. In late April, the House appropriated the money by 51 to 48. The vote divided along partisan and regional lines: all but two southerners opposed the treaty; all but three congressional Federalists supported it; and a majority of middle-state representatives also voted yes. Despite the Federalists' success, their campaign to sway public opinion ironically violated their fundamental government philosophy— that ordinary people should defer to the judgment of elected leaders. The Federalists had won the battle, but in the long run they lost the war, for Republicans ultimately proved far more effective in appealing to the citizenry at large.

Bases of Partisanship

The terms used by Jefferson and Madison (the people versus the aristocrats) or by Hamilton and Washington (true patriots versus subversive rabble) do not adequately explain growing divisions in the electorate. Differences between agrarian and commercial interests do not cover it either, since more than 90 percent of Americans lived in rural areas. Nor did the divisions in the 1790s simply echo the Federalist-Antifederalist debate of 1787–1788. Although most Antifederalists became Republicans, the party's leaders, Madison and Jefferson, had supported the Constitution.

Republicans, especially prominent in the southern and middle states, were confident and optimistic about politics and the economy. Southern planters foresaw a prosperous future based partly on westward expansion, which they expected to dominate. Republicans employed democratic rhetoric to win over small farmers south of New England and non-English ethnic groups, especially Irish, Scots, and Germans. Artisans also joined the coalition. Republicans emphasized developing America's resources and remained sympathetic to France.

Federalists, concentrated among New England commercial interests, came mostly from English stock. They stressed the need for order, hierarchy, and obedience to authority. Wealthy New England merchants aligned with the Federalists, as did the region's farmers who, prevented from expanding production because of New England's poor soil, gravitated toward the more conservative party. To Federalists, potential enemies—internal and external—threatened the nation, requiring an ongoing alliance with Great Britain for protection. Given the dangers posed by European warfare, the Federalists' vision of international affairs may have been accurate. But because the Federalist view held little hope of a better future, Republicans ultimately prevailed.

Washington's Farewell Address

After the treaty debate, wearied by criticism, George Washington decided to retire. In September Washington published his Farewell Address, most of which Hamilton wrote. In it Washington outlined two principles that guided American foreign policy until the late 1940s: to maintain commercial but not political ties to other nations and to enter no permanent alliances. He also stressed America's uniqueness—its exceptionalism—and the need for independent action in foreign affairs, today called unilateralism.

Some historians have interpreted Washington's call for an end to partisan strife as the statement of a man who focused on the good of the whole. But given the impending presidential election, the Farewell Address appears as an attack on the Republican opposition. Washington advocated unity behind the Federalist banner. Both Federalists and Republicans saw themselves as the true heirs of the Revolution and regarded their opponents as misguided, unpatriotic troublemakers.

Election of 1796

The presidential election of 1796 saw the first serious contest for the position. Federalists in Congress put forward Vice President John Adams, with the diplomat Thomas Pinckney as his running mate. Congressional Republicans chose Thomas Jefferson as their presidential candidate; the lawyer, Revolutionary War veteran, and politician Aaron Burr of New York agreed to run for vice president.

In most states, legislatures appointed electors, and the method of voting in the electoral college did not account for the possibility of party slates. The Constitution's drafters had not foreseen the development of competing political organizations, so there was no way to support one person for president and another for vice president. The electors voted for two people. The man with the highest total became president; the second highest, vice president.

This proved to be the Federalists' undoing. Adams won the presidency with seventy-one votes, but Thomas Jefferson won sixty-eight votes, nine more than Pinckney, to become vice president. The incoming administration was thus politically divided. The president and vice president, once allies, eventually became enemies.

JOHN ADAMS AND POLITICAL DISSENT

As president, John Adams never abandoned the outdated notion that the president should be above politics and factionalism. Thus Adams kept Washington's cabinet intact, despite its key members' allegiance to his chief Federalist rival, Alexander Hamilton. Adams was often passive, letting others (usually Hamilton) lead when he should have. But Adams's detachment did enable him to weather the greatest international crisis yet: the Quasi-War with France.

XYZ Affair

The Jay Treaty improved America's relationship with Great Britain, but it provoked the French government to retaliate by ordering its ships to seize American vessels carrying British goods. In response, Congress authorized ship building and stockpiling weapons and ammunition. President Adams also sent three commissioners to Paris to negotiate a settlement. For months, the commissioners sought talks with Talleyrand, the French foreign minister, but Talleyrand's agents demanded a bribe of $250,000 first. The Americans refused. Adams informed Congress of the impasse and recommended increases in defense appropriations.

Convinced that Adams deliberately sabotaged negotiations, congressional Republicans insisted that the commissioners' reports be turned over to Congress.

Adams complied, aware that releasing these dispatches would work to his advantage. He withheld only the names of French agents, referring to them as X, Y, and Z. The revelation that the Americans were treated with contempt stimulated anti-French sentiment in the United States. Cries for war resounded. Congress abrogated the Treaty of Alliance and authorized American ships to seize French vessels.

Quasi-War with France   Thus began an undeclared war with France fought in Caribbean waters between warships of the U.S. Navy and French privateers. Although Americans initially suffered heavy merchant shipping losses, by early 1799 the U.S. Navy established its superiority. Its ships captured eight French privateers and naval vessels, easing the threat to America's Caribbean trade.

The Republicans, who opposed war and sympathized with France, could not quell anti-French feelings. Because Agent Y boasted of a "French party in America," Federalists accused Republicans of traitorous designs. A New York newspaper declared that anyone who remained "lukewarm" after reading the XYZ dispatches "must have a soul black enough to be fit for treason Strategems and spoils."

Alien and Sedition Acts   Now that the country seemed to see the truth of what Federalists argued since the Whiskey Rebellion in 1794—that Republicans were subversive foreign agents—Federalists sought to codify that belief into law. In 1798 the Federalist-controlled Congress adopted four laws known as the Alien and Sedition Acts, intended to suppress dissent and prevent the growth of the Republican faction.

Three of the acts targeted recent immigrants, whom Federalists accurately suspected of having Republican sympathies. The Naturalization Act lengthened the residency period required for citizenship and ordered resident aliens to register with the federal government. The two Alien Acts provided for the detention of enemy aliens in wartime and gave the president authority to deport any alien he deemed dangerous to national security.

The fourth statute, the Sedition Act, outlawed conspiracies to prevent enforcement of federal laws, punishable with five years in prison and a $5,000 fine. And writing, printing, or uttering "false, scandalous and malicious" statements against the government or the president "with intent to defame . . . or to bring them or either of them, into contempt or disrepute" became a crime punishable by up to two years' imprisonment and a fine of $2,000. Today, laws punishing speech alone would be unconstitutional. But in the eighteenth century, when organized political opposition was suspect, many Americans supported the Sedition Act's free speech restrictions. The Sedition Act led to fifteen indictments and ten convictions, including one congressman, Matthew Lyons of Vermont, and several outspoken Republican newspaper editors. One was James Callender, a Scots immigrant and scandalmonger, who relentlessly attacked Federalists while being subsidized by Thomas Jefferson. Callender's exposé forced Alexander Hamilton to admit to an extramarital affair. After turning his attention to President Adams, Callender was convicted, fined, and jailed for nine months, but he continued to produce pro-Jeffersonian writings from the Richmond prison.

Virginia and Kentucky Resolutions

Faced with prosecutions of their allies, Jefferson and Madison sought to combat the acts. Petitioning the Federalist-controlled Congress to repeal the laws would fail. Furthermore, Federalist judges refused to allow accused individuals to question the Sedition Act's constitutionality. Accordingly, the Republican leaders turned to the state legislatures. Concealing their role to avoid being indicted for sedition, Jefferson and Madison drafted resolutions that were introduced into the Kentucky and Virginia legislatures in the fall of 1798. Because a compact among the states created the Constitution, the resolutions contended, people speaking through their states had a right to judge the constitutionality of federal measures. Both pronounced the Alien and Sedition Acts unconstitutional, and thus advanced the doctrine later known as nullification.

Although they stood alone, the Virginia and Kentucky Resolutions had considerable influence. First, they rallied Republican opinion nationwide and placed the opposition party in the revolutionary tradition of resistance to tyrannical authority. Second, the theory of union that they proposed inspired the Hartford Convention of 1814 and southern states' rights advocates in the 1830s and thereafter. Jefferson and Madison identified a key constitutional issue: How far could states go in opposing the national government? The question would not be definitively answered until the Civil War.

Convention of 1800

Federalists split over France. Hamilton and his supporters called for a declaration legitimizing the undeclared naval war. Adams, though, received private signals—among them George Logan's report—that the French government regretted its treatment of the American commissioners.

Adams dispatched William Vans Murray as envoy to Paris to negotiate with Napoleon Bonaparte, France's new leader. The United States sought compensation for ships the French had seized since 1793 and abrogation of the treaty of 1778. The Convention of 1800, which ended the Quasi-War, provided the latter but not the former. Still, it freed the United States to follow the independent diplomatic course Washington urged in his Farewell Address.

THE WEST IN THE NEW NATION

By the end of the eighteenth century, the nation added three states (Vermont, Kentucky, and Tennessee) and more than 1 million people to the nearly 4 million in the 1790 census. It also nominally controlled the land east of the Mississippi River and north of Spanish Florida. Control of the land north of the Ohio River was achieved only after considerable bloodshed, for the land was dominated by a powerful western confederacy of eight Indian nations led by the Miamis.

War in the Northwest Territory

General Arthur St. Clair, first governor of the Northwest Territory, tried to open more land to settlement through treaty negotiations with the western confederacy in early 1789, but negotiations failed. Subsequently, Little Turtle, the confederacy's war

The two chief antagonists at the Battle of Fallen Timbers and negotiators of the Treaty of Greenville (1795). On the left, Little Turtle, the leader of the Miami Confederacy; on the right, General Anthony Wayne. Little Turtle, in a copy of a portrait painted two years later, appears to be wearing a miniature of Wayne on a bear-claw necklace.
(Left: Chicago History Museum / Chicago Historical Society / Neg #ICHi-35980 / Painter, Ralph Dille; right: Independence National Historic Park)

chief, defeated forces led by General Josiah Harmar (1790) and by St. Clair (1791) in battles near the present Indiana and Ohio border. More than six hundred of St. Clair's men died, and more were wounded, in the United States' worst defeat in frontier history.

In 1793 the Miami Confederacy declared that peace would come only if the United States recognized the Ohio River as its northwestern boundary. But the national government refused. A reorganized army under the Revolutionary War hero General Anthony Wayne defeated the confederacy in August 1794 at the Battle of Fallen Timbers (near present-day Toledo, Ohio).

In August 1795, Wayne and the Miami Confederacy agreed to the Treaty of Greenville. The United States gained the right to settle much of what would become Ohio. Indians received the acknowledgment they long sought: the United States accepted the principle of Indian sovereignty, by virtue of residence, over lands native peoples had not ceded. Never again would the U.S. government claim that it acquired Indian territory solely through negotiation with a European or North American country.

Pinckney's Treaty with Spain that year established the 31st parallel as the boundary between the United States and Florida. Spanish influence in the Old Southwest raised questions about the loyalty of American settlers in the region, much of it still unceded and occupied by Creeks, Cherokees, and other Indians. A Southwest Ordinance (1790) attempted to organize the territory; by permitting slavery, it made the region attractive to slaveholders.

"Civilizing" the Indians Increasingly, even Indian peoples came within the orbit of U.S. influence. The nation's stated goal was to "civilize" them. Henry Knox, Washington's secretary of war, contended in 1789, the government should "impart our knowledge of cultivation and the arts to the aboriginals of the country." The first step, Knox suggested, should be to introduce Indians to "a love for exclusive property" by giving livestock to individual Indians. The Indian Trade and Intercourse Act of 1793 codified Knox's plan, promising that the federal government would supply Indians with animals, agricultural implements, and instructors.

The plan incorrectly posited that Indians' traditional commitment to communal landowning could be overcome, and it ignored their centuries-long agricultural experience. Policymakers focused on Indian men: because they hunted, male Indians were "savages" who should be "civilized" by learning to farm. That women traditionally farmed was irrelevant because, to officials, Indian women—like those of European descent—should confine themselves to child rearing, household chores, and home manufacturing.

Iroquois and Cherokees The Iroquois Confederacy was devastated by the war. Restricted to small reservations increasingly surrounded by Anglo-American farmlands in the 1790s, men could no longer hunt and often spent their days in idle carousing. Quaker missionaries started a demonstration farm among the Senecas to teach men to plow, but women showed greater interest. The same was true among the Cherokees of Georgia. As their southern hunting territories were reduced, Cherokee men did begin to raise cattle and hogs, but they startled reformers by treating livestock like wild game, allowing the animals to run free and shooting them when needed. Men also started to plow fields, although women continued to handle cultivation and harvest.

Iroquois men became more receptive to the Quakers' lessons after the spring of 1799, when a Seneca named Handsome Lake experienced a series of visions. Like earlier prophets, Handsome Lake preached that Indian peoples should renounce alcohol, gambling, and other destructive European customs. He directed followers to reorient men's and women's work assignments as the Quakers advocated, as he recognized that only by adopting this European sexual division of labor could the Iroquois retain an autonomous existence.

"REVOLUTIONS" AT THE END OF THE CENTURY

Three events at the end of the eighteenth century were real or potential revolutions: Fries's Rebellion, Gabriel's Rebellion, and the election of Thomas Jefferson. Each mirrored the tensions and uncertainties of the young republic. The Fries rebels resisted national authority to tax. Gabriel and his followers challenged the slave system crucial to the Chesapeake economy. And the venomous presidential election of 1800 exposed a structural flaw in the Constitution that had to be corrected.

Fries's Rebellion

The tax resistance movement named for Revolutionary War veteran John Fries arose in Pennsylvania's Lehigh Valley in 1798–1799 among German American farmers. To finance the Quasi-War, Congress enacted taxes on land, houses, and legal documents. German Americans, imbued with revolutionary ideals (at least two-fifths were veterans like Fries), regarded the taxes as a threat to their liberties and livelihoods. Asserting their right to resist unconstitutional laws, they raised liberty poles, signed petitions to Congress, and nonviolently prevented assessors from evaluating their homes.

A federal judge ordered the arrest of twenty resisters. In response, in March 1799 Fries led 120 militiamen to Bethlehem, where they surrounded the tavern temporarily housing the prisoners. Fearing a violent confrontation, a federal marshal eventually let the men go. Fries and many of his neighbors were arrested and tried; he and two others were convicted of treason; thirty-two more, of violating the Sedition Act. Although Fries and the other "traitors" were sentenced to hang, Adams pardoned them two days before their scheduled execution, concluding they were rioters rather than traitors. But the region's residents remained Republican partisans.

Gabriel's Rebellion

Like their white compatriots, African Americans became familiar with concepts of liberty and equality during the Revolution. They, too, witnessed the benefits of fighting collectively for freedom. Buoyed by news of the successful slave revolt in St. Domingue in 1793, Gabriel, an enslaved Virginia blacksmith, planned the second end-of-the-century revolution.

For months, Gabriel visited Sunday services at black Baptist and Methodist congregations, where bondspeople gathered free of their owners. Gabriel first recruited other skilled African Americans who like himself lived in semifreedom with minimal supervision. Next he enlisted rural slaves. The rebels planned to attack Richmond on the night of August 30, 1800, set fire to the city, seize the state capitol, and capture the governor, James Monroe. At that point, Gabriel believed, other slaves and perhaps poor whites would join in.

Heavy rain forced a postponement. Several planters then learned of the plot. Gabriel avoided arrest for weeks, but militia troops apprehended and interrogated other rebel leaders. Twenty-six rebels, including Gabriel, were hanged. Ironically, only slaves who betrayed their fellows won freedom as a result of the rebellion.

At his trial, one of Gabriel's followers told his judges that, like George Washington, "I have adventured my life in endeavouring to obtain the liberty of my countrymen, and am a willing sacrifice in their cause." Southern state legislatures responded by increasing the severity of slavery laws. Talk of emancipation ceased in the South, and slavery became more firmly entrenched.

Election of 1800

The third end-of-the-century revolution was a Republican takeover—the election of Thomas Jefferson as president and a Congress dominated by Republicans. Prior to November 1800, Federalists and Republicans campaigned for congressional seats and maneuvered to control the electoral college. Both sides wanted to avoid reproducing the divided results of 1796. Republicans again nominated Thomas

Haitian Refugees

Less than a decade after winning independence, the United States confronted its first immigration crisis when in 1789 a slave rebellion broke out in the French colony of St. Domingue (later Haiti). Among the approximately 600,000 residents of St. Domingue in the early 1790s were about 100,000 free people, almost all slaveowners; half were whites, the rest mulattos. When in the wake of the French Revolution those free mulattos sought greater social and political equality, slaves seized the opportunity to revolt. By 1793 they triumphed, led by former slave Toussaint L'Ouverture. In 1804 they ousted the French, establishing the republic of Haiti. Thousands of whites and mulattos, accompanied by as many slaves as they could transport, sought asylum in the United States.

American political leaders feared the consequences of the refugees' arrival. Southern plantation owners worried that slaves so familiar with ideas of freedom and equality would mingle with their bondspeople. Many were uncomfortable with the immigration of numerous free people of color. Most southern states adopted laws forbidding the entry of Haitian slaves and free mulattos, but they were difficult to enforce, as was a similar congressional act. More than 15,000 refugees—white, black, and of mixed-race origins—flooded into the United States and Spanish Louisiana. Many ended up in Virginia or the cities of Charleston, Savannah, and New Orleans.

In New Orleans and Charleston, the influx of mulattos aroused a heightened color consciousness that placed light-skinned people at the top of a hierarchy of people of color. After the United States purchased Louisiana in 1803, the number of free people of color there almost doubled in three years, largely because of a final surge of immigration from Haiti. In Virginia, the revolt inspired local slaves in 1800 to plan the incident now known as Gabriel's Rebellion.

The Haitian refugees thus linked European and African Americans to events in the West Indies.

A free woman of color in Louisiana early in the nineteenth century, possibly one of the refugees from Haiti. Esteban Rodriguez Miró, named governor of Spanish Louisiana in 1782, ordered all slave and free black women to wear head wraps rather than hats—which were reserved for whites—but this woman and many others subverted his order by nominally complying, but nevertheless creating elaborate headdresses.

(Louisiana State Museum)

Dissent During Wartime

The Quasi-War with France in 1798 and 1799 brought the first attempt to suppress dissent. By criminalizing dissenting speech, the Sedition Act of 1798 tried to quiet Republicans' criticism of the war and President John Adams. Fifteen men (including a congressman) were fined and jailed after being convicted under the statute's provisions.

Although Americans might assume that their right to free speech under the First Amendment, now more fully accepted than two centuries ago, protects dissenters during wartime, history suggests otherwise. Every conflict has stimulated efforts by government and individuals to suppress dissenters. During the Civil War, the Union jailed civilian Confederate sympathizers; during the First World War, the government deported immigrant aliens who too vocally criticized the war effort. World War II brought the silencing of isolationists' voices, denying those who opposed American entry into the war public outlets for their ideas.

Americans remain divided over whether the proper course of action during the Vietnam War of the 1960s and 1970s was dissent from, or acquiescence to, government policy. The USA PATRIOT Act, adopted after the September 11, 2001, attacks, removed long-standing restrictions on federal government surveillance of citizens, controversially granting access to library records. Criticism of the Iraq war has raised heated questions: Do newspapers that publish classified information or pictures of abused prisoners overstep their bounds? Can a political figure censure the conduct of the war without seeming unpatriotic?

Freedom of speech is never easy to maintain, and wartime conditions make it harder. When the nation comes under attack, many patriotic Americans argue that dissent should cease. Others contend that people must always have the right to speak freely. Events in the United States since the 9/11 attacks suggest that this legacy remains contentious for the American people.

Jefferson and Aaron Burr; Federalists named John Adams, with Charles Cotesworth Pinckney of South Carolina as vice president. Jefferson and Burr tied with 73 votes, while Adams had 64 and Pinckney 63. Under Article II, Section 1, of the Constitution, the election had to be decided in the existing House of Representatives.

Balloting continued for six days and thirty-five ballots, with Federalists uniformly supporting Burr, and Republicans holding for Jefferson. Finally, James Bayard, a Federalist and the sole congressman from Delaware, brokered a deal that gave Jefferson the presidency on the thirty-sixth ballot. A crucial consequence of the election was the adoption of the Twelfth Amendment, which provided that electors would henceforth cast separate ballots for president and vice president.

The defeated Federalists turned to strengthening their hold on the judiciary. President Adams named his secretary of state, John Marshall, chief justice; Marshall would serve for thirty-four years, leaving a lasting imprint on constitutional interpretation. Adams spent his last hours in office on March 3, 1801, appointing so-called midnight justices to new positions created in the hastily adopted Judiciary Act of 1801, which also reduced the number of Supreme Court justices from six to five. The fiercely partisan Federalists thus hoped to prevent Jefferson from exerting immediate influence on the judicial branch, despite Republican control of the presidency and Congress.

Summary

The first eleven years of government under the Constitution established many enduring precedents for congressional, presidential, and judicial action—among them the establishment of the cabinet, interpretations of key clauses of the Constitution, and stirrings of judicial review of state and federal legislation. Building on successful negotiations with Spain (Pinckney's Treaty), Britain (the Jay Treaty), and France (the Convention of 1800), the United States developed its diplomatic independence.

Yet the 1790s spawned debates over foreign and domestic policy and saw the beginnings of organized factionalism and grassroots politicking, if not yet formal parties. The Whiskey and Fries Rebellions showed that regional conflicts persisted. The waging of an undeclared war against France proved extremely contentious. In 1801, the Jeffersonian ideal of agrarian, decentralized republicanism prevailed over Alexander Hamilton's vision of a powerful centralized economy and strong national government.

Chapter Review

BUILDING A WORKABLE GOVERNMENT

What was the purpose behind the Bill of Rights?

Even after the Constitution was ratified, leaders recognized that tensions still existed over a strong national government versus. the rights of states. While nationalism prevailed, James Madison and others thought that Congress should not ignore amendments proposed in state ratifying conventions that sought to safeguard the rights of the people. As such, he introduced nineteen amendments—ten of which the states ratified—that were added to the Constitution as the Bill of Rights on December 15, 1791. Adopting the Bill of Rights eased Antifederalist concerns about the unwieldy power of the central government and its potential to tyrannize or oppress the people.

DOMESTIC POLICY UNDER WASHINGTON AND HAMILTON

How did the chartering of the Bank of the United States provoke an early constitutional debate?

Treasury Secretary Alexander Hamilton asked Congress to charter a national bank, modeled on England's, which would act as a collecting and disbursing agent for the treasury and the source for national currency. Congress was unsure if the Constitution gave it the power to set up a bank. Some, like Madison and Jefferson, took a strict-constructionist interpretation of the Constitution, arguing that it allowed Congress only to make laws deemed "necessary"—not merely what was desirable. Hamilton took a broad-constructionist view, stating that Congress could use any means not prohibited by the Constitution to achieve a constitutional end. President Washington agreed, and the bill establishing the Bank of the United States became law.

THE FRENCH REVOLUTION AND THE DEVELOPMENT OF PARTISAN POLITICS

Why did U.S. leaders find the rise of political factions disturbing?

In the new republic, leaders had not yet come to understand or embrace dissent as a natural part of democratic government. Factions were seen as linked to monarchies and deemed a sign of corruption in republics. That explains why Washington tried to smooth over discord when Jefferson and Madison critiqued treasury secretary Alexander Hamilton's policies for favoring commercial interests over agriculture. Both sides accused the other of trying to subvert republican principles or destroy the new republic. Similarly, when dozens of Democratic Societies sprang up in the 1790s to protect people's liberties from corrupt rulers, Washington and Hamilton feared their rapid growth as subversive and dangerous.

PARTISAN POLITICS AND RELATIONS WITH GREAT BRITAIN

What fueled the growing partisanship in the new republic at the end of the eighteenth century?

Several different factors divided people and leaders. Debates over who the true patriots were fueled some discord, as did growing differences between agrarian and commercial interests. Republicans optimistically put their faith in the nation's future prosperity, enticing southerners, small farmers, and artisans to ally with them. Federalists, on the other hand, were often New England merchants who sought order and organized authority. Federalists also thought an ongoing alliance with Great Britain would protect their interests from internal and external enemies.

JOHN ADAMS AND POLITICAL DISSENT

What was the underlying purpose of the Alien and Sedition Acts of 1798?

Adopted by the Federalist-controlled Congress, these acts were designed to suppress dissent—still seen as dangerous and subversive rather than a natural part of a republic—and weaken the competing Republican faction. Hence, the acts targeted recent immigrants, typically Republican supporters, by lengthening the residency requirement for citizenship among other rules, as well as allowing the president to detain or deport any alien considered dangerous to national security. The Sedition Act outlawed antigovernment conspiracies and curbed free speech by making the writing or uttering of false or scandalous statements against the government illegal. Both acts enabled Federalists to weaken, silence, and ultimately indict those with whom they disagreed.

THE WEST IN THE NEW NATION

How did the new nation begin to expand its boundaries westward?

The United States controlled the land east of the Mississippi and north of Spanish Florida, and later, through warfare and treaty, managed to extend its northernmost boundary to the Ohio River. Initially, leaders attempted to negotiate for the land; when that failed, war with eight Indian nations ensued, culminating in 1795 with the Treaty of Greenville. This agreement allowed the United States to settle most of what would become Ohio in exchange for acknowledging the principle of Indian sovereignty—by virtue of residence—over lands that had not been ceded.

"REVOLUTIONS" AT THE END OF THE CENTURY

What gave rise to new potential revolutions in America at the end of the eighteenth century?

Three events revealed unresolved issues—and growing tensions—in the new republic. First, Fries's Rebellion questioned the power of the central government to tax, seeing it—much as early revolutionaries had—as a threat to personal liberties and livelihoods. Second, Gabriel's Rebellion of semifree blacks sought to challenge the slave system in the Chesapeake (but ended up inspiring stricter slave laws in the South). And finally the hotly contested 1800 presidential election revealed a structural flaw in the Constitution that would need to be addressed for the new nation to survive. It led to the Twelfth Amendment, which provided that electors cast separate ballots for presidential and vice presidential candidates.

SUGGESTIONS FOR FURTHER READING

Joyce Appleby, *Capitalism and a New Social Order: The Republican Vision of the 1790s* (1984)

Douglas Egerton, *Gabriel's Rebellion: The Virginia Slave Conspiracies of 1800 and 1802* (1993)

Stanley Elkins and Eric McKitrick, *The Age of Federalism, 1788–1800* (1993)

Joseph J. Ellis, *Founding Brothers: The Revolutionary Generation* (2000)

Ronald Hoffman and Peter J. Albert, eds., *Launching the "Extended Republic": The Federalist Era* (1998)

James Horn, Jan Ellen Lewis, and Peter S. Onuf, eds., *The Revolution of 1800: Democracy, Race, and the New Republic* (2002)

Thomas P. Slaughter, *The Whiskey Rebellion* (1986)

Defining the Nation | 1801–1823

E ager to stand apart from the allegedly aristocratic ways of his Federalist predecessors, President Thomas Jefferson displayed impatience for ceremony. But on his first New Year's Day in office, he awaited the presentation of a tribute to his commitment, as one gift's bearer put it, to "defend Republicanism and baffle all the arts of Aristocracy." Crafted in Massachusetts, the belated inaugural gift weighed more than twelve hundred pounds and measured four feet in diameter, bearing the inscription "THE GREATEST CHEESE IN AMERICA— FOR THE GREATEST MAN IN AMERICA."

The mammoth cheese was born the previous July and made by the "Ladies" of Cheshire, Massachusetts, a farming community as resolutely Jeffersonian-Republican as it was Baptist. As members of a religious minority in New England, where Congregationalists dominated the pulpits and statehouses, the Cheshire Baptists celebrated a president whose vision featured both agrarianism and separation of church and state.

Federalist editors said the mammoth cheese's semi-rotten, maggot-infested condition on delivery symbolized the nation under Republican rule. Its existence and size resulted from the excesses of democracy, in which even women and backwoods preachers had roles. Federalists' derision of the mammoth cheese may have backfired, inspiring additional showy expressions of democratic pride. A Philadelphia baker sold Mammoth Bread, while in Washington, a Mammoth Eater consumed forty-two eggs in ten minutes. Two years later, in 1804, a mammoth loaf was served in the Capitol building to a crowd of Federalist-disparaging Republicans, including President Jefferson. Behind such symbolism lay serious political ideologies. Jeffersonsians believed that virtue derived from agricultural endeavors. They thus delighted in the acquisition of the Louisiana Territory, but

This icon will direct you to interactive activities and study materials on A People And A Nation, Brief Edition website: **www.cengage.com/history/norton/ peoplenationbrief8e**

Chronology

1801	Marshall becomes chief justice of the United States.
	Jefferson is inaugurated as first Democratic-Republican president.
1801–05	United States defeats the Barbary states in Tripoli War.
1803	*Marbury v. Madison* establishes judicial review.
	United States purchases the Louisiana Territory from France.
1804	Burr kills Hamilton in a duel.
	Jefferson is reelected president, Clinton vice president.
1804–06	Lewis and Clark explore the Louisiana Territory.
1805	Tenskwatawa emerges as a Shawnee leader.
1807	*Chesapeake* affair almost leads to war with Great Britain.
	Embargo Act halts foreign trade.
1808	Congress bans the importation of slaves to the United States.
	Madison is elected president, Clinton vice president.
1808–13	Tenskwatawa and Tecumseh organize Native American resistance.
1808–15	Embargoes and the War of 1812 secure American sovereignty and stimulate economic development.
1811	Work begins on the federally financed National Road from Cumberland, Maryland, to Wheeling, Virginia.
1812	Madison is reelected president, Gerry vice president.
1812–15	United States and Great Britain fight the War of 1812.
1813	Death of Tecumseh ends effective pan-Indian resistance.
	Boston Manufacturing Company starts a textile mill in Waltham, Massachusetts.
1814	Jackson's defeat of the Red Stick Creeks at the Battle of Horseshoe Bend begins Indian removal from the South.
	Treaty of Ghent ends the War of 1812.
1814–15	Hartford Convention undermines the Federalists.
1815	Battle of New Orleans makes Jackson a national hero.
	First upriver voyage on the Mississippi River by a steamboat occurs.
1815-17	United States experiences a postwar economic boom and Congress-led economic nationalism.
1817	Rush-Bagot Treaty limits British and American naval forces on Lake Champlain and the Great Lakes.
1817–25	The New York State–funded Erie Canal is constructed.
1819	*McCulloch v. Maryland* establishes the supremacy of federal over state law.
	Adams-Onís Treaty with Spain gives Florida to the United States and defines the Louisiana territorial border.
	Missouri applies for statehood with a constitution permitting slavery.
	Financial panic occurs when the Second Bank of the United States calls in debts.
1819–early 20s	United States undergoes its first major depression.
1820–21	Missouri Compromise lays out the rules governing the admission of future slave states carved from the Louisiana Territory.
1823	Monroe Doctrine declares that European nations should stay out of American affairs and that the United States will stay out of European conflicts that do not occur in the Americas.

efforts to expand their agriculturally based "empire of liberty" westward were resisted by Native Americans and their European allies, and sometimes by Federalists. With the War of 1812, the United States began its expansion west. Although that war ended with few issues resolved, it had profound consequences for American development. It secured the United States' status as a sovereign nation, opened up the West for settlement by European Americans and their slaves, and helped spur revolutions in transportation and industry.

Contemporary observers described postwar nationalism as an Era of Good Feelings, but when economic boom turned to bust, nationalistic optimism and unity faded. No issue proved more divisive than slavery in the West, as Missouri's petition to be admitted to the Union revealed.

- **What characterized the two main competing visions for national development?**
- **How did America's relationship with Europe influence political and economic developments?**
- **In what ways did nonvoting Americans—most blacks, women, and Native Americans—take part in defining the new nation?**

POLITICAL VISIONS

In his inaugural address, Jefferson appealed to the electorate not as party members but as citizens with common beliefs: "We are all republicans, we are all federalists. . . . A wise and frugal government, which shall restrain men from injuring one another, which shall leave them free to regulate their pursuits of industry and improvement, and shall not take from the mouth of labor the bread it had earned. This is the sum of good government."

Outgoing president John Adams had already left Washington and did not hear Jefferson's call for unity. Former friends, the two men now disliked each other intensely. Despite Jefferson's inaugural address, the Democratic-Republicans—as the Republicans of the 1790s called themselves—and the Federalists bitterly differed on how society and government should be organized. The Federalists advocated a strong national government to promote economic development. The Democratic-Republicans believed that limited government would foster republican virtue. Nearly two decades later, Jefferson would refer to his election as "the revolution of 1800."

This portrait of President Thomas Jefferson was painted by Rembrandt Peale in 1805. Charles Willson Peale (Rembrandt's father) and his five sons helped establish the reputation of American art in the new nation. Rembrandt Peale achieved fame for his presidential portraits; here he has captured Jefferson in a noble pose without the usual symbols of office or power, befitting the Republican age.   (© Collection of The New-York Historical Society)

Separation of Church and State

In part, the mammoth cheese represented Cheshire farmers' gratitude for Jefferson's commitment to the separation of church and state. A core component of his vision of limited government, Jefferson believed that the Constitution's First Amendment supported a "wall of separation between church and state" and that "religion is a matter which lies solely between Man & his God." New England Baptists hailed Jefferson as a hero, but New England Federalists' worst fears were confirmed. During the election of 1800, Federalists waged a venomous campaign against Jefferson, incorrectly labeling him an atheist. Their rhetoric proved so effective that some New England women hid their Bibles in gardens and wells to foil Democratic-Republicans allegedly bent on confiscating them.

Jefferson took office during a period of religious revivalism, particularly among Methodists and Baptists, whose democratic preaching—all humans, they said, were equal in God's eyes—fed into a growing democratic political culture. Thus, the Cheshire Baptists informed the president that their cheese was made "without a single slave to assist."

Political Mobilization

The revolution of 1800, which gave the Democratic-Republicans majorities in both houses of Congress and the presidency, resulted from an electorate that was limited largely to property-holding men. Under the Constitution, states regulated voting. Nowhere but in New Jersey could women vote, a right granted inadvertently and later revoked. In 1800 free black men who met property qualifications could vote in all states but Delaware, Georgia, South Carolina, and Virginia, but local custom often kept them from exercising that right. Candidates rallied support locally on militia training grounds, in taverns and churches, at court gatherings, and during holiday celebrations. Voters and nonvoters expressed their views by marching in parades, signing petitions, singing, and debating. Perhaps most important, they devoured a growing print culture of pamphlets, broadsides (posters), almanacs, and newspapers.

The Partisan Press

Read aloud in taverns, artisans' workshops, and homes, newspapers gave national importance to local events. In 1800 the nation had 260 newspapers; by 1810 it had 396, virtually all of which were unabashedly partisan.

The parties adopted official organs. After his election, Jefferson persuaded the *National Intelligencer* to move from Philadelphia to Washington, where it became the voice of the Democratic-Republicans. In 1801 Alexander Hamilton launched the *New-York Evening Post* to promote Federalists. Published six or seven times a week, party papers helped feed the growing obsession with partisan politics.

Limited Government

To bring into his administration men who shared his vision of individual liberty, an agrarian republic, and limited government, Jefferson rejected appointments that Adams made during his final days as president and dismissed Federalist customs collectors. He awarded vacant treasury and judicial offices to Republicans. Jefferson, his cabinet, and Congress worked to make the government leaner. If Alexander Hamilton viewed national debt as the engine of economic growth, Jefferson saw it as the source of government corruption. Secretary of the Treasury Albert Gallatin halved the army budget and reduced the 1802 navy budget by two-thirds. He moved to decrease the national debt from $83 million to $57 million, and retire it altogether by 1817. Jefferson closed two of five diplomatic missions abroad, at The Hague and in Berlin. And the Democratic-Republican–controlled Congress oversaw the repeal of all internal taxes, including the despised whiskey tax of 1791.

Along with frugality, ideas of liberty distinguished Democratic-Republicans from Federalists. Opposition to the Alien and Sedition Acts of 1798 united

Republicans. Jefferson now declined to use the acts against opponents and pardoned those convicted under the provisions. Congress let the Sedition Act expire in 1801 and the Alien Act in 1802. Congress also repealed the Naturalization Act of 1798, which required fourteen years of residency for citizenship. The 1802 act that replaced it required five years of residency, loyalty to the Constitution, and the forsaking of foreign allegiances and titles. It would remain the basis of naturalized American citizenship into the twentieth century.

Judicial Politics

To many Democratic-Republicans, the judiciary represented a centralizing and undemocratic force, since judges were appointed rather than elected and served for life. At Jefferson's prompting, the House impeached (indicted) and the Senate convicted Federal District Judge John Pickering of New Hampshire, whose alleged alcoholism made him an easy mark. The House impeached Supreme Court Justice Samuel Chase for judicial misconduct in 1803. A staunch Federalist, Chase pushed for prosecutions under the Sedition Act, campaigned for Adams in 1800, and denounced Jefferson's administration. But Democratic-Republicans failed to muster the two-thirds Senate majority necessary for conviction. The failure to remove Chase preserved the Court's independence and established the precedent that criminal actions, not political disagreements, justified impeachment.

The Marshall Court

Although Jefferson appointed three new Supreme Court justices, the Court remained a Federalist stronghold under his distant cousin John Marshall. Even after Democratic-Republicans achieved a majority of Court seats in 1811, Marshall remained influential as chief justice (1801–1835). Under Marshall, the Supreme Court consistently upheld federal supremacy over the states while protecting the interests of commerce and capital.

Marshall made the Court an equal branch of government. Previously regarded lightly, judicial service became a coveted honor for talented men. Marshall strengthened the Court by having it speak with a unified voice; rather than issuing individual concurring judgments, justices now issued joint majority opinions. From 1801 through 1805, Marshall wrote twenty-four of the Court's twenty-six decisions; through 1810 he wrote 85 percent of the opinions.

Judicial Review

In his last hours in office, Adams named the Federalist William Marbury as justice of the peace in the District of Columbia. Jefferson's secretary of state, James Madison, declined to certify the appointment, so the new president could appoint a Democratic-Republican. Marbury sued for a writ of mandamus (a court order forcing the president to appoint him). If the Supreme Court ruled in Marbury's favor in *Marbury v. Madison,* the president probably would not comply, and the Court had no means to make him. Yet, if the Federalist-dominated bench refused to issue the writ, it would hand the Democratic-Republicans a victory.

Marshall recast the issue to avoid both pitfalls. He ruled that Marbury had a right to his appointment but that the Supreme Court could not compel Madison to honor it because the Constitution did not grant the Court power to issue a writ of mandamus. Without any specific mention in the Constitution, Marshall ruled, the section of the Judiciary Act of 1789 that authorized the Court to issue writs was unconstitutional. Thus the Supreme Court denied itself the power to issue writs of mandamus but established its far greater power to judge the constitutionality of laws. In doing so, Marshall fashioned the theory of judicial review. Because the Constitution was "the supreme law of the land," Marshall wrote, any federal or state act contrary to the Constitution must be null and void. This power of the Supreme Court to determine the constitutionality of legislation and presidential acts enhanced the independence of the judiciary and breathed life into the Constitution.

Election of 1804

In the first election after the Twelfth Amendment's ratification, Jefferson dropped Burr as his running mate and, to have a North-South balance, chose George Clinton of New York. They swamped their opponents—South Carolinian Charles Cotesworth Pinckney and New Yorker Rufus King—in the electoral college by 162 votes to 14, carrying fifteen of the seventeen states.

That 1804 election escalated animosity between Burr and Hamilton, who supported Burr's rival in the New York gubernatorial election. When Hamilton called Burr a liar, Burr challenged him to a duel. Because New York outlawed dueling, the encounter happened in New Jersey. Hamilton decided not to fire, and it cost him his life. New York and New Jersey prosecutors indicted Burr for murder.

Burr fled to the West, where he and Brigadier General James Wilkinson planned to create a new empire by militarily taking what is now Texas and by persuading western territories to leave the United States. Wilkinson, fearful of negative repercussions, revealed the scheme to Jefferson. The president assisted the prosecution in Burr's 1807 trial for treason, which was overseen by Chief Justice Marshall. Prompted by Marshall to use a narrow interpretation of treason, the jury acquitted Burr, who fled to Europe.

NATIONAL EXPANSION WESTWARD

By 1800 hundreds of thousands of white Americans settled in the rich Ohio River and Mississippi River valleys, intruding on Indian lands. In the Northwest they raised foodstuffs, primarily wheat, and in the Southwest they cultivated cotton. During the revolutionary era, cotton production was profitable only for Sea Island planters in South Carolina and Georgia, who grew the long-staple variety. Short-staple cotton, which grew in the interior, was unmarketable because its sticky seeds could be removed only by hand. After the New England inventor Eli Whitney designed a cotton gin in 1793, allowing one person to remove the same number of seeds that previously required fifty people, cultivation of short-staple cotton spread rapidly into Louisiana, Mississippi, Alabama, Arkansas, and Tennessee. The cotton gin greatly increased the demand for slaves, who seeded, tended, and harvested cotton fields.

American settlers depended on free access to the Mississippi River and its Gulf port, New Orleans. "The Mississippi," wrote Secretary of State James Madison, "is to them [western settlers] everything."

Spain, which acquired France's territory west of the Mississippi after the Seven Years' War (1763), secretly transferred it back to France in 1800 and 1801. American officials discovered the transfer only in 1802, when Napoleon seemed poised to re-build a French empire in the New World. American concerns intensified when Spanish officials, on the eve of ceding control to the French, violated Pinckney's treaty by denying Americans the privilege of storing their products at New Orleans prior to transshipment to foreign markets. Western farmers and eastern merchants thought Napoleon had closed the port; they talked war.

To ease the pressure for war and win western farmers' support, Jefferson urged Congress to authorize the call-up of eighty thousand militiamen. He also sent Virginia governor James Monroe to join Robert Livingston in France to buy the port of New Orleans and as much of the Mississippi valley as possible. Arriving in Paris in April 1803, Monroe learned that France had already offered to sell Louisiana to the United States for a mere $15 million. With St. Domingue torn from French control, Napoleon abandoned dreams of a New World empire. He urgently needed money to wage war against Britain. On April 30, Monroe and Livingston signed a treaty buying the 827,000-square-mile territory (see Map 9.1).

The Louisiana Purchase ensured that the United States would control the Mississippi's mouth, pleasing western settlers who relied on the river to market their

Map 9.1   Louisiana Purchase

The Louisiana Purchase (1803) doubled the area of the United States and opened the trans-Mississippi West for American settlement.

goods. It also inspired those who imagined the United States as the nexus of inter-national trade between Europe and Asia. Louisiana promised to fulfill easterners' dreams of cheap, fertile lands. Its vast expanse meant, too, that land could be reserved for Indians displaced by white settlers and their black slaves. But some doubted the purchase's constitutionality, others worried that it belied the Democratic-Republicans' commitment to debt reduction, and some New England Federalists complained that it undermined their commercial interests and threatened the re-public by spreading the population beyond where it could be controlled. Overall, though, the Louisiana Purchase was the most popular achievement of Jefferson's presidency.

Louisiana was not, however, a vast wilderness. When the United States acquired the territory, hundreds of thousands of people living there became American sub-jects, including Native Americans from various nations, as well as people of European and African descent—or, often, a mixture of the two. Around New Orleans, Louisiana's colonial heritage was reflected in its people: creoles of French and Spanish descent; slaves of African descent; free people of color; and Acadians, or Cajuns (descendants of French settlers in eastern Canada), and some Germans and English. The 1810 census reported that 97,000 non-Indians lived in the area. Although Jefferson imagined the West as an "empire of liberty," the free blacks and slaves lost some rights accorded them under French and Spanish law.

Lewis and Clark Expedition

Jefferson had a long-standing interest in the trans-Mississippi West and feared that, if Americans did not claim it, the British, who still controlled present-day Canada and parts of the Pacific Northwest, would. He launched a military-style mission to chart the region's commercial possibilities—its water passages to the Pacific and trading opportunities with Indians—while cataloguing its geography, flora, and fauna.

The expedition, headed by Meriwether Lewis and William Clark, began in May 1804 and lasted for more than two years; it traveled up the Missouri River, across the Rockies, and down the Columbia to the Pacific Ocean—and back. Expedition's mem-bers "discovered" (as they saw it) dozens of previously unknown Indian tribes. Al-though the Corps of Discovery, as the expedition came to be called, was prepared for possible Indian conflict, its goal was peaceable: to foster trade relations, win political allies, and tap into Indians' knowledge of the landscape. Lewis and Clark brought twenty-one bags of gifts for Native American leaders to establish goodwill and stim-ulate interest in trade. Most interactions were cordial, but when Indians were unim-pressed by the gifts, tensions arose.

The Corps of Discovery proved democratic in seating enlisted men on courts-martial and allowing Clark's black slave York and the expedition's female guide and translator, Sacagawea, to vote on where to locate winter quarters in 1805. But, unlike other expedition members, neither York nor Sacagawea drew wages, and when York later demanded his freedom, Clark later wrote to his brother that he gave York "a severe trouncing."

Lewis and Clark failed to discover a Northwest Passage to the Pacific, and the route they mapped across the Rockies proved perilous. But their expedition set the stage for additional government-sponsored exploration.

In their quest for land, white Americans mostly ignored the presence of Native Americans. Although Jefferson displayed more sympathy toward Indians than did many contemporaries—he took interest in their cultures and believed them intellectually equal to whites—he lobbied, unsuccessfully, for a constitutional amendment that would transport them west of the Mississippi into the Louisiana Territory. He became involved in efforts to pressure the Chickasaws to sell their land, and if legal methods failed, he advocated trickery. Traders, he suggested, might run them into debt, which they would have to repay "by a cessation of lands."

Divisions Among Indian Peoples

Some Indian nations adopted white customs as a means of survival and often agreed to sell their lands and move west. These "accommodationists" (or "progressives") were opposed by "traditionalists," who urged adherence to native ways and refused to relinquish their lands. Distinctions between accommodationists and traditionalists were not always so clear-cut, however.

In the early 1800s, two Shawnee brothers, Tenskwatawa (1775–1837) and Tecumseh (1768–1813), led a traditionalist revolt against American encroachment by fostering a pan-Indian federation centered in the Old Northwest and parts of the South. By the 1800s, the Shawnees lost most of their Ohio land, occupying scattered sites there and in the Michigan and Louisiana territories. Despondent, Lalawethika—Tenskwatawa's name as a youth—turned to whiskey and later became a shaman in 1804. When European diseases ravaged his village, he despaired.

Tenskwatawa and Tecumseh

Lalawethika emerged from a battle with illness in 1805 a new man, renamed Tenskwatawa ("The Open Door") or, by whites, the Prophet. Claiming to have died and been resurrected, he traveled in the Ohio River valley as a religious leader, attacking the decline of moral values among Native Americans, warning against whiskey, and condemning intertribal battles. He urged Indians to return to the old ways: to hunt with bows and arrows, not guns; to stop wearing hats; and to give up bread for corn and beans.

By 1808 Tenskwatawa and his older brother Tecumseh talked more about resisting American aggression. They invited all Indians to settle in pan-Indian towns in Indiana, first at Greenville (1806–1808) and then at Prophetstown (1808–1812). This challenged the treaty-making process by denying the claims of Indians who were given the same land under the 1795 Treaty of Greenville. Younger Indians flocked to Tecumseh, the more political of the two brothers.

Convinced that only an Indian federation could stop increasing white settlement, Tecumseh sought to unify northern and southern Indians from Canada to Georgia. Among southern Indians, only one Creek faction welcomed him, but his efforts nonetheless alarmed white settlers and government officials. In November 1811, while Tecumseh was in the South, the Indiana governor William Henry Harrison moved against Tenskwatawa's followers. During the battle of Tippecanoe, the army burned their town; as they fled, the Indians exacted revenge on white settlers. With the stakes raised, Tecumseh entered an alliance with the British. This alliance, along with American neutrality rights on the high seas, propelled the United States toward war with Britain.

THE NATION IN THE ORBIT OF EUROPE

The republic's economy relied heavily on fishing and the carrying trade, in which the American merchant marine transported commodities between nations. Merchants in Boston, Salem, and Philadelphia traded with China, sending cloth and metal to swap for furs with Chinook Indians on the Oregon coast, and then sailing to China to trade for porcelain, tea, and silk. The slave trade lured American ships to Africa. Not long after Jefferson's first inaugural address, the United States was at war with Tripoli—a state along North Africa's Barbary Coast—over a principle that would become a cornerstone of American foreign policy: freedom of the seas. That is, outside national territorial waters, the high seas should be open for free transit.

First Barbary War

In 1801 the bashaw (pasha) of Tripoli declared war on the United States for refusing to pay tribute for safe passage of its ships through the Mediterranean. After two years of stalemate, Jefferson declared a blockade of Tripoli, but when the American frigate *Philadelphia* ran aground in the harbor, its three hundred officers and sailors were imprisoned. Jefferson refused to ransom them, and a small American force accompanied by Arab, Greek, and African mercenaries marched from Egypt to the shores of Tripoli to seize the port of Derne. A treaty ended the war in 1805, but the United States continued to pay tribute to three other Barbary states—Algiers, Morocco, and Tunis—until 1815. In the intervening years, the United States became embroiled in European conflicts.

At first Jefferson distanced the nation from the European turmoil in the wake of the French Revolution. After the Senate ratified the Jay Treaty in 1795, the United States and Great Britain reconciled: Britain withdrew from its western forts on American soil and interfered less in American trade with France. Then, in May 1803, two weeks after Napoleon sold Louisiana to the United States, France was at war against Britain and, later, Britain's allies, Prussia, Austria, and Russia. The United States initially benefited as merchants gained control of most of the West Indian trade. After 1805, however, when Britain defeated French and Spanish fleets at Trafalgar, Britain's Royal Navy tightened its control of the oceans. Two months later, Napoleon crushed the Russian and Austrian armies at Austerlitz. Stalemated, France and Britain launched a commercial war, blockading trade and costing the United States dearly.

Threats to American Sovereignty

To replenish their supply of sailors, British vessels stopped American ships and impressed (forcibly recruited) British deserters, British-born naturalized American seamen, and other sailors suspected of being British. Perhaps six to eight thousand Americans were seized between 1803 and 1812. Alleged deserters—many of them American citizens—faced British courts-martial. Americans saw impressment as an assault on their nation's independence. Americans also resented the British interfering with their West Indian trade and seizing American vessels within U.S. territorial waters.

In April 1806 Congress responded with the Non-Importation Act, barring British manufactured goods from American ports. Because the act exempted most cloth and metal articles, it had little impact on British trade. In November Jefferson suspended the act while the Baltimore lawyer William Pinkney joined James Monroe in London to negotiate a settlement. The treaty they carried home did not mention impressments; hence, the president never submitted it for ratification.

Tense Anglo-American relations came to a head in June 1807 when the USS *Chesapeake*, sailing from Norfolk for the Mediterranean, was stopped by the British frigate *Leopard,* whose officers demanded to search the ship. Refused, the *Leopard* opened fire, killing three Americans and wounding eighteen others. The British then seized four deserters, three of whom held American citizenship; one was hanged. The incident outraged Americans and exposed American military weakness.

The Embargo of 1807

With poor military preparedness, Jefferson responded to the incident with what he called peaceable coercion. In July, the president closed American waters to British warships and increased military and naval expenditures. In December 1807, Jefferson increased economic pressure on Great Britain by invoking the Non-Importation Act, followed by the Embargo Act. The embargo, which forbade all exports from the United States to any country, was designed as a short-term means to avoid war by pressuring Britain and France to respect American rights.

The embargo's biggest economic impact, however, fell on the United States. Exports declined by 80 percent in 1808, squeezing New England shippers and their workers as economic depression set in. Manufacturers fared well as the domestic market became theirs exclusively. Merchants began to shift from shipping to manufacturing. In 1807 there were twenty cotton and woolen mills in New England; by 1813 there were more than two hundred. Merchants willing to engage in smuggling profited enormously.

International Slave Trade

With Jefferson's encouragement, Congress voted in 1807 to abolish the international slave trade as of January 1, 1808—the earliest date permissible under the Constitution. South Carolina alone still allowed the legal importation of slaves, but most of the state's planters favored a ban, fearful of adding to the black population of a state where whites were outnumbered. Congressional debate focused on what should become of Africans imported illegally.

In an effort to win support for measures to end the international slave trade and slavery itself, abolitionists published drawings of the inhumanely cramped slave ships, where each person was allotted a space roughly the size of a coffin. Disease spread rapidly under such conditions, causing many slaves to die before reaching American shores.   (The Huntington Library and Art Collections, San Marino, California)

The final bill provided that smuggled slaves would be sold in accordance with the laws of the state or territory in which they arrived, underscoring that even illegal slaves were property. Had the bill not done so, threatened one Georgia congressman, the result might have been "resistance to the authority of the Government," even civil war.

During the last four months of 1807, sixteen thousand African slaves arrived at Gadsden Wharf in Charleston, where they were detained by merchants eager to wait out the new law's January 1 deadline and net higher prices for their human cargo. Although possibly thousands died in the disease-ridden holding pens before they could be sold, merchants calculated that the increased value of those who survived would outweigh losses. After January 1, 1808, a brisk—and profitable—illegal slave trade took over. In 1819 Congress authorized the president to use force to intercept slave ships along the African coast, but the small American navy could not halt the illicit trade.

Election of 1808

As the 1808 presidential election approached, debate over the embargo heated up. Democratic-Republicans suffered from factional dissent and dissatisfaction in seaboard states hobbled by the trade restrictions. Although nine state legislatures passed resolutions urging Jefferson to run again, the president declined a third term. He supported James Madison, his secretary of state, as the Democratic-Republican candidate. Madison won the endorsement of the party's congressional caucus, and Madison and Clinton headed the ticket. Charles Cotesworth Pinckney and Rufus King again ran on the Federalist ticket.

The younger Federalists, led by Harrison Gray Otis and other Bostonians, played up the widespread disaffection with Democratic-Republican policy, especially the embargo. Pinckney received only forty-seven electoral votes to Madison's 122, but he carried all of New England, except Vermont, and won Delaware. Federalists also gained seats in Congress and captured the New York State legislature. Still, the transition from one Democratic-Republican administration to the next went smoothly.

Women and Politics

Wives eased the transition of newly elected and appointed officials by encouraging political and diplomatic negotiation. This often occurred in social settings, even private homes. As such, personal relationships helped people with divergent interests bridge their ideological divides. Women fostered conversation, providing an ear or a voice for unofficial messages and—in the case of international affairs—standing as surrogates for their nation. Wives' interactions among themselves served political purposes, too: when First Lady Dolley Madison visited congressmen's wives, she cultivated goodwill for her husband while collecting recipes so she could serve regional cuisine at White House functions.

Jeffersonians appealed for women's support of their embargo. Sympathetic women responded by spurning imported fabric and making (or directing their slaves to make) homespun clothing. Federalists, however, encouraged women to keep commerce alive, and sympathetic women bought smuggled goods.

Failed Policies

Under intense domestic opposition, the embargo collapsed. Instead, the Non-Intercourse Act of 1809 reopened trade with all nations except Britain and France and authorized the president to resume trade with those nations once they respected American neutrality rights. In June 1809, President Madison reopened trade with Britain after its minister offered assurances that Britain would repeal restrictions on American trade. His Majesty's government in London, though, repudiated the minister's assurances, and Madison reverted to nonintercourse.

When the Non-Intercourse Act expired in 1810, Congressed substituted Macon's Bill Number 2, which reopened trade with Great Britain and France but provided that, when one nation stopped violating American commercial rights, the president would suspend American commerce with the other. When Napoleon accepted, Madison declared nonintercourse on Great Britain in 1811. Although the French continued to seize American ships, Britain became the focus of American hostility because it dominated the seas.

In spring 1812, the British admiralty ordered its ships not to stop, search, or seize American warships, and in June Britain reopened the seas to American shipping. But before word of this policy change reached America, Congress declared war.

Mr. Madison's War

The House voted 79 to 49 for war; the Senate, 19 to 13. Democratic-Republicans favored war by 98 to 23; Federalists opposed it 39 to 0. Those who favored war, including President Madison, pointed to impressment, violation of neutral trading rights, British alliances with western Indians, and affronts to American independence. Others saw an opportunity to annex British Canada. Most militants were land-hungry southerners and westerners—the War Hawks—led by John C. Calhoun of South Carolina and first-term congressman and House Speaker Henry Clay of Kentucky. Most representatives from the coastal states, especially the Northeast, feared trade disruption and opposed Mr. Madison's War.

Federalists benefited from antiwar sentiment about the War of 1812. They joined renegade Democratic-Republicans in supporting New York City mayor DeWitt Clinton for president in 1812. Clinton lost to Madison by 128 to 89 electoral votes, but Federalists gained some congressional seats and carried many local elections. The pro-war South and the West remained solidly Democratic-Republican.

THE WAR OF 1812

The War of 1812 lasted until 1815, unfolding in skirmishes for which the U.S. armed forces, kept lean by Jeffersonian fiscal policies, were ill prepared. Officers executed campaigns poorly, and the U.S. Navy was no match for the Royal Navy. By 1812 the ten-year-old U.S. Military Academy at West Point produced only eighty-nine regular officers. Senior army officers were aged Revolutionary War veterans or political appointees.

The government's efforts to lure recruits—with sign-up bonuses and promises of three months' pay and rights to purchase 160 acres of western land—met with mixed success. At first, recruitment went well among westerners, motivated by the desire for land, strong anti-Indian sentiment, and fears of Tecumseh's pan-Indian organization. But with pay delays and inadequate supplies, recruitment dwindled. In New England, Federalists discouraged enlistments. Militias in New England and New York often refused to fight outside their own states. Desperate, New York offered freedom to slaves who enlisted, and compensation to their owners, and the U.S. Army made the same offer to slaves in the Old Northwest and Canada. But in the Deep South, fear of arming slaves kept them out of the military except in New Orleans, where a free black militia dated back to the Spanish. The British recruited slaves by promising freedom in exchange for service. In the end, British forces outnumbered American.

Invasion of Canada

Still, Americans expected to take Canada easily. Canada's population was sparse, its army small, and the Great Lakes inaccessible to the Royal Navy. American strategy aimed to split Canadian forces and isolate pro-British Indians, especially Tecumseh, to whom the British promised an Indian nation in the Great Lakes. In July 1812, the U.S. general William Hull, territorial governor of Michigan, marched his troops into Upper Canada. Although his forces outnumbered the British, Hull retreated more than he attacked. He abandoned Mackinac Island and Fort Dearborn and surrendered Fort Detroit, leaving the Midwest exposed. The only bright spot was the September 1812 defense of Fort Harrison in Indiana Territory by Captain Zachary Taylor, who secured the first American land victory. By winter 1812–1813, the British controlled about half of the Old Northwest.

Naval Battles

Despite victories on the Atlantic by the USS *Constitution* (nicknamed Old Ironsides), the USS *Wasp*, and the USS *United States,* the American navy—which began the war with just seventeen ships—could not match the powerful Royal Navy. By 1814, the Royal Navy blockaded nearly all American ports along the Atlantic and Gulf coasts. After 1811, American trade overseas declined by nearly 90 percent, and the loss of customs duties threatened to bankrupt the federal government and prostrate New England.

The contest over the Great Lakes, the key to the war in the Northwest, evolved as a shipbuilding race. Under Master Commandant Oliver Hazard Perry and the shipbuilder Noah Brown, the United States outbuilt the British on Lake Erie and defeated them at the bloody Battle of Put-in-Bay on September 10, 1813, gaining control of Lake Erie.

Burning Capitals

A ragged group of Kentucky militia volunteers, armed with swords and knives, marched 20 to 30 miles a day to join General William Henry Harrison's forces in Ohio. Now 4,500 strong, Harrison's force took Detroit before crossing into Canada, where at the Battle of the Thames they defeated British, Shawnee, and Chippewa forces in October 1813. Among the fallen was Tecumseh. The Americans then razed the Canadian capital of York (now Toronto).

After defeating Napoleon in Europe in April 1814, the British launched a land counteroffensive against the United States, concentrating on Chesapeake Bay. Royal troops occupied Washington, D.C., in August and set it ablaze, leaving the presidential mansion and parts of the city burning all night. The president and cabinet fled. Dolley Madison stayed to oversee the removal of cabinet documents and save a Gilbert Stuart portrait of George Washington.

The British intended the attack as a diversion. The major battle occurred in September 1814 at Baltimore, where Americans held firm. Francis Scott Key, detained on a British ship, watched the bombardment of Fort McHenry and wrote "The Star-Spangled Banner" (which became the national anthem in 1931). The British inflicted heavy damage, but achieved little militarily; their offensive on Lake Champlain also failed. The war reached a stalemate.

War in the Old Southwest

The war's final campaign began with an American attack on the Red Stick Creeks along the Gulf of Mexico and the British around New Orleans. Responding to Tecumseh's call to resist U.S. expansion, in 1813 the Red Sticks attacked Fort Mims, outside Mobile, killing hundreds of white men, women, and children. General Andrew Jackson of Tennessee rallied his militiamen and Indian opponents of the Red Sticks and crushed the Red Sticks at Horseshoe Bend (in present-day Alabama) in March 1814. In the 1814 Treaty of Fort Jackson, the Creeks ceded 23 million acres, about half of their holdings, and withdrew to the southern and western part of Mississippi Territory.

Jackson became a major general, and after seizing Pensacola (in Spanish Florida) and then securing Mobile, Jackson's forces continued to New Orleans. Three weeks later, on January 8, 1815, Jackson's poorly trained army held its ground against two British frontal assaults. At day's end, more than two thousand British soldiers lay dead or wounded, while Americans suffered only twenty-one casualties.

The Battle of New Orleans occurred two weeks after the war's official conclusion: word had not reached the United States that British and American diplomats signed the Treaty of Ghent on December 24, 1814. Still, the Battle of New Orleans catapulted General Andrew Jackson to national prominence.

Treaty of Ghent

The Treaty of Ghent essentially restored the prewar status quo. It provided for an end to hostilities, release of prisoners,

Americans rejoiced that the War of 1812 had reaffirmed their independence from the British monarchy. The sailor's foot here steps on the crown while broken chains of bondage lie nearby. (Picture Research Consultants and Archives)

restoration of conquered territory, and arbitration of boundary disputes. But the United States received no satisfaction on impressment, blockades, or maritime rights for neutrals, and British demands for territorial cessions from Maine to Minnesota went unmet. The British dropped their promise of an independent Indian nation.

Napoleon's defeat allowed the United States to discard its prewar demands, because peace in Europe made impressment and interference with American commerce moot issues. Similarly, war-weary Britain—its treasury nearly depleted—stopped pressing for military victory.

American Sovereignty Reasserted

The War of 1812 affirmed the independence of the American republic and ensured Canada's independence from the United States. Although conflict with Great Britain over trade and territory continued, it never again led to war. The return of peace with Europe also allowed the United States to again focus on the Barbary Coast, where the dey (governor) of Algiers declared war on the United States. In the Second Barbary War, U.S. forces held hundreds of Algerians captive while negotiating a treaty in summer 1815 that forever freed the United States from paying tributes for passage in the Mediterranean. The Second Barbary War reaffirmed America's commitment to freedom of the seas.

Domestic Consequences

With its economy shattered and the War of 1812 stalemated, New England delegates met in Hartford, Connecticut, for three weeks in winter 1814–1815 to discuss revising the national compact or pulling out of the republic. Moderates prevented a resolution of secession—withdrawal from the Union—but delegates condemned the war and the embargo while endorsing constitutional changes to weaken the South and make it harder to declare war. When news arrived of Jackson's New Orleans victory and the Treaty of Ghent, the Hartford Convention made the Federalists look wrong, if not treasonous. By the 1820s, the party faded from the national scene.

With Tecumseh's death, midwestern Indians lost their powerful political and military leader; with the British withdrawal, they lost their strongest ally. Some accommodationists, such as the Cherokees, temporarily flourished in the war's aftermath, but it disarmed traditionalists bent on resisting American expansion. Although the Treaty of Ghent pledged the United States to end hostilities with Indians and restore their prewar "possessions, rights, and privileges," Indians lacked the power to make the United States honor the agreement.

The war's end accelerated three trends that would dominate future decades: westward expansion, industrial takeoff, and the entrenchment of slavery. It opened vast tracts of formerly Indian land for American cotton cultivation in the Old Southwest and for growing wheat in the Old Northwest. The war also stimulated industry as Americans could no longer rely on overseas imports, particularly textiles. The War of 1812 thus fueled the demand for raw cotton, and the newly acquired lands in the Southwest beckoned southerners who migrated either with slaves or with expectations of someday owning slaves.

Industrial Piracy

Great Britain, which in the late eighteenth century pioneered mechanical weaving and power looms, knew the value of its head start in the industrial revolution and prohibited the export of textile technology. But the British-born brothers Samuel and John Slater, their Scottish-born power-loom-builder William Gilmore, and the Bostonians Francis Cabot Lowell and Nathan Appleton evaded British restrictions to establish America's first textile factories.

As an apprentice and then supervisor in a British cotton-spinning factory, Samuel Slater mastered the machinery and the process. To get around British technology laws, Slater emigrated to the United States disguised as a farmer. In 1790 in Pawtucket, Rhode Island, he opened the first water-powered spinning mill in America, rebuilding the machines from memory. With his brother John and Rhode Island partners Moses and Obadiah Brown and William Almy, Slater later built mills in Rhode Island and Massachusetts. In 1815 he hired the recent immigrant William Gilmore to build a water-powered loom like those in Britain. In the 1820s, the Slaters introduced British steam-powered looms.

In 1810, while vacationing in Edinburgh, Scotland, Francis Cabot Lowell met fellow Bostonian Nathan Appleton. Impressed by the British textile mills, they planned to introduce water-powered mechanical weaving into the United States. Lowell went to Britain's textile center in Manchester, visiting and observing the factories by day. At night he sketched from memory the power looms and processes he viewed. Back in the United States, he and others formed the Boston Associates, which created the Waltham-Lowell Mills based on Lowell's industrial piracy. Within a few years, textiles would be a major American industry, and the Boston Associates would dominate it.

Thus the modern American industrial revolution began with international links, not homegrown inventions.

This contemporary painting shows the Boston Manufacturing Company's 1814 textile factory at Waltham, Massachusetts. All manufacturing processes were brought together under one roof, and the company built its first factories in rural New England to tap roaring rivers as a power source. (Gore Place Society, Waltham, Massachusetts)

THE NATIONALIST PROGRAM

In his last year as president, James Madison and the Democratic-Republicans absorbed the Federalist idea that the federal government should encourage economic growth. His agenda, which Henry Clay later called the American System, included a national bank, improved transportation, and a protective tariff—a tax on imported goods to protect American manufacturers from foreign competition. Yet true to his Jeffersonian roots, Madison argued that only a constitutional amendment could authorize the federal government to build local roads and canals.

American System

Clay and other congressional leaders, such as Calhoun of South Carolina, thought the American System would unify the expanding nation, bridging sectional divides. The tariff would stimulate New England industry; those goods would find markets in the South and West. Agricultural products of the South and West—cotton and foodstuffs—would feed New England mills and workers. Manufactured and agricultural products would move along roads and canals which tariff revenues would fund. A national bank would handle the transactions.

In 1816 Congress chartered the Second Bank of the United States (the first bank's charter expired in 1811) to serve as a depository for federal funds and to issue currency, collect taxes, and pay government debts. The Second Bank was responsible, too, for overseeing state and local banks, ensuring that their paper money had backing in specie (precious metals). Like its predecessor, the bank mixed public and private ownership; the government provided one-fifth of the bank's capital and appointed one-fifth of its directors.

Congress also passed the Tariff of 1816, which taxed imported woolens and cottons, iron, leather, hats, paper, and sugar. The tariff divided rather than unified the nation. New England and the western and Middle Atlantic states would benefit from it and so supported it, whereas the southern states would face increased prices on goods they purchased and the possibility that Britain would retaliate with a tariff on cotton and so opposed it.

Southerners such as Calhoun promoted roads and canals to "bind the republic together." However, on March 3, 1817, the day before he left office, President Madison, citing constitutional scruples, vetoed Calhoun's Bonus Bill, which would have authorized federal funding for such public works.

Early Internal Improvements

Federalists and Democratic-Republicans agreed that internal improvements would promote prosperity. Federalists saw roads and canals as a way to spur the nation's commercial development; Jeffersonians, as the route to western expansion and agrarian growth. In 1806 Congress passed (and Jefferson signed into law) a bill authorizing federal funding for the Cumberland Road (later, the National Road) running between Cumberland, Maryland, and Wheeling, Virginia (now West Virginia). In 1820 Congress authorized a survey for the National Road to Columbus, Ohio, which was funded in 1825 and completed in 1833.

Most transportation initiatives were funded by states, private investors, or both. In 1817 New York began construction on the Erie Canal, linking the Great Lakes to the Atlantic seaboard; it was completed in 1825. The South relied mostly on rivergoing steamboats that dominated river trade following Robert Fulton's successful trial of a steam-powered vessel in 1807. By 1817, steamboats made regular trips on the Mississippi. Canals and steamboats greatly reduced the time and cost of transporting western agricultural products to market and fueled westward expansion. Canals expanded commercial networks into regions without natural waterways and would reorient midwestern commerce through the North.

The Era of Good Feelings

Madison's successor, James Monroe, was the third Virginian elected president since 1801. A former senator and twice governor of Virginia, he served under Madison as secretary of state and of war and used his association with Jefferson and Madison to attain the presidency. In 1816 he and his running mate, Daniel Tompkins, trounced the last Federalist presidential nominee, Rufus King, garnering all the electoral votes except those of Federalist strongholds Massachusetts, Connecticut, and Delaware. A Boston newspaper dubbed this one-party period the Era of Good Feelings.

Led by Federalist chief justice John Marshall, the Supreme Court became the bulwark of the nationalist point of view. In *McCulloch v. Maryland* (1819), the Court struck down a Maryland law taxing banks that were not chartered by the Maryland legislature—a law aimed at hindering the Baltimore branch of the Second Bank of the United States. At issue was state versus federal jurisdiction. Writing for a unanimous Court, Marshall asserted the supremacy of the federal government over the states. The Court also unanimously ruled that Congress had the power to charter banks. The Marshall Court thus provided a bulwark for the Federalist view that the federal government could promote interstate commerce.

Government Promotion of Market Expansion

Later Supreme Court cases validated government promotion of economic development and encouraged business enterprise. In *Gibbons v. Ogden* (1824), the Supreme Court overturned the New York law that granted Robert Fulton and Robert Livingston a monopoly on the New York–New Jersey steamboat trade. Chief Justice John Marshall ruled that the federal power to license new enterprises took precedence over New York's grant of monopoly rights and declared that Congress's power under the commerce clause of the Constitution extended to "every species of commercial intercourse." Within two years, the number of steamboats in New York increased from six to forty-three. A later ruling under Chief Justice Roger Taney, *Charles River Bridge v. Warren Bridge* (1837), encouraged new enterprises and technologies by favoring competition over monopoly.

Federal and state courts, in conjunction with state legislatures, also encouraged the proliferation of corporations—organizations holding property and transacting business as if they were individuals. Corporation owners, called shareholders, were granted limited liability, or freedom from personal responsibility for the company's debts beyond their original investment. The government assisted commercial development by expanding the number of U.S. post offices from three thousand in 1815 to fourteen thousand in 1845 and by protecting inventions and domestic industries. Patent laws gave inventors a seventeen-year monopoly on their inventions, and tariffs protected American industry from foreign competition.

Boundary Settlements Monroe's secretary of state, John Quincy Adams, managed foreign policy from 1817 to 1825, stubbornly pushing for expansion, American fishing rights in Atlantic waters, political distance from Europe, and peace. An ardent expansionist, this son of John and Abigail Adams believed that newly acquired territories must come via negotiations, not war, and must bar slavery.

Under Adams's leadership, in 1817 the United States and Great Britain signed the Rush-Bagot Treaty, limiting them to one naval ship each on Lake Champlain and Lake Ontario, and to two ships each on the remaining Great Lakes. This first modern disarmament treaty led to the demilitarization of the United States-Canada border. Adams then pushed for the Convention of 1818, which fixed the U.S.-Canadian boundary from Lake of the Woods in Minnesota westward to the Rockies along the 49th parallel. When they could not agree on the boundary west of the Rockies, the two countries settled on joint occupation of Oregon for ten years (renewed indefinitely in 1827).

Adams's negotiations acquired Florida for the United States. Although the Louisiana Purchase omitted reference to Spanish-ruled West Florida, the United States claimed the territory as far east as the Perdido River (the present-day Florida-Alabama border). During the War of 1812, the United States seized Mobile and the remainder of West Florida, and after the war, Adams claimed East Florida. In 1819 Don Luís de Onís, the Spanish minister to the United States, agreed to cede Florida without payment if the United States renounced its dubious claims to northern Mexico (Texas) and assumed $5 million of claims by American citizens against Spain. The Adams-Onís (or Transcontinental) Treaty also defined the southwestern boundary of the Louisiana Purchase and set the line between Spanish Mexico and Oregon Country at the 42nd parallel.

But Adams's greatest achievement was the Monroe Doctrine. Between 1808 and 1822, the United Provinces of Río de la Plata (present-day northern Argentina, Paraguay, and Uruguay), Chile, Peru, Colombia, and Mexico broke from Spain. In 1822, the United States became the first nation outside Latin America to recognize the new states. But with reactionary regimes ascending in Europe and France now occupying Spain, the United States feared that continental powers would attempt to return the Latin American states to colonial rule.

Monroe Doctrine Monroe's message to Congress in December 1823 became known as the Monroe Doctrine. He announced that the American continents "are henceforth not to be considered subjects for future colonization by any European power." This addressed American anxiety about Latin America and Russian expansion beyond Alaska and its settlements in California. Monroe demanded nonintervention by Europe in the affairs of independent New World nations, and he pledged U.S. noninterference in European affairs, including Europe's existing New World colonies. European nations stayed out of New World affairs because they feared the British Royal Navy, not the United States' proclamations.

SECTIONALISM EXPOSED

The embargo, the War of 1812, and postwar internal improvements helped southern and northern economies develop in different but interrelated ways. While the South would become more dependent on cotton, the North saw an acceleration of industrial development. Although Jeffersonians did not promote industry, a few entrepreneurs did.

Early Industrial Development   Americans relied on British technology to combine the many steps of textile manufacturing—carding (or disentangling) fibers, spinning yarn, and weaving cloth—in one factory. The first American water-powered spinning mill was established in 1790 by Samuel Slater, a British immigrant who reconstructed from memory the complex machines he used in England. But Slater's mill only carded and spun yarn; handweaving it into cloth was often done by farm women seeking extra cash. In 1810 the Bostonian Francis Cabot Lowell visited the British textile center of Manchester, touring factories and later sketching what he had seen. In 1813 he and his business associates founded the Boston Manufacturing Company, uniting all textile manufacturing phases under one roof in Waltham, Massachusetts. A decade later, the Boston Manufacturing Company established a model industrial village—named for its then-deceased founder—along the banks of the Merrimack River. At Lowell, Massachusetts, there would be boarding houses for workers, a healthy alternative to Manchester's tenements and slums.

When the British flooded America with cheap textiles after the War of 1812, Lowell realized the domestic market required protection. He lobbied hard to include cotton textiles in the Tariff of 1816, helping persuade reluctant South Carolinians to support it.

The growth of northern industry was linked to slavery. Much of the capital behind early industrialization came from merchants who partly made their fortunes through the slave trade. Two of the most prominent industries—textiles and shoes—expanded with a growing southern cotton economy. Southern cotton fed northern textile mills, and northern shoe factories sold "Negro brogans" (work shoes) to southern planters.

Panic of 1819   Immediately after the war, the international demand for (and price of) American commodities reached new heights. Poor weather in Europe led to crop failures, which sparked the demand for northern agricultural exports and the South's raw cotton. The demand for American wheat and cotton touched off western land speculation. Speculators raced to buy large tracts of land at modest, government prices and then resell them at a hefty profit to settlers.

Prosperity proved short-lived. By the late 1810s Europeans could grow their own food, and Britain's new Corn Laws established high tariffs on imported foodstuffs—lessening the demand for American agricultural exports. Cotton prices fell in England. Wars in Latin America interfered with mining and reduced the supply of precious metals. European nations hoarded specie; in response, American banks printed paper money and expanded credit. Fearful of inflation, the Second Bank of the United States demanded in 1819 that state banks repay loans in specie. State banks called in the loans and mortgages they made to individuals and companies. Falling prices meant farmers could not pay their mortgages, and plummeting land values—from 50 to 75 percent in portions of the West—meant they could not meet their debts even by selling their farms. The nation's banking system collapsed, triggering a financial panic.

Foreclosures soared. Unemployment skyrocketed, reaching 75 percent in Philadelphia. Workers and their families often could not make it through the winter without charity for food, clothing, and firewood.

Americans everywhere contemplated the virtues and hazards of rapid market expansion, disagreeing on what to blame for its shortcomings. Even as the nation's economy rebounded in the early 1820s, amid a flurry of internal improvement projects, no one could predict in what region or sector the nation's fortunes would lie.

Missouri Compromise

The nation also faced a political crisis in 1819 about slavery's westward expansion. Residents of the Missouri Territory petitioned Congress for admission to the Union with a constitution permitting slavery. Missouri's admission would give slaveholding states a two-vote majority in the Senate and would surely set a precedent for new western states created from the vast Louisiana Purchase. After the War of 1812, the American population surged westward, leading five new states to join the Union: Louisiana (1812), Indiana (1816), Mississippi (1817), Illinois (1818), and Alabama (1819). Of these, Louisiana, Mississippi, and Alabama permitted slavery. Because Missouri was on the same latitude as free Illinois, Indiana, and Ohio, its admission as a slave state would thrust slavery farther northward.

For two and a half years the issue dominated Congress. When Representative James Tallmadge Jr. of New York proposed gradual emancipation in Missouri, some southerners accused the North of threatening to destroy the Union. The House, which had a northern majority, passed the Tallmadge Amendment, but the Senate rejected it.

House Speaker Henry Clay—himself a western slaveholder—suggested a compromise in 1820. Maine, carved out of Massachusetts, would enter as a free state, followed by Missouri as a slave state, maintaining the balance between slave and free states. In the rest of the Louisiana Territory north of Missouri's southern border of 36°30′, slavery would be prohibited forever (see Map 9.2). Thus, the compromise divided the United States into northern and southern regions.

The compromise carried but almost unraveled when Missouri submitted a constitution barring free blacks from entering the state. Opponents contended it violated the federal constitutional provision that citizens of each state were "entitled to all privileges and immunities of citizens in the several States." Proponents countered that many states already barred free blacks. In 1821 Clay proposed a second compromise: Missouri would guarantee that its laws would not discriminate against citizens of other states. (Once admitted to the Union, Missouri twice adopted laws barring free blacks.)

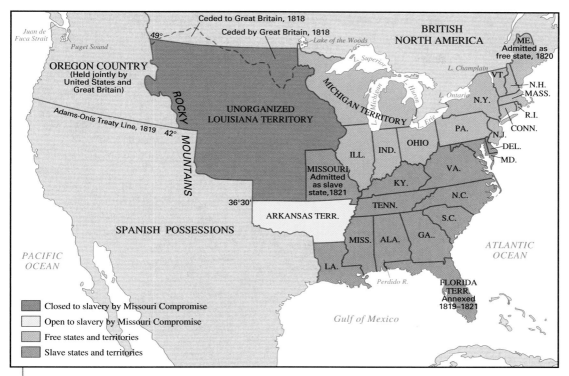

Map 9.2   Missouri Compromise and the State of the Union, 1820

Map labels:

Juan de Fuca Strait
Puget Sound
OREGON COUNTRY (Held jointly by United States and Great Britain)
Ceded to Great Britain, 1818
Ceded by Great Britain, 1818
Lake of the Woods
49°
BRITISH NORTH AMERICA
ME. Admitted as free state, 1820
L. Superior
L. Champlain
VT
ROCKY MOUNTAINS
UNORGANIZED LOUISIANA TERRITORY
MICHIGAN TERRITORY
L. Michigan
L. Huron
L. Ontario
L. Erie
N.H.
MASS.
N.Y.
R.I.
CONN.
PA.
N.J.
DEL.
MD.
Adams-Onís Treaty Line, 1819   42°
OHIO
IND.
ILL.
MISSOURI Admitted as slave state, 1821
KY.
VA.
36°30′
ARKANSAS TERR.
TENN.
N.C.
SPANISH POSSESSIONS
MISS.   ALA.   GA.
S.C.
PACIFIC OCEAN
ATLANTIC OCEAN
LA.
Perdido R.
FLORIDA TERR. Annexed 1819–1821
Gulf of Mexico

Legend:
- Closed to slavery by Missouri Compromise
- Open to slavery by Missouri Compromise
- Free states and territories
- Slave states and territories

Summary

The partisanship of the 1790s made the early republic a period of vigorous political engagement. With a vision of an agrarian nation that protected individual liberty, Jeffersonians promoted a limited national government—one that stayed out of religious affairs and spent little on military forces, diplomatic missions, and economic initiatives. The rival Federalists, who exerted their influence through the judiciary, declared federal supremacy over the states even as the judiciary affirmed its supremacy over other government branches. Federalists hoped a strengthened federal government would help promote commerce and industry.

Jefferson considered the acquisition of the Louisiana Territory and the Corps of Discovery his greatest presidential accomplishments. Americans soon streamed into the Louisiana Territory. More would have gone if not for Indians (and their British allies) and poorly developed transportation routes.

With its economy focused on international shipping, the greatest threats to the United States came from abroad. In its wars with the Barbary states, the United States sought to guard its commerce and ships on the high seas. Although the second war with Britain—the War of 1812—was a military stalemate, it helped inspire a new sense of nationalism and launch an era of American development.

States' Rights and Nullification

The exact nature of the relationship between the states and the federal government was ambiguous under the Constitution, because Constitutional Convention delegates could not agree on whether states or nation should prevail in an irreconcilable conflict. The Tenth Amendment offered a slight clarification: powers not delegated to the central government, it said, were reserved to the states or the people.

When New England Federalists met in Hartford in late 1814 to prepare a list of grievances against Mr. Madison's War, they drew on the doctrine of nullification, first announced sixteen years earlier in the Kentucky and Virginia Resolutions, written by Thomas Jefferson and James Madison. Opposing the Alien and Sedition Acts, these founding fathers asserted that, if the national government assumed powers not delegated to it by the Constitution, states could individually nullify federal actions. Federalist representatives of New England states discussed taking nullification further by seceding. Their formulation of states' rights to nullify federal authority left a legacy that was reinvoked in crises up to the present.

In the following decade, South Carolina nullified federal tariffs, and in 1861 southern states threatened by Abraham Lincoln's election as president claimed the right of secession. Although the Civil War supposedly settled the issue—states could neither nullify federal law nor secede—southern states opposing the Supreme Court's 1954 ruling in favor of school integration again claimed the right to nullify "unauthorized" federal policy within their borders. In the early twenty-first century, as the U.S. Congress failed to muster a two-thirds majority to propose a constitutional amendment banning gay marriage, dozens of states ratified their own such constitutional amendments. The Hartford Convention's legacy provides Americans who dissent from national policy with a model for using state governments as vehicles for protest.

The Treaty of Ghent reaffirmed American independence; thereafter the nation settled disputes with Great Britain at the bargaining table. The war also dealt a serious blow to Indian resistance in the Midwest and Southwest, while accelerating American industrial growth. Federalists' opposition to the war undermined their political credibility, and their party faded from the national political scene by 1820. The absence of well-organized partisan conflict created what contemporaries called an Era of Good Feelings.

Still, competing visions of America's route to prosperity endured. Under Chief Justice John Marshall, the Supreme Court supported the Federalist agenda, issuing rulings that stimulated commerce and industry. The Democratic-Republicans looked, instead, toward the vast and fertile Louisiana Territory. Fearful of European intentions to reassert their influence in the Americas and emboldened by the Louisiana Purchase and acquisition of Florida, President Monroe proclaimed that the United States would not tolerate European intervention in American affairs. But even as its expanding boundaries strengthened the United States' international presence, it threatened new-found political unity at home.

Tensions mounted in 1819, when the postwar economic boom came to a halt and congressmen sharply divided over whether to admit Missouri as a slave state. The compromise brokered by Henry Clay quelled the issue of slavery's expansion, but it did not permanently settle the issue.

Chapter Review

POLITICAL VISIONS

Was Jefferson's election and political vision truly "the revolution of 1800"?

Jefferson considered his election in 1800 a revolution, since it also gave his Democratic-Republican Party a majority in both houses of Congress. That made it easier to enact his vision of limited government, individual liberty (which required the separation of church and state) and an agrarian (versus commercial) republic. While Federalists bitterly opposed Jefferson where they could, he replaced Hamilton with a treasury secretary who would cut the federal budget and decrease the national debt—both signs of corruption to Jefferson and Democratic-Republicans (and Federalists' tools to stimulate the economy). Jefferson also pardoned those convicted under the Alien and Sedition Acts, which he saw as a violation of liberties, and attempted to remove from court appointments people opposed to his brand of politics (but was ultimately unsuccessful, maintaining the Court's independence).

NATIONAL EXPANSION WESTWARD

Why was the Louisiana Purchase among Jefferson's most popular decisions as president?

The purchase of 827,000 square miles of land west of the Mississippi from France doubled the size of the United States, secured American interests from potential European incursion at its inland borders, and opened more land for American settlement (even though Native Americans were already living there). Moreover, by purchasing the land on the other side of the river, the United States controlled access to the Mississippi, which appealed to western settlers who relied on it to get their goods to market. Finally, it fed dreams of cheap, fertile lands for would-be settlers.

THE NATION IN THE ORBIT OF EUROPE

What led to the War of 1812?

Freedom of the seas was the main cause. Ongoing hostilities between European nations spilled over onto American ships, as Great Britain often stopped and seized US ships and forced those aboard into military service. Trade embargoes did little to stop the practice and ultimately hurt American merchants and the U.S. economy. Madison pointed to violation of neutral trading rights, British alliances with western Indians, and affronts to American independence as additional causes, while others saw war as an opportunity to annex British Canada. Although Britain reopened the seas and ordered its ships not to disturb American warships by June of 1812, news of the policy change did not reach America until long after Congress declared war.

THE WAR OF 1812

What were the consequences of the War of 1812?

Although the Treaty of Ghent ended the fighting and restored the prewar status quo, the United States did not get the results it wanted on impressments, blockades, and maritime rights for neutral parties. The war did, however, affirm American independence and guarantee no future battles with Britain over trade or territory. On the home front, the war shattered the U.S. economy and led some New England Federalists to threaten secession, which led to the party's demise when the war soon ended. Indians who had supported the British lost a major ally. And while Indians had their land and rights restored by the Treaty of Ghent, they had no power to enforce it. With the end of war, three trends emerged that were pivotal for the nation's future: westward expansion, the entrenchment of slavery, and industrial development.

THE NATIONALIST PROGRAM

How did the American System mark the triumph of Federalist economic policy?

Long opposed to big government, Democratic-Republicans amended this philosophy to adopt the Federalist notion that the central government should aid economic growth. Their program was dubbed the American System, and included a national bank, development of transportation networks, and a protective tariff that would tax imported goods to protect American products from foreign competitors. Advocates of the American System, such as South Carolina leader John C. Calhoun, believed it could bridge sectional divides and expand the nation. Both parties embraced internal improvements for different reasons: Federalists saw them as spurring commercial development, while Jeffersonians (Democratic-Republicans) thought they would lead to western and agrarian expansion.

SECTIONALISM EXPOSED

How did the admission of new states after the War of 1812 ultimately divide the nation?

The question of slavery's westward expansion sparked controversy in 1819 when the Missouri Territory asked to be admitted as a slave state. Many feared it would give slaveholding states a two-vote congressional majority and would set a precedent for admitting other western states. And since Missouri was on the same latitude as free Illinois, Indiana, and Ohio, its admission as a slave state would move slavery northward. House Speaker Henry Clay suggested the winning compromise: to maintain the balance between free and slave states, Maine would enter as a free state, Missouri as a slave state, and all future new states north of Missouri's 36°30′ border would prohibit slavery. As such, the Missouri Compromise divided the nation into two regions, north and south, according to the politics of slavery.

SUGGESTIONS FOR FURTHER READING

Catherine Allgor, *A Perfect Union: Dolley Madison and the Creation of the American Nation* (2006)

Stephen Aron, *American Confluence: The Missouri Frontier from Borderland to Border State* (2006)

David Edmunds, *Tecumseh and the Quest for Indian Leadership* (2006)

Morton J. Horowitz, *The Transformation of American Law, 1780–1860* (1977)

Reginald Horsman, *The Diplomacy of the Early Republic* (1985)

John Lauritz Larson, *Internal Improvement: National Public Works and the Promise of Popular Government in the United States* (2001)

Peter Onuf and Leonard J. Sadosky, *Jeffersonian America* (2002)

Jeffrey Ostler, *The Plains Sioux and U.S. Colonialism from Lewis and Clark to Wounded Knee* (2004)

Jeffrey Pasley, Andrew Robertson, and David Waldstreicher, eds., *Beyond the Founders: New Approaches to the Political History of the Early American Republic* (2004)

The Rise of the South | 1815–1860

Aslaveholder in debt was a dangerous man, and Pierce Butler was broke. In late winter 1859, fear of disunion dominated national life, and Butler's slave auction had coastal Georgia and South Carolina talking. Butler was the grandson of Major Pierce Butler, a South Carolina senator, wealthy planter, and framer of the Constitution. Butler the younger moved between the family's ostentatious Philadelphia home and fifteen hundred acres of cotton plantations, worked by eight hundred slaves, on Butler Island and St. Simons Island in Georgia. His marriage to famous British actress Fanny Kemble ended in divorce, partly over differences about slavery. By 1859 Butler had squandered $700,000 through speculation and gambling. Most of Butler's Philadelphia properties and possessions were sold to satisfy creditors. Then came the largest slave auction in American history: four hundred thirty-six Butler slaves were taken to Savannah by railroad and steamboat in late February. People of all ages—infants, husbands, wives, children, grandparents—fearfully huddled in horse-and-carriage sheds at the Ten Broeck racetrack. Joseph Bryan, a slave broker and auctioneer, managed the sale. An undercover *New York Tribune* reporter left a detailed account of the auction, held over two days in a driving rainstorm.

If possible, families were sold intact for group prices. Some families of four brought only $1,600 together, while a "prime young man," Abel, netted $1,295 alone. At the end of the second day of what blacks called the weeping time, Butler amassed $303,850 by selling 436 human beings.

In 1815, southern states and territories, with fertile soil and a growing slave labor force to cultivate it, was poised for prosperity and power. New lands were settled, new states were peopled,

This icon will direct you to interactive activities and study materials on A People And A Nation, Brief Edition
website: **www.cengage.com/history/norton/peoplenationbrief8e**

Chronology

1810–20	One lakh thirty-seven thousand slaves are forced to move from the Upper South to Alabama, Mississippi, and other western regions.
1822	Vesey's insurrection plot is discovered in South Carolina.
1830s	Vast majority of African American slaves are native-born in America.
1830s–40s	Cotton trade grows into the largest source of commercial wealth and America's leading export.
1831	Turner leads a violent slave rebellion in Virginia.
1832	Virginia holds the last debate in the South about the future of slavery; gradual abolition is voted down. Dew's proslavery tract *Abolition of Negro Slavery* is published.
1836	Arkansas gains admission to the Union as a slave state.
1839	Mississippi's Married Women's Property Act gives married women some property rights.
1845	Florida and Texas gain admission to the Union as slave states. Douglass's *Narrative of the Life of Frederick Douglass, an American Slave, Written by Himself* is published.
1850	Planters' share of agricultural wealth in the South is 90 to 95 percent.
1850–60	Of some 300,000 slaves who migrate from the Upper to the Lower South, 60 to 70 percent go by outright sale.
1857	Hinton R. Helper's *The Impending Crisis,* denouncing the slave system, is published. George Fitzhugh's *Southern Thought,* an aggressive defense of slavery, is published.
1860	There are 405,751 mulattos in the United States, 12.5 percent of the African American population. Three-quarters of all southern white families own no slaves. South produces the largest cotton crop ever.

and the South emerged as the world's most extensive commercial agricultural economy, linked to an international cotton trade and textile industry. The Old South's wealth came from export crops, land, and slaves, and its population was almost wholly rural. Beyond economics, racial slavery also affected values, customs, laws, class structure, and the region's relationship to the nation and the world. As slaves were increasingly defined as chattel, they struggled to survive and resist, sometimes overtly, but more often in daily life and culture. By 1860 white southerners not only asserted the moral and economic benefits of slavery, but also sought to advance their power over the national government.

- How and why was the Old South a slave society, with slavery permeating every class and group within it, free or unfree?
- How and why did white southerners come to see cotton as "king" of a global economy, and how did the cotton trade's international reach shape southern society from 1815 to 1860?
- How did African American slaves build and sustain a meaningful life and a sense of community amid the potential chaos and destruction of their circumstances?
- How would you weigh the comparative significance of the following central themes in the history of the Old South: class, race, migration, power, liberty, and wealth?

THE "DISTINCTIVE" SOUTH?

Not until the first half of the 1800s did slaveholding states from the Chesapeake and Virginia to Missouri and from Florida across to Texas come to be designated as the South. Today many consider it America's most distinctive region. Historians have long examined how the Old South was like and unlike the rest of the nation. Because of its unique history, has the South, in the words of poet Allen Tate, always been "Uncle Sam's other province"? Analyzing why the South seems more religious, conservative, or tragic than other regions has been an enduring practice in American culture and politics.

American values, such as materialism, individualism, and faith in progress, have been associated with the North and tradition, honor, and family loyalty, with the South. Stereotypes also label the South as static, even backward, and the North as dynamic in the decades before the Civil War. In truth, there were many Souths: low-country rice and cotton regions with dense slave populations, mountainous regions of small farmers, semitropical wetlands in the Southeast, plantation culture in the Cotton Belt and Mississippi valley, tobacco- and wheat-growing regions in Virginia and North Carolina, bustling port cities, and wilderness areas with rare hillfolk homesteads.

South-North Similarity The South shared much in common with the rest of the nation. The geographic sizes of the South and the North were roughly the same. In 1815 white southerners and free northerners shared heroes and ideology from the American Revolution and the War of 1812. They worshiped the same Protestant God as northerners, lived under the same Constitution, and similarly combined nationalism and localism in their attitudes toward government. But as slavery and the plantation economy expanded, the South did not become a land of individual opportunity in the same manner as the North.

Research has shown that, despite enormous cruelties, slavery was a profitable labor system. Southerners and northerners shared an expanding capitalist economy. As it grew, the slave-based economy of money-crop agriculture reflected planters' rational choices. More land and slaves generally converted into more wealth.

By the Civil War in 1860, the distribution of wealth and property in the two sections was almost identical: 50 percent of free adult males owned only 1 percent of real and personal property, and the richest 1 percent owned 27 percent of the wealth. Both North and South had ruling classes. Entrepreneurs in both sections sought their fortunes in an expanding market economy. The southern master class was more likely than propertied northerners to move west in search of profits.

South-North Dissimilarity In terms of differences, the South's climate and longer growing season gave it a rural and agricultural destiny. Many great rivers provided rich soil and transportation routes. The South developed as a biracial society of brutal inequality, where the liberty and wealth of one race depended on the enslavement of another.

Cotton growers spread out over large areas to maximize production and income. Consequently, population density in the South was low; by 1860 there were only 2.3 people per square mile in vast and largely unsettled Texas, 15.6 in Louisiana, and 18.0 in Georgia. The Northeast averaged 65.4 people per square mile. Massachusetts had 153.1 people per square mile, and New York City compressed 86,400 people into each square mile.

Where people were scarce, it was difficult to finance and operate schools, churches, libraries, and even inns and restaurants. Similarly, the South's rural character and sense of the plantation as self-sufficient meant that the region spent little on public health. Southerners were strongly committed to their churches, and some embraced universities, but all such institutions were far less developed than in the North. Factories were rare, because planters invested their capital primarily in slaves. The largest southern industry was lumbering, and the largest factories used slaves to make cigars. The South was slower than the North to develop a unified market economy and a regional transportation network and had only 35 percent of the nation's railroad mileage in 1860.

The Old South never developed its own banking and shipping capacity to any degree, and relied heavily on the North for both. Most southern bank deposits were in the North, and as early as 1822, one-sixth of all southern cotton cleared for Liverpool or Le Havre from the port of New York. With cotton constituting two-fifths of New York's exports, merchants and bankers there became interested in the fate of slavery and cotton prices. In economic conventions from 1837 to 1839, southern delegates debated foreign trade, dependence on northern importers and financiers, and other alleged threats to their commercial independence. But nothing came of these conventions.

The South lagged far behind the North in industrial growth. Its urban centers were mostly ports like New Orleans and Charleston, which became crossroads of commerce and small-scale manufacturing. In the interior were small market towns dependent on agricultural trade. As a system of racial control, slavery did not work well in cities. Lacking manufacturing jobs, the South did not attract immigrants as readily as the North. By 1860 only 13 percent of the nation's foreign-born population lived in slave states.

Like most northerners, antebellum southerners embraced evangelical Christianity. Americans from all regions believed in a personal God and in conversion and piety as the means to salvation. But southern evangelical Baptists and Methodists concentrated on personal rather than social improvement. By the 1830s in the North, evangelicalism was a wellspring of reform movements; but in states where blacks were numerous and unfree, religion, as one scholar has written, preached "a hands-off policy concerning slavery." Moreover, distance and sparse population prevented reform-minded women from developing associations with each other. The reform movements that emerged in the South, such as temperance, focused on personal behavior, not social reform.

A Southern World-View and the Proslavery Argument

In the wake of the American Revolution, Enlightenment ideas of natural rights and equality stimulated antislavery sentiment in the Upper South, produced a brief flurry of manumissions, and inspired hope for gradual emancipation. But that confidence waned in the new nation. As slavery spread, southerners vigorously defended it. In 1816 George Bourne, a Presbyterian minister exiled from Virginia for his antislavery sermons and for the expulsion of slaveholders from his church, charged that, whenever southerners were challenged on slavery, "they were fast choked, for they had a Negro stuck fast in their throats."

By the 1820s, white southerners justified slavery as a positive good, not merely a necessary evil. They used the antiquity of slavery, as well as the Bible's references to

America, 1841, Edward Williams Clay. An idealized portrayal of loyal and contented slaves, likely distributed by northern apologists for slavery. All is well on the plantation as well-dressed slaves dance and express their gratitude to their master and his perfect family. The text includes the old slave saying: "God bless you master! You feed and clothe us. When we are sick you nurse us, and when too old to work, you provide for us!" The master replies piously: "These poor creatures are a sacred legacy from my ancestors and while a dollar is left me, nothing shall be spared to increase their comfort and happiness."   (Library of Congress)

slaveholding, to foster a historical argument for bondage. But at the heart of the proslavery argument was a deep and abiding racism. Whites were the more intellectual race, they deemed, and blacks more inherently physical and therefore destined for labor. In a proslavery tract written in 1851, John Campbell declared that "there is as much difference between the lowest tribe of negroes and the white Frenchman, Englishman, or American, as there is between the monkey and the negro."

Some southerners defended slavery in practical terms; their bondsmen were economic necessities. In 1845 James Henry Hammond of South Carolina argued that slaveholding was a matter of property rights, protected by the Constitution because slaves were legal property. The deepest root of the proslavery argument was a hierarchical view of the social order with slavery prescribed by God or nature. Southerners cherished tradition, believing social change should come slowly, if at all. As Nat Turner's slave rebellion compelled the Virginia legislature to debate the gradual abolition of slavery in 1831–1832, Thomas R. Dew, a slaveholder and professor at the College of William and Mary, contended that "that which is the growth of *ages* may require *ages* to remove." Dew's widely read work, *Abolition of Negro Slavery* (1832), sparked an outpouring of proslavery writing that would intensify over the next thirty years. As slavery expanded westward and fueled national prosperity, Dew cautioned that gradual abolition threatened the South's "irremediable ruin." Dew declared black slavery the basis of the "well-ordered, well-established liberty" of white Americans.

Proslavery advocates invoked natural-law doctrine, arguing that the natural state of humankind was inequality of ability and condition, not equality. Proslavery writers believed that people were born to certain stations in life; they stressed dependence over autonomy and duty over rights as the human condition. As the Virginia writer George Fitzhugh put it in 1854, "Men are not born entitled to equal rights. It would be far nearer the truth to say, that some were born with saddles on their backs, and others booted and spurred to ride them."

Many slaveholders saw themselves in a paternal role, as guardians of a familial relationship between masters and slaves. Although contradicted by countless examples of slave resistance and escape, and slave sales, planters needed to believe in and exerted great energy in constructing the idea of the contented slave.

A Slave Society

In the Old South, whites and blacks grew up, were socialized, married, reared children, worked, conceived of property, and honed even basic habits under the influence of slavery. This was true of slaveholding and nonslaveholding whites, as well as slave and free blacks. Slavery shaped the social structure of the South, fueled its economy, and dominated its politics. The South was interdependent with the North, West, and even Europe in a growing capitalist market system. For its cotton trade, southerners relied on northern banks, northern steamship companies, and northern merchants. But there were elements of that system that southerners increasingly rejected, especially urbanism, wage labor, a broadening right to vote, and threats to their racial and class order.

Americans have long struggled to define what one historian called the "Dixie difference." "The South is both American and something different," writes another historian, "at times a mirror or magnifier of national traits and at other times a counterculture." Distinctive and national, the South's story begins in what we have come to call the *Old South*, a term only conceivable after native peoples were evicted from the region.

SOUTHERN EXPANSION, INDIAN RESISTANCE, AND REMOVAL

When the trans-Appalachian frontier opened after the War of 1812, some 5 to 10 percent of the population moved annually, usually westward. In the first two decades of the century, they poured into the Ohio valley; by the 1820s, they were migrating into the Mississippi River valley and beyond. By 1850 two-thirds of Americans lived west of the Appalachians.

A Southern Westward Movement
After 1820 the heart of cotton cultivation and the slave-based plantation system shifted from southern coastal states to Alabama and the newly settled Mississippi valley—Tennessee, Louisiana, Arkansas, and Mississippi. Slaveholders initiated the move to newer areas of the South, and yeoman farmers followed, also hoping for wealth through cheap land and slaves.

A wave of migration was evident across the Southeast. As early as 1817, a Charleston, South Carolina, newspaper reported that migration out of that state had reached "unprecedented proportions." Almost half of the white people born in South Carolina after 1800 left the state, most for the Southwest. The way to wealth for southern seaboard planters was to go west to grow cotton for the booming world markets, purchasing more land and slaves. The population of Mississippi soared from 73,000 in 1820 to 607,000 in 1850, with African American slaves in the majority. Across the Mississippi River, the population of Arkansas went from 14,000 in 1820 to 210,000 in 1850. By 1835 the American immigrant population in Texas reached 35,000, including 3,000 slaves, outnumbering Mexicans two to one. American settlers declared Texas's independence from Mexico in 1836, spurring further American immigration into the region. By 1845 Texas fever boosted the Anglo population there to 125,000. Statehood that year opened the floodgates to more immigrants and to a confrontation with Mexico that would lead to war.

As the cotton kingdom grew to what southern political leaders dreamed would be national and world dominion, this westward migration, fueled initially by optimistic nationalism, ultimately made migrant planters more sectional and more southern. In time, political dominance in the South migrated westward into the Cotton Belt. By the 1840s and 1850s, capitalist planters, fearful that their slave-based economy was under attack, sought to protect and expand their system. Increasingly, they saw themselves, as one historian has written, less as "landowners who happened to own slaves" than as "slaveholders who happened to own land."

But other Americans already occupied much of the desired land. Before 1830 large swaths of upper Georgia belonged to the Cherokees, and huge regions of Alabama and Mississippi were Creek, Choctaw, or Chickasaw land. Indians were also on the move, but in forced migrations. For most white Americans, Indians were in the way of their growing empire. Taking Indian land, so the reasoning went, reflected the natural course of history and progress: the "civilizers" had to displace the "children of the forest." National leaders provided the rhetoric and justification needed. As president in 1830, Andrew Jackson spoke with certainty about why the Indians must go. "What good man would prefer a country," he asked, "covered with forests and ranged by a few thousand savages to our extensive Republic, studded with cities, towns, and prosperous farms?"

Indian Treaty Making

In theory, under the U.S. Constitution, the federal government recognized Indian sovereignty and treated Indian peoples as foreign nations. Agreements between Indian nations and the United States were signed and ratified like other international treaties. In practice, however, fraud dominated the government's approach to treaty making and Indian sovereignty. As the country expanded, new treaties replaced old ones, shrinking Indian land holdings.

Although Indian resistance persisted against such pressure after the War of 1812, it only delayed their ultimate removal. In the 1820s, native peoples in the middle West, Ohio valley, Mississippi valley, and other parts of the cotton South ceded lands totaling 200 million acres for a pittance.

Indian Accommodation

Increasingly, Indian nations east of the Mississippi sought to survive through accommodation. In the first three decades of the century, the Choctaw, Creek, and Chickasaw peoples in the lower Mississippi became suppliers and traders. Under treaty provisions, trading posts and stores provided Indians with supplies and purchased or bartered Indian-produced goods. The trading posts extended credit to chiefs, who increasingly fell into debt that they could pay off to the federal government only by selling their land.

By 1822 the Choctaw nation sold 13 million acres yet still carried a $13,000 debt. The Indians struggled, increasing agricultural production and hunting, working as farmhands and craftsmen, and selling produce at market stalls in Natchez and New Orleans. As the United States expanded westward, white Americans promoted their assimilation, through education and conversion to Christianity. In 1819, in response to missionary lobbying, Congress appropriated $10,000 annually for "civilization of the tribes adjoining the frontier settlements."

Within five years, thirty-two boarding schools administered by Protestant missionaries enrolled Indian students. They substituted English for Indian languages

The Amistad Case

In April 1839 a Spanish slave ship, *Tecora*, sailed from Lomboko, the region of West Africa that became Sierre Leone. On board were Mende people, captured and sold by their African enemies. In June they arrived in Havana, Cuba, a Spanish colony. Two Spaniards purchased fifty-three of the Mende and sailed aboard *La Amistad* for their plantations elsewhere in Cuba. After three days, the Africans revolted. Led by a man the Spaniards called Joseph Cinque, they killed the captain and seized control of the vessel. They ordered the two Spaniards to take them back to Africa, but the slaveholders tried to reach the American South. Far off course, the *Amistad* was seized by the USS *Washington* in Long Island Sound and brought ashore in Connecticut.

The Amistad Africans soon became a cause for abolitionists and slaveholders, as well as in U.S.-Spanish relations. The Africans were imprisoned in New Haven, and a dispute ensued: Were they slaves and murderers and the property of their Cuban owners, or were they free people exercising their natural rights? Were they Spanish property, seized on the high seas in violation of a 1795 treaty? If a northern state could "free" captive Africans, what did it mean for enslaved African Americans in the South? Connecticut abolitionists went to court, where a U.S. Circuit Court judge dismissed the mutiny and murder charges but refused to release the Africans because their Spanish owners claimed them as property.

Meanwhile, a Yale professor of ancient languages, Josiah Gibbs, visited the captives and learned their words for numbers. In New York he walked along the docks repeating the Mende words until an African seaman, James Covey, responded. Covey journeyed to New Haven, conversed with the jubilant Africans, and soon their tale garnered sympathy throughout New England.

In a new trial, the judge ruled that the Africans were illegally enslaved and ordered them returned to their homeland. Slave trade between Africa and the Americas was outlawed in a treaty between Spain and Great Britain. Spain's lawyers demanded the return of their "merchandise." Needing southern votes to win reelection, President Martin Van Buren supported Spanish claims and advocated the Africans' return to a likely death in Cuba.

The administration appealed to the Supreme Court in February 1841. Arguing the abolitionists' case, former president John Quincy Adams pointed to a copy of the Declaration of Independence on the court wall, invoked the natural rights to life and liberty, and chastised the Van Buren administration. In a 7-to-1 decision, the Court ruled that the Africans were "freeborn."

Fund-raising and speaking tours featuring Cinque financed the return voyage. On November 27, 1841, thirty-five survivors and five American missionaries disembarked for Africa, arriving in Sierre Leone on January 15, 1842. The Amistad case showed how intertwined slavery was with freedom, and the United States with the world. It poisoned diplomatic relations between America and Spain for a generation, and stimulated Christian mission work in Africa.

Amistad Mutiny
(The Granger Collection, New York)

and taught agriculture alongside Christian gospel. But teaching the value of private property did not deter settlers from eyeing Indian land. Wherever native peoples lived, illegal settlers disrupted their lives. The federal government only halfheartedly enforced treaties, as legitimate Indian land rights gave way to the advance of white civilization.

With loss of land came dependency. The Choctaws relied on white Americans for manufactured goods and even food. Disease further facilitated removal of American Indian peoples to western lands. While other groups increased rapidly, the Indian population fell, some nations declining by 50 percent in three decades. The French traveler and author Alexis de Tocqueville concluded, after observing the tragedy of forced Indian removal in 1831, "as they give way or perish, an immense and increasing people fill their place. There is no instance upon record of so prodigious a growth or so rapid a destruction." As many as 100,000 eastern and southern Indian peoples were removed between 1820 and 1850; about 30,000 died in the process.

Removal had a profound impact on all Shawnees, the people of the Prophet and Tecumseh. After giving up 17 million acres in Ohio in a 1795 treaty, the Shawnees scattered to Indiana and eastern Missouri. Many moved to the Kansas territory in 1825. By 1854 Kansas was open to white settlement, and the Shawnees had to cede seven-eighths of their land, or 1.4 million acres. Shawnee men lost their traditional role as providers; their hunting methods and knowledge of woodland animals were useless on the Kansas prairies. As grain became the tribe's dietary staple, Shawnee women played a greater role as providers, supplemented by government aid under treaty provisions. Remarkably, the Shawnees preserved their language and culture despite these devastating dislocations.

Indian Removal as Federal Policy

Cherokees, Creeks, Choctaws, Chickasaws, and Seminoles aggressively resisted white encroachment after the War of 1812 and maintained much of their land. In his last annual message to Congress in late 1824, President James Monroe proposed that all Indians be moved west of the Mississippi River. Monroe considered this an honorable proposal that would protect Indians from invasion and provide them with independence for "improvement and civilization." He believed Indians would willingly accept western land free from white encroachment.

The Cherokees, Creeks, Choctaws, and Chickasaws unanimously rejected Monroe's proposition. In 1789 and 1825 the four nations negotiated thirty treaties with the United States, and they reached their limit. Most wished to remain on what little was left of their ancestral land.

Pressure from Georgia prompted Monroe's policy. In the 1820s, the state accused the federal government of not fulfilling its 1802 promise to remove the Cherokees and Creeks from northwestern Georgia in return for the state's renunciation of its claim to western lands. Georgia remained unsatisfied by Monroe's removal messages and by the Creeks' recalcitrance. In 1826, under federal pressure, the Creek nation ceded all but a small strip of its Georgia acreage, but for Georgians, only their complete removal to the West could resolve the conflict.

In an unsuccessful attempt to hold fast to the remainder of their traditional lands, which were in Alabama, the Creeks radically altered their political structure. In 1829, they abandoned village autonomy for centralized tribal authority and forbade any chief from ceding land. In the end, they lost both their land and their social and political traditions. In 1830, after extensive debate and a narrow vote, Congress passed the Indian Removal Act, authorizing the president to negotiate removal treaties with all tribes east of the Mississippi. The bill, which provided federal funds for relocations, would likely not have passed the House without the additional representation afforded slave states due to the Constitution's three-fifths clause.

Cherokees

No people met the challenge of assimilating to American standards more thoroughly than the Cherokees, whose traditional home centered on eastern Tennessee and northern Alabama and Georgia. Between 1819 and 1829 the tribe became economically self-sufficient and politically self-governing; during this Cherokee renaissance, the nearly fifteen thousand adult Cherokees considered themselves a nation, not a collection of villages. In 1821 and 1822, Sequoyah, a self-educated Cherokee, devised an eighty-six-character phonetic alphabet that made possible a Cherokee-language Bible and a bilingual newspaper, *Cherokee Phoenix* (1828). Between 1820 and 1823, the Cherokees created a formal government with a bicameral legislature and a court system, and in 1827 they adopted a constitution modeled after the United States'.

The Cherokee nation, however, collectively owned all tribal land and forbade land sales to outsiders. Nonetheless, many became individual farmers and slaveholders; by 1833 they held fifteen hundred black slaves. They transformed their economy from hunting, gathering, and subsistence agriculture to commodity trade based on barter, cash, and credit.

But Cherokees' political and economic changes failed to win respect from white southerners. In the 1820s, Georgia pressed them to sell the 7,200 square miles of land they held in the state for $30,000 appropriated by Congress. The Cherokees resisted. Impatient, Georgia annulled the Cherokees' constitution, extended the state's sovereignty over them, prohibited the Cherokee National Council from meeting except to cede land, and ordered their lands seized. The discovery of gold on Cherokee land in 1829 further whetted Georgia's appetite for Cherokee territory.

Cherokee Nation v. Georgia

The Cherokees under Chief John Ross turned to the federal courts to defend their treaty with the United States. In *Cherokee Nation v. Georgia* (1831), Chief Justice John Marshall ruled that under the Constitution an Indian tribe was neither a foreign nation nor a state. Indians' relationship with the United States was "marked," said Marshall, "by cardinal and peculiar distinctions which exist nowhere else." They were deemed "domestic, dependent nations" that were in but not of the United States. Nonetheless, said Marshall, the Indians had an unquestionable right to their lands; they could lose title only by voluntarily giving it up.

A year later, in *Worcester v. Georgia*, Marshall declared that the Indian nation was a distinct political community in which "the laws of Georgia can have no force" and into which Georgians could not enter without permission or treaty. The *Cherokee Phoenix* editor Elias Boudinot called the decision "glorious news." However, President Jackson, whose reputation was built as an Indian fighter, tried to usurp the court's action. Newspapers widely reported that Jackson had said, "John Marshall has made his decision: now let him enforce it." To open up new lands for settlement, Jackson favored expelling the Cherokees.

Georgians, too, refused to comply, and they refused to hear Indians' pleas to share their American dream. A Cherokee census indicated that they owned 33 gristmills, 13 sawmills, 1 powder mill, 69 blacksmith shops, 2 tanneries, 762 looms, 2,486 spinning wheels, 172 wagons, 2,923 plows, 7,683 horses, 22,531 cattle, 46,732 pigs, and 2,566 sheep. "You asked us to form a republican government," declared the Cherokee leader, John Ridge, in 1832. "We did so—adopting your own as a model. You asked us to cultivate the earth, and learn the mechanic arts: We did so. You asked us to learn to read: We did so. You asked us to cast away our idols, and worship your God: We did so." But neither the plow nor the Bible earned the Cherokees respect in the face of the economic, imperial, and racial quests of fellow southerners (see Map 10.1).

Trail of Tears

The Choctaws made the first forced journey from Mississippi and Alabama to the West in the winter of 1831 and 1832. Alexis de Tocqueville was visiting Memphis when they passed through: "The wounded, the sick, newborn babies, and the old men on the point of death. . . . I saw them embark to cross the great river," he wrote. "Neither sob nor complaint rose from that silent assembly." The Creeks in Alabama resisted removal until 1836; a year later the Chickasaws followed.

Some Cherokees believed that further resistance was hopeless and accepted removal, agreeing in 1835 to exchange their southern home for western land in the Treaty of New Echota. Most wanted to stand firm. John Ross, with petitions signed by fifteen thousand Cherokees, lobbied the Senate against ratification of the treaty. He lost. But when evacuation came in 1838, most Cherokees refused to move. President Martin Van Buren sent federal troops; about twenty thousand Cherokees were evicted, held in detention camps, and marched under military escort to Indian Territory in present-day Oklahoma. Nearly one-quarter died of disease and exhaustion on what came to be known as the Trail of Tears.

When the forced march ended, the Indians swapped about 100 million acres east of the Mississippi for 32 million acres west of the river plus $68 million. Forced removal had a disastrous impact on the Cherokees and other displaced Indian nations. In the West they encountered an alien environment. Unable to live off the land, many became dependent on government payments. The Cherokees struggled over their tribal government. In 1839 followers of John Ross assassinated leaders of the protreaty faction. Violence continued sporadically until a new treaty in 1846 imposed a temporary truce. In time the Cherokees reestablished their political institutions and a governing body in Tahlequah, in northeastern Oklahoma.

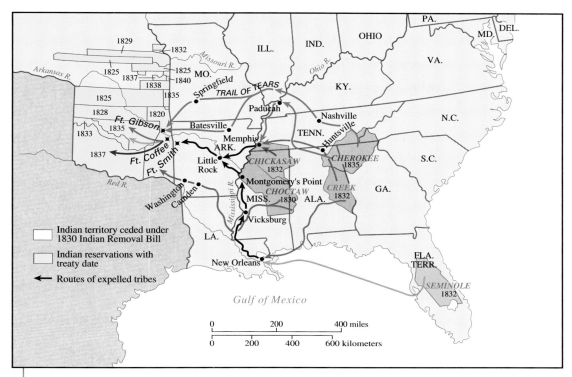

Map 10.1   Removal of Native Americans from the South, 1820–1840

Over a twenty-year period, the federal government and southern states forced Native Americans to exchange their traditional homes for western land. Some tribal groups remained in the South, but most settled in the alien western environment.   (Acknowledgment is due to Martin Gilbert and George Weidenfeld and Nicholson Limited for permission to reproduce this map, taken from *American History Atlas*)

Seminole Wars

In Florida some Seminole leaders agreed in the 1832 Treaty of Payne's Landing to relocate to the West within three years, but others opposed the treaty. A minority under the charismatic leader Osceola refused to vacate and fought the protreaty group. When federal troops were sent to impose removal in 1835, Osceola waged a fierce guerrilla war against them.

The Florida Indians were a varied group that included many Creeks and mixed Indian–African Americans (ex-slaves or descendants of runaway slaves). The U.S. Army, however, considered them all Seminoles. General Thomas Jesup believed that the runaway slave population was the key to the war. "And if it be not speedily put down," he wrote a friend in 1836, "the South will feel the effects of it on their slave population before the end of the next season."

Osceola was captured and died in an army prison in 1838, but Seminoles fought on under Chief Coacoochee (Wild Cat) and other leaders. In 1842 the United States abandoned removal. Most of Osceola's followers agreed to move west to Indian Territory after another war in 1858, but some remained in the Florida Everglades, proud of having resisted.

The Trail of Tears, by twentieth-century Pawnee artist Brummet Echohawk. About twenty thousand Cherokees were evicted in 1838–1839, and about one-quarter of them died on the forced march to present-day Oklahoma.   (Gilcrease Museum, Tulsa, Oklahoma)

LIMITS OF MOBILITY IN A HIERARCHICAL SOCIETY

A large majority of white southerners (three-quarters in 1860) owned no slaves. Some lived in towns and ran stores or businesses, but most were yeoman farmers who owned land and grew their own food. The social distance between poorer whites and the planter class could be great. Still greater was the distance between whites and free blacks. White yeomen, landless whites, and free blacks occupied the broad base of the social pyramid in the Old South.

Yeoman Farmers   After the War of 1812, white farmers, many with no slaves, moved in successive waves down the southern Appalachians into the Gulf lands or through the Cumberland Gap into Kentucky and Tennessee. In large sections of the South, especially inland from the coast and away from large rivers, small, self-sufficient farms were the norm. Lured by stories of good land, many men repeatedly uprooted their wives and children. These farmers were individualistic and hard working. Their status as a numerical majority did not mean that they set the political or economic direction of the slave society. Self-reliant and often isolated, they operated both apart from and within the slave-based staple-crop economy.

On the southern frontier, men cleared fields, built log cabins, and established farms, while their wives labored in the household and patiently re-created the social ties—to relatives, neighbors, fellow churchgoers—that enriched everyone's experience. Women typically dreaded the isolation and loneliness that came with moving to the frontier.

Some yeomen acquired large tracts of level land, purchased slaves, and became planters. They forged part of the new wealth of the cotton-boom states of Mississippi and Louisiana, where mobility into the slaveowning class was possible. Others clung to familiar mountainous areas or sought self-sufficiency. As one historian has written, though they owned no slaves, yeomen were jealous of their independence, and "the household grounded their own claims to masterhood."

Yeoman Folk Culture

Yeomen enjoyed a folk culture based on family, church, and local region. Their speech patterns and inflections recalled their Scots-Irish and Irish backgrounds. They flocked to religious revivals called camp meetings and got together for house-raisings, logrollings, quilting bees, corn-shuckings, and hunting. Such occasions combined work with fun and fellowship, offering food and liquor in abundance.

Demanding work and family responsibilities shaped women's lives. They worked in the fields, but the preparation of food consumed much of women's time. Household tasks continued during frequent pregnancies and childcare. Nursing and medical care also fell to mothers, who relied on folk wisdom. Women, too, wanted to be masters of their household, although it came at the price of their health.

Yeomen's Livelihoods

At age eighteen in 1841, the North Carolinian John F. Flintoff went to Mississippi to seek his fortune. Like other aspiring yeomen, he worked as a slave overseer. Finding it impossible to please his employers, he returned to North Carolina, married, and lived in his parents' house. "Impatient to get along in the world," Flintoff tried Louisiana next and then Mississippi again.

In the Gulf region, routinely first-rate employment alternated with "very low wages." His uncle and other employers found fault with his work, and in 1846 Flintoff concluded that "managing negroes and large farms is soul destroying."

At twenty-six, even before he owned land, Flintoff bought his first slave, "a negro boy 7 years old." Soon he purchased two more children, the cheapest slaves available. Conscious of his status as a slaveowner, Flintoff resented the low wages he was paid. In 1853, with nine young slaves and a growing family, Flintoff was fired by his uncle. He returned to North Carolina, sold some of his slaves, and purchased 124 acres with help from his in-laws. By 1860 he owned animal stock and several slaves and was paying off his debts. As the Civil War approached, he hoped to free his wife from labor and possibly send his sons to college. Although Flintoff demonstrated that a farmer could move in and out of the slaveholding class, he never achieved cotton planter status (owning roughly twenty or more slaves).

Probably more typical of the southern yeoman was Ferdinand L. Steel, who as a young man moved from North Carolina to Tennessee to work as a river boatman but eventually took up farming in Mississippi. Steel rose every day at 5 A.M. and worked until sundown. He and his family raised corn and wheat, though cotton was his cash product: he sold five or six bales (about two thousand pounds) a year to obtain money for sugar, coffee, salt, calico, gunpowder, and a few other store-bought goods. He picked his own cotton and complained that it was brutal and unprofitable work. When cotton prices fell, a small grower like Steel could be driven into debt and lose his farm.

Steel's life in Mississippi in the 1840s survived on a household economy. He made the family's shoes; his wife and sister sewed dresses, shirts, and pantaloons. As the nation fell deeper into crisis over slave labor, this independent southern farmer never came close to owning a slave.

The focus of Steel's life was family and religion. Family members prayed together daily, and he studied Scripture for an hour after lunch. Steel borrowed histories, Latin and Greek grammars, and religious books from his church. Eventually he became a traveling Methodist minister.

Landless Whites

A sizable minority of white southern workers—from 25 to 40 percent—were hired hands who owned no land and worked for others. Their property consisted of a few household items and some animals—usually pigs. The landless included some immigrants, especially Irish, who did heavy and dangerous work, such as building railroads and digging ditches.

In the countryside, white farm laborers struggled to purchase land in the face of low wages or, if they rented, unpredictable market prices for their crops. Scrimping, some climbed into yeomen ranks. When James and Nancy Bennitt of North Carolina succeeded in their ten-year struggle to buy land, they avoided unstable cotton and raised extra corn and wheat for cash.

Herdsmen with pigs and other livestock had a desperate struggle. By 1860, as the South anticipated war to preserve its society, between 300,000 and 400,000 white people in Virginia, North and South Carolina, and Georgia—approximately one-fifth of the total white population—lived in poverty. Land and slaves determined wealth in the Old South, and many whites possessed neither.

Yeomen's Demands and White Class Relations

Class tensions emerged in the western, nonslaveholding parts of the seaboard states by the 1830s. There, yeoman farmers resented their underrepresentation in state legislatures and the corruption in local government. Voters in more recently settled states of the Old Southwest adopted white manhood suffrage and other reforms, including the popular election of governors, legislative apportionment based on white population only, and locally chosen county government. Slaveowners with new wealth, however, knew that a more open government could permit troubling class conflicts and were determined to hold the reins of power.

Historians have offered several explanations why these tensions did not fuel greater conflict between slaveholders and nonslaveholders. One of the most important factors was race. The South's racial ideology stressed the superiority of all whites to blacks. Thus slavery became the basis of equality among whites, and white privilege inflated the status of poor whites, giving them a common interest with the rich. The dream of upward mobility also blunted class conflict. The Old South was a somewhat fluid society in which some people rose in status by acquiring land or slaves and others wished that they could.

Most important, before the Civil War yeomen worked their farms and avoided debt, largely unhindered by slaveholding planters. Likewise, slaveholders pursued their goals independent of yeomen. Suppression of dissent also played an increasing role. After 1830 white southerners who criticized the slave system were intimidated, attacked, legally prosecuted, or rendered politically powerless in a society held together by white racial solidarity.

Still, there were signs that the relative lack of conflict was ending in the late antebellum period. As cotton lands filled up, nonslaveholders faced narrower economic prospects; meanwhile, wealthy planters enjoyed expanding profits. The risks of entering cotton production were becoming too great and the cost of slaves too high for many yeomen to rise in society. From 1830 to 1860 the percentage of white southerners holding slaves declined from 36 to 25 percent. Although slaveowners were a minority in the white population, the planters' share of the South's agricultural wealth remained at 90 to 95 percent.

Anticipating secession and the prospect of a war, slaveowners expressed growing fear about the loyalty of nonslaveholders during the late antebellum years. But in the 1850s slaveowners occupied from 50 to 85 percent of the seats in state legislatures and a similarly high percentage of the South's congressional seats. And planters' interests controlled all other major social institutions, such as churches and colleges.

Free Blacks

The nearly quarter-million free blacks in the South in 1860 often fared little better than slaves. Upper South free blacks were usually descendants of people manumitted by their owners in the 1780s and 1790s. A remarkable number of slaveholders in Virginia and the Chesapeake freed their slaves because of religious principles and revolutionary ideals in the wake of American independence (see Chapter 7). Many blacks also became free as runaways, especially by the 1830s.

Some free blacks worked in towns or cities, but most lived in rural areas and struggled to survive. They usually did not own land and labored in someone else's fields, often beside slaves. By law, free blacks could not own guns, buy liquor, violate curfew, assemble except in church, testify in court, or (throughout the South after 1835) vote. Despite obstacles, a minority bought land, and others found jobs as skilled craftsmen, especially in cities.

A few free blacks prospered and bought slaves. In 1830 there were 3,775 free black slaveholders in the South; 80 percent lived in Louisiana, South Carolina, Virginia, and Maryland, and approximately half of the total lived in New Orleans and Charleston. Most purchased their own wives and children, whom they could not free because laws required newly emancipated blacks to leave their state. To free the family members they purchased, hundreds of black slaveholders petitioned for exemption from the antimanumission laws. At the same time, a few mulattos in New

Orleans were active slave traders. Although rare in the United States, the greed and quest for power that lay at the root of slavery could cross any racial or ethnic barrier.

Free Black Communities

In the Cotton Belt and Gulf regions, a large proportion of free blacks were mulattos, the privileged offspring of wealthy white planters. Not all planters freed their mixed-race offspring, but those who did often gave their children a good education and financial backing. In cities like New Orleans, Charleston, and Mobile, extensive interracial sex, as well as migrations from the Caribbean, produced a mulatto population that was recognized as a distinct class.

Free black communities formed in many southern cities by the 1840s, especially around churches. By the late 1850s, Baltimore had fifteen churches, Louisville nine, and Nashville and St. Louis four each—most of them African Methodist Episcopal. Class and race distinctions were important to southern free blacks, but outside a few cities, most mulattos experienced hardship. In the United States, "one drop" of black "blood" made them black, and potentially enslaveable.

THE PLANTERS' WORLD

At the top of the southern social pyramid were slaveholding planters. Most lived in comfortable farmhouses, not in the opulence legend suggests. The grand plantation mansions with outlying slave quarters, are an enduring symbol of the Old South. But statistics tell the fuller story: in 1850, 50 percent of southern slaveholders had fewer than five slaves, 72 percent had fewer than ten, and 88 percent had fewer than twenty. Thus the average slaveholder was not a wealthy aristocrat but an aspiring farmer.

The Newly Rich

The newly rich Louisiana cotton planter Bennet Barrow was preoccupied in the 1840s with moneymaking. He worried about his cotton crop, yet to overcome his worries, he hunted frequently and had a passion for racing horses and raising hounds. He could report the loss of a slave without feeling, but became emotional when illness afflicted his sporting animals. His strongest feelings surfaced when his horse Jos Bell—equal to "the best Horse in the South"—"broke down running a mile . . . ruined for Ever." The same day, Barrow gave his human property a "general Whipping." In 1841 diary entries he worried about a rumored slave insurrection. When a slave named Ginney Jerry "sherked" his cotton-picking duties and was rumored "about to run off," Barrow whipped him one day and the next.

The richest planters used their wealth to model genteel sophistication. Extended visits, parties, and balls to which women wore the latest fashions provided opportunities for friendship, courtship, and display. These entertainments were important diversions for plantation women, who relished social events to break the monotony of their domestic lives. Yet such socializing also sustained a rigidly gendered society.

Most of the planters in the cotton-boom states of Alabama and Mississippi were newly rich by the 1840s. As one historian put it, "a number of men mounted from log cabin to plantation mansion on a stairway of cotton bales, accumulating slaves as they climbed." But many did not live like rich men. They put their new wealth into cotton acreage and slaves even as they sought refinement and high social status.

The cotton boom in the Mississippi valley created one-generation aristocrats. A case in point is Greenwood Leflore, a Chocktaw chieftain who owned a plantation in Mississippi with four hundred slaves. After selling his cotton on the world market, he spent $10,000 in France to furnish one room of his mansion with hand-woven carpets, furniture upholstered with gold leaf, tables and cabinets ornamented with tortoise-shell inlay, mirrors, paintings, and a clock and candelabra of brass and ebony.

Social Status and Planters' Values

Slave ownership was the main determinant of wealth in the South, and slave labor was the primary means of cultivating cotton and other cash crops on a large scale. Slaves were a commodity and an investment, much like gold; people bought them on speculation, hoping for a steady rise in their market value. Wealth in slaves also translated into political power: a majority of political officeholders were slaveholders, and the most powerful were usually large-scale planters.

The availability of slave labor tended to devalue free labor: where strenuous work under supervision was reserved for an enslaved race, few free people relished it. When Alexis de Tocqueville crossed from Ohio into Kentucky on his travels of 1831, he observed, "On the right bank of the Ohio [River] everything is activity, industry; labor is honoured; there are no slaves. Pass to the left bank and the scene changes so suddenly that you think yourself on the other side of the world; the enterprising spirit is gone. There, work is not only painful; it is shameful." Aristocratic values—lineage, privilege, pride, honor, and refinement of person and manner—commanded respect throughout the South. Many of those qualities were in short supply in the recently settled portions of the cotton kingdom, where frontier values of courage and self-reliance ruled during the 1820s and 1830s. By the 1850s, a settled aristocratic group of planters did predominate in much of the Mississippi valley.

Instead of disappearing, as it had in the North, the Code Duello, which required men to defend their honor through violence, endured in the South. In North Carolina in 1851, wealthy planter Samuel Fleming sought to settle disputes with lawyer William Waightstill Avery by "cowhiding" him in public. Under the code, Avery could redeem his honor violently or brand himself a coward through inaction. Three weeks later, he shot Fleming dead at point-blank range. A jury took ten minutes to find Avery not guilty, and the spectators gave him a standing ovation.

Aristocratic planters expected to wield power and receive deference from poorer whites. But the sternly independent yeoman class resented infringements of their rights, and many belonged to evangelical faiths that exalted simplicity and condemned the planters' wealth. Yeomen sometimes challenged planters' political pretensions. Much of the planters' power and claims to leadership, after all, were built on their assumption of a monopoly on world cotton and a foundation of black slave labor.

King Cotton in a Global Economy

The American South so dominated the world's supply of cotton that southern planters gained enormous confidence that the cotton boom was permanent and that the industrializing nations of England and France would always bow to King Cotton. American cotton production doubled in yield each decade after 1800 and provided three-fourths of the world's supply by the 1840s. Southern staple crops were three-fifths of American exports by 1850, and one of every seven workers in England depended on American cotton for his job. Cotton production made slaves the most valuable financial asset in the United States—greater than banks, railroads, and manufacturing combined. In 1860 dollars, the slaves' total value as property equaled an estimated $3.5 billion ($70 billion in early-twenty-first-century dollars).

"Cotton is King," the *Southern Cultivator* declared in 1859, "and wields an astonishing influence over the world's commerce." Until 1840 the cotton trade furnished much of the export capital that financed northern economic growth. After, the northern economy expanded without dependence on cotton profits. Nevertheless, southern planters and politicians continued to boast of King Cotton's supremacy. "No power on earth dares . . . to make war on cotton," James Hammond lectured the U.S. Senate in 1858. Although the South produced 4.5 million bales in 1861, its greatest crop ever, its world dominance was about to collapse. Thereafter, cotton became a shackle to the South.

Paternalism

Slaveholding men often embraced a paternalistic ideology that justified their dominance over black slaves and white women. They stressed their obligations, viewing themselves as custodians of society and of the black families they owned. The paternalistic planter saw himself not as an oppressor but as the benevolent guardian of an inferior race.

This comforting self-image let rich planters obscure the harsh dimensions of slave treatment. And slaves—accommodating to the realities of power—encouraged their masters to think their benevolence was appreciated. Paternalism also served as a defense against abolitionist criticism. In reality, paternalism grew as a give-and-take relationship between masters and slaves—owners took labor from the bondsmen, while slaves obligated masters to provide them a measure of autonomy and living space.

Relations between men and women in the planter class were similarly defined by paternalism. The upper-class southern woman was raised and educated to be a wife, mother, and subordinate companion to men. South Carolina's Mary Boykin Chesnut wrote of her husband, "He is master of the house. . . . All the comfort of my life depends upon his being in a good humor." Women found it difficult to challenge society's rules on sexual or racial relations.

Planters' daughters usually attended one of the South's rapidly multiplying boarding schools. Typically, the young woman could entertain suitors whom her parents approved, but she quickly had to choose a husband and commit herself to a man whom she generally had known only briefly. Young women had to follow the wishes of their family, especially their father, even if it left them emotionally empty.

On marriage, a planter-class woman ceded to her husband most of her legal rights, becoming part of his family. She was isolated on a large plantation, where she oversaw the cooking and preserving of food, managed the house, supervised the children, and attended sick slaves. These realities were more confining on the frontier, where isolation was greater. Men on plantations could occasionally escape into the public realm—to town, business, or politics. Women could retreat from rural plantation culture only into kinship and associations with other women.

Marriage and Family Among Planters
A perceptive white woman sometimes approached marriage with anxiety. Lucy Breckinridge, a wealthy Virginia girl of twenty, lamented the autonomy she surrendered at the altar. In her diary she recorded: "If [husbands] care for their wives at all it is only as a sort of servant, a being made to attend to their comforts and to keep the children out of the way."

Childbearing often involved grief, poor health, and death. In 1840 the birth rate for white southern women was almost 30 percent higher than the national average. The average southern white woman would bear eight children in 1800; by 1860 the figure decreased to six. Childbirth complications were a major cause of death, occurring twice as often in the hot South as in the Northeast.

Sexual relations between planters and slaves were another problem white women endured but were not supposed to notice. "Violations of the moral law . . . made mulattos as common as blackberries," protested a woman in Georgia, but wives had to play "the ostrich game." In the 1840s and 1850s, as abolitionist attacks on slavery increased, southern men published a barrage of articles stressing that women should not discuss the slavery issue. The *Southern Quarterly Review* declared, "The proper place for a woman is at home. One of her highest privileges, to be politically merged in the existence of her husband."

But a study of women in Petersburg, Virginia, a large tobacco-manufacturing town, revealed behavior that valued financial autonomy. Over several decades before 1860, the proportion of women who never married or did not remarry after a spouse's death grew to exceed 33 percent. Likewise, the number of women who worked for wages, controlled their own property, and ran dressmaking businesses increased. In managing property, these and other women benefited from legal changes enacted to protect families from the husband's indebtedness during business panics and recessions. These reforms gave married women some property rights.

SLAVE LIFE AND LABOR

Slaves provided the physical strength and much of the know-how to build an agricultural empire, but their lives were marked by poverty, coercion, toil, and resentment. They embodied the nation's most basic contradiction: in the world's model republic, slaves were on the wrong side of a brutally unequal power relationship.

Slaves' Everyday Conditions

Beyond bare necessities, southern slaves enjoyed few material comforts. Although they generally had enough to eat, their diet was monotonous and nonnutritious. Clothing was coarse and inexpensive. Few slaves received more than one or two changes of clothing for hot and cold seasons, and one blanket each winter. Children of both sexes ran naked in hot weather and wore long cotton shirts in winter. Many slaves went without shoes until December. Conditions were generally better in cities, where slaves frequently lived in the same dwelling as their owners and were regularly hired out, enabling them to accumulate their own money.

The average slave lived in a crude, one-room cabin. Each dwelling housed one or two families. Crowding and lack of sanitation fostered the spread of infection and such contagious diseases as typhoid fever, malaria, and dysentery. White plantation doctors were hired to care for sick slaves, but some "slave doctors" attained a degree of power in the quarters and with masters by healing through herbalism and spiritualism.

Slave Work Routines

Long hours and large work gangs characterized Gulf Coast cotton districts. Overseers rang the morning bell before dawn, and black people, tools in hand, walked toward the fields. Slaves who cultivated tobacco in the Upper South worked long hours picking the sticky, sometimes noxious, leaves under harsh discipline. As one woman recalled when interviewed in the 1930s, "it was way after sundown fore they could stop that field work. Then they had to hustle to finish their night work [such as watering livestock or cleaning cotton] in time for supper, or go to bed without it."

Working from sun to sun became a norm in much of the South. Profit took precedence over paternalism. Slave women did heavy fieldwork, often as much as the men and even during pregnancy. Old people cared for children, did light chores or carded, ginned, and spun cotton.

By the 1830s planters in the South Carolina and Georgia low country used a task system whereby slaves were assigned measured amounts of work to be performed in a given amount of time. So much cotton on a daily basis was to be picked from a designated field, so many rows hoed or plowed in a specified section. On completion, slaves' time was their own for working garden plots, tending hogs, even hiring out their own labor. From this experience, many slaves developed a sense of property ownership.

Of the 1860 population of 4 million slaves, half were under the age of sixteen. "A child raised every two years," wrote Thomas Jefferson, "is of more profit than the crop of the best laboring man." And in 1858 a slaveowner writing in an agricultural magazine calculated that a slave girl he purchased in 1827 for $400 had borne three sons now worth $3,000 as his working field hands. Slave children gathered kindling, carried water to the fields, swept the yard, lifted cut sugar-cane stalks into carts, stacked wheat, chased birds away from sprouting rice plants, and labored in cotton and tobacco production.

As slave children matured, they faced psychological traumas, including powerlessness and an awareness that their parents could not protect them. They had to fight to keep from internalizing what whites labeled their inferiority. Many former slaves resented their denial of education. And for girls reaching maturity, the potential trauma of sexual abuse loomed over their lives.

Violence and Intimidation Against Slaves

Whites throughout the South believed that slaves "can't be governed except with the whip." One South Carolinian explained to a northern journalist that he whipped his slaves regularly; "the fear of the lash kept them in good order." Evidence suggests that whippings were less frequent on small farms than on large plantations. But beatings symbolized authority to the master and tyranny to slaves, who used them to evaluate a master. Former slaves said a good owner was one who did not "whip too much," whereas a bad owner "whipped till he's bloodied you and blistered you."

The master wielded virtually absolute authority on his plantation. Slaveholders rarely had to answer to the law or state, and courts did not recognize the word of chattel. Pregnant women were whipped, and there were burnings, mutilation, torture, and murder. Yet physical cruelty may have been less prevalent in the United States than in other slaveholding parts of the New World, especially some of the sugar islands of the Caribbean, where death rates were so high that the heavily male slave population shrank in size. In the United States, the slave population experienced a steady natural increase, as births exceeded deaths.

The worst evil of American slavery was the nature of slavery itself: coercion, belonging to another person, virtually no hope for mobility or change. Recalling their time in bondage, some former slaves emphasized the physical abuse, but memories focused on the tyranny of whipping as much as the pain. Delia Garlic made the essential point: "It's bad to belong to folks that own you soul an' body. . . . you couldn't guess the awfulness of it." To be a slave was to be the object of another person's will and material gain, as the saying goes, from the cradle to the grave.

Most American slaves retained their self-respect despite their bondage. They had to be subservient to their masters, but they talked and behaved differently among themselves. In *Narrative of the Life of Frederick Douglass, an American Slave, Written by Himself* (1845), Douglass wrote that most slaves, when asked about "their condition and the character of their masters, almost universally say they are contented, and that their masters are kind." Slaves did this, said Douglass, because they were governed by the maxim that "a still tongue makes a wise head." Slaves often quarreled over who had the best master, but, Douglass remarked, when one had a bad master, he sought a better master; and when he had a better one, he wanted to "be his own master."

Slave-Master Relationships

Some former slaves remembered warm feelings between masters and slaves, but the prevailing attitudes were distrust and antagonism. One woman said her mistress was "a mighty good somebody to belong to" but only "'cause she was raisin' us to work for her." Slaves also resented being used as beasts of burden. One man observed that his master "fed us reg'lar on good, 'stantial food, just like you'd tend to your horse, if you had a real good one."

Slaves were alert to the daily signs of their degraded status. One man recalled the general rule that slaves ate corn bread and owners ate biscuits. If blacks did get biscuits, "the flour that we made the biscuits out of was the third-grade sorts." If the owner took his slaves' garden produce to town to sell, slaves often suspected him of pocketing part of the profits.

Suspicion often grew into hatred. When a yellow fever epidemic struck in 1852, many slaves saw it as God's retribution. An elderly ex-slave named Minnie Fulkes cherished the conviction that God was going to punish white people for their cruelty to blacks. On the plantation, of course, slaves kept such thoughts to themselves and created ways to survive and to sustain their humanity in this world of repression.

SLAVE CULTURE AND RESISTANCE

The resource that enabled slaves to maintain such defiance was their culture: beliefs, values, and practices born of their past and maintained in the present. As best they could, they built a community knit together by stories, music, a religious world-view, leadership, the smells of their cooking, the sounds of their own voices, and the tapping of their feet. "The values expressed in folklore," wrote the African American poet Sterling Brown, provided a "wellspring to which slaves . . . could return in times of doubt to be refreshed."

African Cultural Survival

Slave culture changed significantly after 1808, when Congress banned further importation of slaves and the generations born in Africa died out. For a few years South Carolina reopened the international slave trade, but by the 1830s, the vast majority of slaves in the South were native-born Americans. Yet African influences remained strong. Some slave men plaited their hair into rows and designs; slave women often wore their hair tied in small bunches secured by string or cloth. A few men and many women wrapped their heads in kerchiefs of the styles and colors of West Africa. Some remembered the names of African ancestors passed on by family lore.

Music, religion, and folktales were part of daily life for most slaves. Borrowing from their African background and forging new American folkways, they developed what scholars have called a sacred world-view, which affected work, leisure, and self-understanding. Slaves made musical instruments with carved motifs that resembled African stringed instruments. One visitor to Georgia in the 1860s described a ritual dance of African origin known as the ring shout: "A ring of singers is formed. . . . They then utter a kind of melodious chant, which gradually increases in strength, and in noise, until it fairly shakes the house, and it can be heard for a long distance."

Many slaves continued to believe in spirit possession. While whites believed in ghosts and charms, slaves' beliefs resembled the African concept of the living dead—deceased relatives visit the earth for years until the process of dying is complete. Slaves also practiced conjuration and quasi-magical root medicine. By the 1850s noted conjurers and root doctors were reputed to live in South Carolina, Georgia, Louisiana, and isolated coastal areas with high slave populations.

Slaves increasingly developed a racial identity. In the colonial period, Africans arrived in America from many states and kingdoms, represented in distinctive languages and traditions. Africans arrived in the New World with virtually no concept of race; by the antebellum era, their descendants learned through bitter experience that race was now the defining feature of their lives.

Slaves' Religion and Music

Over time, more and more slaves adopted Christianity, fashioning it into an instrument of support and resistance. Theirs was a religion of justice and deliverance, quite unlike their masters' religious propaganda. "You ought to have heard that preachin'," said one man. "'Obey your master and mistress, don't steal chickens and eggs and meat,' but nary a word about havin' a soul to save." Slaves believed that Jesus cared about their souls and their plight.

Devout men and women worshiped every day, in the field or by the side of the road. Some slaves held secret prayer meetings that lasted far into the night. Many nurtured an unshakable belief that God would end their bondage. This faith—and the emotional release that accompanied worship—sustained them.

Slaves also adapted Christianity to African practices. In West African belief, devotees are possessed by a god so thoroughly that the god's own personality replaces the human personality. In the late antebellum era, Christian slaves experienced possession by the Protestant Holy Spirit. The combination of shouting, singing, and dancing that seemed to overtake black worshipers formed the heart of their religious faith. "The old meeting house caught fire," recalled an ex-slave preacher. "The spirit was there. . . . God saw our need and came to us." Out in brush arbors or in meetinghouses, slaves thrust their arms to heaven, made music with their feet, and sang away their woes.

Rhythm and physical movement were crucial to slaves' religious experience. In black preachers' chanted sermons, which pulled the sinner into a narrative of meanings and cadences en route to conversion, an American tradition was born. The chanted sermon was a scriptural and patterned form that required audience response punctuated by "yes sirs!" and "amens!" But it was in song that slaves left their most sublime gift to American culture.

Through spirituals, slaves tried to impose order on the chaos of their lives. Often referred to later as the *sorrow songs,* slave lyrics covered many themes, especially imminent rebirth. Sadness could immediately give way to joy: "Oh, Freedom": "Oh, Oh, Freedom / Oh, Oh, Freedom over me— / But before I'll be a slave, / I'll be buried in my grave, / And go home to my Lord, / And Be Free!"

Many songs also express intimacy and closeness with God. Some display a rebelliousness, such as the enduring "He said, and if I had my way / If I had my way, if I had my way, / I'd tear this building down!" And some spirituals reached for collective hope in the black community.

> O, gracious Lord! When shall it be,
> That we poor souls shall all be free;
> Lord, break them slavery powers—
> Will you go along with me?
> Lord break them slavery powers,
> Go sound the jubilee!

In many ways, American slaves converted the Christian God to themselves. They sought an alternative world—a home other than the one fate had given them on earth. In variations on the Br'er Rabbit folktales—in which the weak survive by wit and power is reversed—and in songs, they fashioned survival and resistance from their cultural imagination.

The Black Family in Slavery

Although American law did not recognize slave families, slaveowners expected slaves to form families and have children. As a result, there was a normal ratio of men to women, young to old. Studies have shown that, on some of the largest cotton plantations of South Carolina, when masters gave their slaves increased autonomy through the task system, the property accumulation in livestock, tools, and garden produce thus fostered led to more stable and healthier families.

Following African kinship traditions, African Americans avoided marriage between cousins (commonplace among aristocratic slaveowners). By naming their children after relatives of past generations, African Americans emphasized family history. Kinship networks and extended families held life together in many slave communities.

For slave women, sexual abuse and rape by white masters were ever-present threats. By 1860 there were 405,751 mulattos in the United States, making up 12.5 percent of the African American population. White planters were sometimes open with their behavior toward slave women, but not in the way they talked about it. Buying slaves for sex was common at the New Orleans slave market. In what was called the

This photograph of five generations of a slave family, taken in Beaufort, South Carolina, in 1862, is silent but powerful testimony of the importance that enslaved African Americans placed on their ever-threatened family ties.   (Library of Congress)

fancy trade (a fancy was a young, attractive slave girl or woman), females were sold for prices as much as 300 percent higher than the average. At such auctions, slaveholders exhibited some of the ugliest values at the heart of the slave system by paying $3,000 to $5,000 for female "companions."

The Domestic Slave Trade

Slave families most feared and hated separation by violence from those they loved, sexual appropriation, and sale. Many struggled to keep their children together and, after emancipation, to reestablish contact with loved ones lost by forced migration and sale. Between 1820 and 1860, an estimated 2 million slaves were moved into the region from western Georgia to eastern Texas. When the Union Army registered thousands of black marriages in Mississippi and Louisiana in 1864 and 1865, 25 percent of the men over forty reported that they had been forcibly separated from a previous wife. Thousands of black families were disrupted annually to serve the needs of the expanding cotton economy. Many antebellum white southerners made their living from the slave trade. In South Carolina by the 1850s, there were over one hundred slave-trading firms selling approximately 6,500 slaves annually to southwestern states. One estimate from 1858 indicated that slave sales in Richmond, Virginia, netted $4 million that year. A market guide to slave sales that same year in Richmond listed prices for "likely ploughboys," ages twelve to fourteen, at $850 to $1,050; "extra number 1 fieldgirls" at $1,300 to $1,350; and "extra number 1 men" at $1,500.

At slave pens in cities like New Orleans, traders promoted "a large and commodious showroom . . . prepared to accommodate over 200 Negroes for sale." Traders made slaves appear young, healthy, and happy, cutting gray whiskers off men, using paddles as discipline to avoid scarring their merchandise, and forcing people to dance and sing as buyers arrived. When transported to the southwestern markets, slaves were often chained together, making journeys of 500 miles or more on foot.

The complacent mixture of racism and business among traders is evident in their own language. "I refused a girl 20 year[s] old at 700 yesterday," one trader wrote in 1853. "She is very badly whipped but good teeth." Some sales were transacted at owners' requests, often for tragically inhumane reasons. "Bought a cook yesterday that was to go out of state," wrote a trader; "she just made the people mad that was all."

Strategies of Resistance

Slaves brought to their resistance efforts the common sense and determination that characterized their struggle to secure families. The scales weighed against overt revolution, but they seized opportunities to alter work conditions. They sometimes slacked off when they were not watched. Daily discontent and desperation were also manifest in equipment sabotage; carelessness about work; theft of food, livestock, or crops; or getting drunk on stolen liquor. Some slaves who were hired out might hoard their earnings or become recalcitrant. A woman named Ellen, hired as a cook in Tennessee in 1856, quietly put mercury poison into a roasted apple for her unsuspecting mistress. And some slave women resisted by trying to control their own pregnancy, either by avoiding it or by seeking it to improve conditions.

Many male and some female slaves violently attacked overseers or owners. They were customarily secured and flogged, sold away, or hanged. Southern court records

256   CHAPTER 10   THE RISE OF THE SOUTH, 1815–1860

and newspapers contain accounts of resistant slaves who disproved the image of the docile bondsman or woman.

Many slaves attempted to run away to the North, and some received assistance from the loose network known as the Underground Railroad. But it was more common for slaves to run off temporarily and hide in the woods. Approximately 80 percent of runaways were male; children prevented women from fleeing as readily. Fear, disgruntlement over treatment, or family separation might motivate slaves to flee. Only a minority ever made it to freedom in the North, but these fugitives made slavery an insecure institution by the 1850s.

American slavery produced some fearless revolutionaries. Gabriel's Rebellion involved as many as a thousand slaves when it was discovered in 1800, just before it would have exploded in Richmond, Virginia. According to controversial court testimony, a similar conspiracy existed in Charleston in 1822, led by a free black named Denmark Vesey. Born a slave in the Caribbean, Vesey won a lottery of $1,500 in 1799, bought his freedom, and became a religious leader. According to one long-argued interpretation, Vesey was a heroic revolutionary determined to free his people. But, in a recent challenge, the historian Michael Johnson points out that court testimony is the only reliable source on the alleged insurrection. Might the testimony reveal less of reality than of white South Carolina's fears of slave rebellion? The court, says Johnson, built its case on rumors and intimidated witnesses, and "conjured into being" an insurrection that was not truly about to occur. Whatever the facts, thirty-seven "conspirators" were executed, and more than three dozen others were banished from the state.

Nat Turner's Insurrection
The most famous rebel, Nat Turner, struck for freedom in Southampton County, Virginia, in 1831. Turner was a precocious child who learned to read. Encouraged by his first owner to study the Bible, he enjoyed privileges but also endured hard work and changes of masters. Young Nat eventually became a preacher known for eloquence and mysticism. After planning for years, Turner led rebels from farm to farm in the predawn darkness of August 22, 1831. The group severed limbs and crushed skulls with axes or killed victims with guns. Before alarmed planters stopped them, Turner and his followers had in forty-eight hours slaughtered sixty whites. In retaliation whites randomly killed slaves across the region. Turner was caught and hanged. As many as two hundred African Americans, lost their lives as a result of the rebellion.

Nat Turner remains a haunting symbol in America's unresolved history with slavery and discrimination. While in jail, Turner was interviewed by the Virginia lawyer and slaveholder Thomas R. Gray. Their intriguing creation, *The Confessions of Nat Turner,* became a bestseller within a month of Turner's hanging. Gray called the rebel a gloomy fanatic in a manner that made him fascinating and produced one of the most remarkable documents of American slavery. After Turner's insurrection, many states passed stiffened legal codes against black education and religious practice.

Most importantly, in 1832 a shocked Virginia held a legislative and public debate over gradual emancipation. The plan would not have freed any slaves until 1858 and provided that eventually all blacks would be colonized outside Virginia. When the House of Delegates voted, gradual abolition lost, 73 to 58. Virginia merely reinforced its defense of slavery. It was the last time white southerners would debate emancipation.

Reparations for Slavery

How should the United States come to terms with 250 years of racial slavery? Is this period best forgotten as a terrible passage, or does the nation owe a long-overdue debt to black people for their oppression? After emancipation in 1865 and rooted in vague federal promises, many former slaves believed they were entitled to forty acres and a mule, but these never materialized.

In 1897 Callie House, a poor mother of four born in 1865 in a contraband camp for ex-slaves, organized the National Ex-Slave Pension and Bounty Association, modeled after the soldiers' pension system. House traveled across the South, recruiting 250,000 members at 10-cent dues. Her lobbying of the federal government for slave pensions failed; she was accused of mail fraud and imprisoned for one year in 1916.

More recently, a widespread debate over reparations for slavery has emerged. In the rewriting of slavery's history since the 1960s, Americans have learned a great deal about how slave labor created American wealth: how insurance companies insured slaves, how complicit the U.S. government was in slavery's defense and expansion, and how slaves built the U.S. Capitol while their owners received $5 a month for their labor.

The debate is fueled by analogies: reparations paid to Japanese Americans interned during World War II, reparations paid to Native American tribes for stolen land, reparations paid Holocaust survivors and victims of forced labor, and a suit settled in 1999 that will pay roughly $2 billion to some twenty thousand black farmers for discrimination by the Agriculture Department in the early twentieth century.

Some argue that, because there are no living former slaves or slaveholders, reparations can never take the form of money. But in 2002 a lawsuit was filed against three major corporations who allegedly profited from slavery, and the National Reparations Coordinating Committee promises a suit against the U.S. government. Some city councils passed resolutions forcing companies in their jurisdictions to investigate any possible complicity with slave trading or ownership, prompting some firms to establish scholarship programs for African Americans.

Critics argue that resources would be better spent "making sure black kids have a credible education" and rebuilding inner cities. Advocates contend that, when "government participates in a crime against humanity," it is "obliged to make the victims whole." The movement for reparations has sparked broad public debate. The legacy of slavery for a people and a nation promises to become America's most traumatic test of how to reconcile its history with justice.

Summary

During the four decades before the Civil War, the South grew in land, wealth, and power along with the rest of the country. Although southern states were enmeshed in the nation's heritage and political economy, they also developed as a distinctive region, ideologically and economically, because of slavery. More than the North, the antebellum South was a biracial society; whites grew up influenced by black folkways and culture, and blacks, the vast majority of whom were slaves, became cobuilders of a rural, agricultural society.

With the sustained cotton boom, as well as state and federal Indian removal policies, the South grew into a slave society. The coercive influence of slavery affected southern life and politics and increasingly produced a leadership determined to preserve a hierarchical social and racial order. Despite their shared white supremacy, the democratic values of yeomen often clashed with the profit motives of aristocratic planters. The benevolent self-image and paternalistic ideology of slaveholders was tested by slaves' own judgments. African American slaves responded by fashioning a rich folk culture and a religion of deliverance. By 1850, white southerners built one of the last profitable, expanding slave societies on earth. The North, though deeply intertwined with southerners nationally, economically, and through a shared constitutional system and history, grew along different lines, through industrialism and free labor. The clash of these two connected yet divided societies would soon explode over the nation's future.

Chapter Review

THE "DISTINCTIVE" SOUTH

What made the antebellum South different from the North?

Both regions were capitalist and Christian (largely Protestant), and embraced the heroes and causes of the American Revolution. But they differed in their economic development: because of its climate and longer growing season, the South's development was agricultural and rural, whereas the North became increasingly urban and industrial. With a comparatively low population density and people spread out from each other, the South's commercial, educational and health-related institutions lagged. The South was also slower to develop a regional transportation network or market economy and relied on slaves for labor and the North for banking and other financial institutions. The South had fewer urban areas, and those that existed were primarily port cities such as Charleston that provided a link for commerce and small manufacturing. With few labor opportunities, the South also did not attract as many immigrants as the North.

SOUTHERN EXPANSION, INDIAN RESISTANCE, AND REMOVAL

How did Native Americans living in western territories deal with increasing migration by southern whites?

Indians dealt with white encroachment on their land in several ways. Some embraced accommodation, establishing trading posts to exchange supplies with settlers, ultimately falling into heavy debt that could only be repaid by selling their land. Others resisted, rejecting removal/relocation plans that whites offered, and holding fast to their land. The Creeks and Cherokees assimilated to American standards—even changed their political structure to more closely resemble that of whites—in an effort to keep their land. When Congress narrowly passed the Indian Removal Act in 1830, which provided funds to relocate Indians to territory further west, the Cherokees refused to leave and sued the state of Georgia in federal court. While the courts found them entitled to their land, President Jackson sent in troops to evacuate thousands of Cherokees and march them from Georgia to present-day Oklahoma. Many refused to go and were imprisoned; others died of disease and exhaustion on the trek known as the Trail of Tears.

LIMITS OF MOBILITY IN A HIERARCHICAL SOCIETY

What class tensions emerged in the antebellum South?

Although they were fewer in number, the slave-holding planter class occupied the highest rungs of southern society and dominated its political life (controlling up to 85 percent of legislative posts), as well as churches and colleges. Before the 1830s, the vast socioeconomic differences between rich planters and small, independent, nonslaveholding yeomen farmers were mediated by their shared racial status as white. However tensions emerged as yeomen began to resent their underrepresentation in state government and the corruption of local governments. They sought universal manhood suffrage and other reforms, including popular election of governors and legislative apportionment based solely on the white population—all of which planters resisted. Moreover, as cotton farming made land less and less available, nonslaveholders faced fewer opportunities to improve their station, while planters enjoyed greater and greater profits.

THE PLANTERS' WORLD

How did paternalism function on southern plantations?

Paternalism was a belief system that enabled slaveholders to justify their dominance over slaves and white women. In this view, slave owners portrayed themselves as benevolent guardians over their slaves and families—which put them at the helm and required submission of those beneath them. Paternalism denied the truth of slavery's brutality and inhumanity, while providing a counter to abolitionism. As the system developed, it functioned as an exchange in which slaves labored and obligated their owners to provide them with necessities and some autonomy. Between husbands and wives, paternalism gave men control of women's legal rights in marriage—her property became his to manage—and she became his subordinate in every way.

SLAVE LIFE AND LABOR

What was the true nature of the master-slave relationship?

Generally speaking, distrust and antagonism were at the core of most master-slave relationships. For slaves, the vulnerability and frustration of being owned, ruled, and at the mercy of another human being, along with being used as a work-animal, sparked much resentment. Slaves did not trust masters to deal fairly with them in their exchanges. There was also much cruelty and brutality—rather than paternalism—on the part of many owners, including whippings and beatings. Slave families were often separated, as one or more members were sold away to other plantations.

SLAVE CULTURE AND RESISTANCE

How did slaves adapt Christianity and make it their own?

While many slaves maintained and adapted aspects of the African heritage to their new circumstances, they also embraced and remade Christianity as a form of resistance. In secret prayer meetings, slaves focused on justice and deliverance, believing God would liberate them from their servitude and exact retribution from those who unjustly enslaved or abused them. They also merged their Christianity with African practices, adding shouting, singing, dancing, and other rituals to their religious meetings, along with chanted sermons, which were regarded as vital for the conversion experience. Their religious rituals not only attempted to restore order and meaning to their lives but also establish closeness with God and hope for the future. Finally, while prayer meetings were often held in secret, they helped forge relationships and community in slave quarters.

SUGGESTIONS FOR FURTHER READING

Ira Berlin, *Generations of Captivity: A History of African American Slaves* (2003)

David Brion Davis, *Inhuman Bondage: The Rise and Fall of Slavery in the New World* (2006)

Steven Deyle, *Carry Me Back: The Domestic Slave Trade in American Life* (2005)

Drew G. Faust, ed., *The Ideology of Slavery: Proslavery Thought in the Antebellum South, 1830–1860* (1981)

Walter Johnson, *Soul by Soul: Life Inside the Antebellum Slave Market* (1999)

Charles Joyner, *Down by the Riverside: A South Carolina Slave Community* (1984)

James D. Miller, *South by Southwest: Planter Emigration and Identity in the Slave South* (2002)

James Oakes, *Slavery and Freedom: An Interpretation of the Old South* (1991)

Michael O'Brien, *Conjectures of Order: Intellectual Life and the American South, 1810–1860* (2004)

Daniel H. Usner Jr., *American Indians in the Lower Mississippi Valley* (1998)

Jean Fagan Yellin, *Harriet Jacobs: A Life* (2004)

The Modernizing North

CHAPTER 11

1815–1860

After twenty-five days at sea, Mary Ann and James Archbald and their four children arrived in New York on April 17, 1807. The couple left their ancestral homeland in Scotland reluctantly, hoping for a bright future in which their children would be beholden to no one, neither landlord nor employer. They sought the Jeffersonian dream of republican independence.

The Archbalds bought a farm in central New York, along a Hudson River tributary, where they raised sheep, grew hay and vegetables, skinned rabbits for meat and fur, and sold whatever they did not need. Twenty-one years after leaving Scotland, Mary Ann Archbald, in anticipation of their last mortgage payment, declared "being out of debt is, in my estimation, being rich." By then, her sons were young adults with visions of wealth that centered on water, not land.

On April 17, 1817—a decade after the Archbalds arrived on American shores—the New York State legislature authorized construction of a canal connecting Lake Erie to the Hudson River, and surveyors mapped a route through the Archbalds' farm. The sons (one in his early twenties, the other a teenager) helped dig the canal, while Mary Ann and her daughters cooked and cleaned for the twenty Irish laborers whom the sons hired. The Archbald sons tried commercial speculation, borrowing money to buy wheat and lumber in western New York to resell hopefully for substantial profits to merchants in Albany and New York City. As early as 1808 Mary Ann reached an unpleasant conclusion about her new home: "We are a nation of traders in spite of all Mr. Jefferson can say or do."

After the War of 1812, the market economy took off in unanticipated ways. In the North, steamboats, canals, and then

This icon will direct you to interactive activities and study materials on *A People And A Nation, Brief Edition* website: **www.cengage.com/history/norton/ peoplenationbrief8e**

Chronology

1825	Erie Canal is completed.	1837	Panic of 1837 begins economic downturn.
1830	Railroad era begins.	1839–43	Economic depression occurs.
1830s–50s	Urban riots are commonplace.	1842	*Commonwealth v. Hunt* declares strikes lawful.
1834	Women workers strike at Lowell textile mills.	1844	Federal government grant sponsors first telegraph line.
1835	Arkansas passes first women's property law.		Lowell Female Reform Association is formed.
1836	Second Bank of the United States closes.		

railroads remapped the young republic's geography and economy, setting off booms in westward migration, industry, commerce, and urban growth.

Even after the War of 1812, the United States' financial connections to Europe, particularly Britain, remained profound. When Europeans suffered hard times, so did American merchants, manufacturers, farmers, and workers. For wage-earning Americans, economic downturns often meant unemployment and destitution.

Some worried that rapid market expansion threatened the nation's moral fiber. It upset traditional family patterns and relied heavily on unskilled workers—many of whom were immigrants and free African Americans—who seemed unfit for republican citizenship. Commercially minded Americans saw cities as at once exemplars of civilization and breeding grounds of depravity and conflict. Only through strong faith in progress and upward mobility could Americans remain hopeful that the nation's future greatness lay in commercial expansion. They did so partly by articulating a free-labor ideology that rationalized the negative aspects of market expansion while promoting the northern labor system as superior to the South's.

- What factors contributed to the commercialization of northern society, and why did they have less of an influence on the South?
- How did the daily lives—work, family, leisure—of northerners change between 1815 and 1860?
- What factors contributed to rapid urbanization, and how did urban and rural life in the North compare with that in the South?

OR IS IT THE NORTH THAT WAS DISTINCTIVE?

The historian James McPherson has questioned whether it was the *North*—New England, the Middle Atlantic, and the Old Northwest—and not the South that diverged from the norm. At the republic's birth, the two regions had much in common: slavery, ethnic homogeneity, a majority of the population engaged in agriculture, and a small urban population. But that changed with economic development after the War of 1812. State and local governments as well as private entrepreneurs engaged in development, which happened more extensively and rapidly in the North. As the North embraced economic progress, it diverged from the international norm, and, writes McPherson, "hurtled forward toward a future that many Southerners found distasteful if not frightening."

While the South expanded as a slave society, during and after the War of 1812, the North transformed into a market society. With European trade largely cut off during the war, entrepreneurs invested in domestic factories. More men, women, and children began working for wages—rather than on family farms—making the domestic demand for foodstuffs soar. Consequently, farming became commercialized, with farmers abandoning self-sufficiency and specializing in crops that would yield cash on the market. Farmers then used the cash to buy goods they once made for themselves, such as cloth, candles, and soap, as well as some luxuries. In the North, market expansion altered virtually every aspect of life. Some historians see these rapid and pervasive changes as a market revolution.

Preindustrial Farms

At the beginning of the nineteenth century, few yeoman farmers, North or South, were entirely independent. Most practiced mixed agriculture, raising a variety of crops and livestock. When they produced more than they needed, they traded the surplus with neighbors or sold it to local storekeepers. Such transactions often transpired without money; farmers might trade eggs for shoes, or they might labor in a neighbor's fields in exchange for hay. Farmers like James and Mary Ann Archbald engaged in long-distance market exchange, selling farm goods for cash to merchants, who then sent the goods to people hundreds of miles away. Although families like the Archbalds indulged in the occasional luxury, security and debt elimination mattered more than profit.

Family members provided most farm labor, though some yeoman farmers, North and South, relied on slaves or indentured servants. Men and boys worked in the fields, herded livestock, chopped firewood, fished, and hunted. Women and girls tended gardens, milked cows, spun and wove, processed and preserved food, prepared meals, washed clothes, and looked after infants and toddlers.

In their quest for independence, farmers cooperated with one another, lending each other tools, harvesting each other's fields, bartering goods, raising their neighbors' barns, and husking each other's corn. Little cash exchanged hands, mostly because money was scarce. Still, New England farmers kept elaborate account books listing what they owed and were owed, whereas Southern farmers simply made mental notes of debts. In both regions, years might pass without debts being repaid.

In the local economy—where farmers exchanged goods with people they knew—a system of just price prevailed, in which value was calculated on the basis of the amount of labor involved. When the same farmers engaged in long-distance trade—selling goods through a network of merchants who eventually resold them as far away as Europe—they set prices according to what the market would bear.

Preindustrial Artisans

Farmers who lived near towns or villages often purchased crafted goods from local cobblers, saddlers, blacksmiths, gunsmiths, silversmiths, and tailors. Most artisans, though, lived in the nation's seaports, where master craftsmen (businessmen who owned their own shops and tools) employed apprentices and journeymen. Although the vast majority of craftsmen, North and South, were white, free blacks were well represented in some cities' trades, such as tailoring and carpentry in Charleston,

Although separating flax fibers from their woody base could be arduous work, flax-scutching bees—much like corn-husking bees—brought together neighbors for frivolity as well as work.   (National Gallery of Art, Washington, D.C. Gift of Edgar William and Bernice Chrysler Garbisch)

South Carolina. Teenage apprentices lived with masters, who trained, lodged, and fed them in exchange for labor. The master's wife and daughters, cooked, cleaned, and sewed for the workers. When their apprenticeship expired, apprentices became journeymen who earned wages, hoping to save money to open their own shops. The workplace had little division of labor or specialization. For example, a tailor measured, designed, and sewed an entire suit.

Men, women, and children worked long days on farms and in workshops, but the pace was uneven and unregimented. During busy periods, they worked dawn to dusk; work slowed after the harvest or after a large order was completed. Husking bees and barn raisings brought people together to shuck corn and raise buildings, but also to eat, drink, and flirt. Busy periods did not stop artisans from taking grog breaks or reading the newspaper aloud; they might even close their shops to attend a political meeting. Journeymen craftsmen often staggered in late on Monday mornings, if they showed up at all, after carousing on their day off. In this way, workers exerted influence over the workplace.

Early Industrialization Early industry in the United States reorganized daily work routines and market relationships. In the late eighteenth and early nineteenth centuries, a putting-out system developed in the Northeast, particularly Massachusetts, New Jersey, and Pennsylvania. Women and children continued to produce household goods but now a merchant supplied them with raw materials, paid them a wage (usually a price for each piece they produced), and sold their wares in distant markets, pocketing the profits himself. Outwork, as it is sometimes called, appealed to women eager for cash to secure economic independence or save for additional land where their children could set up farms. Particularly in New England—where population density and tired soil constricted farming prospects—the putting-out system provided opportunities to earn money with which to buy cheaper, more fertile western lands.

The earliest factories grew in tandem with the putting-out system. Samuel Slater helped set up the first American water-powered spinning mill in Rhode Island in 1790, using children to card and spin raw cotton into thread. He sent the spun thread to nearby farm families who were paid to weave it into cloth. Although the work remained familiar, women now operated their looms for wages and produced cloth for the market.

THE TRANSPORTATION REVOLUTION

Before the War of 1812, natural waterways provided the most readily available and inexpensive transportation routes for people and goods, but they had limitations. Boatmen poled bateaux (cargo boats) down shallow rivers or floated flatboats down deep ones. Cargo generally moved in one direction—downstream—and most boats were destroyed for lumber at their destination. Upstream commerce was limited.

Roads

Although some roads were built during the colonial and revolutionary eras, they often became obstructed by fallen trees, soaked by mud, or clouded in dust, thereby restricting overland transport. To reduce mud and dust, some turnpike companies built corduroy roads, whose tightly lined-up logs resembled the ribbed fabric. But passengers complained of nausea from being continually jolted, and merchants remained wary of transporting fragile wares by wagon. Land transportation was slow and expensive. In 1800, it cost as much to ship a ton of goods 30 miles into the interior as to ship the same goods from New York to England. The lack of cheap, quick transportation impeded westward expansion and industrial growth.

After the American Revolution, some northern states chartered private stock companies to build turnpikes (toll roads), which expanded commercial possibilities in southern New England and the Middle Atlantic. But during the War of 1812 the lack of a road system in more northerly and southerly reaches constrained the movement of troops and supplies, prompting renewed interest in building roads. Aside from the National Road, financing fell on the states and private investors. The new turnpike companies that emerged did sometimes adopt improvements, such as laying hard crushed-stone surfaces, but many of the newly built roads suffered from the old problems. With natural water routes unpredictable and roads predictably bad, an urgent need arose for better transportation.

Steamboats

The first major innovation was the steamboat. In 1807 Robert Fulton's *Clermont* traveled between New York and Albany on the Hudson River in thirty-two hours, demonstrating the feasibility of steam engines to power boats. After the Supreme Court's 1814 ruling against monopolies in *Gibbons v. Ogden* (1824), steamboat companies flourished on eastern rivers and, to a lesser extent, the Great Lakes. They transported settlers to the Midwest, where they would grow grain and raise pigs. Along western rivers like the Mississippi and the Ohio, steamboats carried midwestern timber and grain and southern cotton to New Orleans, where they were transferred to oceangoing vessels destined for northern and international ports. Privately operated, steamboats became subject to federal regulations after frequent and deadly accidents in which boilers exploded, fires ignited, and boats collided.

Canals

In the late eighteenth and early nineteenth centuries, private companies (sometimes with state subsidies) built small canals to transport goods to and from interior locations. These projects rarely reaped the profits investors sought, making it difficult to court investors for other projects. In 1815 only three canals measured more than 2 miles long; the longest was 27 miles. After Madison's veto of the Bonus Bill dashed New Yorkers' hopes for a canal connecting Lake Erie to the port of New York, Governor DeWitt Clinton pushed successfully for a state-sponsored initiative. The Erie Canal was to run 363 miles between Buffalo and Albany, and was to be 4 feet deep.

Erie Canal

Construction began on July 4, 1817. The canal, its promoters emphasized, would demonstrate how American ingenuity and hard work could overcome any obstacle, including the combined ascent and descent of 680 feet between Buffalo and Albany. Building the canal would help unify the nation and secure its commercial independence from Europe.

Over the next eight years, nearly nine thousand laborers felled forests, shoveled dirt, blasted rock, hauled boulders, rechanneled streams, and molded the canal bed. Stonemasons and carpenters built aqueducts and locks. The work was dangerous, often taking place in malaria- and rattlesnake-infested swamps. Gunpowder explosions blew up some workers along with the rock. Collapsing canal beds smothered others, while some fell to their deaths from aqueducts and locks.

The canal's promoters celebrated the waterway as the work of "republican free men." Although farmers and artisans provided important labor, unskilled laborers—including immigrants and convicts—outnumbered them. Once completed, the Erie Canal relied heavily on child labor. Boys led the horses who pulled the canal boats between the canal's eighty-three locks, while girls cooked and cleaned on the boats. When the canal froze shut during winter, many workers had neither employment nor shelter.

After its completion in November 1825, the Erie Canal became an immediate commercial success. Horse-drawn boats, stacked with bushels of wheat, barrels of oats, and piles of logs, streamed eastward from western New York and Buffalo, where shipments were transferred to canal boat. Forty thousand passengers in 1825 alone traveled on the new waterway. The canal shortened the journey between Buffalo and New York City from twenty to six days and reduced freight charges by nearly 95 percent, thus securing New York City's position as the nation's preeminent port. Goods that were previously unavailable in the nation's interior now could be had easily and cheaply.

By 1840 canals crisscrossed the Northeast and Midwest, and total canal mileage reached 3,300. Fewer canals were dug in the South, where the region's navigable rivers made them less necessary. None of the new canals enjoyed the Erie's financial success. As the high cost of construction combined with economic contraction, investment in canals slumped in the 1830s. Several midwestern states could not repay their canal loans, leading them to bankruptcy or near-bankruptcy. By mid-century the canal era had ended. The Erie Canal (by then twice enlarged and rerouted) continued to prosper and operate until the late twentieth century.

Railroads

The future belonged to railroads. Trains moved faster than canal boats and could operate year-round. Railroads could connect the most remote locations to national markets. By 1860 the United States had 60,000 miles of track, mostly in the North, and railroads dramatically reduced the cost and time of shipping goods by land.

The United States railroad era began in 1830 when Peter Cooper's locomotive, Tom Thumb, steamed along 13 miles of Baltimore & Ohio Railroad track. Not until the 1850s did railroads offer long-distance service at reasonable rates. Even then, lack of a common standard for track width thwarted development of a national system. A journey from Philadelphia to Charleston involved eight different gauges; this meant that passengers and freight had to change trains seven times. Only at Bowling Green, Kentucky, did northern and southern railroads connect. As such, the nation's canals and railroads did little to unite the regions and promote nationalism, as proponents had hoped.

Government Promotion of Internal Improvements

Northern state and local governments and private investors spent substantially more on internal improvements than southerners. Pennsylvania and New York together accounted for half of all state monies invested. Southern states invested in railroads, but—with smaller free populations—they collected fewer taxes and had less to spend.

For capitalists seeking dividends, southern railroads seemed a poor bet. To be profitable for investors and affordable for shippers, trains had to be filled in both directions, transporting southern agricultural goods north and sending northern manufactured goods south. Although planters bought northern ready-made clothes and shoes for slaves, such purchases—made on an annual basis—did not constitute a regular source of incoming freight. Because the wealthiest men lived along rivers and could send their cotton to market on steamboats, they sometimes saw little need for railroads.

The North and South laid roughly the same amount of railroad track per person before the Civil War, but when measured in mileage, the more populous North had tracks that stretched considerably farther, forming an integrated system of local

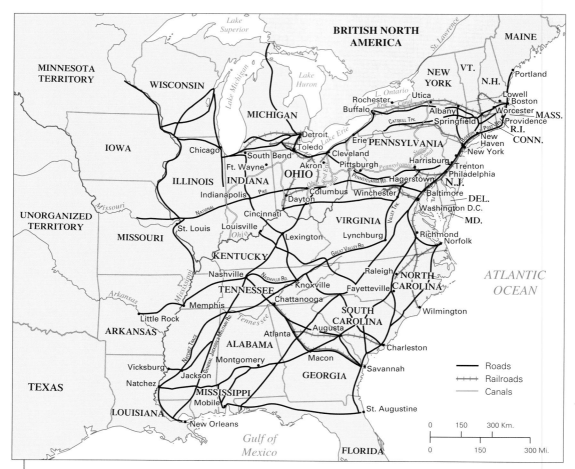

Map 11.1   Major Roads, Canals, and Railroads, 1850

A transportation network linked the seaboard to the interior. Settlers followed those routes westward, and they sent back grain, grain products, and cotton to the port cities.

lines branching off major trunk lines. In the South, railroads remained local. Neither people nor goods moved easily across the South, unless they traveled via steamboat or flatboat along the Mississippi River system, and even then, flooded banks disrupted passage for weeks.

Regional Connections   The North's frenzy of canal and railroad building expanded transportation networks far into the hinterlands. In 1815 nearly all produce from the Old Northwest floated down the Mississippi to New Orleans, tying that region's fortunes to the South. By the 1850s, though, canals and railroads strengthened economic, cultural, and political links between the Old Northwest—particularly the densely populated northern regions—and the Northeast.

Internal improvements hastened westward migration, making western settlement more appealing by providing easy access to eastern markets and the comforts of home. News, visitors, and luxuries now traveled regularly to previously remote areas of the Northeast and Midwest.

With Samuel F. B. Morse's invention of the telegraph in 1844, news traveled almost instantaneously. By 1852 more than 23,000 miles of lines were strung across the nation. The telegraph facilitated the birth of modern business practices involving the coordination of market conditions, production, and supply across great distances.

Ambivalence Toward Progress

Many northerners hailed internal improvements as symbols of progress. Northerners proclaimed that, by building canals and railroads, they had completed God's design for the North American continent. On a more practical level, canals and railroads enabled them to seek better opportunities in the West.

But many northerners worried about the costs of progress. Mary Ann Archbald savored the fresh seafood that now reached her but regretted that her sons turned to speculation. Others decried the enormous numbers of Irish canal diggers and railroad tracklayers, whom they deemed depraved and racially inferior. Still others worried that, by promoting urban growth, transportation innovations fostered social ills.

The degradation of the natural world proved worrisome, too. When streams were rerouted, swamps drained, and forests felled, natural habitats were disturbed, even destroyed. Deprived of waterpower, mills no longer ran. Without forests, wild animals—on which many rural people (Native and European American) had relied for protein—sought homes elsewhere. Fishermen, too, found their sources of protein (and cash) dried up when natural waterways were dammed or rerouted to feed canals.

FACTORIES AND INDUSTRIALIZATION

By dramatically lowering transportation costs, internal improvements facilitated the Northeast's rapid manufacturing and commercial expansion. With the trans-Appalachian West open for settlement, western farmers supplied raw materials and foodstuffs for northeastern factories and workers. They also expanded the domestic market for Northeastern manufactured goods. Focused on cultivating their lands, western settlers preferred to buy rather than make cloth, shoes, and other goods. They needed northeastern iron, too, for farm implements (plows, pitchforks, scythes), nails, and railroad tracks.

One of the oldest industries in North America, iron was centered in Middle Atlantic states, especially Pennsylvania, but stretched to Richmond and Albany. Iron forges, typically small enterprises, flourished wherever ore deposits and fuel sources abounded. During the 1840s, ironworks increasingly shifted from charcoal to coal and then steam to heat their furnaces. But production methods and daily work remained unchanged, with smaller firms remaining more efficient than larger ones.

Factory Work

In other industries, daily life changed dramatically. Much early industrialization involved processing raw materials—milling flour, turning hogs into packaged meat, or sawing lumber. The pork-packing industry illustrates how specialization turned skilled craftsmen into laborers. Traditionally, each butcher cut up an entire pig. Under industrial organization, each worker was assigned a particular task, such as cutting

The United States as a Developing Nation

In the early nineteenth century, the United States was a developing nation, as its economy slowly shifted from agriculture and raw materials to producing manufactured goods. To develop, the United States imported capital to finance international trade, internal improvements, and factories.

American political and economic leaders in the early nineteenth century talked as if they were masters of their own fate. Despite the political independence the United States established after the Revolutionary War and the War of 1812, in many ways, the United States remained economically dependent on Great Britain. Following the War of 1812, 90 percent of all U.S. foreign capital came from Britain, and around 60 percent of British capital exports flowed to the United States. Americans used British capital to develop the canals and railroads. The British invested $7 million in New York State bonds to finance the Erie Canal. Altogether, European investors provided 80 percent of the money to build the Erie.

The United States imported more goods than it exported. Imported capital balanced the trade deficit. As in most developing countries, exports were primarily agricultural commodities; 50 percent of all exports were cotton. British credit financed cotton sales.

U.S. dependency on international capital was highlighted during the Panics of 1819 and 1837. Although these financial crises began in the United States, they were intensified when economic problems in England led investors to pull capital from the United States while merchants demanded that Americans pay their debts to British creditors. Money became tight, and the economy declined.

Thus both economic development and hard times revealed the significance of international capital links to the United States, a developing nation.

Workers near the entrance of the Erie Canal into the Hudson River prepare to ship agricultural products from western New York and the Midwest to the international port of New York.

(© Collection of the New-York Historical Society)

off the right front leg or scooping out the entrails, as the pig moved down a "disassembly line."

The impersonal nature and formal rules of factory work contrasted with the informality of artisan shops and farm households. In large factories, laborers never saw owners, working instead under paid supervisors, nor did they see the final product of their labor. Factory workers lost their sense of autonomy as the bell, steam whistle, or clock governed their day. Jobs were insecure, as competition—particularly from the steady stream of European immigrants, who started arriving in the 1840s—frequently led to replacement by cheaper, less-skilled workers or children. Opportunities for advancement were virtually nil.

At first Americans imported the machines that would make mass production possible or copied British designs. Soon, they built their own. The American System of manufacturing, as the British called it, used precision machinery to produce interchangeable parts. Eli Whitney, the cotton gin's inventor, promoted interchangeable parts in 1798, when he contracted with the federal government to make ten thousand rifles in twenty-eight months. The American System quickly became the machine-tool industry—the manufacture of machines for mass production. With the time and skill involved in manufacturing greatly reduced, the new system permitted mass production of inexpensive but high-quality household items.

Textile Mills

In no industry was mechanization more dramatic than textiles, whose production was centered in New England, near sources of water to power spinning machines and looms. After 1815, New England's rudimentary cotton mills developed into modern factories where machines mass-produced goods. Cotton cloth production rose from 4 million yards in 1817 to 323 million in 1840, and in the mid-1840s, the cotton mills employed approximately eighty thousand operatives; more than half were women.

This young mill girl at Waltham or Lowell, probably in the late 1840s, posed for an early daguerreotype. Her swollen and rough hands contrast with her youth, neat dress, and carefully tied, beribboned hair. Her hands suggest that she worked, as did most twelve- and thirteen-year-olds, as a warper, straightening the strands of cotton or wool as they entered the looms.   (© Mary Evans Picture Library/ The Image Works)

Unable to find enough laborers near mills, managers recruited New England farm daughters, whom they housed in boarding houses in what became known as the Waltham or Lowell plan. People who lived off the land were often suspicious of those who did not—particularly in the young United States, where an agrarian lifestyle was associated with virtue. To ease concerns, mill owners offered paternalistic oversight; they enforced curfews, prohibited alcohol, and required church attendance. Still, the Waltham system offered farm girls opportunities to socialize with other women and gain a sense of independence.

Working conditions in textile mills—the deafening roar of the power looms, long hours, and regimentation—made young women cling to notions their stints were temporary. They used their wages to help their families buy land or send a brother to college, to save for their dowries or education, or to spend on personal items, such as clothing. The average girl arrived at sixteen and stayed five years, usually leaving to get married, often to men they met in town rather than farm boys at home.

Although the Waltham plan drew international attention, more common was the Rhode Island (or Fall River) plan employed by Samuel Slater, among others. Mills hired entire families, whom they lodged in boarding houses. Men often worked farm plots nearby while wives and children worked in the mills, though as the system developed, men worked in the factories, supervising wives and children in family-based work units.

Labor Protests

Life in the textile mills got harder over time. To increase productivity, managers sped up machines and required each worker to operate more machines. Between 1836 and 1850 the number of spindles and looms in Lowell increased 150 and 140 percent, respectively, whereas the number of workers increased by only 50 percent. To boost profits, owners lengthened hours, cut wages, and packed boarding houses.

Workers organized, and in 1834, responding to a 25 percent wage cut, they unsuccessfully turned out (struck) against the Lowell mills. As conditions worsened and strikes failed, workers resisted in new ways. In 1844 Massachusetts mill women formed the Lowell Female Reform Association and joined with other workers to press, unsuccessfully, for state legislation mandating a ten-hour instead of fourteen-hour day.

Women aired their complaints in worker-run newspapers: in 1842, the *Factory Girl* appeared in New Hampshire, the *Wampanoag and Operatives' Journal* in Massachusetts. Two years later, mill workers founded the *Voice of Industry,* nicknamed "the factory girl's voice." The owner-sponsored *Lowell Offering* faced controversy when workers charged that its editors suppressed articles criticizing working conditions.

Worker turnover weakened women's organizational efforts. Few militant native-born mill workers stayed to fight managers and owners, and gradually, fewer New England daughters entered the mills, replaced in the 1850s by Irish immigrants. Technological improvements made the work less skilled and more routine, reducing wages.

Male workers, too, protested changes wrought by the market economy. As voters, they formed labor political parties first in Pennsylvania, New York, and Massachusetts in the 1820s and later elsewhere. They advocated free public education and an end to imprisonment for debt and opposed banks and monopolies. Still aspiring to own land, some advocated for free homesteads.

Labor Unions

Organized labor's greatest achievement came through the courts. When journeyman shoemakers organized during the early 1800s, employers accused them of criminal conspiracy. The cordwainers' (shoemakers') cases between 1806 and 1815 left labor organizations in an uncertain position. Although the courts acknowledged journeymen's right to organize, judges viewed strikes as illegal until a Massachusetts case, *Commonwealth v. Hunt* (1842), ruled that Boston journeyman boot makers could strike "to subserve their own interests."

The first unions arose among urban journeymen in printing, woodworking, shoemaking, and tailoring. Typically local, the strongest sought protection against competition from inferior workmen by regulating apprenticeships and establishing minimum wages. Umbrella organizations of individual craft unions, like the National Trade Union (1834), arose in several cities in the 1820s and 1830s. But the movement fell apart amid wage reductions and unemployment in the hard times of 1839–1843.

Permanent labor organizations were difficult to sustain. Skilled craftsmen looked down on unskilled and semiskilled workers. Moreover, workers divided along ethnic, religious, racial, and gender lines.

CONSUMPTION AND COMMERCIALIZATION

Before the 1820s, women sewed most clothing at home, and some people purchased used clothing. Tailors and seamstresses made wealthy men's and women's clothing to order. By the 1820s and 1830s, much clothing was mass-produced for sale in clothing stores. Measuring was replaced by standard sizes. And now, instead of a tailor's performing every task, the process was divided so one worker cut patterns, another sewed hems, and another fixed buttons. The invention of the sewing machine in 1846 sped the process, especially after it became widely available in the 1850s. Many farm families continued to make their own clothing, but when they could afford to, they bought clothes.

The Garment Industry

Market expansion created a demand for mass-produced clothing. Girls working in factories no longer had time to sew clothes. Young immigrant men, separated from mothers and sisters, had to buy the crudely made, loose-fitting clothing. But the biggest market for ready-made clothes initially was the cotton South. With the success of the textile industry driving up the demand and price for raw cotton, planters bought ready-made shoes and clothes for slaves.

Retailers often bought goods wholesale, though many manufactured shirts and trousers in their own factories. Lewis and Hanford of New York City boasted of cutting more than 100,000 garments in winter 1848–1849. The New York firm did business mostly in the South and owned a retail outlet in New Orleans. While southerners and westerners became involved in the clothing trade, its center remained in New York.

Specialization of Commerce

Commercial specialization transformed some urban traders, especially in New York, into merchant princes. After the Erie Canal opened, New York City became a stop on every major trade route from Europe, southern ports, and the West. Traders sometimes invested in factories, further stimulating urban manufacturing. Some cities specialized: Rochester became a milling center (the Flour City), and Cincinnati (Porkopolis) became the first meatpacking center.

Merchants who engaged in complex commercial transactions required large—mostly male—office staffs. At the bottom were messenger boys, often preteens, who delivered documents. Above them were copyists, who hand-copied documents. Clerks processed documents and did translations. Above them were the bookkeeper and the confidential chief clerk. Those seeking employment in such countinghouses took a course from a writing master. All hoped to rise to partner, although their chances were increasingly slim.

Specialization lagged in small towns, where merchants continued to exchange goods with local farm women, and craftsmen continued to sell finished goods, such as shoes. In some rural areas, peddlers acted as general merchants. But as transportation improved and towns grew, small-town merchants began to specialize.

Commercial Farming

Even amid the manufacturing and commercial boom, agriculture remained the backbone of the economy, North and South. But while the expansion of cotton production in the Southwest brought limited economic change to the rest of the South, in the North, the transportation revolution and market expansion transformed formerly semi-subsistence farms into commercial enterprises. Many families stopped practicing mixed agriculture and began to specialize in cash crops.

By the 1820s, eastern farmers had cultivated nearly all available land, and the uneven terrains did not lend themselves to the new labor-saving farm implements introduced in the 1830s, such as mechanical sowers, reapers, and threshers. Consequently, many northern farmers either moved west or gave up farming for jobs in merchants' houses and factories. Those who remained, however, proved adaptable, their efforts encouraged by state governments that promoted agricultural innovation.

In 1820 about one-third of northern produce was intended for the market, but by 1850 it surpassed 50 percent. As farmers shifted toward market-oriented production, they invested in additional land (buying farms of neighbors who moved west), new equipment, and new labor sources (hired hands). Many New England and Middle Atlantic farm families faced steep competition from midwestern farmers after the Erie Canal's opening, and they began abandoning wheat and corn and turning toward vegetables, fruit, and livestock, especially cattle. Much of what they produced fed the North's growing urban and manufacturing populations.

Farmers financed innovations through land sales and debts. Indeed, increasing land values promised the greatest profit. Farm families who owned land flourished, but by the 1840s it took more than ten years for a laborer in the Northeast to save enough to buy a farm. The number of tenant farmers and hired hands increased, and farmers who previously relied mostly on unpaid family members and enslaved workers now leased portions of their farms or hired waged labor.

Farm Women's Changing Labor

As the commercial economy expanded, rural women added new responsibilities to their substantial chores. Some took in outwork. Many increased production of eggs, dairy products, and garden produce for sale; others raised bees or silkworms.

With New England textile mills producing more finished cloth, farm women and children often abandoned time-consuming spinning and weaving and instead bought factory-produced cloth. With the time saved, women made butter and cheese in large quantities for the market. Some mixed-agriculture farms converted entirely to dairy production, with men taking over formerly female tasks. Canals and railroads carried cheese to eastern ports, where wholesalers sold it worldwide.

Rural Communities   Despite pressure to manage their farms like time-efficient businesses, some farmers clung to old practices of gathering at market, general stores, taverns, and church. They continued barn raisings and husking bees, but by the 1830s, with young women working in textile mills and young men laboring as clerks or factory hands, there were fewer young people at such events.

Farmers continued to swap labor and socialize with neighbors, but they began to reckon debts in dollars. They watched national and international markets more closely. When financial panics hit, cash shortages almost halted business activity, casting many farmers further into debt, even bankruptcy. Faced with potentially losing their land, farmers called in neighbors' debts, sometimes rupturing long-established relationships.

Cycles of Boom and Bust   With market expansion came boom and bust cycles. Prosperity stimulated demand for finished goods, such as clothing and furniture, which led to higher prices and still higher production and to speculation in land. Investment money was plentiful as Americans saved and foreign, mostly British, investors bought U.S. bonds and securities. Then production surpassed demand. Prices and wages fell; land and stock values collapsed, and investment money left the United States. This boom-and-bust cycle touched the whole country, but particularly the Northeast.

Although the 1820s and 1830s were boom times, financial panic triggered a bust in 1837, the year after the Second Bank of the United States closed. Economic contraction remained severe through 1843. Many banks could not repay depositors, and states, facing deficits, defaulted on bonds. European, especially British, investors became suspicious of U.S. loans and withdrew money from the United States.

Hard times had come. "The streets seemed deserted," Sidney George Fisher observed of Philadelphia in 1842. "The largest [merchant] houses are shut up and to rent, there is no business . . . no money, no confidence." New York countinghouses closed their doors. The hungry formed bread lines at soup societies, and beggars crowded the sidewalks. Crowds of laborers demanding their deposits gathered at closed banks. Sheriffs sold seized property at one-quarter of pre–hard-time prices. In smaller cities like Lynn, Massachusetts, shoemakers weathered hard times by fishing and tending gardens, while laborers dug for clams and harvested dandelions. Congress passed the Federal Bankruptcy Law of 1841; by the time the law was repealed two years later, forty-one thousand bankrupts sought protection under its provisions.

FAMILIES IN FLUX

Sweeping changes in the household economy, rural as well as urban, led to new family ideals. In the preindustrial era, families were primarily economic units; now they became a moral and cultural institution. In reality few families could live up to this ideal.

The Ideal Family

In the North, the market economy increasingly separated the home from the workplace, leading to a new middle-class ideal in which men functioned in the public sphere, while women oversaw the private or domestic sphere. The home became, in theory, an emotional retreat from the competitive, selfish business world. Men provided and protected, while women nurtured and guarded the family's morality, ensuring that capitalism's excesses stayed outside the home. Childhood expanded: children remained at home until their late teens or early twenties, and education became important.

This ideal came to be known as separate-sphere ideology, the cult of domesticity, or the cult of true womanhood. Although it rigidly separated male and female spheres, this ideology elevated domestic responsibilities. In her widely read *Treatise on Domestic Economy* (1841), Catharine Beecher approached housekeeping as a science while trumpeting mothers' role as moral guardians. Beecher maintained that women's natural superiority as moral, nurturing caregivers suited them for teaching (when single) and parenting (once married). Beecher insisted that the private sphere be elevated to the same status as the public.

Shrinking Families

These new domestic ideals depended on smaller families, enabling parents, particularly mothers, to give children better attention, education, and financial help. Urban families produced fewer household goods, and commercial farmers, unlike self-sufficient ones, relied on hired laborers rather than family members. Although smaller families resulted partly from first marriages' occurring at a later age, they also resulted from planning, made easier when cheap rubber condoms became available in the 1850s. Some women chose, too, to end accidental pregnancies with abortion.

In 1800 American women bore seven or eight children; by 1860 they had five or six. This decline occurred even though immigrants with large-family traditions were settling in the United States; thus the birth rate among native-born women declined more sharply.

Few northern women could fulfill the middle-class ideal of separate spheres. Most wage-earning women provided essential income for their families and could not stay home. Yet middle-class reformers mistook poverty for immorality, condemning working mothers for letting their children work or scavenge rather than attend school. Middle-class women could stay home, but new standards of cleanliness and comfort drained their time. Women's contributions to their families were assessed in moral, not economic, terms. Working inside their homes, women could not devote themselves primarily to childrearing, making the ideals of the cult of domesticity impossible for even middle-class families.

Women's Paid Labor

In working-class families, women left home as early as age twelve, earning wages most of their lives, with short respites for bearing and rearing children. Unmarried girls and women worked primarily as domestic servants or in factories; married and widowed women worked as laundresses, seamstresses, and cooks. Some hawked food and wares on city streets, others did piecework, and some became prostitutes. Few could support themselves or a family comfortably.

If middle-class girls left home to work—in New England's textile mills, in new urban stores as clerks—it was only briefly, before marriage. Otherwise, teaching was the only occupation consistent with genteel femininity. In 1823 Catharine and Mary Beecher established the Hartford Female Seminary, adding history and science to the traditional women's curriculum of domestic arts and religion. A decade later, Catharine Beecher successfully campaigned for teacher-training schools for women. Single, these women would not need to earn as much as their male counterparts, whom she presumed to be married. Unmarried women earned half the salary of male teachers. By 1850 schoolteaching had become a woman's profession.

The proportion of single women in the population increased significantly in the nineteenth century. As more young men headed west, some eastern communities had a disproportionate number of young women. Other women chose to remain independent. Because women's work was often poorly paid, those who forswore marriage faced serious challenges; many single women could not support themselves without charitable or family assistance.

THE GROWTH OF CITIES

The most rapid urbanization occurred between 1820 and 1860. The percentage of people living in urban areas (defined by a population of 2,500 or more) grew from 7 percent in 1820 to nearly 20 percent in 1860. The greatest growth took place in the Northeast and the Midwest. Although most northerners continued to live on farms or in small villages, cities boomed. Many urban residents were temporary—soon moving to another city or the countryside—and many were immigrants.

Urban Boom

In 1820 the United States had thirteen places with a population greater than 10,000; in 1860 it had ninety-three (see Map 11.2). New York City, already the nation's largest city in 1820, saw its population grow from 123,709 people to 813,669 in 1860. Philadelphia, the nation's second-largest city, saw its population multiply ninefold in that forty-year period. In 1815 Rochester, New York, had just 300 residents. By 1830, the Erie Canal turned the sleepy agricultural town into the nation's twenty-fifth-largest city, with a population of just over 9,000.

Cities expanded geographically, too. Until 1830, New Yorkers could walk the entire length of the city in an hour. In 1825 Fourteenth Street was the city's northern boundary. By 1860, Forty-second Street was the city's northern limit. Public transit made city expansion possible. By the 1850s, all big cities had horse-drawn streetcars, allowing wealthier residents who could afford the fare to settle on the cities' outskirts.

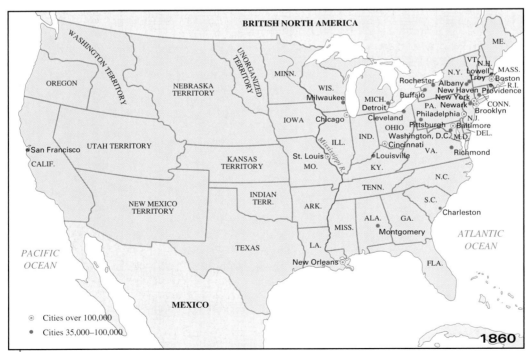

Map 11.2   Major American Cities in 1830 and 1860

The number of Americans who lived in cities increased rapidly between 1820 and 1860, and the number of large cities grew as well. In 1820 only New York City had a population exceeding 100,000; forty years later, eight more cities had surpassed that level.

Cities sustained the North's market revolution by serving as transportation hubs, commercial centers, and sometimes manufacturing sites. Some cities grew up with manufacturing. The Boston Manufacturing Company selected the site for Lowell, Massachusetts, because of its proximity to the Merrimack River, which could power the company's textile mill. Incorporated in 1826, by the 1850s it was the second-largest city in New England. Although most early manufacturing took place in rural areas, some cities, such as New York, experienced what historians call metropolitan industrialization. Most early ready-made clothing, for example, was produced as outwork by women in tenements throughout New York City. In 1860, 25,000 women worked in manufacturing jobs in New York City, constituting a quarter of the labor force; two-thirds worked in the garment industry.

Municipal Services

Northern cities developed elaborate municipal services but lacked taxing power to provide them for everyone. At best, they could tax property adjoining new sewers, paved streets, and water mains. New services and basic sanitation depended on residents' ability to pay. Another solution was to charter private companies to sell basic services. Baltimore first chartered a private gas company for lights in 1816. By mid-century every major city was lit by a private gas supplier. Private firms lacked the capital to build adequate water systems and laid pipe only in commercial and well-to-do residential areas. Supplying water ultimately fell to city governments.

Extremes of Wealth

Wealth was increasingly concentrated in fewer hands. By 1860 the top 5 percent of American families owned more than half of the nation's wealth, and the top 10 percent

This gouache, attributed to Nicholino Calyo, depicts the Haight family in their drawing room in 1848. Richard K. Wright was a wealthy New York City merchant, trading internationally, as the globe in the foreground suggests. Sarah Rogers Haight was a famous beauty and socialite, and the family's clothing, art, library, and furniture all stand in sharp contrast to the poverty, homelessness, and orphans found on the city's streets. (Museum of the City of New York, Bequest of Elizabeth Cushing Iselin)

owned nearly three-quarters. In the South, income extremes were most apparent on rural plantations, but in the North, economic inequities were most evident in cities.

A number of factors contributed to widespread poverty in America's industrial cities: poor wages, the lack of full-time employment, and the increasingly widespread employment of women and children, which further drove down wages for everyone. Women and children did not need a living wage because they were—employers rationalized—dependent, meaning that they could rely on men to support them. In reality, not all women or children had men to support them, nor did men's wages always prove adequate.

New York provides a striking example. Houses built for two families often held four. Some families took in lodgers to pay the rent; such crowding encouraged poorer New Yorkers to head outdoors. But poor neighborhoods were filthy. Excess sewage from outhouses drained into ditches that carried urine and fecal matter into the streets. People piled garbage into gutters, backyards, or alleys. Pigs, geese, dogs, and vultures scavenged the streets, while rats roamed under wooden sidewalks and through large buildings. Typhoid, dysentery, malaria, and tuberculosis regularly visited the poorer sections of cities. Cholera epidemics struck in 1831, 1849, and 1866.

Just beyond poor neighborhoods, the wealthy lived in lavish mansions and escaped to country estates during summer's brutal heat or epidemics. Much of this wealth was inherited. Rich New Yorkers increased their fortunes by investing in commerce and manufacturing.

The middle class was larger than the wealthy elite but substantially smaller than the working classes. They were businessmen, traders, and professionals, and the rapid turn toward industrialization and commercial specialization made them a larger presence in northern cities than in southern ones. Middle-class families enjoyed new consumer items: wool carpeting, fine wallpaper, and rooms full of furniture. Houses were large, often from four to six rooms. By the 1840s and 1850s, middle-class families used indoor toilets that were mechanical, though not yet flushing. These families formed the backbone of urban clubs, filled the family pews in church, and sent their sons to college.

Immigration

Many of the urban poor were immigrants. The 5 million immigrants to the United States between 1830 and 1860 outnumbered the country's population in 1790. During peak pre–Civil War immigration (1847–1857), 3.3 million immigrants entered the United States, including 1.3 million Irish and 1.1 million Germans (see Figure 11.1). By 1860, 15 percent of the white population was foreign-born, with 90 percent of immigrants living in northern states.

Various factors pushed Europeans from their homes and pulled them to the northern United States. In Ireland, the potato famine (1845–1850)—a period of widespread starvation caused by a diseased potato crop—drove millions from their homeland. Although economic conditions pushed most Germans, some were political refugees—liberals, freethinkers, Socialists, communists, and anarchists. Employers, states, and shipping companies promoted opportunities in the United States to Europeans, with the message: work and prosper in America or starve in Europe.

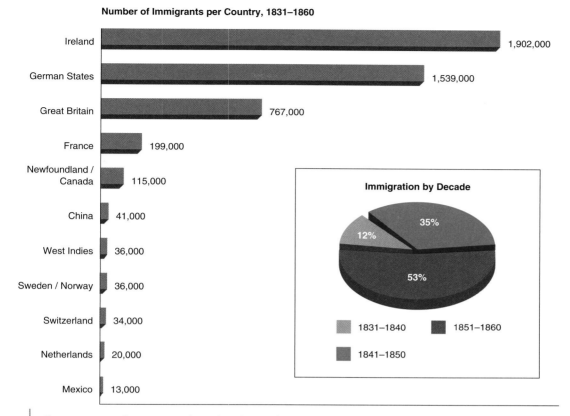

Number of Immigrants per Country, 1831–1860

Country	Number
Ireland	1,902,000
German States	1,539,000
Great Britain	767,000
France	199,000
Newfoundland / Canada	115,000
China	41,000
West Indies	36,000
Sweden / Norway	36,000
Switzerland	34,000
Netherlands	20,000
Mexico	13,000

Immigration by Decade

35% 1851–1860
12% 1831–1840
53% 1841–1850

Figure 11.1   Major Sources of Immigration to the United States, 1831–1860

Most immigrants came from two areas: Great Britain, of which Ireland was a part, and the German states. These two areas sent more immigrants between 1830 and 1860 than the inhabitants of the United States enumerated at the first census in 1790. By 1860, 15 percent of the white population was of foreign birth.   (Data from Stephan Thernstrom, ed., *Harvard Encyclopedia of American Ethnic Groups* [Cambridge, MA, and London: Harvard University Press, 1980], 1047)

Once in the United States, immigrants often became disillusioned, and hundreds of thousands returned home.

Many early immigrants lived or worked in rural areas. Like the Archbalds, a few settled on farms and bought land. Others worked as hired farmhands, canal diggers, or railroad tracklayers, often hoping to buy land later. But by the 1840s and 1850s—when record numbers of immigrants arrived—the prospects of buying land became more remote.

By 1860 most immigrants settled in cities, often the port at which they arrived. The most destitute could not afford the fare to places farther inland. Others had resources but fell victim to swindlers. Cities' ethnic flair induced some to stay put. In 1855, 52 percent of New York's 623,000 inhabitants were immigrants, 28 percent from Ireland and 16 percent from German states. Throughout the 1850s about 35 percent of Boston was foreign-born; more than two-thirds were Irish.

Most of the new Irish immigrants were young, poor, Roman Catholics from rural districts. Women found work as domestic servants or millhands, while men

worked in construction or transportation. Most Germans came with enough resources to head to states such as Ohio, Illinois, Wisconsin, and Missouri. Although
some southern cities like Charleston and Savannah had Irish immigrants, European
immigrants, with aversions to slavery and semitropical heat, settled in the Northeast
or Midwest.

Ethnic Tensions

Anxieties over the era's economic changes fueled tension
between native-born Americans and immigrants, particularly Irish Catholics. Native-born workers blamed immi-
grants for scarce jobs and low wages. Middle-class whites blamed them for poverty
and crime and believed immigrants' moral depravity—not poor wages—led to poverty.

White northerners often portrayed Irish immigrants as nonwhite, as African in
appearance. But Irish and African Americans did not develop a sense of solidarity.
Instead, some of the era's most virulent riots erupted between Irish immigrants and
African Americans.

Anti-Catholicism also became strident in the 1830s. In Boston, anti-Catholic
riots occurred frequently. Nearby Charlestown, Massachusetts, saw a mob burn a
convent in 1834. In Philadelphia a crowd attacked priests and nuns and vandalized
churches in 1844, and in Lawrence, Massachusetts, a mob leveled the Irish neighborhood in 1854. Riots between native-born and Irish Catholic workers also erupted
along canals and railroads, but urban riots attracted more newspaper attention,
fueling fears that cities were depraved places.

Protestant German immigrants fared better than the Irish. Because Germans
generally arrived with resources and skills, Americans stereotyped them as hard
working. But non-Protestant Germans—Catholics and Jews (whom white Americans
considered a separate race)—frequently encountered racial and religious prejudice.

Irish Catholics usually lived in their own neighborhoods, where they set up
churches and schools. In larger cities, immigrants from the same German states clustered together. Immigrants set up social clubs and mutual-aid societies.

People of Color

African Americans also forged their own communities and
culture. As late as the 1830s, many remained enslaved in
New York and New Jersey, but the numbers of free African
Americans grew steadily, and by 1860 nearly 250,000 (many of them refugees from
southern slavery) lived in the urban North. African Methodist Episcopal churches
and preachers helped foster a sense of community among African Americans.

White racism impinged on northern African Americans' lives. Streetcars, hotels,
restaurants, and theaters could turn away African Americans without legal penalty.
City laws barred African Americans from public buildings. Even where laws were
liberal, whites' attitudes constrained African Americans' opportunities. In Massachusetts, for example, African Americans enjoyed more legal rights than anywhere
else. But laws protecting civil and political rights could not make whites shop at
black businesses.

African Americans were excluded from factory and clerical jobs. Women worked
as house servants, cooks, washerwomen, and child nurses. Most African American
men worked as construction workers, porters, longshoremen, or day laborers—all

A Mixed Economy

Should the U.S. government run, regulate, or leave to the market system healthcare, Social Security and private pensions, corporate concentration, and stock trading and investments? To what degree should the government be responsible for the well-being of the economy and individuals?

In the early nineteenth century, government played an active role as federal and state governments built roads and canals, developed harbors, and operated post offices and the early telegraph. Government stimulated and regulated the private sector. In chartering corporations and banks and in land sales and grants, the United States created an infrastructure that paved the way for the market economy and industrialization.

In the late nineteenth century, advocates of laissez-faire, or hands-off government, challenged the pre–Civil War active government. Laissez-faire dominated until the 1880s and 1890s, when large corporations and trusts accumulated so much power that governments stepped in to regulate railroads and business concentration. After the turn of the century, the federal government extended regulation to food, drugs, working conditions, and fair business practices. Federal regulation and private initiative were innovatively combined in the Federal Reserve System, created in 1913, as a public system for overseeing currency and banking which left control in private hands. After a revival of laissez-faire in the 1920s, the Great Depression of the 1930s and World War II led the federal government to establish the modern welfare state, which operates through a mixed public and private structure.

Americans today still debate the appropriate role of government. Conservatives argue that regulation hampers individual freedom and distorts supply and demand. Advocates of an activist government argue that only government has the power to check economic concentration and protect health, safety, and the environment. This debate is a legacy from antebellum America.

Summary

During the first half of the nineteenth century, the North became enmeshed in commercial culture, as northern states and capitalists invested heavily in internal improvements. Most northerners shifted toward commercial farming or, in smaller numbers, industrial wage labor. Farmers specialized in cash crops, while their children often worked in factories or countinghouses.

To many northerners, the market economy symbolized progress, bringing easier access to cheap western lands, employment for surplus farm laborers, and the commercial availability of goods that had once been time-consuming to produce. But the market economy also led to increased specialization, a depersonalized workplace, and a sharper divide between work and leisure. The market economy tied northerners more directly to fluctuating national and international markets, and during economic downturns, many northern families experienced destitution.

With less need for children's labor, northerners began producing smaller families. Even as working-class children worked, middle-class families created a model of childhood that had parents shielding children from the world's dangers. Mothers, in theory, became moral guardians, keeping the home safe from the new economy's competitiveness and selfishness. In reality, few women could devote themselves entirely to nurturing children and husbands.

Immigrants and free African Americans generally performed the lowest-paying work, and many native-born whites blamed them for problems spurred by rapid economic change. Anti-immigrant (especially anti-Catholic) and antiblack riots became commonplace. Immigrants and African Americans responded by forming their own communities.

Cities came to symbolize the possibilities and limits of market expansion. Urban areas were marked by extremes of wealth, vibrant working-class cultures as well as poverty and crime. To reconcile these seeming contradictions, middle-class northerners articulated a free-labor ideology, touting the possibility for upward mobility in a competitive marketplace. This ideology would become central to northern regional identity.

Chapter Review

OR IS IT THE NORTH THAT WAS DISTINCTIVE?

What happened to the North and South economically after the War of 1812?

The South continued as an agricultural region and expanded its slave system, while the North transformed quickly into a market economy. With the war cutting off European trade, northern entrepreneurs invested in domestic production and factories. Former artisans and farmers increasingly shifted from producers to wage workers. Commercial farming emerged in the North to meet the growing demand for foodstuffs that was created when people shifted from farming to factory jobs. Those farmers who remained in agriculture shifted to cash crops. Early forms of market changes came from piece work or outwork, where manufacturers hired women and children in their homes to produce goods, often paying them for each piece produced. By 1790, the first spinning mills were opened in Rhode Island.

THE TRANSPORTATION REVOLUTION

Why did the canal era end after just a few decades?

Initially, canals were hailed for transporting goods to and from interior regions at much lower costs and faster timetables than overland routes, with the Erie Canal the largest of its kind and the greatest success story. But by the mid-nineteenth century, the canal heyday was over, as high construction costs combined with economic downturns to make them less desirable. The focus of transportation development shifted to railroads, which were quicker, easier, and cheaper to build; could move far more people and goods for far less money; and unlike canals, could operate year-round.

FACTORIES AND INDUSTRIALIZATION

How was factory work different from the work life people previously knew?

The artisan shops and family farms that pre-dated factories had fewer formal rules and less structure than the factories that arose in the late eighteenth and early nineteenth centuries. Artisans and farmers saw themselves as producers, in charge of their labor and its outcome and working side-by-side with hired helpers. In factories, workers never saw owners, and worked for wages under the watchful eye of supervisors with strict rules and a clock governing their day. There was no job security, and factory workers were often replaced by cheaper immigrant and women workers. Whereas artisan apprentices worked to learn a trade with the hope of setting up their own businesses, there was little or no opportunity for advancement in factories.

CONSUMPTION AND COMMERCIALIZATION

How did farm women's work change as the commercial economy expanded?

Along with their regular farm and household duties, rural women took on new responsibilities to help pay for some of the items they now bought (such as textiles) instead of bartering for or making on their own. Some took in outwork; others increased production of eggs, milk, butter, and produce and other items for sale in the market. Daughters were often sent to work in textile mills, sending part of their wages home to aid their families.

FAMILIES IN FLUX

What roles did families play in the new industrial era?

Before the rise of the market economy, families were the center of production and economic activity. As industrialization took hold, however, new ideals transformed families into moral and cultural institutions. Men, particularly middle-class men, occupied the public sphere, providing for and protecting their families. In this new "separate spheres" ideology, women's roles were confined to the home, and they were charged with making it a retreat for husbands and children from the harshness of economic life. This ideology, which elevated women's domestic roles, was later dubbed *the cult of domesticity* or *the cult of true womanhood*.

THE GROWTH OF CITIES

What contributed to increasing poverty in new urban areas of the Northeast and Midwest?

There were several causes for widespread poverty in industrial cities: poor wages, the lack of full-time employment, and the increasing employment of women and children, which drove down wages for everyone. Massive immigration between 1830 and 1860 also swelled the ranks of the poor, who often began their life in U.S. cities, such as New York. In urban areas, the poor doubled up in apartments or rented out rooms to lodgers to make ends meet. Without the ability to pay for city services, garbage and excess human waste piled high, contributing to disease and epidemics through the middle of the nineteenth century.

SUGGESTIONS FOR FURTHER READING

Hal Barron, *Those Who Stayed Behind: Rural Society in Nineteenth-Century New England* (1984)

Jeanne Boydston, *Home and Work: Housework, Wages, and the Ideology of Labor in the Early Republic* (1990)

Christopher Clark, *The Roots of Rural Capitalism: Western Massachusetts, 1780–1860* (1990)

Nancy Cott, *The Bonds of Womanhood: "Women's Sphere" in New England, 1780–1835* (1977)

Bruce Laurie, *Artisans into Workers: Labor in Nineteenth-Century America* (1989)

Winifred Barr Rothenberg, *From Market-Places to Market Economy: The Transformation of Rural Massachusetts, 1750–1850* (1994)

Mary Ryan, *Cradle of the Middle Class: The Family in Oneida County, New York, 1790–1865* (1981)

Carol Sheriff, *The Artificial River: The Erie Canal and the Paradox of Progress, 1817–1862* (1996)

Christine Stansell, *City of Women: Sex and Class in New York, 1789–1860* (1986)

George Rogers Taylor, *The Transportation Revolution, 1815–1860* (1951)

Reform and Politics in the Age of Jackson

CHAPTER 12

1824–1845

The twenty-eight-year-old millhand steadied himself atop a cliff in Paterson, New Jersey; peered down the seventy-foot precipice to the river below; then leapt into the water. He resurfaced to cheers for his death-defying stunt and what it symbolized. It was September 1827, and Sam Patch—who had worked in mills since he was eight years old—was making a point.

Jumping from waterfalls had long been a pastime among boys working in textile mills. But Patch considered it an art imbued with political meaning. He timed his Paterson leap to steal the show from Timothy B. Crane, an entrepreneur who dreamed up Forest Garden, a pleasure park offering respectable ladies and gentlemen a respite from the mill town. To reach the park, which was formerly open to everyone, visitors now had to cross a toll bridge. The toll would raise revenue to sustain the park, but, more important, as Crane saw it, it would keep out the riffraff.

Patch and the mill hands understood that the riffraff meant *them*. Forest Garden symbolized a world in which manual labor was devalued, in which artisans became workers, in which industrialists and entrepreneurs increasingly held themselves as morally superior to wage earners. In previous months, town residents attacked (physically and verbally) the park, its workers, its buildings, and Crane. When Crane planned elaborate celebrations marking the toll bridge's completion, Patch determined to assert the pride of workers who made the industrial revolution possible.

In the two years following his Paterson leap—before his last, fatal jump at the 125-foot Genesee Falls in Rochester, New York—Sam Patch became a professional waterfall jumper. Even as some dismissed his leaps as drunken stunts, he costumed

This icon will direct you to interactive activities and study materials on A People And A Nation, Brief Edition
website: **www.cengage.com/history/norton/ peoplenationbrief8e**

Chronology

1790s–1840s	Second Great Awakening spreads religious fervor.
1820s	Reformers in New York and Pennsylvania establish model penitentiaries.
1824	No presidential candidate wins a majority in the electoral college.
1825	House of Representatives elects Adams president.
1826	American Society for the Promotion of Temperance is founded.
1828	Tariff of Abominations is passed.
	Jackson is elected president.
1830s–40s	Democratic-Whig competition gets in the second party system.
1831	Garrison begins the abolitionist newspaper *The Liberator*.
	Antimasons are the first political party to hold a national convention.
1832	Jackson vetoes rechartering the Second Bank of the United States.
	Jackson is reelected president.
1832–33	South Carolina nullifies the Tariffs of 1828 and 1832, prompting a nullification crisis.
1836	Specie Circular ends the credit purchase of public lands.
	Van Buren is elected president.
1837	*Caroline* affair sparks tension with Britain.
	Financial panic ends the boom of the 1830s.
1838–39	United States and Canada mobilize militias over Maine–New Brunswick border dispute.
1839–43	Hard times spread unemployment and deflation.
1840	Whigs win the presidency under Harrison.
1841	Tyler assumes the presidency after Harrison's death.
1848	Woman's Rights Convention at Seneca Falls, New York, calls for woman suffrage.

himself in the symbolic clothing of the textile spinner and associated socially and politically with a raucous crowd of skilled operatives. His flaunting of middle-class values caught the attention of the political press, organs for the era's two main political parties—the Whigs and Jacksonian Democrats. To Whigs, Patch exemplified what was, in one editor's words, "wrong with democracy," whereas Jacksonians labeled him a heroic artisan. In 1833 Philadelphia presented President Andrew Jackson with a horse, which he named Sam Patch.

Like Patch, many Americans sought to reaffirm control over their lives in an era of rapid economic and social changes. The market economy, growing wealth and inequality, immigration, the westward thrust of slavery, and territorial expansion contributed to Americans' hopes and fears. But Americans often divided over what defined progress, what constituted a social ill, and how those ills should be remedied.

To quell anxieties, many turned to evangelical religion and, in the North, reform movements. Believing in human perfectibility, reformers worked to free individuals and society from sin. In the Northeast and Midwest, people organized to end prostitution and alcohol abuse, improve prison and asylum conditions, and establish public schools. Other reformers created utopian communities. Opponents of slavery and proponents of women's rights, meanwhile, sought to radically alter the application of the revolutionary declaration that "all men are created equal."

Evangelical reformers generally aligned with the Whig Party, but Jacksonian Democrats, too, were concerned with social problems, mostly class inequities. They disliked middle-class reformers who told working-class men and women how to live, and they opposed privileges bestowed by government policies and institutions, such as the Second Bank of the United States. Yet when it came to slavery, the national parties often remained silent to keep sectional conflict submerged.

Democrats and Whigs held distinct positions on most other issues. Democrats emphasized that the best government is that which governs least, whereas Whigs championed a strong federal government. Democrats focused on the nation's agricultural expansion west, whereas Whigs promoted industrial and commercial growth in the East. They hoped to bring growth through high protective tariffs, centralized banking, and federal funding for internal improvements. Together, Democrats and Whigs constituted what is often called the second party system.

- **What were the evils in society that reformers hoped to eliminate, and what motivated them to do so?**
- **What was the relationship between reform and politics?**
- **What were the main issues dividing Democrats and Whigs?**

FROM REVIVAL TO REFORM

Religious revivals in the late eighteenth and early nineteenth centuries—sometimes called the Second Great Awakening for their resemblance to the eighteenth-century Great Awakening—raised people's hopes for the Second Coming of the Christian messiah and the establishment of God's kingdom on earth. Revivalists resolved to speed the millennium, or the thousand years of peace on earth that would accompany Christ's Second Coming, by combating sin. They urged individuals to renounce sins, such as drinking, swearing, and licentiousness, and aid in combating social evils, including slavery. Not until all Americans were converted would Christ make his Second Coming.

Revivalists strove for large-scale conversions. Rural women, men, and children traveled to camp meetings, where they listened to fiery sermons day and night delivered from hastily constructed platforms and tents in forests or fields. In cities, women in particular attended daily church services and prayer meetings, sometimes for months. Converts vowed to live sanctified lives and help others see the light.

Revivals

The most famous revival was at Cane Ridge, Kentucky, in August 1801. An estimated twenty-five thousand people attended at a time when Kentucky's largest city, Lexington, had barely two thousand inhabitants. The call to repentance and conversion invigorated southern Protestantism. Although laws often restricted or outlawed black churches and preachers, particularly after Nat Turner's 1831 revolt, black and mixed churches flourished locally. During the 1840s and 1850s, though, as slavery was publically debated, southern Presbyterian, Baptist, and Methodist churches seceded from their denominations' national conferences. For these churches' leaders, slavery did not impede human perfectibility but ensured it, as benevolent masters guided Africans to Christ.

Revivalists believed in individual self-improvement, but northern revivalists also emphasized communal improvement. Wherever they preached, northern evangelists generated new religious groups and voluntary reform societies. Preachers like Lyman

Samuel Waldo and William Jewett's oil portrait of Charles Finney around 1834 captures Finney at his peak. The charismatic Finney mesmerized his audiences, and contemporaries credited him with converting 500,000 people.   (Oberlin College Archives, Oberlin, Ohio)

Beecher, who began in New England before moving to Cincinnati, and Charles Finney, who traveled the canals and roads linking the Northeast to the Midwest, argued that "God has made man a moral free agent," that Christians were not doomed by original sin, and that anyone could achieve salvation. Revivalism had a strong base among Methodists and Baptists, whose denominational structures maximized democratic participation and drew ministers from ordinary folk.

Finney achieved his greatest successes in those parts of western New York experiencing rapid changes in transportation and industrialization—what he called the Burned-Over District because of the region's intense evangelical fires. Rapid change raised fears of the social evils that might accompany economic progress. Many individuals worried, too, about their economic fate in an era of booms and busts.

When northern revivalist preachers emphasized good works—that is, good deeds and piety—they helped ignite social reform movements, which began in the Burned-Over District and spread to New England, the Middle Atlantic, and the upper Midwest. These associations shared a commitment to human perfectibility and often turned to the same wealthy men for financial resources and advice.

Moral Reform

Those resources allowed them to use the era's new technologies—steam presses and railroads. By mass-producing pamphlets and newspapers for distribution far into the nation's interior, reformers spread their message throughout the Northeast and Midwest. With canals and railroads making travel easier, reformers could attend annual conventions and host speakers from distant places. Most reform organizations sponsored weekly newspapers, creating a virtual reform community.

While industrialists and merchants provided financial resources for evangelical reform, wives and daughters solicited new members and circulated petitions. Women, more than men, felt responsible for counteracting the expanding market economy's social evils. Evangelical reformers broadened the cult of domesticity's role for women as moral guardians beyond the home into the public realm. Women would help run reformatories for wayward youth or establish orphan asylums. Participation in reform movements gave some women a sense of purpose outside the home. Although some elite women in Upper South cities formed and joined reform societies, moral reform was primarily a northeastern and midwestern phenomenon.

For women and some men, particularly non–property owners who could not vote, reform led to political action. In 1830, as female reformers in New York City organized a shelter for prostitutes, they publicized the names of brothel clients to shame men who contributed to the women's waywardness. They then organized themselves into the Female Moral Reform Society, and by 1840 the society had

555 affiliated chapters nationwide. It soon lobbied successfully for criminal sanctions in New York State against men who seduced women into prostitution.

Penitentiaries and Asylums

Rather than simply punishing criminals, reformers tried to transform them into productive members of society. Their model penitentiaries aimed to rehabilitate criminals through disciplined regimens.

Other reformers sought to improve treatment of the mentally ill, who were frequently imprisoned, put in cages or dark dungeons, chained to walls, brutalized, or held in solitary confinement. The leader of this crusade, Dorothea Dix, exemplifies the reformer who started with a religious belief in human perfectibility and moved into social, then political action. Investigating asylums, petitioning the Massachusetts legislature, and lobbying other states and Congress, Dix pushed twenty-eight states to build institutions for the mentally ill by 1860.

Temperance

Temperance advocates, who railed against alcoholic beverages, likewise crossed from the personal into the political sphere. Drinking was widespread in the early nineteenth century, when men like Sam Patch gathered in public houses and inns to drink whiskey, rum, and hard cider. Respectable women did not drink in public, but many tippled alcohol-based patent medicines promoted as cure-alls.

Evangelicals considered drinking sinful, and in many denominations, forsaking alcohol was part of conversion. Preachers condemned alcohol for violating the Sabbath—workers' one day off, which some spent at the public house. Factory owners claimed alcohol made workers unreliable. Civic leaders connected alcohol with crime. Middle-class reformers, often women, condemned it for diverting men from family responsibilities and making them more likely to be abusive. In the early 1840s, thousands of women formed Martha Washington societies to reform alcoholics, raise children as teetotalers, and spread the temperance message.

As the temperance movement grew, its goal shifted from moderation to abstinence to prohibition. By the mid-1830s, five thousand state and local temperance societies touted teetotalism, and more than a million people had pledged abstinence. Per capita consumption of alcohol fell from five gallons per year in 1800 to below two gallons in the 1840s. The American Society for the Promotion of Temperance, organized in 1826, pushed for legislation ending alcohol manufacture and sale. In 1851 Maine became the first state to ban alcohol except for medicinal purposes, and by 1855 similar laws were enacted throughout New England, New York, Pennsylvania, and the Midwest.

The temperance campaign had an anti-immigrant and anti-Catholic strain to it. Along the nation's canals, reformers lamented the hundreds of taverns catering to Irish workers, and in the cities, they expressed outrage at the Sunday tradition of German families' gathering at beer gardens. Their efforts had some success, as Catholics pledged abstinence and formed organizations such as the St. Mary's Mutual Benevolence Total Abstinence Society in Boston.

But many workers—Protestants as well as Catholics—rejected middle-class temperance campaigns. Workers agreed that poverty and crime were problems but blamed poor wages, not drinking habits. Even some who abstained from alcohol opposed prohibition, believing that drinking should be a matter of self-control, not state coercion.

Public Schools

Protestants and Catholics differed over education as well. Public education almost always included religious education, but when teachers taught Protestant beliefs and used the King James Bible, Catholics established their own schools. Some Protestants feared that Catholics would never be assimilated into American culture and charged Catholics with plotting to impose papal control. Still, public education touched more Americans than any other reform movement.

Horace Mann, a Massachusetts lawyer and reformer from humble beginnings, advocated free, tax-supported education to replace church and private schools. Universal education, Mann proposed, would end crime and help Americanize immigrants.

During Mann's tenure as secretary of the Massachusetts Board of Education from 1837 to 1848, Massachusetts led the common school movement which established teacher training, lengthened the school year, and raised teachers' salaries to make the profession more attractive. Adhering to notions that women had special claims to morality and could be paid less than men, Mann envisioned a system in which women educated future clerks, farmers, and workers with a practical curriculum that stressed geography, arithmetic, and science. Education reformers believed that individuals could educate themselves out of their circumstances.

With the expansion of public education, by 1850 the majority of native-born white Americans were literate. Power printing presses and better transportation enabled a wide distribution of religious and secular publications.

COMMUNITARIAN EXPERIMENTS

Some idealists dreamed of an entirely new social order. They established dozens of utopian communities based on religious principles, a resistance to the market economy's excessive individualism, or both. Some groups, like the Shakers, originated in eighteenth-century Europe, while others, like the Mormons, arose from the Second Great Awakening. Utopian communities attempted to recapture what they perceived as the communal nature of the past, even while offering radical departures from marriage and child-rearing practices.

Utopian Communities

The Shakers, the largest of the communal utopian experiments, reached their peak between 1820 and 1860, when six thousand members lived in twenty settlements in eight states. Shaker communities emphasized agriculture and handcrafts, contrasting with the new factory regime. Many were profitable enterprises. But the Shakers were essentially a spiritual community. Founded in England in 1772 by Mother Ann Lee, their name derived from their worship service, which included shaking their bodies. Ann Lee's children died in infancy, and she believed their deaths were retribution for her sin of intercourse; thus she advocated celibacy. After imprisonment in England in 1773–1774, she settled in America.

Shakers lived communally, with men and women in separate quarters; individual families were abolished. Leadership was shared equally between men and women. Many Shaker settlements became temporary refuges for orphans, widows, runaways, abused wives, and unemployed workers. Their settlements depended on new recruits, not only because celibacy meant that they could not reproduce themselves but also because some members soon left, unsuited to communal living or the Shakers' spiritual message.

Other influential utopian communities also sought to resist social change. John Humphrey Noyes, a lawyer converted by Finney's revivals, established two perfectionist communities, first in Putney, Vermont, in 1835, and then—after being indicted for adultery—in Oneida, New York, in 1848. Noyes advocated communal property ownership, communal child rearing, and "complex marriage," in which all men were married to all women but women were free to reject sexual propositions. In the Oneida colony, pregnancies were to be planned; couples would apply to Noyes for permission to have a child, or Noyes would assign two people to reproduce. Robert Dale Owen's community in New Harmony, Indiana (1825–1828), abolished private property and advocated communal child rearing. The Fourierists, named after French philosopher Charles Fourier, established more than two dozen northeastern and midwestern communities that resisted the individualism of market society and promoted sexual equality.

The most famous Fourier community was Brook Farm in West Roxbury, Massachusetts. Inspired by transcendentalism—the belief that the physical world is secondary to the spiritual realm, which humans can reach only by intuition—Brook Farm's rural communalism combined spirituality, manual labor, intellectual life, and play. Founded in 1841 by Unitarian minister George Ripley, a literary critic and friend of transcendentalist essayist Ralph Waldo Emerson, Brook Farm attracted farmers, craftsmen, and writers, among them novelist Nathaniel Hawthorne. In 1845 Brook Farm's hundred members organized into phalanxes (working-living units) following Fourier's model. As regimentation replaced individualism, membership dropped. A year after a disastrous fire in 1846, the experiment collapsed.

American Renaissance Though short-lived, Brook Farm was crucial to the flowering of national literature. During these years, Hawthorne, Emerson, Margaret Fuller, Henry David Thoreau, Herman Melville, and others launched a literary outpouring known today as the American Renaissance. Their work was distinctively American and an outgrowth of the European romantic movement. Themes were universal, their settings and characters American. Hawthorne, for instance, used Puritan New England as a backdrop.

Essayist Ralph Waldo Emerson was the prime mover of the American Renaissance and a pillar of transcendentalism. Emerson followed his father and grandfather into the ministry but quit his Boston Unitarian pulpit in 1831. After a two-year sojourn in Europe, he returned to lecture and write, preaching individualism and self-reliance. Widely admired, he influenced Thoreau, Fuller, Hawthorne, and other members of Brook Farm.

Mormons

No communitarian experiment had a more lasting influence than the Church of Jesus Christ of Latter-Day Saints, whose members were known as Mormons. During the religious ferment of the 1820s in western New York, Joseph Smith, a young farmer, reported that an angel called Moroni had given him divinely engraved gold plates. Smith published his revelations as the *Book of Mormon* and organized a church in 1830. The next year, the community moved to Ohio to build a New Jerusalem and await the Second Coming of Jesus.

But angry mobs drove the Mormons from Ohio, and they settled in Missouri. Anti-Mormons charged that Mormonism was a scam by Joseph Smith. Opponents feared Mormon economic and political power. In 1838 Missouri's governor charged Smith with fomenting insurrection and gathered evidence to indict him and other leaders for treason.

Smith and his followers resettled in Nauvoo, Illinois. The state legislature gave them a city charter that made them self-governing. But again the community met antagonism, especially after Smith introduced polygamy in 1841, allowing men several wives. The next year Smith became mayor, and this consolidation of power further antagonized opponents, including former Mormons. In 1844, after Smith and his brother were charged with treason and jailed, then murdered, the Mormons left Illinois to seek security in the western wilderness. Under Brigham Young's leadership, they set up a cooperative community in the Great Salt Lake valley.

There, the Mormons distributed agricultural land according to family size. An extensive irrigation system transformed the arid valley into a rich oasis. As the colony developed, church elders gained control of water, trade, industry, and the territorial government of Utah.

ABOLITIONISM

Like reformers and utopians, evangelical abolitionists tried to eradicate a communal sin suffusing American society: slavery. Inspired by the Second Great Awakening, their efforts built on an earlier generation of antislavery activists.

Early Abolitionism and Colonization

From the nation's earliest days—in places like Philadelphia, New York, Albany, Boston, and Nantucket—free blacks formed societies to petition legislatures, seek judicial redress, stage public marches, and publish tracts chronicling the horrors of bondage. African American abolitionists wrote about slavery's devastating impact on black and white families, advocated an end to slavery, assisted fugitive slaves, and promoted legal equality for free blacks. By 1830 there were fifty African American abolitionist societies in the United States. David Walker, a southern-born free African American, captured white Americans' attention with his *Appeal . . . to the Colored Citizens* (1829). He advocated the violent overthrow of slavery, triggering fear throughout the white South and the North.

Early white antislavery advocates pressed for gradual abolition and an end to the international slave trade. After the American Revolution, abolitionists united in places like Boston and Philadelphia, with its large population of Quakers, whose religious beliefs emphasized human equality. Although they aided African Americans seeking freedom through judicial decisions, their assumptions about blacks' racial inferiority made them stop short of advocating equal rights. Early white abolitionists were typically wealthy men who excluded women, African Americans, and nonelites from their societies.

Elites often supported colonization, which crystallized in 1816 with the organization of the American Colonization Society. Its members planned to purchase and relocate American slaves and free blacks to Africa or the Caribbean. Supporters included Thomas Jefferson, James Madison, James Monroe, and Henry Clay. In 1824 the society founded Liberia, on Africa's west coast, and established a settlement for willing African Americans, resettling nearly twelve thousand by 1860. Some colonizationists aimed to strengthen slavery by ridding the South of troublesome slaves or to purge the North of African Americans. Although some African Americans supported the movement, black abolitionists generally denounced it.

In the early 1830s, a new group of more radical white abolitionists—most prominently, William Lloyd Garrison—demanded immediate, complete, and uncompensated emancipation. Garrison began publishing his abolitionist newspaper, *The Liberator*, in 1831, two years before founding the American Antislavery Society, the era's largest abolitionist organization.

Immediatism

Immediatists believed slavery was a sin needing urgent eradication. They were influenced by African American abolitionist societies and by evangelicals' notion that humans, not God, determined their spiritual fate by opting for good or evil. When all humans had chosen good over evil, the millennium would come. For every day that slavery continued, then, the millennium was delayed.

Because the millennium depended on *all* hearts having been won over to Christ, Garrison's brand of abolitionism focused on moral suasion. He and his followers hoped to bring about emancipation by winning over slaveowners and other white Americans who supported or tolerated slavery. Evangelical abolitionism depended, then, on large numbers of ministers and laypeople spreading the word nationwide.

The Lane Debates

In 1829 Congregationalists and Presbyterians founded the Lane Seminary in Cincinnati to train ministers. With Lyman Beecher as president, it drew students from North and South and encouraged "people of color" to apply. After Theodore Weld, one of Charles Finney's converts, arrived at Lane in 1833, he organized the Lane Debates, eighteen days of discussion among students and faculty about colonization and immediatism. Immediatism won.

Led by Weld, the Lane students and faculty founded an antislavery society and reached out to the growing African American population of Cincinnati. Fearful of disorder, white business leaders protested the antislavery society. Lane's trustees responded by banning antislavery organizations on campus and barring further debate on slavery. Beecher supported the trustees. Weld and the other Lane Rebels left and the following year enrolled in a new seminary at Oberlin, a northern Ohio town founded as a Christian perfectionist settlement. The new seminary would become the first college to admit women and one of the first to admit African Americans.

The International Antislavery Movement

The heart of the international antislavery movement had been Great Britain, but in the 1830s many of Britain's antislavery societies thought that their work was finished and disbanded. The international slave trade greatly diminished, and in 1833 Parliament ended slavery in the British Empire. Abolitionism in the United States was growing, and American abolitionists revived the international antislavery movement.

American abolitionism in the 1830s was invigorated by the militancy of black abolitionists and by William Lloyd Garrison's conversion to immediatism. Seeking to raise money and to pressure the United States to abolish slavery, African American abolitionists in the 1840s toured Britain regularly. Ex-slaves recounted their experiences of slavery and bared their scarred bodies.

After the fugitive slave Moses Gandy toured England, he published his autobiography, the first of dozens of slave narratives published in London. The next year, 1845, Frederick Douglass began a nineteen-month tour, giving three hundred lectures in Britain.

In 1849 the black abolitionists William Wells Brown, Alexander Crummell, and J. W. C. Pennington were among twenty American delegates at the international Paris Peace Conference. Brown's lecture tour in Britain became a five-year exile because, after passage of the 1850 Fugitive Slave Law, he feared being sent back to slavery if he returned to the United States. In 1854 he became free when British abolitionists purchased his freedom.

Gandy, Douglass, Brown, and other former slaves energized the British and Foreign Anti-Slavery Society, founded in 1839, and hundreds of militant local societies. By the early 1850s, abolitionists helped abolish slavery in Colombia, Argentina, Venezuela, and Peru. In the United States, black abolitionists were instrumental in reviving the worldwide antislavery movement and, as advocates of women's rights, international peace, temperance, and other reforms, linking Americans to other worldwide reform movements.

William Wells Brown's autobiography stirred abolitionists in the United States and England. In 1849 Brown was among the American delegates to the Paris Peace Conference, then spent the next five years as an exile in Britain, fearing being sent back to slavery under the 1850 Fugitive Slave Act. He returned to the United States only after British abolitionists purchased his freedom from his former master.
(Documenting the American South [http://docsouth.unc.edu], The University of North Carolina at Chapel Hill Libraries)

The American Antislavery Society

By 1838, at its peak, the society had 2,000 local affiliates and over 300,000 members. In contrast to earlier white abolitionists, the immediatists welcomed men and women of all races and classes. Lydia Maria Child, Maria Chapman, and Lucretia Mott served on its executive committee; Child edited its official paper, the *National Anti-Slavery Standard*, from 1841 to 1843, and Chapman coedited it from 1844 until 1848.

With the great postal campaign in 1835, the society flooded the mails with antislavery tracts. Women went door to door in northern and midwestern communities collecting signatures on antislavery petitions; by 1838 more than 400,000 petitions were sent to Congress. Abolitionist-minded women met in sewing circles, where they made clothes for fugitive slaves while organizing activities, such as antislavery fairs at which they sold goods—often hand-made items—donating the proceeds to antislavery causes.

African American Abolitionists

Even as white abolitionist societies included African Americans and sponsored speaking tours by former slaves, African Americans continued independent efforts to end slavery and improve free African Americans' status into the 1840s and 1850s. Former slaves—most famously, Frederick Douglass, Henry Bibb, Harriet Tubman, and Sojourner Truth—fought slavery through speeches, publications, and participation in a secret network known as the Underground Railroad, which spirited enslaved men, women, and children to freedom. By the thousands, African Americans established churches, founded moral reform societies, published newspapers, created schools and orphanages, and held conventions.

Opposition to Abolitionism

The immediatists' success at winning converts gave rise to a virulent opposition. In the South, mobs blocked the distribution of antislavery tracts. The state of South Carolina intercepted and burned abolitionist literature, and in 1835 proslavery assailants killed four abolitionists in South Carolina and Louisiana, as well as forty people allegedly plotting a slave rebellion in Mississippi and Louisiana.

White northerners who opposed abolition recognized cotton's vital role in the nation's economy and feared that emancipation would prompt an influx of freed slaves into their region. They believed blacks to be inherently inferior and incapable of the virtue and diligence required of freedom and citizenship.

The North saw its share of antiabolitionist violence. In Boston, David Walker died under mysterious circumstances in 1830, after a bounty was put on his head. Of northerners who despised abolitionists, most were commercial and political elites with strong connections to the southern cotton economy and political connections to leading southerners. Northern gentlemen incited antiabolitionist riots. Mob violence peaked in 1835, with more than fifty riots aimed

Women played an activist role in reform, especially in abolitionism. A rare daguerreotype from August 1850 shows women and men, including Frederick Douglass, on the podium at an abolitionist rally in Cazenovia, New York. (Collection of J. Paul Getty Museum, Los Angeles, California)

at abolitionists or African Americans. In 1837 in Alton, Illinois, a mob murdered the abolitionist editor Elijah P. Lovejoy and rioters sacked his printing office, and in 1838, Philadelphia rioters hurled stones at three thousand black and white women attending the Anti-Slavery Convention of American Women at the new Pennsylvania Hall, constructed to house abolitionist meetings and an abolitionist bookstore, before torching the building itself.

Moral Suasion Versus Political Action

Violence made some immediatists question moral suasion as a tactic. James G. Birney, the son of a Kentucky slave-owner, embraced immediatism but sought to elect abolitionists who would push for antislavery legislation. Those who favored a political solution saw little room for women within the movement. To involve women violated the natural order of things while detracting from the ultimate goal: freedom for slaves.

Thus, when William Lloyd Garrison, an ardent women's rights supporter, endorsed Abby Kelly's appointment to the business committee of the American Anti-Slavery Society in 1840, he provoked an irreparable split in the abolitionist movement. Arthur Tappan and Theodore Weld led a dissident group that formed the new American and Foreign Anti-Slavery Society. That society established a new political party: the Liberty Party, which nominated Birney for president in 1840 and 1844.

Although committed to immediate abolitionism, Liberty Party members doubted the federal government had the authority to abolish slavery. It was up to the states to determine the legality of slavery. They felt the government could act in the western territories, however, and demanded that new territories prohibit slavery. Prominent black abolitionists, including Frederick Douglass, endorsed the party, whose leaders also emphasized combating northern prejudice.

WOMEN'S RIGHTS

At the first World Anti-Slavery Convention in London in 1840, abolitionists Lucretia Mott and Elizabeth Cady Stanton were dismayed when female abolitionists were denied seats in the convention's main hall; eight years later, the two helped organize the first American women's rights convention. Born to a South Carolina slaveholding family, Angelina and Sarah Grimké moved north and became active in abolitionism. After critics attacked them for speaking to audiences that included men, the sisters began advocating for women's legal and social equality.

Religious revivals helped women see themselves as inherently equal to men, and reform movements brought middle-class women into the public sphere. Female reformers' lobbying helped to effect legal change, and some women believed the next step was citizenship rights for women.

Legal Rights

After independence, American states carried over traditional English marriage law, which gave husbands familial control. Men owned their wives' property, were legal guardians of their children, and owned whatever family members produced or earned.

A father had the legal authority to oppose his daughter's choice of husband, though by 1800 most women chose their spouses.

Married women made modest gains in property and spousal rights after 1830. Arkansas in 1835 passed the first married women's property law, and by 1860 sixteen more states followed. In those states, women could own and convey property and write wills. When a wife inherited property, it was hers, though money she earned still belonged to her husband. Such laws were popular among wealthy Americans who hoped to protect family fortunes during economic downturns; property in a woman's name was safe from her husband's creditors. In the 1830s, states also added cruelty and desertion as grounds for divorce.

Radical reformers argued that marriage constituted a form of bondage. Lucy Stone, an outspoken critic of marriage, consented to wed fellow abolitionist Henry Blackwell only if shecould eschew a vow of obedience and keep her own name.

Political Rights

The women's movement was launched in July 1848, when Elizabeth Cady Stanton, Lucretia Mott, Mary Ann McClintock, Martha Wright, and Jane Hunt organized the first Woman's Rights Convention at Seneca Falls, New York, where three hundred women and men demanded women's social and economic equality. Their Declaration of Sentiments, modeled on the Declaration of Independence, broadcast the injustices suffered by women and proclaimed "All men and women are created equal." The similarities between abolitionism and women's rights led reformers, including Stone and Blackwell, and former slaves like Sojourner Truth, to work for both movements. Some men supported women's rights, notably William Lloyd Garrison and Frederick Douglass, but most men opposed female suffrage. The Seneca Falls' suffrage resolution passed only after Frederick Douglass passionately defended it. In 1851 Elizabeth Cady Stanton joined with temperance advocate Susan B. Anthony to advocate persistently for women's voting rights.

JACKSONIANISM AND PARTY POLITICS

Like reformers, politicians sought to control the direction of the expanding nation. As suffrage laws changed, they reached out to an increasingly broad-based electorate. Hotly contested elections drew the interest and participation of voters and nonvoters alike.

Expanding Political Participation

Property restrictions for voters remained in only seven of twenty-six states by 1840. Some states even allowed foreign nationals who officially declared their intention of becoming American citizens to vote. The net effect was that between 1824 and 1828 the number of votes cast in presidential elections tripled, from 360,000 to over 1.1 million. The proportion of eligible voters who cast ballots also grew, from about 27 percent in 1824 to more than 80 percent in 1840.

The selection of presidential electors also became more democratic. Previously a caucus of party leaders in most states picked them, but by 1824 eighteen out of twenty-four states chose electors by popular vote. Consequently, politicians augmented

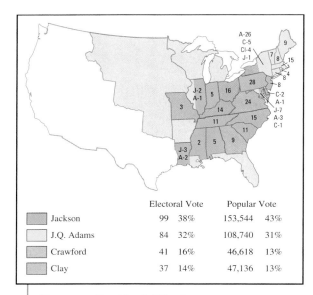

	Electoral Vote		Popular Vote	
Jackson	99	38%	153,544	43%
J.Q. Adams	84	32%	108,740	31%
Crawford	41	16%	46,618	13%
Clay	37	14%	47,136	13%

Map 12.1   Presidential Election, 1824

Andrew Jackson led in both electoral and popular votes but failed to win a majority of electoral college votes. The House elected John Quincy Adams president.

Presidential candidate Andrew Jackson is portrayed on a trinket or sewing box in 1824. This is an example both of how campaigns entered popular culture and of the active role of women, excluded from voting, in politics. (Collection of David J. and Janice L. Frent)

appeals to voters, and the 1824 election saw the end of the congressional caucus, when House and Senate members of the same political party united to select their candidate.

Election of 1824

As a result, five Democratic-Republican candidates ran for president in 1824. The poorly attended Republican caucus chose William H. Crawford of Georgia, secretary of the treasury, as its candidate. Instead of Congress, state legislatures now nominated candidates, offering the expanded electorate a slate of sectional candidates. John Quincy Adams drew support from New England, while westerners backed House Speaker Henry Clay of Kentucky. Some southerners at first supported Secretary of War John C. Calhoun, who later ran for the vice presidency instead. The Tennessee legislature nominated military hero Andrew Jackson.

Jackson led in electoral and popular votes, but no candidate received a majority in the electoral college. Adams finished second. Under the Constitution, the House of Representatives, voting by state delegation, one vote to a state, would select the next president from among the three electoral vote leaders. With the fewest votes, Clay was dropped. Crawford, disabled by a stroke, never received consideration. Clay backed Adams, who won with thirteen of the twenty-four state delegations and became president (see Map 12.1). Adams appointed Clay as secretary of state, the steppingstone to the presidency.

Angry Jacksonians denounced the election as a corrupt bargain, claiming that Adams had stolen the presidency by promising Clay a cabinet position for his votes. The Republican Party split. The Adams wing emerged as the National Republicans, and the Jacksonians became the Democrats.

Adams proposed a strong nationalist policy incorporating Clay's American System of protective tariffs, a national bank, and internal improvements. Adams believed the federal government's active role should extend to education, science, and the arts. He proposed a national university in Washington, D.C. Brilliant as a diplomat and secretary of state, Adams fared less well as chief executive.

Election of 1828

The 1828 election pitted Adams against Jackson. Andrew Jackson was born in South Carolina in 1767 and rose from humble beginnings to become a wealthy Tennessee planter and slaveholder. Jackson was the first American president from the West. Having served in the Revolution as a boy, Jackson claimed a connection to the founding generation. In the Tennessee militia, General Jackson led the campaign to remove Creeks from the Alabama and Georgia frontier. He burst onto the national scene in 1815 as the hero of the Battle of New Orleans and enhanced his glory in an 1818 expedition against Seminoles in Spanish Florida. Jackson served as congressman and senator from Tennessee and the first territorial governor of Florida (1821).

Jackson's proponents accused Adams of stealing the 1824 election and, when he was envoy to Russia, of securing prostitutes for the czar. Anti-Jacksonians published reports that Jackson's wife, Rachel, married Jackson before her divorce from her first husband was final. In 1806, while defending Rachel's integrity, Jackson killed a man during a duel, and the cry of "murderer!" haunted the election.

Although Adams held the states he won in 1824, his opposition was now unified behind a single candidate, and Jackson swamped him, polling 56 percent of the popular vote and winning the electoral college by 178 to 83 votes (see Map 12.2). Through a lavishly financed coalition of state parties, political leaders, and newspaper editors, a popular movement had elected the president. The Democratic Party became the first well-organized national political party in the United States.

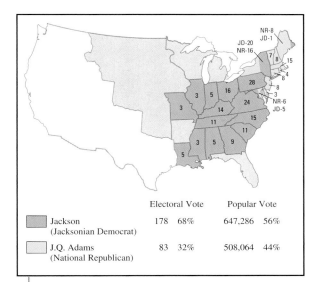

	Electoral Vote		Popular Vote	
Jackson (Jacksonian Democrat)	178	68%	647,286	56%
J.Q. Adams (National Republican)	83	32%	508,064	44%

Map 12.2   Presidential Election, 1828
Andrew Jackson avenged his 1824 loss of the presidency, sweeping the election in 1828.

Democrats

Democrats shared a commitment to the Jeffersonian concept of an agrarian society. They viewed a strong central government as the enemy of individual liberty and believed government intervention in the economy benefited special-interest groups and created corporate monopolies. They sought to end federal support of banks and corporations and restrict paper currency. Jackson and his supporters also opposed reform movements as interfering with individual liberty. When it came to westward expansion, though, Jackson and his followers wanted federal intervention. It was Jackson who initiated Indian removal despite northeastern reformers' protests.

By restraining government and emphasizing individualism, Jacksonians sought to restore traditional republican virtues, such as self-discipline and self-reliance, undermined by economic and social change. Jackson advocated for popular government and declared that sovereignty resided with the people, not with the states or courts.

Like Jefferson, Jackson strengthened the executive branch even as he advocated limited government. In combining the roles of party leader and chief of state, he centralized power in the White House. He relied on political friends, his Kitchen Cabinet, for advice, only rarely consulting his official cabinet. Rotating officeholders, Jackson claimed, made government more responsive to the public and allowed him to appoint loyal Democrats, a practice his critics called the spoils system, in which the victor rewards supporters. The spoils system, opponents charged, corrupted the government because appointments were based on loyalty, not competency.

King Andrew

Opponents mocked Jackson as King Andrew I, charging him with abuse of power by ignoring the Supreme Court's ruling on Cherokee rights, sidestepping his cabinet, and replacing experienced officeholders with his cronies.

Jackson frequently used the veto to promote limited government. In 1830 he vetoed the Maysville Road bill, which would have funded construction of a 60-mile turnpike from Maysville to Lexington, Kentucky. A federally subsidized internal improvement in one state was unconstitutional, he insisted; states should handle such projects. The veto undermined Clay's American System and embarrassed Clay because the project was in his home district.

The first six presidents vetoed nine bills; Jackson vetoed twelve. Previous presidents believed that vetoes were justified only on constitutional grounds; Jackson considered policy disagreements legitimate grounds. He made the veto a weapon for controlling Congress, because representatives and senators had to weigh the prospect of a veto as they deliberated.

FEDERALISM AT ISSUE: THE NULLIFICATION AND BANK CONTROVERSIES

The slave South feared federal power and no state more so than South Carolina, where the planter class was strongest and slavery most concentrated. Southerners resented protectionist tariffs, which in 1824 and 1828 protected manufactures by imposing import duties on manufactured cloth and iron. In protecting northern factories, the tariff raised the costs of manufactured goods to southerners, who labeled the 1828 tariff the Tariff of Abominations.

Nullification

South Carolina's political leaders rejected the 1828 tariff, invoking the doctrine of nullification, which proffered that states had the right to overrule, or nullify, federal legislation. Nullification was based on the Virginia and Kentucky Resolutions of 1798, stating that states, representing the people, have a right to judge the constitutionality of federal actions. Jackson's vice president, John C. Calhoun of South Carolina, argued in his unsigned *Exposition and Protest* that, in any disagreement between the federal government and a state, a special state convention should decide the conflict by either nullifying or affirming federal law.

As Jackson's running mate in 1828, Calhoun avoided endorsing nullification and embarrassing the Democratic ticket; he also hoped to win Jackson's support as the Democratic presidential heir apparent. Thus, in early 1830, Calhoun presided silently over the Senate when Massachusetts Senator Daniel Webster and South Carolina Senator Robert Y. Hayne debated states' rights. The debate started over a resolution to restrict western land sales but soon touched on the tariff. Hayne charged that the North was threatening to bring disunity. Webster defended New England and the republic, keeping nullification supporters on the defensive.

Though sympathetic to states' rights and distrustful of the federal government, Jackson rejected state sovereignty. Believing in the Union, he shared Webster's dread of nullification. The president made his position clear at a Jefferson Day dinner with the toast "Our Federal Union, it must and shall be preserved." Vice President Calhoun toasted "The Federal Union—next to our liberty the most dear," revealing his adherence to states' rights. Calhoun and Jackson grew apart, and Jackson looked to Secretary of State Martin Van Buren as his successor.

Tension resumed when Congress passed a new tariff in 1832, reducing some duties but retaining high taxes on imported iron, cottons, and woolens. Although a majority of southern representatives supported the new tariff, South Carolinians refused to go along. They feared the act could set a precedent for legislation on slavery. In November 1832 a South Carolina state convention nullified the 1828 and the 1832 tariffs, declaring it unlawful for federal officials to collect duties in the state.

The Force Act

In December Jackson issued a proclamation opposing nullification. He moved troops to federal forts in South Carolina and prepared U.S. marshals to collect the duties. At Jackson's request, Congress passed the Force Act, authorizing the president to call up troops but offering a way to avoid force by collecting duties before foreign ships reached Charleston's harbor. Jackson extended an olive branch by recommending tariff reductions.

Calhoun, disturbed by South Carolina's drift toward separatism, resigned as vice president and was soon elected to represent South Carolina in the U.S. Senate. There he worked with Henry Clay on the compromise Tariff of 1833. Quickly passed by Congress and signed by the president, the new tariff lengthened the list of duty-free items and reduced duties over nine years. Satisfied, South Carolina repealed its nullification law.

Nullification offered a genuine debate on the nature and principles of the republic. Each side believed it was upholding the Constitution. South Carolina opposed the tyranny of the federal government and manufacturing interests. Jackson fought the tyranny of South Carolina, which threatened to split the republic. It took the crisis over a central bank to define federal government's powers more clearly.

Second Bank of the United States

The Second Bank of the United States' twenty-year charter was scheduled to expire in 1836. The bank served as a depository for federal funds and provided business credit. Its bank notes circulated as currency nationwide; they could be readily exchanged for gold. Through its twenty-five branch offices, the Second Bank acted as a clearinghouse for state banks, refusing bank notes from state banks lacking sufficient gold reserves. But by presenting a state bank's notes for redemption all at once, the Second Bank could ruin a state bank. Moreover, with less money in reserve, state banks found themselves unable to compete with the Second Bank.

Many state governments regarded the national bank as unresponsive to local needs. Westerners and urban workers bitterly remembered the bank's conservative credit policies during the Panic of 1819. As a private, profit-making institution, its policies reflected its owners' interests, especially the president, Nicholas Biddle. The bank became the prime issue in the 1832 presidential campaign.

Antimasonry

The national political convention was the innovation of the Antimason Party, which started in upstate New York in the mid-1820s as a grassroots movement against Freemasonry, a secret male fraternity of middle- and upper-class men prominent in commerce and civic affairs. Opponents claimed Masons colluded to bestow business and political favors on each other. Evangelicals considered Masons sacrilegious, claiming that Masonry encouraged men to neglect their families for alcohol and ribald entertainment. In the 1828 presidential election, the Antimasons opposed Jackson, himself a Mason. They held the first national political convention in Baltimore in 1831, nominating William Wirt of Maryland for president and Amos Ellmaker of Pennsylvania for vice president.

Election of 1832

Following the Antimasons' lead, the Democrats and National Republicans also held conventions. Democrats reaffirmed Jackson for president and nominated Martin Van Buren of New York for vice president. The National Republican convention selected Clay and John Sergeant of Pennsylvania. The Independent Democrats ran John Floyd and Henry Lee of Virginia.

Jacksonians denounced the bank as a vehicle for special privilege, while Republicans supported it within their plan for economic nationalism. The bank's charter was valid until 1836, but Clay persuaded Biddle to ask Congress to approve an early rechartering. If Jackson signed the rechartering bill, then Clay could attack the president's inconsistency. If Jackson vetoed it, Clay hoped voters would favor him instead. The plan backfired. The president vetoed the bill with a message appealing to voters who feared that rapid economic development spread advantages undemocratically. Jackson took a strong stand against special interests that tried to use the government to their own unfair advantage and won 54 percent of the popular vote to Clay's 37 percent; in the electoral college, he captured 76 percent of electors. The Antimasons won only Vermont.

Jackson's Second Term

Jackson moved in 1833 to dismantle the Second Bank and deposited federal funds in state-chartered banks. Without federal money, the Second Bank shriveled, becoming a Pennsylvania-chartered private bank in 1836. Five years later it closed.

Congress passed the Deposit Act of 1836 with Jackson's support. It authorized the secretary of the treasury to designate one bank per state and territory to provide services formerly performed by the Bank of the United States. The act provided that federal surpluses over $5 million be distributed to states as interest-free loans beginning in 1837. These loans were never repaid.

The surplus derived from wholesale speculation in public lands: speculators borrowed money to purchase public land, used the land as collateral for credit to buy additional acreage, and repeated the cycle. Between 1834 and 1836, federal receipts from land sales rose from $5 million to $25 million. State banks providing the loans issued bank notes. Jackson feared that the speculative craze threatened the stability of state banks and undermined settlers, who could not compete with speculators for the best land.

Specie Circular

With his opposition to paper currency, the president ordered Treasury Secretary Levi Woodbury to issue the Specie Circular. It provided that after August 1836 only specie—gold or silver—or Virginia scrip (paper money) would be accepted as payment for land. By ending credit sales, it significantly reduced purchases of public land and the federal budget surplus. Consequently, the government suspended payments to states.

The policy was a disaster. Although federal land sales fell, speculation continued. The increased demand for specie squeezed banks, and many suspended the redemption of bank notes for specie. Credit contracted further as banks issued fewer notes and made fewer loans. More important, the Specie Circular was similar to a bill defeated in the Senate three months earlier, so Jackson used presidential powers to override legislative will. In the waning days of Jackson's administration, Congress voted to repeal the circular, but the president pocket-vetoed the bill by holding it unsigned until Congress adjourned. In May 1838, a joint resolution of Congress overturned the circular. Sales of land resumed, and speculative fervor ended.

THE WHIG CHALLENGE AND THE SECOND PARTY SYSTEM

In the 1830s, the Democrats' opponents, including remnants of the National Republican and Antimason Parties, joined to become the Whig Party. Resentful of Jackson's domination of Congress, Whigs borrowed the name of the eighteenth-century British party that opposed the tyranny of Hanoverian monarchs. They, too, were the loyal opposition. From 1834 through the 1840s, the Whigs and the Democrats competed on nearly equal footing, and each drew supporters from all regions. The second party system was more intense and better organized than what scholars have labeled as the first party system of Democratic-Republicans versus Federalists.

Whigs and Reformers

Whigs favored economic expansion through an activist government. They supported corporate charters, a national bank, and paper currency; Democrats opposed all three. Whigs professed a strong belief in progress and perfectibility, and favored public schools, prison and asylum reform, and temperance. Whigs did not object to helping special interests if it promoted the general welfare. The chartering of corporations, they argued, expanded economic opportunity for everyone. Democrats, distrustful of concentrated economic power, held to the Jeffersonian principle of limited government.

Whigs stressed a harmony of interests among all classes as well as equal opportunity. Democrats saw society divided into the haves and have nots and embraced equal rights. They championed heroic artisans like Sam Patch, whereas Whigs preferred to see society ruled from the top down. Whigs believed in free-labor ideology and thought that society's wealthy and powerful had risen by their own merits.

Whigs' support for moral reform won over evangelical Protestants. Methodists and Baptists were overwhelmingly Whigs, as were the small number of free black voters. In many locales the membership rolls of reform societies overlapped those of the party. Whigs' rallies resembled camp meetings, their speeches employed pulpit rhetoric, and their programs embodied perfectionist beliefs.

By appealing to evangelicals, Whigs alienated other faiths. The evangelicals' ideal Christian state had no room for nonevangelical Protestants, Catholics, Mormons, or religious freethinkers. Those groups opposed Sabbath laws and temperance legislation and preferred to keep religion and politics separate. Consequently, more than 95 percent of Irish Catholics, 90 percent of Reformed Dutch, and 80 percent of German Catholics voted Democratic.

Thus, Whigs appealed to those who benefited from the era's economic changes, whereas Democrats remained committed to agrarian expansion. Whigs drew antislavery supporters as well northern businessmen and workers pledged to good relations with the South. Well-settled slaveowners, especially in the Upper South, voted Whig, as did black New Englanders. Both favored halting slavery's westward expansion. Democrats' promises to open additional lands for settlement attracted yeoman farmers, wage earners, frontier slaveowners, and immigrants. With such broad voter coalitions, there was room within each party for a spectrum of beliefs, particularly about slavery.

Some politicians went to extremes to keep slavery out of the national debate. In response to the American Anti-Slavery Society's petitioning campaign, the House of Representatives in 1836 adopted what abolitionists labeled *the gag rule,* which automatically tabled abolitionist petitions. Defending the right of petition, former president John Quincy Adams, now a representative from Massachusetts, spoke against the gag rule, which was repealed in 1844.

Election of 1836

Vice President Martin Van Buren headed the Democratic ticket in the 1836 presidential election. Van Buren was a career politician who built a political machine—the Albany Regency—in New York and then joined Jackson's cabinet in 1829, first as secretary of state and then as American minister to Great Britain.

Not yet a national party, in 1836 Whigs entered three sectional candidates: Daniel Webster (New England), Hugh White (the South), and William Henry Harrison (the West). Van Buren comfortably captured the electoral college even though he had only a twenty-five thousand–vote lead. No vice-presidential candidate received a majority of electoral votes, and for the only time, the Senate decided a vice-presidential race, selecting Democratic candidate Richard M. Johnson of Kentucky.

Van Buren and Hard Times

Van Buren took office weeks before the American credit system collapsed. In response to the Specie Circular, New York banks stopped redeeming paper currency with gold in mid-1837. Soon all banks suspended payments in hard coin. A downward economic spiral began. Credit contraction made things worse. After a brief recovery, hard times persisted from 1839 until 1843.

Van Buren cut federal spending, causing prices to drop further, and he opposed a national bank, which would have expanded credit. The president proposed a new regional treasury system for government deposits that became law in 1840. Treasury branches would accept and disperse only gold and silver coin. Increasing the demand for hard coin accelerated price deflation. Whigs favored new banks, more paper currency, and readily available corporate and bank charters. As the party of hard money, Democrats favored eliminating paper currency, and by the mid-1840s most favored eliminating bank corporations.

Anglo-American Tensions

Amid hard times came renewed Anglo-American tensions. After the privately owned steamer *Caroline* carried supplies to aid an unsuccessful Canadian uprising against Great Britain, British loyalists burned the ship, killing an American. Britain refused to apologize, and American newspapers called for revenge. Fearing war, President Van Buren posted troops at the border to discourage vigilante retaliation. Tensions subsided in late 1840 when New York arrested a Canadian deemed responsible for the American's death. The alleged murderer was acquitted. Had the verdict gone otherwise, Lord Palmerston, the British foreign minister, might have sought war.

An old border dispute between Maine and New Brunswick also disrupted Anglo-American relations. When Canadian lumbermen cut trees in the disputed region in winter 1838–1839, a Maine posse assembled to expel them. The lumbermen captured the posse, both sides mobilized militias, and Congress authorized a call-up of fifty thousand men. General Scott was dispatched to Aroostook, Maine, where he arranged a truce. The Webster-Ashburton Treaty (1842) settled the boundaries between Maine and New Brunswick and along the Great Lakes.

William Henry Harrison and the Election of 1840

With the nation facing hard times, Whigs felt confident about the 1840 election. Their strategy was to maintain loyal supporters and win independents by blaming hardship on Democrats. Whigs rallied behind military hero, General William Henry Harrison, conqueror of the Shawnees at Tippecanoe Creek in 1811. Democrats renominated President Van Buren, and the Liberty Party ran James Birney.

Harrison and his running mate, John Tyler of Virginia, ran a people's crusade against the aristocratic president in the Palace. Although from a Virginia plantation family, Harrison presented

Even as the Whigs opposed the Democrats, they adopted many of the Democrats' campaign techniques, appealing to the common man with their log cabin and cider campaign of 1840. The band in this street scene is riding a wagon decorated with a log-cabin painting. The campaign's excitement appealed to voters and nonvoters alike, and 80 percent of eligible voters cast ballots. (Franklin D. Roosevelt Library, Hyde Park, New York)

himself as an ordinary farmer. Whigs wooed voters with huge rallies, parades, songs, posters, campaign mementos, and a party newspaper, *The Log Cabin*. Roughly 80 percent of eligible voters cast ballots. Harrison won the popular vote by a narrow margin but swept the electoral college by 234 to 60.

Immediately after taking office in 1841, President Harrison convened a special session of Congress to pass the Whig program: repealing the independent treasury system, creating a new national bank, and passing a higher protective tariff. But sixty-eight-year-old Harrison caught pneumonia and died within a month of his inauguration. The Constitution did not stipulate what should happen, but Tyler took possession of executive powers and set a precedent that would not be codified in the Constitution until the twentieth century with the Twenty-fifth Amendment.

President Tyler

Tyler became more a Democrat than a Whig. He repeatedly vetoed Clay's protective tariffs, internal improvements, and bills aimed at reviving the Bank of the United States. Two days after Tyler's second veto of a bank bill, the entire cabinet except Secretary of State Daniel Webster resigned, and he left after negotiating the Webster-Ashburton treaty. Disgusted Whigs referred to Tyler as His Accidency.

Like Jackson, Tyler expanded presidential powers and emphasized westward expansion. During his presidency, the United States negotiated its first treaties with China, and Tyler expanded the Monroe Doctrine to include Hawaii. More than anything else, Tyler's vision fixed on Texas and the westward expansion of slavery.

Summary

Religion and reform shaped politics from 1824 through the 1840s. Driven by a belief in human perfectibility, many evangelicals, especially women, worked to right the wrongs of American society. They hoped to trigger the millennium, the thousand years of peace on earth that would accompany Christ's Second Coming. Some utopians joined experimental communities that modeled radical alternatives to existing society. Abolitionists worked to perfect American society through the eradication of slavery. As women entered the public sphere as reformers and abolitionists, some embraced women's rights.

Struggles between the National Republicans and Democrats, then between Democrats and Whigs, stimulated interest in political issues. Both parties built strong organizations and favored economic expansion but by different means: Whigs advocated centralized government, whereas Democrats advocated limited government and agricultural expansion. Controversies over the Second Bank of the United States and nullification exposed different interpretations of the nation's founding principles.

The late 1830s and early 1840s would be a period of uncertainty: the economy experienced a period of bust; tensions with the British resurfaced; and a president died in office. John Tyler's vision of American greatness depended on westward expansion.

The Bible Belt

Had an eighteenth-century visitor to North America asked for the Bible belt, she would have been directed to New England, whose colonies were founded for religious purposes. By the 1830s, the South was the most churched and devout region. The Second Great Awakening, beginning in 1801, spread quickly through the South. By the 1830s, more than half of white and one-quarter of black southerners had a conversion experience. Embracing the Bible as God's word revealed, the South became known as the Bible belt.

Southern Protestant liturgy and cadences were as much African as European; thus southern and northern denominations grew apart. They separated in the 1840s, when Southern Baptists and Methodists withdrew from the national organizations that had barred slaveowners from church offices. Presbyterians withdrew later.

Protestantism dominated, making the South more religiously homogeneous than other regions. Mostly evangelical, southern religion emphasized conversion and a personal battle against sin. By the twentieth century, fundamentalism, which stressed a literal reading of the Bible, reinforced resistance to modernism. Yet southern Protestantism lost ground in opposing evolution and by allying with anti-immigrant groups.

Evangelicalism rose again in the 1960s, especially after the Catholic John F. Kennedy won the Democratic presidential nomination. Many evangelicals moved to the Republican Party, and in 1964 the Republican Barry Goldwater won the Bible belt states. His conservative rhetoric resonated with southerners concerned about desegregation and eroding religious values. *Time* called 1976 the Year of the Evangelical when the born-again Southern Baptist Jimmy Carter became president.

In the 1980s and 1990s, the Bible belt became the base of evangelical political action led by the Moral Majority. Religious and cultural issues rallied southern evangelicals defending the traditional family; advocating prayer in schools; and opposing abortion, the Equal Rights Amendment, and gay rights legislation. In the 2006 midterm elections, dissatisfaction with the Iraq war cost Republicans control of both houses of Congress, but most Bible belt states stuck with the party. Thus the revivals that began in Kentucky in 1801 have rippled across the South for two centuries, shaping the distinctive southern blend of culture and politics.

Chapter Review

FROM REVIVAL TO REFORM

How did religious revival movements lead to social reform?

Ministers and preachers in the Second Great Awakening focused on the importance of good works in gaining salvation in the afterlife. The more they told listeners that how they lived would make a difference in whether they entered God's Kingdom, the more they inspired social and moral reform. Women were often a major force in reform movements, expanding their domestic roles in the home into efforts to counteract the evils of the market economy. Reform goals included reformatories for wayward youth, orphan asylums, rehabilitation for criminals, temperance, and improvements in education.

COMMUNITARIAN EXPERIMENTS

What were the goals of utopian communities?

Often inspired by religious revivalism, the utopian movement sought to hold the line on the rapid social change that members found disturbing, in particular, the rising market economy's excessive individualism. They wanted to recapture the so-called communal nature of the past, and at the same time reshape marriage, child rearing, and other social arrangements. The Shakers, for example, built a profitable community around agriculture and handcrafts, but also abolished individual families in favor of men and women living in separate quarters and sharing leadership. The Oneida community centered on communal property ownership, communal child-rearing, and "complex marriage" in which all men were married to all women. The Fourierists included writers and intellectuals who inspired an American renaissance in literature and the arts, with Brook Farm in West Roxbury, Massachusetts, its most famous community. During its brief existence, the community embraced transcendentalism, the notion that the physical world is secondary to the spiritual realm.

ABOLITIONISM

How did the Second Great Awakening transform the antislavery movement?

Abolitionism dates back to the nation's earliest days, when efforts to end slavery were initiated by both free blacks and elite whites. After 1830, however, evangelical abolitionists seeking to eradicate America's sins focused on slavery with renewed vigor. The activist and newspaper editor William Lloyd Garrison led a new, more radical strain of abolitionism known as "immediatism," which called for the immediate and complete end of slavery without compensating slave owners. Immediatists shared the evangelical belief that people determined their spiritual fate through good or evil acts and that by ending slavery, they could bring about the millennium, or Christ's return to earth. Unlike earlier movements, these abolitionists relied on participation of ministers and many others, and as such encouraged women to not only join but serve on executive committees.

WOMEN'S RIGHTS

What inspired the rise of the women's movement in the mid-nineteenth century?

The religious revivals of the Second Great Awakening provided the first impetus for a later women's movement by encouraging women to see themselves as equal spiritually to men and urging them to take part in reforming society. Women's growing participation in the antislavery movement had many seeing parallels between slave bondage and marriage as a form of bondage, as well as their own lack of citizenship rights. Traditional marriage law, borrowed from the English, gave husbands control over the family, including wives' property and earnings. Eight years after being denied a seat at the World Anti-Slavery Convention because of their sex, Elizabeth Cady Stanton and Lucretia Mott joined others in holding the first Woman's Rights Convention in 1848 at Seneca Falls, N.Y. There, three hundred participants outlined their demands for political and social equality, including the right to vote, in their Declaration of Rights and Sentiments, a document that paralleled the Declaration of Independence.

JACKSONIANISM AND PARTY POLITICS

How did changing demographics influence the outcome of the 1824 presidential election and the future of political parties?

As suffrage laws changed to eliminate land requirements and allow immigrants to vote, the number of eligible voters tripled from 1824 to 1828. Politicians broadened their outreach to these new voters and successfully urged states to shift from appointing presidential electors to the more democratic popular vote. That, combined with the end of candidate selection by congressional caucus, meant that five Democratic-Republican candidates ran for president in 1824. Although Andrew Jackson led in both electoral and popular vote, no one had a clear majority, leaving the House of Representatives to choose the president. Its members chose second place John Quincy Adams, which led to charges of election-stealing and divided the party into the National Republicans (behind Adams) and the Democrats (behind Jackson). With two parties and only two candidates in the 1828 election, Jackson handily won the presidency, and the Democratic Party became the first well-organized national political party in the United States.

FEDERALISM AT ISSUE: THE NULLIFICATION AND BANK CONTROVERSIES

What was at issue in the Nullification Controversy?

At the core of the Nullification Controversy were differing interpretations of the Constitution regarding federal power and states' rights. The doctrine of nullification, which stated that states could overrule federal legislation, was based on the Virginia and Kentucky Resolutions of 1798, which argued that states could judge whether federal actions were constitutional, and ultimately nullify federal laws that did not pass the test. President Jackson rejected state sovereignty and saw nullification as leading to disunion. When South Carolina nullified a federal tariff, Jackson moved troops in to collect the duties. As a compromise, the tariff was reduced and South Carolina withdrew its nullification. But the debate on the nature of the republic and of federal power continued.

THE WHIG CHALLENGE AND THE SECOND PARTY SYSTEM

How did the Whigs and Democrats differ on the role of government in the economy?

Unlike the Democrats, Whigs embraced an activist government and had no problem with government aiding special interests as long as the public benefited as well. Democrats believed in the Jefferson model of limited government. Whigs thought government should be ruled from the top-down, and they embraced the notion of a meritocracy—that the wealthy obtained their status and power through their own hard work. Democrats saw the world divided into "haves" and "have nots" and sought equal rights for all to restore some form of balance. Whigs supported corporate charters, a national bank, and paper currency; Democrats opposed all three.

SUGGESTIONS FOR FURTHER READING

Michael F. Holt, *The Rise and Fall of the American Whig Party: Jacksonian Politics and the Onset of the Civil War* (1999)

Julie Roy Jeffrey, *The Great Silent Army of Abolitionism: Ordinary Women in the Antislavery Movement* (1998)

Curtis D. Johnson, *Redeeming America: Evangelicals and the Road to Civil War* (1993)

Paul E. Johnson, *Sam Patch, the Famous Jumper* (2003)

Steven Mintz, *Moralists and Modernizers: America's Pre–Civil War Reformers* (1995)

Richard S. Newman, *The Transformation of American Abolitionism: Fighting Slavery in the Early Republic* (2002)

Harry L. Watson, *Liberty and Power: The Politics of Jacksonian America* (1990)

Sean Wilentz, *The Rise and Fall of American Democracy: Jefferson to Lincoln* (2005)

The Contested West | 1815–1860

To eight-year-old Henry Clay Bruce, moving west was an adventure. In April 1844, the Virginia boy began a 1,500-mile, two-month trip to his new home in Missouri. Henry marveled at the beautiful terrain, impressive towns, and the steamboat ride from Louisville to St. Louis. Once in Missouri, Henry noticed how much the West differed from the East. Farms were far apart, and the countryside abounded with wild fruits, game, and fish. But rattlesnakes, wolves, and vicious hogs kept Henry and his playmates from straying far from home.

A slave boy, Henry made the trip with his mother and siblings after the plantation owner Jack Perkinson decided to seek a new beginning in the West. Pettis Perkinson (Jack's brother and Henry's owner) and three other white Virginians crammed their families, slaves, and belongings into three wagons. In Missouri, Pettis took up residence with Jack Perkinson, who—according to Henry—yelled at and whipped his slaves.

Henry's first year in Missouri was as carefree as a slave child's life could be. The boy fished, hunted (with dogs, not guns), and gathered prairie chicken eggs. But by age nine, Henry was hired out, first to a brick maker, then to a tobacco factory. He worked sunup to sundown, and when he did not meet his bosses' expectations, he was whipped.

Meanwhile, Pettis Perkinson decided to return to Virginia, later sending for some of his slaves, including Henry. The slaves' work would be less arduous in Virginia, but that was small compensation for having to leave behind loved ones in Missouri.

Again Pettis Perkinson grew weary of Virginia and renewed his quest for opportunity in the West, this time in Mississippi. But cotton plantation life suited neither Henry nor his master, who now decided—to his slaves' joy—to give Missouri another chance.

This icon will direct you to interactive activities and study materials on A People And A Nation, Brief Edition
website: **www.cengage.com/history/norton/peoplenationbrief8e**

Chronology

1812	Congress establishes the General Land Office.	**1840–60**	250,000 to 500,000 migrants travel overland to the Far West.
1820	Congress lowers the price of public lands.	**1841**	Log Cabin Bill allows settlers to claim 160 acres of public land on credit.
1821	William Becknell charts the Santa Fe Trail. Mexico becomes an independent nation.	**1844**	Presidential campaign features annexation of Texas.
1823	Mexico allows Stephen Austin to settle U.S. citizens in Mexico.	**1845**	Democratic editor coins the term *manifest destiny*. Texas is annexed by joint resolution of Congress (March 1) and becomes twenty-eighth state (December 29).
1824	Congressional General Survey Act empowers the military to chart transportation routes. Jedediah Smith publicizes the South Pass to the Far West. Indian Office (later Bureau of Indian Affairs) is established.	**1846–48**	War occurs with Mexico.
1825–32	*Empresario* contracts are signed for American settlement of Texas.	**1847**	Mormons settle in Great Salt Lake valley.
		1848	Gold is discovered in California.
1826	Fredonia rebellion fails in Texas.	**1849–50s**	Farmers and prospectors stream into the Great Plains and Far West.
1830	Indian Removal Act is passed (see Chapter 10).	**1855**	Massacre of Indians at Ash Hollow triggers warfare between the Sioux and the United States.
1832	Black Hawk War occurs.	**1857–58**	Mormons and the U.S. Army engage in armed conflict.
1834	Cyrus McCormick patents the mechanical reaper.	**1862**	Homestead Act allots 160 acres of free land to those who improve it.
1836	Lone Star Republic is founded. U.S. Army Corps of Topographical Engineers is established.		

Two years later, the restless Perkinson set his eyes farther west, on Texas. Henry, now in his late teens, and his brothers refused to go. Although livid, Pettis Perkinson preferred to abandon his plans than deal with recalcitrant slaves. Henry became the foreman on Perkinson's Missouri farm, where he remained until escaping amid the Civil War to the free state of Kansas in 1864. More than twenty years after leaving Virginia, Henry Clay Bruce finally found the freedom and opportunity that led so many to the West.

In 1820 about 20 percent of the nation's population lived west of the Appalachian Mountains. By 1860 nearly 50 percent did. Most whites and free blacks moved west seeking better opportunities. They envisioned enormous tracts of fertile and uncultivated land or, beginning in the late 1840s, gold or silver mines that promised quick riches. Some saw opportunities for lumbering or ranching or selling goods or services to farmers, miners, lumbermen, and cattlemen.

Men often decided to head west without consulting their wives and children, and slaves' wishes received even less consideration. Nor did western settlers consider the Indian peoples already living there.

The federal government sponsored westward exploration, made laws regulating settlement and the establishment of territorial governments, surveyed and fixed prices on public lands, and sold land. It also invested in transportation routes and established a military presence to assist white settlers.

In the 1820s, the Mexican government, too, aided westward expansion by encouraging Anglo-American settlement in its northern borderlands—something it would later regret. U.S. settlers vied with the region's other inhabitants—Indians, Hispanics, and people of mixed heritage—for land and natural resources. A decade later, Mexico's northern province of Texas declared its independence and sought annexation by the United States. Thus began heightened tensions between the United States and Mexico and within the United States, as Texas's future became entangled with slavery.

For some white Americans, mostly southerners, the ability to own slaves in the West represented freedom. For others, from both the North and the South, slavery's westward expansion frustrated dreams for a new beginning in a region free from slavery's degrading influence on white labor. Even as political parties tried to avoid the slavery issue, they took distinct stands on westward expansion's role in the nation's economic development. Once the spotlight trained on Texas, political leaders would find it increasingly difficult to disentangle westward expansion and slavery.

With each passing decade, conflict—between expectations and reality, between people with different aspirations and world-views—increasingly defined life in the West. By the mid-1840s, western events would aggravate long-simmering discord between southern and northern political interests.

- **How did tensions in the modernizing North and the slave South influence western migration and settlement?**
- **How did public, private, and individual initiatives work together to shape the West's development?**
- **What motivated cooperation in the West, and what spurred conflict?**

THE WEST IN THE AMERICAN IMAGINATION

For historian Frederick Jackson Turner, writing in the late nineteenth century, the western frontier, with its abundant free land, was the "meeting point between savagery and civilization." It bred American democracy, shaped the American character, and made the United States exceptional. Modern historians generally eschew the notion of American exceptionalism, stressing instead the complex connections between the United States and the world. Although today's scholars reject the racialist assumptions of Turner's definition of *frontier,* some see value in the term when understood as a meeting place of different cultures. Others see the West as a place, not a process, though they disagree about what delineates it.

Defining the West   For early-nineteenth-century Americans of European descent, the West included anything west of the Appalachian Mountains. It represented the future—a place where they might seek economic and social betterment, typically through land ownership. The West seemed to have so much land that even the poor might acquire a farm. Men who already owned land, like Pettis Perkinson, looked westward for cheaper, bigger, and more fertile landholdings. With the discovery of gold in California in 1848, the West became a place to strike it rich. Other people, though, went west only under

Map 13.1 Westward Expansion, 1800–1860
Through exploration, purchase, war, and treaty, the United States became a continental nation, stretching from the Atlantic to the Pacific.

Legend:
- U.S. territory, 1783
- Louisiana Purchase, 1803
- Florida annexed, 1819–1821
- Texas, 1845
- Oregon Country, 1846
- Mexican Cession, 1848
- Gadsden Purchase, 1853
- States admitted, 1800–1860
- Western trails

the threat of force, including enslaved persons as well as Indians removed from their eastern homelands by the U.S. military.

To many, the concept of the West would have been baffling. Emigrants from Mexico and Central or South America traveled northward to reach what European Americans called the West. The twenty-five thousand or so Chinese who went to California during the 1850s traveled eastward from Asia. Some Indians and French Canadians journeyed southward to the West. All arrived in the western portion of the North American continent because of factors that pushed and pulled them.

Frontier Literature

For European Americans, Daniel Boone became the archetypical frontiersman, a man whose daring individualism opened the Eden-like West for virtuous and hard-working freedom lovers. Through biographies, Boone became a familiar figure in American and European households. The mythical Boone lived in the wilderness and shrank from society. He single-handedly overpowered bears and Indians but also became the pathfinder for civilization. As a friend wrote, he blazed a trail for millions "to a Land flowing with milk and honey." By borrowing Biblical language—the land of milk and honey referred to the Promised Land that God promised beleaguered Israelites—Boone's friend suggested he was a Moses leading his people to a land of abundance.

With the invention of the steam press in the early 1830s, western adventure stories were cheap and widely read. Davy Crockett, another real-life figure turned into mythical hero, was featured in many of them. Crockett first fought the Creeks under Andrew Jackson but later championed Indian rights. After he died defending the Alamo mission during Texas's fight for independence (1836), Crockett appeared in stories portraying the West as a place where one escaped from civilized society and fought Indians and Mexicans. But even in this western myth, the American West symbolized what white Americans saw as their nation's core value: freedom.

Western Art

In artists' renderings, the West was sometimes an untamed wilderness inhabited by savages (noble or otherwise) and sometimes a cultivated garden, a land of milk and honey where the Jeffersonian agrarian dream was realized. Either way, artwork often revealed more about white Americans' ideals that about the West itself.

The first Anglo-American artists to travel west were Samuel Seymour and Titian Ramsay Peale, whom the federal government hired to accompany explorer Stephen H. Long to the Rocky Mountains in 1820. They pioneered an influential genre: facsimiles in government reports. Between 1840 and 1860, Congress published nearly sixty works on western exploration, featuring hundreds of lithographs and engravings of the region's plants, animals, and people. Some of these reports became bestsellers.

Although government reports often faithfully reproduced original paintings, they sometimes made telling alterations. When Richard Kern accompanied explorer James H. Simpson in 1849 to the Southwest, for example, he painted a Navajo man

In one of his most famous portraits, George Catlin painted Wi-Jun-Jon, an Assiniboine Indian, both before and after he had mingled with white men. In the before stance, the Indian is a dignified, peace-pipe-bearing warrior; in the after portrait, the corrupted Indian has abandoned dignity for vanity and his peace pipe for a cigar.   (Smithsonian American Art Museum, Washington, D.C./Art Resource, NY)

in a submissive pose. The reproduction transformed the man's pose into a rebellious one. In other cases, the government reports changed artists' depictions of Indian-occupied landscapes into empty terrain free for the taking.

Artists portrayed their subjects through the lens of their own cultural assumptions, and commercial artists produced what they thought the public craved. When George Catlin traveled west in the immediate aftermath of the 1830 Indian Removal Act, Catlin painted with a moral in mind. Indians came in two varieties—those who preserved their original, almost noble qualities of freedom and moderation and those who, after coming in contact with whites, had become dissolute. Indians, he implied, would benefit from removal from white Americans' corrupting influence.

Countering the Myths   Western reality often clashed with promoters' promises, and disappointed settlers sometimes tried to clarify matters for future migrants. Rebecca Burlend and her family, for example, were lured to Illinois by a fellow Englishman's letters extolling "a land flowing with milk and honey." Later Burlend wrote with her son *A True Picture of Emigration* (1831), which described Illinois's hardships—intemperate weather, difficult working conditions, and swindlers. The Burlends did not discourage emigration, but substituted a realistic for a rosy description.

EXPANSION AND RESISTANCE IN THE OLD NORTHWEST

In the 1820s and 1830s, settlers streamed into the Old Northwest and the Old Southwest by foot, horseback, wagon, canal boat, steamboat, or a combination of means. Many people, like Pettis Perkinson and his slaves, moved several times, and when opportunities failed to materialize, some returned home.

In the first federal census of 1790, the Northwest Territory's white population numbered a few hundred people. By 1860 nearly 7 million people called it home. Between 1810 and 1830, the population of Ohio more than quadrupled, while Indiana and Illinois grew fourteenfold and thirteenfold, respectively. Michigan's population multiplied fiftyfold between 1820 and 1850. Migration accounted for most of this growth. Once in the Old Northwest, people did not stay put. Geographic mobility, the search for better opportunities, and connections to the market economy came to define the region that became the Midwest.

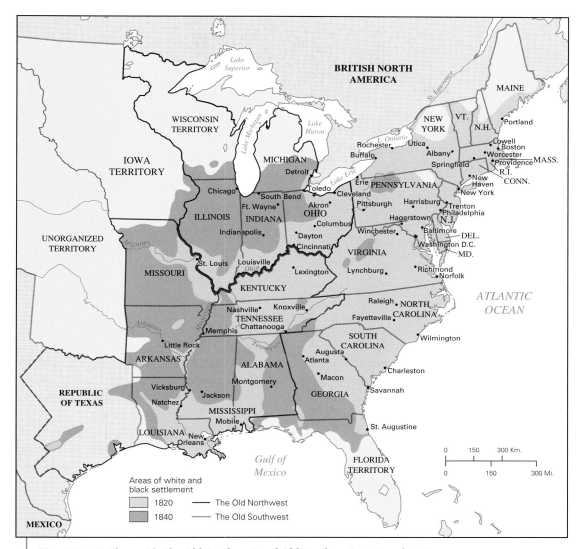

Map 13.2   Settlement in the Old Southwest and Old Northwest, 1820 and 1840

Removal of Indians and a growing transportation network opened up land to white and black settlers in the regions known as the Old Southwest and the Old Northwest, as the U.S. population grew from 9.6 million in 1820 to 17.1 million in 1840.

Deciding Where to Move   Moving west meant leaving behind worn-out soil and areas where little land was available for purchase, but it also meant leaving behind family, friends, and communities. The trip promised to be arduous, as did the backbreaking labor of clearing land for cultivation. But what if the soil proved less fertile than anticipated? What if neighbors proved unfriendly, or worse? What if homesickness became unbearable?

Settlers tried to control as many variables as possible. Like Pettis Perkinson, people often relocated to where they had relatives or friends and traveled with people they knew. They sought areas with familiar climates. The legal status of slavery also

In 1834 Karl Bodmer painted a farm on the Illinois Prairie, depicting the more permanent, if still modest, structures that farmers built after the initial urgency to clear fields for cultivation had subsided.   (© Collection of The New-York Historical Society)

influenced where people settled. Some white southerners, tired of the social and political power of the planter elite, sought areas free from slavery—or at least where plantations did not dominate. Many others went west to increase their chances of owning slaves or of owning more slaves. White northerners mostly hoped to distance themselves from slavery, not out of sympathy for slaves but because they, too, detested the economic and political power of elite slaveowners. Many northerners hoped to settle in areas free of *any* black people. In the 1850s, many midwestern states passed "black laws" prohibiting African Americans, free or enslaved, from living within their boundaries. Ironically, many free blacks migrated west believing that the region would be less prejudiced than the East.

Between 1815 and 1860, few western migrants settled on the Great Plains, a region reserved for Indians until the 1850s, and few easterners risked the journey to California and Oregon before the completion of the transcontinental railroad in 1869. At first the Southwest appealed most to settlers, but after 1820, the Midwest— with its better-developed transportation routes, democratic access to economic markets, smaller African American population, cheaper average landholding, and climatic similarity to New England and northern Europe—drew more settlers. The Midwest's thriving transportation hubs also made good first stops for western migrants lacking cash to purchase land. They found work unloading canal boats, planting and harvesting wheat, grinding wheat into flour, sawing trees into lumber, or, more often, a combination of these seasonal jobs. With the Old Northwest's population growing fast, white southerners became increasingly worried about congressional representation and slavery laws.

Indian Removal and Resistance

In the Midwest and the Southwest, white settlement depended on the removal of Indians. Even as the U.S. Army escorted Indians out of the Old Southwest, the federal government arranged eighty-six treaties between 1829 and 1851 in which northeastern

Indian nations relinquished land titles in exchange for lands west of the Mississippi River.

Some northern Indians evaded removal, including the Miamis in Indiana, the Ottawas and Chippewas in the upper Midwest, and the Winnebagos in southern Wisconsin. In 1840, chiefs of the Miamis acceded to pressure to exchange 500,000 acres of land in Indiana for 500,000 acres in Indian Country. Under the treaty, their people had five years to move or be escorted west by federal troops. But about half of the Miami nation dodged the soldiers, and many of those who made the trek later returned. In Wisconsin, some Winnebagos eluded removal or returned to Wisconsin after being escorted west of the Mississippi.

Black Hawk War

In a series of treaties between 1804 and 1830, Sauks (or "Sacs") and Fox leaders exchanged tribal lands in northwestern Illinois and southwestern Wisconsin for lands across the Mississippi River in Iowa Territory. The Sauk warrior Black Hawk disputed the validity of the treaties, and in 1832 he led Sauk and Fox families to Illinois, panicking white settlers. The state's governor called up the militia, who were joined by militia units from surrounding states and territories and U.S. Army regular soldiers. Over the next several months, hundreds of Indians and dozens of whites died under often-gruesome circumstances in the Black Hawk War. As the Sauks and Fox tried to flee across the Mississippi, they were fired on by American soldiers. Those who survived the river crossing were met with gunfire by Lakota (Sioux) warriors allied with the Americans.

Black Hawk surrendered, and U.S. officials undertook to impress on him and other leaders the futility of resistance. After being imprisoned, then sent to Washington, D.C., along a route meant to underscore the immense size and population of the United States, and imprisoned again, the Indians were returned to their homes. The Black Hawk War marked the end of militant Indian uprisings in the Old Northwest.

Selling the West

Land speculators, developers of "paper towns" (towns that existed on paper only), steamboat companies, and manufacturers of farming implements promoted the Midwest as tranquil place of unbounded opportunity. Land proprietors emphasized the region's connections to eastern ways of life and markets. They knew that, when families relocated in the West, they did not seek to escape civilization. Settlement in the West generally followed connections to national and international markets. Eastern farmers, hoping to escape tired soil or tenancy, sought fertile lands on which to grow commercial crops. Labor-saving devices, such as Cyrus McCormick's reaper (1834) and John Deere's steel plow (1837), made the West more alluring. McCormick, a Virginia inventor, patented a horse-drawn reaper that allowed two men to harvest the same number of acres of wheat that previously required between four and sixteen men. The reaper's efficiency achieved its greatest payoffs on the large, flat prairie lands, so McCormick relocated his factory to Chicago in 1847. Without John Deere's steel plow, which could break through tough grass and roots without constant cleaning, "breaking the plains" might not have been possible.

MᶜCORMICKS MACHINES.

In his advertisements, Cyrus McCormick portrayed his reapers as turning the West into a place of prosperity and leisure.   (The Center for American History, The University of Texas at Austin)

Clearing the Land

After locating a suitable land claim, settlers constructed a rudimentary cabin if one did not exist. Time did not permit more elaborate structures, because first they had to clear the land. At the rate of five to ten acres a year, the average family needed ten years to fully clear a farm. Prairie land took less time, though throughout the 1850s, many farmers considered lands free of timber to be deserts, unfit for cultivation.

Whereas farming attracted families, lumbering and mining appealed mostly to single young men. By the 1840s, as forests became depleted in the eastern United States and Canada, northeastern lumber companies and laborers migrated to Wisconsin, Michigan, and Minnesota. Recently arrived Scandinavians and French Canadians also worked in the lumber industry. As Great Lakes' forests thinned, lumbermen moved on again—some to the Gulf states' pine forests, some to Canada, and some to the Far West, where Mexicans in California and British in Canada had already established flourishing lumber industries. With the rapid growth of California's cities following the 1849 Gold Rush, timber demand soared, drawing midwestern lumbermen farther west.

Midwestern cities nurtured the settlement of the surrounding countryside. Steamboats turned river settlements like Louisville and Cincinnati into commercial centers, while Chicago, Detroit, and Cleveland grew up on the banks of the Great Lakes. By the mid-nineteenth century, Chicago, with its railroads, stockyards, and grain elevators, was positioned to dominate the region's economy; western farmers transported livestock and grain by rail to that city, where pigs became packed meat and grain became flour before being shipped east. The promise of future flour and future pigs gave rise to commodities markets. Some of the world's most sophisticated and speculative economic practices started in Chicago.

THE FEDERAL GOVERNMENT AND WESTWARD EXPANSION

Few white Americans considered settling in the West before the region had been explored, surveyed, and civilized, which meant Indian removal and the establishment of churches, businesses, and American legal structures. Wide-scale settlement became possible only with the sponsorship of the federal government.

Artist Alfred Jacob Miller portrayed a marriage *à la façon du pays* ("in the custom of the country") in which an Indian woman is given in marriage by her father to a *métis* man at a Rocky Mountain *rendezvous* in 1837. (Library of Congress)

The Fur Trade

Fur trappers were among the first white Americans in the trans-Appalachian West, but their lives bore faint resemblance to their mythical representation as mountain men who lived off the land, trapped beaver, cast off civilization, and dared to go where whites never trod. Although many had little contact with American society, fur trappers lived among Indians, became multilingual, and often married Indian women, who became their business partners, finishing pelts and helping smooth trade relations between their husbands and their native communities. The children of such marriages—*métis* or *mestizos* (people of mixed Indian and European heritage)—added to the cultural complexity of the West.

The fur trade was an international business, with many pelts from the American interior reaching Europe and Asia. Beginning in the 1820s, trappers and traders came together annually for a *rendezvous*—a multiday gathering at which they traded fur for guns, tobacco, and beads that they could later exchange with Indians while also sharing stories and alcohol and gambling. Modeled on similar Indian gatherings that had occurred for generations, the rendezvous brought together Americans, Indians, Mexicans, and people of mixed heritage from all over the West—from as far north as Canada and as far south as Mexico. Rendezvous took place in remote mountain locations, but they were cosmopolitan affairs.

By the 1840s, the American fur trade was in decline. Beavers had been overhunted, and fashions shifted toward silk rather than fur for hat making. One legacy of the fur trade was the devastating effect on native peoples of diseases introduced by mountain men. Another was the development of trails that crossed the trans-Mississippi West.

Transcontinental Exploration

A desire for quicker and safer routes for transporting furs and other goods to trading posts drove much early exploration. In 1821, the merchant William Becknell helped chart the Santa Fe Trail running between Missouri and Santa Fe, New Mexico, where it connected to the Chihuahua Trail running into Mexico, allowing American and

Map 13.3 Western Indians and Routes of Exploration

Although western explorers believed they were discovering new routes and places, Indians had long lived in most of the areas through which explorers traveled.

Mexican merchants to develop a vibrant trade. In 1824, the fur trader Jedediah Smith rediscovered the South Pass, a 20-mile break in the Rocky Mountains in present-day Wyoming previously known only to Native Americans and some Pacific Fur Company trappers. The South Pass became the route followed by most people headed overland to California and Oregon.

Gold in California

When James Marshall discovered gold in Sutter's Mill, California, in January 1848, word spread quickly worldwide. Within a year, tens of thousands of adventurers from other countries rushed to California, making it one of the most cosmopolitan places in North America.

In an era before the telegraph crossed the oceans, it is surprising how fast the news traveled. Mexicans heard of the gold strike first. Next, word spread to Chile, Peru, and throughout South America; then across the Pacific to Hawai'i, China, and Australia; and on to Europe—Ireland, France, and the German states. Overland travelers brought the news south to Baja California and Sonora in Mexico. By spring 1849 some six thousand Mexicans were panning for gold; many came seasonally, spreading news of California every trip home.

Sailing ships brought news of California gold to Hawai'i. The newspaper *Honolulu Polynesian* announced it in the kingdom on June 24, 1848. Gold seekers and merchants sailed to California, and regular steamship service between Hawai'i and California began in 1853.

A ship brought news of California gold discoveries to Valparaiso, Chile, in August 1848. People in Chile's cities talked feverishly about gold, and newspapers kept pace. Before year's end, two thousand Chileans left for California.

Word of gold reached Australia in December 1848, and by 1850 every ship in Sydney Harbour was destined for California. News reached China in mid-1848. After the upheavals of the Taiping Revolution in 1850, Chinese migration soared. By the mid-1850s, one in five gold miners was Chinese.

In 1850 the new state of California had nearly 40 percent foreign-born inhabitants, the majority non-European. Through word of mouth, rumor, letters home, and newspaper reports, the 1848 gold discovery linked California to millions of people around the globe.

This 1855 Frank Marryat drawing of a San Francisco saloon dramatizes the international nature of the California gold rush. Like theater performers, the patrons of the saloon dress their parts as Yankees, Mexicans, Asians, and South Americans.

(© Collection of the New York Historical Society)

Lewis and Clark's Corps of Discovery was only the first of many federally sponsored expeditions to chart the trans-Mississippi West. Some expeditions sought to establish cordial relations with Indian groups with whom Americans might trade or enter military alliances; others were scientific, exploring native inhabitants, flora, and fauna. But they were always also commercial. Like Lewis and Clark, later explorers hoped to locate land, water, and rail routes that would allow American businessmen and farmers to engage in national and international trade.

In 1805 the U.S. Army dispatched Zebulon Pike to find the source of the Mississippi and a navigable route west. Along the way, he was to research natural resources and native peoples and foster diplomatic relationships with Indian leaders. Before the Supreme Court ruled in *Johnson v. M'Intosh* (1823) that Indians did not own land but merely had a "right of occupancy," government officials instructed Pike and other explorers to purchase lands for military garrisons.

Although Pike failed to identify the Mississippi's source and had only limited success in cultivating relationships and purchasing land, he gathered important information about the terrain. When Pike and his men wandered into Spanish territory to the south, military officials held him captive for months in Mexico, inadvertently showing him areas he might not have explored himself. After his release, Pike wrote about a potential market in southwestern cities. The province of Tejas (Texas), with its fertile soil and rich grasslands, enchanted him. But Pike dismissed the other northern provinces of Mexico, whose boundaries stretched to present-day Nevada and Utah, as unsuitable for cultivation by civilized people. In 1820 the army explorer Stephen Long similarly branded modern-day Oklahoma, Kansas, and Nebraska as the Great American Desert, incapable of cultivation. Until the 1850s, when a transcontinental railroad was planned, this desert was reserved for Indian settlement.

In 1838 Congress established the U.S. Army Corps of Topographical Engineers to systematically explore the West. As a second lieutenant in that corps, John C. Frémont undertook three expeditions to the region between the upper Mississippi and Missouri rivers, the Rockies, the Great Basin, Oregon, and California. He helped

Charles Koppel portrayed the Colorado Desert and Signal Mountain for the *Pacific Railway Reports* (1853). The desert appears vast and unlimited, and those who travel through it are advancing into the unknown.   (The Center for American History, The University of Texas at Austin)

survey the Oregon Trail. Aided by his wife, Jessie Benton Frémont, Frémont published bestselling accounts of his explorations. The Corps of Topographical Engineers' most significant contributions came in the 1850s with its surveying of possible routes for a transcontinental railroad.

A Military Presence

The army also helped ready the West for settlement. With the General Survey Act of 1824, Congress empowered the military to chart transportation improvements vital to the nation's military protection or commercial growth. Army engineers helped design state- and privately sponsored roads, canals, and railroads, and soldiers cleared forests and laid roadbeds. A related bill in 1824 authorized the army to improve the Ohio and Mississippi Rivers, and a later amendment did the same for the Missouri.

By the 1850s, 90 percent of the U.S. military was stationed west of the Mississippi River. When Indians refused to relinquish their lands, the army escorted them westward; when they harmed whites or their property, the army waged war. The army sometimes destroyed the crops and buildings of white squatters who refused to vacate lands they did not own. But, primarily, the army presence assisted overland migration. Army forts intimidated Indians, defended settlers from Indian attacks, and supplied information and provisions. In theory, the army was also supposed to protect Indians by driving settlers off Indian lands and enforcing laws prohibiting alcohol sales to Indians. Yet the army's small size made it impossible to enforce such policies even when officers were disposed to do so.

The Office of Indian Affairs handled the government's other interactions with Indians, including negotiating treaties, managing schools, and overseeing trade. Created in 1824 as part of the War Department, the Indian Office cooperated with the military in removing Indians from lands needed for American expansion and in protecting citizens who relocated. In 1849 the Indian Office became part of the newly established Department of the Interior, and it soon shifted from removal to civilization, through a reservation system. Whereas some Indians accepted reservations as protection from white incursion, others rejected them, sometimes setting off deadly intratribal disagreements.

Public Lands

The federal government controlled vast tracts of land, procured either from the states' cessions of their western claims after the Revolution or through treaties with foreign powers, including Indian nations. The General Land Office, established in 1812 as part of the Treasury Department, handled the distribution of those lands. Its earliest policies divided western lands into 640-acre tracts to be auctioned at a minimum $2 an acre. These policies favored speculators—who bought up millions of acres—over individual, cash-poor farmers. Many settlers became squatters, prompting Congress in 1820 to lower land prices to $1.25 per acre and sell tracts as small as 80 acres. Twelve years later, it sold 40-acre tracts. Yet it also demanded that the land be bought outright; few would-be western settlers (particularly in the aftermath of the Panic of 1819) had enough cash to purchase government land. Because speculators sold land on credit, many small-time farmers bought from them at inflated prices.

Farmers pressed for a federal policy of preemption—the right to settle on land without obtaining title, improve it, and buy it later at the legal minimum price ($1.25). Some states offered land through preemption, and Congress occasionally authorized preemption of federal land in the 1820s and 1830s. But there was no general preemption law until the so-called Log Cabin Bill in 1841, and that applied to surveyed land only. Preemption extended to unsurveyed lands with the Homestead Act of 1862, which deemed that land would be provided free to any U.S. citizen (or foreigner who declared the intention of becoming a citizen) after residing on it for five years and improving it. Alternatively, settlers could buy land outright at $1.25 an acre after six months of living on it, which allowed them to use the land as collateral for loans for additional land, farming supplies, or machinery.

THE SOUTHWESTERN BORDERLANDS

Along the southwestern border of the Louisiana Territory were vast provinces under the domain of first Spain and then, after 1821, the newly independent nation of Mexico. New Mexico, with commercial centers in Albuquerque and Santa Fe, remained under

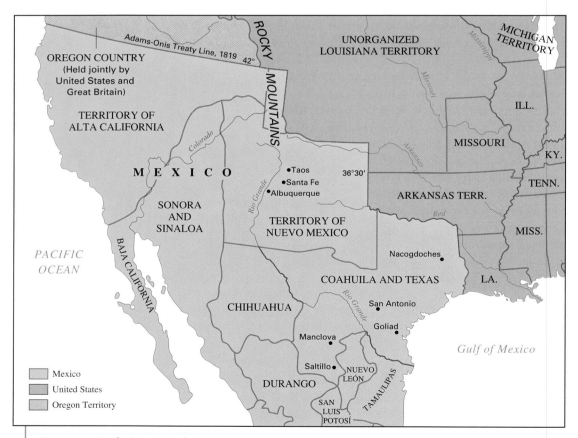

Map 13.4   Mexico's Far North

What is now considered the American Southwest was made up of the northern provinces of Mexico until the United States conquered the territory during the Mexican War (1846–1848).

Mexican control until the United States conquered the territory during its War with Mexico. Texas became an autonomous state in 1824, giving it greater independence from federal authorities in Mexico City than New Mexico enjoyed. This situation helped foster Texas's struggle for national independence and then annexation to the United States; this returned the divisive issue of slavery to the center of American politics.

Southwestern Slavery

Slavery existed in the Southwest for centuries. As practiced by Spaniards and indigenous peoples—the Apaches, Comanches, Kiowas, Navajos, Utes, and Pueblos—slavery centered on capturing women and children, who were then assimilated into their captors' communities, where they provided labor and status while aiding economic and diplomatic exchanges with their former communities.

This system was built on racial mixing, which was anathema to most white Americans. As white slaveholders from the Southeast pushed into Mexican territory during the 1820s and 1830s, they often justified their conquest in racial terms. The region's Hispanic settlers, they reasoned, had been rendered lazy and barbarous by racial intermixing and were thus destined to be supplanted.

The New Mexican Frontier

When Mexico gained independence from Spain in 1821, New Mexico's Hispanic population outnumbered indigenous Pueblo peoples by three to one. There were 28,000 Hispanics, including people born in Spain and *criollos*, people born in New Spain to parents of Spanish descent. Most New Mexicans engaged in irrigated agriculture. To the north of Santa Fe, they worked small plots of land, but to the south, larger farms and ranches predominated. Rancheros became wealthy by selling wool and corn in distant markets and by using unpaid laborers, often relatives, bound by debt. Threatened by the province's raiding Indian tribes—the Apaches, Utes, Navajos, and sometimes the Comanches—Hispanics, Pueblos, and *mestizos* sometimes united in defense. But their numerical superiority allowed Hispanics to take over many Pueblo villages and lands in the rich northern river valleys.

The Santa Fe Trail caused a commercial explosion in New Mexico, doubling the value of imports in two years. Whereas the Spanish tried to keep foreigners out, the Mexican government offered enormous land grants to Anglo-American and French entrepreneurs, hoping they would develop the region's industry and agriculture, and strengthen commercial ties with the United States.

While commercial relationships grew, few Americans settled in New Mexico during the 1820s and 1830s. The best lands were occupied by Indians and Hispanics. And Americans seeking cheap, fertile land could find it in Texas.

The Texas Frontier

In 1821, indigenous Indians remained the dominant group in Texas, although there were also immigrant Indians, Hispanics, Anglos, and *mestizos*. Of the thirty thousand indigenous people, most were Comanches. To identify distinctive Indian groups, though, belies the intermarriage and cultural exchange among them. Indians married Indians from other nations, as well as Europeans and African Americans.

As Indian groups competed for the region's resources, intermittent warfare resulted. Comanches hunted bison or stole horses, livestock, and crops from their enemies, the Pawnees, Arapahos, and Cheyennes. Smaller groups such as the Wichitas and Caddos grew corn, beans, squash, and pumpkin. When crops failed, these Indian farmers turned to bison hunting, sometimes triggering conflict with the Comanches.

Tensions increased around the time of Mexican independence, when the first of another ten thousand Indians migrated into the region. From the Old Northwest came Shawnees and Kickapoos—former members of Tecumseh's confederacy. From the Old Southwest came Cherokees, Creeks, Choctaws, Chickasaws, and Seminoles. As Indian newcomers competed for land and animals, they came into conflict with established Indian groups, such as the Comanches. Many immigrant Indians had adopted European clothing and European ideas about land and race. They saw land as a commodity, and some owned African American slaves. They often dismissed as savage the indigenous Indians who hunted bison and wore their skins. But such contempt did not guarantee an affinity for Anglo-Americans; many immigrant Indians resented those who had evicted them from their homelands.

Tejanos

Hispanic peoples had been in Texas since the 1500s, establishing missions and presidios, but by 1820 they numbered only five thousand. Most raised livestock on ranches, while others traded with Indians. Because they were so distant from the Spanish colonial capital in Mexico City, they formed a distinctive identity, seeing themselves as *Tejanos* (or Texans). Many intermarried with Indians.

In the years after the War of 1812, Anglo-Americans began entering Texas. They traded manufactured goods—guns, ammunition, and kettles—for animal hides,

This depiction of San Antonio residents going to a ball, circa 1848, represents the vibrant cultural life in early Texas society.   (Daughters of the Republic of Texas Library)

horses, and mules. Although some Anglos settled in Texas, more came and went along the Santa Fe and Chihuahua Trails. These Anglo newcomers largely supplanted the Tejanos as the Indians' trading partners, and the economic fortunes of the region's tribes became increasingly oriented toward the United States.

American *Empresarios*

In the 1820s, Americans began settling in Texas under an *empresario* system. The first arrangement was made by Moses Austin, a Missouri miner and trader, who approached Spanish authorities in Mexico City in January 1821 with a settlement plan. The Spanish considered Texas a buffer between hostile Indians and the United States and wanted it populated. They gave Austin a land grant of approximately 200,000 acres along the Brazos River in exchange for his promise to bring three hundred Catholic families and no slaves. Before Austin could act, he died. Mexico won its independence from Spain in September 1821.

Austin's son, Stephen, took up his father's scheme and pressed the new Mexican government to honor the grant, which it did in 1823, provided that Austin give up his American citizenship and become a Mexican national. By 1825 Stephen Austin brought two thousand white people and four hundred contract laborers of African descent. With ninety-nine-year contracts, these African Americans were slaves by another name. Still, Austin's success encouraged the Mexican government to contract with Austin to bring nine hundred families.

Satisfied with the Austin experiment, in 1824 Mexico passed a Colonization Law providing land and tax incentives to future foreign settlers. Details were left up to individual Mexican states. Coahuila y Texas specified that the head of a family could obtain 4,428 acres of grazing or 177 acres of farming land. The land was cheap, and could be paid in installments over six years, with nothing due until the fourth year. To be eligible, foreigners had to be upstanding Christians and had to establish permanent residency. The Coahuila y Texas government provided additional land to settlers who married Mexican women.

Most U.S. citizens who settled in Mexico did so under an *empresario,* or immigration agent, who selected moral colonists, distributed lands, and enforced regulations. In exchange, he received nearly twenty-five thousand acres of grazing land and one thousand acres of farming land for every hundred families he settled. Between 1825 and 1832, approximately twenty-four *empresario* contracts (seventeen of which went to Anglo-Americans) were signed covering eight thousand families total. The land grants enveloped almost all of present-day Texas.

Some Anglo-Americans who emigrated to Texas in the 1820s were pushed from the United States by the Panic of 1819 and pulled to Texas by cheap land and, especially, generous credit terms. Despite Mexican efforts to encourage assimilation with Mexicans of Spanish origin in Texas, Americans tended to settle in separate communities. Anglo-Americans outnumbered the Tejanos two to one. Authorities worried that transplanted Americans would try to make Texas part of the United States.

Texas Politics

In 1826 an *empresario* named Haden Edwards called for an independent Texas, which he named the Fredonia Republic. Other *empresarios,* seeing advantages in peaceful relations with the Mexican government, resisted Edwards's movement. Although the Fredonia revolt failed, Mexican authorities dreaded what it might foreshadow.

Consequently, in 1830, Mexican authorities terminated legal immigration from the United States while encouraging immigration from Europe and other parts of Mexico. They also prohibited American slaves from entering Texas, a provision that brought Texas in line with the rest of Mexico, where slavery had been outlawed the previous year. These laws did not keep Americans and their slaves from coming; soon they controlled most of the Texas coastline and Texas's U.S. border. Mexican authorities repealed the anti-immigration law in 1833, reasoning that it discouraged upstanding settlers without deterring undesirables. By 1835 the population of Texas was nearly thirty thousand, with Americans outnumbering Tejanos seven to one.

Among white Texans, some, like Stephen Austin, favored staying in Mexico and demanding more autonomy, the legalization of slavery, and free trade with the United States. Others pushed for Texas to secede from Mexico and request annexation by the United States. In 1835 the secessionists overtook a Mexican military installation charged with collecting taxes at Galveston Bay. Austin advocated a peaceful resolution, but, suspicious, Mexican authorities jailed him for eighteen months, which converted him to the independence cause.

The Lone Star Republic With discontent over Texas increasing throughout Mexico, the Mexican president General Santa Anna declared himself dictator and marched his army toward Texas. Fearing that Santa Anna would free their slaves, Texans rebelled. After initial defeats at the Alamo mission in San Antonio and at Goliad in March 1836, the Texans won the conflict by year's end. They declared themselves the Lone Star Republic and elected Sam Houston as president. The Texas constitution legalized slavery and banned free blacks.

Texas then faced the challenge of nation building, which to its leaders involved Indian removal. When Indians refused to leave, Mirabeau Lamar, the nation's second

Like George Allen, many Texas settlers relied on slave labor to work their fields and maintain their households. (Texas Memorial Museum, University of Texas at Austin)

president, mobilized the Texas Rangers—mounted nonuniformed militia—to drive them out through terror. The Rangers raided Indian villages, where they robbed, raped, and murdered. This "ethnic cleansing," as one historian labeled it, ultimately cleared native settlers out to make room for white Americans and their African American slaves.

MIGRATION TO THE FAR WEST

In the following decade, more Americans moved to the Far West, even though California and Utah were part of Mexico. Some sought religious freedom or Christian converts, but most sought fertile farmland.

Western Missionaries Catholic missionaries—Americans, Europeans, and converted Indians—maintained a strong presence in the Far West even after a Mexican law secularized the California missions in 1833, using them to organize Indian labor. The missionaries ministered to Catholic immigrants, worked—with some success—to convert Indians and encouraged specifically Roman Catholic colonies.

In the Pacific Northwest, Catholics vied directly with Protestant missionaries for Indian souls. Under the auspices of the American Board of Commissioners for Foreign Missions, two missionary couples—credited as being the first white migrants along the Oregon Trail—traveled to the Pacific Northwest in 1836. Narcissa and Marcus Whitman built a meetinghouse for Cayuse Indians in Waiilatpu, near present-day Walla Walla, Washington, while Eliza and Henry Spalding worked to convert the Nez Percé at Lapwai, in what is now Idaho. With their air of cultural superiority, the Whitmans were unable to convert the Cayuses and focused instead on the white migrants flowing into Oregon in the 1840s.

Tensions escalated when a devastating measles epidemic struck in 1847, and the Cayuses saw it as a calculated assault on their people. They retaliated by murdering the Whitmans and twelve other missionaries. The Spaldings abandoned their successful mission, blamed Catholics for inciting the massacre, and became farmers in Oregon, not returning to Lapwai for another fifteen years.

Mormons Persecuted in Missouri and Illinois, the Mormons followed Brigham Young to their Promised Land in the Great Salt Lake valley. The region was still under Mexican control but about to become part of the U.S. territory of Utah. As non-Mormons began to settle in Utah, Young diluted their influence by attracting new Mormon settlers to what he called the state of Deseret.

Mormons prospered by providing services and supplies to California-bound settlers and miners. Young discouraged *gentiles* (his term for non-Mormons) from settling in Deseret and advocated boycotts of gentile businesses. When in 1852 the Mormons openly sanctioned polygamy, animosity toward them increased nationwide. In June 1857, President James Buchanan dispatched twenty-five hundred federal troops to suppress an alleged Mormon rebellion.

Anxious over their own safety and eager to maintain peace with neighboring Indians, some Mormons joined Paiutes in attacking a passing wagon train of non-Mormon migrants from Arkansas and Missouri. Approximately 120 men, women, and children died in the so-called Mountain Meadows Massacre in August 1857. In the next two years, the U.S. Army and the Mormons engaged in armed conflict, though there were no fatalities.

Oregon and California Trails

In the twenty years after 1840, between 250,000 and 500,000 men, women, and children walked across much of the continent, usually taking seven months. Although they traveled armed, most of their encounters with Indians were peaceful, if tense.

Overlanders began their journeys at one of the so-called jumping-off points—towns such as Independence, St. Joseph, and Westport Landing—along the Missouri River, where they bought supplies for the 2,000-mile trip. While miners frequently traveled alone or with other fortune-seeking young men, farmers traveled with their families, often in wagon trains of relatives, neighbors, church members, and other acquaintances.

They tried to time their departures to be late enough to find forage grass for their oxen and livestock, but not so late that they would encounter the treacherous snows of the Rockies and Sierra Nevada. They trudged alongside their wagons on average 15 miles a day, in weather from freezing cold to blistering heat. Men generally tended livestock, while women set up camp, prepared meals, and tended children.

Indians were usually peaceful, and during the trails' early days, they provided food and information or ferried migrants across rivers. In exchange, migrants offered blankets, knives, metal pots, tobacco, ornamental beads, and other items. When exchanges went bad—due to misunderstanding or attempts to swindle one or the other—tensions mounted.

This rare stereocard shows an emigrant train, including two women and possibly a child, dwarfed by the natural landscape in Strawberry Valley, California, in the 1860s. (Library of Congress)

Livestock theft persistently aggravated migrants, who blamed Indians even though white thieves stole livestock, too. Indians who took livestock often did so when whites failed to offer gifts in exchange for grazing rights. The so-called Mormon Cow Incident (or the Grattan Massacre) forever altered relationships along the Oregon Trail.

In August 1854, a Lakota in present-day Wyoming slaughtered a cow that strayed from a nearby Mormon camp. When Lakota leaders offered compensation for the cow, U.S. Army Lieutenant John Grattan, seeking to set an example, refused. Grattan ordered his men to shoot, and when a Lakota chief fell dead, Indians returned fire, killing Grattan and his twenty-nine men. The following year General William Harney led six hundred soldiers to a village near Ash Hollow, where migrants and Indians traded for many years. When Indian leaders refused to surrender anyone to Harney, he ordered his men to fire. Thirty minutes later, eighty-seven Indians lay dead, and seventy women and children were taken prisoner. The event disrupted peace along the trail and ignited nearly two decades of warfare between the Lakotas and the U.S. Army.

Indian Treaties

Still, the Indian Office negotiated treaties to keep Indians—and their intertribal conflicts—from interfering with western migration and commerce. The Fort Laramie Treaty of 1851 (or the Horse Creek Council Treaty) was signed by the United States and eight northern Plains tribes—the Lakotas, Cheyennes, Arapahos, Crows, Assinaboines, Gros-Ventres, Mandans, and Arrickaras—who occupied the Platte River valley through which the three great overland routes westward—the Oregon, California, and Mormon Trails—all passed. Two years later, in 1853, the United States signed a treaty with three southwestern nations, the Comanches, Kiowas, and Apaches, who lived

Established in 1834, Fort Laramie—pictured here three years later by Alfred Jacob Miller—served as a fur-trading site, where Indians and trappers of European or mixed heritage came together not only to exchange goods but also to socialize. In 1849, as interactions between Indians and overland migrants to Oregon grew increasingly tense, the U.S. Army took over the fort, now designed to protect overland emigrants. Located in eastern Wyoming, the fort stood at the beginning of the Oregon Trail. (The Walters Art Museum, Baltimore)

near the Santa Fe Trail. Under both treaties, Indians agreed to maintain intertribal peace, recognize government-delineated tribal boundaries, allow the United States to construct roads and forts within those boundaries, refrain from depredations against western migrants, and issue restitution for any depredations committed. In return, they would receive annual allotments from the U.S. government for ten years, paid with provisions, domestic animals, and agricultural implements.

Contrary to U.S. expectations, Indian chiefs did not believe treaties were perpetually binding. Government officials, meanwhile, promised allotments but did little to ensure their timely arrival, often leaving Indians starving. Treaties did not end intertribal warfare, nor did they fully secure overlanders' safety. Instead, they represented the U.S. government's effort to promote expansion and protect its westward-bound citizens.

Ecological Consequences of Cultural Contact

Armed conflict took relatively few lives compared to cholera, smallpox, and other maladies. The trails' jumping-off points bred disease, which migrants carried with them, inadvertently infecting Indians with whom they traded. Fearful of infection, Indians and migrants increasingly shied away from trading relationships.

The bison provided protein to Plains Indians and held spiritual significance. Many Native Americans blamed the migrants for the bison's disappearance, even though most overlanders never laid eyes on a buffalo. By the time the overland migration reached its peak in the late 1840s and 1850s, the herds had already been overhunted, partly by Native Americans. The surviving bison scattered to areas where the grass was safe from the appetites and trampling feet of overlanders' livestock. On rare occasions when wagon trains stumbled on bison herds, men rushed to live out frontier fantasies and shot the animals. Overlanders hunted other animals for sport, too, leaving behind rotting carcasses of antelopes, wolves, bears, and birds—animals that held spiritual significance for many Native Americans.

The vibrant trade in bison hides prompted both Indians and whites to overhunt the American bison, leading to near extinction for the animal by the latter part of the nineteenth century.   (Library of Congress)

Gold Rush

In January 1848, John Wilson Marshall discovered gold in a shallow tributary to the American River near present-day Sacramento, California. During the next year, tens of thousands of forty-niners rushed to California, where they practiced placer mining, panning and dredging for gold in the hope of instant riches.

Some did make fortunes. Peter Brown, a black man from St. Genevieve, Missouri, wrote his wife in 1851 that "California is the best country in the world to make money. It is also the best place for black folks on the globe." He had earned $300 in two months. Most forty-niners, however, never found enough gold to pay their expenses. With their dreams dashed, many forty-niners took wage-paying jobs with large mining companies that used dangerous machinery to cut deep into the earth's surface.

As a remote Mexican province, California had a chain of small settlements surrounded by military forts (presidios) and missions. It was inhabited mostly by Indians, with a small number of Mexican *rancheros,* who raised cattle and sheep on enormous landholdings worked by coerced Indians. With the arrival of the forty-niners came the great California agricultural boom. Wheat became the preferred crop; it required minimal investment, was easily planted, and offered a quick return. Unlike the family farms of the Midwest and Oregon, California's large-scale wheat farming relied largely on bonded Indian laborers.

Map 13.5   The California Gold Rush
Gold was discovered at Sutter's Mill in 1848, sparking the California gold rush that took place mostly along the western foothills of the Sierra Nevada mountains.

Mining Settlements

Mining areas experienced a commercial and industrial boom, as enterprising merchants rushed to supply, feed, and clothe new settlers. Among them was Levi Strauss, a German Jewish immigrant, whose tough mining pants found a ready market among the prospectors. Because men greatly outnumbered women, women's skills were in demand. Even as men set up all-male households and performed traditionally female tasks, women received high fees for cooking, laundering, and sewing. Women also ran boarding houses, hotels, and brothels.

Cities sprang up. In 1848 San Francisco had been a small mission settlement of about one thousand Mexicans, Anglos, soldiers, friars, and Indians. With the gold rush, it became a city, ballooning to thirty-five thousand people in 1850. It was the West Coast gateway to the interior, and ships bringing people and supplies jammed the harbor. Although California was admitted into the Union as a free state in 1850, its legislature soon passed "An Act for the Government and Protection of Indians" that essentially legalized the enslavement of Indians. The practice of using enslaved Indians in the California mines between 1849 and 1851 ended only when newly arrived miners brutally attacked Indian workers, believing they degraded white labor and gave an unfair advantage to established miners. Those slaves who survived the violence became field workers and house servants. Between 1821 and 1860, the Indian population of California fell from 200,000 to 30,000, as Indians died from disease, starvation, and violence. Because masters separated male and female workers, Indians failed to reproduce in large numbers.

THE POLITICS OF TERRITORIAL EXPANSION

With Americans moving west in numbers that would shift the locus of political power, Democratic and Whig politicians tried, unsuccessfully, to keep the slavery issue out of the politics of territorial expansion. Westward expansion was central to Democratic ideology, which saw the West's fertile and abundant lands as essential for creating a society in which white men could establish independent livelihoods and receive equal rights, freed from the undue influence of established slaveholders or urban elites. Whigs were more suspicious of rapid westward expansion, though they welcomed the commercial opportunities it might bring. Instead, they pushed harder for industrial and commercial development within the nation's current boundaries.

The Texas issue made it impossible for politicians to disentangle westward expansion and slavery. Soon after establishing the Lone Star Republic, Sam Houston approached American authorities to propose annexation as a state. But a new slave state would upset the balance of slave and free states in the Senate. Neither Whigs nor Democrats, wary of causing sectional divisions within their ranks, were inclined to confront the issue. In the 1830s, Democratic presidents Andrew Jackson and Martin Van Buren—one a strong slavery proponent, the other a mild opponent—sidestepped the issue. But by the mid-1840s—with cotton cultivation expanding—some Democratic politicians equated Texas annexation with the nation's manifest destiny.

Manifest Destiny

The belief that American expansion westward and southward was inevitable, just, and divinely ordained dated to the nation's founding but was first labeled manifest destiny in 1845 by John L. O'Sullivan, editor of the *United States Magazine and Democratic Review*. O'Sullivan claimed that Texas annexation would be "the fulfillment of our manifest destiny to overspread the continent allotted by Providence for the free development of our yearly multiplying millions." Manifest destiny implied that Americans had a God-given right, perhaps even an obligation, to expand their republican and Christian institutions to less fortunate and less civilized peoples. Implicit in the idea of manifest destiny was the belief that American Indians and Hispanics, much like people of African descent, were inferior peoples best controlled or conquered. Manifest destiny motivated few Americans to pack their wagons and head westward. It did, however, provide a political rationale for territorial expansion.

In June 1846, expansionists, including John C. Frémont, staged an armed rebellion and declared California an independent republic. Because the U.S. military soon conquered California in its War with Mexico, the Bear Flag Rebellion—so named for the symbol on the revolutionaries' flag—was short-lived but inflamed racial tensions in California.

Fifty-Four Forty or Fight

Britain and the United States had jointly occupied the disputed Oregon Territory since 1818. Beginning with John Quincy Adams's administration, the United States tried

This 1845 portrayal of Oregon City, the western terminus of the Oregon Trail, was provided by a British army officer sent to investigate the influence of large-scale American immigration into a territory jointly occupied by Great Britain and the United States. After the Oregon Treaty (1846) drew the boundary between British and American territory at the forty-ninth parallel, Oregon City became the capital of the Oregon Territory from 1848 to 1851.   (Library of Congress)

to fix the boundary at the 49th parallel, but Britain wanted access to Puget Sound and the Columbia River. In the early 1840s, expansionists demanded the entire Oregon Country for the United States, up to its northernmost border at latitude 54°40′. Soon "fifty-four forty or fight" became their rallying cry.

President Tyler wanted both Oregon and Texas, but Texas was his obsession. He argued that slavery's expansion would spread the nation's black population more thinly, allowing for the institution's gradual demise. But when word leaked out that Secretary of State John Calhoun had written to the British minister in Washington justifying Texas annexation as a way of protecting slavery, the Senate rejected annexation in 1844 by a vote of 35 to 16.

Polk and the Election of 1844

Worried southern Democrats persuaded their party's 1844 convention to require that the presidential nominee receive two-thirds of the convention votes, effectively giving the southern states a veto and allowing them to block the nomination of Martin Van Buren, an opponent of annexation. Instead, the party ran Young Hickory, House Speaker James K. Polk, an avid expansionist and slaveholding cotton planter from Tennessee. The Democratic platform, designed to appeal to voters across regional lines, called for occupation of the entire Oregon Territory and annexation of Texas. The Whigs, who nominated Henry Clay, argued that the Democrats' belligerent nationalism would lead to war with Great Britain, Mexico, or both. Clay favored expansion through negotiation, whereas many northern Whigs opposed annexation altogether, fearful that it would add slave states and strain relations with vital trading partners. Polk won the election by 170 electoral votes to 105, though with a margin of just 38,000 out of 2.7 million popular votes.

Annexation of Texas   Interpreting Polk's victory as a mandate for annexation, President Tyler proposed that Texas be admitted to the Union by joint resolution of Congress. The usual method of annexation, by treaty negotiation, required a two-thirds vote in the Senate, which differences over slavery prevented. A joint resolution required only a simple majority in each house. On March 1, 1845, the resolution passed the House by 120 to 98 and the Senate by 27 to 25. Three days before leaving office, Tyler signed the measure. Mexico, which had never recognized Texas independence, broke relations with the United States. In October Texas citizens ratified annexation, and Texas joined the Union, with a constitution permitting slavery, in December 1845. The nation was on the brink of war with Mexico. That conflict—like none other before it—would expose the inextricable relationships among westward expansion, slavery, and sectional discord.

Summary

Encouraged by literary and artistic images of the frontier as a place of natural abundance and opportunity, easterners by the millions poured into the Old Southwest and Old Northwest in the early decades of the nineteenth century. The federal government promoted westward expansion via support for transportation improvements, surveying, cheap land, and protection from Indians. Still, western migrants did not always find what they were seeking. Some returned home, some moved to new locations, and some stayed in the West, where they reluctantly abandoned their dreams of economic independence.

African American slaves were moved westward by their owners in enormous numbers between 1820 and 1860. Native Americans saw their lands and livelihoods constricted and their environments altered dramatically, threatening their economic and spiritual lives. Some Indians responded to white incursion through accommodation and peaceful overtures; others resisted. For Indians in Texas and California, white incursions brought devastation.

While beliefs about Native Americans' supposed inferiority allowed many white Americans to rationalize the Indians' fate, the white Americans' attitudes toward black people and slavery drove where they settled in the West. Those who believed that slavery degraded white labor headed along a northern trajectory, whereas those who dreamed of slave ownership headed southward, where they clashed with yet another group they deemed racially inferior: Mexicans. When American settlers in Texas achieved their independence from Mexico, legalized slavery, and applied for annexation by the United States, they brought the divisive issue of slavery's westward expansion to the surface of American politics. Although Democratic politicians at first tried to maintain a geographic equilibrium by proposing an ambitious territorial agenda in Oregon as well, it would be Texas's annexation that set the stage for military conflict, the addition of vast territories in the Southwest, and reinvigorated sectional conflict.

Descendants of Early Latino Settlers

Current census figures identify Latinos as the largest racial or ethnic minority in the United States. The news media focus on such topics as the growing number of documented and undocumented Latino immigrants, their increasing social impact, and their occasionally difficult relationships with African Americans. Yet all the attention surrounding recent arrivals overlooks the sizable number who are descended from people whose residency in North America predated the existence of the United States.

When the region stretching from eastern Texas to California was acquired by the United States in the 1840s, its population included not only indigenous Indian nations but also thousands of people with at least partial European ancestry, primarily Spanish or Portuguese. Their descendants have included such U.S. legislators as Senator Dennis Chávez (who served from 1936 to 1962) and Congressman Manuel Luján (1969–1988). Their families have resided in what is now U.S. territory for up to fourteen generations.

Persuasive evidence suggests that many of the early Iberian settlers in New Mexico were *conversos,* or of New Christian descent, that is, people whose Jewish ancestors converted to Catholicism in the fifteenth century to avoid religious persecution. After Jews were expelled from Spain and Portugal in 1492, many fled throughout the Spanish empire. Some participated in Juan de Oñate's 1598 expedition to New Mexico. There, many secretly maintained such Jewish customs as Sabbath observances and food restrictions. Today, some Latino residents of New Mexico have acknowledged their *converso* roots and reclaimed a Jewish identity.

All long-standing Latino citizens of the United States, not just those of *converso* descent, have given the nation an important multicultural legacy.

Chapter Review

THE WEST IN THE AMERICAN IMAGINATION

What were the myths that helped shape American perceptions of the West?

In dime store novels, artists' paintings, and materials recruiting settlers, the West was depicted as a place of abundant land where anyone could seek to better themselves. It was also seen as untamed, and frontiersmen like Daniel Boone were portrayed as having the courage and independent spirit needed to tame and open the West to other freedom lovers. The mythical Daniel Boone overpowered Indians and civilized the terrain for settlement. The West effectively symbolized core American values of freedom, independence, and the opportunity.

EXPANSION AND RESISTANCE IN THE OLD NORTHWEST

What made the Midwest appealing to white settlers?

Migrants who headed west in search of a better life often chose the Midwest because they wanted a region with the same features and conveniences they had come to know. The Midwest, unlike the Plains and Southwest, had better-developed transportation routes, easier access to markets, a smaller African American population, and cheaper landholdings, and were similar to New England in climate. The region proved a good first stop for those who did not yet have enough cash to purchase land; in the Midwest they could obtain jobs unloading canal boats, or working in farms or mills, before moving on.

THE FEDERAL GOVERNMENT AND WESTWARD EXPANSION

How did the federal government sponsor and speed up westward expansion?

Federal Indian and land policies, particularly Indian removal from desirable lands, did much to encourage white movement into the West. Many whites, in fact, awaited government efforts to clear lands before moving there. The government funded exploration of the West in search of the best location for a transcontinental railroad. Army engineers helped design roads, canals, and railroads, while soldiers cleared forests and did other work. The military also removed Indians from lands that whites desired, defended settlers from Indian attacks, or pushed squatters from land they did not own. Sales of government-controlled land also encouraged settlement.

THE SOUTHWESTERN BORDERLANDS

What factors led Texas to break away from Mexico?

For decades prior to 1836, Americans moved into Texas, and their numbers increased in 1824 when a newly-independent Mexico encouraged further settlement by offering tax incentives and land grants to foreigners—who need be Christians willing to establish permanent residences to qualify. The land grants given covered most of present-day Texas and were populated by U.S. citizens pushed from their homeland by depressed economic conditions. Most were unwilling to assimilate, and Mexican officials rightly feared that the transplanted Americans would seek to annex Texas to the United States. Beginning in 1826, there were calls for an independent Texas under the name "Fredonia Republic"; and as the proportion of Americans to Tejanos reached 7 to 1 in 1835, calls for secession heightened, culminating in battles and the eventual declaration of Texas as the Lone Star Republic in 1836.

MIGRATION TO THE FAR WEST

How did the gold rush impact the development of the Far West?

As miners flooded into California seeking gold, an agricultural boom emerged, with wheat becoming the main crop often farmed by Indian slaves. Wherever mining areas sprung up, a commercial and industrial boom usually followed, as merchants rose to provide necessities and other goods to new settlers. Cities also grew up fast; San Francisco went from one thousand people in 1848 to thirty-five thousand two years later. While California was admitted as a free state that year, it quickly legalized the enslavement of Indians, using them to work the mines and later in fields or homes.

THE POLITICS OF TERRITORIAL EXPANSION

How was Manifest Destiny a factor in the U.S. War with Mexico?

Manifest Destiny was the belief that U.S. westward expansion was not only inevitable but divinely ordained as the nation's mission to spread its Christian and republican institutions as widely as possible. First articulated in 1845, its proponents saw the annexation of Texas as part of a broader mission to occupy the entire continent. The subtext of Manifest Destiny was the superiority of whites over Indians, Hispanics, and people of African descent, and as such, conquering land occupied by Mexico—such as Texas and California—was seen as just. When President Tyler sought annexation of Texas via joint resolution of Congress and a vote by Texans, Mexico broke off relations with the United States and the two nations moved toward war.

SUGGESTIONS FOR FURTHER READING

Gary Clayton Anderson, *The Conquest of Texas: Ethnic Cleansing in the Promised Land, 1820–1875* (2005)

Stuart Banner, *How the Indians Lost Their Land: Law and Power on the Frontier* (2005)

James F. Brooks, *Captives and Cousins: Slavery, Kinship, and Community in the Southwest Borderlands* (2002)

Andrew R. L. Cayton and Peter S. Onuf, *The Midwest and the Nation: Rethinking the History of an American Region* (1990)

Robert V. Hine and John Mack Faragher, *The American West: A New Interpretive History* (2000)

Albert L. Hurtado, *Indian Survival on the California Frontier* (1998)

Susan L. Johnson, *Roaring Camp: The Social World of the California Gold Rush* (2000)

Andrés Reséndez, *Changing National Identities at the Frontier: Texas and New Mexico, 1800–1850* (2005)

Michael L. Tate, *Indians and Emigrants: Encounters on the Overland Trails* (2006)

Richard White, *"It's Your Misfortune and None of My Own": A New History of the American West* (1991)

Slavery and America's Future: The Road to War

On a stiflingly hot evening, June 16, 1858, Abraham Lincoln, a former one-term congressman, stepped onto the platform of the legislative chamber in the Springfield, Illinois, state house to accept the Republican Party's nomination for the U.S. Senate, running against America's leading Democrat, the incumbent Stephen A. Douglas. At six feet, four inches, Lincoln towered over the packed hall. The nation was at a historic crossroads, and he worked on this speech for weeks, delivering his poetic prose with intellectual power. "Slavery agitation" had convulsed American politics and exploded in guerrilla war in Kansas. "It will not cease," ventured Lincoln, "until a crisis shall have been reached, and passed." Then, in familiar biblical imagery, he gave the crisis its unforgettable metaphor:

> "A house divided against itself cannot stand." I believe this government cannot endure permanently half slave and half free. . . . It will become *all* one thing, or *all* the other. Either the *opponents* of slavery will arrest the further spread of it, and place it where the public mind shall rest in the belief that it is in the course of ultimate extinction; or its *advocates* will push it forward, till it shall become alike lawful in *all* the States, *old* as well as *new*—North as well as South.

Lincoln contended that a conspiracy—a "design" led by the Democratic Party's "chief bosses"—sought to make slavery a *national* institution. He charged Douglas with not caring "whether slavery be voted down or voted up."

In the ensuing campaign, Lincoln and Douglas squared off over the issues dividing the country: the westward expansion of slavery, the character of federal authority over property in slaves, whether the Declaration of Independence signaled racial equality, and ultimately the moral integrity and future of the American republic. Reluctantly, Douglas agreed to seven debates,

This icon will direct you to interactive activities and study materials on *A People And A Nation*, Brief Edition website: **www.cengage.com/history/norton/ peoplenationbrief8e**

Chronology

1846	War with Mexico begins.	**1857**	*Dred Scott v. Sanford* endorses southern views on black citizenship and slavery in the territories.
	Oregon Treaty is negotiated.		
	Wilmot Proviso inflames sectional divisions.		Economic panic and widespread unemployment begin.
1847	Cass proposes the idea of popular sovereignty.	**1858**	Kansas voters reject the Lecompton Constitution.
1848	Treaty of Guadalupe Hidalgo gives the United States new territory in the Southwest.		Lincoln-Douglas debates attract attention.
	Free-Soil Party is formed.		Douglas contends popular sovereignty prevails over the *Dred Scott* decision in the territories.
	Taylor is elected president.	**1859**	Brown raids Harpers Ferry.
	Gold is discovered in California, which later applies for admission to Union as a free state.	**1860**	Democratic Party splits in two; southern Democrats demand a constitutional guarantee for the territories.
1850	Compromise of 1850, containing the controversial Fugitive Slave Act, passes.		Lincoln is elected president in a divided, sectional election.
1852	Stowe publishes *Uncle Tom's Cabin.*		Crittenden Compromise fails.
	Pierce is elected president.		South Carolina secedes from the Union.
1854	"Appeal of the Independent Democrats" is published.	**1861**	Six more Deep South states secede.
	Kansas-Nebraska Act wins approval and ignites controversy.		Confederacy is established at Montgomery, Alabama.
	Republican Party is formed.		Attack on Fort Sumter begins the Civil War.
	Return of the fugitive Burns to slavery in Virginia.		Four states in the Upper South join the Confederacy.
1856	Bleeding Kansas troubles nation.		
	Brooks attacks Sumner in Senate chamber.		
	Buchanan is elected president, but the Republican Frémont wins most northern states.		

one in each congressional district of Illinois, except Chicago and Springfield, where the candidates had already appeared.

The Lincoln-Douglas debates were three-hour marathons of confrontation, political analysis, and theater, with the candidates speaking in long addresses and rebuttals. Tens of thousands of people attended these outdoor events, arriving by foot, wagon, or train and accompanied by brass bands. Perhaps never before or since have Americans demonstrated such an appetite for democratic engagement. As Douglas accused his opponent and all Republicans of being abolitionists and favoring racial equality, Lincoln was forced to admit that he opposed social equality between whites and blacks. He embraced, however, the natural-rights doctrine of the Declaration of Independence and condemned slavery as an evil that must be constrained. Lincoln insisted on stopping slavery's expansion, while maintaining that the federal government could not legally end it in the South. A foot shorter than Lincoln, better dressed, and resplendent in oratorical manner, Douglas appealed to racial prejudice and to a vague unionism. Lincoln cast the election as a moral choice between free-labor–Free-Soil doctrine and a republic ultimately dominated by slaveholders and their abettors, determined to erase ordinary citizens' liberties.

Of the quarter-million votes cast, Lincoln received four thousand more than Douglas. But senators were elected by state legislatures, and with an outdated apportionment, Democrats maintained a 54-to-46 margin to return Douglas to the U.S. Senate. Lincoln would be heard from again, however.

Well before 1858, conflict and violence were enveloping the nation. In the Kansas Territory, open warfare exploded between proslavery and antislavery settlers. On the floor of the U.S. Senate, a southern representative had beaten a northern senator senseless. A new fugitive slave law sent thousands of free and fugitive blacks fleeing into Canada in fear for their lives. The Supreme Court issued a dramatic decision about slavery's constitutionality in westward expansion, as well as the status of African American citizenship, to the delight of most southerners and the dread of many northerners. And the abolitionist John Brown was planning a raid into Virginia to start a slave rebellion.

As the 1850s advanced, divergent economic and political aims, which had long been held in check, now flew apart over the issue of slavery. Political parties fractured, replaced by a realignment that reinforced sectional interests. Each time the nation expanded, it confronted a thorny issue: should new territories and states be slave or free?

North and South, a feeling grew that America's future was at stake—the character of its economy, its labor system, its definition of constitutional liberty, and its racial self-definition. Blacks could take heart that political strife over slavery might lead to their liberation. In 1855 Frederick Douglass spoke for the enslaved when he wrote that "the thought of only being a creature of the present and the past, troubled me, and I longed to have a future—a future with hope in it."

- **After 1845, how and why did westward expansion become so intertwined with the future of slavery and freedom?**
- **During the 1850s, why did Americans (white males, virtually all of whom could vote, and blacks, few of whom had the franchise) seem to care so deeply about electoral politics?**
- **What were the long-term and immediate causes of the Civil War?**

THE WAR WITH MEXICO AND ITS CONSEQUENCES

In the 1840s, territorial expansion surged forward under President James K. Polk of North Carolina. The annexation of Texas just before his inauguration did not make war with Mexico inevitable, but several of Polk's decisions did. Mexico broke off relations with the United States, and during the annexation process, Polk urged Texans to seize all the land to the Rio Grande and claim the river as their southern and western border. Mexico held that the Nueces River was the border; hence, the stage was set for conflict. In his determination to fulfill the nation's manifest destiny over the continent, Polk wanted Mexico's territory to the Pacific and all of the Oregon Country. He and his expansionist cabinet achieved their goals but were largely unaware of the cost in domestic harmony.

Oregon

During the 1844 campaign, Polk's supporters threatened war with Great Britain to gain Oregon. Not wanting to fight Mexico and Great Britain at the same time, Polk sought diplomacy in the Northwest, where America and Britain had jointly occupied disputed territory since 1819. Dropping the demand for a boundary at latitude 54°40′, he convinced the British to accept the 49th parallel. In 1846, the Oregon Treaty gave the United States present-day Oregon, Washington, and Idaho, and parts of Wyoming and Montana. Thus a new era of land acquisition and conquest began under the eleventh president, who was the sixth to be a slaveholder and who, through an agent, secretly bought and sold slaves from the White House.

Mr. Polk's War

Toward Mexico Polk was more aggressive. In early 1846 he ordered American troops under Old Rough and Ready, General Zachary Taylor, to defend the contested border of the Rio Grande across from the town of Matamoros, Mexico. Polk saw California as the prize, and he attempted to buy from Mexico a huge tract of land extending to the Pacific, to no avail. After a three-week standoff, on April 24, 1846, Mexican cavalry ambushed a U.S. cavalry unit on the north side of the river; eleven Americans were killed, and sixty-three were captured. On April 26, Taylor sent a dispatch to Washington, D.C., announcing, "Hostilities may now be considered as commenced."

Polk then drafted a message to Congress: Mexico had "passed the boundary of the United States, invaded our territory and shed American blood on American soil." Polk deceptively declared that "war exists by the act of Mexico itself." Two days later, on May 13, the House recognized a state of war with Mexico by a vote of 174 to 14, and the Senate, by 40 to 2. Because Polk withheld key facts, the reality of what happened on the Rio Grande was not known. Manifest destiny launched the United States into its first major war on foreign territory.

Foreign War and the Popular Imagination

The idea of war unleashed public celebrations in southern cities, such as Richmond and Louisville, and northern cities, such as Philadelphia and New York. After news came of General Taylor's first victories at Palo Alto and Resaca de la Palma, volunteers swarmed recruiting stations. The New York writer Herman Melville remarked that "nothing is talked of but the 'Halls of the Montezumas.'" Publishers rushed books about Mexican geography into print. And new daily newspapers boosted sales by giving the war a romantic appeal.

Here was an adventurous war of conquest, the fulfillment of an Anglo-Saxon–Christian destiny to possess the North American continent and to civilize the semi-Indian Mexicans. Racism fueled the expansionist spirit. In 1846 an Illinois newspaper justified the war by labeling Mexicans as "reptiles in the path of progressive democracy." Because of newspapers, the War with Mexico became the first national event experienced with immediacy. War correspondents reported on battles, and ships from Vera Cruz on the Gulf Coast of Mexico carried news dispatches to New Orleans. Near war's end, news traveled by telegraph in only three days from New Orleans to Washington, D.C.

The war spawned an outpouring of poetry, song, drama, travel literature, and lithographs that glorified the conflict. But not everyone cheered. The abolitionist James Russell Lowell considered the war a "national crime committed in behoof of slavery, our common sin." Even the proslavery spokesman John C. Calhoun feared expansionism's perils.

Conquest

Early in the war, U.S. forces made significant gains. In May 1846 Polk ordered Colonel Stephen Kearny and a small detachment to invade the remote provinces of New Mexico and California. Taking Santa Fe, Kearny pushed into California, where he joined forces with two U.S. naval units and American settlers led by Captain John C. Frémont. General Zachary Taylor's forces attacked Monterrey, which surrendered in September, securing northeastern Mexico.

New Mexico did not prove easy for U.S. forces. In January 1847, in Taos, northwest of Santa Fe, Hispanics and Indians led by Pablo Montoya and Tomás Romero rebelled against the Americans and killed government officials. In what became known as the Taos Revolt, some 500 Mexican and Indian insurgents laid siege to a mill in Arroyo Hondo, outside Taos. The U.S. command swiftly suppressed the revolt, and the insurgents retreated to a thick-walled church in Taos Pueblo. With cannon, the U.S. Army killed 150 and captured 400 rebels. After many arrests, approximately twenty-eight insurgent leaders were hanged in the Taos plaza, ending bloody resistance to U.S. occupation.

Before the end of 1846, American forces also established dominion over California. Because losses on the periphery had not broken Mexican resistance, General Winfield Scott carried the war to the enemy's heartland. He led fourteen thousand men toward Mexico City in what proved to be the war's decisive campaign. Outnumbered and threatened by yellow fever, Scott's men repeatedly discovered flanking routes around their foes. After several hard-fought battles, U.S. troops captured the Mexican capital.

Treaty of Guadalupe Hidalgo

Representatives of both countries signed the Treaty of Guadalupe Hidalgo in February 1848. The United States gained California and New Mexico (including present-day Nevada, Utah, and Arizona, and parts of Colorado and Wyoming) and recognition of the Rio Grande as Texas's southern boundary. The American government agreed to settle the claims of its citizens (mostly Texans) against Mexico ($3.2 million) and to pay Mexico a mere $15 million. The costs of the war included the deaths of thirteen thousand Americans (mostly from disease) and fifty thousand Mexicans. Enmity between Mexico and the United States endured into the twentieth century. Domestically, southwesterners and most southern planters embraced the war; New Englanders opposed it. Whigs in Congress charged that Polk, a Democrat, provoked an unnecessary war and usurped the power of Congress. Abolitionists and a minority of antislavery Whigs charged that the war was a plot to extend slavery.

Slave Power Conspiracy

These charges fed northern fear of the Slave Power. Abolitionists had long warned of a slaveholding oligarchy that would dominate the nation through its hold on federal power. Slaveholders gained control of the South by suppressing dissent, and they forced a gag rule on Congress in 1836. To many white northerners, even those who had no problem with slavery, this battle over free speech made the idea of a Slave Power credible. The War with Mexico deepened such fears, as antislavery northerners wondered if it had been launched to acquire vast, new slave territory.

At first, some southern Whigs attacked the Democratic president for causing the war, and few southern congressmen saw slavery as the paramount issue. Many whites North and South feared that large land seizures would bring nonwhite Mexicans into the United States and upset the racial order. An Indiana politician did not want "any mixed races in our Union, nor men of any color except white, unless they be slaves."

Wilmot Proviso

In August 1846, David Wilmot, a Pennsylvania Democrat, proposed an amendment, or proviso, to a military appropriations bill: that "neither slavery nor involuntary servitude shall ever exist" in any territory gained from Mexico. Although the proviso was never passed, its repeated introduction by northerners transformed the debate over slavery's expansion. Southerners intensified efforts to protect slavery's future. John C. Calhoun insisted that the territories belonged to all the states, and the federal government could not limit slavery there.

This position, often called state sovereignty, was a radical reversal of history. In 1787 the Confederation Congress discouraged if not fully excluded slavery from the Northwest Territory (see pages 169–70?), Article IV of the U.S. Constitution authorized Congress to make "all needful rules and regulations" for the territories, and the Missouri Compromise barred slavery from most of the Louisiana Purchase. Now, southern leaders demanded future guarantees for slavery.

In the North, the Wilmot Proviso became a rallying cry for abolitionists. While fourteen state legislatures endorsed it, not all of its supporters were abolitionists. David Wilmot was neither an abolitionist nor an antislavery Whig. Instead, his goal was to defend "the rights of white freemen" and to obtain California "for free white labor."

As Wilmot demonstrated, it was possible to be a racist and an opponent of slavery. The vast majority of white northerners were not active abolitionists, and their desire to keep the West slavery-free was often matched by their desire to keep blacks from settling there. At stake was the free individual's access to social mobility through acquisition of land in the West. Slave labor, thousands of northerners soon believed, would degrade the toil of free men and render them unemployable. The West must therefore be kept free of slaves.

The Election of 1848 and Popular Sovereignty

The divisive slavery question infested national politics. After Polk renounced a second term as president, the Democrats nominated Senator Lewis Cass of Michigan for president and General William Butler of Kentucky for vice president. In 1847 Cass, a party loyalist who had served in Jackson's cabinet, devised the idea of popular sovereignty, letting residents in the western territories decide the slavery question for themselves. His party's platform declared that Congress lacked the power to interfere with slavery's expansion. The Whigs nominated General Zachary Taylor, a southern slaveholder and war hero; the New York Congressman Millard Fillmore was his running mate. The Whig convention similarly denied congressional power over slavery in the territories.

TABLE 14.1   New Political Parties

Party	Period of Influence	Area of Influence	Outcome
Liberty Party	1839–1848	North	Merged with other antislavery groups to form Free-Soil Party
Free-Soil Party	1848–1854	North	Merged with Republican Party
Know-Nothings (American Party)	1853–1856	Nationwide	Disappeared, freeing most to join Republican Party
Republican Party	1854–present	North (later nationwide)	Became rival of Democratic Party and won presidency in 1860

Many southern Democrats distrusted Cass and voted for Taylor because he was a slaveholder. New York Democrats committed to the Wilmot Proviso rebelled against Cass and nominated former president Martin Van Buren. Antislavery Whigs and former Liberty Party supporters joined them to form the Free-Soil Party (see Table 14.1). This party, which sought to restrict slavery's expansion to western territories and whose slogan was "Free Soil, Free Speech, Free Labor, and Free Men," won almost 300,000 northern votes. Taylor polled 1.4 million votes to Cass's 1.2 million and won the White House, but the results were ominous.

Like politics, religious denominations split into northern and southern wings. Many Protestants feared that God would either destroy the national sin of slavery or help the South defend it as part of the divine order. As the 1850s dawned, the legacies of the War with Mexico and the conflicts of 1848 threatened the nature of the Union.

1850: COMPROMISE OR ARMISTICE?

More than eighty thousand Americans flooded into California during the 1849 gold rush. With Congress unable to agree on a governing formula for the territories, President Taylor urged settlers to apply for admission to the Union. They did, proposing a state constitution that banned slavery. Because California's admission as a free state would upset the sectional balance in the Senate (the ratio of slave to free states was fifteen to fifteen), southern politicians wanted to postpone admission and make California a slave territory or at least extend the Missouri Compromise.

Debate over Slavery in the Territories Twice before—in 1820 and 1833—Henry Clay, the venerable Whig leader and Great Pacificator, had shaped sectional compromise; now he struggled one last time to preserve the nation. In winter 1850, Clay and Senator Stephen A. Douglas of Illinois, the Little Giant, steered their compromise package through Senate debate and amendment.

The problems were numerous. Would California or part of it become a free state? How should the territory acquired from Mexico be organized? Texas, which allowed slavery, claimed areas extending as far west as Santa Fe. Southerners complained that fugitive slaves were not being returned as the Constitution required, and northerners objected to the sale of human beings in the nation's capital. Eight years earlier, in *Prigg v. Pennsylvania* (1842), the Supreme Court ruled that enforcement of the Constitution's fugitive slave clause was a federal obligation. The Court further ruled that states could not exact measures, often called personal liberty laws, banning the seizure and removal of a fugitive. Most troublesome, however, was the status of slavery in the territories.

Clay and Douglas discovered in Lewis Cass's idea of popular sovereignty what one historian called a "charm of ambiguity." Ultimately Congress would have to approve statehood for a territory, but "in the meantime," said Cass, it should allow the people living there "to regulate their own concerns in their own way."

To avoid dissension within their party, northern and southern Democrats explained Cass's statement to constituents in incompatible ways. Southerners claimed that neither Congress nor a territorial legislature could bar slavery. Northerners, however, insisted that Americans living in a territory were entitled to self-government and thus could outlaw slavery.

The cause of compromise gained a powerful supporter when on March 7 Senator Daniel Webster committed his prestige and eloquence to Clay's bill. Abandoning his earlier support for the Wilmot Proviso, Webster urged northerners not to "taunt or reproach" the South with antislavery measures. He warned southern firebrands that disunion inevitably would cause violence and destruction. Many of Webster's former abolitionist friends in New England condemned him for his compromise efforts and accused him of going over to the Devil.

Only three days earlier, with equal drama, Calhoun was carried from his sickbed to advocate against the compromise. With Calhoun unable to speak, Senator James Mason of Virginia read his address, which predicted disunion if southern demands went unanswered, frightening some into supporting compromise.

Months later, when Clay and Douglas brought their legislative package to a vote, it lost. With Clay sick, Douglas reintroduced the compromise measures one at a time. Douglas realized that because southerners favored some bills and northerners the rest, the small majority for compromise could be achieved only on each distinct issue. The strategy worked and the Compromise of 1850 became law.

Compromise of 1850   The compromise had five essential measures.

1. California became a free state.
2. The Texas boundary was set at its then-current limits (see Map 14.1), and the United States paid Texas $10 million for the loss of New Mexico Territory.
3. The territories of New Mexico and Utah were organized on the basis of popular sovereignty.
4. The fugitive slave law was strengthened.
5. The slave trade was abolished in the District of Columbia.

At best, the Compromise of 1850 was an artful evasion. Douglas found a way to pass the five proposals without convincing northerners and southerners to agree on fundamentals. The compromise bought time for the nation, but it did not resolve territorial questions.

The compromise had two flaws. The first concerned the ambiguity of popular sovereignty. Southerners insisted on no prohibition of slavery during the territorial

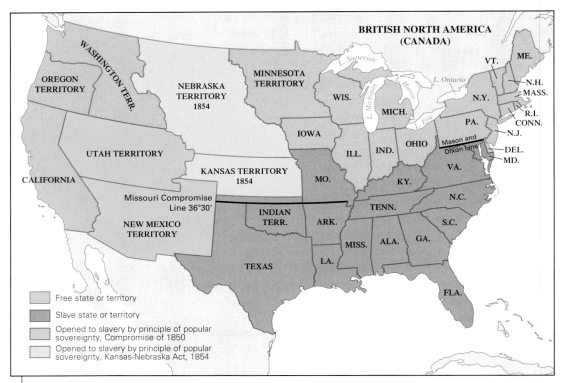

Map 14.1   The Kansas-Nebraska Act and Slavery Expansion, 1854

The vote on the Kansas-Nebraska Act in the House of Representatives (see also Table 14.2 on page 357) demonstrates the sectionalization of American politics due to the slavery question.

stage, and northerners declared that settlers could bar slavery whenever they wished. The compromise allowed for the appeal of a territorial legislature's action to the Supreme Court.

Fugitive Slave Act

The second flaw lay in the Fugitive Slave Act, which gave new—and controversial—protection to slavery. The law empowered slaveowners to go into state courts to present evidence that a slave had escaped. The resulting transcript and description of the fugitive would serve as legal proof of slave status, even in free states and territories. Court officials adjudicated the identity of the person described, not whether he or she was indeed a slave. The law made it a felony to harbor fugitives and stated that northern citizens could be summoned to hunt fugitives. U.S. marshals received $10 if the alleged fugitive was returned, $5 if not returned.

Abolitionist newspapers attacked the Fugitive Slave Act as a violation of American rights. Why were alleged fugitives denied a trial by jury? Why would northerners be arrested if they harbored runaways? These questions convinced some northerners that free blacks were vulnerable to kidnapping and enslavement. An estimated twenty thousand blacks fled to Canada.

Between 1850 and 1854, protests and violent resistance to slave catchers occurred in northern towns. Sometimes a captured fugitive was broken out of jail by abolitionists, as in the 1851 Boston case of Shadrach Minkins, who was spirited by wagons and trains to Montreal, Canada. That same year, the small black community in Lancaster County, Pennsylvania, defended four escaped slaves from a federal posse charged with reenslaving them. At this Christiana riot, fugitives shot and killed Edward Gorsuch, the Maryland slaveowner who sought the return of his property. A headline reporting the Christiana affair screamed, "Civil War, The First Blow Struck!"*

Many abolitionists became convinced that violence was a legitimate means of opposing slavery. In an 1854 column, Frederick Douglass said that the only way to make the fugitive slave law a dead letter was to make a "few dead slave catchers."

Uncle Tom's Cabin

Around this time, Harriet Beecher Stowe, whose New England family produced prominent ministers, wrote a novel portraying the humanity and suffering of slaves. Her story, *Uncle Tom's Cabin,* was serialized in 1851 and published as a book in 1852. It touched millions of northerners with its tale of a slave mother's dash to freedom with her child across the frozen Ohio River. Stowe also portrayed slavery's evil effects on slaveholders, indicting the institution more harshly than southerners caught in its web. Moreover, Stowe exposed northern racism and complicity with slavery by making the worst slaveholder a man of New England birth.

By mid-1853, the book sold over 1 million copies. Its popularity alarmed southern whites, who saw their way of life threatened. Behind the South's claims about territorial rights lay the fear that, if nearby areas outlawed slavery, they would become bases from which abolitionism would spread into slave states.

Some twenty proslavery novels were published in the 1850s as responses to *Uncle Tom's Cabin.* Most paled in comparison to Stowe's masterpiece, but southern writers defended their system as more humane than wage labor. In awkward stories, such as J. W. Page's *Uncle Robin in His Cabin and Tom Without One in Boston,* slaves were induced to run away by visiting abolitionists, and then starved in northern cities.

The Underground Railroad

By the 1850s, slaveholders were especially disturbed about the Underground Railroad, a loose, illegal network that spirited runaways to freedom. Thousands of slaves escaped by these often disorganized routes, but largely through their own wits and courage, with assistance from blacks in northern cities. Lewis Hayden in Boston; David Ruggles in New York; William Still in Philadelphia; John Parker in Ripley, Ohio; and Jacob Gibbs in Washington, D.C. were among the many black abolitionists who managed fugitive slave escapes through their regions.

Harriet Tubman, herself an escapee in 1848, returned to her native Maryland and Virginia at least a dozen times and secretly helped as many as three hundred slaves, some her family members, to freedom. Outraged Maryland planters offered a $40,000 reward for her capture.

In Ohio, white abolitionists, often Quakers, joined with blacks to help slaves cross the river to freedom. The Underground Railroad also had numerous maritime routes, as coastal slaves escaped aboard ships from Virginia, the Carolinas, or New

---

*A headline from the Lancaster, Pennsylvania, *Saturday Express,* reporting on the Christiana Affair screamed "Civil War! The first blow struck!"

In *Still Life of Harriet Tubman with Bible and Candle*, we see the youthful, calm, determined leader of the Underground Railroad. Appearing gentle, Tubman was in her own way a revolutionary who liberated nearly three hundred of her people.
(© psihoyos.com / Science Faction)

Orleans and ended up in northern port cities, the Caribbean, or England. Many slaves from the Lower South and Texas escaped to Mexico, which abolished slavery in 1829. Some joined Seminole communities in Florida, where they fought with them against the U.S. Army in the Seminole Wars of 1835–1842 and 1855–1858.

Slave escapes were a testament to human courage and the will for freedom. They never reached the scale believed by angry slaveholders or bragged about by northern towns and local historical societies today. But, in reality and legend, the Underground Railroad applied pressure to the institution of slavery and gave slaves hope.

Election of 1852 and the Collapse of Compromise

The 1852 election gave southern leaders hope that under a new president, slavery would be secure. Franklin Pierce, a New Hampshire Democrat, won easily over the Whig presidential nominee, General Winfield Scott. Pierce defended each section's rights as essential to national unity, and southerners hoped that his support for the Compromise of 1850 might end the ongoing crisis.

President Pierce's embrace of the compromise appalled many northerners. His enforcement of the Fugitive Slave Act provoked fear of the Slave Power, especially in the case of the fugitive slave Anthony Burns, who fled Virginia in 1852. In Boston, thinking he was safe, Burns began a new life. But in 1854 federal marshals placed him under guard in Boston's courthouse. An interracial crowd of abolitionists attacked the courthouse, killing a jailer while attempting to free Burns.

Pierce telegraphed local officials to "incur any expense to insure the execution of the law" and sent troops to Boston. Soldiers marched Burns to Boston harbor, while Burns's supporters draped the streets in black and hung American flags at half-mast. At a cost of $100,000, a single black man was returned to slavery.

This demonstration of federal support for slavery radicalized opinion, even among conservatives. Juries refused to convict the abolitionists who stormed the Boston courthouse, and New England states passed personal liberty laws that absolved local judges from enforcing the Fugitive Slave Act, in effect nullifying federal authority. What northerners now saw as evidence of a dominating Slave Power, slaveholders saw as legal defense of their rights.

Pierce confronted sectional conflict at every turn. His proposal for a transcontinental railroad stalled when congressmen fought over its location, North or South. An annexation treaty with Hawai'i failed because southern senators would not vote for another free state, while efforts to acquire slaveholding Cuba angered northerners. Events in the Pacific fueled debate over just how far American expansion should extend. With two orchestrated landings in the Bay of Tokyo, in 1853 and 1854, Commodore Matthew Perry established U.S. intentions to trade with Japan, whether that country wanted it or not. Offended, the Japanese were nonetheless impressed with Perry's steam-powered warships, the first they had seen. Perry's Treaty of Kanagawa in March 1854 negotiated two ports as coaling stations for American ships, but the sought-after trading arrangements were slow in coming.

Back home, another territorial bill threw Congress and the nation into greater turmoil, and the Compromise of 1850 collapsed.

SLAVERY EXPANSION AND COLLAPSE OF THE PARTY SYSTEM

The new controversy began in a surprising way. Stephen A. Douglas introduced a bill to establish the Kansas and Nebraska Territories. Ambitious for the presidency, Douglas did not think slavery would be a problem and was willing to risk some controversy to economically aid his home state of Illinois. A transcontinental railroad would encourage Great Plains settlement and stimulate the Illinois economy, but no company would build a railroad before Congress organized the territories it would cross. Thus interest in promoting a railroad drove Douglas to introduce a bill that inflamed sectional passions.

Kansas-Nebraska Act The Kansas-Nebraska Act exposed conflicting interpretations of popular sovereignty. Douglas's bill left "all questions pertaining to slavery in the Territories . . . to the people residing therein." Northerners and southerners, however, still disagreed over what territorial settlers could constitutionally do. Moreover, the Kansas and Nebraska Territories lay within the Louisiana Purchase, and the Missouri Compromise prohibited slavery there from latitude 36°30′ north to the Canadian border. If popular sovereignty were applied in Kansas and Nebraska, it would mean that the Missouri Compromise was no longer valid.

Southern congressmen, anxious to establish slaveholders' right to take slaves into any territory, pressed Douglas for an explicit repeal of the 36°30′ limitation in exchange for their support. During a carriage ride with the Kentucky senator Archibald Dixon, Douglas conceded: "I will incorporate it in my bill, though I know it will raise a hell of a storm."

Douglas may have hoped that climate and soil conditions would keep slavery out of Kansas and Nebraska; nonetheless, his bill allowed slavery on land from which it had been prohibited for thirty-four years. Many Free-Soilers and antislavery forces considered this turn of events a betrayal of trust. The bill became law in May 1854 by a vote that demonstrated the dangerous sectionalization of American politics (see Map 14.1 and Table 14.2).

TABLE 14.2   **The Vote on the Kansas-Nebraska Act**

	Aye	Nay
The vote was 113 to 100 in favor.		
Northern Democrats	44	42
Southern Democrats	57	2
Northern Whigs	0	45
Southern Whigs	12	7
Northern Free-Soilers	0	4

Opposition to the Fugitive Slave Act grew; between 1855 and 1859, Connecticut, Rhode Island, Massachusetts, Michigan, Maine, Ohio, and Wisconsin passed personal-liberty laws. These laws enraged southerners by providing counsel for alleged fugitives and requiring trial by jury. The Kansas-Nebraska Act had a devastating impact on political parties. The weakened Whig Party broke into northern and southern wings. The Democrats survived, but their support in the North plummeted in the 1854 elections. Northern Democrats lost sixty-six of their ninety-one congressional seats and lost control of all but two free-state legislatures.

Birth of the Republican Party

The beneficiary of northern voters' wrath was a new political party. During debate on the Kansas-Nebraska Act, six congressmen—most prominently, Joshua Giddings, Salmon Chase, and Charles Sumner—published an "Appeal of the Independent Democrats." In it, they attacked Douglas's legislation as a violation of the Missouri Compromise and a "criminal betrayal of precious rights" that would make free territory a "dreary region of despotism." Their appeal tapped a reservoir of northern concerns, cogently expressed by Illinois's Abraham Lincoln.

Although Lincoln did not condemn southerners, he exposed the meaning of the Kansas-Nebraska Act. Lincoln argued that the founders, from love of liberty, banned slavery from the Northwest Territory, kept the word *slavery* out of the Constitution, and treated it as a cancer on the republic. Rather than encouraging liberty, the Kansas-Nebraska Act promised to extend slavery. America's future, Lincoln warned, was being mortgaged to slavery.

Thousands of white northerners agreed. During summer and fall 1854, antislavery Whigs and Democrats, Free-Soilers, and reformers throughout the Old Northwest formed the new Republican Party, dedicated to keeping slavery from the territories. Republicans' influence rapidly spread to the East. They won a stunning victory in the 1854 elections, capturing a majority of northern House seats and leading roughly a quarter of northern Democrats to desert their party.

For the first time, too, a sectional party gained power in the political system. The Whigs were gone, and Democrats struggled to maintain national membership. The emergence of the Republican coalition of antislavery interests is the most rapid transformation in party allegiance in American history.

Know-Nothings

Republicans drew into their coalition a growing nativist movement that called itself the American Party, or Know-Nothings (because initial members kept their purposes secret, answering "I know nothing" to questions). This group exploited fear of foreigners and Catholics. Between 1848 and 1860, nearly 3.5 million immigrants entered the United States—proportionally the heaviest influx of foreigners in American history. Democrats courted these new citizens, but many native-born Anglo-Saxon Protestants feared that Irish and German Catholics would owe primary allegiance to the pope in Rome.

In 1854 anti-immigrant fears made the Know-Nothings successful in some northern states, particularly Massachusetts, where they elected 11 congressmen, a governor, all state officers, all state senators, and all but 2 of 378 state representatives.

The temperance movement also gained ground early in the 1850s with promises to stamp out the evils associated with liquor and immigrants (a pointedly anti-Irish campaign). The Know-Nothings strove to reinforce Protestant morality and restrict voting and office holding to the native-born. As the Whig Party vanished, the Know-Nothings filled the void, but, like the Whigs, the Know-Nothings could not keep their northern and southern wings together due to the slavery expansion issue. They dissolved after 1856. Instead, Republicans wooed nativists with temperance ordinances and laws postponing suffrage for naturalized citizens (see Table 14.1).

Party Realignment and the Republicans' Appeal

The Whig Party's demise ensured a major realignment of the political system. Immigration, temperance, homestead bills, the tariff, and internal improvements were crucial issues for voters during the 1850s. Commercial agriculture was booming in the Ohio–Mississippi–Great Lakes area, but residents desired more canals, roads, and river and harbor improvements. Because credit was scarce, a homestead program—the idea that western land should be free to individuals who would farm it and make a home on it—attracted many voters. Republicans appealed strongly to those interested in the economic development of the West, promising internal improvements and land grants, as well as higher tariffs to protect industry.

Partisan ideological appeals became the currency of the realigned political system. As Republicans preached "Free Soil, Free Labor, Free Men," they conveyed many northerners' self-image. These phrases resonated with traditional ideals of equality, liberty, and opportunity under self-government—the heritage of republicanism. Invoking that heritage also undercut charges that the Republican Party was radical and abolitionist.

The northern economy was booming, and thousands of migrants moved west to establish farms and communities. Midwesterners multiplied their yields using new machines, such as mechanical reapers. Railroads were carrying crops to urban markets. And industry was making available goods that had recently been unaffordable for most people.

Republican Ideology

To many people, especially northerners, the key to progress appeared to be free labor—the dignity of work and prospect of opportunity. Any hard-working and virtuous man, it was thought, could improve his condition and achieve economic independence. Republicans argued that the South, with little industry and slave labor, was backward by comparison.

Traditional republicanism hailed the virtuous common man as the nation's backbone. In Abraham Lincoln, a man of humble origins who became a successful lawyer and political leader, Republicans had a symbol of that tradition. They portrayed their party as the guardian of economic opportunity, giving individuals a chance to work, acquire land, and attain success.

At stake in the crises of the 1850s were two competing definitions of liberty: southern planters' claims of their liberty to own and transport their slaves nationwide, and northern workers' and farmers' claims of their liberty to seek a new start on free land, unimpeded by a system that defined labor as slave and black.

Annexation of Cuba

One of the most contentious issues in antebellum American foreign relations was the annexation of Cuba. As a strategic bulwark against Britain and France in the Western Hemisphere, for its sugar wealth, and as a slave society that might reinforce southern slavery, the Spanish-controlled island fired the imagination of manifest destiny. In the early republic, Presidents Thomas Jefferson and James Madison explored acquisition. John Quincy Adams, as secretary of state in 1823, considered Cuba "indispensable to the continuance . . . of the Union."

Until the 1840s, the United States supported Spanish rule for stability and the preservation of slavery. Southerners feared a second Haiti if Cuba became independent through revolution. The prospect of slave insurrection and the spread of abolitionism throughout the upper Caribbean and the Deep South drove many southerners and three Democratic administrations to pursue acquisition of Cuba. Slaveholding politicians viewed Cuba as critical to expansion.

In 1848 President Polk authorized $100 million to purchase Cuba. The Spanish foreign minister, however, told Polk's emissary that his government would rather see Cuba "sunk in the ocean" than sell it to the United States. During the Kansas-Nebraska Act crisis in 1854, as President Pierce revived the annexation scheme, some southerners planned to seize Cuba by force. Although the expedition never embarked, its prospect outraged antislavery Republicans eager to halt slavery's expansion and protect free labor.

Yet another aggressive American design on Cuba emerged in the Ostend Manifesto in October 1854. Written after a meeting among the American foreign ministers to Britain, France, and Spain, the document advocated conquest of Cuba if it could not be purchased. But antislavery northerners saw schemes of the Slave Power. The Ostend controversy forced temporary abandonment of annexation efforts, but as the fires in Bleeding Kansas subsided in 1858, President Buchanan reignited Cuba fever. A fierce Senate debate over another purchase offer in early 1859 ended in bitter division over the extension of slavery's domain.

The failure of Cuban annexation was intertwined with the meaning of the United States as a slaveholding republic. "I want Cuba . . . for the planting or spreading of slavery," said the Mississippian Albert G. Brown in 1858. In America's links to the world—90 miles from the Florida coast—just as in domestic affairs, the expansion of slavery poisoned the body politic.

Despite the failure of filibustering expeditions, the effort to annex Cuba continued throughout James Buchanan's presidential administration. This cartoon portrays Sam Houston, the famed Texan and proponent of American expansion, rowing the boat for a harpoonist in quest of the whale, Cuba. The dream of appropriating Cuba to the United States died very hard in the antebellum era. *Vanity Fair,* June 1860.

(© Bettmann/Corbis)

Opposition to the extension of slavery helped create the Republican Party, but members carefully broadened their appeal by adopting other causes. Their coalition ideology consisted of several elements: resentment of southern political power, devotion to unionism, opposition to slavery based on a belief in free-labor, and moral revulsion to slavery and racial prejudice. As the *New York Tribune* editor Horace Greeley wrote in 1860, "an Anti-Slavery man per se cannot be elected." But, "a Tariff, River-and-Harbor, Pacific Railroad, Free Homestead man, may succeed although he is Anti-Slavery."

Southern Democrats
In the South, the disintegration of the Whig Party left many at loose ends politically, including wealthy planters, smaller slaveholders, and urban businessmen. In the tense atmosphere of sectional crisis, southerners were highly susceptible to strong states' rights positions and the defense of slavery. Hence, most formerly Whig slaveholders joined the Democratic Party.

Since Andrew Jackson's day, however, nonslaveholding yeomen had been the heart of the Democratic Party. Democratic politicians, though often slaveowners, lauded the common man and claimed to advance his interests. According to the southern version of republicanism, white citizens in slave society enjoyed liberty and equality because black people were enslaved. Jefferson Davis explained in 1851 that in the South, slavery elevated every white to "stand upon the broad level of equality with the rich man." To retain the support of ordinary whites, southern Democrats appealed to racism, asking: "Shall negroes govern white men, or white men govern negroes?"

Racial fears and traditional political loyalties kept the political alliance between yeoman farmers and planters intact through the 1850s. Across class lines, white southerners united against what they perceived as the Republican Party's capacity to cause slave unrest. In the South, no viable party emerged to replace the Whigs, and political realignment sharpened sectional identity.

Political leaders of both sections used race in their arguments about opportunity. The *Montgomery* (Alabama) *Mail* warned southern whites in 1860 that Republicans intended "to free the negroes and force amalgamation between them and the children of the poor men of the South." Republicans warned northern workers that if slavery entered the territories, the reservoir of opportunity would be poisoned.

Bleeding Kansas
The Kansas-Nebraska Act spawned violence as land-hungry partisans clashed in Kansas Territory. Abolitionists and religious groups sent armed Free-Soil settlers; southerners sent reinforcements to establish slavery and prevent "northern hordes" from stealing Kansas. Conflicts led to bloodshed, and soon the nation was talking about Bleeding Kansas.

Politics in the territory resembled war more than democracy. During 1855 elections for a territorial legislature, thousands of proslavery Missourians—known as Border Ruffians—invaded the polls and ran up a fraudulent majority for proslavery candidates. They murdered and intimidated free-state settlers. The resulting legislature legalized slavery. Free-Soilers responded with an unauthorized convention at which they created their own government and constitution.

In May, a proslavery posse sent to arrest Free-Soil leaders sacked the town of Lawrence, Kansas, killing several people and destroying a hotel. In revenge, the radical abolitionist John Brown and his followers murdered five proslavery settlers living along Pottawatomie Creek. The victims' heads and limbs were hacked by heavy broadswords. Brown did not wield a sword, but he fired a fatal shot into the head of one foe. Soon, armed bands of guerrillas battled over land claims and slavery.

Violence touched the U.S. Senate in May 1856, when Charles Sumner of Massachusetts denounced "the Crime against Kansas." Radically opposed to slavery, Sumner assailed the president, the South, and Senator Andrew P. Butler of South Carolina. Butler's cousin, Representative Preston Brooks, approached Sumner, raised his cane in defense of his kin's honor, and beat Sumner on the head.

Shocked northerners recoiled from another seeming case of wanton southern violence and assault on free speech. William Cullen Bryant, editor of the *New York Evening Post,* asked, "Has it come to this, that we must speak with bated breath in the presence of our southern masters?" Popular opinion in Massachusetts supported Sumner; South Carolina voters reelected Brooks.

Election of 1856

The election of 1856 reflected extreme polarization. For their nominee, Democrats chose James Buchanan of Pennsylvania, who, as ambassador to Britain for four years, was uninvolved in territorial controversies. Superior organization helped Buchanan win 1.8 million votes and the election, but he owed his victory to southern support. Hence, he was labeled "a northern man with southern principles."

Eleven of sixteen free states voted against Buchanan, and Democrats did not regain those states for decades. The Republican candidate, John C. Frémont, won those eleven free states and 1.3 million votes; Republicans became the dominant party in the North after only two years of existence. The coming battle would pit a sectional Republican Party against an increasingly divided Democratic Party, with voter turnouts as high as 75 to 80 percent in many states.

SLAVERY AND THE NATION'S FUTURE

For years Congress tried to settle the slavery issue. In 1857 the Supreme Court attempted to definitively silence controversy.

Dred Scott Case

A Missouri slave named Dred Scott and his wife, Harriet Robinson Scott, sued for their freedom. Scott argued that his former owner, an army surgeon, had taken him into and kept him for years in Illinois, a free state, and taken him to Fort Snelling in the Minnesota Territory, from which slavery was banned by the Missouri Compromise. Scott first won and then lost his case on appeal in the Supreme Court.

Harriet and Dred Scott were legally married at Fort Snelling in 1836 when Dred was forty and Harriet seventeen. She had lived as a slave on free soil for about five years and had four children, also born on free soil: two sons who died in infancy and two daughters, Eliza and Lizzie, who lived. The quest for freedom papers through a lawsuit—begun in 1846 as two cases, one in his name and one in hers—possibly came as much from Harriet's desire to protect her teenage daughters from potential sale as from the aging Dred. Indeed, her legal case may have been stronger than Dred's, but lawyers subsumed her case into his during the eleven-year appeal process.

With hesitation, the Supreme Court agreed to hear *Dred Scott v. Sanford*. Two northern justices indicated that they would dissent from the assigned opinion and argue for Scott's freedom and the constitutionality of the Missouri Compromise. Their decision emboldened southerners on the Court, who were eager to declare the 1820 geographical restriction on slavery unconstitutional. Several justices felt they should resolve sectional strife once and for all.

In March 1857, Chief Justice Roger B. Taney of Maryland delivered the majority opinion of a divided Court (the vote was 7 to 2). Taney declared that Scott was not a citizen of the United States or Missouri, that residence in free territory did not make Scott free, and that Congress had no power to bar slavery from any territory. The decision not only overturned a thirty-seven year-old sectional compromise, it also invalidated the Wilmot Proviso and popular sovereignty.

The Slave Power seemed to have won a major constitutional victory. African Americans were especially dismayed, for Taney's decision asserted that the founders never intended for blacks to be citizens. Taney was mistaken, however. African Americans had been citizens in several original states and had voted.

Nevertheless, the ruling seemed to shut the door permanently on black hopes for justice. In northern black communities, rage and despair prevailed. Many

Dred Scott and his wife, from Frank Leslie's Illustrated Newspaper.
(Library of Congress)

fugitive slaves sought refuge in Canada; others considered the Caribbean or even Africa. One black abolitionist said that the *Dred Scott* decision made slavery "the supreme law of the land." In this state of social dislocation and fear, blacks contemplated whether they had any future in the United States.

Northern whites who rejected the decision were suspicious of the circumstances that produced it. Five of the nine justices were southerners; three northern justices dissented or refused to concur in parts of the decision. The only northerner who supported Taney's opinion, Justice Robert Grier of Pennsylvania, was close to President Buchanan. In fact, Buchanan secretly applied improper but effective influence on him.

The decision seemed to confirm every northern charge against the aggressive Slave Power. The *Cincinnati Freeman* asked, "What security have the Germans and the Irish that their children will not, within a hundred years, be reduced to slavery in this land of their adoption?"

Abraham Lincoln and the Slave Power

Republican politicians used these fears to strengthen their antislavery coalition. Abraham Lincoln declared as early as 1854 that the nation wanted the territories put to best use as "homes of free white people. This they cannot be, to any considerable extent, if slavery shall be planted within them."

More important, Lincoln warned of slavery's increasing control over the nation. While the founders recognized slavery's existence, the public, Lincoln argued in the "House Divided" speech of 1858, believed that slavery would die naturally or by legislation. The next step in the unfolding Slave Power conspiracy, Lincoln alleged, would be a Supreme Court decision "declaring that the Constitution does not permit a State to exclude slavery from its limits." Indeed, lawsuits soon challenged state laws that freed slaves brought within their borders.

By endorsing the South's doctrine of state sovereignty, the Court had in effect declared that the Republican Party's central position—no extension of slavery—was unconstitutional. Republicans could only repudiate the decision, appealing to a higher law or hope to change the personnel of the Court. They did both and gained politically as fear of the Slave Power grew.

Lecompton Constitution and Disharmony Among Democrats

Northern voters were alarmed by the prospect that the territories would be opened to slavery. To retain their support, northern Democrats like Stephen Douglas had to reassure these voters. Yet, given his presidential ambitions, Douglas could not alienate southern Democrats.

Douglas chose to stand by popular sovereignty, even if the result angered southerners. In 1857 Kansans voted on a proslavery constitution drafted at Lecompton. It was defeated by more than ten thousand votes in a referendum boycotted by most proslavery voters. Kansans did not want slavery, yet President Buchanan tried to force the Lecompton Constitution through Congress to hastily organize the territory.

Never had the Slave Power's influence over the government seemed more blatant; the Buchanan administration and southerners demanded a proslavery outcome, contrary to majority will in Kansas. Douglas threw his weight against the Lecompton Constitution, infuriating southern Democrats like Senator Albert G. Brown of Mississippi. Increasingly, though, many southerners believed that their sectional rights would be safe only in a separate nation. And northern Democrats, led by Douglas, found it harder to support the territorial protection for slavery that southern Democrats insisted was a constitutional right.

DISUNION

But in the late 1850s, most Americans were not always caught up in the slavery crisis. Daily, they were preoccupied with personal affairs, especially the economic panic that began in spring 1857. In the Midwest, clerks, mechanics, domestics, railroad hands, and lumber camp workers lost jobs by the thousands. Bankers did not know what to do about a weak credit system caused by frenzied western land speculation earlier in the decade. In parts of the South, such as Georgia, the panic intensified class divisions between upcountry yeomen and coastal slaveholding planters. Farmers blamed the tight money policies of Georgia's budding commercial banking system on wealthy planters who controlled the state's Democratic Party.

The panic was caused by several shortcomings of the unregulated American banking system, by speculation in western lands and railroads, and by a weak and overburdened credit system. By 1858 Philadelphia had 40,000 unemployed workers and New York City, nearly 100,000. Fear of bread riots and class warfare gripped many northern cities. Blame for the crisis became sectionalized, as southerners saw their system justified by the temporary collapse of industrial prosperity and northerners feared further incursions of the Slave Power on an insecure future.

John Brown's Raid on Harpers Ferry

Born in Connecticut in 1800, John Brown was raised by staunchly religious antislavery parents. Between 1820 and 1855, he engaged in some twenty business ventures, failing in nearly all of them. In his abolitionism, Brown relied on an Old Testament conception of justice—"an eye for an eye"—and he believed that slavery was an unjustifiable state of war conducted by one group against another. He also believed that violence in a righteous cause was a holy act. To Brown, the destruction of slavery in America required revolutionary ideology and revolutionary acts.

On October 16, 1859, Brown led a small band of eighteen whites and blacks in an attack on the federal arsenal at Harpers Ferry, Virginia. Hoping to trigger a slave rebellion, Brown failed and was quickly captured. In a celebrated trial in November and a widely publicized execution in December in Charles Town, Virginia, Brown became one of the most enduring martyrs, as well as villains, of American history. White southerners' outrage intensified when they learned first that Brown received financial backing from several prominent abolitionists, and second that such northern intellectuals as Ralph Waldo Emerson and Henry David Thoreau praised Brown as a holy warrior. The South almost universally interpreted Brown's attack at Harpers Ferry as an act of terrorism and the fulfillment of their dread of abolition emissaries who would infiltrate the region to incite slave rebellion. When Brown went to the gallows, he handed a note to his jailer with the famous prediction "I John Brown am now quite certain that the crimes of this guilty land will never be purged away, but with blood.

Election of 1860

Many Americans believed that the election of 1860 would decide the Union's fate. Until that election the Democratic Party was the only party that was truly national in scope, often, as one Mississippi editor wrote, waving "the olive branch over the troubled waters of politics." But, at its 1860 convention in Charleston, South Carolina, the Democratic Party split.

Stephen Douglas wanted his party's presidential nomination, but he feared alienating northern voters by accepting the southern position on the territories. Southern Democrats, however, insisted on recognition of their rights, as defined by the *Dred Scott* decision. When Douglas obtained a majority for his version of the platform, delegates from the Deep South walked out. Compromise attempts failed, and the Democrats presented two nominees: Douglas for the northern wing and Vice President John C. Breckinridge of Kentucky for the southern.

Republicans nominated Abraham Lincoln, a reflection of the Midwest's growing power. Lincoln was also perceived as more moderate on slavery than the early front runner, Senator William H. Seward of New York. A Constitutional Union Party nominated John Bell of Tennessee.

Bell's only issue in the campaign was preserving the Union, appealing to history, sentiment, and moderation to hold the country together. Douglas sought to unite his northern and southern supporters, while Breckinridge backed away from the appearance of extremism, and his supporters in several states stressed his unionism. Although Lincoln and the Republicans denied any intent to interfere with slavery where it existed, they stood firm against its extension into the territories.

The 1860 election was sectional in character, and the only one in American history in which the losers refused to accept the result. Lincoln won, but Douglas, Breckinridge, and Bell together received a majority of the votes. Douglas had broad-based support but won few states. Breckinridge carried nine southern states in the Deep South. Bell won pluralities in Virginia, Kentucky, and Tennessee. Lincoln prevailed in the North, but in the four slave states that remained loyal to the Union (Missouri, Kentucky, Maryland, and Delaware—the border states) he gained only a plurality (see Table 14.3). Lincoln's victory was won in the electoral college. He polled only 40 percent of the total vote and was not even on the ballot in ten slave states.

Opposition to slavery's extension was the core issue for Lincoln and the Republican Party. And abolitionists and Free-Soil supporters in the North held them to it. Meanwhile, in the South, proslavery advocates and secessionists whipped up public opinion and demanded that state conventions assemble to consider secession.

Lincoln did not soften his party's position on the territories. Although many conservative Republicans—eastern businessmen and former Whigs who did not feel strongly about slavery—hoped for a compromise, the original and most committed Republicans—old Free-Soilers and antislavery Whigs—held firm on slavery expansion.

In winter 1860–1861, the Kentucky senator John J. Crittenden offered a late-hour compromise. Hoping to avert disunion, Crittenden proposed that the two sections divide the territories between them at the Missouri Compromise line, 36°30′. When Lincoln ruled out concessions on the territorial issue, Crittenden's peacemaking effort collapsed.

TABLE 14.3   Presidential Vote in 1860 (by State)

Lincoln (Republican)*	Carried all northern states and all electoral votes except three in New Jersey
Breckinridge (Southern Democrat)	Carried all slave states except Virginia, Kentucky, Tennessee, Missouri
Bell (Constitutional Union)	Carried Virginia, Kentucky, Tennessee
Douglas (Northern Democrat)	Carried only Missouri

*Lincoln received only 26,000 votes in the entire South and was not even on the ballot in ten slave states. Breckinridge was not on the ballot in three northern states.

R. H. Howell, after Henry Cleenewerck, *The First Flag of Independence Raised in the South*. Lithograph, Savannah, Georgia, 1860. On the night of November 8, 1860, a huge crowd gathered in Johnson Square, Savannah, to protest Lincoln's election victory. The special banner on the obelisk reads "Our Motto Southern Rights, Equality of the States, Don't Tread on Me," drawing on traditions from the Revolutionary War.
(Library of Congress)

Secession and the Confederate States of America

Meanwhile, on December 20, 1860, South Carolina passed an ordinance of secession. Secession strategists concentrated on the most extreme proslavery state, hoping that South Carolina's move would induce other states to follow toward disunion.

No longer was secession unthinkable; secessionists now argued that other states should follow suit and that those favoring compromise could make a better deal outside the Union than in it.

Southern extremists called separate state conventions and passed secession ordinances in Mississippi, Florida, Alabama, Georgia, Louisiana, and Texas. By February 1861 these states joined South Carolina to form a new government in Montgomery, Alabama: the Confederate States of America. The delegates at Montgomery chose Jefferson Davis of Mississippi as their president, and the Confederacy began to function independently of the United States.

This apparent unanimity of action was deceiving. Many southerners who voted in the 1860 U.S. presidential election stayed home a few months later rather than vote for delegates who would decide on secession. And in some state conventions the secession vote was close—decided by overrepresentation of plantation districts. Four Upper South states—Virginia, North Carolina, Tennessee, and Arkansas—rejected secession and did not join the Confederacy until after fighting commenced. In the border states, popular sentiment was divided; minorities in Kentucky and Missouri tried to secede, but these slave states ultimately came under Union control, along with Maryland and Delaware (see Map 14.2).

Secession posed new and troubling issues for southerners, especially the possibility of war. Analysis of election returns from 1860 and 1861 indicates that slaveholders and nonslaveholders were beginning to part company politically.

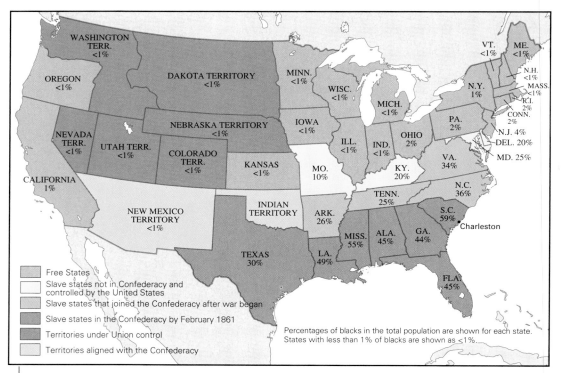

Map 14.2   The Divided Nation—Slave and Free Areas, 1861

After fighting began, the Upper South joined the Deep South in the Confederacy. How does the nation's pattern of division correspond to the distribution of slavery and the percentage of blacks in the population?

Slaveholding counties strongly supported secession. But most counties with few slaves took an antisecession position or were staunchly Unionist (see Figure 14.1). With war looming, yeomen were beginning to ask themselves how far they would go to support slavery and slaveowners.

In speeches and writings, secession commissioners from the seven seceded states revealed why the Deep South broke away. Repeatedly they stressed independence as the only way to preserve white racial security and the slave system. On "slavery," said the Alabama commissioner, Stephen Hale, to the Kentucky legislature, rested "the wealth and prosperity of the southern people." Only secession, Hale contended, could sustain the "heaven-ordained superiority of the white over the black race."

Fort Sumter and Outbreak of War

The dilemma facing President Lincoln on inauguration day in March 1861 was how to maintain the authority of the federal government without provoking war. His solution: by holding onto forts in the states that left the Union, he could assert federal sovereignty while waiting for a restoration. But Jefferson Davis could not claim to lead a sovereign nation if the Confederate ports were under foreign (that is, U.S.) control. The two sides collided in the early morning of April 12, 1861, at Fort Sumter in Charleston harbor. When a federal garrison there ran low on food, Lincoln notified South Carolinians that he was sending a supply ship. For the

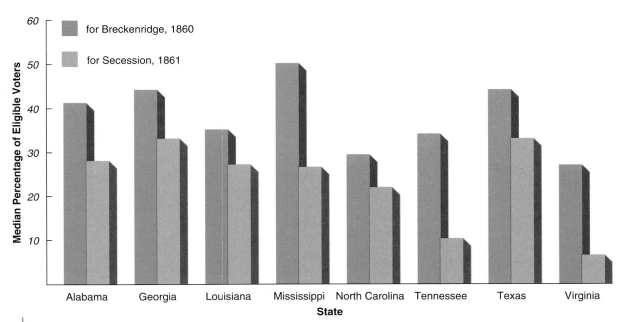

Figure 14.1   Voting Returns of Counties with Few Slaveholders, Eight Southern States, 1860 and 1861
This graph depicts voting in counties whose percentage of slaveholders ranked them among the lower half of the counties in their state. How does voters' support for secession in 1861 compare with support for John Breckinridge, the southern Democratic candidate in 1860? Why was their support for secession so weak? At this time counties with many slaveholders were giving increased support to secession.

Montgomery government, the alternatives were to attack the fort or acquiesce to Lincoln's authority. The secretary of war ordered local commanders to obtain a surrender or attack the fort. After two days of heavy bombardment, the federal garrison surrendered. Confederates permitted U.S. troops to sail away on unarmed vessels while Charlestonians celebrated. The Civil War—the bloodiest war in America's history—had begun.

Causation

Historians have long debated the causes of the Civil War. Some have interpreted it as the clash of two civilizations on divergent historical trajectories. But the issues dividing Americans in 1861 were fundamental to the republic's future. Republican ideology tended toward abolishing slavery, even though Republicans denied such intentions. Southern ideology led to establishing slavery everywhere, though southern leaders, too, denied such motives.

These positions hardened in American political life during the decade and a half before secession. In a postelection letter to his friend Alexander Stephens of Georgia, soon to be vice president of the Confederacy, Lincoln stated, "You think slavery is right and ought to be expanded; while we think it is wrong and ought to be restricted. That I suppose is the rub." Without slavery, there would have been no war. Many Americans still believe that the war was about states' rights. But the significance of states' rights is always in the cause in which it is employed. To borrow from Douglass, it is the meaning within the fight that we must understand.

Terrorist or Freedom Fighter?

The greatest significance of John Brown's 1859 raid on Harpers Ferry rests in its hold on American memory. Brown has been at once one of the most beloved and loathed figures in American history. In the song that bears his name, "John Brown's Body," a popular marching tune during the Civil War, his "soul goes marching on."

In the wake of his execution, in painting, song, and poetry people constructed a John Brown mythology. Was he a Christ-like figure who died for the nation's sins, who had to commit crimes to expose the nation's larger crime? Or was he a terrorist, who murdered according to his vision of God's will? Brown can be inspiring and disturbing, a warrior saint and a monster. He represents the highest ideals and the most ruthless deeds. He killed for justice and was hanged as a traitor. Over the years many organizations have adopted John Brown as their justifying symbol, from left-wing students opposing American foreign policy to current anti-abortion groups who target clinics and doctors. In today's world, terrorism and revolutionary violence are often in the news. Suicide bombers attack buses in Israel; a federal building exploded in Oklahoma City; Al Qaeda operatives blew up trains in Madrid; American embassies are attacked in Africa and Europe; on September 11, 2001, four hijacked passenger airplanes became weapons of death that brought terrorism to American soil as never before; and in Iraq an insurgency resists American occupation, as a country falls into sectarian civil war between Shi'ites and Sunnis. The story of John Brown's 1859 raid forces us to ask when and how revolutionary violence—for political or spiritual end—is justified. That is his legacy for a people and a nation.

Summary

The War with Mexico fostered massive land acquisition, which forced a debate about slavery in the West. The Compromise of 1850 attempted to settle the dispute but only exacerbated sectional tensions, leading to the fateful Kansas-Nebraska Act of 1854, which tore asunder the political party system and gave birth to an antislavery coalition. With Bleeding Kansas and the *Dred Scott* decision by 1857, Americans faced clear and dangerous choices about the future of labor and the meaning of liberty in an expanding society. Finally, by 1859, when the radical abolitionist John Brown attacked Harpers Ferry to foment a slave insurrection, southerners and northerners began viewing each other in conspiratorial terms. Meanwhile, African Americans, slave and free, fled from slave catchers and expected violent resolutions to their dreams of freedom in America.

Throughout the 1840s and 1850s, many able leaders worked to avert disunion. Secession dismayed northern editors and voters and plunged some planters into depression. Paul Cameron, the largest slaveowner in North Carolina, confessed to being "very unhappy. I love the Union." Many blacks, however, shared Frederick Douglass's outlook. "The contest must now be decided," he wrote in March 1861, "and decided forever, which of the two, Freedom or Slavery, shall give law to this Republic."

Why had all efforts to prevent war failed? The emotions bound up in attacking and defending slavery's future were too powerful, and the interests it affected too vital for compromise. During the 1850s, every southern victory in territorial expansion increased fear of the Slave Power, and each new expression of Free-Soil sentiment prompted slaveholders to harden their demands. In the profoundest sense, slavery was the root of the war. As a people and a nation, Americans reached the most fateful turning point in their history. Resolution would come from the battlefield.

Chapter Review

THE WAR WITH MEXICO AND ITS CONSEQUENCES

How did Polk make the war with Mexico inevitable?

President Polk wanted to expand America's borders into territory occupied by Great Britain and Mexico. He negotiated with Great Britain, securing for America the Oregon territory it desired, but he was aggressive in his dealings with Mexico. He supported annexation of Texas and contested the U.S. border with Mexico. Finally, Polk attempted to buy a tract of land extending into California, but when Mexico refused, he sent in troops. A three-day stand-off resulted in the temporary retreat of U.S. cavalry, but also the onset of war with Mexico.

1850: COMPROMISE OR ARMISTICE?

What were the two troubling flaws inherent in the Compromise of 1850?

The Compromise of 1850 attempted to resolve the debate between the North and South over slavery in the territories. In the end it only furthered controversy. First, it left the definition of popular sovereignty unclear so that southerners could interpret it to mean that a region could not ban slavery during the territorial stage, whereas northerners believed it was up to the people to decide. Second, the Fugitive Slave Act enabled slave owners to present evidence in state courts that a slave had escaped, which would then serve as proof of slave status even in free states and territories—and without investigation into its truth. Abolitionists feared that free blacks would be vulnerable to kidnapping and enslavement. Moreover, the law made it a felony to harbor fugitives and said northerners could be compelled to hunt runaway slaves.

SLAVERY EXPANSION AND COLLAPSE OF THE PARTY SYSTEM

How did slavery fuel the collapse of the party system?

It came in the form of the Kansas-Nebraska Act, which ultimately eroded the 1850 Compromise, and prompted sectional divisions within the political parties that led to each party's breakdown. The act established the Kansas and Nebraska territories, but it applied popular sovereignty to let the territories decide what to do about slavery. Northerners argued that since the territories were within the Louisiana Purchase, they were subject to the Missouri Compromise (which prohibited slavery from latitude 36°30′ north to the Canadian border). When the Act was passed in 1854, sectional divisions intensified. The weakened Whig Party split into northern and southern wings. Democrats' support in the North plummeted, costing them most of their congressional seats and control of all but two state legislatures. In late 1854, antislavery Whigs and Democrats, Free-Soilers, and reformers throughout the Old Northwest formed the new Republican Party to keep slavery from the territories.

SLAVERY AND THE NATION'S FUTURE

How did the issue of slavery—and the Dred Scott decision—further divide the nation?

The Dred Scott decision validated northern fears of a southern slave power, and inspired new fears about the territories being open to slavery. The Supreme Court was ultimately stacked in favor of the southern position on slavery and its extension into the new territories. Five of the nine justices were southerners. The court's decision in the Dred Scott case—that Scott was a slave despite the fact that he lived in the free territory of Missouri and that Congress could not make any laws that barred slavery—invalidated popular sovereignty, the Wilmot Proviso, and the Missouri Compromise.

DISUNION

What were the final straws leading to secession and the dissolution of the Union?

Lincoln's contested election by his Democratic rivals, along with the inability to reach a compromise on the extension of slavery in the territories, ultimately fueled the movement to secede. When Lincoln rejected a compromise that would divide the territories into slave and free at the Missouri Compromise line (36°30′), hopes for preventing secession collapsed. South Carolina passed the first secession ordinance in December 1860; Mississippi, Florida, Alabama, Georgia, Louisiana, and Texas followed. A month after Lincoln's inauguration, these states established their own national capitol in Montgomery, Alabama, dubbing themselves the Confederate States of America.

SUGGESTIONS FOR FURTHER READING

Edward L. Ayers, *What Caused the Civil War: Reflections on the South and Southern History* (2005)

Richard J. Carwardine, *Lincoln* (2003)

Charles Dew, *Apostles of Disunion: Southern Secession Commissioners and the Causes of the Civil War* (2001)

Nicole Etcheson, *Bleeding Kansas: Contested Liberty in the Civil War Era* (2004)

Don E. Fehrenbacher, *The Slaveholding Republic: An Account of the United States Government's Relations to Slavery* (2001)

Eric Foner, *Free Soil, Free Labor, Free Men: The Ideology of the Republican Party* (1970)

Robert W. Johannsen, *To the Halls of the Montezumas: The Mexican War and the American Imagination* (1985)

Michael A. Morrison, *Slavery and the American West: The Eclipse of Manifest Destiny and the Coming of the Civil War* (1997)

David S. Reynolds, *John Brown, Abolitionist: The Man Who Killed Slavery, Sparked the Civil War, and Seeded Civil Rights* (2005)

Richard H. Sewell, *Ballots for Freedom: Antislavery Politics in the United States* (1976)

Transforming Fire: The Civil War

S lave pens were the ugly crossroads of American history. Wallace Turnage, a seventeen-year-old slave from a cotton plantation in Pickens County, Alabama, entered wartime Mobile in December 1862 through the slave traders' yard; he would leave Mobile from that same yard twenty months later.

Turnage was born on a tobacco farm near Snow Hill, North Carolina, in 1846. In mid-1860, as the nation teetered on disunion, he was sold to a Richmond, Virginia, slave trader named Hector Davis. Turnage worked in Davis's three-story slave jail, organizing daily auctions until he was sold for $1,000 in 1861 to a cotton planter from Pickens County, Alabama. Frequently whipped, the desperate teenager tried four times over the next two years to escape to Mississippi. He was captured each time and returned to his owner.

Frustrated, his owner sold Turnage for $2,000 at the Mobile slave traders' yard to a wealthy merchant in the port city. During 1864, as Mobile came under siege, its slaves were enlisted to build trenchworks. Turnage did many urban tasks for his new owner's family, including driving their carriage on errands.

In early August, Turnage crashed the old carriage on a Mobile street. In anger, his owner took him to the slave pen, hiring the jailer to administer thirty lashes in the whipping house. Stripped naked, his hands tied in ropes, Turnage was hoisted up on a hook on the wall. When it was over, his owner instructed Wallace to walk home. Instead, Turnage "took courage," as he wrote in his postwar narrative, and walked southwest through the Confederate encampment. The soldiers mistook the bloodied and tattered black teenager for one among hundreds of slaves who did camp labor.

For the next three weeks, Turnage crawled and waded for 25 miles through the snake-infested swamps of the Foul River estuary, down the west edge of Mobile Bay. Nearly starved and

This icon will direct you to interactive activities and study materials on *A People And A Nation*, Brief Edition website: **www.cengage.com/history/norton/peoplenationbrief8e**

Chronology

1861	Battle of Bull Run occurs.
	McClellan organizes the Union Army.
	Union blockade begins.
	U.S. Congress passes the first confiscation act.
	Trent affair occurs.
1862	Union captures Fort Henry and Fort Donelson.
	U.S. Navy captures New Orleans.
	Battle of Shiloh shows the war's destructiveness.
	Confederacy enacts conscription.
	McClellan's Peninsula Campaign fails to take Richmond.
	U.S. Congress passes the second confiscation act, initiating emancipation.
	Confederacy mounts an offensive in Maryland and Kentucky.
	Battle of Antietam ends Lee's drive into Maryland in September.
	British intervention in the war on the Confederate side is averted.
1863	Emancipation Proclamation takes effect.
	U.S. Congress passes the National Banking Act.
	Union enacts conscription.
	African American soldiers join the Union Army.
	Food riots occur in southern cities.
	Battle of Chancellorsville ends in Confederate victory but Jackson's death.

	Union wins key victories at Vicksburg and Gettysburg.
	Draft riots take place in New York City.
	Battle of Chattanooga leaves the South vulnerable to Sherman's march into Georgia.
1864	Battles of the Wilderness and Spotsylvania produce heavy casualties on both sides in the efforts to capture and to defend Richmond.
	Battle of Cold Harbor continues the carnage in Virginia.
	Lincoln requests a Republican Party plank abolishing slavery.
	Sherman captures Atlanta.
	Confederacy begins to collapse on the home front.
	Lincoln wins reelection, eliminating any Confederate hopes for a negotiated end to war.
	Jefferson Davis proposes emancipation within the Confederacy.
	Sherman marches through Georgia to the sea.
1865	Sherman marches through the Carolinas.
	U.S. Congress approves the Thirteenth Amendment.
	Lee abandons Richmond and Petersburg.
	Lee surrenders at Appomattox Court House.
	Lincoln is assassinated.
	Death toll in war reaches 620,000.

narrowly escaping Confederate patrols, Turnage made it to Cedar Point, where he could see Dauphin Island, now occupied by Union forces. Alligators swam nearby, as Turnage hid from Confederates in a swampy den. He remembered: "It was death to go back and it was death to stay there and freedom was before me."

Then, Turnage noticed an old rowboat that rolled in with the tide. The veteran runaway began to row out into the bay. He suddenly "heard the crash of oars and behold there was eight Yankees in a boat." Turnage jumped into the Union gunboat. For a stunning few moments, he remembered, the oarsmen "were struck with silence" by the frail young black man crouched before them. Turnage looked back at Confederate soldiers on the shore. Then he took his first breaths of freedom.

The Civil War brought astonishing changes to individuals and daily life, North and South. Millions of men were swept into training camps and regiments. Armies numbering in the hundreds of thousands marched over the South, devastating the countryside. Families struggled to survive without men; businesses tried to cope with fewer workers. Women took on extra responsibilities and moved into new workforce jobs, with many becoming nurses and hospital workers.

But southerners also experienced utter defeat. For most, wealth changed to poverty as countless farms were ruined. Late in the war, many southerners yearned only for an end to inflation, shortages, slave escapes, and the death that touched most families. Southern slaves did not always encounter sympathetic liberators such as those who aided Turnage, fed and clothed him, and took him before a Union general, where the freedman could either join a black regiment or become a white officer's camp servant. Until war's end, Turnage cooked for a Maryland captain.

In the North, farm boys and mechanics would be asked for heretofore unimagined sacrifices. Businessmen, however, found new profits in war. The conflict ensured vast government expenditures and lucrative federal contracts. "The battle of Bull Run," predicted an eminent financier in *Harper's Monthly*, "makes the fortune of every man in Wall Street who is not a natural idiot."

Change was most drastic in the South, where secessionists launched a conservative revolution for their section's national independence. Born of states' rights doctrine, the Confederacy had to be transformed into a centralized nation to fight a vast war. Southern whites feared that a peacetime government of Republicans would interfere with slavery and ruin plantation life. Instead, their actions led to a war that turned southern society upside down and imperiled the existence of slavery.

The war created social strains in both North and South. To the alarm of many, the powers of the federal government and of the president increased during the war. Dissent flourished in the North, and antiwar sentiment occasionally erupted into violence. Disaffection was strongest, though, in the Confederacy, where poverty and class resentment threatened the South from within as federal armies assailed it from without.

The Civil War forced a social and political revolution regarding race. It compelled leaders and citizens to finally face the question of slavery. And blacks embraced the most fundamental turning point in their experience as Americans.

- How and why did the Civil War bring social transformations to both South and North?
- How did the war to preserve the Union or for southern independence become the war to free the slaves?
- By 1865, when Americans on all sides searched for the *meaning* of the war they had just fought, what might some of their answers have been?

AMERICA GOES TO WAR, 1861–1862

The onset of hostilities sparked patriotic sentiments, speeches, and ceremonies across the North and South. Northern communities raised companies of volunteers eager to save the Union. Southern recruits boasted of whipping the Yankees and returning home before Christmas. Southern women sewed dashing uniforms for men who would soon be lucky to wear drab gray or butternut homespun. Americans went to war in 1861 filled with romantic notions.

First Battle of Bull Run Through spring 1861, both sides scrambled to organize and train their undisciplined armies. On July 21, 1861, the first battle took place outside Manassas Junction, Virginia, near a stream called Bull Run. General Irvin McDowell and thirty thousand Union troops attacked General P. G. T. Beauregard's twenty-two thousand southerners. Federal forces gained ground, until they ran into a line of Virginia troops under General Thomas "Stonewall" Jackson. Jackson's line held, and the arrival of nine thousand Confederate reinforcements won the day for the South. Union troops fled to Washington.

The unexpected rout at Bull Run proved that although the United States enjoyed an enormous advantage in resources, victory would not be easy. Pro-Union feeling was growing in western Virginia, and loyalties were divided in the four border slave states—Missouri, Kentucky, Maryland, and Delaware. But the rest of the Upper South—the states of North Carolina, Virginia, Tennessee, and Arkansas—joined the Confederacy. Half a million southerners volunteered to fight—so many that the Confederate government could hardly arm them all. The United States therefore undertook a massive mobilization of troops around Washington, D.C.

Lincoln gave command of the army to General George B. McClellan, who proved better at organization and training than fighting. McClellan devoted fall and winter 1861 to readying a force of a quarter-million men to take Richmond, the Confederate capital.

Grand Strategy

While McClellan prepared, the Union began to implement other parts of its strategy, which called for a blockade of southern ports and capture of the Mississippi River. Like a constricting snake, this Anaconda plan would strangle the Confederacy. The Union Navy initially had too few ships to patrol 3,550 miles of coastline. Gradually, the navy increased the blockade's effectiveness, though it never stopped southern commerce completely.

The Confederate strategy was essentially defensive, given the South's claim of independence and the North's resource advantage (see Figure 15.1). But Jefferson Davis called the southern strategy an offensive defensive, taking advantage of opportunities to attack and using its interior transportation lines to concentrate troops at

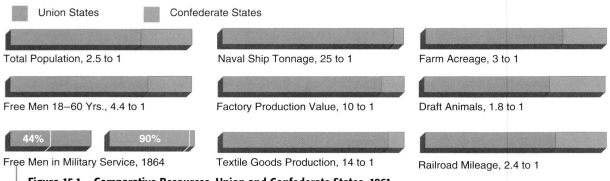

Figure 15.1   Comparative Resources, Union and Confederate States, 1861
The North had vastly superior resources. Although the North's advantages in manpower and industrial capacity proved very important, the South still had to be conquered, its society and its will crushed.
(*The Times Atlas of World History.* Time Books, London, 1978. Used with permission.)

crucial points. The Confederacy did not need to conquer the North; the Union, however, required conquest of the South.

Both sides slighted the importance of the West, that vast expanse between Virginia and the Mississippi River and beyond. Guerrilla warfare broke out in 1861 in politically divided Missouri, and key locations along the Mississippi and other western rivers would prove crucial prizes in the North's eventual victory. Beyond the Mississippi, the Confederacy hoped to gain an advantage by negotiating treaties with the Creeks, Choctaws, Chickasaws, Cherokees, Seminoles, and smaller groups of Plains Indians. Meanwhile, the Republican U.S. Congress carved the West into territories in anticipation of state making. For most Indians west of the Mississippi, the Civil War launched nearly three decades of an enveloping strategy of conquest, relocation, and slaughter.

Union Naval Campaign

The last half of 1861 brought no major land battles, but in late summer, Union naval forces captured Cape Hatteras and Hilton Head, one of the Sea Islands off Port Royal, South Carolina. A few months later, federal naval operations established significant beachheads along the Confederate coastline, including vital points in North Carolina, as well as Fort Pulaski, which defended Savannah.

The coastal victories off South Carolina foreshadowed a revolution in slave society. As federal gunboats approached, planters abandoned their land and fled. The Confederate cavalry tried to round up slaves and move them to the interior. But thousands of slaves greeted what they hoped to be freedom with rejoicing and broke the hated cotton gins. Some entered their master's homes and took clothing and furniture. Many runaways poured into Union lines. Unwilling at first to wage a war against slavery, the federal government did not acknowledge the slaves' freedom, though it used their labor. These emancipated slaves, defined by Union officers as war contraband (confiscated enemy property), forced first a debate within the Union Army and government over how to treat the freedmen, and then an attempt to harness their labor and military power.

Spring 1862 brought southerners stronger evidence of the war's gravity. In March, two ironclad ships—the *Monitor* (a Union warship) and the *Merrimack* (a Union ship seized by the Confederacy)—fought off the coast of Virginia. Their battle, though indecisive, ushered in a new era in naval design. In April, Union ships commanded by Admiral David Farragut smashed through log booms blocking the Mississippi River and moved upstream to capture New Orleans. The South's greatest seaport and slave-trading center was now in federal hands.

War in the Far West

Farther west, three Confederate regiments were organized, mostly of Cherokees, but a Union victory at Elkhorn Tavern, Arkansas, shattered southern control of the region. Thereafter, dissension within Native American groups and a Union victory the following year at Honey Springs, Arkansas, reduced Confederate operations in Indian Territory to guerrilla raids.

In the westernmost campaign of the war, from February to May 1862, some three thousand Confederate and four thousand Union forces fought to control New Mexico Territory. The Confederate invasion aimed to seize the trade riches of the

Santa Fe Trail and take possession of gold mines in Colorado and California. But Colorado and New Mexico Unionists fought back, and in a series of battles at Glorieta Pass, 20 miles east of Santa Fe, on March 26 through 28, they blocked the Confederates. By May 1, Confederate forces straggled down the Rio Grande River into Texas, abandoning efforts to take New Mexico.

Grant's Tennessee Campaign and the Battle of Shiloh

Meanwhile, in February 1862, forces in northern Tennessee won significant victories for the Union. A Union commander named Ulysses S. Grant saw the strategic importance of Fort Henry and Fort Donelson, the Confederate outposts guarding the Tennessee and Cumberland Rivers. In just ten days he seized the forts, completely cutting off the Confederates and demanding unconditional surrender of Fort Donelson. A path into Tennessee, Alabama, and Mississippi was now open to the Union Army.

Grant moved into southern Tennessee and the first of the war's shockingly bloody encounters, the Battle of Shiloh. On April 6, Confederate general Albert Sidney Johnston caught federal troops with their backs to the Tennessee River awaiting reinforcements. The Confederates attacked and inflicted heavy damage all day. Close to victory, General Johnston was killed. Union reinforcements arrived that night. The next day the battle turned, and after ten hours of combat, the Confederates withdrew.

Neither side won a decisive victory at Shiloh, yet losses were staggering and the Confederates were forced to retreat into northern Mississippi. Northern troops lost thirteen thousand men (killed, wounded, or captured) out of sixty-three thousand; southerners sacrificed eleven thousand out of forty thousand. Total casualties in this battle exceeded those in all three of America's previous wars combined. Before Shiloh, Grant hoped that southerners would soon tire of the conflict. After Shiloh, he recalled in his 1885 memoir, he "gave up all idea of saving the Union except by complete conquest." Memories of the Shiloh battlefield would haunt the surviving soldiers for the rest of their lives.

McClellan and the Peninsula Campaign

On the Virginia front, President Lincoln had problems with General McClellan. Only thirty-six, McClellan had achieved success as an army officer and railroad president. Habitually overestimating the size of enemy forces, he called repeatedly for reinforcements and ignored Lincoln's directions to advance. McClellan advocated a war of limited aims that would lead to a quick reunion. He intended neither disruption of slavery nor war on noncombatants. McClellan finally sailed his troops down the Chesapeake, landing them on the peninsula between the York and James Rivers, and advanced on Richmond.

After a bloody battle at Fair Oaks from May 31 through June 1, the federal armies moved to within 7 miles of the Confederate capital. The Confederate commanding general, Joseph E. Johnston, was badly wounded at Fair Oaks, and President Jefferson Davis placed his chief military adviser, Robert E. Lee, in command. The fifty-five-year-old Lee was an aristocratic Virginian, a lifelong military officer, and a veteran of distinction from the War with Mexico. Although he initially opposed secession, Lee gave his allegiance to his state and became a staunch Confederate. He soon foiled McClellan's legions.

First, Lee sent Stonewall Jackson's corps of seventeen thousand northwest into the Shenandoah valley behind Union forces, where they threatened Washington, D.C., and drew some federal troops away from Richmond to protect their own capital. Further, in mid-June, in an extraordinary four-day ride around the Union Army, Confederate cavalry under J. E. B. Stuart confirmed the exposed position of McClellan's army north of the Chickahominy River. In the Seven Days Battles from June 26 through July 1, Lee struck at McClellan's army. Lee's daring move of taking the majority of his army northeast and attacking the Union right flank, while leaving only a small force to defend Richmond, forced McClellan to retreat toward the James River.

During the sustained fighting of the Seven Days, Union forces suffered 20,614 casualties and the Confederates, 15,849. By August 3, McClellan withdrew his army to the environs of Washington. Richmond remained safe for almost two more years.

In October 1862 in New York City, photographer Mathew Brady opened an exhibition of photographs from the Battle of Antietam. Although few knew it, Brady's vision was very poor, and this photograph of Confederate dead was actually made by his assistants, Alexander Gardner and James F. Gibson.   (Library of Congress)

Confederate Offensive in Maryland and Kentucky

Buoyed by these results, Jefferson Davis conceived an ambitious plan to gain wartime advantage and recognition by European nations. He ordered a general offensive, sending Lee north into Maryland and Generals Kirby Smith and Braxton Bragg into Kentucky. Calling on residents of Maryland and Kentucky, still slave states, to make peace with his government, Davis also invited northwestern states like Indiana, which sent much of their trade down the Mississippi to New Orleans, to leave the Union. This was a coordinated effort to take the war to the North and force both a military and a political turning point.

The plan was promising, but the offensive ultimately failed. Lee's forces achieved a striking success at the battle of Second Bull Run, August 29 through 30. The entire Union army retreated to the federal capital. Thousands of wounded occupied schools and churches, and two thousand suffered on cots in the U.S. Capitol rotunda.

But in the bloodiest day of the war, September 17, 1862, McClellan turned Lee back from Sharpsburg, Maryland. In this Battle of Antietam, five thousand men died and another eighteen thousand were wounded. McClellan intercepted a battle order, wrapped around cigars for each Confederate corps commander and lost by a courier. But McClellan moved slowly, failed to use his larger forces in simultaneous attacks, and allowed Lee's stricken army to retreat across the Potomac. Lincoln removed McClellan from command.

In Kentucky, Generals Smith and Bragg secured Lexington and Frankfort, but their effort to force the Yankees back to the Ohio River was stopped at the Battle of Perryville on October 8. Bragg's army retreated into Tennessee, where from December 31, 1862, to January 2, 1863, they fought an indecisive but bloody battle at Murfreesboro. Casualties exceeded even those of Shiloh.

Outnumbered and disadvantaged, the South could not continue the offensive. Davis admitted to Confederate representatives that southerners were entering "the darkest and most dangerous period we have yet had."

But 1862 also brought painful lessons to the North. On December 13, Union general Ambrose Burnside, now in command of the Army of the Potomac, unwisely ordered his soldiers to attack Lee's army, which held fortified positions at Fredericksburg, Virginia. Lee's men performed efficiently in killing northerners, and Burnside's repeated assaults up Marye's Heights shocked his opponents, killing 1,300 and wounding 9,600 Union soldiers. The scale of carnage now challenged people on both sides to question the meaning of the war and what they would endure to win it.

WAR TRANSFORMS THE SOUTH

One of the first traditions to fall was the southern preference for local and limited government. States' rights had been a formative ideology for the Confederacy, but state governments were weak operations. To withstand the North's massive power, Jefferson Davis saw the necessity of centralization and moved to thwart the separate aims of states.

The Confederacy and Centralization

Davis brought all arms, supplies, and troops under his control. But by early 1862 the scope and duration of the conflict required more recruits. Tens of thousands of Confederate soldiers volunteered for just one year's service, planning to return home in spring to plant their crops. Faced with a critical troop shortage, in April 1862 the Confederate government enacted the first national conscription (draft) law in American history.

Davis adopted a firm leadership role toward the Confederate Congress, which raised taxes and later passed a tax-in-kind—a tax paid in farm products. Nearly 4,500 agents dispersed to collect the tax. Where opposition arose, the government suspended the writ of habeas corpus (which prevented individuals from being held without trial) and imposed martial law. Still, this tax system proved inadequate for the South's war effort.

To replace the food that men in uniform would have grown, Davis exhorted state governments to require farmers to switch from cash crops to food crops. But army food and labor shortages continued. The War Department impressed slaves to work on fortifications, and after 1861, officers raided farms and carted away grain, meat, wagons, and draft animals to feed the troops. Such raids caused increased hardship and resentment for women managing farms without husbands and sons.

Soon the Confederate administration in Richmond gained control over the southern economy. The Confederate Congress also gave the central government almost complete control of the railroads. A large bureaucracy of over seventy thousand civilians administered these operations. By the war's end, the southern bureaucracy was larger in proportion to population than its northern counterpart.

Confederate Nationalism

Historians have long argued over whether the Confederacy itself was a rebellion, a revolution, or the creation of a genuine nation. Whatever the label, Confederates created a culture and ideology of nationalism. In flags, songs, language, seals, school readers, and other national characteristics, Confederates created their own story and identity.

Southerners believed that the Confederacy was the true legacy of the American Revolution—a bulwark against centralized power that was in keeping with the war for independence. To southerners, theirs was a continuing revolution against the excesses of Yankee democracy, and George Washington (a Virginian) on horseback formed the center of the Confederacy's official seal.

Also central to Confederate nationalism was a refurbished defense of slavery as a benign, protective institution, complete with the image of the faithful slave. In wartime schoolbooks, children were instructed in the divinely inspired, paternalistic character of slavery. A poem popular among whites captured an old slave's rejection of the Emancipation Proclamation.

> Now, Massa, dis is berry fine, dese words
> You've spoke to me,
> No doubt you mean it kindly, but ole Dinah
> Won't be free . . .
> Ole Massa's berry good to me—and though I am
> His slave,
> He treats me like I'se kin to him—and I would
> Rather have
> A home in Massa's cabin, and eat his black
> Bread too,
> Dan leave ole Massa's children and go and
> Lib wid you.

This and other forms of Confederate nationalism collapsed in the war's final year. But it would reappear in the postwar period.

Southern Cities and Industry

Clerks and subordinate officials crowded towns and cities where Confederate departments had offices. Clerks had always been males, but now government girls staffed the Confederate bureaucracy. The sudden migration overwhelmed the housing supply and stimulated new construction. Richmond's population increased 250 percent. Mobile's population jumped from twenty-nine thousand to forty-one thousand; and ten thousand people poured into war-related industries in little Selma, Alabama.

As the Union blockade disrupted imports, the traditionally agricultural South forged new industries. Many planters shared Davis's hope that industrialization would bring "deliverance . . . from all commercial dependence" on the North or the world. Indeed, the Confederacy achieved tremendous industrial development. Chief of Ordnance Josiah Gorgas increased the capacity of Richmond's Tredegar Iron Works and other factories so that by 1865 his Ordnance Bureau was supplying all

Confederate small arms and ammunition. The government constructed new railroad lines and ironworks, using slaves relocated from farms and plantations.

Changing Roles of Women

White women, restricted to narrow roles in antebellum society, gained new responsibilities in wartime. The wives and mothers of soldiers now headed households and performed men's work, including raising crops and tending animals. Women in nonslaveowning families cultivated fields, while wealthier women acted as overseers and managed fieldwork. In cities, white women—previously all but excluded from the labor force—found respectable paying jobs, often in the Confederate bureaucracy. And female schoolteachers appeared in the South for the first time.

Patriotic sacrifice appealed to some women; others resented their new burdens. A Texas woman who struggled to discipline slaves pronounced herself "sick of trying to do a man's business." Others grew angry over shortages and resented contact with lower-class women. Some scorned the war and demanded that their men return to provide for their families.

Human Suffering, Hoarding, and Inflation

For millions of southerners, the war brought privation and suffering. Mass poverty descended on a large minority of the white population, as many yeoman families lost their breadwinners to the army. Women sought help from relatives, neighbors, friends, anyone. Sometimes they pleaded with the Confederate government to discharge their husbands.

The South was in many places so sparsely populated that the conscription of one craftsman could wreak hardship on an entire county. Often people begged together for the exemption or discharge of the local miller, neighborhood tanner, wheelwright, or physician. Most serious, however, was the loss of a blacksmith, who could repair farming tools.

The blockade of Confederate shipping created shortages of important supplies—salt, sugar, coffee, nails—and speculation and hoarding made shortages worse. Greedy businessmen cornered the supply of some commodities; prosperous citizens stocked up on food. The *Richmond Enquirer* criticized a planter who purchased so many supplies that his "lawn and paths looked like a wharf covered with a ship's loads."

Inflation raged out of control, fueled by the Confederate government's heavy borrowing and inadequate taxes, until prices increased almost 7,000 percent. Inflation particularly imperiled urban dwellers without their own food sources. As early as 1861 and 1862, officials predicted that "women and children are bound to come to suffering if not starvation." Hoarding continued, and a rudimentary relief program organized by the Confederacy failed to meet the need.

Inequities of the Confederate Draft

Not all classes sacrificed equally. The Confederate government's policies decidedly favored the upper class. Until the last year of the war, for example, prosperous southerners could avoid military service by hiring substitutes. Well over fifty thousand upper-class southerners purchased substitutes, despite skyrocketing prices that reached

$5,000 or $6,000 per man. Mary Boykin Chesnut knew of one aristocrat who "spent a fortune in substitutes. . . . He is at the end of his row now, for all able-bodied men are ordered to the front."

Anger at such discrimination exploded in October 1862, when the Confederate Congress exempted from military duty anyone who was supervising at least twenty slaves. Protests poured in from across the Confederacy, and North Carolina's legislators condemned the law. Its defenders argued, however, that exemption preserved order and aided food production, and the statute remained on the books.

This Twenty Negro law is indicative of the racial fears many Confederates felt as the war threatened to overturn southern society. But it also fueled desertion and stimulated Unionism in nonslaveholding regions of the South. In Jones County, Mississippi, a wooded area with few slaves or plantations, Newt Knight, a Confederate soldier, led renegades who took over the county, declared allegiance to the Union, and called their district the Free State of Jones. They held out for the remainder of the war as an enclave of Union sympathizers.

The bitterness of letters to Confederate officials suggests the depth of the dissension and class anger. One woman swore to the secretary of war that, unless help was provided to poverty-stricken wives and mothers, "an allwise god . . . will send down his fury . . . [on] those that are in power."

WARTIME NORTHERN ECONOMY AND SOCIETY

War brought change in the North as well. Factories and citizens' associations geared up to support the war, and the federal government and its executive branch gained new powers. Idealism and greed flourished together, and the northern economy proved its awesome productivity. Unlike the South, northern farms and factories weathered the war unharmed.

Northern Business, Industry, and Agriculture

At first the war was a shock to business. Northern firms lost southern markets, and many companies changed their products and found new customers. Southern debts became uncollectible, jeopardizing northern merchants and western banks. In farming regions, families struggled with an aggravated labor shortage caused by army enlistments. Cotton mills lacked cotton, construction declined, and shoe manufacturers sold few of the cheap shoes that planters bought for slaves. Some businesses never recovered.

Certain entrepreneurs, such as wool producers, benefited from shortages of competing products, and soaring demand for war-related goods swept some businesses to new success. The Treasury issued $3.2 billion in bonds and paper money called greenbacks, and the War Department spent over $360 million in revenues from new taxes, including the first income tax. Government contracts soon totaled more than $1 billion.

Secretary of War Edwin M. Stanton's list of the supplies needed by the Ordnance Department indicates the scope of government demand: "7,892 cannon, 11,787 artillery carriages, 4,022,130 small-arms, . . . 1,022,176,474 cartridges for small-arms, 1,220,555,435 percussion caps, . . . 26,440,054 pounds of gunpowder, . . . and

90,416,295 pounds of lead." The government also purchased huge quantities of uniforms, boots, food, camp equipment, saddles, ships, and other necessities. War-related spending revived business in many northern states and saved Massachusetts shoe manufacturers from ruin.

The story of Jay Cooke, a wealthy New York financier, best illustrates the wartime partnership between business and government. Cooke earned hefty commissions marketing government bonds to finance the war. But the financier's profit served the Union cause, as the interests of capitalism and government merged in American history's first era of big government.

War aided heavy industries in the North as well, especially iron and steel production. Although new railroad construction slowed, the manufacture of rails actually increased with demand for repairs. Of future significance was the railroad industry's adoption of a standard gauge (width) for track, which created a unified transportation system.

The northern economy also grew because of a complementary relationship between agriculture and industry. Wartime recruitment and conscription gave western farmers an added incentive to purchase labor-saving machinery. The shift from human labor to machines created new markets for industry and expanded the food supply. Cyrus and William McCormick built an industrial empire in Chicago from the sale of their reapers. Between 1862 and 1864, the manufacture of mowers and reapers doubled to 70,000 yearly; by war's end, 375,000 reapers were in use, triple the number in 1861. Thus northern farm families whose breadwinners went to war did not suffer as much their counterparts in the South.

Northern Workers' Militancy

Northern industrial and urban workers did not fare as well. After the initial slump, jobs became plentiful, but inflation ate up much of a worker's paycheck. The price of coffee tripled; the price of rice and sugar doubled; and between 1860 and 1864, consumer prices rose at least 76 percent, while daily wages rose only 42 percent. Workers' families consequently suffered a substantial decline in their standard of living.

Industrial workers also lost job security. To increase production, some employers replaced workers with labor-saving machines. Others urged the government to promote immigration to secure cheap labor. Workers responded by forming unions and sometimes striking. Indeed, thirteen occupational groups—including tailors, coal miners, and railway engineers—formed national unions during the Civil War, and the number of strikes climbed.

Manufacturers viewed labor activism as a threat and formed statewide or craft-based associations to pool information. They shared blacklists of union members and required new workers to sign yellow dog contracts (promises not to join a union). To put down strikes, they hired strikebreakers from among blacks, immigrants, and women, and sometimes used federal troops.

Labor militancy, however, had little impact on employer profits or profiteering on government contracts. With an immense demand for army supplies, unscrupulous businessmen sold clothing and blankets made of "shoddy"—wool fibers reclaimed from rags or worn cloth. Shoddy goods often came apart in the rain; most of the shoes purchased early in the war were worthless. Contractors sold inferior guns for double the usual price and passed off tainted meat as good. Rampant corruption led to a year-long investigation by the House of Representatives.

Economic Nationalism and Government-Business Partnership

Legitimate enterprises also made healthy profits. The output of woolen mills increased so dramatically that industry dividends nearly tripled. Some cotton mills made record profits, even while reducing output. Brokerage houses earned unheard-of commissions. Railroads increased their business so much that railroad stocks skyrocketed.

Railroads were a leading beneficiary of government largesse. With southern representatives absent from Congress, the northern route of the transcontinental railroad prevailed. In 1862 and 1864, Congress chartered two corporations, the Union Pacific Railroad and the Central Pacific Railroad, and assisted them in connecting Omaha, Nebraska, with Sacramento, California. For each mile of track laid, the railroads received a loan of from $16,000 to $48,000 in government bonds plus 20 square miles of land along a free 400-foot-wide right of way. Overall, the two corporations gained approximately 20 million acres and nearly $60 million in loans.

Other businessmen benefited handsomely from the Morrill Land Grant Act (1862). To promote public education in agriculture, engineering, and military science, Congress granted each state thirty thousand acres of federal land for each of its congressional districts. The law eventually fostered sixty-nine colleges and universities, and early on enriched a few prominent speculators. Similarly, the Homestead Act of 1862 offered cheap and sometimes free land to people who would settle the West and improve their property.

Before the war, banks operating under state charters issued seven thousand different kinds of currency notes, which were difficult to distinguish from forgeries. During the war, Congress and the Treasury Department established a national banking system to issue national bank notes, and by 1865 most state banks were forced by a prohibitive tax to join the national system. This created sounder currency but also inflexibility in the money supply and an eastern-oriented financial structure.

In the excitement of wartime moneymaking, an eagerness to display one's wealth flourished in the largest cities. *Harper's Monthly* reported that "the men button their waistcoats with diamonds . . . and the women powder their hair with gold and silver dust." The *New York Herald* noted: "This war has entirely changed the American character. . . . The individual who makes the most money—no matter how—and spends the most—no matter for what—is considered the greatest man."

The Union Cause

In the first two years of the war, northern morale remained remarkably high for a cause that today may seem abstract—the Union—but at the time meant preservation of a social and political order that people cherished.

Secular and church leaders supported the Union, and many churches endorsed it as God's cause. One Methodist newspaper described the war as a contest between "equalizing, humanizing Christianity" and "disunion, war, selfishness, [and] slavery." Abolitionists campaigned to turn the war into a crusade against slavery. Free black communities and churches both black and white sent clothing, ministers and teachers to aid slaves who flocked to the Union lines. Indeed, thousands of northern blacks volunteered to join the war effort in spite of the initial rejection they received from the Lincoln administration. Thus in wartime northern society, materialism and greed flourished alongside idealism, religious conviction, and self-sacrifice.

Northern Women on Home Front and Battlefront

Northern women, like their southern counterparts, took on new roles. They organized over ten thousand soldiers' aid societies, rolled bandages, and raised $3 million for injured troops. Women pressed for the first trained ambulance corps in the Union Army, and they formed the backbone of the U.S. Sanitary Commission, a civilian agency recognized by the War Department in 1861, which provided nutritional and medical aid to soldiers. Although most of its officers were men, the bulk of the volunteers who ran its seven thousand auxiliaries were women. Women organized elaborate sanitary fairs all across the North to raise money and awareness for soldiers' health and hygiene.

Approximately 3,200 women also served as nurses in frontline hospitals. Yet women had to fight to serve; the professionalization of medicine since the Revolution created a medical system dominated by men, who often did not want women's aid. Even Clara Barton, famous for her working in the worst hospitals at the front, was ousted from her post in 1863. But women such as Dorothea Dix, who sought to reform asylums for the insane, and the Illinois widow Mary Ann Bickerdyke, who served in Sherman's army in the West, established a heroic tradition for Civil War nurses. They also advanced the professionalization of nursing, as several nursing schools were established in northern cities during or after the war.

Women also wrote sentimental war poetry, short stories, novels, and songs that reached thousands of readers in illustrated weeklies, monthly periodicals, and special story papers. In many stories, female characters seek recognition for their loyal service to the Union, while others probe the suffering and death of loved ones. Louisa May Alcott, arrived at her nursing job in Washington, D.C., after the horrific Union defeat at Fredericksburg in December 1862. From her six weeks' experience (she quit because of illness), she later wrote *Hospital Sketches* (1863), providing northern readers a view of the hospitals where loved ones agonized and perished.

By 1863 many women found the liberation of slaves an inspiring subject, as Julia Ward Howe did in her "Battle Hymn of the Republic": "As He died to make men holy/Let us die to make men free."

Walt Whitman's War

The poet Walt Whitman recorded his experiences as a volunteer nurse in Washington, D.C. As he dressed wounds and comforted suffering men, Whitman found "the marrow of the tragedy concentrated in those Army Hospitals." But he also found inspiration in such suffering and a deepening faith in American democracy. In "The Wound Dresser," Whitman meditated unforgettably on the deaths he witnessed:

On, on I go, (open doors of time! open hospital doors!)
The crush'd head I dress, (poor crazed hand tear not the bandage away,)

Nurse Anne Bell.
(U.S. Army Center of Military
History)

The neck of the cavalry-man with the bullet through and through I examine,
Hard the breathing rattles, quite glazed already the eye, yet life struggles hard,
(Come sweet death! be persuaded O beautiful death! In mercy come quickly.)

Indeed, the scale of death in this war shocked many Americans into believing that
the conflict had to be for purposes larger than themselves.

THE ADVENT OF EMANCIPATION

Soldiers and civilians on both sides may have possessed fierce loyalty to their respective wartime cause, but the governments of the United States and the Confederacy
lacked clarity about the war's purpose. Throughout the war's early months, Davis
and Lincoln avoided references to slavery. Davis realized that emphasis on the issue
could increase class conflict in the South. Instead, he told southerners that they were
fighting for constitutional liberty: northerners betrayed the founders' legacy, and
southerners seceded to preserve it.

Lincoln had his reasons for avoiding slavery. It was crucial at first not to antag-
onize the Union's border slave states, whose loyalty was tenuous. Lincoln also
hoped that a pro-Union majority would assert itself in the South and help coax the
South back into the Union. And there were powerful political considerations. Some
Republicans burned with moral outrage over slavery; others were frankly racist,
dedicated to protecting free whites from the Slave Power and the competition of
cheap slave labor. No Republican or northern consensus on slavery existed early in
the war.

Lincoln and Emancipation

Lincoln's compassion, humility, and moral anguish during the war were evident in his speeches and writings. But as a politician, Lincoln distinguished between his convictions and his official acts. The latter were calculated for maximum advantage.

Many blacks attacked Lincoln furiously during the war's first year because of his refusal to convert the struggle into an abolition war. When Lincoln countermanded General John C. Frémont's order of liberation for slaves owned by disloyal masters in Missouri in September 1861, the *Anglo-African* declared that the president "hurls back into the hell of slavery thousands . . . rightfully set free." As late as July 1862, Frederick Douglass characterized administration policy as reconstruction of "the old union on the old and corrupting basis of compromise, by which slavery shall retain all the power that it ever had." Douglass wanted slavery destroyed and the Constitution rewritten in the name of human equality. Within a year, just such a profound result began to take place.

Lincoln first substantively broached the subject of slavery in March 1862, when he proposed that states consider emancipation. He asked Congress to promise aid to any state that emancipated, appealing especially to border state representatives. What Lincoln proposed was gradual emancipation, with compensation for slaveholders and colonization of freed slaves outside the United States.

Until well into 1864, Lincoln's administration promoted an impractical scheme to colonize 4.2 million freed slaves in Central America or the Caribbean. He was as yet unconvinced that America could become a biracial society, and he feared that white northerners might not support a war for black freedom. Black abolitionists vehemently opposed the Lincoln administration's machinations.

A group of congressional Republicans known as the Radicals—led by George Julian, Charles Sumner, and Thaddeus Stevens—dedicated themselves to a war for emancipation. They were instrumental in creating a special House-Senate committee on the conduct of the war, which investigated Union reverses, sought to improve wartime efficiency war effort, and prodded the president to take stronger measures against slavery.

Confiscation Acts

In August 1861, at the Radicals' instigation, Congress passed its first confiscation act. Designed to punish Confederates, the law confiscated all property used for "insurrectionary purposes." A second confiscation act (July 1862) confiscated the property of anyone who supported the rebellion, even those who merely resided in the South and paid Confederate taxes. Their slaves were declared "forever free of their servitude."

In summer 1862, Lincoln stood by his proposal of voluntary gradual emancipation and made no effort to enforce the second confiscation act. In protest, Horace Greeley, editor of the powerful *New York Tribune,* published an open letter to the president entitled "The Prayer of Twenty Millions." Greeley declared, "Mr. President, there is not one . . . intelligent champion of the Union cause who does not feel that all attempts to put down the Rebellion and at the same time uphold its inciting cause are preposterous and futile." Lincoln offered a calculated reply. He disagreed with those who would make slavery the paramount issue of the war and said,

"If I could save the Union without freeing any slave I would do it, and if I could save it by freeing all the slaves I would do it; and if I could save it by freeing some and leaving others alone I would also do that. What I do about slavery, and the colored race, I do because I believe it helps to save the Union."

But Lincoln had already decided to issue a presidential Emancipation Proclamation. He was waiting for a Union victory so it would not appear an act of desperation. The letter to Greeley was an integral part of Lincoln's approach to the future of slavery. Lincoln was concerned with conditioning public and international opinion for the coming social revolution.

Emancipation Proclamations

On September 22, 1862, shortly after Union success at the Battle of Antietam, Lincoln issued the first part of his two-part proclamation. Invoking his powers as commander-in-chief, he announced that on January 1, 1863, he would emancipate the slaves in the states "in rebellion" (those lacking legitimate representatives in the U.S. Congress by January). Thus his September 1862 proclamation was less a declaration of the right of slaves to be free than a threat to southerners: unless they put down their arms and returned to Congress, they would lose their slaves. Lincoln had little expectation that southerners would give up, but he carefully offered them the option.

In the fateful January 1, 1863, proclamation, Lincoln declared that "all persons held as slaves" in areas in rebellion "shall be then, thenceforward, and forever free." But he excepted every Confederate county or city that had fallen under Union control. Those areas, he declared, "are, for the present, left precisely as if this proclamation were not issued." Nor did Lincoln liberate slaves in the border slave states that remained in the Union. "The President . . . has proclaimed emancipation only where he has notoriously no power to execute it," charged the anti-administration *New York World.*

But Lincoln was worried about the constitutionality of his acts, and he anticipated that after the war, southerners might sue for restoration of their property. Making the liberation of the slaves "a fit and necessary war measure" raised a variety of legal questions: Would it expire with the suppression of a rebellion? The proclamation did little to clarify the status of freed slaves, but it did open the possibility of military service for blacks.

If as a legal document the Emancipation Proclamation was wanting, as a moral and political document it had great meaning. Because the proclamation defined the war as a war against slavery, congressional Radicals could applaud it. Yet at the same time it protected Lincoln's position with conservatives, enabling him to retreat and forcing no immediate changes on the border slave states.

Most important, though, thousands of slaves had already reached Union lines across the South. They voted with their feet for emancipation well before the proclamation. And now, every advance of federal forces into slave society was a liberating step.

Across the North and in Union-occupied sections of the South, blacks and their white allies celebrated the Emancipation Proclamation. At a large contraband camp in Washington, D.C., some six hundred black men, women, and children gathered at the superintendent's headquarters on New Year's Eve and sang through the night. In chorus after chorus of "Go Down, Moses," they announced the magnitude of their painful but beautiful exodus.

African American Recruits

The need for men soon convinced the administration to recruit northern and southern blacks for the Union Army. By the spring of 1863, African American troops were answering the call of a dozen or more black recruiters in northern cities and towns. Lincoln came to see black soldiers as "the great available and yet unavailed of force for restoring the Union."

African American leaders hoped that military service would secure equal rights for their people. Once the black soldier had fought for the Union, wrote Frederick Douglass, "there is no power on earth which can deny that he has earned the right of citizenship in the United States."

In June 1864, with thousands of former slaves in blue uniforms, Lincoln gave his support to a constitutional ban on slavery. On the eve of the Republican national convention, Lincoln called on the party to "put into the platform as the keystone, the amendment of the Constitution abolishing and prohibiting slavery forever." The party promptly called for the Thirteenth Amendment, which passed in early 1865 and went to the states for ratification. The war to save the Union had become a war to free the slaves.

Who Freed the Slaves?

It has long been debated whether Abraham Lincoln deserved the label (one he never claimed for himself) of Great Emancipator. Was Lincoln ultimately a reluctant emancipator, following rather than leading Congress and public opinion? Or did Lincoln give essential presidential leadership by going slow but, once moving, never backpedaling on black freedom? Once he focused on the unconditional surrender of the Confederates, Lincoln made slavery's destruction central to the war's purpose.

Others have argued, however, that the slaves were central in achieving their own freedom. When they were in proximity to war zones, slaves fled by the thousands. Some worked as camp laborers for the Union armies, and eventually more than 180,000 black men served in the Union Army and Navy. Some found freedom as individuals in 1861, and some not until 1865, as refugees trekking to contraband camps.

Nonetheless, emancipation was a historical confluence of a policy directed by and dependent on the military authority of the president; and the will and courage for self-emancipation. Wallace Turnage's escape in Mobile Bay in 1864 shows how emancipation could result from both a slave's own heroism and Union forces. Most blacks comprehended their freedom as given and taken, but also as their human right. "I now dreaded the gun and handcuffs . . . no more," recalled Turnage. "I could now speak my opinion . . . to men of all grades and colors."

A Confederate Plan of Emancipation

Before the war was over, the Confederacy, too, addressed emancipation. Late in the war Jefferson Davis was willing to sacrifice slavery to achieve independence. He proposed that the Confederate government purchase 40,000 slaves to work as army laborers, with a promise of freedom at the end of their service. He then called for the recruitment and arming of slaves as soldiers, who likewise would gain their freedom at war's end, as would their wives and children. Bitter debate over Davis's plan resounded through the Confederacy. When the Confederate Congress finally approved slave enlistments in March 1865, owners had to comply only on a voluntary basis. With manpower shortages, General Lee supported the idea of slave soldiers, while most Confederate slaveholders and editors vehemently opposed the enlistment plan. Supporters hoped to fight to a stalemate, achieve independence, and control the postwar racial order through their limited wartime emancipation schemes, but it was too late. By contrast, Lincoln's Emancipation Proclamation stimulated a vital infusion of forces into the Union armies; 134,000 former slaves (and 52,000 free blacks) fought for freedom and the Union. Their participation was pivotal in the northern victory.

THE SOLDIERS' WAR

Military service altered soldiers' lives. Enlistment submerged young men in large organizations whose military discipline ignored their individuality. It molded men on both sides so thoroughly that they came to resemble one another more than civilians back home. Many soldiers forged bonds with their fellows and a connection to a noble purpose that they cherished for years afterward.

Union soldiers may have sensed most clearly the massive scale of modern war. The average soldier was between eighteen and twenty-one, joining large armies with extensive bureaucracies. By late 1861 there were 640,000 volunteers, a stupendous increase over the regular army of 20,000 men.

Hospitals and Camp Life

Soldiers benefited from certain new products, such as canned condensed milk, but blankets, clothing, and arms were often of poor quality. Hospitals were badly managed at first. Rules of hygiene in large camps were scarcely enforced. Water supplies were unsafe and typhoid common. About 57,000 men died from dysentery and diarrhea; 224,000 Union troops died from disease or accidents, double the 110,100 who died from battle. Confederate troops were less well supplied, and they had no sanitary commission. Still, an extensive hospital network, aided by white female volunteers and black female slaves, sprang up.

On both sides, troops quickly learned that soldiering was far from glorious. Fighting, wrote a North Carolina volunteer in 1863, taught him "the realities of a soldier's life. . . . Without time to wash our clothes or our persons . . . the whole army became lousy more or less with body lice." Union troops skirmished against lice by boiling their clothes, but to little avail.

War soon exposed them to the blasted bodies of their friends and comrades. "It is a sad sight to see the dead and if possible more sad to see the wounded—shot in every possible way you can imagine."

Still, as campaigns dragged on, most soldiers who did not desert grew determined to see the struggle through. "We now, like true Soldiers go determined not to yield one inch," wrote a New York corporal. When at last the war was over, "it seemed like breaking up a family to separate," one man observed.

The Rifled Musket

Advances in technology made the Civil War particularly deadly. The most important were the rifle and the minié ball. Bullets fired from a smoothbore musket were not accurate at distances over eighty yards. Cutting spiraled grooves inside the barrel gave the projectile greater accuracy, but rifles remained difficult to use until the Frenchman Claude Minié and the American James Burton developed a new bullet that expanded on firing and flew accurately. With these bullets, rifles were deadly at four hundred yards and useful up to one thousand yards.

This meant that soldiers assaulting a position defended by riflemen were in greater peril. While artillery now fired from a safe distance, there was no substitute for the infantry assault or the popular turning movements aimed at an enemy's flank. Thus advancing soldiers exposed themselves repeatedly to accurate rifle fire. With only rudimentary medical knowledge, even minor wounds often led to amputation and death through infection. Never before in Europe or America had such massive forces pummeled each other with weapons of such destructive power.

The Black Soldier's Fight for Manhood

At the outset of the war, racism in the Union Army was strong. Most white soldiers wanted nothing to do with black people and regarded them as inferior. For many, acceptance of black troops grew only because they could do heavy labor and "stop Bullets as well as white people." A popular song celebrated "Sambo's Right to Be Kilt" as the only justification for black enlistments.

But white officers who volunteered to lead segregated black units to gain promotion found that experience altered their opinions. After one month with black troops, a white captain informed his wife, "I have a more elevated opinion of their abilities than I ever had before. I know that many of them are vastly the superiors of those . . . who would condemn them all to a life of brutal degradation." Black troops had a mission to destroy slavery and demonstrate their equality. "When Rebellion is crushed," wrote a black volunteer from Connecticut, "who will be more proud than I to say, 'I was one of the first of the despised race to leave the free North with a rifle on my shoulder.'" Corporal James Henry Gooding of Massachusetts's black Fifty-fourth Regiment explained that his unit intended "to live down all prejudice against its color, by a determination to do well in any position it is put."

Indeed, blacks and whites of the Fifty-fourth Massachusetts forged deep bonds. Just before the regiment launched its costly assault on Fort Wagner in Charleston harbor in July 1863, a black soldier called to abolitionist Colonel Robert Gould Shaw, who would perish that day, "Colonel, I will stay by you till I die." The Fort Wagner assault was celebrated for demonstrating the valor of black men, but this bloody chapter in the history of American racism also proved that black men had to die in battle to be acknowledged as men.

Such valor emerged despite persistent discrimination. Off-duty black soldiers were sometimes attacked by northern mobs; on duty, they did most of the heavy labor. The Union government, moreover, paid white privates $13 per month plus a clothing allowance of $3.50, whereas black privates earned only $10 per month less $3 for clothing. Outraged, several regiments refused to accept any pay, and Congress eventually remedied the inequity.

1863: The Tide of Battle Turns

The fighting in spring and summer of 1863 did not settle the war, but it suggested the outcome. The campaigns began in a deceptively positive way for Confederates, as Lee's army performed brilliantly in battles in central Virginia.

Battle of Chancellorsville

On May 2 and 3, west of Fredericksburg, Virginia, some 130,000 members of the Union Army of the Potomac bore down on fewer than 60,000 Confederates. Boldly, Lee and Stonewall Jackson divided their forces, ordering 30,000 men under Jackson on a day-long march westward to prepare a flank attack.

Arriving at their position in late afternoon, Jackson's seasoned foot cavalry found unprepared Union troops smoking and playing cards. The Confederate attack drove the right side of the Union Army back. Eager to press his advantage, Jackson rode forward with a few officers to study the ground. Returning at twilight, southern troops mistook them for federals and fired, fatally wounding their commander. The next day, Union forces left in defeat. Southern forces won at Chancellorsville, but it cost them Stonewall Jackson, who would remain a legend in Confederate memory.

Siege of Vicksburg

July brought crushing defeats for the Confederacy in two critical battles—Vicksburg and Gettysburg—that damaged Confederate hopes for independence. Vicksburg was the last major fortification on the Mississippi River in southern hands. General Ulysses S. Grant laid siege to Vicksburg in May, bottling up the defending army of General John Pemberton. If Vicksburg fell, Union forces would control the river, cutting the Confederacy in two and gaining an open path into its interior. To stave off such a result, Jefferson Davis put General Joseph E. Johnston in charge there and beseeched him to aid Pemberton. Meanwhile, General Robert E. Lee proposed a Confederate invasion of the North, which, though it would not relieve Vicksburg, could stun the North and possibly lead to peace. By invading the North a second time, Lee hoped to move from war-weary Virginia, garner civilian support in Maryland, win a vital victory on northern soil, threaten major cities, and thereby force a Union capitulation.

As Lee's emboldened army advanced through western Maryland and into Pennsylvania, Confederate prospects along the Mississippi darkened. Davis repeatedly wired General Johnston, urging him to attack Grant's army. Johnston, however, considered "saving Vicksburg hopeless." Grant's men, meanwhile, were supplying themselves from the abundant crops of the Mississippi River valley and could continue their siege indefinitely.

Battle of Gettysburg

On July 4, 1863, Vicksburg's commander surrendered. The same day, a battle that had been raging for three days concluded at Gettysburg, Pennsylvania (see Map 15.1). On July 1, Confederate forces hunting for a supply of shoes collided with the Union Army. Heavy fighting on the second day left federal forces in possession of high

Map 15.1   Battle of Gettysburg
In the war's greatest battle, fought around a small market town in southern Pennsylvania, Lee's invasion of the North was repulsed. Union forces had the advantage of high ground, shorter lines, and superior numbers. The casualties for the two armies—dead, wounded, and missing—exceeded fifty thousand men.

ground along Cemetery Ridge, where they were shielded by a stone wall and had a clear view of their foe across almost a mile of open field.

Undaunted, Lee believed his reinforced troops could break the Union line, and on July 3 he ordered an assault. Virginians under General George E. Pickett and North Carolinians under General James Pettigrew marched up the slope in a doomed assault known as Pickett's Charge. They breached the enemy's line briefly, but most fell in heavy slaughter. On July 4 Lee withdrew, having suffered almost four thousand dead and about twenty-four thousand missing and wounded. The Confederate general blamed himself and offered to resign, but President Davis refused. The Confederacy had reached what many consider its high water mark at Gettysburg.

After Gettysburg and Vicksburg, the Confederacy was split; west of the Mississippi, General E. Kirby Smith had to operate on his own, independent of Richmond. Moreover, the heartland of Louisiana, Tennessee, and Mississippi lay exposed to invasion. Lee's northern defeat ended major southern offensive actions. Severely weakened, the Confederacy thenceforth relied on a prolonged defense. By wearing down northern morale, the South might yet win, but its prospects were darker than before.

DISUNITY: SOUTH, NORTH, AND WEST

Northern and southern governments waged the final two years of the war with increasing opposition at home. The gigantic costs of a civil war fed the unrest. But protest also arose from stresses in the regions' various social structures.

Union Occupation Zones

Wherever Union forces invaded, they imposed a military occupation consisting of three zones: garrisoned towns, with many troops in control of civilian and economic life; the Confederate frontier, areas still under southern control but with some federal military penetration; and no man's lands, regions between the two armies, beyond Confederate authority and under frequent Union patrols.

As many as one hundred southern towns were garrisoned, causing severe social disruption. Large sections of Tennessee, Virginia, Louisiana, Mississippi, and Georgia were occupied and suffered food shortages, crop and property destruction, disease, roadway banditry, guerrilla warfare, summary executions, and the random flow of escaped slaves. After two years of occupation, a southern white woman wrote to a kinsman about their native Clarksville, Tennessee: "It is nothing but a dirty hole filled . . . with niggers and Yankees."

Disintegration of Confederate Unity

Vastly disadvantaged in industrial capacity, natural resources, and labor, southerners felt the cost of the war more painfully than northerners. And internally, the southern class system threatened the Confederate cause.

Planters were increasingly opposed to their own government. Along with new taxation, Confederate military authorities impressed slaves to build fortifications. And when Union forces advanced, Confederate commanders burned cotton stores that lay in the enemy's path, enraging planters about such losses to their agricultural production and finances.

The increasing size and power of the Richmond government also alarmed planters. The Confederate constitution granted substantial powers to the central government, especially in war time. But many planters took the position articulated by R. B. Rhett, editor of the *Charleston Mercury,* that the Confederate constitution "leaves the States untouched in their Sovereignty, and commits to the Confederate Government only a few simple objects, and a few simple powers to enforce them."

Confused and embittered planters struck out at Jefferson Davis. Conscription, thundered Georgia's Governor James E. Brown, was "subversive of [Georgia's] sovereignty, and at war with all the principles for the support of which Georgia entered into this revolution." To frustrate the law, Brown ordered local enrollment officials not to cooperate with the Confederacy. Southern courts ultimately upheld Davis's power to conscript. Though Davis was devoted to southern independence, some of Davis's actions earned him the hatred of influential citizens.

Food Riots in Southern Cities

Widespread hunger and suffering sparked food riots in spring 1863 in Atlanta, Macon, Columbus, and Augusta, Georgia, and in Salisbury and High Point, North Carolina. On April 2 a crowd assembled in Richmond to demand relief. A passerby asked a young girl, "Is there some celebration?" "We are starving," replied the girl. "We are going to the bakeries and each of us will take a loaf of bread." That action fueled a riot that Davis ordered quelled at gunpoint.

Throughout the rural South, ordinary people resisted more quietly—by refusing to cooperate with conscription, tax collection, and impressments of food. Farmers who did provide food for the army refused to accept payment in certificates of credit or government bonds, as required by law. Conscription officers increasingly found no one to draft, and in some areas, tax agents were killed.

Austere and private by nature, Jefferson Davis was ill equipped to deal with such discontent. Often he buried himself in military affairs or administrative details. His class perspective also distanced him from common people's suffering. While his social circle in Richmond dined on duck and oysters, ordinary southerners went hungry. Failing to connect with plain folk, Davis thus lost their support.

Desertions from the Confederate Army

Such discontent affected the Confederate armies. Worried about their loved ones and resentful of what they saw as a rich man's war, large numbers of men abandoned the armies, supported by friends and neighbors. Mary Chesnut observed a man being dragged back to the army as his wife looked on. "Desert agin, Jake!" she cried.

Desertion did not become a serious problem for the Confederacy until mid-1862, and stiffer policing solved the problem that year. But from 1863 on, the number of men on duty fell rapidly. By mid-1863, John A. Campbell, the South's assistant secretary of war, estimated that 40,000 to 50,000 troops were absent without leave and that 100,000 were evading duty. By November 1863, one-third of the army could not be accounted for.

The defeats at Gettysburg and Vicksburg dealt a heavy blow to Confederate morale. Desperate, President Davis and several state governors resorted to racial scare tactics to drive southern whites to further sacrifice. Defeat, Davis warned, would mean "extermination of yourselves, your wives, and children." Mississippi governor Charles Clark predicted "elevation of the black race to a position of equality—aye, of superiority, that will make them your masters and rulers."

Internal disintegration of the Confederacy quickened. A few newspapers began to call openly for peace. Similar proposals, presented as plans for independence on honorable terms, were made in several state legislatures. Confederate leaders were losing the people's support. It is remarkable how long and effectively the Confederacy sustained a military effort facing such internal division.

Antiwar Sentiment, South and North

In North Carolina, William W. Holden, a popular Democratic politician and editor, led a growing peace movement. Over one hundred public meetings supporting peace negotiations took place during summer 1863. In Georgia early in 1864, Governor Brown and Alexander H. Stephens, vice president of the Confederacy, led a similar effort. Ultimately, the lack of a two-party system made questionable the legitimacy of any government criticism.

In the 1863 congressional elections, secessionists and supporters of the administration lost seats to men not identified with the government. In the last years of the war, Davis's support in the Confederate Congress dwindled. Some newspaper editors and soldiers, especially in Lee's Army of Northern Virginia, kept the Confederacy alive despite disintegrating popular support.

By 1864 southerners everywhere were giving up the struggle. Deserters dominated whole towns and counties. Active dissent was particularly common in upland and mountain regions, where Union support always held fast.

Opposition to the war, though less extreme, existed in the North as well. Alarm intensified over the growing centralization of government. The draft sparked protest, especially among poor citizens, and the Union Army struggled with a troubling desertion rate. But with vast human resources, the Union government's effectiveness was never threatened. Fresh recruits were always available, especially after black enlistments in 1863.

Moreover, unlike Davis, Lincoln knew how to connect with ordinary citizens. The daily carnage, tortuous political problems, and ceaseless criticism weighed heavily on him, and he communicated his suffering in public letters to newspapers and private ones to soldiers' families. His moving words helped contain northern discontent, though they could not stop it.

Peace Democrats

Much of the wartime protest in the North was political. The Democratic Party fought to regain power by blaming Lincoln for the war's death toll, the expansion of federal powers, inflation, the high tariff, and the emancipation of blacks. Its leaders called for an end to the war and reunion on the basis of "the Constitution as it is and the Union as it was." Democrats denounced conscription and martial law and defended states' rights. They charged that Republican policies were designed to flood the North with blacks, depriving white males of their status, their jobs, and their women. In the 1862 congressional elections, Democrats made a strong comeback, with peace Democrats wielding influence in New York State and majorities in the legislatures of Illinois and Indiana.

Led by outspoken men like Representative Clement L. Vallandigham of Ohio, the peace Democrats became highly visible. Vallandigham criticized Lincoln as a dictator who suspended the writ of habeas corpus without congressional authority and arrested thousands of innocent citizens. He urged voters to depose King Abraham. Vallandigham's attacks seemed so damaging to the war effort that military authorities arrested him for treason. Lincoln wisely decided against punishment—and martyr's status—for the Ohioan and exiled him to the Confederacy. (Eventually Vallandigham returned to the North through Canada.)

Lincoln believed that antiwar Democrats were linked to secret organizations harboring traitorous ideas, and encouraged draft resistance, discouraged enlistment, sabotaged communications, and plotted to aid the Confederacy. Republicans sometimes branded them—and by extension the peace Democrats—as Copperheads, after the poisonous snake. Although Confederate agents were active in the North and Canada, they never genuinely threatened the Union war effort.

New York City Draft Riots

Although many soldiers risked their lives willingly, others sought to avoid service. Under the 1863 draft law, a draftee could stay home by providing a substitute or paying a $300 commutation fee. Many wealthy men chose these options, and with demand high, clubs, cities, and states provided the money for others to escape conscription. In all, 118,000 substitutes were provided and 87,000 commutations paid before Congress ended the commutation system in 1864.

Urban poor and immigrants in strongly Democratic areas were especially hostile to conscription. The North's poor viewed the system as discriminatory, and many immigrants suspected (wrongly, on the whole) that they were disproportionately called. (Approximately 200,000 men born in Germany and 150,000 born in Ireland served in the Union Army.)

As a result, enrolling officers received rough treatment in many northern areas, and riots occurred in New Jersey, Ohio, Indiana, Pennsylvania, Illinois, and Wisconsin. The most serious violence happened in New York City in July 1863. The war was unpopular there, and racial, ethnic, and class tensions ran high. Shippers had recently broken a longshoremen's strike by hiring black strikebreakers. Working-class New Yorkers feared an inflow of black labor from the South and regarded blacks as the cause of the war. Poor Irish resented being forced to serve in place of others who could afford to avoid the draft.

Military police officers were attacked first; then mobs crying, "Down with the rich" looted wealthy homes and stores. But blacks became the special target, as mobs ransacked African American neighborhoods, beating and murdering people in the streets and burning an orphan asylum. At least seventy-four people died during the three days of violence. Army units dispatched from Gettysburg ended this tragic event.

War Against Indians in the Far West

A civil war of another kind raged on the Great Plains and in the Southwest. By 1864 U.S. troops under the command of Colonel John Chivington waged full-scale war against the Sioux, Arapahos, and Cheyennes to eradicate Indian title to eastern Colorado. Indian chiefs sought peace, but American commanders had orders to "burn villages and kill Cheyennes." A Cheyenne chief, Lean Bear, was shot as he rode toward U.S. troops, holding papers he received from President Lincoln during a visit to Washington, D.C. Another chief, Black Kettle, was told by the U.S. command that his people would find safe haven in Sand Creek, Colorado. Instead, on November 29, 1864, 700 cavalrymen, many drunk, attacked the Cheyenne village. With many Indian men absent hunting, the slaughter at the Sand Creek Massacre included 105 Cheyenne women and children and 28 men. American soldiers scalped and mutilated victims, carrying women's body parts on their saddles or hats back to Denver.

In the New Mexico and Arizona Territories, an authoritarian and brutal commander, General James Carleton, waged war on the Apaches and the Navajos. For generations both tribes raided the region's Pueblo and Hispanic peoples to maintain their security and economy. During the Civil War years, Anglo-American farms also became Indian targets. In 1863 the New Mexico Volunteers, commanded by former mountain man Kit Carson, defeated the Mescalero Apaches and forced them onto a reservation at Bosque Redondo in the Pecos River valley.

But the Navajos resisted. Carson destroyed their' livestock, orchards, and crops, causing the starving Navajos to surrender for food in January 1864. Three-quarters of the 12,000 Navajos were forced to march 400 miles (the Long Walk) to the Bosque Redondo Reservation, suffering malnutrition and death along the way. Permitted to return to a fraction of their homelands later in 1868, the Navajos never forgot the federal government's ruthless policies of removal and eradication of Indian peoples.

Election of 1864

Back east, war-weariness reached a peak in summer 1864, when the Democratic Party nominated popular general George B. McClellan for president and inserted a peace plank into its platform. Written by Vallandigham, it called for an armistice and spoke vaguely about preserving the Union. Democrats made racist appeals to white insecurity, calling Lincoln Abe the nigger-lover. No incumbent president had been reelected since 1832, and some Republicans worked to dump Lincoln from their ticket, favoring Salmon P. Chase or John C. Frémont, although little came of either effort.

With the fall of Atlanta and Union victories in the Shenandoah valley by early September, Lincoln's prospects rose. A decisive factor: eighteen states allowed troops to vote at the front. Lincoln received 78 percent of the soldier vote. With 55 percent of the popular vote, Lincoln's reelection—a referendum on the war and emancipation—crushed southern morale. Without this political outcome, a Union military victory and a redefined nation might never have happened.

1864–1865: THE FINAL TEST OF WILLS

The Confederates could still have won their version of victory in the war's final year if military stalemate and northern antiwar sentiment had forced a negotiated settlement. But northern determination prevailed.

Northern Diplomatic Strategy

From the outset, the North pursued one paramount goal: to prevent recognition of the Confederacy by European nations. Foreign recognition would belie Lincoln's claim that the United States was fighting an illegal rebellion and might lead to the financial and military aid that could ensure Confederate independence. Both England and France stood to benefit from a divided and weakened America. Thus, Lincoln and Secretary of State Seward needed to avoid serious military defeats and controversies with European powers.

Since the textile industry employed one-fifth of the British population, southerners banked on British recognition of the Confederacy. But at the beginning of the war, British mills had a 50 percent surplus of cotton, and they later found new supplies in India, Egypt, and Brazil. The British government flirted with recognition of the Confederacy but awaited southern battlefield successes. France was unwilling to act without Britain. Confederate agents purchased arms and supplies in Europe and obtained loans from European financiers, but they never achieved a diplomatic breakthrough.

An acute crisis occurred in 1861 when the overzealous commander of an American frigate stopped the British steamer *Trent* and moved two Confederate ambassadors, James Mason and John Slidell, to a Boston prison. The British interpreted the capture as a violation of freedom of the seas and demanded the prisoners' release. Lincoln and Seward waited until northern public opinion cooled before releasing them. The incident strained U.S.-British relations.

Then the sale to the Confederacy of warships constructed in England sparked protest from U.S. ambassador Charles Francis Adams. Over twenty-two months, the English-built ship, the *Alabama*, destroyed or captured more than sixty U.S. ships.

Battlefield Stalemate and a Union Strategy for Victory

On the battlefield, northern victory was far from won in 1864. General Nathaniel Banks's Red River campaign to capture more of Louisiana and Texas fell apart, and the capture of Mobile Bay in August did not cause the city to fall. Union general William Tecumseh Sherman soon brought total war to the southern heartland. On the eastern front during winter 1863–1864, the two armies in Virginia settled into a stalemate awaiting another northern spring offensive.

Military authorities have historically agreed that deep invasion is risky: the farther an army penetrates enemy territory, the more vulnerable its communications and

The Civil War in Britain

Because of the direct reliance of the British textile industry on southern cotton (cut off by the war), the American war was significant in Britain's economy and domestic politics. The British aristocracy and most cotton mill owners were pro-Confederate and proslavery, whereas clergymen, shopkeepers, artisans, and radical politicians worked for the causes of Union and emancipation. Most British workers saw their future at stake in a war for slave emancipation. Freedom to the huge British working class (who could not vote) meant basic political and civil rights, as well as secure jobs in an industrializing economy.

English aristocrats saw Americans as untutored and took satisfaction in America's troubles. Conservatives believed in the superiority of the British system of government and looked askance at America's leveling tendencies. And some aristocratic British Liberals sympathized with the Confederacy's demand for order and independence. English racism also intensified, exemplified by the popularity of minstrelsy and the employment of science in racial theory.

The British propaganda war over the American conflict was intensely debated: public meetings organized by both sides were huge affairs, with competing banners, carts and floats, orators, and resolutions. In a press war the British argued over when rebellion is justified, whether secession was right or legal, whether slavery was at the heart of the conflict, and especially over the democratic image of America. This bitter debate became a test of reform in Britain: those eager for a broadened franchise and increased democracy there were pro-Union, and those who preferred Britain's class-ridden political system favored the Confederacy.

The nature of the internal British debate was symbolized by the dozens of African Americans who served as pro-Union agents in England. The most popular was William Andrew Jackson, Confederate president Jefferson Davis's former coachman, who escaped from Richmond in September 1862. At British public meetings, Jackson countered pro-Confederate arguments that the war was not about slavery.

In the end, the British government did not recognize the Confederacy, and by 1864 English cotton lords found new sources in Egypt and India. But in this link between America and its English roots at its time of greatest travail, we can see the Civil War's international significance.

KING COTTON BOUND;
OR, THE MODERN PROMETHEUS.

Some southern leaders pronounced that cotton was king and would bring Britain to their cause. This British cartoon shows King Cotton brought down in chains by the American eagle, anticipating the cotton famine to follow and the intense debate in Great Britain over the nature and meaning of the American Civil War.

(The Granger Collection, New York)

supply lines become. Moreover, observed the Prussian expert Karl von Clausewitz, if the invader encounters a truly national resistance, his troops will be "everywhere exposed to attacks by an insurgent population."

General Grant, by now in command of the entire federal army, tested southern will with massive raids. Grant proposed to use armies to destroy Confederate railroads, thus ruining the enemy's transportation and economy. Union troops would live off the land while destroying resources useful to the Confederate military and to the civilian population. After General George H. Thomas's troops won the Battle of Chattanooga in November 1863, Georgia's heartland lay open. Grant entrusted General Sherman with 100,000 men for an invasion toward Atlanta's rail center.

Fall of Atlanta

Jefferson Davis positioned General Joseph E. Johnston's army in Sherman's path. Davis's political strategy for 1864 was to demonstrate Confederate military strength and defend Atlanta. When General Johnston slowly but steadily fell back toward Atlanta, Davis anxiously sought assurances that Atlanta would be held. From a military viewpoint, Johnston maneuvered skillfully. But when Johnston fell silent and continued to retreat, Davis replaced him with the one-legged General John Hood, who knew his job was to fight.

Hood attacked but was beaten, and Sherman's army occupied Atlanta on September 2, 1864. The victory buoyed northern spirits and ensured Lincoln's reelection. Davis exhorted southerners to fight on. Hood's army marched north to cut Sherman's supply lines and force him to withdraw, but Sherman marched sixty thousand of his men to the sea (see Map 15.2).

Sherman's March to the Sea

Sherman's army was formidable, composed almost entirely of battle-tested veterans and officers who rose through the ranks from the midwestern states. Before the march, army doctors weeded out men who were weak or sick. Although many harbored racist attitudes, most now supported emancipation because, as one said, "Slavery stands in the way of putting down the rebellion."

As Sherman's men moved across Georgia, they cut a path 50 to 60 miles wide and more than 200 miles long. The destruction they caused was awesome; indeed, it was Sherman's campaign that later prompted historians to deem this the first modern total war. A Georgia woman described the Burnt Country this way: "The fields were trampled down and the road was lined with carcasses of horses, hogs, and cattle that the invaders, unable either to consume or to carry with them, had wantonly shot down to starve our people."

After reaching Savannah in December, Sherman marched his armies into the Carolinas. To soldiers, South Carolina was the root of secession. They burned and destroyed as they marched, encountering little resistance. The opposing army of General Johnston was small, but Sherman's men should have faced guerrilla raids and attacks by local defense units. The absence of both led South Carolina's James Chesnut Jr. (a politician and the husband of Mary Chesnut) to write that

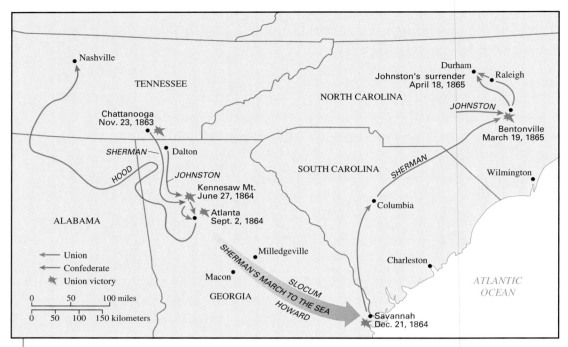

Map 15.2 Sherman's March to the Sea

The Deep South proved a decisive theater at the end of the war. From Chattanooga, Union forces drove into Georgia, capturing Atlanta. Following the fall of Atlanta, General Sherman embarked on his march of destruction through Georgia to the coast and then northward through the Carolinas.

his state "was shamefully and unnecessarily lost." Southerners lost the will to continue.

In Georgia, as many as nineteen thousand slaves followed the marauding Union troops. Others remained on the plantations to await the war's end, because of either wariness of whites or negative experiences with federal soldiers. The destruction of food harmed slaves along with white rebels, and many blacks lost livestock, clothing, crops, and other valuables to their liberators.

Virginia's Bloody Soil   Throughout spring and summer 1864, intent on capturing Richmond, Grant hurled his troops at Lee's army and suffered appalling losses: almost eighteen thousand casualties in the Battle of the Wilderness, more than eight thousand at Spotsylvania, and twelve thousand in only a few hours at Cold Harbor.

Before the assault at Cold Harbor, Union troops pinned scraps of paper bearing their names and addresses to their backs, certain they would be mowed down as they rushed Lee's trenches. In four weeks in May and June, Grant lost as many men as were enrolled in Lee's entire army. From early May until July, when Union forces fought from forests west of Fredericksburg to Petersburg, south of Richmond, the two armies engaged each other nearly every day. Wagon trains carrying thousands of Union wounded crawled back toward Washington.

Undaunted, Grant kept up the pressure. Although costly, these battles enabled eventual victory: Lee's army shrank until offensive action was no longer possible, while Grant's army kept replenishing itself with new recruits. The siege of Petersburg, with the armies facing each other in miles of trenches, lasted throughout winter 1864–1865.

Surrender at Appomattox

With the numerical superiority of Grant's army now greater than two to one, Confederate defeat was inevitable. On April 2, 1865, Lee abandoned Richmond and Petersburg. On April 9, he surrendered at Appomattox Court House. Grant treated his rival respectfully and paroled the defeated troops, allowing cavalrymen to keep their horses. Within weeks, Johnston surrendered to Sherman in North Carolina, and Davis, who had fled Richmond, was captured in Georgia. The war was over; the North rejoiced, and most southerners fell into despair.

Lincoln lived to see but a few days of the war's aftermath. On the evening of April 14, he accompanied his wife to Ford's Theatre in Washington. There, John Wilkes Booth, an embittered southern sympathizer, shot the president in the head at point-blank range. Lincoln died the next day. Twelve days later, troops tracked down and killed Booth. Relief at the war's end mingled with a renewed sense of loss and anxiety about the future.

Financial Tally

U.S. loans and taxes during the conflict totaled almost $3 billion, and interest on the war debt was $2.8 billion. The Confederacy borrowed over $2 billion but lost far more in the destruction of homes, crops, livestock, and other property. Union troops looted factories and put two-thirds of the South's railroad system out of service.

THE FUNERAL OF PRESIDENT LINCOLN, NEW YORK, APRIL 25TH 1865.
PASSING UNION SQUARE.

The death of President Lincoln caused a vast outpouring of grief in the North. As this Currier and Ives print shows, his funeral train stopped at several cities on its way to Illinois, to allow local services to be held.
(Anne S.K. Brown Military Collection, Brown University Library)

Estimates of the total cost of the war exceed $20 billion—five times the total expenditures of the federal government from its creation until 1861. By 1865 the federal government's spending soared to twenty times the prewar level and accounted for over 26 percent of the gross national product. Many changes were more or less permanent, as wartime measures left the government deeply involved in manufacturing, banking, and transportation.

Death Toll

More men died in the Civil War than in all other American wars combined until Vietnam. The total number of casualties exceeded 1 million—frightfully high for a nation of 31 million people. Approximately 360,000 Union soldiers died, 110,000 of them from battle wounds. Another 275,175 Union soldiers were wounded but survived. On the Confederate side, an estimated 260,000 lost their lives, and almost as many suffered wounds. Of an estimated 194,743 northerners in southern prisons, 30,218 died; of 214,865 southerners in northern prisons, 25,976 died. The prison story fueled mutual accusations for decades over starvation and brutal treatment.

Summary

The Civil War altered American society forever. Although precise figures are unavailable, it appears that 700,000 to 800,000 men served in the Confederate armies. Far more, possibly 2.3 million, served in the Union armies. All were taken from home and family; their lives, if they survived, were permanently altered. During the war, northern and southern women took on new roles to support the war effort.

Industrialization and economic enterprises grew exponentially with the war. Ordinary citizens' futures were increasingly tied to huge organizations. Under Republican leadership, the federal government expanded its power to preserve the Union and extend freedom. A social revolution and government authority emancipated the slaves.

It was unclear at war's end how or whether the nation would use its power to protect former slaves' rights. The war left many unanswered questions: How would white southerners, embittered and impoverished, respond to efforts to reconstruct the nation? How would the country care for the maimed, the orphans, the farm widows? What would be the place of black men and women in America?

In the West, a second civil war resulted in a conquest of southwestern Indians by U.S. troops and land-hungry settlers. On the diplomatic front, the Union government managed to keep Great Britain and other foreign powers out of the war. Dissent played a crucial role in the Confederacy's collapse, where the Union was only marginally affected by sabotage and draft riots.

In the Civil War, Americans underwent a dramatic transformation. White southerners experienced defeat that few other Americans ever faced. Blacks were moving proudly but anxiously from slavery to freedom. White northerners were self-conscious victors in a massive war for the nation's existence and for new definitions of freedom. The war would leave a compelling memory in American hearts and minds for generations.

"Big Government"

In 1995 President Bill Clinton declared that "the era of big government is over." Before him, President Ronald Reagan achieved considerable political success denouncing big-government programs. Whether the federal government ought to be the agent of social change, citizen welfare, and legal protection has been among the most polarizing questions in American political culture since at least the New Deal of the 1930s. But when did big government really begin?

One answer is with the Lincoln administration and Republican policies during the Civil War. Facing the demands of war, Republicans created an activist federal government, rooted in the harmony of interests among capitalism, free labor, and government power. Indeed, with agricultural legislation, an income tax, land grant colleges, higher tariffs, the Homestead Act, and railroad subsidies, the federal government permanently entered the nation's economy.

The powers of the federal government and the president grew steadily during the crisis. In one striking exercise of executive power, Lincoln suspended the writ of habeas corpus for everyone living between Washington, D.C., and Philadelphia. The president sought to ensure the loyalty of Maryland, which surrounded the capital on three sides. Later, with congressional approval, Lincoln repeatedly suspended habeas corpus and invoked martial law. Between fifteen and twenty thousand U.S. citizens were arrested on suspicion of disloyal acts and speech. Through such measures Lincoln expanded the powers of wartime presidents.

Above all, the Emancipation Proclamation and the Union military's prosecution of a war to destroy slavery was the most aggressive use of federal power. The Republicans' push for the Thirteenth Amendment to abolish slavery also stood as evidence of the advance of federal over state authority.

Today, Lincoln's legacy is richly controversial because of his exercise of such power. His admirers have honored him for his vision in taking the nation to a new birth of freedom in the crucible of total war. But critics have attacked him as the great centralizer, the father of big government. Ironically, twenty-first-century conservative Republicans crave the mantle of the party of Lincoln while denouncing the activist, regulatory government that Lincoln championed. As long as Americans debate the size and function of their federal government, they are replaying a chief Civil War legacy.

Chapter Review

AMERICA GOES TO WAR, 1861–1862

How did the North's naval victories trigger a revolution in slave society?

As federal gunboats drew near the South Carolina coast, planters fled their land. Confederate soldiers were unable to round up slaves, who, in their hopes that this signaled their freedom, broke cotton gins, stole clothing and furniture from masters' homes, and ran away to join the Union army. While the Union at first did not acknowledge the slaves as free, it did put them to work for the Union army.

WAR TRANSFORMS THE SOUTH

What happened to the South's embrace of state sovereignty during the war?

State power ultimately succumbed to a central authority. To maintain the war effort, the Confederacy centralized its operations, troops, and supplies, seeing the efforts of individual states as likely to fragment the greater cause. President Jefferson Davis took a firm leadership role toward the Confederate Congress and urged state governments to require farmers to switch from cash crops to food production. The central government assumed control of the southern economy and nearly complete control of the railroads. The Southern bureaucracy ironically became larger than its northern counterpart and provided new opportunities for women to work in government jobs.

WARTIME NORTHERN ECONOMY AND SOCIETY

How did the war affect workers in the North?

While many businesses weathered the initial slump and saw profits soar, northern industrial and urban workers enjoyed more job opportunities and higher wages but saw inflation devour much of their earnings. Consumer price hikes were nearly twice the rate of workers' salary increases, and workers' families saw their standard of living decline. Industrial workers were often replaced by labor-saving machines or cheap immigrant workers. While workers in several industries often went out on strike, manufacturers responded with blacklists or by requiring workers to sign "yellow dog" contracts promising not to join a union.

THE ADVENT OF EMANCIPATION

Why did Lincoln and Davis both avoid discussing slavery in the early days of the war?

Davis feared that the issue would increase class conflict in the South and preferred to point out that they were fighting to preserve their constitutional liberties against northerners. Lincoln avoided the topic of slavery to keep from antagonizing the Union's border states, whose loyalty he sought. He also hoped to inspire a pro-Union majority in the South that might bring the region back to the Union. Avoiding the topic was also politically expedient, since no Republican or northern consensus on slavery existed early in the war. When Lincoln first addressed emancipation in March 1862, he proposed gradual emancipation with payment for slaveholders and colonization for freed slaves outside the United States. Even the Emancipation Proclamation only promised freedom to slaves within confederate borders and exempted confederate cities that had fallen to Union control.

THE SOLDIERS' WAR

What changed white military leaders' minds about black soldiers?

Simply witnessing the bravery and determination of black units was enough to change white officers' opinions of the segregated black units they led. Black soldiers, too, felt they were fighting prejudice by their actions and proving their legitimate claim to freedom. In truth, black soldiers' willingness to die in battle was what earned the respect of white men. Many black and white soldiers who fought together did forge deep ties, especially those of the ill-fated 54th Massachusetts regiment.

1863: THE TIDE OF BATTLE TURNS

What turned the tide of war toward Union victory?

Battles at Vicksburg and Gettysburg changed the course of war from a possible Confederate victory to one assured for the Union. Vicksburg was the last major fortification on the Mississippi River in southern hands, while Gettysburg marked Lee's attempts to break the Union line and invade the North. Both battles produced heavy losses, but also left the Confederate army divided, so that west of the Mississippi General E. Kirby Smith operated alone, while Louisiana, Tennessee, and Mississippi were vulnerable to invasions. After Gettysburg, there were no more Confederate offensive moves; severely weakened, the Confederate army could only act defensively.

DISUNITY: SOUTH, NORTH, AND WEST

What were the causes of wartime dissent in the South?

Class divisions in the South fueled opposition to Confederate authority and its wartime operations. Planters opposed new taxation and the impressments of their slaves to build fortifications. They also disliked the fact that Confederate commanders burned planters' cotton stores as Union soldiers advanced. In addition, they rejected the increasing size and power of the central government in Richmond and conscription for military service. Outside the planter class, many people refused to comply with conscription, taxation, or the demand to provide food for soldiers. The ability of wealthy people to buy their way out of military service by hiring substitutes fueled resentment among soldiers, some of whom abandoned the army.

1864–1865: THE FINAL TEST OF WILLS

Why was it so crucial to northern military strategy that Europe remain neutral during the Civil War?

Lincoln felt that if foreign countries recognized the Confederacy, it would legitimize what Lincoln considered to be an illegal rebellion. He also feared it could lead to military and financial aid that would facilitate a Confederate victory and its ultimate independence. The president knew that both England and France would gain by a divided America, but France would not act without Britain, and Britain wasn't making a move until there were major southern battlefield successes. While England's relationship with southern textile mills made the confederacy hopeful for an alliance, Britain's large cotton surplus and new supplies in India, Egypt, and Brazil kept them from doing more than selling arms and supplies or offering loans.

SUGGESTIONS FOR FURTHER READING

Stephen V. Ash, *When the Yankees Came: Conflict and Chaos in the Occupied South* (1995)

Edward L. Ayers, *In the Presence of Mine Enemies: War in the Heart of America, 1859–1863* (2002)

Ira Berlin et al., eds., *Freedom: A Documentary History of Emancipation, 1861–1867,* 3 vols. (1979–1982)

David W. Blight, *Frederick Douglass' Civil War: Keeping Faith in Jubilee* (1989)

Alice Fahs, *The Imagined Civil War: Popular Literature of the North and South* (2001)

Drew G. Faust, *Mothers of Invention: Women of the Slaveholding South in the Civil War* (1996)

William W. Freehling, *The South vs. the South* (2001)

Gary W. Gallagher, *The Confederate War* (1997)

Bruce Levine, *Confederate Emancipation: Southern Plans to Free and Arm Slaves During the Civil War* (2006)

James M. McPherson, *Battle Cry of Freedom: The Civil War Era* (1987)

Philip S. Paludan, *"A People's Contest": The Union and the Civil War* (1989)

Heather Cox Richardson, *The Greatest Nation on Earth: Republican Economic Policies During the Civil War* (1997)

Reconstruction: An Unfinished Revolution

The lower half of secession's seedbed, Charleston, South Carolina, lay in ruin when most of the white population evacuated on February 18, 1865. A prolonged bombardment by Union forces around Charleston harbor destroyed many of the low-country planters' town homes. Fires broke out everywhere, ignited in bales of cotton stockpiled in public squares. To many observers, the flames were the funeral pyres of a dying civilization.

The Union's Twenty-first U.S. Colored Regiment received Charleston's surrender from its mayor. For black Charlestonians, most of whom were former slaves, this was a time to celebrate freedom and rebirth. The city's freedpeople converted Confederate ruin into a vision of Reconstruction based on Union victory and black liberation.

During the war's final year, the Confederates transformed the planters' Race Course, a horseracing track, and its famed Jockey Club, into a prison. Kept outdoors in the middle of the track, 257 Union soldiers died of exposure and disease and were buried in a mass grave behind the judges' stand. After the city fell, in April more than twenty black workmen reinterred the dead in marked graves. On the archway over the cemetery's entrance they painted the inscription Martyrs of the Race Course.

On May 1, 1865, ten thousand people marched around the planters' Race Course, led by three thousand children carrying roses and singing "John Brown's Body." Black women with baskets of flowers and wreaths, came next and then black men. The parade concluded with black and white Union regiments and white missionaries and teachers. At the gravesite, five black ministers read from Scripture, and a black children's choir sang "America," "We'll Rally 'Round the Flag," "The Star-Spangled

This icon will direct you to interactive activities and study materials on A People And A Nation, Brief Edition
website: **www.cengage.com/history/norton/ peoplenationbrief8e**

Chronology

1865	Johnson begins rapid and lenient Reconstruction.	**1871**	Congress passes the second Enforcement Act and Ku Klux Klan Act.
	Confederate leaders regain power.		Treaty with England settles the *Alabama* claims.
	White southern governments pass restrictive black codes.	**1872**	Amnesty Act frees almost all remaining Confederates from restrictions on holding office.
	Congress refuses to seat southern representatives.		Grant is reelected.
	Thirteenth Amendment, abolishing slavery, is ratified.	**1873**	*Slaughter-House* cases limit the power of the Fourteenth Amendment.
1866	Congress passes the Civil Rights Act and renewal of the Freedmen's Bureau over Johnson's veto.		Panic of 1873 leads to widespread unemployment and labor strife.
	Congress approves the Fourteenth Amendment.	**1874**	Democrats win a majority in the House of Representatives.
	Most southern states reject the Fourteenth Amendment.	**1875**	Several Grant appointees are indicted for corruption.
	In *Ex parte Milligan* the Supreme Court reasserts its influence.		Congress passes a weak Civil Rights Act.
1867	Congress passes the First Reconstruction Act and Tenure of Office Act.		Democratic Party increases control of the southern states with white supremacy campaigns.
	Seward arranges the purchase of Alaska.	**1876**	*U.S. v. Cruikshank* further weakens the Fourteenth Amendment.
	Constitutional conventions called in the southern states.		Presidential election is disputed.
1868	House impeaches and Senate acquits Johnson.	**1877**	Congress elects Hayes president.
	Most southern states readmitted to the Union under the Radical plan.		"Home rule" returns to three remaining southern states not yet controlled by Democrats; Reconstruction is considered over.
	Fourteenth Amendment is ratified.		
	Grant is elected president.		
1869	Congress approves the Fifteenth Amendment (ratified in 1870).		

Banner," and Negro spirituals. When the ceremony ended, the crowd retired to the Race Course for speeches, picnics, and military festivities.

African Americans founded this Decoration Day—now Memorial Day—as a day to remember those who perished in the war. In their vision, it was the Independence Day of a Second American Revolution.

The Civil War and its aftermath wrought unprecedented changes in American society, law, and politics, but the underlying realities of economic power, racism, and judicial conservatism limited Reconstruction's revolutionary potential. The nation had to determine the nature of federal-state relations, whether confiscated land could be redistributed, and how to bring justice to freedpeople and aggrieved white southerners. Americans also had to heal psychologically from a bloody and fratricidal war. How they negotiated the relationship between healing and justice would determine the extent of change during Reconstruction.

The turmoil wrought by Reconstruction was most evident in national politics, as Lincoln's successor, Andrew Johnson, fought with Congress over Reconstruction policies. Although a southerner, Johnson disliked the South's wealthy planters, and his early moves suggested that he would be tough on "traitors." By late 1865, however, Johnson became the protector of southern interests. Jefferson Davis stayed in prison for two years, but Johnson pardoned other rebel leaders and allowed them to occupy high offices. He also ordered plantations returned to the original owners, including the abandoned coastal lands of Georgia and South Carolina on which forty thousand freed men and women settled early in 1865, by order of General William Tecumseh Sherman.

Johnson imagined a rapid restoration of the South to the Union rather than the fundamental reconstruction that Republican congressmen favored. Between 1866 and 1868, the president and the Republican leadership in Congress battled over how to put the United States back together again. Before it ended, Congress impeached the president and enfranchised freed men and gave them a role in reconstructing the South. The nation also adopted the Fourteenth and Fifteenth Amendments, ensuring equal protection of the law, citizenship, and universal manhood suffrage. But the cause of equal rights for African Americans fell almost as fast as it had risen.

By 1869 the Ku Klux Klan employed extensive violence to thwart Reconstruction and undermine black freedom. As white Democrats in the South took over state governments, they encountered little opposition. Moreover, the wartime industrial boom created new opportunities and priorities. The West, with its seemingly limitless potential and its wars against Indians, drew American resources as never before. Political corruption became a nationwide scandal, and bribery a way of doing business.

The white South's desire to reclaim control of its states and of race relations overwhelmed the national interest in stopping it. Thus Reconstruction became a revolution eclipsed, leaving legacies with which the nation has struggled ever since.

- **Should the Reconstruction era be considered the Second American Revolution? By what criteria should we make such a judgment?**
- **What were the origins and meanings of the Fourteenth Amendment in the 1860s? What is its significance today?**
- **Reconstruction is judged to have ended in 1877. Over the course of the 1870s, what caused its end?**

WARTIME RECONSTRUCTION

Reconstruction of the Union was an issue in 1863, well before the war ended. Specifically, four vexing problems compelled early thinking and would haunt the Reconstruction era. First, who would rule in the South once it was defeated? Second, who would rule in the federal government—Congress or the president? Third, what were the dimensions of black freedom, and what rights under law would freed men enjoy? And fourth, would Reconstruction be a preservation of the old republic or a second revolution, inventing a new republic?

Lincoln's 10 Percent Plan

Abraham Lincoln had never been antisouthern. His worst fear was that the war would collapse into guerrilla warfare by surviving bands of Confederates. Lincoln insisted on leniency for southern soldiers once they surrendered. In his Second Inaugural Address, delivered a month before his assassination, Lincoln promised "malice toward none; with charity for all."

Lincoln planned early for a swift and moderate Reconstruction process. In his 1863 Proclamation of Amnesty and Reconstruction, he proposed to replace majority rule with "loyal rule" to reconstruct southern state governments, and to pardon ex-Confederates except the highest-ranking military and civilian officers. Once 10 percent of a given state's voting population in the 1860 general election had taken an oath to the United States and established a government, the new state would be recognized. Lincoln did not consult Congress in these plans, and "loyal" assemblies (known as Lincoln governments) were created in Louisiana, Tennessee, and Arkansas in 1864, states largely occupied by Union troops on which they depended for survival.

Congress and the Wade-Davis Bill

Congress responded with hostility to Lincoln's moves to readmit southern states quickly. Led by Pennsylvania's Thaddeus Stevens in the House and Massachusetts's Charles Sumner in the Senate, Radical Republicans were strong proponents of emancipation and aggressive prosecution of the war and now proposed a longer and harsher Reconstruction. Stevens advocated a conquered provinces theory, arguing that southerners organized as a foreign nation to make war on the United States. They, therefore, must be treated as conquered foreign lands and returned to the status of unorganized territories before their readmission could be entertained.

In July 1864, the Wade-Davis bill, sponsored by Ohio senator Benjamin Wade and Maryland congressman Henry W. Davis, emerged from Congress with three specific conditions for southern readmission.

1. There had to be a majority of white male citizens participating in the creation of a new government.
2. To vote or be a delegate to constitutional conventions, men had to take an iron-clad oath declaring that they never aided the Confederate war effort.
3. All officers above the rank of lieutenant and all civil officials in the Confederacy would be disfranchised and deemed "not a citizen of the United States."

Lincoln pocket-vetoed the bill and issued a conciliatory proclamation that he would not be inflexibly committed to any one plan of Reconstruction.

This exchange occurred when the war's outcome and Lincoln's reelection were still in doubt. On August 5, Radical Republicans issued the "Wade-Davis Manifesto" to newspapers, accusing Lincoln of usurpation of presidential powers and disgraceful leniency toward an eventually conquered South. Lincoln saw Reconstruction as a means of weakening the Confederacy and winning the war; the Radicals saw it as a transformation of the nation's political and racial order.

Thirteenth Amendment

In early 1865, Congress and Lincoln joined in two important measures that recognized slavery's centrality to the war. On January 31, Congress passed the Thirteenth Amendment, which first, abolished involuntary servitude and second, declared that Congress shall have the power to enforce this outcome by appropriate legislation. When the measure passed by 119 to 56, just 2 votes more than the necessary two-thirds, Congress rejoiced.

The Thirteenth Amendment emerged from congressional debate and considerable petitioning and public advocacy. One of the first and most remarkable petitions for a constitutional amendment abolishing slavery was submitted in 1864 by Elizabeth Cady Stanton, Susan B. Anthony, and the Women's Loyal National League. Women throughout the Union accumulated thousands of signatures. It was a long road from the Emancipation Proclamation to the Thirteenth Amendment, through treacherous constitutional theory about individual property rights, beliefs that the sacred document (the Constitution) ought never be altered, and partisan politics.

Freedmen's Bureau

On March 3, 1865, Congress created the Bureau of Refugees, Freedmen, and Abandoned Lands—the Freedmen's Bureau, an unprecedented federal agency of social uplift. With thousands of refugees in the South, the government continued what private freed men's aid societies started in 1862. In its four-year existence, the Freedmen's Bureau supplied food and medical services, built several thousand schools and some colleges, negotiated several hundred thousand employment contracts between freed men and their former masters, and tried to manage confiscated land.

The bureau was a controversial aspect of Reconstruction. Southern whites hated it, and politicians divided over its constitutionality. Some bureau agents were devoted to freed men's rights; others exploited the chaos of the postwar South. The war prompted an eternal question of republics: what are the social welfare obligations of the state toward its people, and what do people owe their governments in return? Apart from conquest and displacement of the eastern Indians, Americans were inexperienced at the Freedmen's Bureau's task—social reform through military occupation.

Ruins and Enmity

In 1865, with the war's devastation, America was a land with ruins. Some of its cities lay in rubble; large stretches of the southern countryside were depopulated and defoliated; and thousands of people, white and black, were refugees. Many white refugees faced starvation. Of the approximately 18,300,000 rations distributed across the South in the first three years of the Freedmen's Bureau, 5,230,000 went to whites.

In October 1865, after a five-month imprisonment in Boston, former Confederate vice president Alexander H. Stephens rode a train southward. When he reached northern Georgia, his native state, he expressed shock: "War has left a terrible impression. . . . Fences gone, fields all a-waste, houses burnt." A northern journalist visiting Richmond that fall observed a city "mourning for her sins . . . in dust and ashes." Every northern traveler experienced hatred from white southerners. A North Carolina innkeeper told a journalist that Yankees killed his sons, burned his house, and stole his slaves and left him "one inestimable privilege . . . to hate 'em."

THE MEANINGS OF FREEDOM

Black southerners entered life after slavery with hope and circumspection. A Texas man recalled his father's telling him, "Our forever was going to be spent living among the Southerners, after they got licked." Often the changes freed men and women valued most were personal—alterations in employer or living arrangements.

The Armed Slave, William Sprang, oil on canvas, c. 1865. This remarkable painting depicts an African American veteran soldier, musket with fixed bayonet leaning against the wall, cigar in hand indicating a new life of safety and leisure, and reading a book to demonstrate his embrace of education and freedom. The man's visage leaves the impression of satisfaction and dignity. (Civil War Museum of Philadelphia)

The Feel of Freedom

For America's former slaves, Reconstruction meant a chance to explore freedom. Former slaves remembered singing into the night after federal troops, who confirmed rumors of their emancipation, reached their plantations. A few people gave in to the desire to do what was forbidden before. One angry grandmother dropped her hoe and confronted her mistress with, "I'm free! Ain't got to work for you no more!" Another man recalled that he and others "started on the move," either to search for family members or just to start fresh.

As slaves they learned to expect hostility from white people; they did not presume it would instantly disappear. Many freedpeople evaluated potential employers carefully. After searching for better circumstances, a majority of blacks eventually settled as agricultural workers on their former farms or plantations. But they relocated their houses and tried to control the conditions of their labor.

Reunion of African American Families

Throughout the South, former slaves focused on reuniting their families, separated during slavery by sale or hardship and during the war by dislocation and emancipation. By relying on the black community for help and by placing ads in black newspapers well into the 1880s, some succeeded, while others searched in vain.

Husbands and wives who belonged to different masters could finally establish homes together and raise their own children. When her old master claimed a right to whip her children, a mother informed him that "he warn't goin' to brush none of her chilluns no more." Freed men and women were tired of punishment.

Blacks' Search for Independence

Many black people wanted to minimize contact with whites because, as Reverend Garrison Frazier told General Sherman in January 1865, "There is a prejudice against us . . . that will take years to get over." As such, blacks abandoned slave quarters and fanned out to distant corners of the land they worked. Some described moving "across the creek" or building a "saplin house . . . back in the woods." Other rural dwellers established small, all-black settlements that still exist along the South's back roads.

Freedpeople's Desire for Land

In addition to a fair employer, freed men and women most wanted to own land, which represented self-sufficiency and compensation for generations of bondage. General Sherman's special Field Order Number 15, issued in February 1865, set aside 400,000 acres in the Sea Islands for exclusive settlement by freedpeople. Hope swelled among ex-slaves as forty-acre plots and mules were promised. But President Johnson ordered them removed in October and the land returned to its original owners under army enforcement. The U.S. government eventually sold thousands of acres in the Sea Islands, 90 percent of which went to wealthy northern investors.

Most members of both political parties opposed land redistribution to the freed men. Even northern reformers who administered the Sea Islands during the war showed little sympathy for black aspirations. The former Sea Island slaves wanted to establish small, self-sufficient farms. Northern soldiers, officials, and missionaries of both races brought education and aid to the freed men but also insisted that they grow cotton. They emphasized profit, cash crops, and competitive capitalism.

Black Embrace of Education

Blacks hungered for education that previously belonged only to whites. With freedom, they started schools, and on log seats and dirt floors, freed men and women studied in old almanacs and discarded dictionaries. Young children brought infants to school with them, and adults attended at night or after "the crops were laid by." Despite their poverty, many blacks paid tuition, typically $1 or $1.50 a month—which constituted major portions of a person's agricultural wages and totaled more than $1 million by 1870.

In its brief life, the Freedmen's Bureau founded over four thousand schools, and northern reformers established others through private philanthropy. The Yankee schoolmarm—selfless and religious—became an agent of progress in many southern communities. By 1877, more than 600,000 African Americans broke with their past by enrolling in elementary school.

Blacks and their white allies also established colleges and universities to train teachers, ministers, and future leaders. The American Missionary Association founded seven colleges, including Fisk and Atlanta Universities, between 1866 and 1869. The Freedmen's Bureau helped establish Howard University in Washington, D.C., and northern religious groups, such as the Methodists, Baptists, and Congregationalists, supported seminaries and teachers' colleges.

During Reconstruction, African American leaders were often highly educated members of the prewar elite of free people of color. Francis Cardozo, who held various offices in South Carolina, attended universities in Scotland and England. P. B. S. Pinchback, who became lieutenant governor of Louisiana, was the son of a planter who sent him to school in Cincinnati.

Growth of Black Churches

Freed from slavery's restrictions, blacks could build their own institutions. The secret churches of slavery came into the open; in communities throughout the South, ex-slaves started a *brush arbor*—a shelter with leaves for a roof, where freed men and women worshiped.

Within a few years, independent branches of the Methodist and Baptist denominations attracted most black Christians in the South. By 1877 in South Carolina, the African Methodist Episcopal (A.M.E.) Church had one thousand ministers, forty-four thousand members and a school of theology, while the A.M.E. Zion Church had forty-five thousand members. In these churches, some of which became the wealthiest and most autonomous institutions in black life, freedpeople created enduring communities.

Rise of the Sharecropping System Since most former slaves lacked money to buy land, they preferred the next best thing: renting. But the South had few sources of credit, and few whites would rent to blacks.

Consequently, black farmers and white landowners turned to sharecropping, a system in which a landlord or merchant furnished food and supplies, such as draft animals and seed, to farmers who worked the land. The owners and merchants were repaid with part of the crops. Although landowners tried to set the laborers' share at a low level, sharecroppers would resist or move from year to year. As the system matured during the 1870s and 1880s, most sharecroppers worked on *halves*—half for the owner and half for themselves.

The sharecropping system, which materialized as early as 1868, originated as a compromise between former slaves and white landowners. It eased landowners' problems with cash and credit and provided a permanent, dependent labor force; blacks accepted it because it freed them from daily supervision. But sharecropping proved to be a disaster. Owners and merchants developed a monopoly over the agricultural economy, as sharecroppers faced ever-increasing debt.

The fundamental problem was that southern farmers still concentrated on cotton. In freedom, black women often stayed away from cotton picking to concentrate on domestic chores, especially given the diminishing incentives of the cotton system. By 1878 the South recovered its prewar share of British cotton purchases. But even as southerners grew more cotton, their reward diminished. Cotton prices began a long decline, as world demand fell off.

Thus southern agriculture slipped into depression. Black sharecroppers struggled under growing debt which bound them to landowners and to furnishing merchants almost as oppressively as slavery had bound them to masters. Many white farmers gradually lost their land and became sharecroppers. By the end of Reconstruction, over one-third of all southern farms were worked by sharecropping tenants, white and black.

JOHNSON'S RECONSTRUCTION PLAN

Many people expected President Andrew Johnson's Reconstruction policies to be harsh. Throughout his career in Tennessee he criticized wealthy planters and championed small farmers. When an assassin's bullet thrust Johnson into the presidency, former slaveowners feared their treatment in Johnson's hands. When northern Radicals suggested the exile or execution of ten or twelve leading rebels, Johnson replied, "How are you going to pick out so small a number?"

Andrew Johnson of Tennessee

Like Lincoln, Johnson moved from obscurity to power. With no formal education, he became a tailor's apprentice. But from 1829, while in his twenties, he held nearly every office in Tennessee politics: alderman, state representative, congressman, two terms as governor, and U.S. senator by 1857. Although elected as a Democrat, Johnson was the only senator from a seceded state who refused to leave the Union. Lincoln appointed him war governor of Tennessee in 1862, hence his symbolic place on the ticket in the president's 1864 bid for reelection.

Although a Unionist, Johnson's political beliefs made him an old Jacksonian Democrat. Before the war, he supported tax-funded public schools and homestead legislation, fashioning himself as a champion of the common man. Johnson advocated limited government and was an ardent states' rightist. His philosophy toward Reconstruction may be summed up his slogan: "The Constitution as it is, and the Union as it was."

Through 1865 Johnson alone controlled Reconstruction policy; Congress recessed before he became president in April and did not reconvene until December. Johnson formed new state governments in the South by using his power to grant pardons and extended easy terms to former Confederates.

Johnson's Racial Views

Johnson had owned house slaves, although he was not a planter. He accepted emancipation but did not believe that black suffrage could be imposed on a southern state by the federal government; this set him on a collision course with the Radicals. Johnson was a thoroughgoing white supremacist. He declared in his annual message of 1867 that blacks possessed less "capacity for government than any other race of people. . . . Wherever they have been left to their own devices they have shown a constant tendency to relapse into barbarism."

Such racial views affected Johnson's policies. Where whites were concerned, however, Johnson proposed rules that would keep the wealthy planter class at least temporarily out of power.

Johnson's Pardon Policy

White southerners were required to swear an oath of loyalty to gain amnesty, but Johnson barred from the oath former federal officials, high-ranking Confederate officers, and political leaders or graduates of West Point or Annapolis who joined the Confederacy. He also added ex-Confederates whose taxable property was worth more than $20,000. These individuals had to apply to the president for pardon. The president, it seemed, sought revenge on the old planter elite and the promotion of a new yeomen leadership.

Johnson appointed provisional governors, who began the Reconstruction process by calling state constitutional conventions. The delegates had to draft new constitutions that eliminated slavery and invalidated secession. After ratification, new governments could be elected, and states would be restored to the Union. But only southerners who had taken the oath of amnesty and were eligible to vote on the day the state seceded could participate. Thus unpardoned whites and former slaves were ineligible.

Presidential Reconstruction

The old white leadership proved resilient; prominent Confederates won elections and turned up in appointive offices. Then Johnson started pardoning planters and leading rebels. By September 1865, hundreds of pardons were issued in one day. These pardons, plus the return of planters' abandoned lands, restored the old elite to power and made Johnson seem the South's champion.

Why did Johnson allow the planters to regain power? He may have enjoyed turning proud planters into pardon seekers. He also sought a rapid Reconstruction to deny the Radicals an opportunity for more thorough racial and political changes in the South. Plus, Johnson needed southern support in the 1866 elections; hence, he declared Reconstruction complete only eight months after Appomattox. In December 1865, many Confederate congressmen claimed seats in the U.S. Congress, including former Confederate vice president Alexander Stephens, who was now Georgia's senator-elect.

Black Codes

Furthermore, to define the status of freed men and women and control their labor, some legislatures substituted the word *freedmen* for *slaves* in the old slave codes. These new black codes compelled former slaves to carry passes, observe a curfew, and live in housing provided by a landowner. Vagrancy laws and restrictive labor contracts bound freedpeople to plantations, and antienticement laws punished anyone luring these workers to other employment. State-supported schools and orphanages excluded blacks.

It seemed to northerners that the South was intent on returning African Americans to servitude and that Johnson's Reconstruction policy held no one responsible for the war. Thus the Republican majority in Congress halted Johnson's plan, and the House and Senate did not admit newly elected southern representatives. Instead, they challenged the president's authority and established a joint committee to investigate a new direction for Reconstruction.

THE CONGRESSIONAL RECONSTRUCTION PLAN

The Constitution mentioned neither secession nor reunion, but it gave Congress the primary role in admitting states. Moreover, the Constitution declared that the United States shall guarantee to each state a "republican form of government." This provision, legislators believed, gave them the authority to devise Reconstruction policies.

The key question: What had rebellion done to the relationship between southern states and the Union? Congressmen who favored vigorous Reconstruction measures argued that the war had broken the Union and that the South was subject to the victor's will. Moderate congressmen held that states forfeited their rights through rebellion and thus came under congressional supervision.

The Radicals

Northern Democrats, weakened by their opposition to the war in its final year, denounced racial equality and supported Johnson's policies. Conservative Republicans, despite their party loyalty, favored a limited federal role in Reconstruction. Although a minority, the Radical Republicans, led by Thaddeus Stevens, Charles Sumner, and George Julian, sought to democratize the South, establish public education, and ensure freedpeople's rights. They favored black suffrage and some land confiscation and redistribution and were willing to exclude the South from the Union for years to achieve their goals.

The Radicals brought a new civic vision to American life; they wanted to create an activist federal government and the beginnings of racial equality. A large group of moderate Republicans, led by Lyman Trumbull, opposed Johnson's leniency but wanted to restrain the Radicals. They were, however, committed to federalizing the enforcement of civil, if not political, rights for the freedmen.

With the 1866 elections looming, Johnson and the Democrats sabotaged the possibility of a conservative coalition by refusing to cooperate with conservative or moderate Republicans. They insisted that Reconstruction was over, that the new state governments were legitimate, and that southern representatives should be admitted to Congress. The Radicals' influence grew with Johnson's intransigence.

Congress Versus Johnson

Republicans believed they reached a compromise with Johnson in spring 1866 in which Johnson would modify his program by extending the Freedmen's Bureau for another year and passing a civil rights bill to counteract the black codes. This would force southern courts to practice equality under scrutiny of the federal judiciary. Its

In 1866, as Congress reviewed the progress of Reconstruction, news from the South had a considerable impact. Violence against black people, like the riot in Memphis depicted here, helped convince northern legislators that they had to modify President Johnson's policies. (Library of Congress)

provisions applied to public, not private, acts of discrimination. The Civil Rights Bill of 1866 was the first statutory definition of the rights of American citizens.

Johnson, however, vetoed both bills; they became law when Congress overrode his veto. Because the civil rights bill defined U.S. citizens as native-born persons who were taxed, Johnson claimed that it discriminated against "large numbers of intelligent, worthy, and patriotic foreigners . . . in favor of the negro."

All hope of presidential-congressional cooperation was dead. In 1866 newspapers reported daily violations of blacks' rights in the South and carried alarming accounts of antiblack violence. In Memphis, forty blacks were killed and twelve schools burned by white mobs, and in New Orleans, the toll was thirty-four African Americans dead and two hundred wounded. Violence convinced Republicans and the northern public that more needed to be done. A new Republican plan focused on the Fourteenth Amendment to the Constitution.

Fourteenth Amendment

Of the five sections of the Fourteenth Amendment, the first would have the greatest legal significance. It conferred citizenship on "all persons born or naturalized in the United States" and prohibited states from abridging their constitutional "privileges and immunities" (see the appendix for the Constitution and all amendments). It also barred states from taking a person's life, liberty, or property "without due process of law" and from denying "equal protection of the laws." These phrases have become powerful guarantees of African Americans' civil rights and the rights of all citizens, except Indians, who were not granted citizenship rights until 1924.

Republicans almost universally agreed on the amendment's second and third sections. The fourth declared the Confederate debt null and void and guaranteed the United States' war debt. Northerners rejected paying taxes to reimburse those who financed a rebellion, and business groups agreed on the necessity of upholding the U.S. government's credit. The second and third sections barred Confederate leaders from holding state and federal office. Only Congress, by a two-thirds vote of each house, could remove the penalty, thereby guaranteeing some punishment for Confederate leaders.

The second section of the amendment also dealt with representation and embodied the compromises that produced the document. Northerners disagreed about whether blacks should have the right to vote. In truth, public will, North and South, lagged behind the amendment's egalitarian spirit. Many northern states still maintained black disfranchisement laws during Reconstruction.

Emancipation ended the three-fifths clause for the purpose of counting blacks, which would have increased southern representation. Thus the postwar South stood to gain power in Congress, and if white southerners did not allow blacks to vote, former secessionists would derive the political benefit from emancipation. Consequently, Republicans determined that, if a southern state did not grant black men the vote, their representation would be reduced proportionally.

The Fourteenth Amendment specified for the first time that voters were male. As such, it damaged the women's rights movement. Advocates of women's equality worked with abolitionists for decades, often subordinating their cause to the slaves'. During the drafting of the Fourteenth Amendment, however, some leaders, such as

Elizabeth Cady Stanton and Susan B. Anthony, ended their alliance with abolitionists and fought for women, infusing new life into the women's rights movement. Other women activists, however, argued that it was "the Negro's hour." Many former male abolitionists, white and black, were willing to delay woman's suffrage to secure freed men the vote.

The South's and Johnson's Defiance

Johnson tried to block the Fourteenth Amendment. He urged state legislatures in the South to vote against ratification, and all but Tennessee rejected the amendment by a wide margin.

To present his case to northerners, Johnson organized a National Union Convention. He boarded a special train for a "swing around the circle" that carried his message into the Northeast, the Midwest, and then back to Washington. Increasingly, audiences rejected his views, jeering at him. Johnson handed out American flags with thirty-six rather than twenty-five stars, declaring the Union already restored, and he labeled the Radicals traitors for attempting to take over Reconstruction.

In the 1866 elections radical and moderate Republicans whom Johnson denounced won reelection by large margins, and the Republican majority grew to two-thirds of both houses of Congress. The North had spoken clearly: Johnson's policies of states' rights and white supremacy were giving the advantage to rebels and traitors. Thus Republican congressional leaders won a mandate to pursue their Reconstruction plan.

But nothing could be accomplished as long as the Johnson governments existed and the southern electorate remained exclusively white. Republicans resolved to form new state governments in the South and enfranchise the freed men.

Reconstruction Acts of 1867–1868

After embittered debate, the First Reconstruction Act passed in March 1867. This plan, under which the southern states were readmitted to the Union, incorporated only part of the Radical program. Union generals, commanding small garrisons and charged with supervising elections, assumed control in five military districts in the South (see Map 16.1). Confederate leaders designated in the Fourteenth Amendment were barred from voting until new state constitutions were ratified and freed men were guaranteed the right to vote. In addition, each southern state was required to ratify the Fourteenth Amendment and its new constitution by majority vote and submit that constitution to Congress for approval (see Table 16.1).

The Second, Third, and Fourth Reconstruction Acts, passed between March 1867 and March 1868, provided the details for voter registration boards, the adoption of constitutions, and the administration of good faith oaths by white southerners.

Failure of Land Redistribution

The Radicals halted Johnson, but they had hoped Congress could do much more. Thaddeus Stevens, for example, argued that economic opportunity was essential to the freedmen. He drew up a plan for extensive confiscation and redistribution of land, but it was never realized.

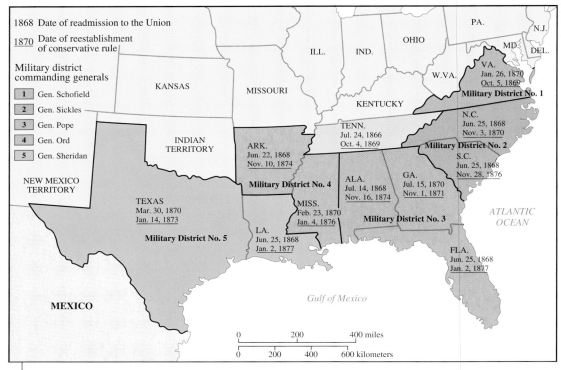

1868 Date of readmission to the Union

1870 Date of reestablishment of conservative rule

Military district commanding generals
- 1 Gen. Schofield
- 2 Gen. Sickles
- 3 Gen. Pope
- 4 Gen. Ord
- 5 Gen. Sheridan

Map 16.1   The Reconstruction

This map shows the five military districts established when Congress passed the Reconstruction Act of 1867. As the dates within each state indicate, conservative Democratic forces quickly regained control of government in four southern states. So-called Radical Reconstruction was curtailed in most of the others, as factions within the weakened Republican Party began to cooperate with conservative Democrats.

TABLE 16.1   Plans for Reconstruction Compared

	Johnson's Plan	Radicals' Plan	Fourteenth Amendment	Reconstruction Act of 1867
Voting	Whites only can vote; high-ranking Confederate leaders must seek pardons.	Give vote to black males.	Southern whites may decide but can lose representation if they deny black suffrage.	Black men gain vote; whites barred from office by Fourteenth Amendment cannot vote while new state governments are being formed.
Officeholding	Many prominent Confederates regain power.	Only loyal white and black males are eligible.	Confederate leaders barred until Congress votes amnesty.	Fourteenth Amendment in effect.
Time Out of Union	Brief.	Several years; until South is thoroughly democratized.	Brief.	3–5 years after war.
Other Change in Southern Society	Little; gain of power by yeomen not realized; emancipation grudgingly accepted, but no black civil or political rights.	Expand public education; confiscate land and provide farms for freedmen; expansion of activist federal government.	Probably slight, depending on enforcement.	Considerable, depending on action of new state governments.

Racial fears and an American obsession with the sanctity of private property made land redistribution unpopular. Thus black farmers were forced to seek work in a hostile environment in which landowners opposed their acquisition of land.

Constitutional Crisis

To restrict Johnson's influence and safeguard its plan, Congress passed several controversial laws. First, it limited Johnson's power over the army by requiring the president to issue military orders through the general of the army, Ulysses S. Grant. Then Congress passed the Tenure of Office Act, which gave the Senate power to approve changes in the president's cabinet. Designed to protect Secretary of War Stanton, a Radical sympathizer, this law violated the tradition of presidents controlling cabinet appointments. All of these measures, along with the Reconstruction Acts, were passed by a two-thirds override of presidential vetoes.

In response, Johnson limited the power of military commanders in the South and increased the powers of the civil governments he created in 1865. Then he removed military officers who were enforcing Congress's new law, preferring commanders who allowed disqualified Confederates to vote. Finally, he tried to remove Secretary of War Stanton, pushing the confrontation to its climax.

Impeachment of President Johnson

Impeachment is a political procedure provided for in the Constitution as a remedy for crimes or serious abuses of power by presidents, federal judges, and other high government officials. Those who are impeached (judged or politically indicted) in the House are then tried in the Senate. Twice in 1867, the House Judiciary Committee considered impeachment of Johnson, first rejecting it and then recommending it by a 5-to-4 vote, which was defeated by the House. After Johnson tried to remove Stanton, however, a third attempt to impeach him carried in early 1868. The indictment concentrated on his violation of the Tenure of Office Act, though modern scholars regard his efforts to obstruct enforcement of the Reconstruction Act of 1867 as a more serious offense.

Johnson's trial in the Senate lasted more than three months. The prosecution, led by Radicals, attempted to prove that Johnson was guilty of "high crimes and misdemeanors." But they also argued that the trial was a means to judge Johnson's performance. The Senate rejected such reasoning, which could have made removal from office a political weapon against any chief executive who disagreed with Congress. The prosecution fell one vote short of the necessary two-thirds majority needed to convict Johnson. He remained in office, politically weakened.

Election of 1868

In the 1868 presidential election, Ulysses S. Grant, running as a Republican, defeated Horatio Seymour, a New York Democrat. Grant was not a Radical, but his platform supported congressional Reconstruction and endorsed black suffrage in the South. (Significantly, Republicans stopped short of endorsing black suffrage in the North.) The Democrats denounced Reconstruction and preached white supremacy, conducting the most openly racist campaign in American history. Both

A Republican Party brass band in action during the 1868 election campaign in Baton Rouge, Louisiana. The Union regimental colors and soldiers' caps demonstrate the strong federal presence in the South at this pivotal moment in radical Reconstruction.
(Andrew D. Lytle Collection, Louisiana and Lower Mississippi Valley Collections, LSU Libraries, Louisiana State University, Baton Rouge, Louisiana)

sides waved the "bloody shirt," blaming each other for the war's sacrifices. By associating with rebellion and Johnson's repudiated program, the Democrats were defeated in all but eight states, though the popular vote was close. Blacks voted en masse for General Grant.

In office Grant vacillated in dealing with the southern states, sometimes defending Republican regimes and sometimes currying favor with Democrats. Occasionally Grant called out federal troops to stop violence or enforce Congressional acts, but he never imposed a military occupation on the South. Rapid demobilization reduced a federal army of more than 1 million to fifty-seven thousand within a year of the surrender at Appomattox. Thereafter, the number of troops in the South declined until in 1874 there were only four thousand in southern states outside Texas. The legend of military rule, so important to southern claims of victimization during Reconstruction, was steeped in myth.

Fifteenth Amendment   In 1869 the Radicals pushed through the Fifteenth Amendment, the final major measure in Reconstruction's constitutional revolution. It forbade states to deny the right to vote "on account of race, color, or previous condition of servitude." Such wording did not guarantee the right to vote and left states free to restrict suffrage on other grounds. Northern states could deny suffrage to women and certain men— Chinese immigrants, illiterates, and those too poor to pay poll taxes. With passage of the Fifteenth Amendment in 1870, many Americans, especially northerners, considered Reconstruction completed.

RECONSTRUCTION POLITICS AND ECONOMY IN THE SOUTH

From the start, white southerners resisted Reconstruction and opposed emancipation, as evident in the black codes. The former planter class proved especially unbending because of their tremendous financial loss in slaves. For many poor whites who never owned slaves, destitution, plummeting agricultural prices, disease, and the uncertainties of a growing urban industrialization drove them off land, toward cities, and into hatred of black equality.

White Resistance   Some planters attempted to postpone freedom by denying or misrepresenting events. Former slaves reported that their owners didn't tell them it was freedom or wouldn't let them go. To hold onto their workers, some landowners claimed control over black children and used guardianship and apprentice laws to bind black families to the plantation. While a few planters divided up plots among their slaves, most condemned the notion of blacks as landowners.

Adamant resistance by whites soon manifested itself in other ways, including violence. A local North Carolina magistrate clubbed a black man on a public street, and in several states bands of Regulators terrorized blacks who displayed any independence. After President Johnson encouraged the South to resist congressional Reconstruction, many white conservatives captured the new state governments, while others boycotted the polls to defeat Congress's plans.

Black Voters and the Southern Republican Party   Enthusiastically blacks went to the polls, voting Republican, as one man said, to "stick to the end with the party that freed me." Illiteracy did not keep them (or uneducated whites) from making intelligent choices. Mississippi's William Henry could read only "a little," but he said, "We saw D. Sledge vote; he owned half the county. We knowed he voted Democratic so we voted the other ticket so it would be Republican." Women, who could not vote, encouraged husbands and sons, and preachers exhorted congregations to use the franchise.

Thanks to a large black turnout and the restrictions on prominent Confederates, a new southern Republican Party came to power in the 1868–1870 constitutional conventions. Republican delegates consisted of a sizable black contingent (265 of the more than 1,000 delegates throughout the South), northerners who moved to the South, and native southern whites seeking change. The new constitutions they drafted were more democratic than anything previously adopted in the South. They eliminated property qualifications for voting and holding office, turned many appointed offices into elective posts, and provided for public schools and institutions to care for the mentally ill, the blind, the deaf, the destitute, and the orphaned.

The conventions broadened women's rights in property holding and divorce. Usually the goal was not equality but providing relief to thousands of suffering debtors. Since husbands usually contracted the debts, giving women legal control over their own property provided some protection for their families.

Triumph of Republican Governments

Under these new constitutions, southern states elected Republican-controlled governments. For the first time, state legislators in 1868 included black southerners. Contrary to what white southerners later claimed, Republican state governments did not disfranchise ex-Confederates as a group. James Lynch, a leading black politician from Mississippi, saw disfranchising whites as foolish. Landless former slaves "must be in friendly relations with the great body of the whites in the state," he explained. "Otherwise . . . peace can be maintained only by a standing army." Despised and lacking power, southern Republicans strove for safe ways to gain a foothold in a depressed economy.

Far from being vindictive toward the race that enslaved them, most southern blacks appealed to whites to be fair. Hence, the South's Republican Party condemned itself to defeat if white voters would not cooperate. Within a few years most fledgling Republican parties in the southern states would be struggling for survival against violent white hostility.

Industrialization and Mill Towns

Reconstruction governments promoted industry via loans, subsidies, and short-term exemptions from taxation. The southern railroad system was rebuilt and expanded, and coal and iron mining made possible Birmingham's steel plants. Between 1860 and 1880, the number of manufacturing establishments in the South nearly doubled.

This emphasis on big business, however, produced higher state debts and taxes, drew money away from schools and other programs, and multiplied possibilities for corruption. The alliance between business and government often operated at the expense of farmers and laborers. It also doomed Republicans to failure in building support among poorer whites.

Poverty remained the lot of many southern whites. The war caused a massive loss of income-producing wealth, such as livestock, and a steep decline in land values. From 1860 to 1880, the South's share of per capita income fell to 51 percent of the national average. In many regions the old planter class still had the best land and access to credit or markets.

As poor whites and blacks found farming less tenable, they moved to cities and mill towns. Industrialization did not sweep the South as it did the North, but it laid deep roots. Attracting textile mills to southern towns became a competitive crusade. In 1860 the South counted some 10,000 mill workers; by 1880, the number grew to 16,741; and by century's end to 97,559. Many poor southerners moved from farmer to mill worker or other low-income urban wage earner job.

Republicans and Racial Equality

Whites who controlled the southern Republican Party were reluctant to allow blacks a share of offices proportionate to their electoral strength. Aware of their weakness, black leaders did not push hard for revolutionary change. Instead, they led efforts to establish public schools, though without pressing for integrated facilities. In 1870 South Carolina passed the first comprehensive school law in the South. By 1875, 50 percent of that state's black school-age children were enrolled in school, and approximately one-third of the three thousand teachers were black.

Those African American politicians who did fight for civil rights and integration were typically from cities such as New Orleans or Mobile, where large populations of light-skinned free blacks existed before the war. Their experience made them sensitive to issues of status. Laws requiring equal accommodations were passed but often went unenforced.

Economic progress, particularly land ownership, was a major concern for most freedpeople. Land reform failed because in most states whites were the majority, and former slaveowners controlled the best land and financial resources. Much land did fall into state hands for nonpayment of taxes and was sold in small lots. But most freed men had too little cash to bid against investors or speculators. Any widespread redistribution of land had to arise from Congress, which never supported such action.

Myth of Negro Rule

Within a few years, white hostility to congressional Reconstruction increasingly prevailed. Conservatives who long wanted to fight Reconstruction through economic pressure and racist propaganda began to do so. Charging that the South had been turned over to ignorant blacks, conservatives used black domination as a rallying cry for a return to white supremacy.

Such attacks were part of the growing myth of Negro rule, which would become a central theme in battles over the memory of Reconstruction. African Americans participated in politics but hardly dominated. They were a majority in only two of ten state constitutional conventions. In the state legislatures, only in South Carolina's lower house did blacks constitute a majority. Sixteen blacks won seats in Congress before Reconstruction was over. Only eighteen served in a high state office, such as lieutenant governor, treasurer, superintendent of education, or secretary of state, but none became governor.

Some four hundred blacks served in political office during the Reconstruction era, an enormous achievement. Elected officials, such as Robert Smalls in South Carolina, labored for cheaper land prices, better healthcare, access to schools, and the enforcement of civil rights. In this way, the black politicians of Reconstruction took heroic first steps in America's long civil rights movement.

Carpetbaggers and Scalawags

Conservative propaganda also assailed the allies of black Republicans. They denounced northern whites as *carpetbaggers*, greedy crooks planning to pour stolen tax revenues into their luggage made of carpet material.

In fact, most northerners who settled in the South had come seeking business opportunities, as schoolteachers, or to find a warmer climate; most never entered politics. Those who did generally wanted to democratize the South and introduce northern ways, such as industry and public education.

In addition to tagging northern interlopers as carpetbaggers, conservatives invented the term *scalawag* to discredit native white southerners cooperating with the Republicans, as many, including wealthy men, did. Most scalawags were yeoman farmers from mountain areas and nonslaveholding districts who were Unionists under the Confederacy. They hoped to benefit from the education and opportunities Republicans promoted. Sometimes joining with freed men, they pursued common class interests to make headway against long-dominant planters. Initially promising, over time most of these black-white coalitions floundered due to racism.

Tax Policy and Corruption as Political Wedges

Republicans wanted to repair the war's destruction, stimulate industry, and support such new ventures as public schools, all of which required tax monies. But the Civil War damaged the South's tax base. Hundreds of thousands of citizens lost much of their property—slaves, money, livestock, and buildings—to the war. Tax increases (sales, excise, and property) were necessary for even traditional services. Inevitably, Republican tax policies aroused strong opposition, especially among yeomen.

Corruption charges also plagued Republicans. Many carpetbaggers and black politicians engaged in fraudulent schemes or sold their votes, participating in what scholars recognize as a nationwide corruption surge in an age ruled by spoilsmen. Corruption crossed party lines, but the Democrats pinned the blame on unqualified blacks and greedy carpetbaggers among southern Republicans.

Ku Klux Klan

Republican leaders also allowed factionalism along racial and class lines to undermine party unity. At the same time, the Ku Klux Klan, a secret veterans' club that began in Tennessee in 1866, spread through the South, quickly becoming a terrorist organization. Klansmen sought to frustrate Reconstruction and keep the freed men in subjection with ongoing nighttime harassment, whippings, beatings, rapes, and murders.

Although the Klan tormented blacks, its main purpose was political. Lawless nightriders targeted active Republicans, killing leading whites and blacks in several states. After freed men who worked for a South Carolina scalawag started voting, terrorists visited the plantation and, as one victim noted, "whipped every . . . [black] man they could lay their hands on." Klansmen also attacked Union League clubs—Republican organizations that mobilized the black vote—and schoolteachers who aided freed men.

Specific social forces shaped and directed Klan violence, with Alamance and Caswell Counties in North Carolina receiving the worst of it. Slim Republican majorities there rested on cooperation between black voters and white yeomen. Together, these black and white Republicans ousted long-entrenched officials. The wealthy and powerful men who lost their accustomed political control were the Klan's county officers and local chieftains. By intimidation and murder, the Klan weakened the Republican coalition and restored a Democratic majority.

Klan violence injured Republicans across the South. One of every ten black delegates to the 1867–1868 state constitutional conventions was attacked, seven fatally. In one judicial district of North Carolina, the Ku Klux Klan was responsible for twelve murders, over seven hundred beatings, along with many cases of rape and arson. A single attack on Republicans in Eutaw, Alabama, left four blacks dead and fifty-four wounded. According to historian Eric Foner, the Klan "made it virtually impossible for Republicans to campaign or vote in large parts of Georgia."

Thus Republican mistakes, racial hostility, and terror brought down the Republican regimes. In most states, Radical Reconstruction lasted only a few years (see Map 16.1). The most enduring failure of Reconstruction, however, was that it did not alter the South's social structure or its distribution of wealth and power.

RETREAT FROM RECONSTRUCTION

During the 1870s, northerners lost the political will to sustain Reconstruction, as they confronted vast economic and social transformations in their region and the West. Radical Republicans like Albion Tourgée, a former Union soldier who moved to North Carolina and was elected a judge, condemned Congress's timidity. He and many African Americans believed that, during Reconstruction, the North "threw all the Negroes on the world without any way of getting along." As the North lost interest in the South's dilemmas, Reconstruction collapsed.

Political Implications of Klan Terrorism

Whites in the old Confederacy referred to this decline of Reconstruction as southern redemption. During the 1870s, "redeemer" Democrats claimed to be the South's saviors from alleged black domination and carpetbag rule, as the party regained control of the South.

Meanwhile, in 1870 and 1871 the Ku Klux Klan's violent campaigns forced Congress to pass two Enforcement Acts and an anti-Klan law. These laws made actions by individuals against the civil and political rights of others a federal criminal offense. They also provided for election supervisors and permitted martial law and suspension of the writ of habeas corpus to combat murders, beatings, and Klan threats. In 1872 and 1873, Mississippi and the Carolinas saw many prosecutions; but in other states, the laws were ignored. Southern juries sometimes refused to convict Klansmen; less than half of the 3,310 cases ended in convictions. Although many Klansmen fled their state to avoid prosecution, and the Klan officially disbanded, paramilitary organizations known as Rifle Clubs and Red Shirts often took the Klan's place.

Still, there were ominous signs that the North's commitment to racial justice was fading, as some influential Republicans opposed the anti-Klan laws. Rejecting other Republicans' arguments that the Thirteenth, Fourteenth, and Fifteenth Amendments made the federal government the protector of citizens' rights, dissenters charged that Congress was infringing on states' rights. This foreshadowed a general revolt within Republican ranks in 1872.

Industrial Expansion and Reconstruction in the North

Immigration and industrialization surged in the North. Between 1865 and 1873, 3 million immigrants entered the country, most settling in the industrial cities of the North and West. In that eight-year period, industrial production increased by 75 percent. For the first time, nonagricultural workers outnumbered farmers, and wage earners outnumbered independent craftsmen. Government policies encouraged this rapid growth, as low taxes on investment and high tariffs on manufactured goods helped create a new class of powerful industrialists, especially railroad entrepreneurs.

From 1865 to 1873, 35,000 miles of new track were laid; this fueled the banking industry and made Wall Street the center of American capitalism. Eastern railroad magnates, such as Thomas Scott of the Pennsylvania Railroad, created economic empires with the assistance of huge government subsidies of cash and land. Railroad corporations also bought up mining operations, granaries, and lumber companies. Big business now employed lobbyists to curry favor with government. Corruption ran rampant, with some congressmen and legislators paid retainers of major companies.

As captains of industry amassed unprecedented fortunes, gross economic inequality polarized American society. The workforce, worried a prominent Massachusetts business leader, was in a "transition state . . . living in boarding houses" and becoming a "permanent factory population." In New York and Philadelphia, workers increasingly lived in unhealthy tenement housing. Thousands would list themselves on the census as common laborer or general jobber. Concerned, in 1868 Republicans passed an eight-hour workday bill that applied to federal workers. The labor question (see Chapter 18) now preoccupied northerners far more than the southern or the freed men question.

Then the Panic of 1873 ushered in over five years of economic contraction. Three million people lost their jobs, especially in cities. Workers and farmers desperately needed cash and sought easy-money policies to spur economic expansion. Businessmen, disturbed by the strikes and industrial violence that accompanied the panic, defended property rights and demanded sound money policies. The chasm between wealthy industrialists and farmers and workers widened.

Liberal Republican Revolt

Disenchanted with Reconstruction, a largely northern group calling itself the Liberal Republicans bolted the party in 1872 and nominated Horace Greeley, editor of the *New York Tribune,* for president. A varied group, Liberal Republicans included foes of corruption and advocates of a lower tariff. Two popular and widespread issues united them: distaste for federal intervention in the South and an elitist desire to let market forces and the "best men" determine policy.

The Grants' Tour of the World

On May 17, 1877, two weeks after his presidency ended, Ulysses S. Grant and his wife Julia embarked from Philadelphia on a twenty-six month world tour. Portrayed as a private vacation, the trip was meant to help dissipate the taint of corruption in Grant's second term. The small entourage included John Russell Young, a reporter for the *New York Herald* who recorded the journey in the two-volume, illustrated *Around the World with General Grant*.

The Grants spent months in England attending an array of banquets, one with Queen Victoria. In Newcastle, thousands of workingmen conducted a massive parade in Grant's honor. Grant was viewed as the savior of the American nation, the liberator of slaves, and a celebrity.

Every royal or republican head of a European state hosted the Grants, including the heads of state of Belgium, France, Switzerland, Italy, Russia, Poland, Austria, and Spain. The Grants next went to Egypt and then traveled by train to the Indian Ocean, where they embarked for India. They encountered British imperialism in Bombay, and that of the French in Saigon. The grand excursion went to China and Japan. The Grants enjoyed a rare audience with Japan's Emperor Mutsuhito and found Japan "beautiful beyond description."

The Grants landed in San Francisco in late June 1879. The reason for the prolonged trip: Grant sought publicity abroad to convince his countrymen back home that they should reelect him president in 1880. But he developed no compelling reason why Americans should choose him again. He spent his final years a war hero and a national symbol. No American president would again establish such personal links to the world until Woodrow Wilson after World War I.

On their tour of the world, Ulysses and Julia Grant sat with companions and guides in front of the Great Hypostyle Hall at the Temple of Amon-Ra in Karnak at Luxor, Egypt, 1878. The Grants' extraordinary tour included many such photo opportunities, often depicting the plebeian American president's presence in exotic places with unusual people. Whether he liked it or not, Grant was a world celebrity.

(Library of Congress)

The Democrats also nominated Greeley in 1872, but it was not enough to keep Grant from reelection. Greeley's campaign for North-South reunion was a harbinger of the future in American politics. Organized Blue-Gray fraternalism (gatherings of Union and Confederate veterans) began as early as 1874. Grant continued to avoid confrontation with white southerners and in 1875 refused a desperate request from Mississippi's governor for troops to quell racial and political terrorism there.

Grant made several poor appointments that fueled public dissatisfaction with his administration. His secretary of war, his private secretary, and officials in the Treasury and Navy Departments were involved in bribery or tax-cheating scandals. Instead of exposing the corruption, Grant defended the culprits. In 1874, the Democrats recaptured the House of Representatives, signaling the end of the Radical Republican vision of Reconstruction.

General Amnesty

Democratic gains in Congress weakened legislative resolve on southern issues. Congress already lifted the political disabilities of the Fourteenth Amendment from many former Confederates. In 1872 it adopted an Amnesty Act, which pardoned most of the remaining rebels. In 1875 Congress passed a Civil Rights Act, partly in tribute to the recently deceased Charles Sumner, purporting to guarantee black people equal accommodations in public places, but the bill was watered down and contained no enforcement provisions. (The Supreme Court later struck down this law;)

Democrats regained control of four state governments before 1872 and eight by late January 1876 (see Map 16.1). In the North, Democrats successfully stressed the failure and scandals of Reconstruction governments. Sectional reconciliation now seemed crucial for commerce. The nation was expanding westward, and the South was a new investment frontier.

The West, Race, and Reconstruction

As the Fourteenth Amendment and other enactments granted blacks the beginnings of citizenship, other non-whites faced continued persecution. Across the West, the federal government pursued a containment policy against Native Americans. In California, where white farmers and ranchers often forced Indians into captive labor, some civilians practiced Indian hunting. By 1880, thirty years of violence left an estimated forty-five hundred California Indians dead at the hands of white settlers.

In California and other states of the Far West, few whites objected to the Chinese immigrants who did the dangerous work of building railroads through the Rocky Mountains. But when the Chinese competed for urban, industrial jobs, conflict erupted. Anticoolie clubs appeared in California in the 1870s seeking laws against Chinese labor, inciting racism, and organizing brutal attacks on Chinese workers and the factories that employed them. Western politicians sought white votes by pandering to prejudice, and in 1879 the new California constitution denied Chinese the vote.

Viewing America from coast to coast, the Civil War and Reconstruction years dismantled racial slavery and fostered a volatile new racial complexity, especially in the West. Some African Americans, despite generations of mixture with Native Americans, asserted that they were more like whites than uncivilized Indians, while others, like the Creek freed men of Indian Territory, sought an Indian identity. In Texas, whites, Indians, blacks, and Hispanics had mixed for decades, and by the 1870s forced reconsideration in law and custom of who exactly who was white.

America was undergoing what one historian has called a reconstruction of the concept of race itself. The turbulence of the expanding West reinforced the new nationalism and the reconciliation of North and South based on a resurgent white supremacy.

Foreign Expansion

In 1867 new expansion pressures led Secretary of State William H. Seward to purchase Alaska from Russia, adding vast new territory to the United States (see Chapter 22). Opponents ridiculed Seward's $7.2 million venture, but Seward convinced important congressmen of Alaska's economic potential, and other lawmakers favored the dawning of friendship with Russia.

Also in 1867 the United States took control of the Midway Islands, a thousand miles northwest of Hawai'i. Through diplomacy, Seward and his successor, Hamilton Fish, resolved wartime grievances with Great Britain by arranging a financial settlement for damage done by the *Alabama* and other cruisers built in England and sold to the Confederacy. Sectional reconciliation in Reconstruction America would serve new ambitions for world commerce and expansion.

Judicial Retreat from Reconstruction

Meanwhile, the Supreme Court played its part in the northern retreat from Reconstruction. During the Civil War, the Court was cautious and inactive. Reaction to the *Dred Scott* decision (1857) was so vehement and the Union's wartime emergency so great, that the Court had avoided interference with government actions. But that changed in 1866 when *Ex parte Milligan* reached the Court.

Lambdin P. Milligan of Indiana plotted to free Confederate prisoners of war and overthrow state governments. Consequently, a military court sentenced Milligan, a civilian, to death. Milligan challenged the military tribunal's authority, claiming he was entitled to a civil trial. The Supreme Court declared that military trials were illegal when civil courts were functioning. It seemed the Court intended to reassert its authority.

In the 1870s the Court renewed its challenge to Congress's actions when it narrowed the meaning of the Fourteenth Amendment. The *Slaughter-House* cases (1873) began in 1869, when the Louisiana legislature granted one company a monopoly on livestock slaughtering in New Orleans. Rival butchers sued, and their attorney, former Supreme Court justice John A. Campbell, argued that Louisiana violated the rights of some citizens in favor of others. The Fourteenth Amendment, Campbell contended, had brought individual rights under federal protection.

But in the *Slaughter-House* decision, the Supreme Court dealt a blow to the scope of the Fourteenth Amendment. It declared state citizenship and national citizenship separate. National citizenship involved only matters such as the right to travel freely from state to state, and only such narrow rights, held the Court, were protected by the Fourteenth Amendment.

Shrinking from a role as "perpetual censor upon all legislation of the States, on the civil rights of their own citizens," the Court's majority declared that the framers of the recent amendments had not intended to "destroy" the federal system, in which the states exercised "powers for domestic and local government, including the regulation of civil rights." Thus the justices severely limited the amendment's potential for safeguarding the rights of black citizens—its original intent.

The next day the Court decided *Bradwell v. Illinois,* a case in which Myra Bradwell, a female attorney, was denied the right to practice law in Illinois because she was married woman, and hence not a free agent. Using the Fourteenth Amendment, Bradwell's attorneys contended that the state had unconstitutionally abridged her "privileges and immunities" as a citizen. The Supreme Court disagreed, declaring it was a woman's "paramount destiny . . . to fulfill the noble and benign offices of wife and mother."

In 1876 the Court further weakened the Reconstruction era amendments. In *U.S. v. Cruikshank* the Court overruled the conviction under the 1870 Enforcement Act of Louisiana whites who attacked a meeting of blacks and conspired to deprive them of their rights. The justices ruled that the Fourteenth Amendment did not give the federal government power to act against these whites. The duty of protecting citizens' equal rights, the Court said, "rests alone with the States." Such judicial conservatism blunted the revolutionary potential in the Civil War amendments into the next century.

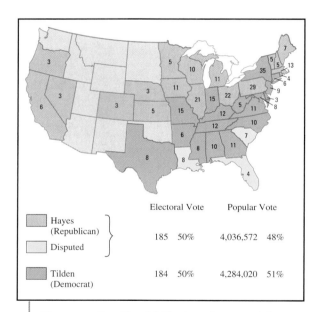

	Electoral Vote	Popular Vote
Hayes (Republican)		
Disputed	185 50%	4,036,572 48%
Tilden (Democrat)	184 50%	4,284,020 51%

Map 16.2   Presidential Election of 1876 and the Compromise of 1877

In 1876 a combination of solid southern support and Democratic gains in the North gave Samuel Tilden the majority of popular votes, but Rutherford B. Hayes won the disputed election in the electoral college, after a deal satisfied Democratic wishes for an end to Reconstruction.

Disputed Election of 1876 and Compromise of 1877

The results of the disputed presidential election of 1876 confirmed that economic issues predominated and that the North was no longer pursuing the goals of reconstruction. Samuel J. Tilden, the Democratic governor of New York, ran strongly in the South and needed one electoral vote to triumph over Rutherford B. Hayes, the Republican nominee. Nineteen electoral votes from Louisiana, South Carolina, and Florida (the only southern states not yet under Democratic rule) were disputed; both Democrats and Republicans claimed to have won those states despite fraud committed by their opponents (see Map 16.2).

To resolve this unprecedented situation, Congress established a fifteen-member electoral commission, balanced between Democrats and Republicans. Because Republicans held the majority in Congress, they prevailed, 8 to 7, on every attempt to count the returns. Hayes would become president if Congress accepted the commission's findings.

But Democrats controlled the House and could filibuster to block action on the vote. Many citizens worried about another civil war, as some southerners vowed "Tilden or Fight!" Finally, Democrats acquiesced in the election of Hayes based on a deal cut between Hayes's supporters and southerners who wanted federal aid to railroads, internal improvements, and removal of troops from southern states. Northern and southern Democrats simply decided not to contest the election of a Republican who was not going to continue Reconstruction.

Southern Democrats rejoiced that Reconstruction was over, but African Americans grieved over the betrayal of their hopes for equality. In a Fourth of July speech in Washington, D.C., in 1875, Frederick Douglass looked back on fifteen years of unparalleled change for his people and worried about the hold of white supremacy on America's historical memory: "If war among the whites brought peace and liberty to the blacks, what will peace among the whites bring?"

Summary

Reconstruction was an era of tragic aspirations and failures but also of unprecedented legal, political, and social change. The Union victory brought increased federal power, stronger nationalism, sweeping federal intervention in the southern states, and landmark constitutional amendments. But northern commitment to make these changes eroded, leaving the revolution unfinished. The early promise for new lives and liberties among freedpeople had fallen, at least temporarily, by the wayside.

The North had embraced emancipation, black suffrage, and constitutional alterations strengthening the central government, primarily to defeat the rebellion. As wartime pressures declined, Americans, especially northerners, retreated from Reconstruction. The American people and the courts maintained a preference for state authority and a distrust of federal power, while free-labor ideology stressed respect for property and individual self-reliance. Racism transformed into Klan terror and theories of black degeneration.

New challenges to American society gradually overwhelmed the aims of Reconstruction. Industrialization promised prosperity but also wrought increased exploitation of labor. Moreover, industry laid the foundation for an enlarged American role in international affairs.

In the wake of the Civil War, Americans faced two profound tasks—healing and dispensing justice. Making sectional reunion compatible with black freedom and equality overwhelmed American politics, and the nation faced much of this dilemma more than a century later.

The Lost Cause

All major wars compel a struggle over their memory. After the Civil War, white southerners and their northern allies constructed a Lost Cause tradition, a potent and racially exclusive version of the war and Reconstruction which persists today.

The Lost Cause emerged among ex-Confederates as a mourning ritual and a psychological response to the trauma of defeat. But it also took root in selective reinterpretations of the war's causes; southern resistance to Reconstruction; doctrines of white supremacy; and a mythic, nostalgic popular culture among northerners and southerners. Lost Cause advocates—from high-ranking officers to common soldiers—argued that the war had never been about slavery, that Confederates only lost to Yankee numbers and resources, and that the nation should reconcile by equally honoring southern and northern sacrifice. In the industrial, urban, multiethnic America of the emerging twentieth century, images of benevolent Southern masters and faithful slaves and of Robert E. Lee as America's truest Christian soldier provided a sentimentalized road to reunion. These images reverberated in Jim Crow America, and they endure in modern tastes for Civil War memorabilia and uses of the Confederate flag to oppose civil rights and affirmative action.

From 1865 to the 1880s, this Confederate legend was forged by wartime participants determined to vindicate the Confederacy. By the 1890s, however, Lost Cause culture emerged especially with the United Daughters of the Confederacy. Elite southern white women built monuments, lobbied congressmen, delivered lectures, ran contests for schoolchildren, and strove to control the content of history textbooks in the service of an exalted South. Above all, Lost Causers advocated what one historian has called a "victory narrative." This new victory was the nation's triumph over the racial revolution and constitutional transformations of Reconstruction.

In his 1881 memoir, Jefferson Davis declared the Lost Cause not lost: "Well may we rejoice in the regained possession of self-government. . . . This is the great victory . . . a total non-interference by the Federal government in the domestic affairs of the States."

Chapter Review

WARTIME RECONSTRUCTION

Which two political acts recognized the centrality of slavery to the war?

Passage of the Thirteenth Amendment and establishment of the Freedmen's Bureau in early 1865 sent a clear signal that slavery was a major cause for the Civil War. The Thirteenth Amendment first abolished slavery ("involuntary servitude") and second gave Congress the power to enforce it. Then, a few months later in March, Congress established the Bureau of Refugees, Freedmen and Abandoned Lands, known as the Freedmen's Bureau, to help former slaves. During its four years as a federal agency, it supplied food and medical services, built thousands of schools and colleges, negotiated job contracts between former slaves and masters, and managed confiscated lands.

THE MEANINGS OF FREEDOM

How did blacks exert their newfound freedom?

With emancipation, former slaves sought to reunite families broken apart through slave sales. Community also became important, as they built their own churches that ultimately served to unify racial ties. Seeking greater control over their work lives, African Americans wanted fairer employers and hoped to own land; when that was not possible, they rented land from former masters under the sharecropping system, in which they paid for supplies and rent by giving owners' half their crops on average. Former slaves also embraced the education that had been denied them under slavery and started schools, colleges, and universities throughout the South or attended those launched by the Freedman's Bureau.

JOHNSON'S RECONSTRUCTION PLAN

What was Johnson's vision for Reconstruction?

Johnson's approach to Reconstruction could be summed up in a single quote: "The Constitution as it is, and the Union as it was." As president, he controlled Reconstruction policy through 1865, pardoning former Confederates and reestablishing state governments in the South. Despising the planter class, he initially insisted that ex-Confederates with property worth more than $20,000 apply directly to him for pardons. Gradually, Johnson pardoned planters, too, which restored the former elite to power, possibly because he wanted to block Radical Republicans from implementing extensive and racial political changes in the South. Deeply racist, Johnson remained silent when southern states implemented black codes to restrict former slaves' freedom by requiring them to carry passes, obey curfew laws, and live in housing provided by a landowner. Nonetheless, after just eight months, Johnson declared Reconstruction was completed.

THE CONGRESSIONAL RECONSTRUCTION PLAN

What made Radical Reconstruction different from Johnson's plan?

Radical Republicans in Congress were upset at Johnson's moderate approach, which seemed to hold no one responsible for the war and re-established racial hierarchies and the southern elite. Initially a minority, the Radicals' popularity grew as Johnson increasingly dug in his heels. Radicals wanted to democratize the South through black suffrage, civil rights, and land confiscation and redistribution. They secured passage of the Fourteenth Amendment, which conferred citizenship on "all persons born or naturalized in the United States," and granted voting rights to males. They also passed four strident Reconstruction acts with strict and detailed plans for readmitting southern states to the Union. They barred ex-Confederates from voting until freedmen could and outlined the rules for voter registration boards and the adoption of state constitutions. Unpopular, land redistribution never materialized, but in 1869, Radicals pushed through their final measure, the Fifteenth Amendment, which prohibited states from denying the vote based on "race, color, or previous condition of servitude."

RECONSTRUCTION POLITICS AND ECONOMY IN THE SOUTH

How did black voters in the early days of Reconstruction transform the South?

With a large black voter turnout and prominent confederates barred from the polls and political positions, a new southern variant on the Republican Party came to power during the 1868 to 1870 state constitutional conventions. Their constitutions were highly democratic, eliminating property qualifications for voting and political office, shifting some appointed offices to elected ones, and establishing public schools. They also gave women greater rights in terms of property-holding and divorce. Blacks became state legislators for the first time in 1868. Angry whites charged they were being ruled by negroes, and some resorted to violent resistance. In truth, while blacks did play a greater role in government, they remained a minority.

RETREAT FROM RECONSTRUCTION

What led the North to lose interest in reconstructing the South?

First, northerners became disillusioned with Reconstruction, including some who thought federal expansion had cut too far into states rights. Second, economic and social changes in the North and West forced legislators to focus on their regional concerns. While immigration and industrialization made northern economies boom from 1865 to 1873, it also widened the gap between the richest and the poorest and created a powerful new class of industrialists. But when the Panic of 1873 brought hard times and job losses, interest in Reconstruction faded beside regional economic concerns. The Supreme Court also played a role, challenging congressional Reconstruction in several decisions. The Court ultimately narrowed the meaning of the Fourteenth Amendment by declaring state and national citizenship as separate issues and limited the amendment's ability to safeguard black citizens, as it was intended to do.

SUGGESTIONS FOR FURTHER READING

David W. Blight, *Race and Reunion: The Civil War in American Memory* (2001)

W. E. B. Du Bois, *Black Reconstruction in America* (1935)

Eric Foner, *Reconstruction: America's Unfinished Revolution, 1863–1877* (1988)

William Gillette, *Retreat from Reconstruction, 1869–1879* (1980)

Steven Hahn, *A Nation Under Our Feet: Black Political Struggles in the Rural South from Slavery to the Great Migration* (2003)

Gerald Jaynes, *Branches Without Roots: The Genesis of the Black Working Class in the American South, 1862–1882* (1986)

Michael Perman, *The Road to Redemption* (1984)

George Rable, *But There Was No Peace* (1984)

Heather Richardson, *The Death of Reconstruction* (2001)

Elliot West, "Reconstructing Race," *Western Historical Quarterly* (Spring 2003)

DECLARATION OF INDEPENDENCE
IN CONGRESS, JULY 4, 1776

When, in the course of human events, it becomes necessary for one people to dissolve the political bonds which have connected them with another, and to assume, among the powers of the earth, the separate and equal station to which the laws of nature and of nature's God entitle them, a decent respect to the opinions of mankind requires that they should declare the causes which impel them to the separation.

We hold these truths to be self-evident: That all men are created equal; that they are endowed by their Creator with certain unalienable rights; that among these are life, liberty, and the pursuit of happiness; that, to secure these rights, governments are instituted among men, deriving their just powers from the consent of the governed; that whenever any form of government becomes destructive of these ends, it is the right of the people to alter or to abolish it, and to institute new government, laying its foundation on such principles, and organizing its powers in such form, as to them shall seem most likely to effect their safety and happiness. Prudence, indeed, will dictate that governments long established should not be changed for light and transient causes; and accordingly all experience hath shown that mankind are more disposed to suffer, while evils are sufferable, than to right themselves by abolishing the forms to which they are accustomed. But when a long train of abuses and usurpations, pursuing invariably the same object, evinces a design to reduce them under absolute despotism, it is their right, it is their duty, to throw off such government, and to provide new guards for their future security. Such has been the patient sufferance of these colonies; and such is now the necessity which constrains them to alter their former systems of government. The history of the present King of Great Britain is a history of repeated injuries and usurpations, all having in direct object the establishment of an absolute tyranny over these states. To prove this, let facts be submitted to a candid world.

He has refused his assent to laws, the most wholesome and necessary for the public good.

He has forbidden his governors to pass laws of immediate and pressing importance, unless suspended in their operation till his assent should be obtained; and, when so suspended, he has utterly neglected to attend to them.

He has refused to pass other laws for the accommodation of large districts of people, unless those people would relinquish the right of representation in the legislature, a right inestimable to them, and formidable to tyrants only.

He has called together legislative bodies at places unusual, uncomfortable, and distant from the depository of their public records, for the sole purpose of fatiguing them into compliance with his measures.

He has dissolved representative houses repeatedly, for opposing, with manly firmness, his invasions on the rights of the people.

He has refused for a long time, after such dissolutions, to cause others to be elected; whereby the legislative powers, incapable of annihilation, have returned to the people at large for their exercise; the state remaining, in the mean time, exposed to all the dangers of invasions from without and convulsions within.

He has endeavored to prevent the population of these states; for that purpose obstructing the laws for naturalization of foreigners; refusing to pass others to encourage their migration hither, and raising the conditions of new appropriations of lands.

He has obstructed the administration of justice, by refusing his assent to laws for establishing judiciary powers.

He has made judges dependent on his will alone, for the tenure of their offices, and the amount and payment of their salaries.

He has erected a multitude of new offices, and sent hither swarms of officers to harass our people and eat out their substance.

He has kept among us, in times of peace, standing armies, without the consent of our legislatures.

He has affected to render the military independent of, and superior to, the civil power.

He has combined with others to subject us to a jurisdiction foreign to our constitution, and unacknowledged by our laws, giving his assent to their acts of pretended legislation:

For quartering large bodies of armed troops among us;

For protecting them, by a mock trial, from punishment for any murders which they should commit on the inhabitants of these states;

For cutting off our trade with all parts of the world;

For imposing taxes on us without our consent;

For depriving us, in many cases, of the benefits of trial by jury;

For transporting us beyond seas, to be tried for pretended offenses;

For abolishing the free system of English laws in a neighboring province, establishing therein an arbitrary government, and enlarging its boundaries, so as to render it at once an example and fit instrument for introducing the same absolute rule into these colonies;

For taking away our charters, abolishing our most valuable laws, and altering fundamentally the forms of our governments;

For suspending our own legislatures, and declaring themselves invested with power to legislate for us in all cases whatsoever.

He has abdicated government here, by declaring us out of his protection and waging war against us.

He has plundered our seas, ravaged our coasts, burned our towns, and destroyed the lives of our people.

He is at this time transporting large armies of foreign mercenaries to complete the works of death, desolation, and tyranny already begun with circumstances of cruelty and perfidy scarcely paralleled in the most barbarous ages, and totally unworthy the head of a civilized nation.

He has constrained our fellow-citizens, taken captive on the high seas, to bear arms against their country, to become the executioners of their friends and brethren, or to fall themselves by their hands.

He has excited domestic insurrection among us, and has endeavored to bring on the inhabitants of our frontiers the merciless Indian savages, whose known rule of warfare is an undistinguished destruction of all ages, sexes, and conditions.

In every stage of these oppressions we have petitioned for redress in the most humble terms; our repeated petitions have been answered only by repeated injury. A prince, whose character is thus marked by every act which may define a tyrant, is unfit to be the ruler of a free people.

Nor have we been wanting in our attentions to our British brethren. We have warned them, from time to time, of attempts by their legislature to extend an unwarrantable jurisdiction over us. We have reminded them of the circumstances of our emigration and settlement here. We have appealed to their native justice and magnanimity; and we have conjured them, by the ties of our common kindred, to disavow these usurpations, which would inevitably interrupt our connections and correspondence. They, too, have been deaf to the voice of justice and of consanguinity. We must, therefore, acquiesce in the necessity which denounces our separation, and hold them, as we hold the rest of mankind, enemies in war, in peace friends.

We, therefore, the representatives of the United States of America, in General Congress assembled, appealing to the Supreme Judge of the world for the rectitude of our intentions, do, in the name and by the authority of the good people of these colonies, solemnly publish and declare, that these United Colonies are, and of right ought to be, FREE AND INDEPENDENT STATES; that they are absolved from all allegiance to the British crown, and that all political connection between them and the state of Great Britain is, and ought to be, totally dissolved; and that, as free and independent states, they have full power to levy war, conclude peace, contract alliances, establish commerce, and do all other acts and things which independent states may of right do. And for the support of this declaration, with a firm reliance on the protection of Divine Providence, we mutually pledge to each other our lives, our fortunes, and our sacred honor.

ARTICLES OF CONFEDERATION

(The text of the Articles of Confederation can be found at cengage.com/ history/norton/peoplenationbrief8e)

CONSTITUTION OF THE UNITED STATES OF AMERICA AND AMENDMENTS*

Preamble

We the people of the United States, in order to form a more perfect union, establish justice, insure domestic tranquillity, provide for the common defense, promote the general welfare, and secure the blessings of liberty to ourselves and our posterity, do ordain and establish this Constitution for the United States of America.

Article I

Section 1 All legislative powers herein granted shall be vested in a Congress of the United States, which shall consist of a Senate and a House of Representatives.

---

* Passages no longer in effect are printed in italic type.

Section 2 The House of Representatives shall be composed of members chosen every second year by the people of the several States, and the electors in each State shall have the qualifications requisite for electors of the most numerous branch of the State Legislature.

No person shall be a Representative who shall not have attained to the age of twenty-five years, and been seven years a citizen of the United States, and who shall not, when elected, be an inhabitant of that State in which he shall be chosen.

Representatives and direct taxes shall be apportioned among the several States which may be included within this Union, according to their respective numbers, *which shall be determined by adding to the whole number of free persons, including those bound to service for a term of years and excluding Indians not taxed, three-fifths of all other persons.* The actual enumeration shall be made within three years after the first meeting of the Congress of the United States, and within every subsequent term of ten years, in such manner as they shall by law direct. The number of Representatives shall not exceed one for every thirty thousand, but each State shall have at least one Representative; *and until such enumeration shall be made, the State of New Hampshire shall be entitled to choose three, Massachusetts eight, Rhode Island and Providence Plantations one, Connecticut five, New York six, New Jersey four, Pennsylvania eight, Delaware one, Maryland six, Virginia ten, North Carolina five, South Carolina five, and Georgia three.*

When vacancies happen in the representation from any State, the Executive authority thereof shall issue writs of election to fill such vacancies.

The House of Representatives shall choose their Speaker and other officers; and shall have the sole power of impeachment.

Section 3 The Senate of the United States shall be composed of two Senators from each State, *chosen by the legislature thereof,* for six years; and each Senator shall have one vote.

Immediately after they shall be assembled in consequence of the first election, they shall be divided as equally as may be into three classes. The seats of the Senators of the first class shall be vacated at the expiration of the second year, of the second class at the expiration of the fourth year, and of the third class at the expiration of the sixth year, so that one-third may be chosen every second year; *and if vacancies happen by resignation or otherwise, during the recess of the legislature of any State, the Executive thereof may make temporary appointments until the next meeting of the legislature, which shall then fill such vacancies.*

No person shall be a Senator who shall not have attained to the age of thirty years, and been nine years a citizen of the United States, and who shall not, when elected, be an inhabitant of that State for which he shall be chosen.

The Vice-President of the United States shall be President of the Senate, but shall have no vote, unless they be equally divided.

The Senate shall choose their other officers, and also a President *pro tempore,* in the absence of the Vice-President, or when he shall exercise the office of President of the United States.

The Senate shall have the sole power to try all impeachments. When sitting for that purpose, they shall be on oath or affirmation. When the President of the United States is tried, the Chief Justice shall preside: and no person shall be convicted without the concurrence of two-thirds of the members present.

Judgment in cases of impeachment shall not extend further than to removal from the office, and disqualification to hold and enjoy any office of honor, trust or profit under the United States: but the party convicted shall nevertheless be liable and subject to indictment, trial, judgment and punishment, according to law.

Section 4 The times, places and manner of holding elections for Senators and Representatives shall be prescribed in each State by the legislature thereof; but the Congress may at any time by law make or alter such regulations, except as to the places of choosing Senators.

The Congress shall assemble at least once in every year, and such meeting *shall be on the first Monday in December, unless they shall by law appoint a different day.*

Section 5 Each house shall be the judge of the elections, returns and qualifications of its own members, and a majority of each shall constitute a quorum to do business; but a smaller number may adjourn from day to day, and may be authorized to compel the attendance of absent members, in such manner, and under such penalties, as each house may provide.

Each house may determine the rules of its proceedings, punish its members for disorderly behavior, and with the concurrence of two-thirds, expel a member.

Each house shall keep a journal of its proceedings, and from time to time publish the same, excepting such parts as may in their judgment require secrecy; and the yeas and nays of the members of either house on any question shall, at the desire of one-fifth of those present, be entered on the journal.

Neither house, during the session of Congress, shall, without the consent of the other, adjourn for more than three days, nor to any other place than that in which the two houses shall be sitting.

Section 6 The Senators and Representatives shall receive a compensation for their services, to be ascertained by law and paid out of the treasury of the United States. They shall in all cases except treason, felony and breach of the peace, be privileged from arrest during their attendance at the session of their respective houses, and in going to and returning from the same; and for any speech or debate in either house, they shall not be questioned in any other place.

No Senator or Representative shall, during the time for which he was elected, be appointed to any civil office under the authority of the United States, which shall have been created, or the emoluments whereof shall have been increased, during such time; and no person holding any office under the United States shall be a member of either house during his continuance in office.

Section 7 All bills for raising revenue shall originate in the House of Representatives; but the Senate may propose or concur with amendments as on other bills.

Every bill which shall have passed the House of Representatives and the Senate, shall, before it become a law, be presented to the President of the United States; if he approve he shall sign it, but if not he shall return it with objections to that house in which it originated, who shall enter the objections at large on their journal, and proceed to reconsider it. If after such reconsideration two-thirds of that house shall agree to pass the bill, it shall be sent, together with the objections, to the other house, by which it shall likewise be reconsidered, and, if approved by two-thirds of that house, it shall become a law. But in all such cases the votes of both houses shall be determined by yeas and nays, and the names of the persons voting for and against the bill shall be entered on the journal of each house respectively. If any bill shall not be returned by the President within ten days (Sundays excepted) after it shall have been presented to him, the same shall be a law, in like manner as if he had signed it, unless the Congress by their adjournment prevent its return, in which case it shall not be a law.

Every order, resolution, or vote to which the concurrence of the Senate and House of Representatives may be necessary (except on a question of adjournment) shall be presented to the President of the United States; and before the same shall take effect, shall be approved by him, or being disapproved by him, shall be repassed by two-thirds of the Senate and House of Representatives, according to the rules and limitations prescribed in the case of a bill.

Section 8 The Congress shall have power

To lay and collect taxes, duties, imposts, and excises, to pay the debts and provide for the common defense and general welfare of the United States; but all duties, imposts and excises shall be uniform throughout the United States;

To borrow money on the credit of the United States;

To regulate commerce with foreign nations, and among the several States, and with the Indian tribes;

To establish an uniform rule of naturalization, and uniform laws on the subject of bankruptcies throughout the United States;

To coin money, regulate the value thereof, and of foreign coin, and fix the standard of weights and measures;

To provide for the punishment of counterfeiting the securities and current coin of the United States;

To establish post offices and post roads;

To promote the progress of science and useful arts by securing for limited times to authors and inventors the exclusive right to their respective writings and discoveries;

To constitute tribunals inferior to the Supreme Court;

To define and punish piracies and felonies committed on the high seas and offenses against the law of nations;

To declare war, grant letters of marque and reprisal, and make rules concerning captures on land and water;

To raise and support armies, but no appropriation of money to that use shall be for a longer term than two years;

To provide and maintain a navy;

To make rules for the government and regulation of the land and naval forces;

To provide for calling forth the militia to execute the laws of the Union, suppress insurrections, and repel invasions;

To provide for organizing, arming, and disciplining the militia, and for governing such part of them as may be employed in the service of the United States, reserving to the States respectively the appointment of the officers, and the authority of training the militia according to the discipline prescribed by Congress;

To exercise exclusive legislation in all cases whatsoever, over such district (not exceeding ten miles square) as may, by cession of particular States, and the acceptance of Congress, become the seat of government of the United States, and to exercise like authority over all places purchased by the consent of the legislature of the State, in which the same shall be, for erection of forts, magazines, arsenals, dockyards, and other needful buildings;—and

To make all laws which shall be necessary and proper for carrying into execution the foregoing powers, and all other powers vested by this Constitution in the government of the United States, or in any department or officer thereof.

Section 9 The migration or importation of such persons as any of the States now existing shall think proper to admit shall not be prohibited by the Congress prior to the year 1808; but a tax or duty may be imposed on such importation, not exceeding $10 for each person.

The privilege of the writ of habeas corpus shall not be suspended, unless when in cases of rebellion or invasion the public safety may require it.

No bill of attainder or ex post facto law shall be passed.

No capitation, or other direct, tax shall be laid, unless in proportion to the census or enumeration herein before directed to be taken.

No tax or duty shall be laid on articles exported from any State.

No preference shall be given by any regulation of commerce or revenue to the ports of one State over those of another; nor shall vessels bound to, or from, one State, be obliged to enter, clear, or pay duties in another.

No money shall be drawn from the treasury, but in consequence of appropriations made by law; and a regular statement and account of the receipts and expenditures of all public money shall be published from time to time.

No title of nobility shall be granted by the United States: and no person holding any office of profit or trust under them, shall, without the consent of the Congress, accept of any present, emolument, office, or title, of any kind whatever, from any king, prince, or foreign state.

Section 10 No State shall enter into any treaty, alliance, or confederation; grant letters of marque and reprisal; coin money; emit bills of credit; make anything but gold and silver coin a tender in payment of debts; pass any bill of attainder, ex post facto law, or law impairing the obligation of contracts, or grant any title of nobility.

No State shall, without the consent of Congress, lay any imposts or duties on imports or exports, except what may be absolutely necessary for executing its inspection laws: and the net produce of all duties and imposts, laid by any State on imports or exports, shall be for the use of the treasury of the United States; and all such laws shall be subject to the revision and control of the Congress.

No State shall, without the consent of Congress, lay any duty of tonnage, keep troops or ships of war in time of peace, enter into any agreement or compact with another State, or with a foreign power, or engage in war, unless actually invaded, or in such imminent danger as will not admit of delay.

Article II

Section 1 The executive power shall be vested in a President of the United States of America. He shall hold his office during the term of four years, and, together with the Vice-President, chosen for the same term, be elected as follows:

Each State shall appoint, in such manner as the legislature thereof may direct, a number of electors, equal to the whole number of Senators and Representatives to which the State may be entitled in the Congress; but no Senator or Representative, or person holding an office of trust or profit under the United States, shall be appointed an elector.

The electors shall meet in their respective States, and vote by ballot for two persons, of whom one at least shall not be an inhabitant of the same State with themselves. And they shall make a list of all the persons voted for, and of the number of votes for each; which list they shall sign and certify, and transmit sealed to the seat of government of the United States, directed to the President of the Senate. The President of the Senate shall, in the presence of the Senate and House of Representatives, open all the certificates, and the votes shall then be counted. The person having the greatest number of votes shall be the President, if such number be a majority of the whole number of electors appointed; and if there be more than one who have such majority, and have an equal number of votes, then the House of Representatives shall immediately choose by ballot one of them for President; and if no person have a majority, then from the five highest on the list said house shall in like manner choose the President. But in choosing the President the votes shall be taken by States, the representation from each State having one vote; a quorum for this purpose shall consist of a member or members from two-thirds of the States, and a majority of all the States shall be necessary to a choice. In every case, after the choice of the President, the person having the greatest number of votes of the electors shall be the Vice-President. But if there should remain two or more who have equal votes, the Senate shall choose from them by ballot the Vice-President.

The Congress may determine the time of choosing the electors and the day on which they shall give their votes; which day shall be the same throughout the United States.

No person except a natural-born citizen, *or a citizen of the United States at the time of the adoption of this Constitution,* shall be eligible to the office of President; neither shall any person be eligible to that office who shall not have attained to the age of thirty-five years, and been fourteen years a resident within the United States.

In cases of the removal of the President from office or of his death, resignation, or inability to discharge the powers and duties of the said office, the same shall devolve on the Vice-President, and the Congress may by law provide for the case of removal, death, resignation, or inability, both of the President and Vice-President, declaring what officer shall then act as President, and such officer shall act accordingly, until the disability be removed, or a President shall be elected.

The President shall, at stated times, receive for his services a compensation, which shall neither be increased nor diminished during the period for which he shall have been elected, and he shall not receive within that period any other emolument from the United States, or any of them.

Before he enter on the execution of his office, he shall take the following oath or affirmation:—"I do solemnly swear (or affirm) that I will faithfully execute the office of the President of the United States, and will to the best of my ability preserve, protect and defend the Constitution of the United States."

Section 2 The President shall be commander in chief of the army and navy of the United States, and of the militia of the several States, when called into the actual service of the United States; he may require the opinion, in writing, of the principal officer in each of the executive departments, upon any subject relating to the duties of their respective offices, and he shall have power to grant reprieves and pardons for offenses against the United States, except in cases of impeachment.

He shall have power, by and with the advice and consent of the Senate, to make treaties, provided two-thirds of the Senators present concur; and he shall nominate, and by and with the advice and consent of the Senate, shall appoint ambassadors, other public ministers and consuls, judges of the Supreme Court, and all other officers of the United States, whose appointments are not herein otherwise provided for, and which shall be established by law: but Congress may by law vest the appointment of such inferior officers, as they think proper, in the President alone, in the courts of law, or in the heads of departments.

The President shall have power to fill up all vacancies that may happen during the recess of the Senate, by granting commissions which shall expire at the end of their next session.

Section 3 He shall from time to time give to the Congress information of the state of the Union, and recommend to their consideration such measures as he shall judge necessary and expedient; he may, on extraordinary occasions, convene both houses, or either of them, and in case of disagreement between them, with respect to the time of adjournment, he may adjourn them to such time as he shall think proper; he shall receive ambassadors and other public ministers; he shall take care that the laws be faithfully executed, and shall commission all the officers of the United States.

Section 4 The President, Vice-President and all civil officers of the United States shall be removed from office on impeachment for, and on conviction of, treason, bribery, or other high crimes and misdemeanors.

Article III

Section 1 The judicial power of the United States shall be vested in one Supreme Court, and in such inferior courts as the Congress may from time to time ordain and establish. The judges, both of the Supreme and inferior courts, shall hold their offices during good behavior, and shall, at stated times, receive for their services a compensation which shall not be diminished during their continuance in office.

Section 2 The judicial power shall extend to all cases, in law and equity, arising under this Constitution, the laws of the United States, and treaties made, or which shall be made, under their authority;—to all cases affecting ambassadors, other public ministers and consuls;—to all cases of admiralty and maritime jurisdiction;—to controversies to which the United States shall be a party;—to controversies between two or more States;—*between a State and citizens of another State;*—between citizens of different States;—between citizens of the same State claiming lands under grants of different States, and between a State, or the citizens thereof, and foreign states, citizens or subjects.

In all cases affecting ambassadors, other public ministers and consuls, and those in which a State shall be party, the Supreme Court shall have original jurisdiction. In all the other cases before mentioned, the Supreme Court shall have appellate jurisdiction, both as to law and fact, with such exceptions, and under such regulations, as the Congress shall make.

The trial of all crimes, except in cases of impeachment, shall be by jury; and such trial shall be held in the State where said crimes shall have been committed; but when not committed within any State, the trial shall be at such place or places as the Congress may by law have directed.

Section 3 Treason against the United States shall consist only in levying war against them, or in adhering to their enemies, giving them aid and comfort. No person shall be convicted of treason unless on the testimony of two witnesses to the same overt act, or on confession in open court.

The Congress shall have power to declare the punishment of treason, but no attainder of treason shall work corruption of blood, or forfeiture except during the life of the person attainted.

Article IV

Section 1 Full faith and credit shall be given in each State to the public acts, records, and judicial proceedings of every other State. And the Congress may by general laws prescribe the manner in which such acts, records, and proceedings shall be proved, and the effect thereof.

Section 2 The citizens of each State shall be entitled to all privileges and immunities of citizens in the several States.

A person charged in any State with treason, felony, or other crime, who shall flee from justice, and be found in another State, shall on demand of the executive authority of the State from which he fled, be delivered up, to be removed to the State having jurisdiction of the crime.

No person held to service or labor in one State, under the laws thereof, escaping into another, shall, in consequence of any law or regulation therein, be discharged from such service or labor, but shall be delivered up on claim of the party to whom such service or labor may be due.

Section 3 New States may be admitted by the Congress into this Union; but no new State shall be formed or erected within the jurisdiction of any other State; nor any State be formed by the junction of two or more States, or parts of States, without the consent of the legislatures of the States concerned as well as of the Congress.

The Congress shall have power to dispose of and make all needful rules and regulations respecting the territory or other property belonging to the United States; and nothing in this Constitution shall be so construed as to prejudice any claims of the United States, or of any particular State.

Section 4 The United States shall guarantee to every State in this Union a republican form of government, and shall protect each of them against invasion; and on application of the legislature, or of the executive (when the legislature cannot be convened), against domestic violence.

Article V

The Congress, whenever two-thirds of both houses shall deem it necessary, shall propose amendments to this Constitution, or, on the application of the legislatures of two-thirds of the several States, shall call a convention for proposing amendments, which, in either case, shall be valid to all intents and purposes, as part of this Constitution, when ratified by the legislatures of three-fourths of the several States, or by conventions in three-fourths thereof, as the one or the other mode of ratification may be proposed by the Congress; provided *that no amendments which may be made prior to the year one thousand eight hundred and eight shall in any manner affect the first and fourth clauses in the ninth section of the first article;* and that no State, without its consent, shall be deprived of its equal suffrage in the Senate.

Article VI

All debts contracted and engagements entered into, before the adoption of this Constitution, shall be as valid against the United States under this Constitution, as under the Confederation.

This Constitution, and the laws of the United States which shall be made in pursuance thereof; and all treaties made, or which shall be made, under the authority of the United States, shall be the supreme law of the land; and the judges in every State shall be bound thereby, anything in the Constitution or laws of any State to the contrary notwithstanding.

The Senators and Representatives before mentioned, and the members of the several State legislatures, and all executive and judicial officers, both of the United States and of the several States, shall be bound by oath or affirmation to support this Constitution; but no religious test shall ever be required as a qualification to any office or public trust under the United States.

Article VII

The ratification of the conventions of nine States shall be sufficient for the establishment of this Constitution between the States so ratifying the same.

Done in Convention by the unanimous consent of the States present, the seventeenth day of September in the year of our Lord one thousand seven hundred and eighty-seven and of the Independence of the United States of America the twelfth. In witness whereof we have hereunto subscribed our names.

AMENDMENTS TO THE CONSTITUTION*

Amendment I

Congress shall make no law respecting an establishment of religion, or prohibiting the free exercise thereof; or abridging the freedom of speech, or of the press; or the right of the people peaceably to assemble, and to petition the government for a redress of grievances.

Amendment II

A well-regulated militia being necessary to the security of a free State, the right of the people to keep and bear arms shall not be infringed.

Amendment III

No soldier shall, in time of peace, be quartered in any house without the consent of the owner, nor in time of war, but in a manner to be prescribed by law.

Amendment IV

The right of the people to be secure in their persons, houses, papers, and effects, against unreasonable searches and seizures, shall not be violated, and no warrants shall issue but upon probable cause, supported by oath or affirmation, and particularly describing the place to be searched, and the persons or things to be seized.

---

*The first ten Amendments (the Bill of Rights) were adopted in 1791.

Amendment V

No person shall be held to answer for a capital, or otherwise infamous crime, unless on a presentment or indictment of a grand jury, except in cases arising in the land or naval forces, or in the militia, when in actual service in time of war or public danger; nor shall any person be subject for the same offense to be twice put in jeopardy of life or limb; nor shall be compelled in any criminal case to be a witness against himself, nor be deprived of life, liberty, or property, without due process of law; nor shall private property be taken for public use without just compensation.

Amendment VI

In all criminal prosecutions, the accused shall enjoy the right to a speedy and public trial, by an impartial jury of the State and district wherein the crime shall have been committed, which district shall have been previously ascertained by law, and to be informed of the nature and cause of the accusation; to be confronted with the witnesses against him; to have compulsory process for obtaining witnesses in his favor, and to have the assistance of counsel for his defense.

Amendment VII

In suits at common law, where the value in controversy shall exceed twenty dollars, the right of trial by jury shall be preserved, and no fact tried by a jury shall be otherwise reexamined in any court of the United States, than according to the rules of the common law.

Amendment VIII

Excessive bail shall not be required, nor excessive fines imposed, nor cruel and unusual punishments inflicted.

Amendment IX

The enumeration in the Constitution, of certain rights, shall not be construed to deny or disparage others retained by the people.

Amendment X

The powers not delegated to the United States by the Constitution, nor prohibited by it to the States, are reserved to the States respectively, or to the people.

Amendment XI

[Adopted 1798]

The judicial power of the United States shall not be construed to extend to any suit in law or equity, commenced or prosecuted against one of the United States by citizens of another State, or by citizens or subjects of any foreign state.

Amendment XII

[Adopted 1804]

The electors shall meet in their respective States, and vote by ballot for President and Vice-President, one of whom, at least, shall not be an inhabitant of the same State with themselves; they shall name in their ballots the person voted for as President, and in distinct ballots the person voted for as Vice-President, and they shall make distinct lists of all persons voted for as President, and of all persons voted for as Vice-President, and of the number of votes for each, which lists they shall sign and certify, and transmit sealed to the seat of government of the United States, directed to the President of the Senate;—the President of the Senate shall, in the presence of the Senate and House of Representatives, open all the certificates and the votes shall then be counted;—the person having the greatest number of votes for President shall be the President, if such number be a majority of the whole number of electors appointed; and if no person have such majority, then from the persons having the highest numbers not exceeding three on the list of those voted for as President, the House of Representatives shall choose immediately, by ballot, the President. But in choosing the President, the votes shall be taken by States, the representation from each State having one vote; a quorum for this purpose shall consist of a member or members from two-thirds of the States, and a majority of all the States shall be necessary to a choice. And if the House of Representatives shall not choose a President whenever the right of choice shall devolve upon them, before *the fourth day of March* next following, then the Vice-President shall act as President, as in the case of the death or other constitutional disability of the President.

The person having the greatest number of votes as Vice-President shall be the Vice-President, if such number be a majority of the whole number of electors appointed; and if no person have a majority, then from the two highest numbers on the list the Senate shall choose the Vice-President; a quorum for the purpose shall consist of two-thirds of the whole number of Senators, and a majority of the whole number shall be necessary to a choice. But no person constitutionally ineligible to the office of President shall be eligible to that of Vice-President of the United States.

Amendment XIII

[Adopted 1865]

Section 1 Neither slavery nor involuntary servitude, except as a punishment for crime whereof the party shall have been duly convicted, shall exist within the United States, or any place subject to their jurisdiction.

Section 2 Congress shall have power to enforce this article by appropriate legislation.

Amendment XIV

[Adopted 1868]

Section 1 All persons born or naturalized in the United States, and subject to the jurisdiction thereof, are citizens of the United States and of the State wherein they reside. No State shall make or enforce any law which shall abridge the privileges or immunities of citizens of the United States; nor shall any State deprive any person of life, liberty, or property, without due process of law; nor deny to any person within its jurisdiction the equal protection of the laws.

Section 2 Representatives shall be apportioned among the several States according to their respective numbers, counting the whole number of persons in each State, excluding Indians not taxed. But when the right to vote at any election for the choice of Electors for President and Vice-President of the United States, Representatives in Congress, the executive and judicial officers of a State, or the members of the legislature thereof, is denied to any of the male inhabitants of such State, being twenty-one years of age and citizens of the United States, or in any way abridged, except for participation in rebellion, or other crime, the basis of representation therein shall be reduced in the proportion which the number of such male citizens shall bear to the whole number of male citizens twenty-one years of age in such State.

Section 3 No person shall be a Senator or Representative in Congress, or Elector of President and Vice-President, or hold any office, civil or military, under the United States, or under any State, who, having previously taken an oath, as a member of Congress, or as an officer of the United States, or as a member of any State legislature, or as an executive or judicial officer of any State, to support the Constitution of the United States, shall have engaged in insurrection or rebellion against the same, or given aid or comfort to the enemies thereof. Congress may, by a vote of two-thirds of each house, remove such disability.

Section 4 The validity of the public debt of the United States, authorized by law, including debts incurred for payment of pensions and bounties for services in suppressing insurrection or rebellion, shall not be questioned. But neither the United States nor any State shall assume or pay any debt or obligation incurred in aid of insurrection or rebellion against the United States, or any claim for the loss of emancipation of any slave; but all such debts, obligations, and claims shall be held illegal and void.

Section 5 The Congress shall have power to enforce, by appropriate legislation, the provisions of this article.

Amendment XV
[Adopted 1870]

Section 1 The right of citizens of the United States to vote shall not be denied or abridged by the United States or by any State on account of race, color, or previous condition of servitude.

Section 2 The Congress shall have power to enforce this article by appropriate legislation.

Amendment XVI
[Adopted 1913]

The Congress shall have power to lay and collect taxes on incomes, from whatever source derived, without apportionment among the several States, and without regard to any census or enumeration.

Amendment XVII
[Adopted 1913]

Section 1 The Senate of the United States shall be composed of two Senators from each State, elected by the people thereof, for six years; and each Senator shall have one vote. The electors in each State shall have the qualifications requisite for electors of [voters for] the most numerous branch of the State legislatures.

Section 2 When vacancies happen in the representation of any State in the Senate, the executive authority of such State shall issue writs of election to fill such vacancies: Provided, that the Legislature of any State may empower the executive thereof to make temporary appointments until the people fill the vacancies by election as the Legislature may direct.

Section 3 This amendment shall not be so construed as to affect the election or term of any Senator chosen before it becomes valid as part of the Constitution.

Amendment XVIII

[Adopted 1919; Repealed 1933]

Section 1 After one year from the ratification of this article the manufacture, sale, or transportation of intoxicating liquors within, the importation thereof into, or the exportation thereof from the United States and all territory subject to the jurisdiction thereof, for beverage purposes, is hereby prohibited.

Section 2 The Congress and the several States shall have concurrent power to enforce this article by appropriate legislation.

Section 3 This article shall be inoperative unless it shall have been ratified as an amendment to the Constitution by the legislatures of the several States, as provided by the Constitution, within seven years from the date of the submission thereof to the States by the Congress.

Amendment XIX

[Adopted 1920]

Section 1 The right of citizens of the United States to vote shall not be denied or abridged by the United States or by any State on account of sex.

Section 2 The Congress shall have power to enforce this article by appropriate legislation.

Amendment XX

[Adopted 1933]

Section 1 The terms of the President and Vice-President shall end at noon on the 20th day of January, and the terms of Senators and Representatives at noon on the 3rd day of January, of the years in which such terms would have ended if this article had not been ratified; and the terms of their successors shall then begin.

Section 2 The Congress shall assemble at least once in every year, and such meeting shall begin at noon on the 3d day of January, unless they shall by law appoint a different day.

Section 3 If, at the time fixed for the beginning of the term of the President, the President-elect shall have died, the Vice-President–elect shall become President. If a President shall not have been chosen before the time fixed for the beginning of his term, or if the President-elect shall have failed to qualify, then the Vice-President–elect shall act as President until a President shall have qualified; and the Congress may by law provide for the case wherein neither a President-elect nor a Vice-President–elect shall have qualified, declaring who shall then act as President, or the manner in which one who is to act shall be selected, and such persons shall act accordingly until a President or Vice-President shall have qualified.

Section 4 The Congress may by law provide for the case of the death of any of the persons from whom the House of Representatives may choose a President whenever the right of choice shall have devolved upon them, and for the case of the death of any of the persons from whom the Senate may choose a Vice-President whenever the right of choice shall have devolved upon them.

Section 5 Sections 1 and 2 shall take effect on the 15th day of October following the ratification of this article.

Section 6 This article shall be inoperative unless it shall have been ratified as an amendment to the Constitution by the Legislatures of three-fourths of the several States within seven years from the date of its submission.

Amendment XXI

[Adopted 1933]

Section 1 The eighteenth article of amendment to the Constitution of the United States is hereby repealed.

Section 2 The transportation or importation into any State, Territory, or Possession of the United States for delivery or use therein of intoxicating liquors, in violation of the laws thereof, is hereby prohibited.

Section 3 This article shall be inoperative unless it shall have been ratified as an amendment to the Constitution by conventions in the several States, as provided in the Constitution, within seven years from the date of submission thereof to the States by the Congress.

Amendment XXII

[Adopted 1951]

Section 1 No person shall be elected to the office of President more than twice, and no person who has held the office of President, or acted as President, for more than two years of a term to which some other person was elected President shall be elected to the office of President more than once. But this article shall not apply to any person holding the office of President when this article was proposed by the Congress, and shall not prevent any person who may be holding the office of President, or acting as President, during the term within which this article becomes operative from holding the office of President or acting as President during the remainder of such term.

Section 2 This article shall be inoperative unless it shall have been ratified as an amendment to the Constitution by the legislatures of three-fourths of the several States within seven years from the date of its submission to the States by the Congress.

[Adopted 1961]

Amendment XXIII

Section 1 The District constituting the seat of Government of the United States shall appoint in such manner as the Congress may direct:

A number of electors of President and Vice-President equal to the whole number of Senators and Representatives in Congress to which the District would be entitled if it were a State, but in no event more than the least populous State; they shall be in addition to those appointed by the States, but they shall be considered for the purposes of the election of President and Vice-President, to be electors appointed by a State; and they shall meet in the District and perform such duties as provided by the twelfth article of amendment.

Section 2 The Congress shall have the power to enforce this article by appropriate legislation.

[Adopted 1964]

Amendment XXIV

Section 1 The right of citizens of the United States to vote in any primary or other election for President or Vice-President, for electors for President or Vice-President, or for Senator or Representative in Congress, shall not be denied or abridged by the United States or any State by reason of failure to pay any poll tax or other tax.

Section 2 The Congress shall have the power to enforce this article by appropriate legislation.

[Adopted 1967]

Amendment XXV

Section 1 In case of the removal of the President from office or of his death or resignation, the Vice-President shall become President.

Section 2 Whenever there is a vacancy in the office of the Vice-President, the President shall nominate a Vice-President who shall take office upon confirmation by a majority vote of both Houses of Congress.

Section 3 Whenever the President transmits to the President pro tempore of the Senate and the Speaker of the House of Representatives his written declaration that he is unable to discharge the powers and duties of his office, and until he transmits to them a written declaration to the contrary, such powers and duties shall be discharged by the Vice-President as Acting President.

Section 4 Whenever the Vice-President and a majority of either the principal officers of the executive departments or of such other body as Congress may by law provide, transmit to the President pro tempore of the Senate and the Speaker of the House of Representatives their written declaration that the President is unable to discharge the powers and duties of his office, the Vice-President shall immediately assume the powers and duties of the office as Acting President.

Thereafter, when the President transmits to the President pro tempore of the Senate and the Speaker of the House of Representatives his written declaration that no inability exists, he shall resume the powers and duties of his office unless the Vice-President and a majority of either the principal officers of the executive department[s] or of such other body as Congress may by law provide, transmit within four days to the President pro tempore of the Senate and the Speaker of the House of Representatives their written declaration that the President is unable to discharge the powers and duties of his office. Thereupon Congress shall decide the issue, assembling within forty-eight hours for that purpose if not in session. If the Congress, within twenty-one days after receipt of the latter written declaration, or, if Congress is not in session, within twenty-one days after Congress is required to assemble, determines by two-thirds vote of both Houses that the President is unable to discharge the powers and duties of his office, the Vice-President shall continue to discharge the same as Acting President; otherwise, the President shall resume the powers and duties of his office.

Amendment XXVI

[Adopted 1971]

Section 1 The right of citizens of the United States, who are eighteen years of age or older, to vote shall not be denied or abridged by the United States or by any State on account of age.

Section 2 The Congress shall have power to enforce this article by appropriate legislation.

Amendment XXVII

[Adopted 1992]

No law, varying the compensation for the services of the Senators and Representatives, shall take effect, until an election of Representatives shall have intervened.

Presidential Elections

Year	Number of States	Candidates	Parties	Popular Vote	% of Popular Vote	Electoral Vote	% Voter Partici-pation[a]
1789	10	**George Washington**	No party			69	
		John Adams	designations			34	
		Other candidates				35	
1792	15	**George Washington**	No party			132	
		John Adams	designations			77	
		George Clinton				50	
		Other candidates				5	
1796	16	**John Adams**	Federalist			71	
		Thomas Jefferson	Democratic-Republican			68	
		Thomas Pinckney	Federalist			59	
		Aaron Burr	Democratic-Republican			30	
		Other candidates				48	
1800	16	**Thomas Jefferson**	Democratic-Republican			73	
		Aaron Burr	Democratic-Republican			73	
		John Adams	Federalist			65	
		Charles C. Pinckney	Federalist			64	
		John Jay	Federalist			1	
1804	17	**Thomas Jefferson**	Democratic-Republican			162	
		Charles C. Pinckney	Federalist			14	
1808	17	**James Madison**	Democratic-Republican			122	
		Charles C. Pinckney	Federalist			47	
		George Clinton	Democratic-Republican			6	
1812	18	**James Madison**	Democratic-Republican			128	
		DeWitt Clinton	Federalist			89	
1816	19	**James Monroe**	Democratic-Republican			183	
		Rufus King	Federalist			34	
1820	24	**James Monroe**	Democratic-Republican			231	
		John Quincy Adams	Independent Republican			1	

Presidential Elections (*continued*)

Year	Number of States	Candidates	Parties	Popular Vote	% of Popular Vote	Electoral Vote	% Voter Participation[a]
1824	24	**John Quincy Adams**	Democratic-Republican	108,740	30.5	84	26.9
		Andrew Jackson	Democratic-Republican	153,544	43.1	99	
		Henry Clay	Democratic-Republican	47,136	13.2	37	
		William H. Crawford	Democratic-Republican	46,618	13.1	41	
1828	24	**Andrew Jackson**	Democratic	647,286	56.0	178	57.6
		John Quincy Adams	National Republican	508,064	44.0	83	
1832	24	**Andrew Jackson**	Democratic	701,780	54.2	219	55.4
		Henry Clay	National Republican	484,205	37.4	49	
		Other candidates		107,988	8.0	18	
1836	26	**Martin Van Buren**	Democratic	764,176	50.8	170	57.8
		William H. Harrison	Whig	550,816	36.6	73	
		Hugh L. White	Whig	146,107	9.7	26	
1840	26	**William H. Harrison**	Whig	1,274,624	53.1	234	80.2
		Martin Van Buren	Democratic	1,127,781	46.9	60	
1844	26	**James K. Polk**	Democratic	1,338,464	49.6	170	78.9
		Henry Clay	Whig	1,300,097	48.1	105	
		James G. Birney	Liberty	62,300	2.3		
1848	30	**Zachary Taylor**	Whig	1,360,967	47.4	163	72.7
		Lewis Cass	Democratic	1,222,342	42.5	127	
		Martin Van Buren	Free Soil	291,263	10.1		
1852	31	**Franklin Pierce**	Democratic	1,601,117	50.9	254	69.6
		Winfield Scott	Whig	1,385,453	44.1	42	
		John P. Hale	Free Soil	155,825	5.0		
1856	31	**James Buchanan**	Democratic	1,832,955	45.3	174	78.9
		John C. Frémont	Republican	1,339,932	33.1	114	
		Millard Fillmore	American	871,731	21.6	8	
1860	33	**Abraham Lincoln**	Republican	1,865,593	39.8	180	81.2
		Stephen A. Douglas	Democratic	1,382,713	29.5	12	
		John C. Breckinridge	Democratic	848,356	18.1	72	
		John Bell	Constitutional Union	592,906	12.6	39	
1864	36	**Abraham Lincoln**	Republican	2,206,938	55.0	212	73.8
		George B. McClellan	Democratic	1,803,787	45.0	21	
1868	37	**Ulysses S. Grant**	Republican	3,013,421	52.7	214	78.1
		Horatio Seymour	Democratic	2,706,829	47.3	80	

Presidential Elections (*continued*)

Year	Number of States	Candidates	Parties	Popular Vote	% of Popular Vote	Elec- toral Vote	% Voter Partici- pation[a]
1872	37	**Ulysses S. Grant**	Republican	3,596,745	55.6	286	71.3
		Horace Greeley	Democratic	2,843,446	43.9	[b]	
1876	38	**Rutherford B. Hayes**	Republican	4,036,572	48.0	185	81.8
		Samuel J. Tilden	Democratic	4,284,020	51.0	184	
1880	38	**James A. Garfield**	Republican	4,453,295	48.5	214	79.4
		Winfield S. Hancock	Democratic	4,414,082	48.1	155	
		James B. Weaver	Greenback- Labor	308,578	3.4		
1884	38	**Grover Cleveland**	Democratic	4,879,507	48.5	219	77.5
		James G. Blaine	Republican	4,850,293	48.2	182	
		Benjamin F. Butler	Greenback- Labor	175,370	1.8		
		John P. St. John	Prohibition	150,369	1.5		
1888	38	**Benjamin Harrison**	Republican	5,447,129	47.9	233	79.3
		Grover Cleveland	Democratic	5,537,857	48.6	168	
		Clinton B. Fisk	Prohibition	249,506	2.2		
		Anson J. Streeter	Union Labor	146,935	1.3		
1892	44	**Grover Cleveland**	Democratic	5,555,426	46.1	277	74.7
		Benjamin Harrison	Republican	5,182,690	43.0	145	
		James B. Weaver	People's	1,029,846	8.5	22	
		John Bidwell	Prohibition	264,133	2.2		
1896	45	**William McKinley**	Republican	7,102,246	51.1	271	79.3
		William J. Bryan	Democratic	6,492,559	47.7	176	
1900	45	**William McKinley**	Republican	7,218,491	51.7	292	73.2
		William J. Bryan	Democratic; Populist	6,356,734	45.5	155	
		John C. Wooley	Prohibition	208,914	1.5		
1904	45	**Theodore Roosevelt**	Republican	7,628,461	57.4	336	65.2
		Alton B. Parker	Democratic	5,084,223	37.6	140	
		Eugene V. Debs	Socialist	402,283	3.0		
		Silas C. Swallow	Prohibition	258,536	1.9		
1908	46	**William H. Taft**	Republican	7,675,320	51.6	321	65.4
		William J. Bryan	Democratic	6,412,294	43.1	162	
		Eugene V. Debs	Socialist	420,793	2.8		
		Eugene W. Chafin	Prohibition	253,840	1.7		
1912	48	**Woodrow Wilson**	Democratic	6,296,547	41.9	435	58.8
		Theodore Roosevelt	Progressive	4,118,571	27.4	88	
		William H. Taft	Republican	3,486,720	23.2	8	
		Eugene V. Debs	Socialist	900,672	6.0		
		Eugene W. Chafin	Prohibition	206,275	1.4		

Presidential Elections (*continued*)

Year	Number of States	Candidates	Parties	Popular Vote	% of Popular Vote	Electoral Vote	% Voter Participation[a]
1916	48	**Woodrow Wilson**	Democratic	9,127,695	49.4	277	61.6
		Charles E. Hughes	Republican	8,533,507	46.2	254	
		A. L. Benson	Socialist	585,113	3.2		
		J. Frank Hanly	Prohibition	220,506	1.2		
1920	48	**Warren G. Harding**	Republican	16,143,407	60.4	404	49.2
		James M. Cox	Democratic	9,130,328	34.2	127	
		Eugene V. Debs	Socialist	919,799	3.4		
		P. P. Christensen	Farmer-Labor	265,411	1.0		
1924	48	**Calvin Coolidge**	Republican	15,718,211	54.0	382	48.9
		John W. Davis	Democratic	8,385,283	28.8	136	
		Robert M. La Follette	Progressive	4,831,289	16.6	13	
1928	48	**Herbert C. Hoover**	Republican	21,391,993	58.2	444	56.9
		Alfred E. Smith	Democratic	15,016,169	40.9	87	
1932	48	**Franklin D. Roosevelt**	Democratic	22,809,638	57.4	472	56.9
		Herbert C. Hoover	Republican	15,758,901	39.7	59	
		Norman Thomas	Socialist	881,951	2.2		
1936	48	**Franklin D. Roosevelt**	Democratic	27,752,869	60.8	523	61.0
		Alfred M. Landon	Republican	16,674,665	36.5	8	
		William Lemke	Union	882,479	1.9		
1940	48	**Franklin D. Roosevelt**	Democratic	27,307,819	54.8	449	62.5
		Wendell L. Willkie	Republican	22,321,018	44.8	82	
1944	48	**Franklin D. Roosevelt**	Democratic	25,606,585	53.5	432	55.9
		Thomas E. Dewey	Republican	22,014,745	46.0	99	
1948	48	**Harry S Truman**	Democratic	24,179,345	49.6	303	53.0
		Thomas E. Dewey	Republican	21,991,291	45.1	189	
		J. Strom Thurmond	States' Rights	1,176,125	2.4	39	
		Henry A. Wallace	Progressive	1,157,326	2.4		
1952	48	**Dwight D. Eisenhower**	Republican	33,936,234	55.1	442	63.3
		Adlai E. Stevenson	Democratic	27,314,992	44.4	89	
1956	48	**Dwight D. Eisenhower**	Republican	35,590,472	57.6	457	60.6
		Adlai E. Stevenson	Democratic	26,022,752	42.1	73	
1960	50	**John F. Kennedy**	Democratic	34,226,731	49.7	303	62.8
		Richard M. Nixon	Republican	34,108,157	49.5	219	
1964	50	**Lyndon B. Johnson**	Democratic	43,129,566	61.1	486	61.7
		Barry M. Goldwater	Republican	27,178,188	38.5	52	
1968	50	**Richard M. Nixon**	Republican	31,785,480	43.4	301	60.6
		Hubert H. Humphrey	Democratic	31,275,166	42.7	191	
		George C. Wallace	American Independent	9,906,473	13.5	46	

Presidential Elections (*continued*)

Year	Number of States	Candidates	Parties	Popular Vote	% of Popular Vote	Electoral Vote	% Voter Participation[a]
1972	50	Richard M. Nixon	Republican	47,169,911	60.7	520	55.2
		George S. McGovern	Democratic	29,170,383	37.5	17	
		John G. Schmitz	American	1,099,482	1.4		
1976	50	James E. Carter	Democratic	40,830,763	50.1	297	53.5
		Gerald R. Ford	Republican	39,147,793	48.0	240	
1980	50	Ronald W. Reagan	Republican	43,904,153	50.7	489	52.6
		James E. Carter	Democratic	35,483,883	41.0	49	
		John B. Anderson	Independent	5,720,060	6.6		
		Ed Clark	Libertarian	921,299	1.1		
1984	50	Ronald W. Reagan	Republican	54,455,075	58.8	525	53.3
		Walter F. Mondale	Democratic	37,577,185	40.6	13	
1988	50	George H. W. Bush	Republican	48,886,097	53.4	426	50.1
		Michael S. Dukakis	Democratic	41,809,074	45.6	111[c]	
1992	50	William J. Clinton	Democratic	44,909,326	43.0	370	55.2
		George H. W. Bush	Republican	39,103,882	37.4	168	
		H. Ross Perot	Independent	19,741,048	18.9		
1996	50	William J. Clinton	Democratic	47,402,357	49.2	379	49.1
		Robert J. Dole	Republican	39,196,755	40.7	159	
		H. Ross Perot	Reform	8,085,402	8.4		
		Ralph Nader	Green	684,902	0.7		
2000	50	George W. Bush	Republican	50,455,156	47.9	271	51.2
		Albert Gore	Democratic	50,992,335	48.4	266	
		Ralph Nader	Green	2,882,955	2.7		
2004	50	George W. Bush	Republican	62,039,073	50.7	286	55.3
		John F. Kerry	Democratic	59,027,478	48.2	251	
		Ralph Nader	Independent	240,896	0.2		
2008	50	Barack Obama	Democratic	66,882,230	53.0	365	61.7
		John McCain	Republican	58,343,671	46.0	173	
		Ralph Nader	Independent	705,200	0.55		

Candidates receiving less than 1 percent of the popular vote have been omitted. Thus the percentage of popular vote given for any election year may not total 100 percent.
   Before the passage of the Twelfth Amendment in 1804, the electoral college voted for two presidential candidates; the runner-up became vice president.
   Before 1824, most presidential electors were chosen by state legislatures, not by popular vote.

[a]Percent of voting-age population casting ballots.
[b]Greeley died shortly after the election; the electors supporting him then divided their votes among minor candidates.
[c]One elector from West Virginia cast her electoral college presidential ballot for Lloyd Bentsen, the Democratic Party's vice-presidential candidate.

Presidents and Vice Presidents

1. President	George Washington	1789–1797	
Vice President	John Adams	1789–1797	
2. President	John Adams	1797–1801	
Vice President	Thomas Jefferson	1797–1801	
3. President	Thomas Jefferson	1801–1809	
Vice President	Aaron Burr	1801–1805	
Vice President	George Clinton	1805–1809	
4. President	James Madison	1809–1817	
Vice President	George Clinton	1809–1813	
Vice President	Elbridge Gerry	1813–1817	
5. President	James Monroe	1817–1825	
Vice President	Daniel Tompkins	1817–1825	
6. President	John Quincy Adams	1825–1829	
Vice President	John C. Calhoun	1825–1829	
7. President	Andrew Jackson	1829–1837	
Vice President	John C. Calhoun	1829–1833	
Vice President	Martin Van Buren	1833–1837	
8. President	Martin Van Buren	1837–1841	
Vice President	Richard M. Johnson	1837–1841	
9. President	William H. Harrison	1841	
Vice President	John Tyler	1841	
10. President	John Tyler	1841–1845	
Vice President	None		
11. President	James K. Polk	1845–1849	
Vice President	George M. Dallas	1845–1849	
12. President	Zachary Taylor	1849–1850	
Vice President	Millard Fillmore	1849–1850	
13. President	Millard Fillmore	1850–1853	
Vice President	None		
14. President	Franklin Pierce	1853–1857	
Vice President	William R. King	1853–1857	
15. President	James Buchanan	1857–1861	
Vice President	John C. Breckinridge	1857–1861	
16. President	Abraham Lincoln	1861–1865	
Vice President	Hannibal Hamlin	1861–1865	
Vice President	Andrew Johnson	1865	
17. President	Andrew Johnson	1865–1869	
Vice President	None		
18. President	Ulysses S. Grant	1869–1877	
Vice President	Schuyler Colfax	1869–1873	
Vice President	Henry Wilson	1873–1877	
19. President	Rutherford B. Hayes	1877–1881	
Vice President	William A. Wheeler	1877–1881	
20. President	James A. Garfield	1881	
Vice President	Chester A. Arthur	1881	
21. President	Chester A. Arthur	1881–1885	
Vice President	None		
22. President	Grover Cleveland	1885–1889	
Vice President	Thomas A. Hendricks	1885–1889	
23. President	Benjamin Harrison	1889–1893	
Vice President	Levi P. Morton	1889–1893	
24. President	Grover Cleveland	1893–1897	
Vice President	Adlai E. Stevenson	1893–1897	
25. President	William McKinley	1897–1901	
Vice President	Garret A. Hobart	1897–1901	
Vice President	Theodore Roosevelt	1901	
26. President	Theodore Roosevelt	1901–1909	
Vice President	Charles Fairbanks	1905–1909	
27. President	William H. Taft	1909–1913	
Vice President	James S. Sherman	1909–1913	
28. President	Woodrow Wilson	1913–1921	
Vice President	Thomas R. Marshall	1913–1921	
29. President	Warren G. Harding	1921–1923	
Vice President	Calvin Coolidge	1921–1923	
30. President	Calvin Coolidge	1923–1929	
Vice President	Charles G. Dawes	1925–1929	
31. President	Herbert C. Hoover	1929–1933	
Vice President	Charles Curtis	1929–1933	
32. President	Franklin D. Roosevelt	1933–1945	
Vice President	John N. Garner	1933–1941	
Vice President	Henry A. Wallace	1941–1945	
Vice President	Harry S Truman	1945	
33. President	Harry S Truman	1945–1953	
Vice President	Alben W. Barkley	1949–1953	
34. President	Dwight D. Eisenhower	1953–1961	
Vice President	Richard M. Nixon	1953–1961	

35. President	**John F. Kennedy**	1961–1963
Vice President	Lyndon B. Johnson	1961–1963
36. President	**Lyndon B. Johnson**	1963–1969
Vice President	Hubert H. Humphrey	1965–1969
37. President	**Richard M. Nixon**	1969–1974
Vice President	Spiro T. Agnew	1969–1973
Vice President	Gerald R. Ford	1973–1974
38. President	**Gerald R. Ford**	1974–1977
Vice President	Nelson A. Rockefeller	1974–1977
39. President	**James E. Carter**	1977–1981
Vice President	Walter F. Mondale	1977–1981

40. President	**Ronald W. Reagan**	1981–1989
Vice President	George H. W. Bush	1981–1989
41. President	**George H. W. Bush**	1989–1993
Vice President	J. Danforth Quayle	1989–1993
42. President	**William J. Clinton**	1993–2001
Vice President	Albert Gore	1993–2001
43. President	**George W. Bush**	2001–2009
Vice President	Richard Cheney	2001–2009
44. President	**Barack Obama**	2009–
Vice President	Joseph Biden	2009–

For a complete list of Presidents, Vice Presidents, and Cabinet Members, go to cengage.com/history/norton/peoplenationbrief8e

Justices of the Supreme Court

	Term of Service	Years of Service	Life Span		Term of Service	Years of Service	Life Span
John Jay	1789–1795	5	1745–1829	William Strong	1870–1880	10	1808–1895
John Rutledge	1789–1791	1	1739–1800	Joseph P. Bradley	1870–1892	22	1813–1892
William Cushing	1789–1810	20	1732–1810	Ward Hunt	1873–1882	9	1810–1886
James Wilson	1789–1798	8	1742–1798	Morrison R. Waite	1874–1888	14	1816–1888
John Blair	1789–1796	6	1732–1800	John M. Harlan	1877–1911	34	1833–1911
Robert H. Harrison	1789–1790	–	1745–1790	William B. Woods	1880–1887	7	1824–1887
James Iredell	1790–1799	9	1751–1799	Stanley Mathews	1881–1889	7	1824–1889
Thomas Johnson	1791–1793	1	1732–1819	Horace Gray	1882–1902	20	1828–1902
William Paterson	1793–1806	13	1745–1806	Samuel Blatchford	1882–1893	11	1820–1893
John Rutledge*	1795	–	1739–1800	Lucius Q. C. Lamar	1888–1893	5	1825–1893
Samuel Chase	1796–1811	15	1741–1811	Melville W. Fuller	1888–1910	21	1833–1910
Oliver Ellsworth	1796–1800	4	1745–1807	David J. Brewer	1890–1910	20	1837–1910
Bushrod Washington	1798–1829	31	1762–1829	Henry B. Brown	1890–1906	16	1836–1913
Alfred Moore	1799–1804	4	1755–1810	George Shiras Jr.	1892–1903	10	1832–1924
John Marshall	1801–1835	34	1755–1835	Howell E. Jackson	1893–1895	2	1832–1895
William Johnson	1804–1834	30	1771–1834	Edward D. White	1894–1910	16	1845–1921
H. Brockholst Livingston	1806–1823	16	1757–1823	Rufus W. Peckham	1895–1909	14	1838–1909
Thomas Todd	1807–1826	18	1765–1826	Joseph McKenna	1898–1925	26	1843–1926
Joseph Story	1811–1845	33	1779–1845	Oliver W. Holmes	1902–1932	30	1841–1935
Gabriel Duval	1811–1835	24	1752–1844	William D. Day	1903–1922	19	1849–1923
Smith Thompson	1823–1843	20	1768–1843	William H. Moody	1906–1910	3	1853–1917
Robert Trimble	1826–1828	2	1777–1828	Horace H. Lurton	1910–1914	4	1844–1914
John McLean	1829–1861	32	1785–1861	Charles E. Hughes	1910–1916	5	1862–1948
Henry Baldwin	1830–1844	14	1780–1844	Willis Van Devanter	1911–1937	26	1859–1941
James M. Wayne	1835–1867	32	1790–1867	Joseph R. Lamar	1911–1916	5	1857–1916
Roger B. Taney	1836–1864	28	1777–1864	Edward D. White	1910–1921	11	1845–1921
Philip P. Barbour	1836–1841	4	1783–1841	Mahlon Pitney	1912–1922	10	1858–1924
John Catron	1837–1865	28	1786–1865	James C. McReynolds	1914–1941	26	1862–1946
John McKinley	1837–1852	15	1780–1852	Louis D. Brandeis	1916–1939	22	1856–1941
Peter V. Daniel	1841–1860	19	1784–1860	John H. Clarke	1916–1922	6	1857–1945
Samuel Nelson	1845–1872	27	1792–1873	William H. Taft	1921–1930	8	1857–1930
Levi Woodbury	1845–1851	5	1789–1851	George Sutherland	1922–1938	15	1862–1942
Robert C. Grier	1846–1870	23	1794–1870	Pierce Butler	1922–1939	16	1866–1939
Benjamin R. Curtis	1851–1857	6	1809–1874	Edward T. Sanford	1923–1930	7	1865–1930
John A. Campbell	1853–1861	8	1811–1889	Harlan F. Stone	1925–1941	16	1872–1946
Nathan Clifford	1858–1881	23	1803–1881	Charles E. Hughes	1930–1941	11	1862–1948
Noah H. Swayne	1862–1881	18	1804–1884	Owen J. Roberts	1930–1945	15	1875–1955
Samuel F. Miller	1862–1890	28	1816–1890	Benjamin N. Cardozo	1932–1938	6	1870–1938
David Davis	1862–1877	14	1815–1886	Hugo L. Black	1937–1971	34	1886–1971
Stephen J. Field	1863–1897	34	1816–1899	Stanley F. Reed	1938–1957	19	1884–1980
Salmon P. Chase	1864–1873	8	1808–1873	Felix Frankfurter	1939–1962	23	1882–1965

	Term of Service	Years of Service	Life Span		Term of Service	Years of Service	Life Span
William O. Douglas	1939–1975	36	1898–1980	Abe Fortas	1965–1969	4	1910–1982
Frank Murphy	1940–1949	9	1890–1949	Thurgood Marshall	1967–1991	24	1908–1993
Harlan F. Stone	1941–1946	5	1872–1946	*Warren C. Burger*	1969–1986	17	1907–1995
James F. Byrnes	1941–1942	1	1879–1972	Harry A. Blackmun	1970–1994	24	1908–1998
Robert H. Jackson	1941–1954	13	1892–1954	Lewis F. Powell Jr.	1972–1987	15	1907–1998
Wiley B. Rutledge	1943–1949	6	1894–1949	*William H. Rehnquist*	1972–2005	33	1924–2005
Harold H. Burton	1945–1958	13	1888–1964	John P. Stevens III	1975–	–	1920–
Fred M. Vinson	1946–1953	7	1890–1953	Sandra Day O'Connor	1981–	–	1930–
Tom C. Clark	1949–1967	18	1899–1977	Antonin Scalia	1986–	–	1936–
Sherman Minton	1949–1956	7	1890–1965	Anthony M. Kennedy	1988–	–	1936–
Earl Warren	1953–1969	16	1891–1974	David H. Souter	1990–	–	1939–
John Marshall Harlan	1955–1971	16	1899–1971	Clarence Thomas	1991–	–	1948–
William J. Brennan Jr.	1956–1990	34	1906–1997	Ruth Bader Ginsburg	1993–	–	1933–
Charles E. Whittaker	1957–1962	5	1901–1973	Stephen Breyer	1994–	–	1938–
Potter Stewart	1958–1981	23	1915–1985	John G. Roberts	2005–	–	1955–
Byron R. White	1962–1993	31	1917–	Samuel A. Alito, Jr.	2006–	–	1950–
Arthur J. Goldberg	1962–1965	3	1908–1990				

Note: Chief justices are in italics.

*Appointed and served one term, but not confirmed by the Senate.